BATMAN CHRONICLES

VOLUME FOUR

SUSTAINABLE FORESTRY INITIATIVE
Certified Fiber Sourcing
www.sfiprogram.org
Fiber used in this product line meets the sourcing requirements
of the SFI program. www.sfiprogram.org PWC-SFICOC-260

Cover art by Bob Kane.

BATMAN CHRONICLES

VOLUME FOUR

BATMAN CREATED BY BOB KANE

*ALL STORIES WRITTEN BY BILL FINGER. ALL COVERS AND STORIES PENCILLED BY BOB KANE
AND INKED BY JERRY ROBINSON AND GEORGE ROUSSOS UNLESS OTHERWISE NOTED.*

**These stories were originally untitled and are
titled here for reader convenience.*

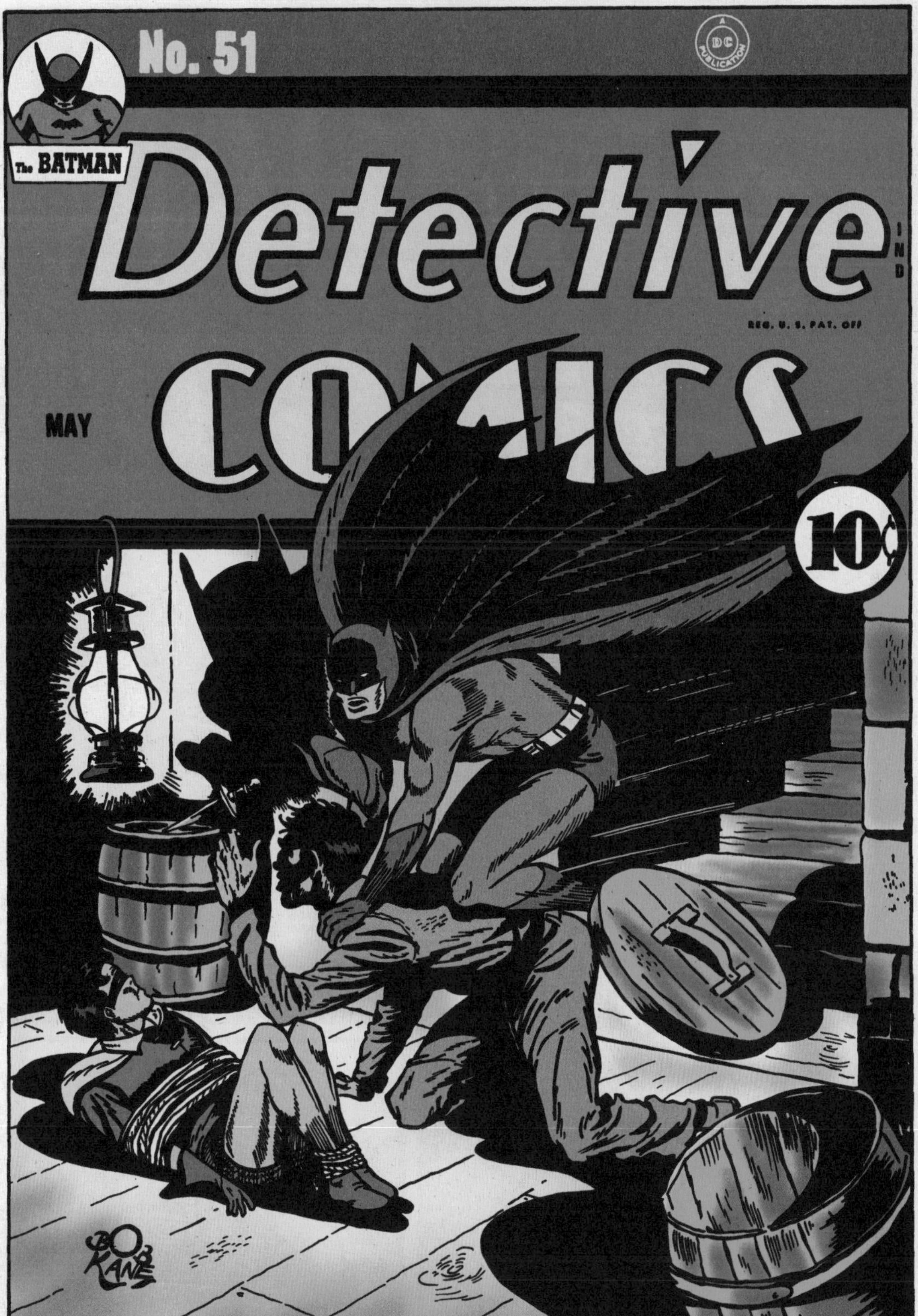
No. 51
A DC PUBLICATION
The BATMAN
Detective
REG. U. S. PAT. OFF
COMICS
MAY
10¢
BOB KANE

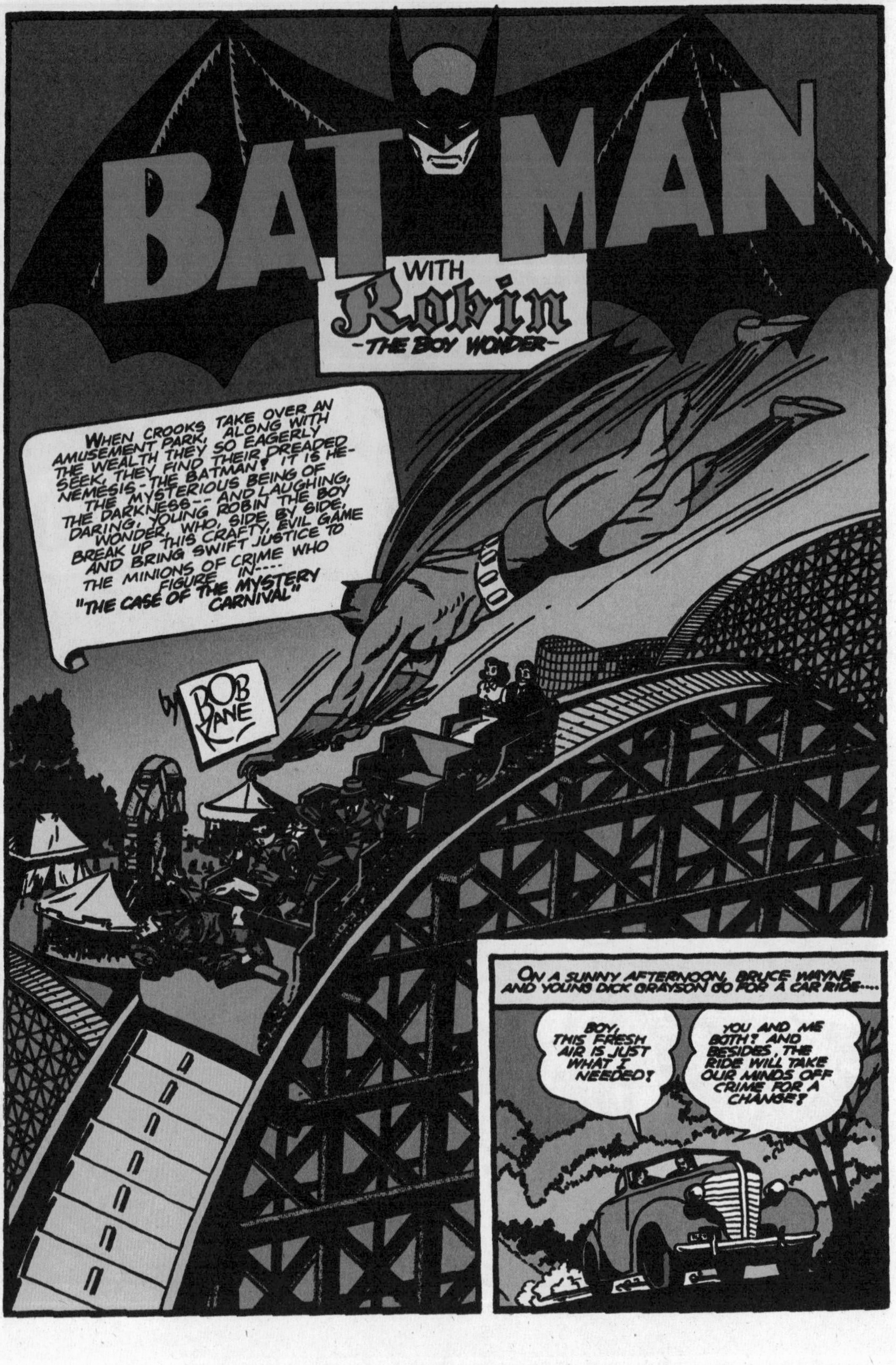
BATMAN
WITH Robin -THE BOY WONDER-
WHEN CROOKS TAKE OVER AN AMUSEMENT PARK, ALONG WITH THE WEALTH THEY SO EAGERLY SEEK, THEY FIND THEIR DREADED NEMESIS - THE BATMAN! IT IS HE - THE MYSTERIOUS BEING OF THE DARKNESS -- AND LAUGHING, DARING, YOUNG ROBIN THE BOY WONDER, WHO, SIDE BY SIDE, BREAK UP THIS CRAFTY, EVIL GAME AND BRING SWIFT JUSTICE TO THE MINIONS OF CRIME WHO FIGURE IN---- "THE CASE OF THE MYSTERY CARNIVAL"
by BOB KANE
ON A SUNNY AFTERNOON, BRUCE WAYNE AND YOUNG DICK GRAYSON GO FOR A CAR RIDE....
BOY, THIS FRESH AIR IS JUST WHAT I NEEDED!
YOU AND ME BOTH! AND BESIDES, THE RIDE WILL TAKE OUR MINDS OFF CRIME FOR A CHANGE!

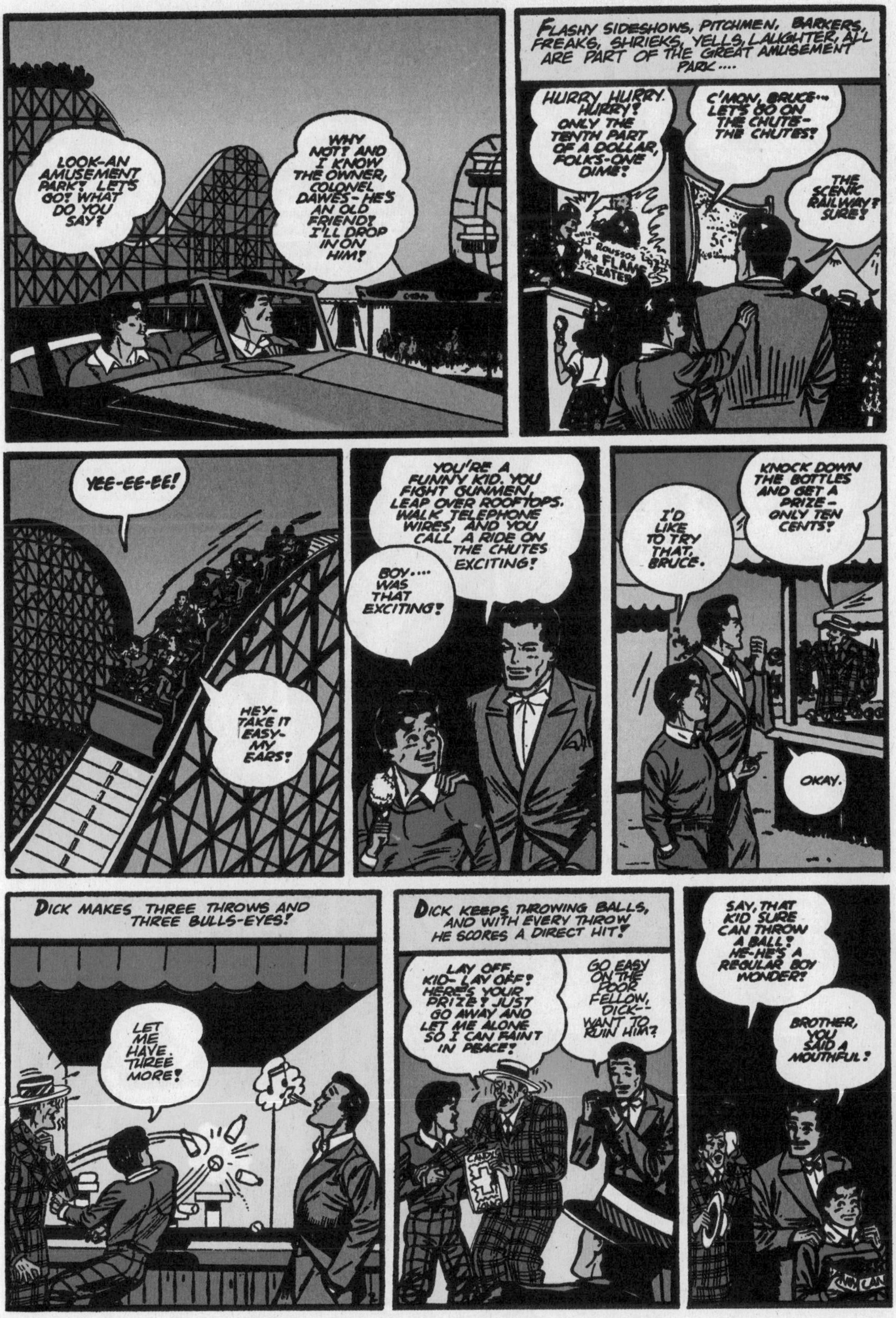

LOOK-AN AMUSEMENT PARK! LET'S GO! WHAT DO YOU SAY?
WHY NOT? AND I KNOW THE OWNER, COLONEL DAWES- HE'S AN OLD FRIEND! I'LL DROP IN ON HIM!
FLASHY SIDESHOWS, PITCHMEN, BARKERS, FREAKS, SHRIEKS, YELLS, LAUGHTER, ALL ARE PART OF THE GREAT AMUSEMENT PARK....
HURRY HURRY HURRY! ONLY THE TENTH PART OF A DOLLAR, FOLKS-ONE DIME!
C'MON, BRUCE... LET'S GO ON THE CHUTE-THE CHUTES!
THE SCENIC RAILWAY? SURE!
YEE-EE-EE!
HEY-TAKE IT EASY-MY EARS!
YOU'RE A FUNNY KID. YOU FIGHT GUNMEN, LEAP OVER ROOFTOPS, WALK TELEPHONE WIRES, AND YOU CALL A RIDE ON THE CHUTES EXCITING!
BOY.... WAS THAT EXCITING!
KNOCK DOWN THE BOTTLES AND GET A PRIZE-ONLY TEN CENTS!
I'D LIKE TO TRY THAT, BRUCE.
OKAY.
DICK MAKES THREE THROWS AND THREE BULLS-EYES!
LET ME HAVE THREE MORE!
DICK KEEPS THROWING BALLS, AND WITH EVERY THROW HE SCORES A DIRECT HIT!
LAY OFF, KID- LAY OFF! HERE'S YOUR PRIZE! JUST GO AWAY AND LET ME ALONE SO I CAN FAINT IN PEACE!
GO EASY ON THE POOR FELLOW, DICK-- WANT TO RUIN HIM?
SAY, THAT KID SURE CAN THROW A BALL! HE-HE'S A REGULAR BOY WONDER!
BROTHER, YOU SAID A MOUTHFUL!

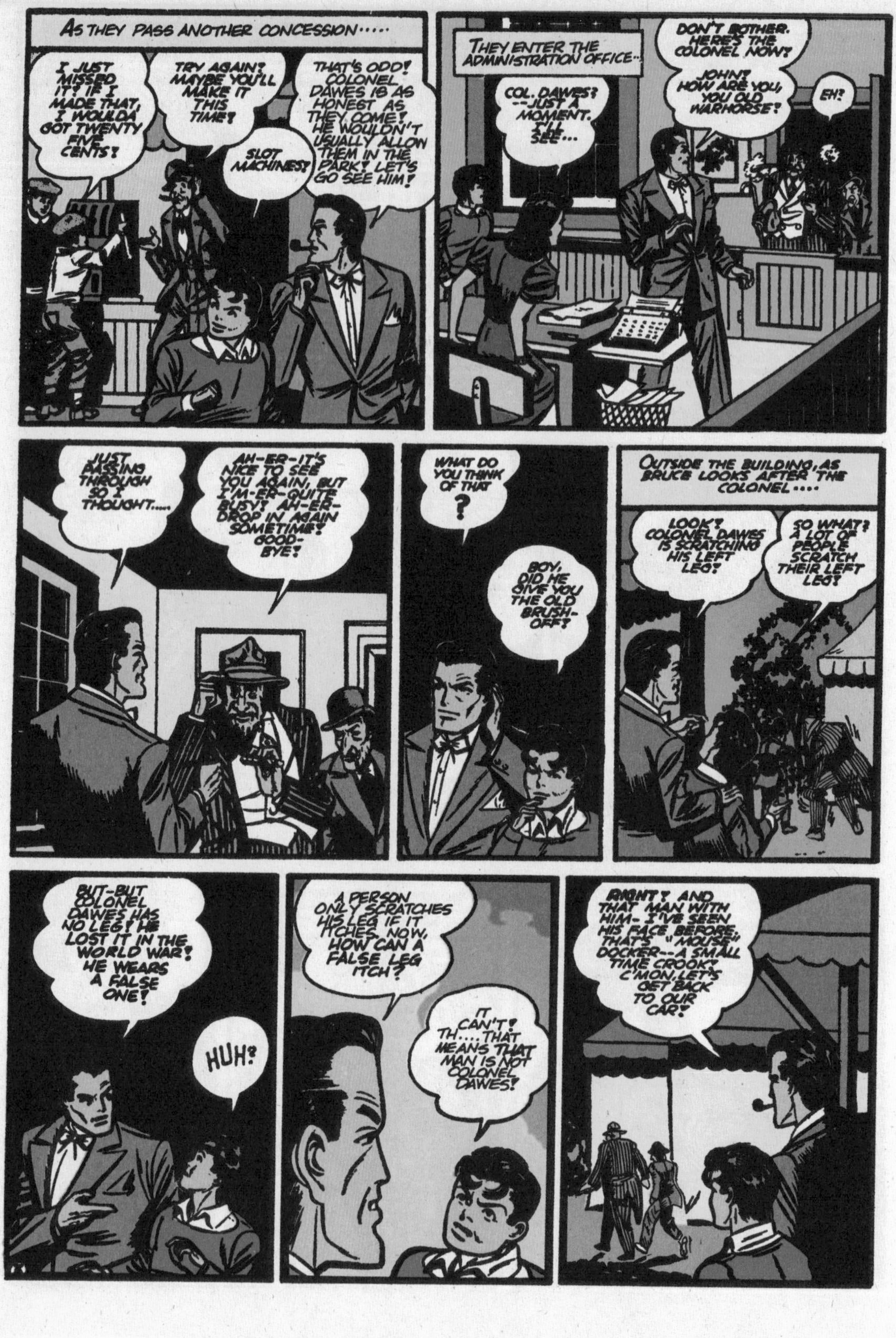
AS THEY PASS ANOTHER CONCESSION.....
I JUST MISSED IT! IF I MADE THAT, I WOULDA GOT TWENTY FIVE CENTS!
TRY AGAIN! MAYBE YOU'LL MAKE IT THIS TIME!
SLOT MACHINES!
THAT'S ODD! COLONEL DAWES IS AS HONEST AS THEY COME! HE WOULDN'T USUALLY ALLOW THEM IN THE PARK! LET'S GO SEE HIM!
THEY ENTER THE ADMINISTRATION OFFICE...
COL. DAWES? --JUST A MOMENT. I'LL SEE...
DON'T BOTHER. HERE'S THE COLONEL NOW!
JOHN! HOW ARE YOU, YOU OLD WARHORSE!
EH?
JUST PASSING THROUGH SO I THOUGHT.....
AH-ER-IT'S NICE TO SEE YOU AGAIN, BUT I'M-ER-QUITE BUSY! AH-ER-DROP IN AGAIN SOMETIME! GOOD-BYE!
WHAT DO YOU THINK OF THAT ?
BOY, DID HE GIVE YOU THE OLD BRUSH-OFF!
OUTSIDE THE BUILDING, AS BRUCE LOOKS AFTER THE COLONEL....
LOOK! COLONEL DAWES IS SCRATCHING HIS LEFT LEG!
SO WHAT? A LOT OF PEOPLE SCRATCH THEIR LEFT LEG!
BUT-BUT COLONEL DAWES HAS NO LEG! HE LOST IT IN THE WORLD WAR! HE WEARS A FALSE ONE!
HUH?
A PERSON ONLY SCRATCHES HIS LEG IF IT ITCHES. NOW, HOW CAN A FALSE LEG ITCH?
IT CAN'T! TH....THAT MEANS THAT MAN IS NOT COLONEL DAWES!
RIGHT! AND THAT MAN WITH HIM- I'VE SEEN HIS FACE BEFORE. THAT'S "MOUSE" DOCKER--A SMALL TIME CROOK! C'MON, LET'S GET BACK TO OUR CAR!

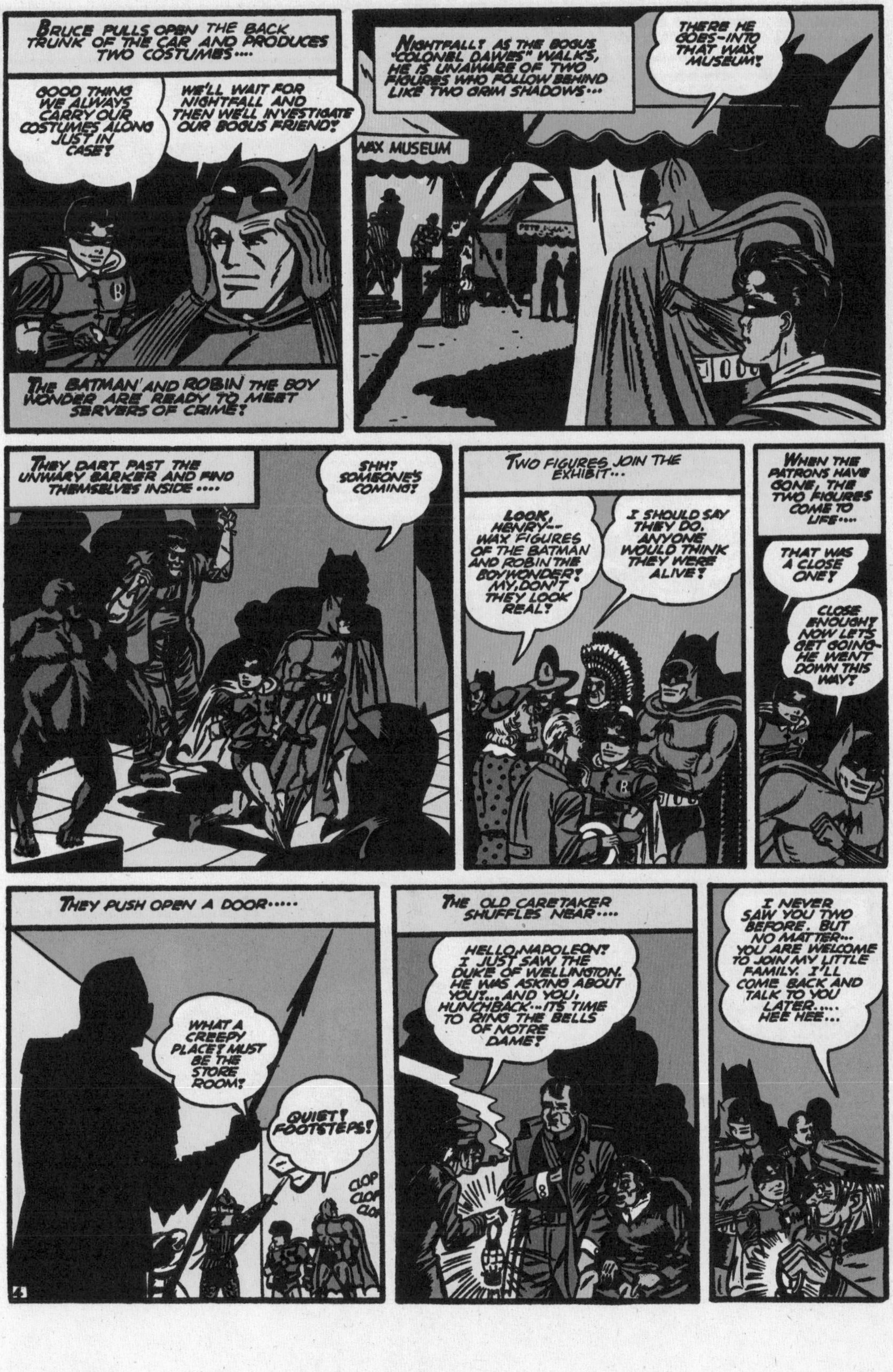
BRUCE PULLS OPEN THE BACK TRUNK OF THE CAR AND PRODUCES TWO COSTUMES....
GOOD THING WE ALWAYS CARRY OUR COSTUMES ALONG JUST IN CASE!
WE'LL WAIT FOR NIGHTFALL AND THEN WE'LL INVESTIGATE OUR BOGUS FRIEND!
THE BATMAN AND ROBIN THE BOY WONDER ARE READY TO MEET SERVERS OF CRIME!
NIGHTFALL! AS THE BOGUS "COLONEL DAWES" WALKS, HE IS UNAWARE OF TWO FIGURES WHO FOLLOW BEHIND LIKE TWO GRIM SHADOWS...
THERE HE GOES-INTO THAT WAX MUSEUM!
WAX MUSEUM
THEY DART PAST THE UNWARY BARKER AND FIND THEMSELVES INSIDE....
SHH! SOMEONE'S COMING!
TWO FIGURES JOIN THE EXHIBIT...
LOOK, HENRY-- WAX FIGURES OF THE BATMAN AND ROBIN THE BOY WONDER! MY, DON'T THEY LOOK REAL!
I SHOULD SAY THEY DO. ANYONE WOULD THINK THEY WERE ALIVE!
WHEN THE PATRONS HAVE GONE, THE TWO FIGURES COME TO LIFE....
THAT WAS A CLOSE ONE!
CLOSE ENOUGH! NOW LET'S GET GOING- HE WENT DOWN THIS WAY!
THEY PUSH OPEN A DOOR.....
WHAT A CREEPY PLACE! MUST BE THE STORE ROOM!
QUIET! FOOTSTEPS!
CLOP CLOP CLO
4
THE OLD CARETAKER SHUFFLES NEAR....
HELLO, NAPOLEON! I JUST SAW THE DUKE OF WELLINGTON. HE WAS ASKING ABOUT YOU!... AND YOU, HUNCHBACK-- ITS TIME TO RING THE BELLS OF NOTRE DAME!
I NEVER SAW YOU TWO BEFORE. BUT NO MATTER... YOU ARE WELCOME TO JOIN MY LITTLE FAMILY. I'LL COME BACK AND TALK TO YOU LATER..... HEE HEE...

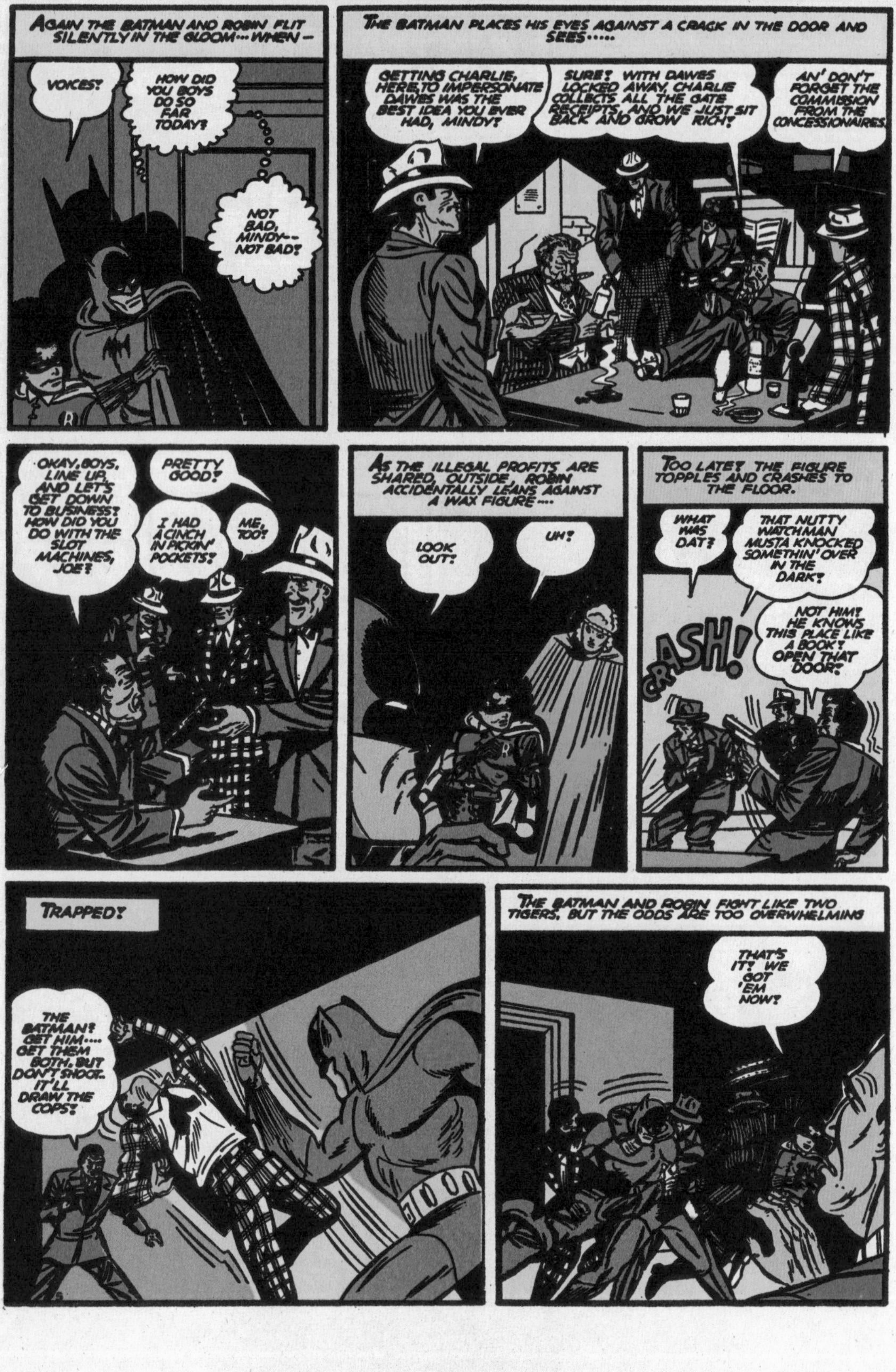
AGAIN THE BATMAN AND ROBIN FLIT SILENTLY IN THE GLOOM... WHEN—
VOICES!
HOW DID YOU BOYS DO SO FAR TODAY?
NOT BAD, MINDY-- NOT BAD!
THE BATMAN PLACES HIS EYES AGAINST A CRACK IN THE DOOR AND SEES.....
GETTING CHARLIE, HERE,TO IMPERSONATE DAWES WAS THE BEST IDEA YOU EVER HAD, MINDY!
SURE! WITH DAWES LOCKED AWAY, CHARLIE COLLECTS ALL THE GATE RECEIPTS, AND WE JUST SIT BACK AND GROW RICH!
AN' DON'T FORGET THE COMMISSION FROM THE CONCESSIONAIRES.
OKAY, BOYS, LINE UP, AND LET'S GET DOWN TO BUSINESS! HOW DID YOU DO WITH THE SLOT MACHINES, JOE?
PRETTY GOOD!
I HAD A CINCH IN PICKIN' POCKETS!
ME, TOO!
AS THE ILLEGAL PROFITS ARE SHARED, OUTSIDE, ROBIN ACCIDENTALLY LEANS AGAINST A WAX FIGURE....
LOOK OUT!
UH!
TOO LATE! THE FIGURE TOPPLES AND CRASHES TO THE FLOOR.
WHAT WAS DAT?
THAT NUTTY WATCHMAN MUSTA KNOCKED SOMETHIN' OVER IN THE DARK!
CRASH!
NOT HIM! HE KNOWS THIS PLACE LIKE A BOOK! OPEN THAT DOOR!
TRAPPED!
THE BATMAN! GET HIM.... GET THEM BOTH. BUT DON'T SHOOT. IT'LL DRAW THE COPS!
THE BATMAN AND ROBIN FIGHT LIKE TWO TIGERS. BUT THE ODDS ARE TOO OVERWHELMING
THAT'S IT! WE GOT 'EM NOW!

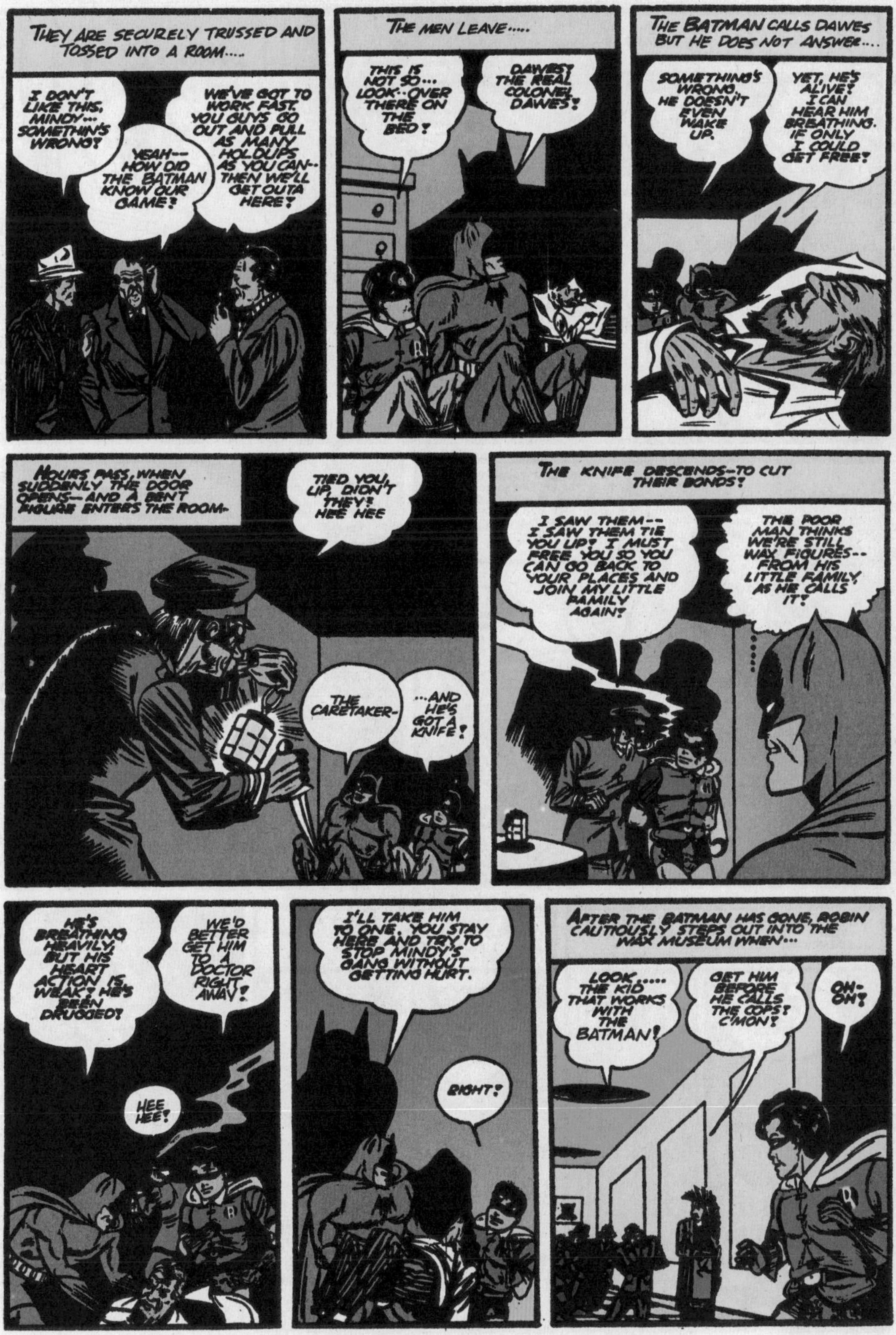
THEY ARE SECURELY TRUSSED AND TOSSED INTO A ROOM.....
I DON'T LIKE THIS, MINDY... SOMETHIN'S WRONG!
YEAH-- HOW DID THE BATMAN KNOW OUR GAME?
WE'VE GOT TO WORK FAST. YOU GUYS GO OUT AND PULL AS MANY HOLDUPS AS YOU CAN-- THEN WE'LL GET OUTA HERE!
THE MEN LEAVE.....
THIS IS NOT SO... LOOK--OVER THERE ON THE BED!
DAWES! THE REAL COLONEL DAWES!
THE BATMAN CALLS DAWES BUT HE DOES NOT ANSWER....
SOMETHING'S WRONG. HE DOESN'T EVEN WAKE UP.
YET, HE'S ALIVE! I CAN HEAR HIM BREATHING. IF ONLY I COULD GET FREE!
HOURS PASS, WHEN SUDDENLY THE DOOR OPENS-- AND A BENT FIGURE ENTERS THE ROOM-
TIED YOU, UP, DIDN'T THEY! HEE HEE
THE CARETAKER-
...AND HE'S GOT A KNIFE!
THE KNIFE DESCENDS--TO CUT THEIR BONDS!
I SAW THEM-- I SAW THEM TIE YOU UP! I MUST FREE YOU SO YOU CAN GO BACK TO YOUR PLACES AND JOIN MY LITTLE FAMILY AGAIN!
THE POOR MAN THINKS WE'RE STILL WAX FIGURES-- FROM HIS LITTLE FAMILY, AS HE CALLS IT!
HE'S BREATHING HEAVILY, BUT HIS HEART ACTION IS WEAK! HE'S BEEN DRUGGED!
WE'D BETTER GET HIM TO A DOCTOR RIGHT AWAY!
HEE HEE!
I'LL TAKE HIM TO ONE. YOU STAY HERE AND TRY TO STOP MINDY'S GANG WITHOUT GETTING HURT.
RIGHT!
AFTER THE BATMAN HAS GONE, ROBIN CAUTIOUSLY STEPS OUT INTO THE WAX MUSEUM WHEN...
LOOK..... THE KID THAT WORKS WITH THE BATMAN!
GET HIM BEFORE HE CALLS THE COPS! C'MON!
OH-OH!

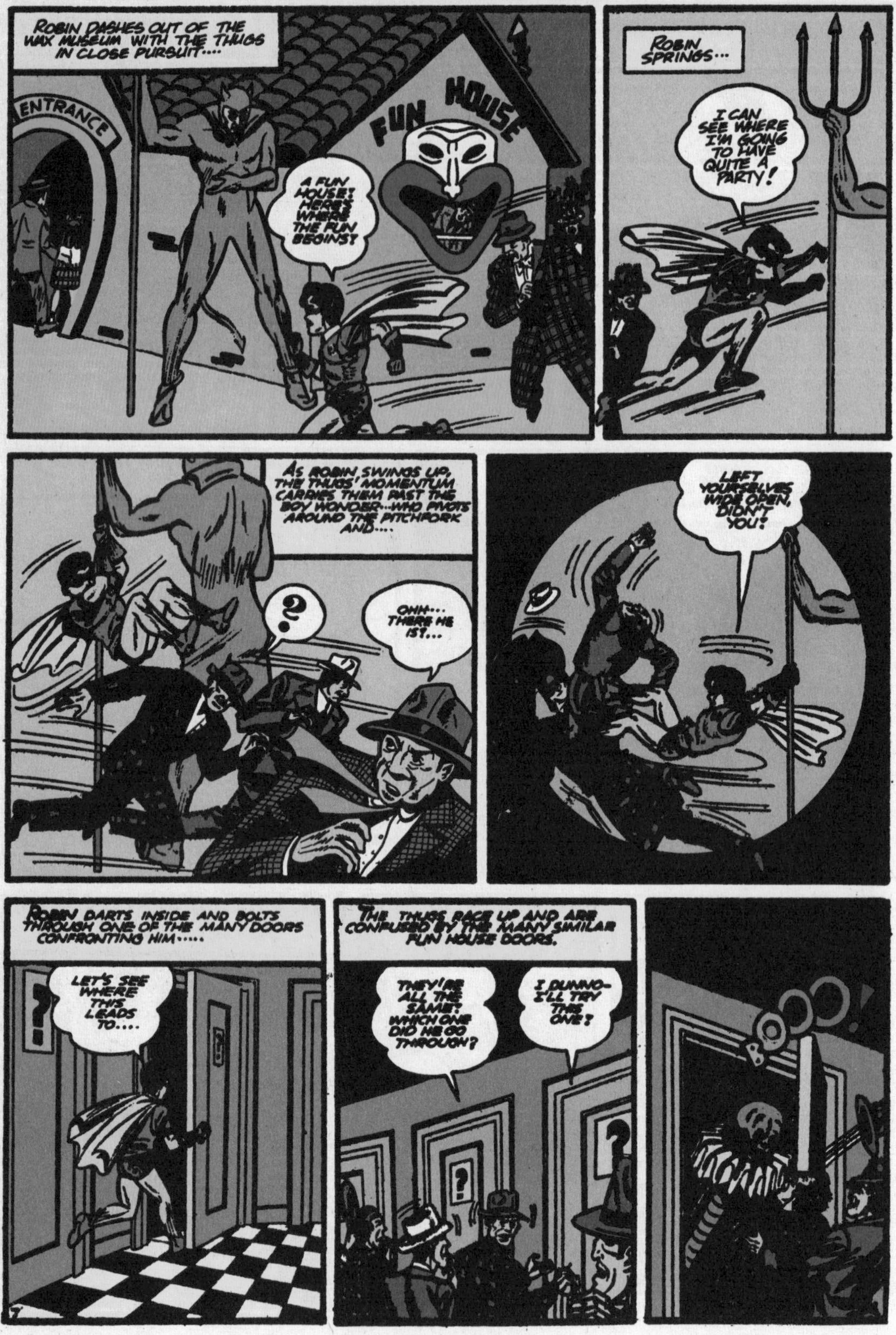
ROBIN DASHES OUT OF THE WAX MUSEUM WITH THE THUGS IN CLOSE PURSUIT....
ENTRANCE
FUN HOUSE
A FUN HOUSE! HERE'S WHERE THE FUN BEGINS!
ROBIN SPRINGS...
I CAN SEE WHERE I'M GOING TO HAVE QUITE A PARTY!
AS ROBIN SWINGS UP, THE THUGS' MOMENTUM CARRIES THEM PAST THE BOY WONDER...WHO PIVOTS AROUND THE PITCHFORK AND....
?
OHH... THERE HE IS!...
LEFT YOURSELVES WIDE OPEN, DIDN'T YOU?
ROBIN DARTS INSIDE AND BOLTS THROUGH ONE OF THE MANY DOORS CONFRONTING HIM.....
LET'S SEE WHERE THIS LEADS TO....
THE THUGS RACE UP AND ARE CONFUSED BY THE MANY SIMILAR FUN HOUSE DOORS.
THEY'RE ALL THE SAME! WHICH ONE DID HE GO THROUGH?
I DUNNO-- I'LL TRY THIS ONE!

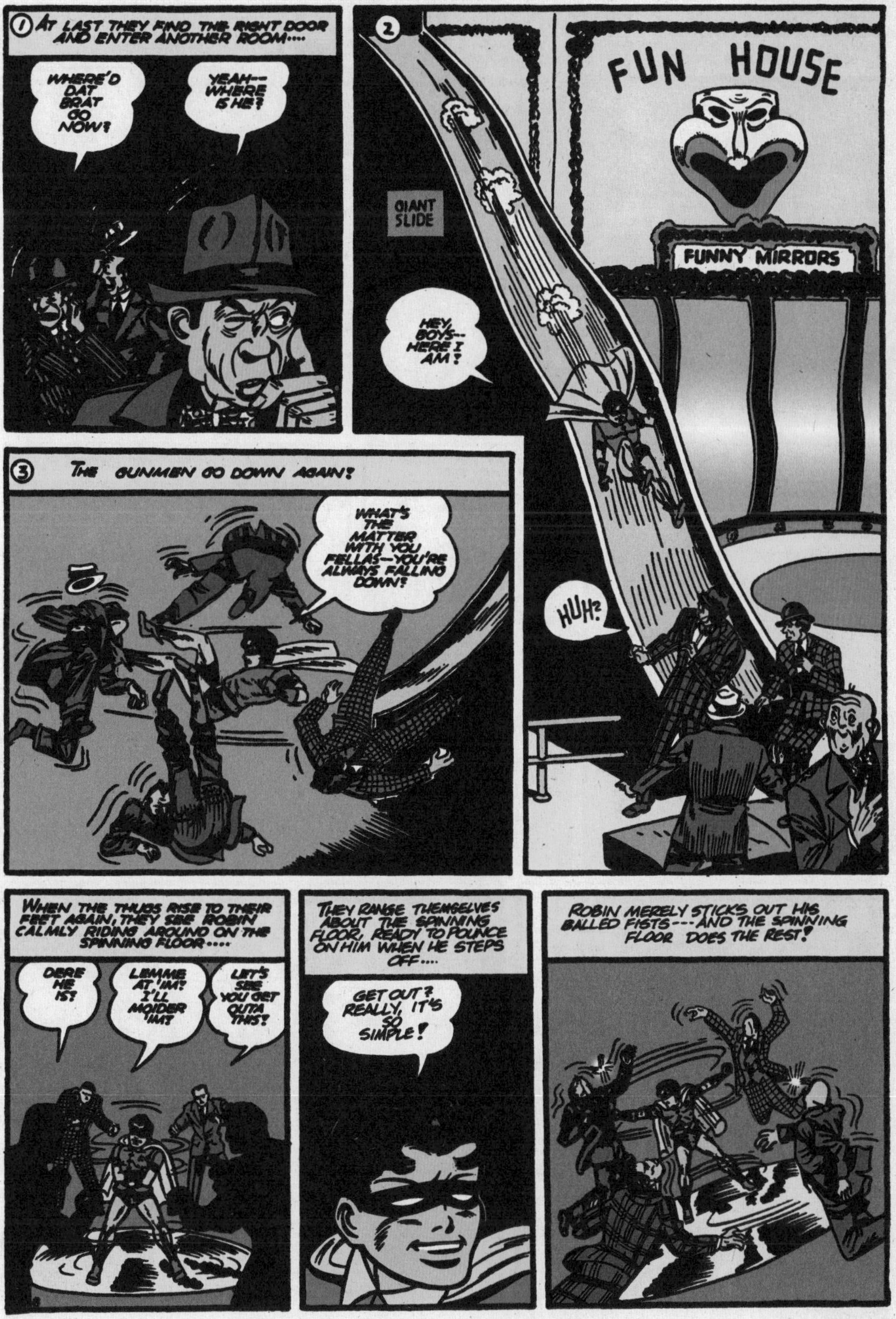
1 AT LAST THEY FIND THE RIGHT DOOR AND ENTER ANOTHER ROOM....
WHERE'D DAT BRAT GO NOW?
YEAH-- WHERE IS HE?
2
FUN HOUSE
GIANT SLIDE
FUNNY MIRRORS
HEY, BOYS-- HERE I AM!
HUH?
3 THE GUNMEN GO DOWN AGAIN!
WHAT'S THE MATTER WITH YOU FELLAS--YOU'RE ALWAYS FALLING DOWN!
WHEN THE THUGS RISE TO THEIR FEET AGAIN, THEY SEE ROBIN CALMLY RIDING AROUND ON THE SPINNING FLOOR....
DERE HE IS!
LEMME AT 'IM! I'LL MOIDER 'IM!
LET'S SEE YOU GET OUTA THIS!
THEY RANGE THEMSELVES ABOUT THE SPINNING FLOOR, READY TO POUNCE ON HIM WHEN HE STEPS OFF....
GET OUT? REALLY, IT'S SO SIMPLE!
ROBIN MERELY STICKS OUT HIS BALLED FISTS---AND THE SPINNING FLOOR DOES THE REST!

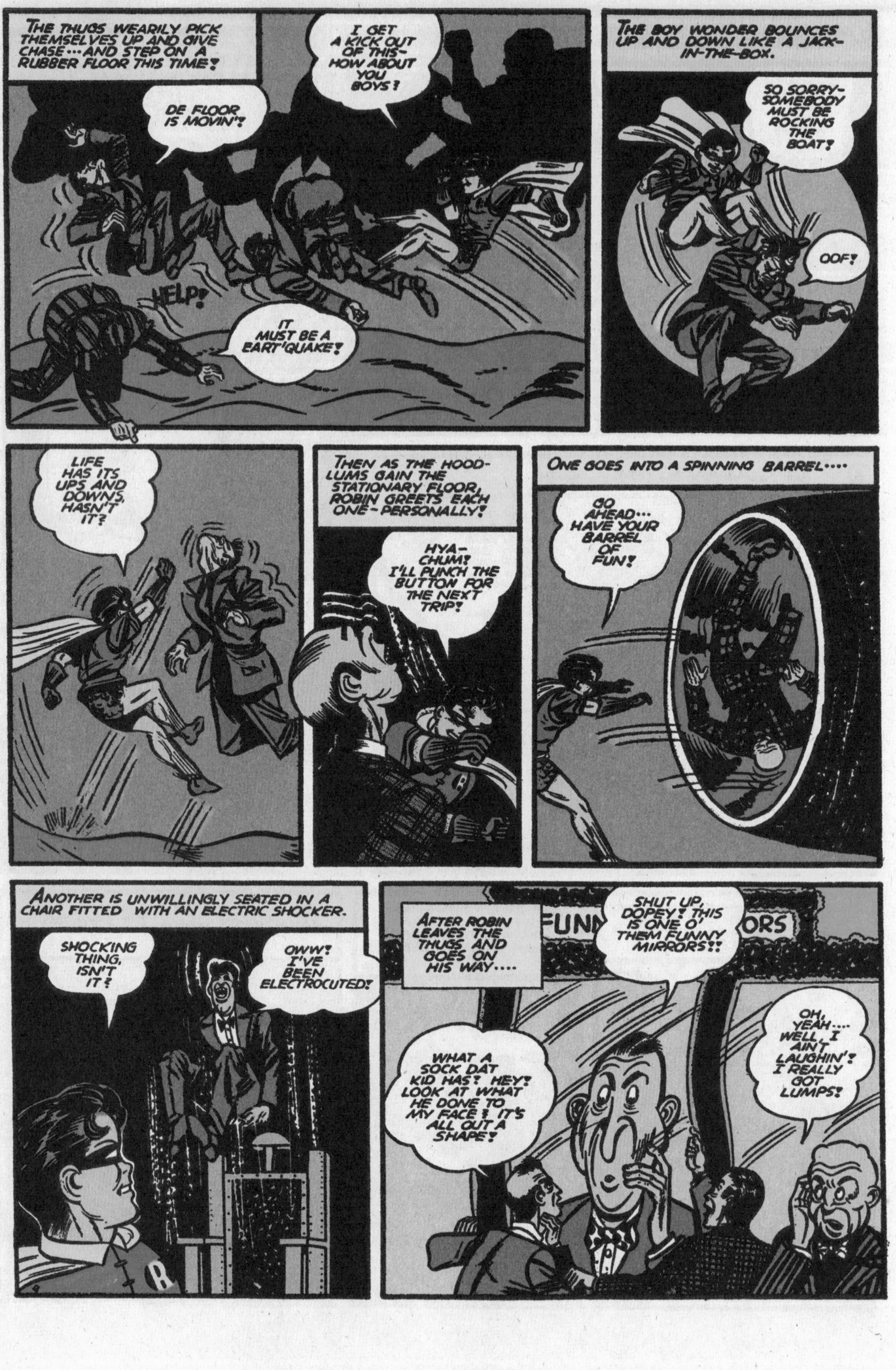
THE THUGS WEARILY PICK THEMSELVES UP AND GIVE CHASE... AND STEP ON A RUBBER FLOOR THIS TIME!
I GET A KICK OUT OF THIS-HOW ABOUT YOU BOYS?
DE FLOOR IS MOVIN'!
HELP!
IT MUST BE A EART'QUAKE!
THE BOY WONDER BOUNCES UP AND DOWN LIKE A JACK-IN-THE-BOX.
SO SORRY-SOMEBODY MUST BE ROCKING THE BOAT!
OOF!
LIFE HAS ITS UPS AND DOWNS, HASN'T IT?
THEN AS THE HOODLUMS GAIN THE STATIONARY FLOOR, ROBIN GREETS EACH ONE-PERSONALLY!
HYA-CHUM! I'LL PUNCH THE BUTTON FOR THE NEXT TRIP!
ONE GOES INTO A SPINNING BARREL....
GO AHEAD... HAVE YOUR BARREL OF FUN!
ANOTHER IS UNWILLINGLY SEATED IN A CHAIR FITTED WITH AN ELECTRIC SHOCKER.
SHOCKING THING, ISN'T IT?
OWW! I'VE BEEN ELECTROCUTED!
AFTER ROBIN LEAVES THE THUGS AND GOES ON HIS WAY....
SHUT UP, DOPEY! THIS IS ONE O' THEM FUNNY MIRRORS!!
WHAT A SOCK DAT KID HAS! HEY! LOOK AT WHAT HE DONE TO MY FACE! IT'S ALL OUT A SHAPE!
OH, YEAH.... WELL, I AIN'T LAUGHIN'! I REALLY GOT LUMPS!

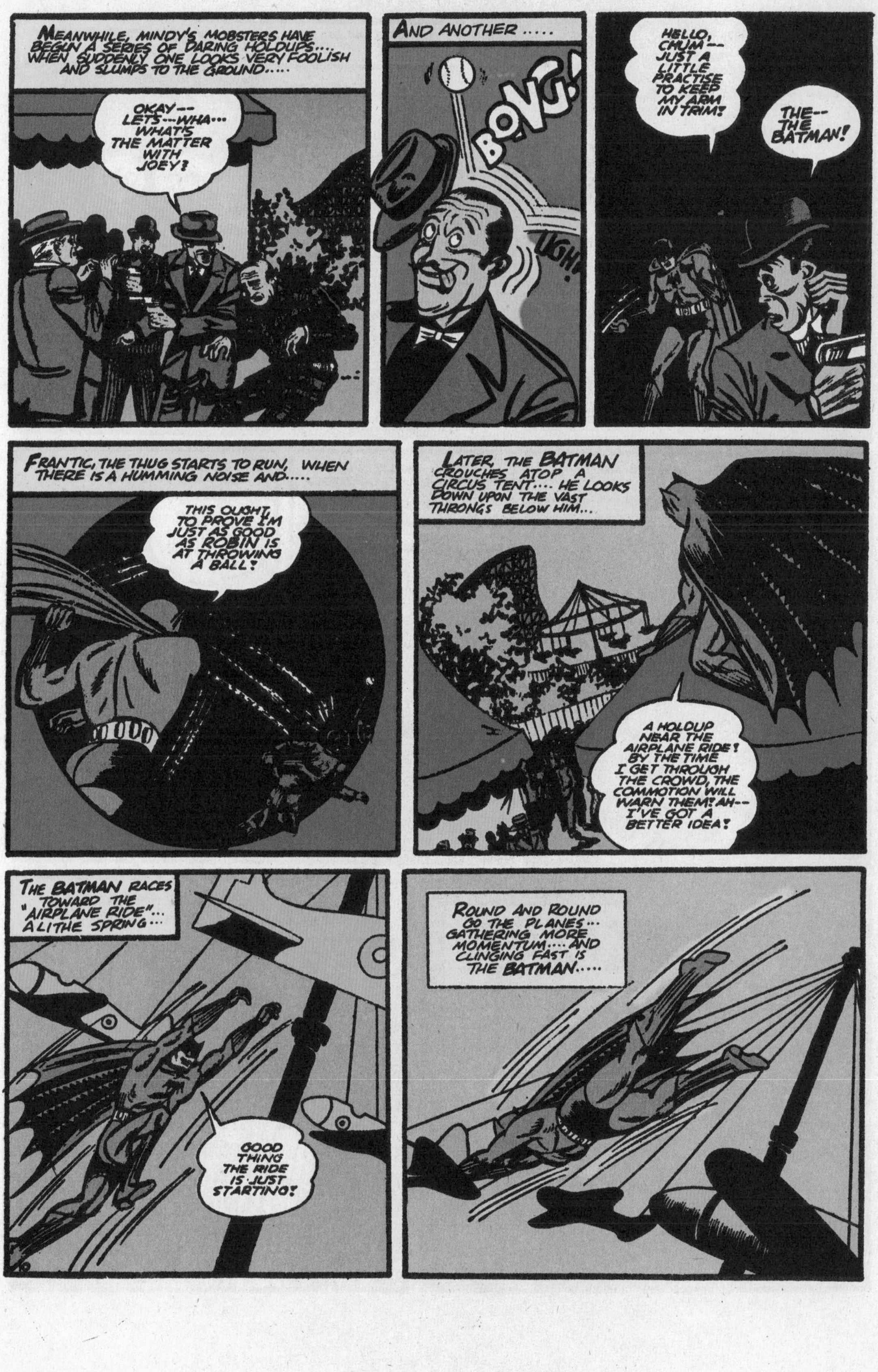
MEANWHILE, MINDY'S MOBSTERS HAVE BEGUN A SERIES OF DARING HOLDUPS.... WHEN SUDDENLY ONE LOOKS VERY FOOLISH AND SLUMPS TO THE GROUND....
OKAY-- LETS--WHA... WHAT'S THE MATTER WITH JOEY?
AND ANOTHER .....
BONG!
UGH!
HELLO, CHUM-- JUST A LITTLE PRACTISE TO KEEP MY ARM IN TRIM!
THE-- THE BATMAN!
FRANTIC, THE THUG STARTS TO RUN, WHEN THERE IS A HUMMING NOISE AND.....
THIS OUGHT TO PROVE I'M JUST AS GOOD AS ROBIN IS AT THROWING A BALL!
LATER, THE BATMAN CROUCHES ATOP A CIRCUS TENT.... HE LOOKS DOWN UPON THE VAST THRONGS BELOW HIM...
A HOLDUP NEAR THE AIRPLANE RIDE! BY THE TIME I GET THROUGH THE CROWD, THE COMMOTION WILL WARN THEM! AH-- I'VE GOT A BETTER IDEA!
THE BATMAN RACES TOWARD THE "AIRPLANE RIDE"... A LITHE SPRING...
GOOD THING THE RIDE IS JUST STARTING!
ROUND AND ROUND GO THE PLANES... GATHERING MORE MOMENTUM.... AND CLINGING FAST IS THE BATMAN.....

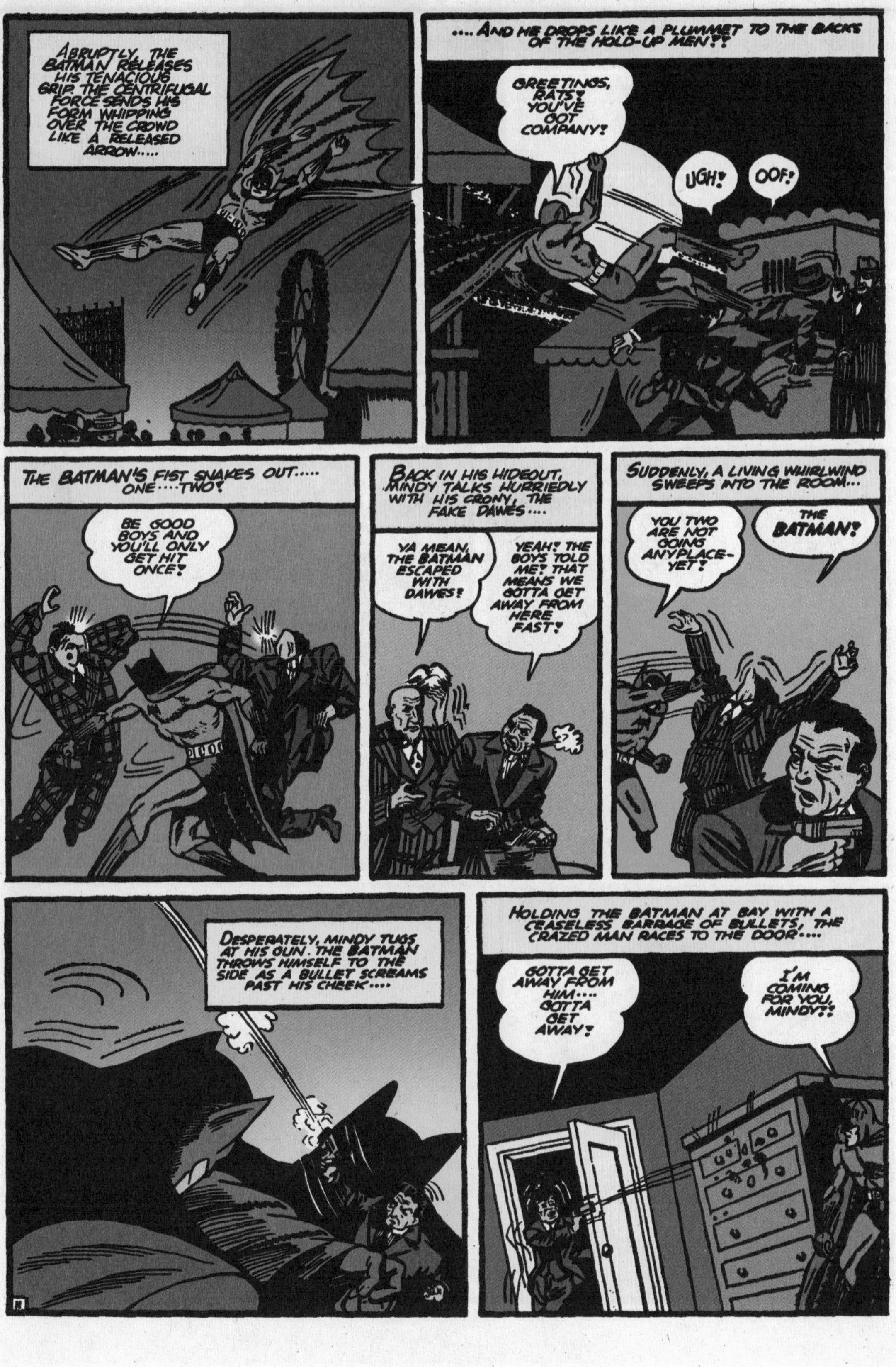
ABRUPTLY, THE BATMAN RELEASES HIS TENACIOUS GRIP. THE CENTRIFUGAL FORCE SENDS HIS FORM WHIPPING OVER THE CROWD LIKE A RELEASED ARROW.....
.... AND HE DROPS LIKE A PLUMMET TO THE BACKS OF THE HOLD-UP MEN!!
GREETINGS, RATS! YOU'VE GOT COMPANY!
UGH!
OOF!
THE BATMAN'S FIST SNAKES OUT..... ONE.... TWO!
BE GOOD BOYS AND YOU'LL ONLY GET HIT ONCE!
BACK IN HIS HIDEOUT, MINDY TALKS HURRIEDLY WITH HIS CRONY, THE FAKE DAWES....
YA MEAN, THE BATMAN ESCAPED WITH DAWES!
YEAH! THE BOYS TOLD ME! THAT MEANS WE GOTTA GET AWAY FROM HERE FAST!
SUDDENLY, A LIVING WHIRLWIND SWEEPS INTO THE ROOM...
YOU TWO ARE NOT GOING ANYPLACE- YET!
THE BATMAN!
DESPERATELY, MINDY TUGS AT HIS GUN. THE BATMAN THROWS HIMSELF TO THE SIDE AS A BULLET SCREAMS PAST HIS CHEEK....
HOLDING THE BATMAN AT BAY WITH A CEASELESS BARRAGE OF BULLETS, THE CRAZED MAN RACES TO THE DOOR....
GOTTA GET AWAY FROM HIM.... GOTTA GET AWAY!
I'M COMING FOR YOU, MINDY!!

His terror growing, Mindy darts toward the scenic railway, hoping to shake his relentless pursuer....

HERE-- A DOLLAR--I WANT THE WHOLE CAR TO MYSELF...START HER OFF RIGHT NOW!

YES, SIR!

TOO LATE?

GOT TO GET UP TO HIM. THE FERRIS WHEEL-- THAT WILL DO IT!

The Batman leaps toward a rising car of the Ferris Wheel .....

COME TO POPPA!

Up--up--up goes the Batman as the car ascends.

The car reaches it's highest point. The Batman flings himself toward the scenic railway structure....

I'D BETTER NOT MISS!

...And his fists close vise-like about a supporting beam?

NOW FOR MINDY?

The Batman climbs to the upper portion of the railway and waits for the car Mindy is on.....

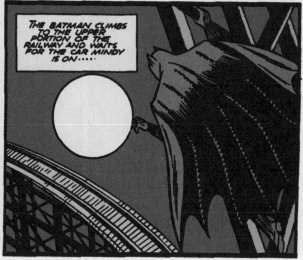

17

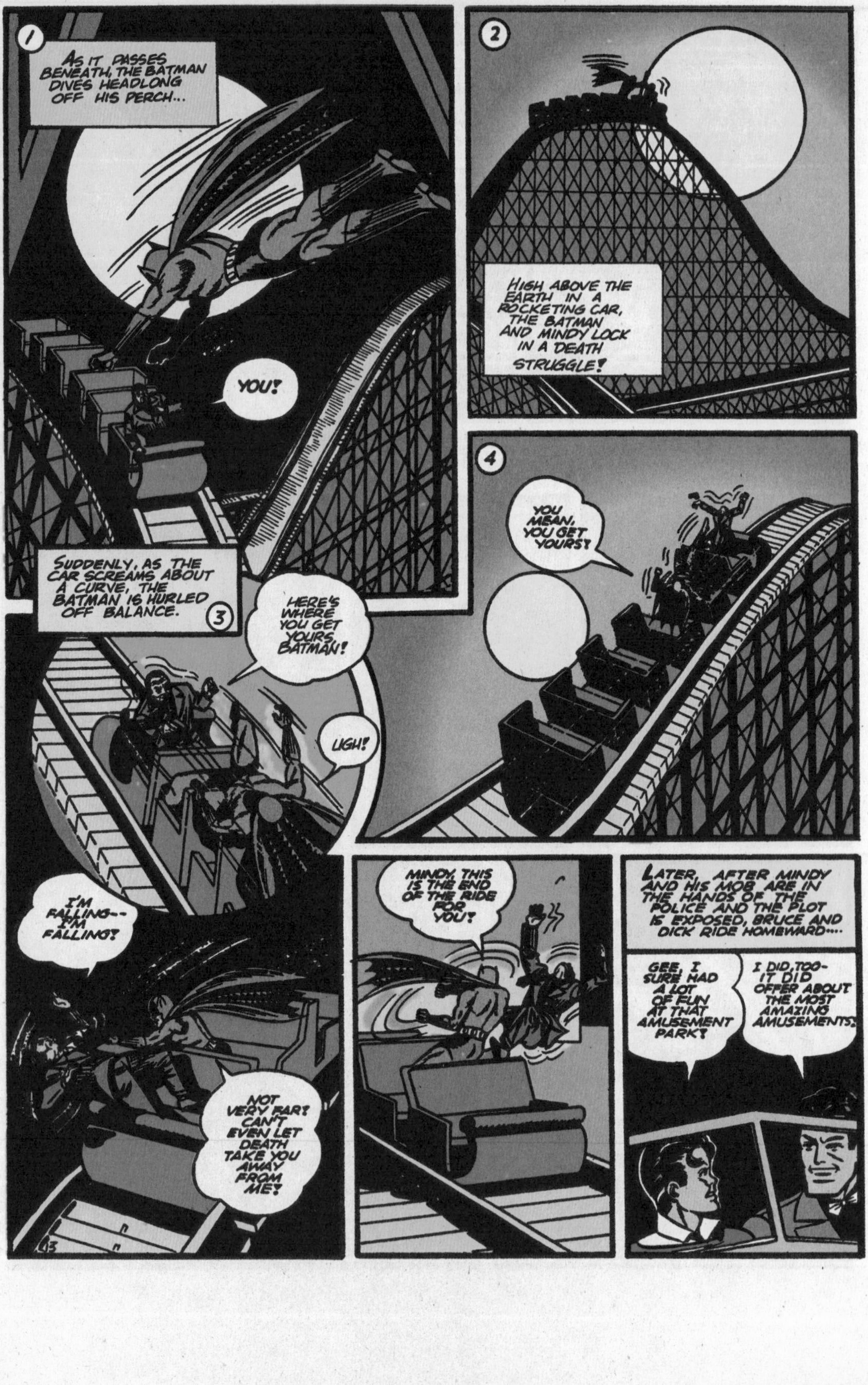

AS IT PASSES BENEATH, THE BATMAN DIVES HEADLONG OFF HIS PERCH...
YOU!
HIGH ABOVE THE EARTH IN A ROCKETING CAR, THE BATMAN AND MINDY LOCK IN A DEATH STRUGGLE!
SUDDENLY, AS THE CAR SCREAMS ABOUT A CURVE, THE BATMAN IS HURLED OFF BALANCE.
HERE'S WHERE YOU GET YOURS, BATMAN!
UGH!
YOU MEAN, YOU GET YOURS!
I'M FALLING-- I'M FALLING!
NOT VERY FAR! CAN'T EVEN LET DEATH TAKE YOU AWAY FROM ME!
MINDY, THIS IS THE END OF THE RIDE FOR YOU!
LATER, AFTER MINDY AND HIS MOB ARE IN THE HANDS OF THE POLICE AND THE PLOT IS EXPOSED, BRUCE AND DICK RIDE HOMEWARD....
GEE, I SURE HAD A LOT OF FUN AT THAT AMUSEMENT PARK!
I DID, TOO-- IT DID OFFER ABOUT THE MOST AMAZING AMUSEMENTS!

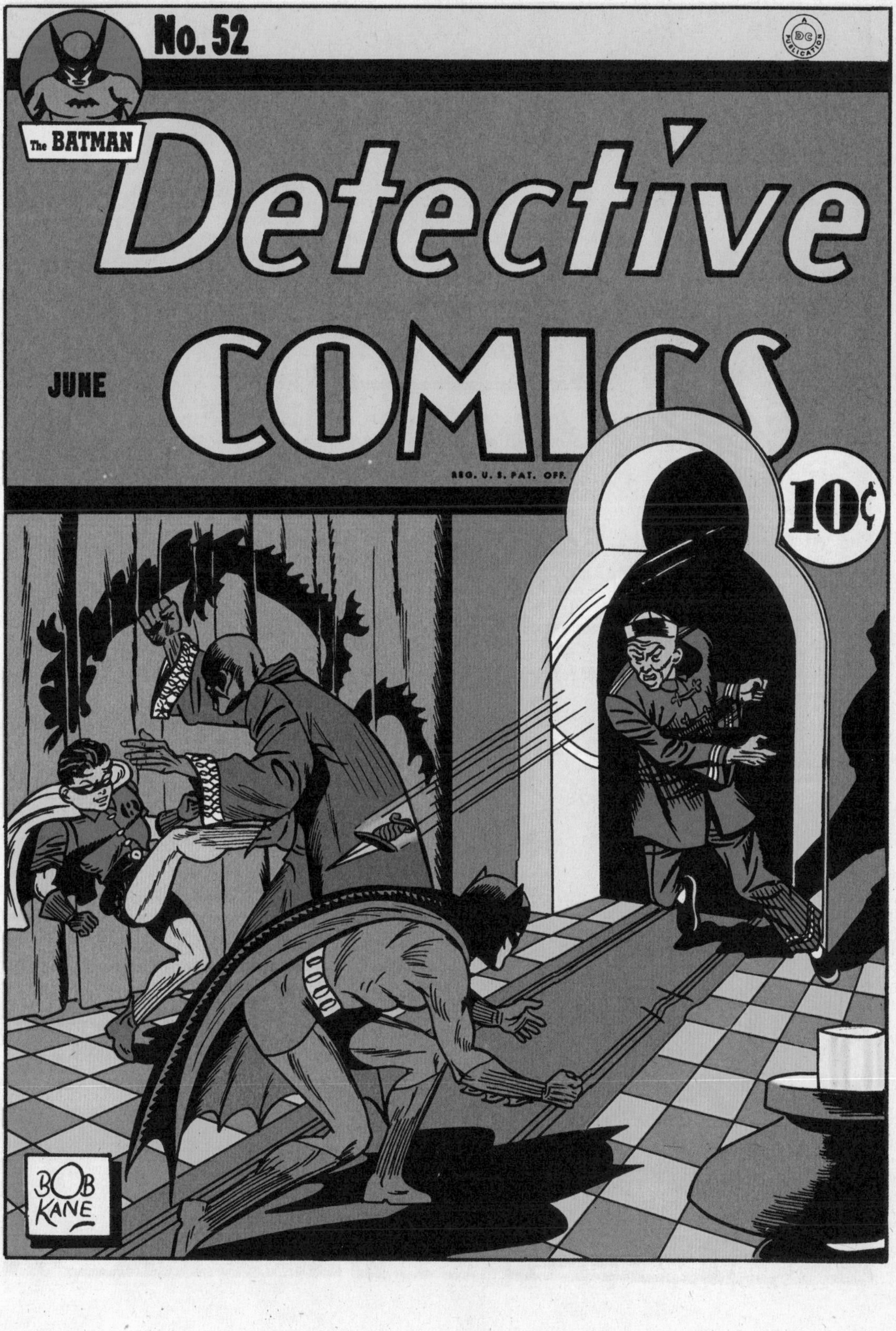
No. 52
A DC PUBLICATION
The BATMAN
Detective
COMICS
JUNE
REG. U. S. PAT. OFF.
10¢
BOB KANE

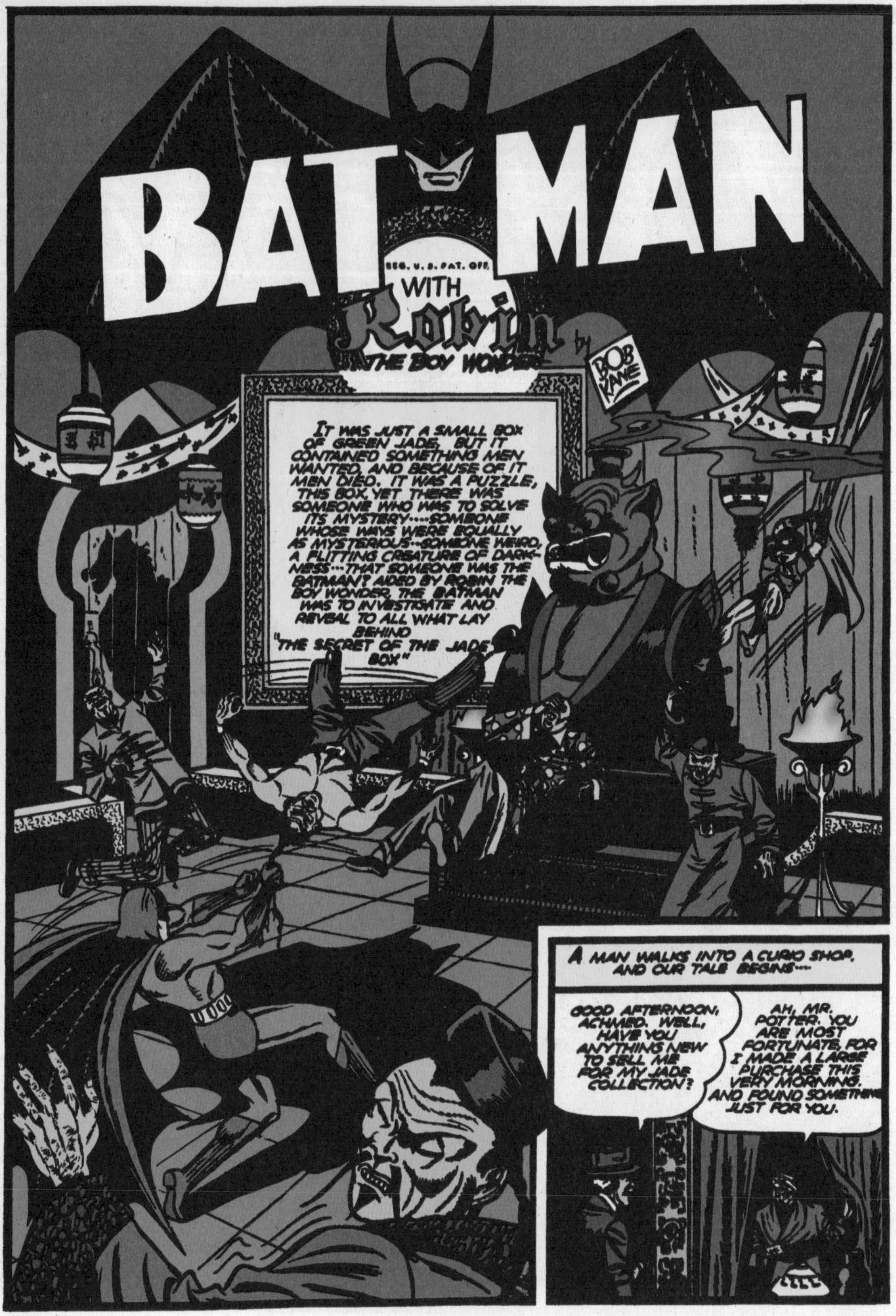
BATMAN
REG. U. S. PAT. OFF.
WITH Robin THE BOY WONDER
by BOB KANE
IT WAS JUST A SMALL BOX OF GREEN JADE, BUT IT CONTAINED SOMETHING MEN WANTED, AND BECAUSE OF IT MEN DIED. IT WAS A PUZZLE, THIS BOX, YET THERE WAS SOMEONE WHO WAS TO SOLVE ITS MYSTERY----SOMEONE WHOSE WAYS WERE EQUALLY AS MYSTERIOUS--SOMEONE WEIRD, A FLITTING CREATURE OF DARKNESS---THAT SOMEONE WAS THE BATMAN! AIDED BY ROBIN THE BOY WONDER, THE BATMAN WAS TO INVESTIGATE AND REVEAL TO ALL WHAT LAY BEHIND "THE SECRET OF THE JADE BOX"
A MAN WALKS INTO A CURIO SHOP, AND OUR TALE BEGINS----
GOOD AFTERNOON, ACHMED. WELL, HAVE YOU ANYTHING NEW TO SELL ME FOR MY JADE COLLECTION?
AH, MR. POTTER. YOU ARE MOST FORTUNATE, FOR I MADE A LARGE PURCHASE THIS VERY MORNING, AND FOUND SOMETHING JUST FOR YOU.

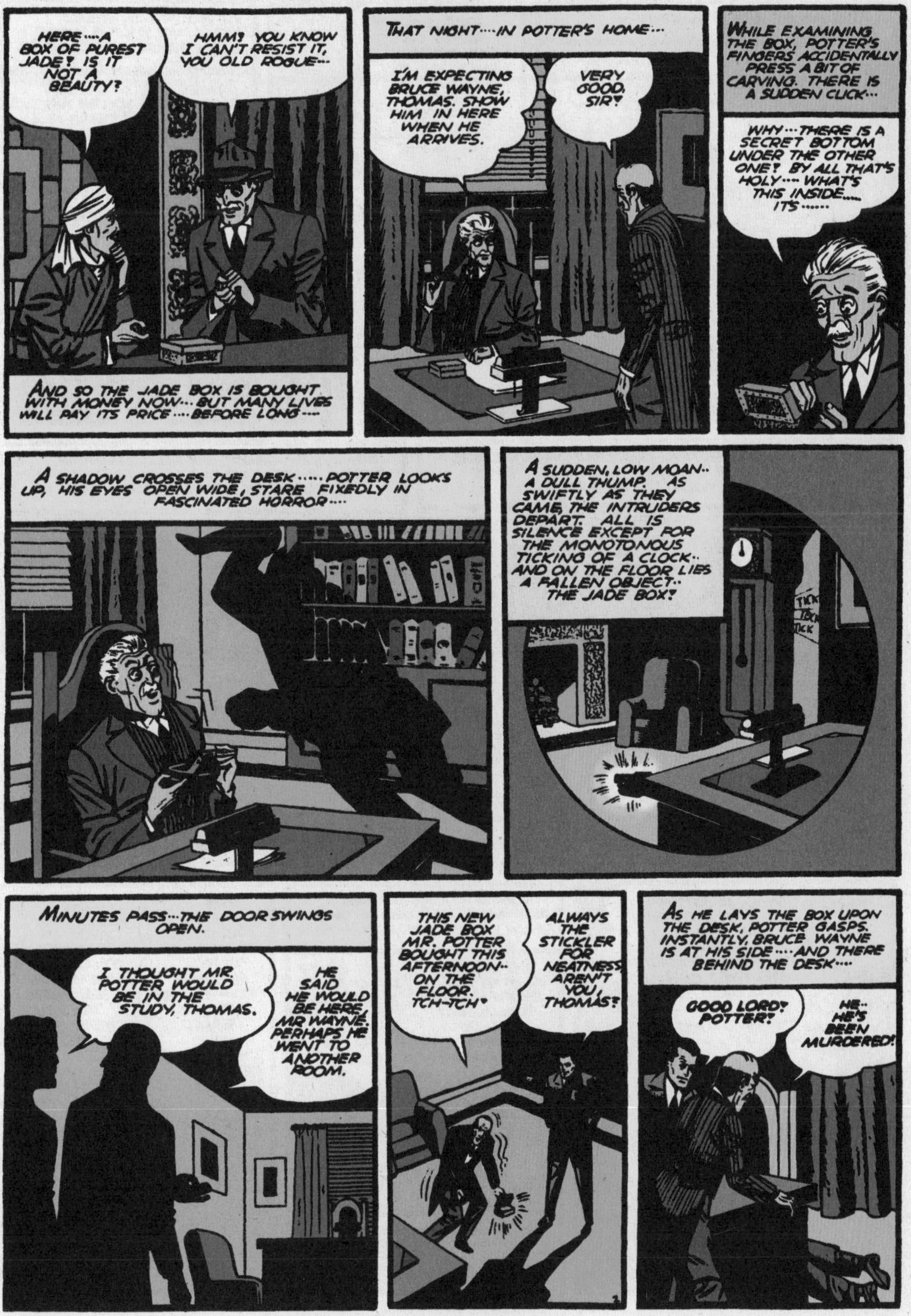
HERE....A BOX OF PUREST JADE! IS IT NOT A BEAUTY?
HMM! YOU KNOW I CAN'T RESIST IT, YOU OLD ROGUE--
AND SO THE JADE BOX IS BOUGHT WITH MONEY NOW... BUT MANY LIVES WILL PAY ITS PRICE....BEFORE LONG----
THAT NIGHT....IN POTTER'S HOME...
I'M EXPECTING BRUCE WAYNE, THOMAS. SHOW HIM IN HERE WHEN HE ARRIVES.
VERY GOOD, SIR!
WHILE EXAMINING THE BOX, POTTER'S FINGERS ACCIDENTALLY PRESS A BIT OF CARVING. THERE IS A SUDDEN CLICK...
WHY...THERE IS A SECRET BOTTOM UNDER THE OTHER ONE! BY ALL THAT'S HOLY.... WHAT'S THIS INSIDE..... IT'S......
A SHADOW CROSSES THE DESK..... POTTER LOOKS UP, HIS EYES OPEN WIDE, STARE FIXEDLY IN FASCINATED HORROR....
A SUDDEN, LOW MOAN.. A DULL THUMP. AS SWIFTLY AS THEY CAME, THE INTRUDERS DEPART. ALL IS SILENCE EXCEPT FOR THE MONOTONOUS TICKING OF A CLOCK.. AND ON THE FLOOR LIES A FALLEN OBJECT.. THE JADE BOX!
TKK
TKK
TKK
MINUTES PASS...THE DOOR SWINGS OPEN.
I THOUGHT MR. POTTER WOULD BE IN THE STUDY, THOMAS.
HE SAID HE WOULD BE HERE, MR WAYNE. PERHAPS HE WENT TO ANOTHER ROOM.
THIS NEW JADE BOX MR. POTTER BOUGHT THIS AFTERNOON.. ON THE FLOOR. TCH-TCH!
ALWAYS THE STICKLER FOR NEATNESS AREN'T YOU, THOMAS?
AS HE LAYS THE BOX UPON THE DESK, POTTER GASPS. INSTANTLY, BRUCE WAYNE IS AT HIS SIDE....AND THERE BEHIND THE DESK....
GOOD LORD! POTTER!
HE.. HE'S BEEN MURDERED!

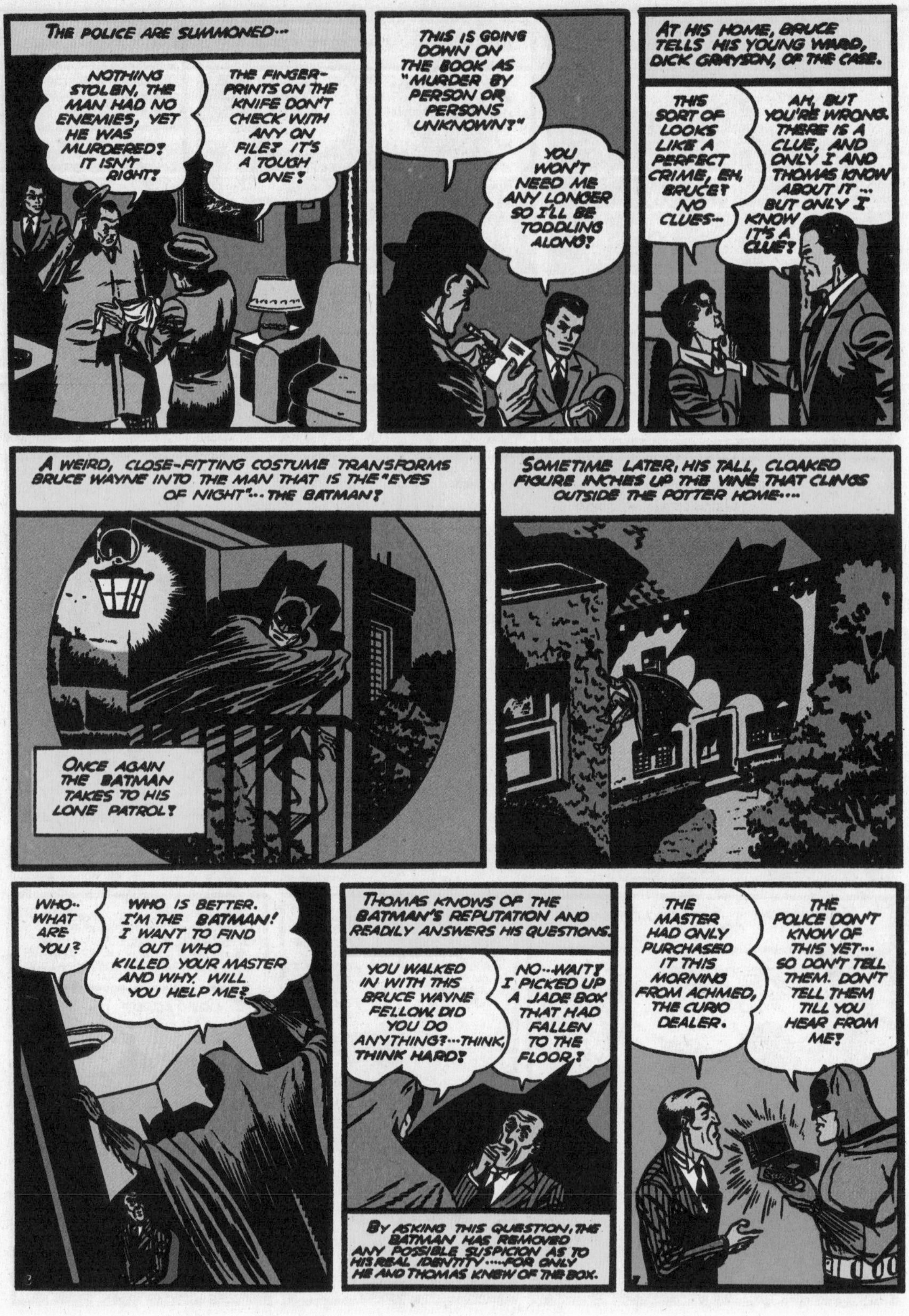
THE POLICE ARE SUMMONED...
NOTHING STOLEN, THE MAN HAD NO ENEMIES, YET HE WAS MURDERED! IT ISN'T RIGHT!
THE FINGER-PRINTS ON THE KNIFE DON'T CHECK WITH ANY ON FILE! IT'S A TOUGH ONE!
THIS IS GOING DOWN ON THE BOOK AS "MURDER BY PERSON OR PERSONS UNKNOWN!"
YOU WON'T NEED ME ANY LONGER SO I'LL BE TODDLING ALONG!
AT HIS HOME, BRUCE TELLS HIS YOUNG WARD, DICK GRAYSON, OF THE CASE.
THIS SORT OF LOOKS LIKE A PERFECT CRIME, EH, BRUCE? NO CLUES...
AH, BUT YOU'RE WRONG. THERE IS A CLUE, AND ONLY I AND THOMAS KNOW ABOUT IT... BUT ONLY I KNOW IT'S A CLUE!
A WEIRD, CLOSE-FITTING COSTUME TRANSFORMS BRUCE WAYNE INTO THE MAN THAT IS THE "EYES OF NIGHT"... THE BATMAN!
ONCE AGAIN THE BATMAN TAKES TO HIS LONE PATROL!
SOMETIME LATER, HIS TALL, CLOAKED FIGURE INCHES UP THE VINE THAT CLINGS OUTSIDE THE POTTER HOME....
WHO-- WHAT ARE YOU?
WHO IS BETTER. I'M THE BATMAN! I WANT TO FIND OUT WHO KILLED YOUR MASTER AND WHY. WILL YOU HELP ME?
THOMAS KNOWS OF THE BATMAN'S REPUTATION AND READILY ANSWERS HIS QUESTIONS.
YOU WALKED IN WITH THIS BRUCE WAYNE FELLOW. DID YOU DO ANYTHING?...THINK, THINK HARD!
NO...WAIT! I PICKED UP A JADE BOX THAT HAD FALLEN TO THE FLOOR!
BY ASKING THIS QUESTION, THE BATMAN HAS REMOVED ANY POSSIBLE SUSPICION AS TO HIS REAL IDENTITY ....FOR ONLY HE AND THOMAS KNEW OF THE BOX.
THE MASTER HAD ONLY PURCHASED IT THIS MORNING FROM ACHMED, THE CURIO DEALER.
THE POLICE DON'T KNOW OF THIS YET... SO DON'T TELL THEM. DON'T TELL THEM TILL YOU HEAR FROM ME!

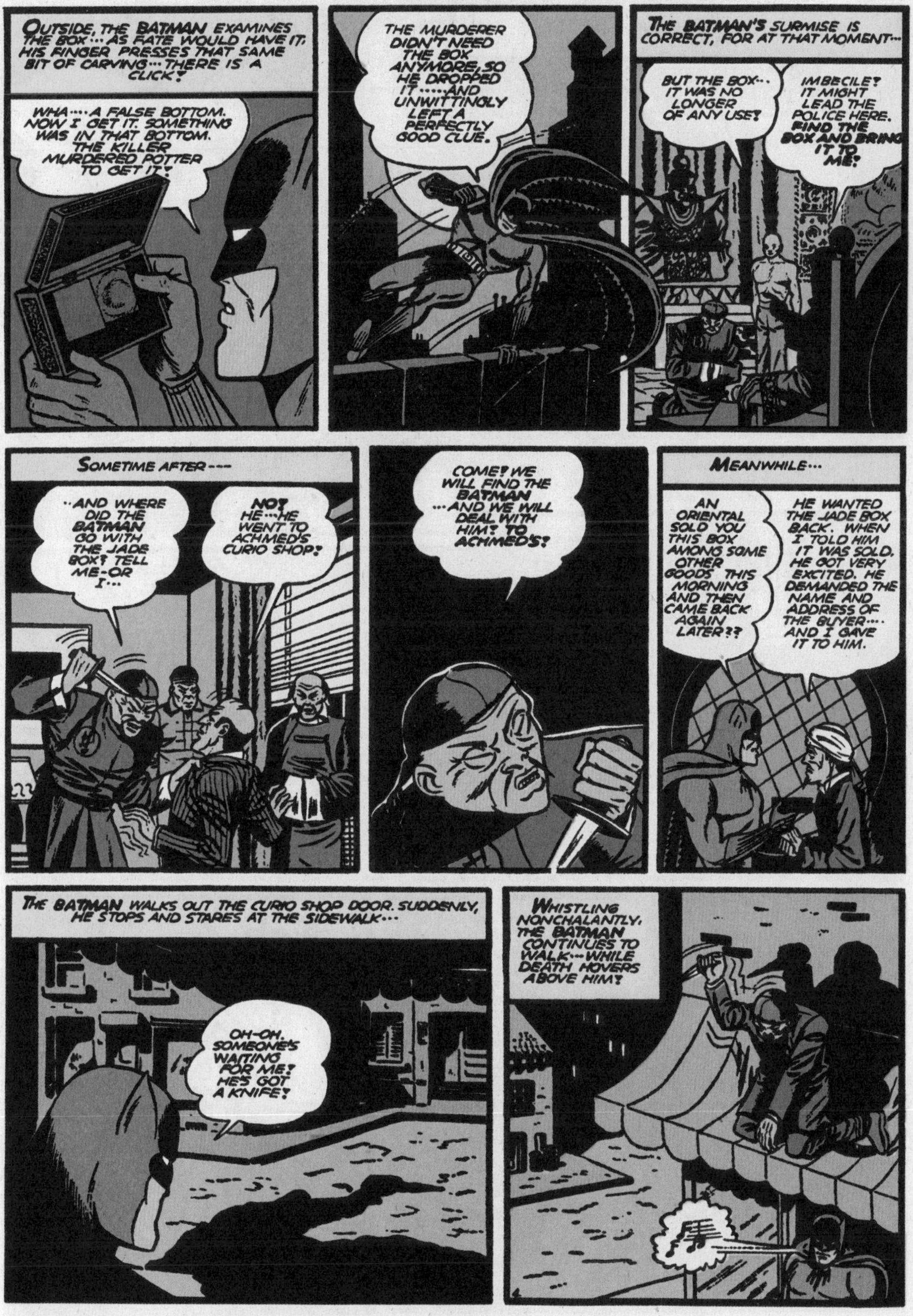

OUTSIDE, THE BATMAN EXAMINES THE BOX... AS FATE WOULD HAVE IT, HIS FINGER PRESSES THAT SAME BIT OF CARVING... THERE IS A CLICK!
WHA.... A FALSE BOTTOM. NOW I GET IT. SOMETHING WAS IN THAT BOTTOM. THE KILLER MURDERED POTTER TO GET IT!
THE MURDERER DIDN'T NEED THE BOX ANYMORE, SO HE DROPPED IT.....AND UNWITTINGLY LEFT A PERFECTLY GOOD CLUE.
THE BATMAN'S SURMISE IS CORRECT, FOR AT THAT MOMENT...
BUT THE BOX.. IT WAS NO LONGER OF ANY USE!
IMBECILE! IT MIGHT LEAD THE POLICE HERE. FIND THE BOX AND BRING IT TO ME!
SOMETIME AFTER---
..AND WHERE DID THE BATMAN GO WITH THE JADE BOX? TELL ME-OR I...
NO! HE...HE WENT TO ACHMED'S CURIO SHOP!
COME! WE WILL FIND THE BATMAN ...AND WE WILL DEAL WITH HIM! TO ACHMED'S!
MEANWHILE...
AN ORIENTAL SOLD YOU THIS BOX AMONG SOME OTHER GOODS THIS MORNING AND THEN CAME BACK AGAIN LATER??
HE WANTED THE JADE BOX BACK. WHEN I TOLD HIM IT WAS SOLD, HE GOT VERY EXCITED. HE DEMANDED THE NAME AND ADDRESS OF THE BUYER... AND I GAVE IT TO HIM.
THE BATMAN WALKS OUT THE CURIO SHOP DOOR. SUDDENLY, HE STOPS AND STARES AT THE SIDEWALK...
OH-OH. SOMEONE'S WAITING FOR ME! HE'S GOT A KNIFE!
WHISTLING NONCHALANTLY, THE BATMAN CONTINUES TO WALK...WHILE DEATH HOVERS ABOVE HIM!

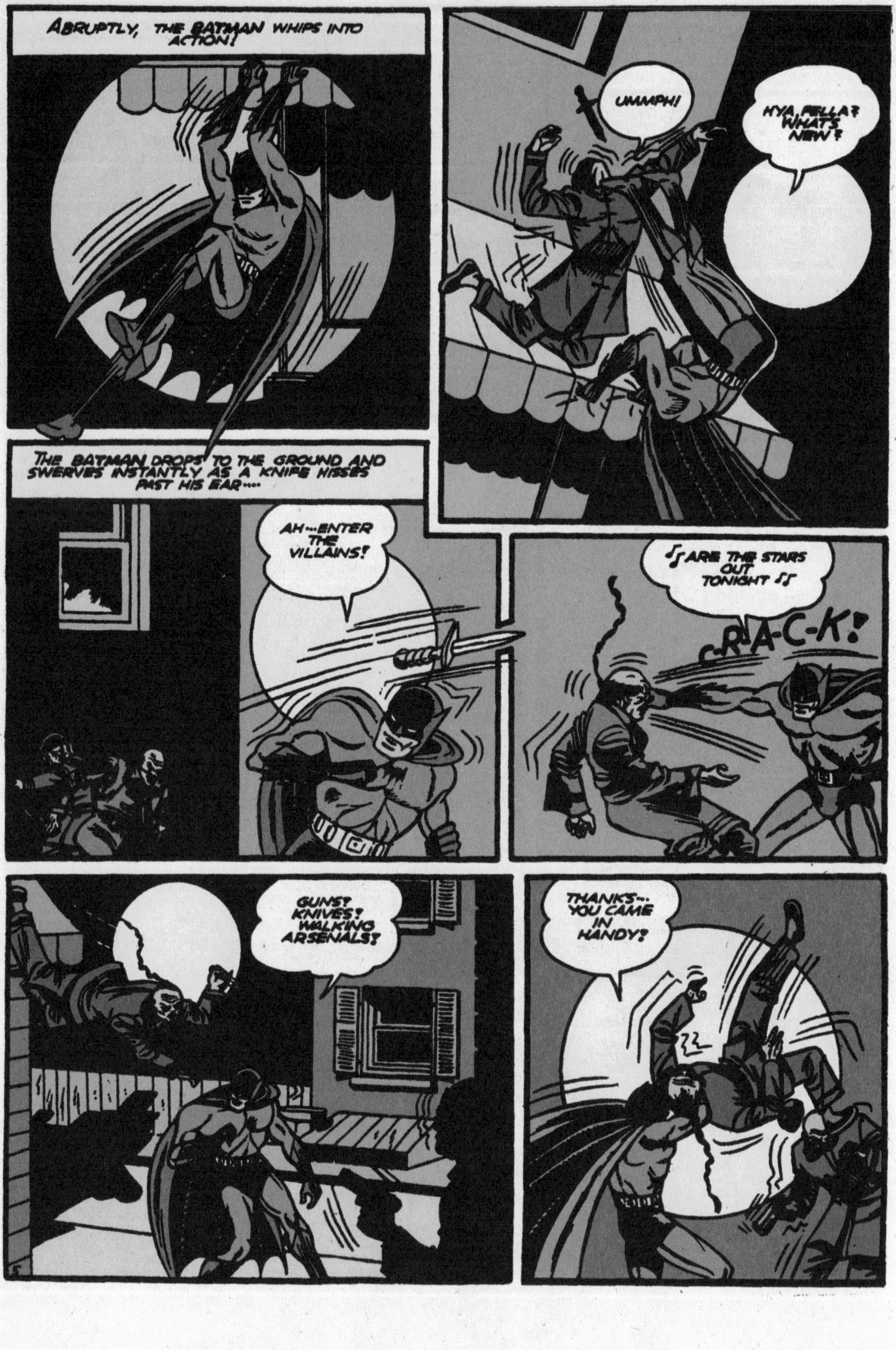
ABRUPTLY, THE BATMAN WHIPS INTO ACTION!
UMMPH!
HYA FELLA? WHAT'S NEW?
THE BATMAN DROPS TO THE GROUND AND SWERVES INSTANTLY AS A KNIFE HISSES PAST HIS EAR....
AH...ENTER THE VILLAINS!
♫ ARE THE STARS OUT TONIGHT ♫
C-R-A-C-K!
GUNS? KNIVES? WALKING ARSENALS?
THANKS... YOU CAME IN HANDY?

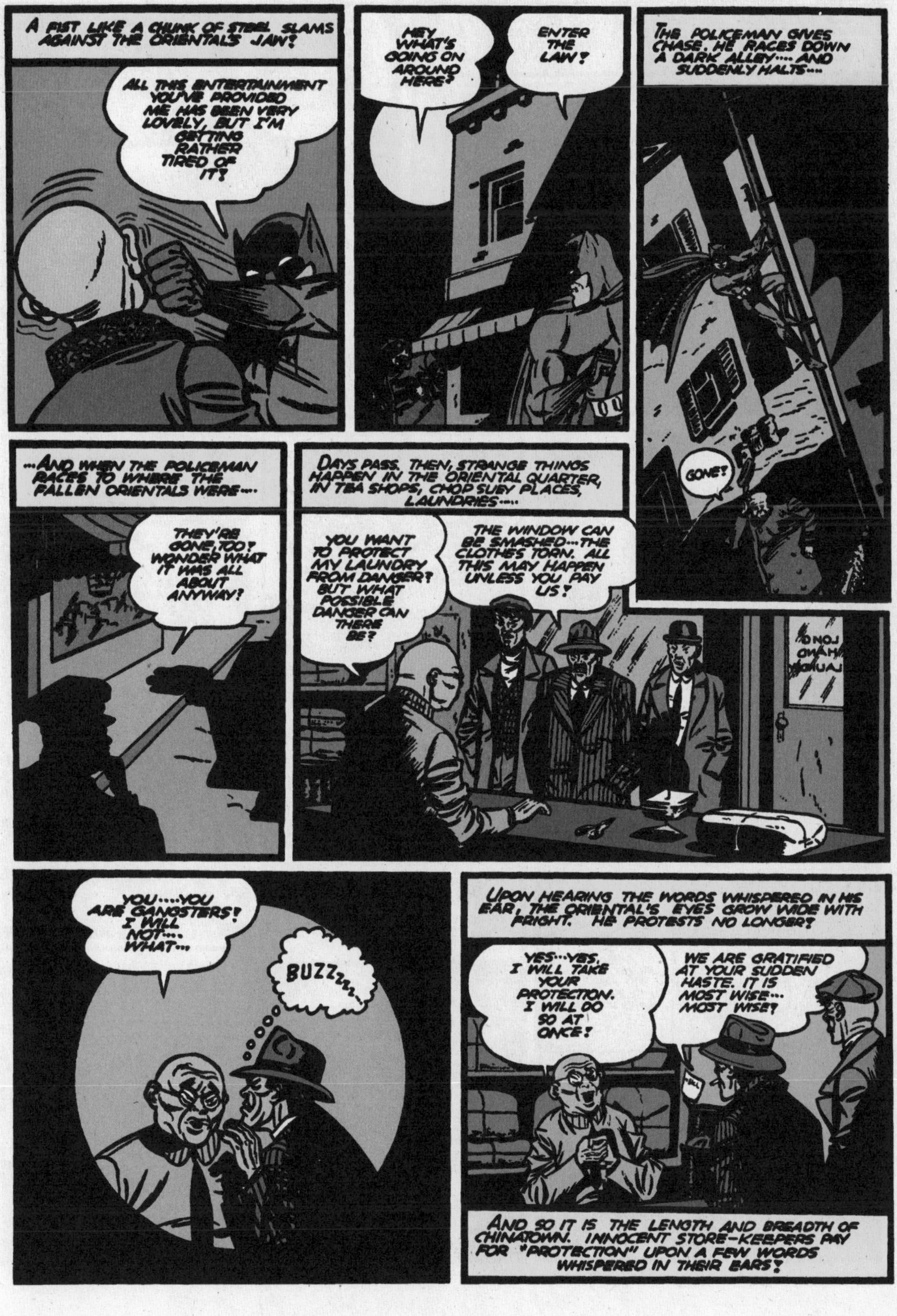
A FIST LIKE A CHUNK OF STEEL SLAMS AGAINST THE ORIENTAL'S JAW!
ALL THIS ENTERTAINMENT YOU'VE PROVIDED ME HAS BEEN VERY LOVELY, BUT I'M GETTING RATHER TIRED OF IT!
HEY WHAT'S GOING ON AROUND HERE?
ENTER THE LAW!
THE POLICEMAN GIVES CHASE. HE RACES DOWN A DARK ALLEY.... AND SUDDENLY HALTS...
GONE?
...AND WHEN THE POLICEMAN RACES TO WHERE THE FALLEN ORIENTALS WERE....
THEY'RE GONE, TOO! WONDER WHAT IT WAS ALL ABOUT ANYWAY?
DAYS PASS. THEN, STRANGE THINGS HAPPEN IN THE ORIENTAL QUARTER, IN TEA SHOPS, CHOP SUEY PLACES, LAUNDRIES....
YOU WANT TO PROTECT MY LAUNDRY FROM DANGER? BUT WHAT POSSIBLE DANGER CAN THERE BE?
THE WINDOW CAN BE SMASHED...THE CLOTHES TORN. ALL THIS MAY HAPPEN UNLESS YOU PAY US!
YOU....YOU ARE GANGSTERS! I WILL NOT.... WHAT...
BUZZzz..
UPON HEARING THE WORDS WHISPERED IN HIS EAR, THE ORIENTAL'S EYES GROW WIDE WITH FRIGHT. HE PROTESTS NO LONGER!
YES...YES. I WILL TAKE YOUR PROTECTION. I WILL DO SO AT ONCE!
WE ARE GRATIFIED AT YOUR SUDDEN HASTE. IT IS MOST WISE... MOST WISE!
AND SO IT IS THE LENGTH AND BREADTH OF CHINATOWN. INNOCENT STORE-KEEPERS PAY FOR "PROTECTION" UPON A FEW WORDS WHISPERED IN THEIR EARS!

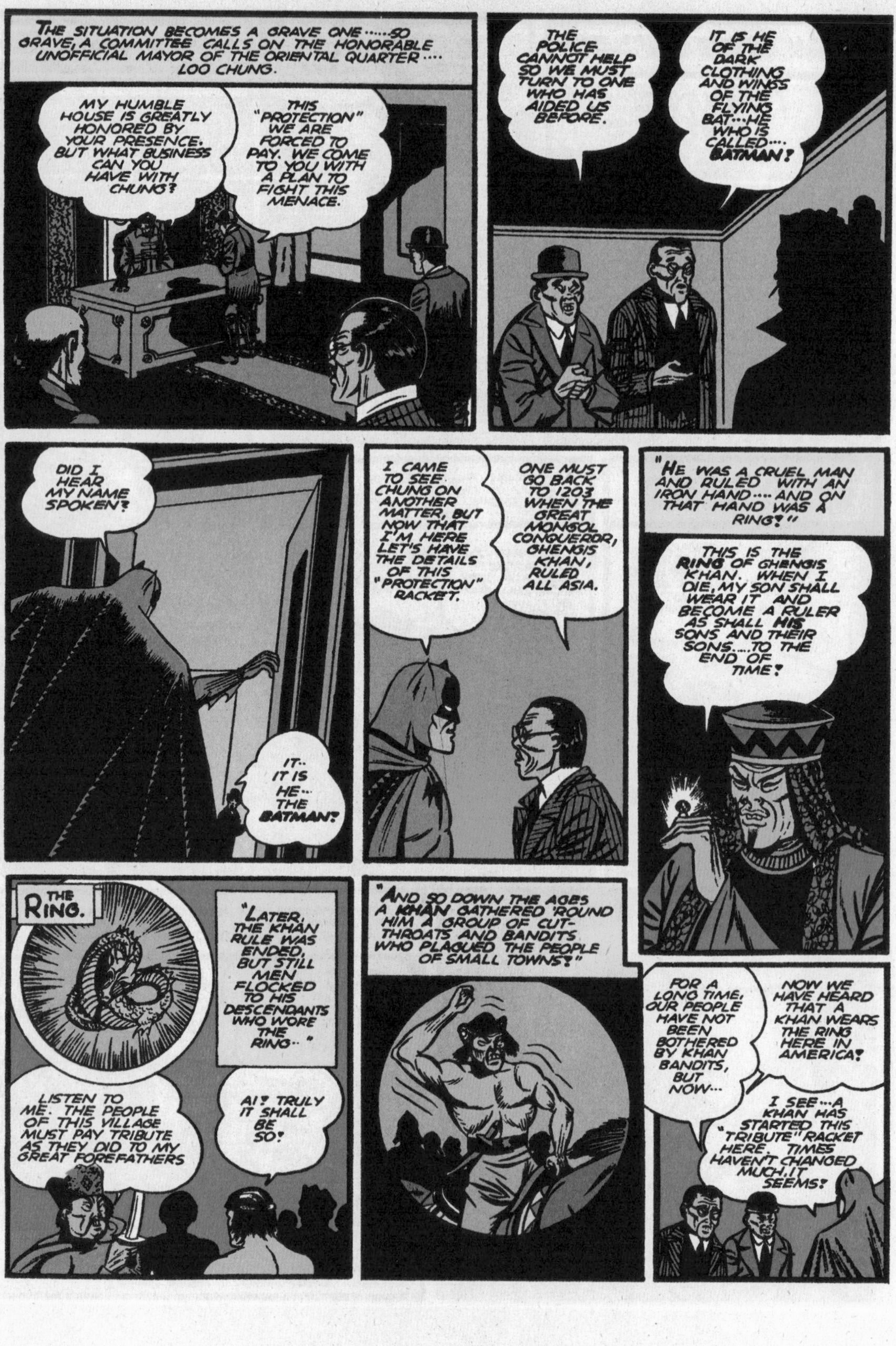
THE SITUATION BECOMES A GRAVE ONE......SO GRAVE, A COMMITTEE CALLS ON THE HONORABLE UNOFFICIAL MAYOR OF THE ORIENTAL QUARTER.... LOO CHUNG.
MY HUMBLE HOUSE IS GREATLY HONORED BY YOUR PRESENCE. BUT WHAT BUSINESS CAN YOU HAVE WITH CHUNG?
THIS "PROTECTION" WE ARE FORCED TO PAY. WE COME TO YOU WITH A PLAN TO FIGHT THIS MENACE.
THE POLICE CANNOT HELP SO WE MUST TURN TO ONE WHO HAS AIDED US BEFORE.
IT IS HE OF THE DARK CLOTHING AND WINGS OF THE FLYING BAT...HE WHO IS CALLED.... BATMAN!
DID I HEAR MY NAME SPOKEN?
IT.. IT IS HE.. THE BATMAN!
I CAME TO SEE CHUNG ON ANOTHER MATTER, BUT NOW THAT I'M HERE LET'S HAVE THE DETAILS OF THIS "PROTECTION" RACKET.
ONE MUST GO BACK TO 1203 WHEN THE GREAT MONGOL CONQUEROR, GHENGIS KHAN, RULED ALL ASIA.
"HE WAS A CRUEL MAN AND RULED WITH AN IRON HAND.... AND ON THAT HAND WAS A RING!"
THIS IS THE RING OF GHENGIS KHAN. WHEN I DIE, MY SON SHALL WEAR IT AND BECOME A RULER AS SHALL HIS SONS AND THEIR SONS.....TO THE END OF TIME!
THE RING.
"LATER, THE KHAN RULE WAS ENDED, BUT STILL MEN FLOCKED TO HIS DESCENDANTS WHO WORE THE RING.."
LISTEN TO ME. THE PEOPLE OF THIS VILLAGE MUST PAY TRIBUTE AS THEY DID TO MY GREAT FOREFATHERS
AI! TRULY IT SHALL BE SO!
"AND SO DOWN THE AGES A KHAN GATHERED 'ROUND HIM A GROUP OF CUT-THROATS AND BANDITS WHO PLAGUED THE PEOPLE OF SMALL TOWNS!"
FOR A LONG TIME, OUR PEOPLE HAVE NOT BEEN BOTHERED BY KHAN BANDITS, BUT NOW...
NOW WE HAVE HEARD THAT A KHAN WEARS THE RING HERE IN AMERICA!
I SEE...A KHAN HAS STARTED THIS "TRIBUTE" RACKET HERE. TIMES HAVEN'T CHANGED MUCH, IT SEEMS!

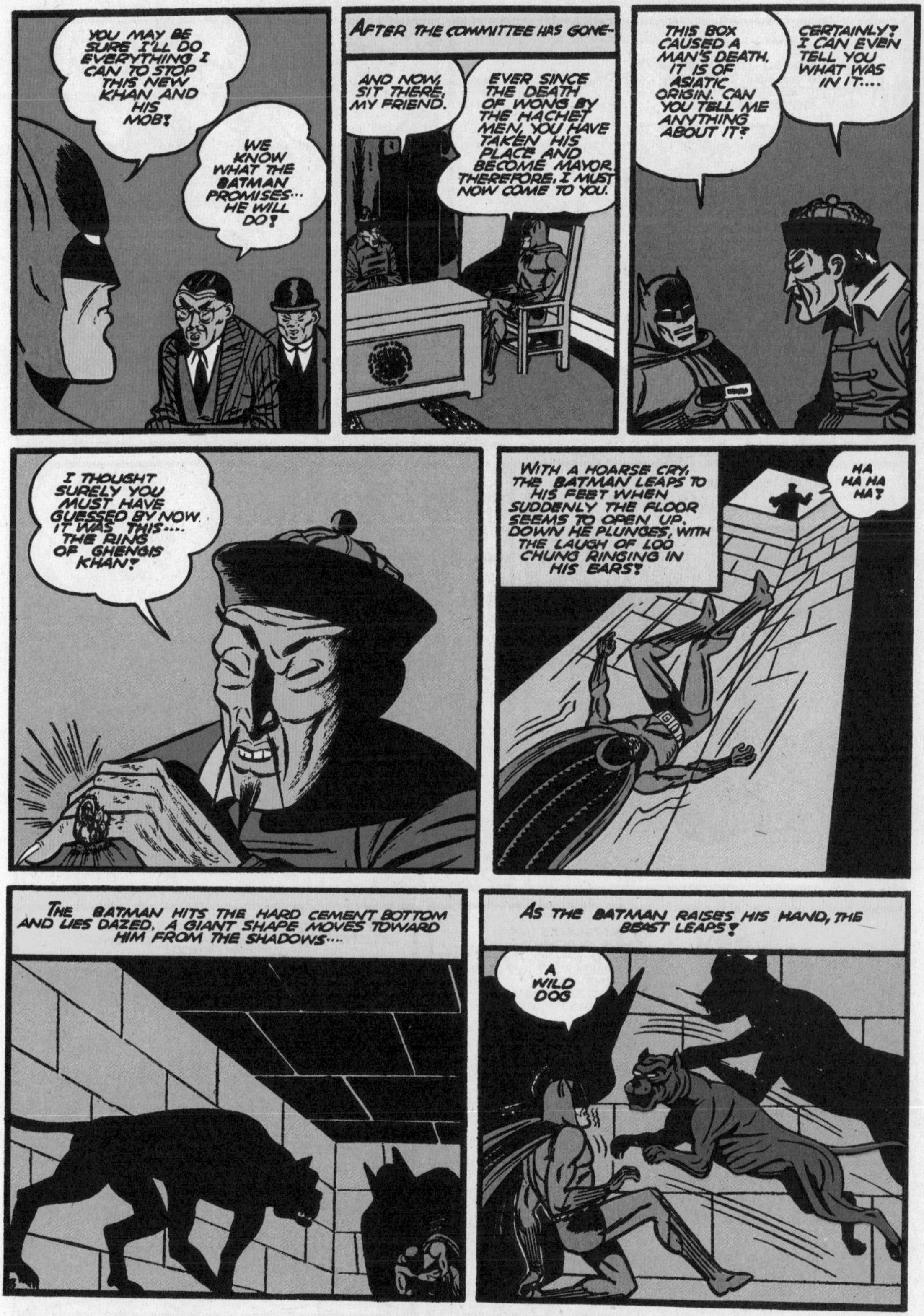
YOU MAY BE SURE I'LL DO EVERYTHING I CAN TO STOP THIS NEW KHAN AND HIS MOB!
WE KNOW WHAT THE BATMAN PROMISES... HE WILL DO!
AFTER THE COMMITTEE HAS GONE-
AND NOW, SIT THERE, MY FRIEND.
EVER SINCE THE DEATH OF WONG BY THE HACHET MEN, YOU HAVE TAKEN HIS PLACE AND BECOME MAYOR. THEREFORE, I MUST NOW COME TO YOU.
THIS BOX CAUSED A MAN'S DEATH. IT IS OF ASIATIC ORIGIN. CAN YOU TELL ME ANYTHING ABOUT IT?
CERTAINLY! I CAN EVEN TELL YOU WHAT WAS IN IT....
I THOUGHT SURELY YOU MUST HAVE GUESSED BY NOW. IT WAS THIS.... THE RING OF GHENGIS KHAN!
WITH A HOARSE CRY, THE BATMAN LEAPS TO HIS FEET WHEN SUDDENLY THE FLOOR SEEMS TO OPEN UP. DOWN HE PLUNGES, WITH THE LAUGH OF LOO CHUNG RINGING IN HIS EARS!
HA HA HA HA!
THE BATMAN HITS THE HARD CEMENT BOTTOM AND LIES DAZED. A GIANT SHAPE MOVES TOWARD HIM FROM THE SHADOWS....
AS THE BATMAN RAISES HIS HAND, THE BEAST LEAPS!
A WILD DOG

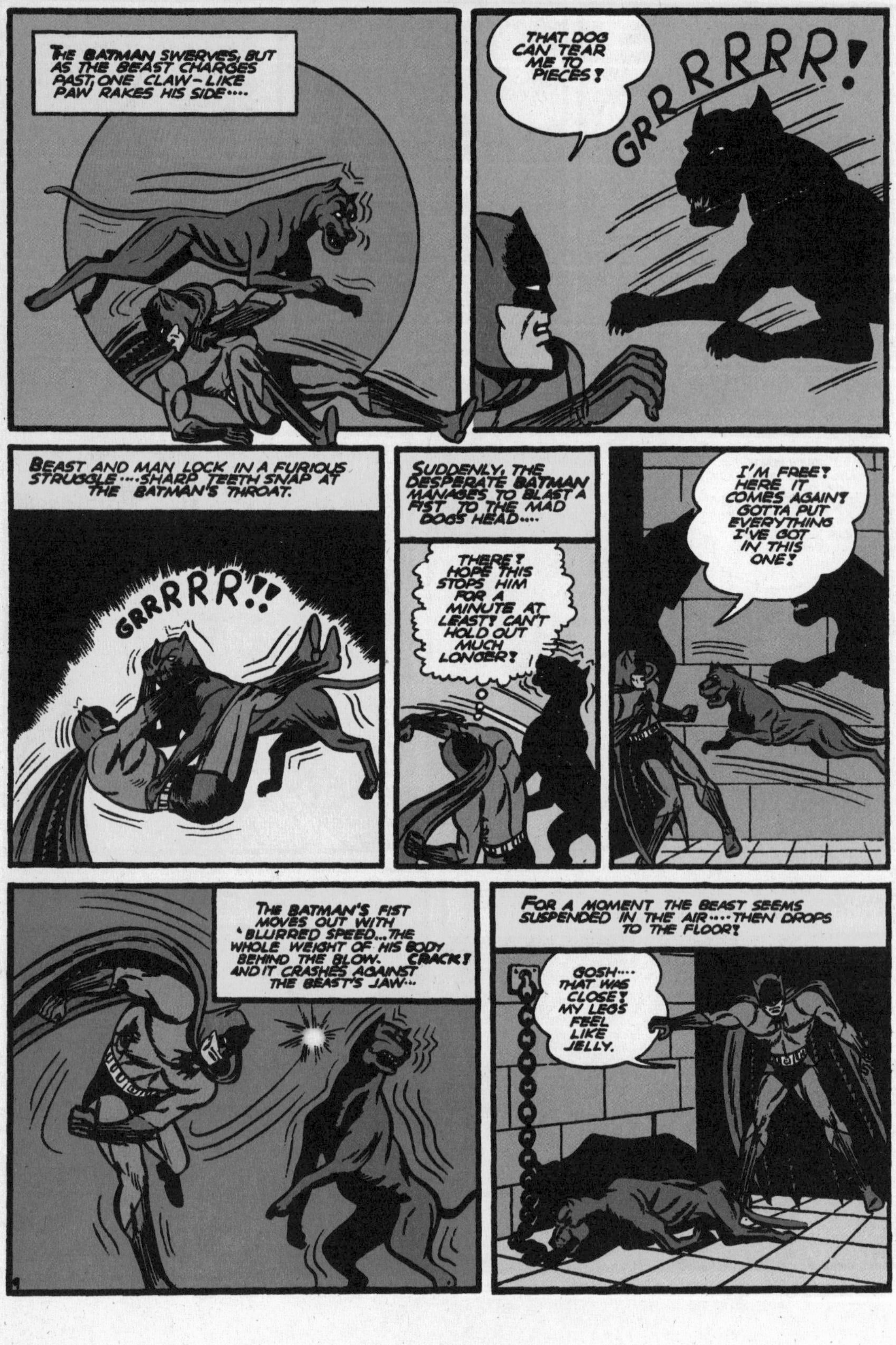
THE BATMAN SWERVES, BUT AS THE BEAST CHARGES PAST, ONE CLAW-LIKE PAW RAKES HIS SIDE....
THAT DOG CAN TEAR ME TO PIECES!
GRRRRRRR!
BEAST AND MAN LOCK IN A FURIOUS STRUGGLE....SHARP TEETH SNAP AT THE BATMAN'S THROAT.
GRRRRR!!
SUDDENLY, THE DESPERATE BATMAN MANAGES TO BLAST A FIST TO THE MAD DOG'S HEAD....
THERE! HOPE THIS STOPS HIM FOR A MINUTE AT LEAST! CAN'T HOLD OUT MUCH LONGER!
I'M FREE! HERE IT COMES AGAIN! GOTTA PUT EVERYTHING I'VE GOT IN THIS ONE!
THE BATMAN'S FIST MOVES OUT WITH BLURRED SPEED...THE WHOLE WEIGHT OF HIS BODY BEHIND THE BLOW. CRACK! AND IT CRASHES AGAINST THE BEAST'S JAW...
FOR A MOMENT THE BEAST SEEMS SUSPENDED IN THE AIR....THEN DROPS TO THE FLOOR!
GOSH.... THAT WAS CLOSE! MY LEGS FEEL LIKE JELLY.

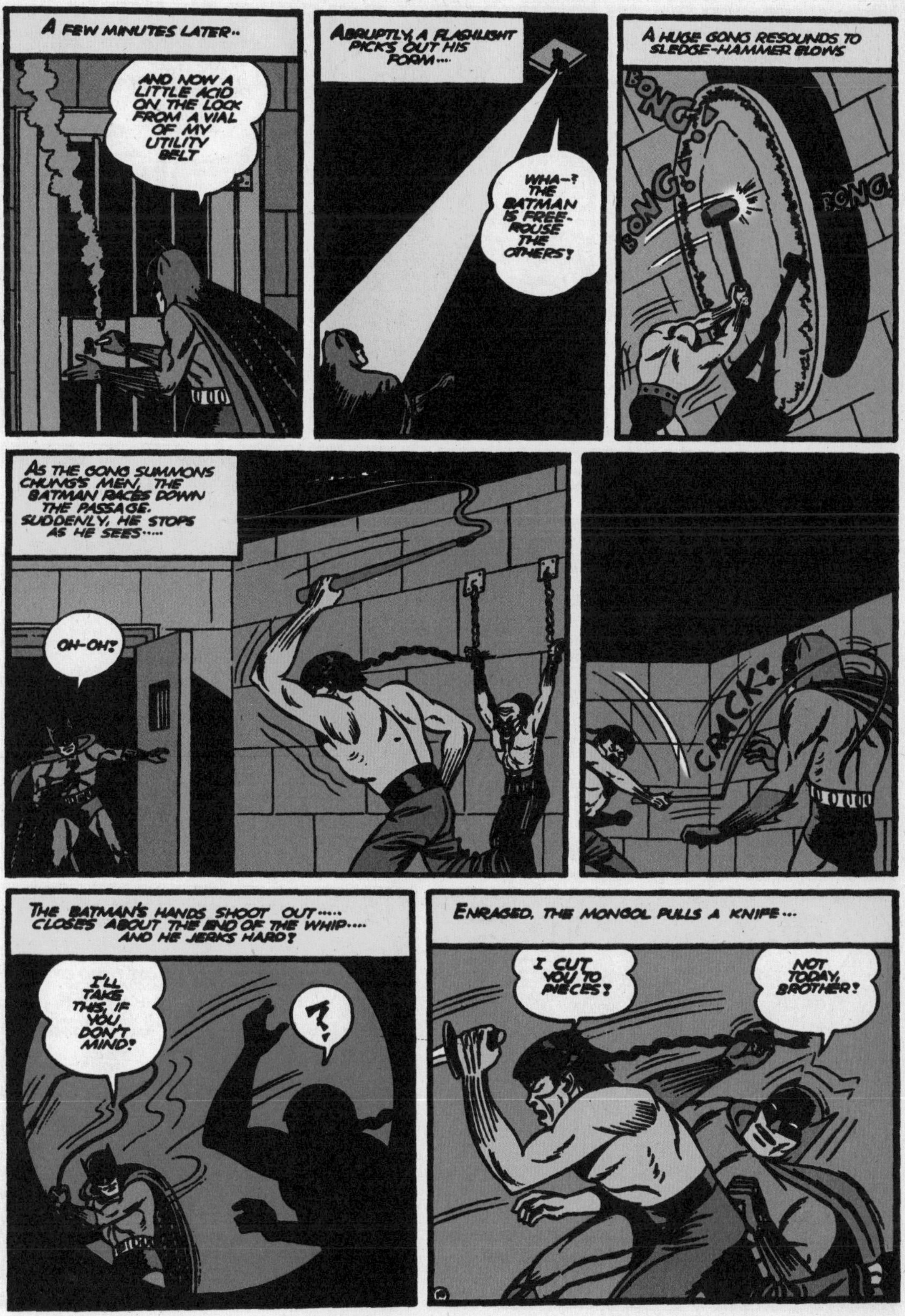
A FEW MINUTES LATER..
AND NOW A LITTLE ACID ON THE LOCK FROM A VIAL OF MY UTILITY BELT
ABRUPTLY, A FLASHLIGHT PICKS OUT HIS FORM....
WHA-? THE BATMAN IS FREE-ROUSE THE OTHERS!
A HUGE GONG RESOUNDS TO SLEDGE-HAMMER BLOWS
BONG!
BONG!
BONG!
BONG!
AS THE GONG SUMMONS CHUNG'S MEN, THE BATMAN RACES DOWN THE PASSAGE. SUDDENLY, HE STOPS AS HE SEES....
OH-OH!
CRACK!
THE BATMAN'S HANDS SHOOT OUT..... CLOSES ABOUT THE END OF THE WHIP.... AND HE JERKS HARD!
I'LL TAKE THIS, IF YOU DON'T MIND!
?
ENRAGED, THE MONGOL PULLS A KNIFE...
I CUT YOU TO PIECES!
NOT TODAY, BROTHER!

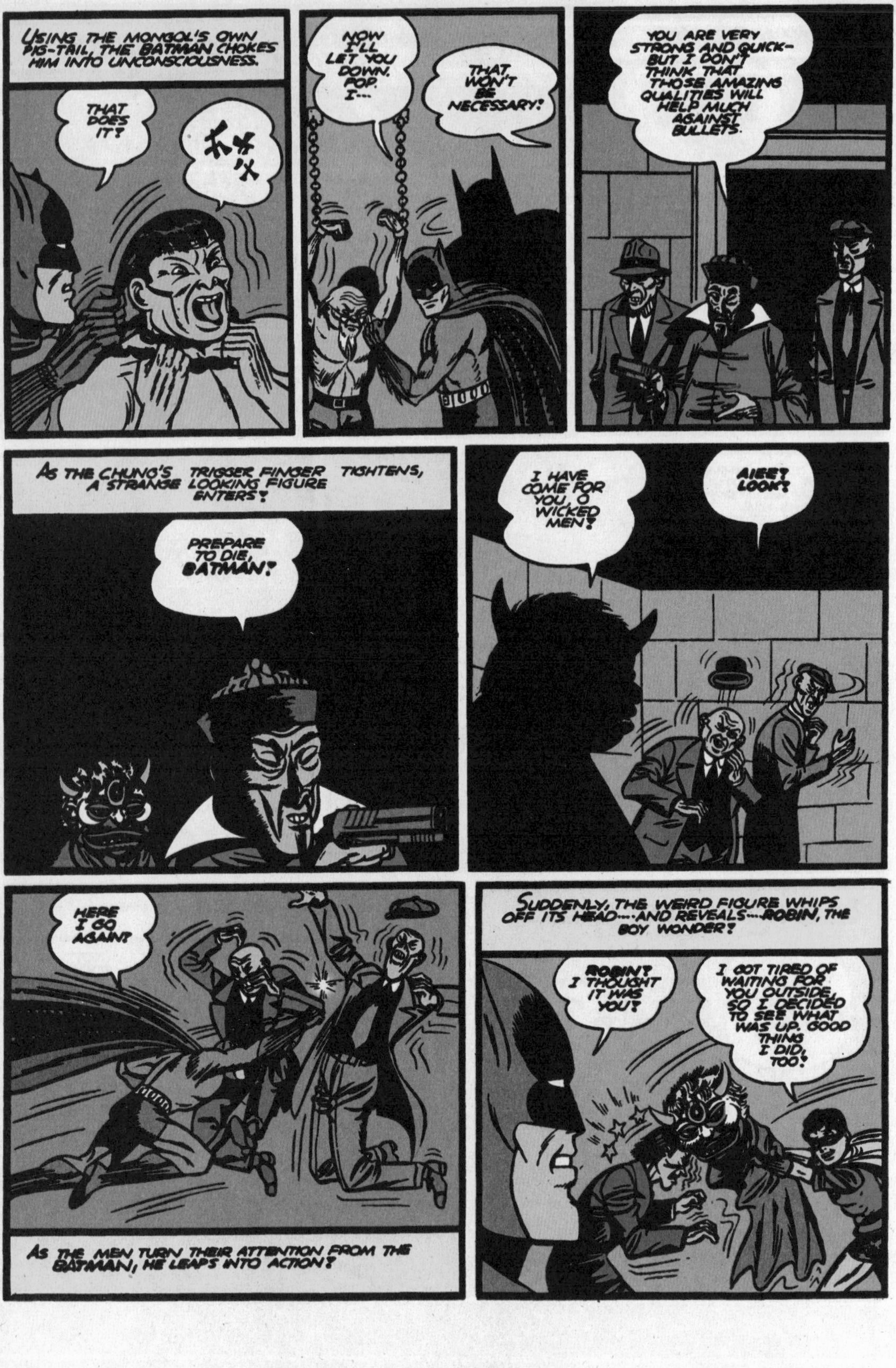
USING THE MONGOL'S OWN PIG-TAIL, THE BATMAN CHOKES HIM INTO UNCONSCIOUSNESS.
THAT DOES IT!
NOW I'LL LET YOU DOWN, POP. I---
THAT WON'T BE NECESSARY!
YOU ARE VERY STRONG AND QUICK-- BUT I DON'T THINK THAT THOSE AMAZING QUALITIES WILL HELP MUCH AGAINST BULLETS.
AS THE CHUNG'S TRIGGER FINGER TIGHTENS, A STRANGE LOOKING FIGURE ENTERS!
PREPARE TO DIE, BATMAN!
I HAVE COME FOR YOU, O WICKED MEN!
AIEE! LOOK!
HERE I GO AGAIN!
AS THE MEN TURN THEIR ATTENTION FROM THE BATMAN, HE LEAPS INTO ACTION!
SUDDENLY, THE WEIRD FIGURE WHIPS OFF ITS HEAD---AND REVEALS---ROBIN, THE BOY WONDER!
ROBIN! I THOUGHT IT WAS YOU!
I GOT TIRED OF WAITING FOR YOU OUTSIDE, SO I DECIDED TO SEE WHAT WAS UP. GOOD THING I DID, TOO!

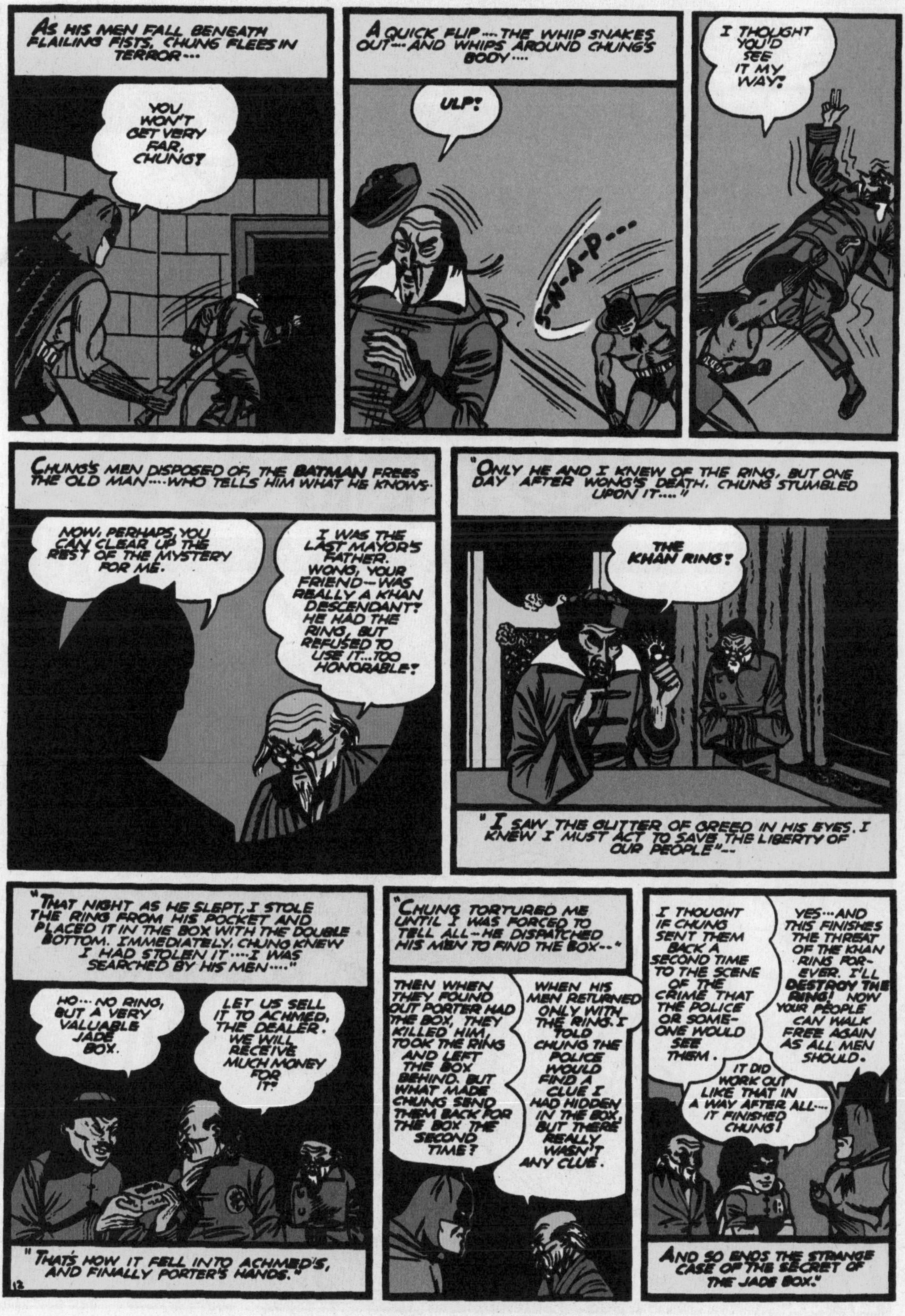
AS HIS MEN FALL BENEATH FLAILING FISTS, CHUNG FLEES IN TERROR...
YOU WON'T GET VERY FAR, CHUNG!
A QUICK FLIP.... THE WHIP SNAKES OUT... AND WHIPS AROUND CHUNG'S BODY....
ULP!
S-N-A-P...
I THOUGHT YOU'D SEE IT MY WAY!
CHUNG'S MEN DISPOSED OF, THE BATMAN FREES THE OLD MAN.... WHO TELLS HIM WHAT HE KNOWS.
NOW, PERHAPS YOU CAN CLEAR UP THE REST OF THE MYSTERY FOR ME.
I WAS THE LAST MAYOR'S FATHER. WONG, YOUR FRIEND--WAS REALLY A KHAN DESCENDANT! HE HAD THE RING, BUT REFUSED TO USE IT...TOO HONORABLE!
"ONLY HE AND I KNEW OF THE RING, BUT ONE DAY AFTER WONG'S DEATH, CHUNG STUMBLED UPON IT...."
THE KHAN RING!
"I SAW THE GLITTER OF GREED IN HIS EYES. I KNEW I MUST ACT TO SAVE THE LIBERTY OF OUR PEOPLE"--
"THAT NIGHT AS HE SLEPT, I STOLE THE RING FROM HIS POCKET AND PLACED IT IN THE BOX WITH THE DOUBLE BOTTOM. IMMEDIATELY, CHUNG KNEW I HAD STOLEN IT.... I WAS SEARCHED BY HIS MEN...."
HO... NO RING, BUT A VERY VALUABLE JADE BOX.
LET US SELL IT TO ACHMED, THE DEALER. WE WILL RECEIVE MUCH MONEY FOR IT!
"THAT'S HOW IT FELL INTO ACHMED'S, AND FINALLY PORTER'S HANDS."
12
"CHUNG TORTURED ME UNTIL I WAS FORCED TO TELL ALL--HE DISPATCHED HIS MEN TO FIND THE BOX--"
THEN WHEN THEY FOUND OUT PORTER HAD THE BOX, THEY KILLED HIM, TOOK THE RING AND LEFT THE BOX BEHIND. BUT WHAT MADE CHUNG SEND THEM BACK FOR THE BOX THE SECOND TIME?
WHEN HIS MEN RETURNED ONLY WITH THE RING, I TOLD CHUNG THE POLICE WOULD FIND A CLUE I HAD HIDDEN IN THE BOX, BUT THERE REALLY WASN'T ANY CLUE.
I THOUGHT IF CHUNG SENT THEM BACK A SECOND TIME TO THE SCENE OF THE CRIME THAT THE POLICE OR SOME-ONE WOULD SEE THEM.
YES...AND THIS FINISHES THE THREAT OF THE KHAN RING FOR-EVER. I'LL DESTROY THE RING! NOW YOUR PEOPLE CAN WALK FREE AGAIN AS ALL MEN SHOULD.
IT DID WORK OUT LIKE THAT IN A WAY AFTER ALL.... IT FINISHED CHUNG!
AND SO ENDS THE STRANGE CASE OF THE SECRET OF THE JADE BOX."

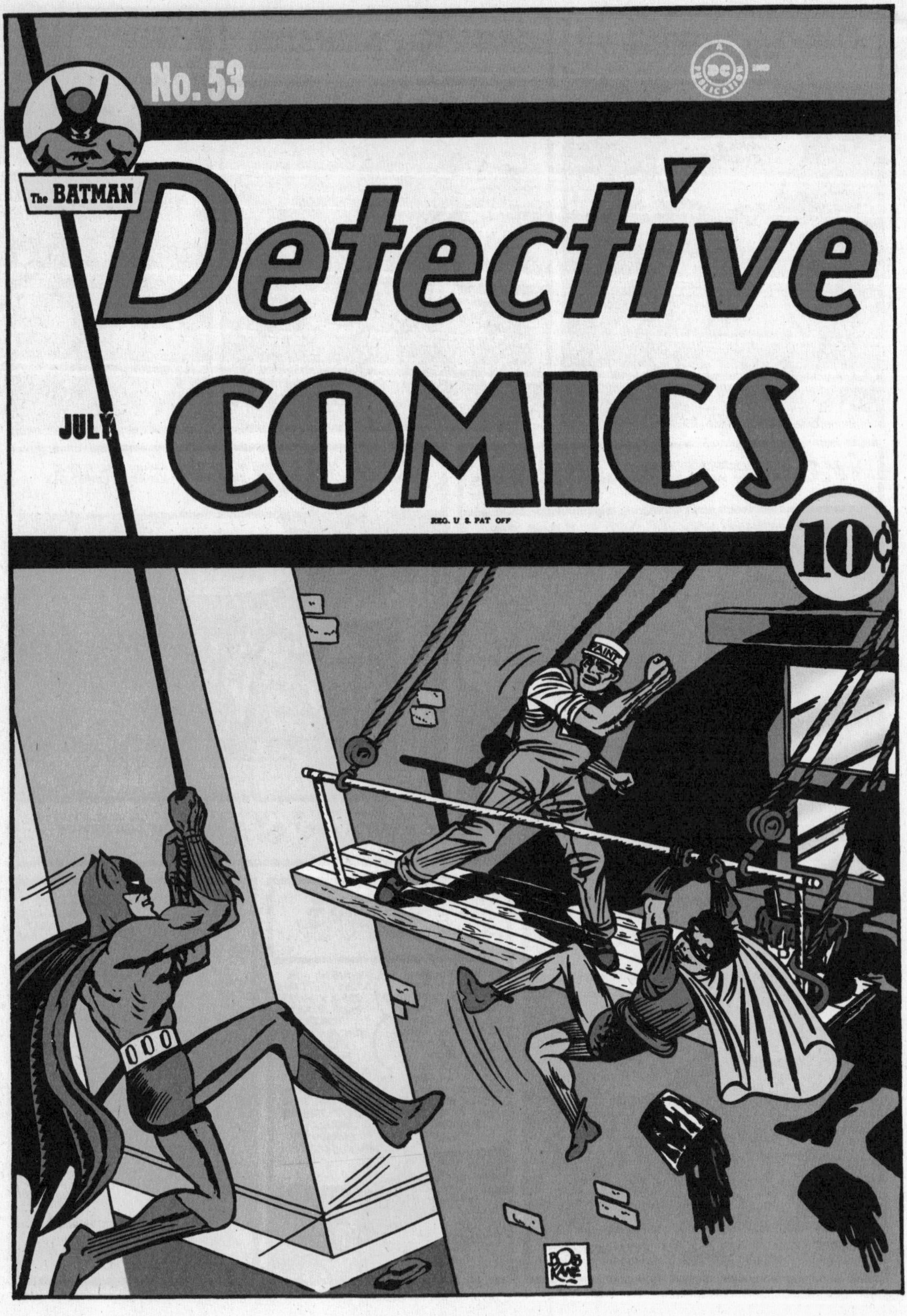
No. 53
A DC PUBLICATION
The BATMAN
Detective
JULY
COMICS
REG. U S. PAT OFF
10¢
PAINT
BOB KANE

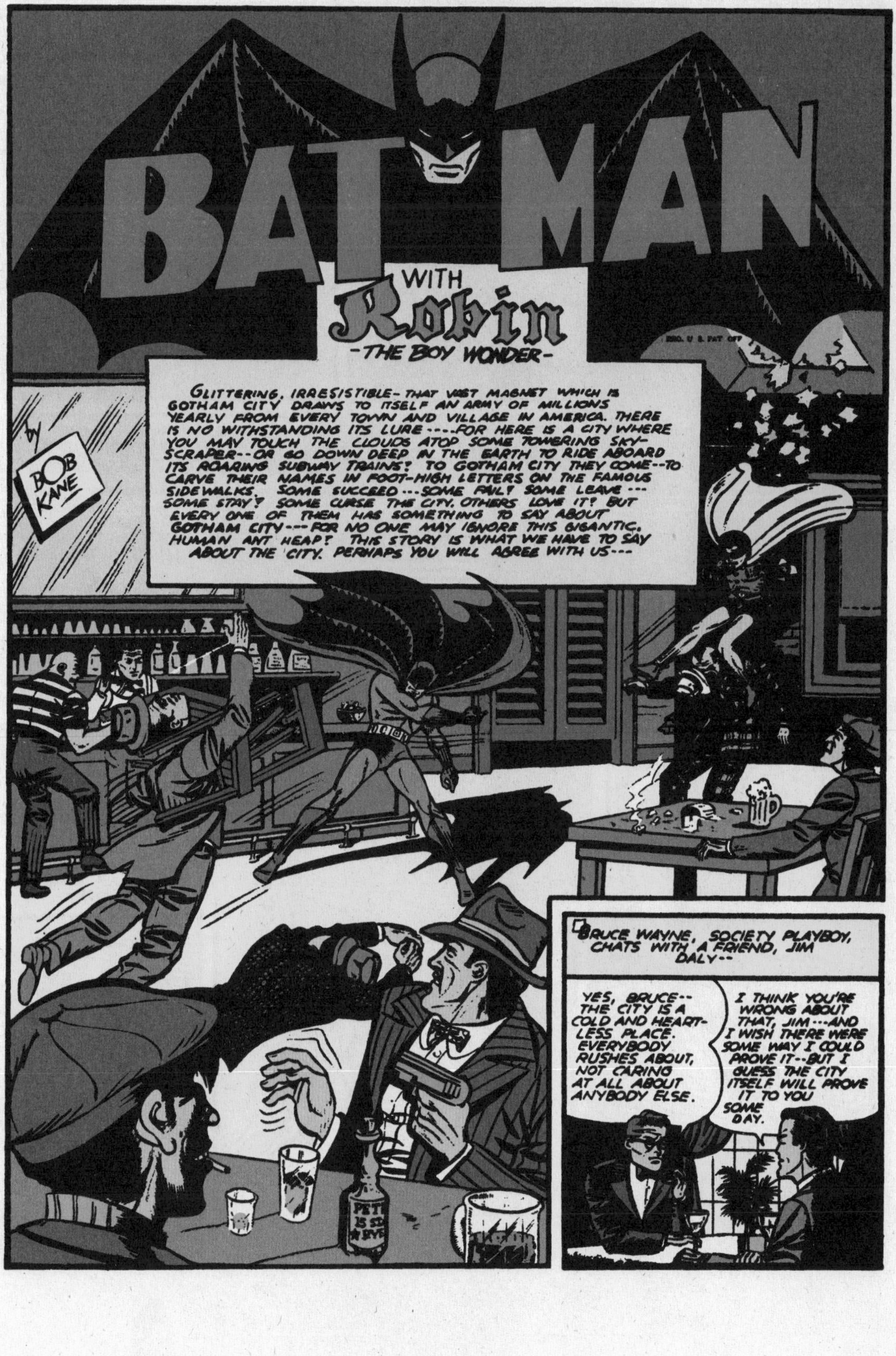
BATMAN
WITH
Robin
-THE BOY WONDER-
GLITTERING, IRRESISTIBLE- THAT VAST MAGNET WHICH IS GOTHAM CITY DRAWS TO ITSELF AN ARMY OF MILLIONS YEARLY FROM EVERY TOWN AND VILLAGE IN AMERICA. THERE IS NO WITHSTANDING ITS LURE----FOR HERE IS A CITY WHERE YOU MAY TOUCH THE CLOUDS ATOP SOME TOWERING SKY-SCRAPER--OR GO DOWN DEEP IN THE EARTH TO RIDE ABOARD ITS ROARING SUBWAY TRAINS! TO GOTHAM CITY THEY COME--TO CARVE THEIR NAMES IN FOOT-HIGH LETTERS ON THE FAMOUS SIDEWALKS. SOME SUCCEED---SOME FAIL! SOME LEAVE---SOME STAY! SOME CURSE THE CITY, OTHERS LOVE IT! BUT EVERY ONE OF THEM HAS SOMETHING TO SAY ABOUT GOTHAM CITY---FOR NO ONE MAY IGNORE THIS GIGANTIC, HUMAN ANT HEAP! THIS STORY IS WHAT WE HAVE TO SAY ABOUT THE CITY. PERHAPS YOU WILL AGREE WITH US---
by BOB KANE
BRUCE WAYNE, SOCIETY PLAYBOY, CHATS WITH A FRIEND, JIM DALY--
YES, BRUCE--THE CITY IS A COLD AND HEARTLESS PLACE. EVERYBODY RUSHES ABOUT, NOT CARING AT ALL ABOUT ANYBODY ELSE.
I THINK YOU'RE WRONG ABOUT THAT, JIM---AND I WISH THERE WERE SOME WAY I COULD PROVE IT--BUT I GUESS THE CITY ITSELF WILL PROVE IT TO YOU SOME DAY.

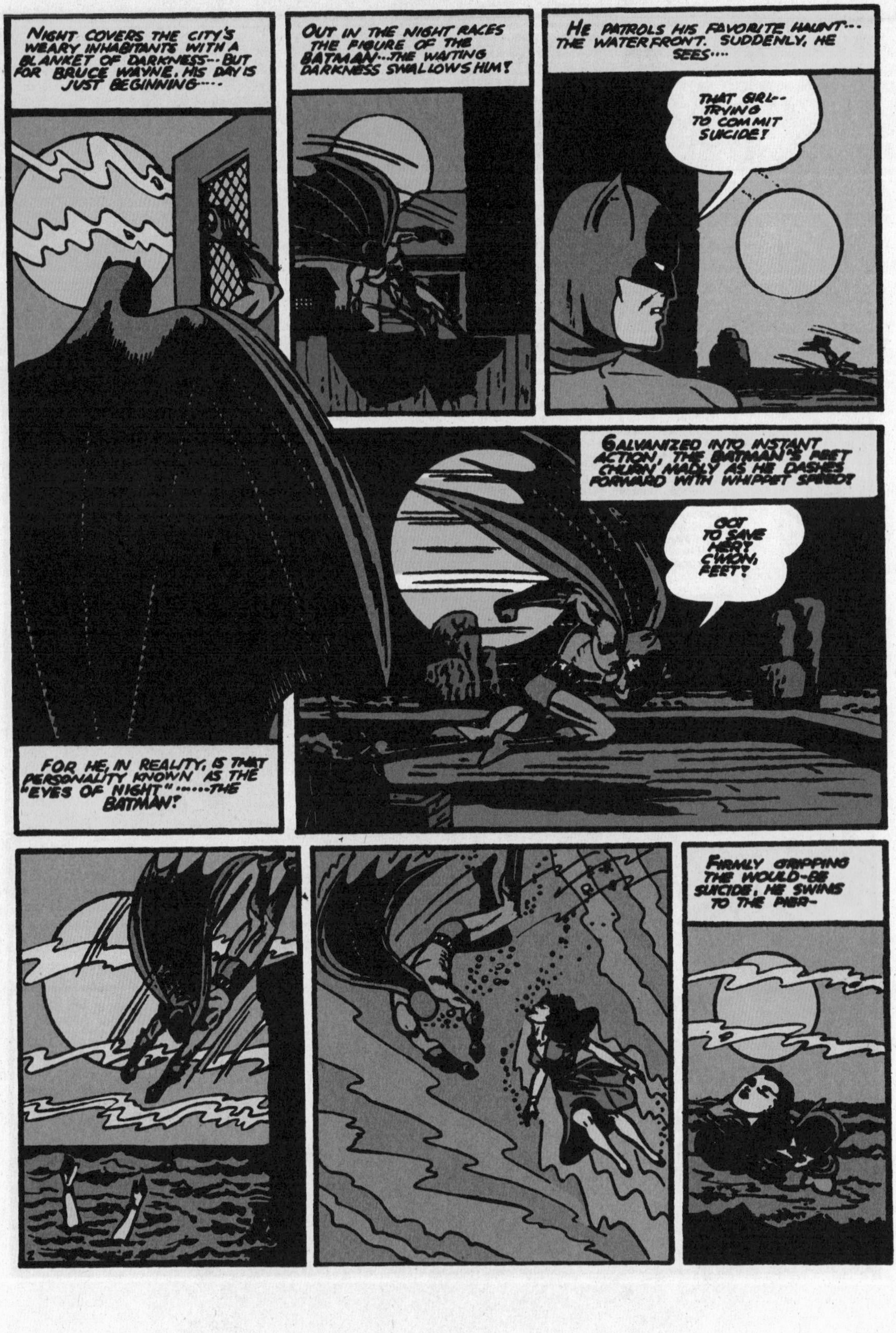
NIGHT COVERS THE CITY'S WEARY INHABITANTS WITH A BLANKET OF DARKNESS-- BUT FOR BRUCE WAYNE, HIS DAY IS JUST BEGINNING....
OUT IN THE NIGHT RACES THE FIGURE OF THE BATMAN...THE WAITING DARKNESS SWALLOWS HIM!
HE PATROLS HIS FAVORITE HAUNT... THE WATERFRONT. SUDDENLY, HE SEES....
THAT GIRL-- TRYING TO COMMIT SUICIDE!
FOR HE, IN REALITY, IS THAT PERSONALITY KNOWN AS THE "EYES OF NIGHT"......THE BATMAN!
GALVANIZED INTO INSTANT ACTION, THE BATMAN'S FEET 'CHURN' MADLY AS HE DASHES FORWARD WITH WHIPPET SPEED!
GOT TO SAVE HER! C'MON, FEET!
FIRMLY GRIPPING THE WOULD-BE SUICIDE, HE SWIMS TO THE PIER--

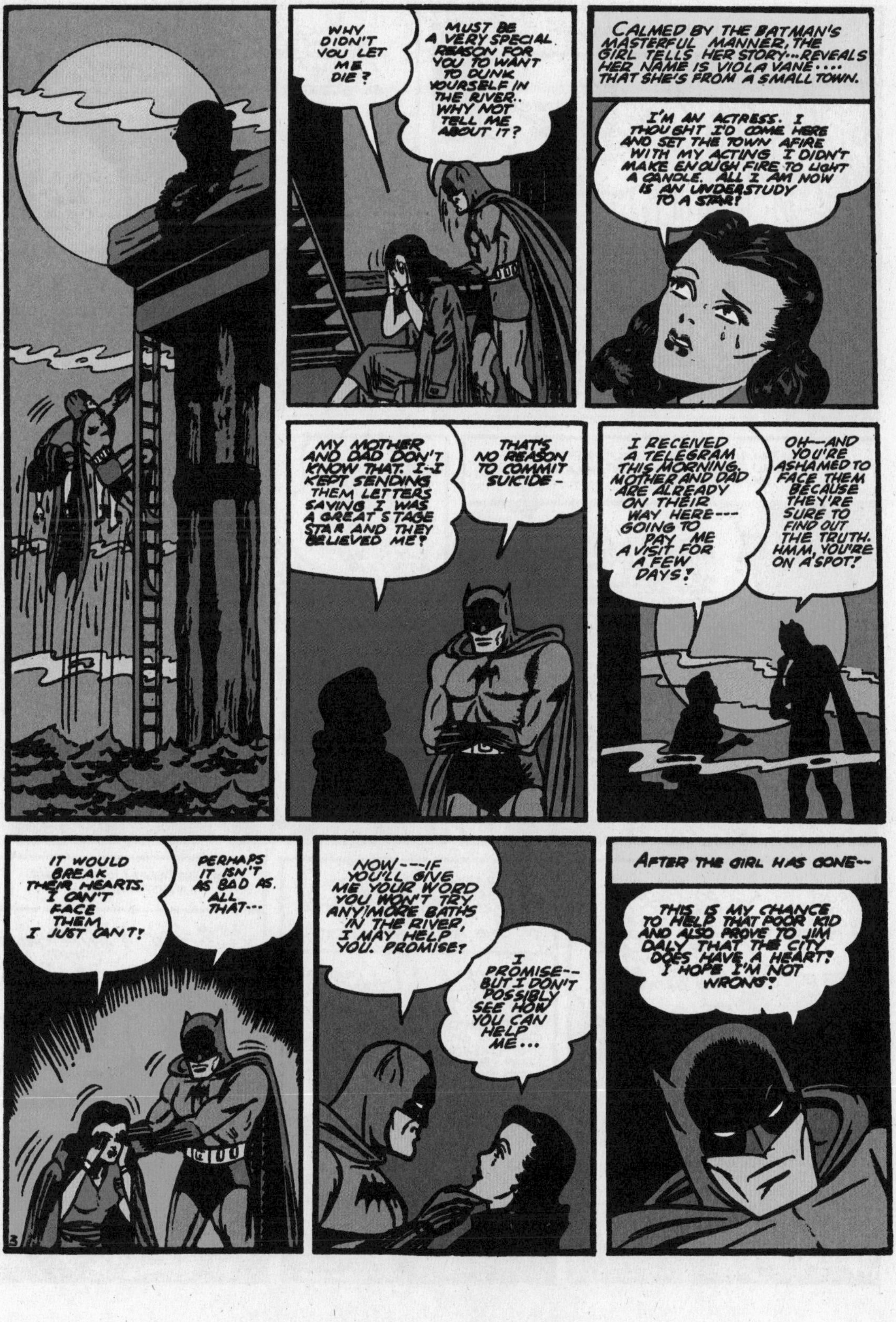
WHY DIDN'T YOU LET ME DIE ?
MUST BE A VERY SPECIAL REASON FOR YOU TO WANT TO DUNK YOURSELF IN THE RIVER.. WHY NOT TELL ME ABOUT IT?
CALMED BY THE BATMAN'S MASTERFUL MANNER, THE GIRL TELLS HER STORY...REVEALS HER NAME IS VIOLA VANE.... THAT SHE'S FROM A SMALL TOWN.
I'M AN ACTRESS. I THOUGHT I'D COME HERE AND SET THE TOWN AFIRE WITH MY ACTING. I DIDN'T MAKE ENOUGH FIRE TO LIGHT A CANDLE. ALL I AM NOW IS AN UNDERSTUDY TO A STAR!
MY MOTHER AND DAD DON'T KNOW THAT. I--I KEPT SENDING THEM LETTERS SAYING I WAS A GREAT STAGE STAR AND THEY BELIEVED ME!
THAT'S NO REASON TO COMMIT SUICIDE -
I RECEIVED A TELEGRAM THIS MORNING. MOTHER AND DAD ARE ALREADY ON THEIR WAY HERE--- GOING TO PAY ME A VISIT FOR A FEW DAYS!
OH---AND YOU'RE ASHAMED TO FACE THEM BECAUSE THEY'RE SURE TO FIND OUT THE TRUTH. HMM, YOU'RE ON A SPOT!
IT WOULD BREAK THEIR HEARTS. I CAN'T FACE THEM. I JUST CAN'T!
PERHAPS IT ISN'T AS BAD AS ALL THAT---
NOW---IF YOU'LL GIVE ME YOUR WORD YOU WON'T TRY ANYMORE BATHS IN THE RIVER, I MAY HELP YOU. PROMISE?
I PROMISE-- BUT I DON'T POSSIBLY SEE HOW YOU CAN HELP ME...
AFTER THE GIRL HAS GONE--
THIS IS MY CHANCE TO HELP THAT POOR KID AND ALSO PROVE TO JIM DALY THAT THE CITY DOES HAVE A HEART! I HOPE I'M NOT WRONG!

LATER IN THE NIGHTCLUB---

AND NOW A LITTLE SURPRISE, CUSTOMERS. WE PRESENT FOR THE FIRST TIME---

THANKS FOR THE INTRODUCTION! I REALLY DIDN'T EXPECT IT!

LOOK! THE BATMAN!

DON'T TELL ME HE'S PART OF THE FLOOR SHOW---

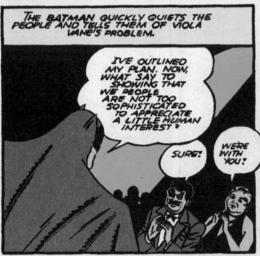

THE BATMAN QUICKLY QUIETS THE PEOPLE AND TELLS THEM OF VIOLA VANE'S PROBLEM.

I'VE OUTLINED MY PLAN. NOW, WHAT SAY TO SHOWING THAT WE PEOPLE ARE NOT TOO SOPHISTICATED TO APPRECIATE A LITTLE HUMAN INTEREST?

SURE!

WE'RE WITH YOU!

THE GIRL WILL NEED AN ESCORT, SOMEONE HANDSOME, WEALTHY, AND GOOD-NATURED ENOUGH TO PLAY ALONG WITH OUR PLAN.

I KNOW JUST THE FELLOW! HE'S A BIT LAZY, BUT WEALTHY AND GOOD LOOKING.

HIS NAME IS BRUCE WAYNE!

GULP--THAT'S ME!

THIS BRUCE WAYNE FELLOW WILL BE PERFECT!

HMM! IF I DO ESCORT HER ABOUT, I CAN KEEP AN EYE ON HER IN PLACES I COULDN'T BE SEEN AS THE BATMAN!

ALL RIGHT! I'LL HUNT UP THIS BRUCE WAYNE FELLOW. MEANWHILE-- SPREAD THE WORD ABOUT, LET EVERYONE KNOW ABOUT THE PLAN!

THE BATMAN GOES FROM NIGHTSPOT TO NIGHTSPOT TELLING EVERYONE OF VIOLA VANE. THEN HE CALLS ON THE RADIO NETWORKS.

THE WHOLE TOWN WILL SOON KNOW ABOUT IT, BUT IF YOU BROAD-CAST IT ON THE RADIO, THE GIRL'S PARENTS MIGHT HEAR IT AND---

I UNDER-STAND. YOU MAY REST ASSURED WE WILL NOT BROAD-CAST ANY-THING PER-TAINING TO THE GIRL.

THE BATMAN VISITS THE NEWSPAPERS---

NOW IF YOU SHOULD WRITE THE STORY IN THE PAPERS, THE GIRL'S PARENTS MIGHT READ IT AND---YOU CAN GUESS THE REST!

MACK, IF ANY REPORTER BRINGS IN THE STORY ABOUT VIOLA VANE, KILL IT. THIS IS ONE STORY WE'RE NOT PRINTING!

RIGHT, MR. ROBINSON.

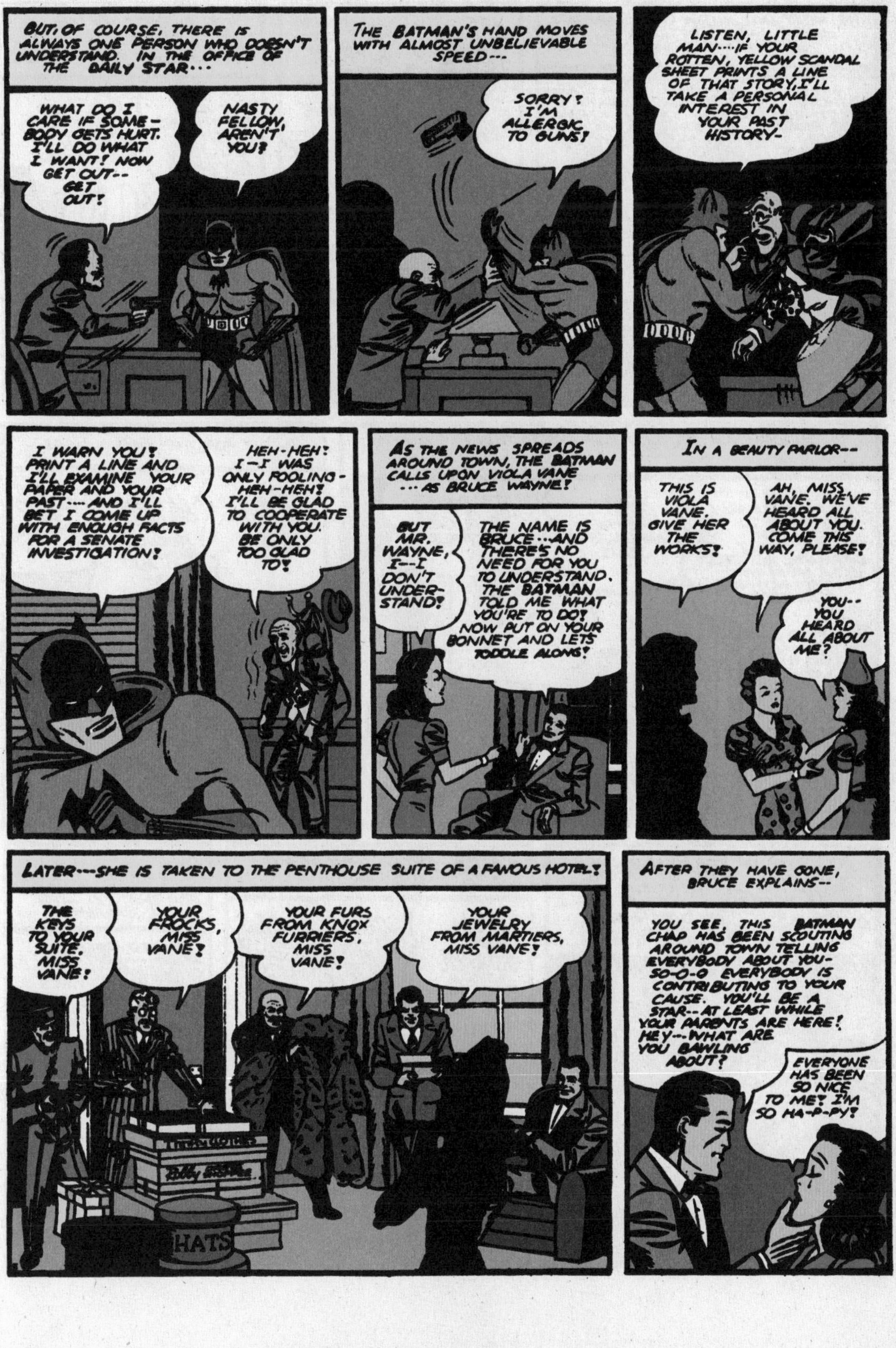
BUT, OF COURSE, THERE IS ALWAYS ONE PERSON WHO DOESN'T UNDERSTAND. IN THE OFFICE OF THE DAILY STAR...
WHAT DO I CARE IF SOMEBODY GETS HURT. I'LL DO WHAT I WANT! NOW GET OUT-- GET OUT!
NASTY FELLOW, AREN'T YOU?
THE BATMAN'S HAND MOVES WITH ALMOST UNBELIEVABLE SPEED---
SORRY? I'M ALLERGIC TO GUNS!
LISTEN, LITTLE MAN----IF YOUR ROTTEN, YELLOW SCANDAL SHEET PRINTS A LINE OF THAT STORY, I'LL TAKE A PERSONAL INTEREST IN YOUR PAST HISTORY-
I WARN YOU! PRINT A LINE AND I'LL EXAMINE YOUR PAPER AND YOUR PAST---AND I'LL BET I COME UP WITH ENOUGH FACTS FOR A SENATE INVESTIGATION!
HEH-HEH! I--I WAS ONLY FOOLING-HEH-HEH! I'LL BE GLAD TO COOPERATE WITH YOU. BE ONLY TOO GLAD TO!
AS THE NEWS SPREADS AROUND TOWN, THE BATMAN CALLS UPON VIOLA VANE ---AS BRUCE WAYNE!
BUT MR. WAYNE, I--I DON'T UNDERSTAND!
THE NAME IS BRUCE---AND THERE'S NO NEED FOR YOU TO UNDERSTAND. THE BATMAN TOLD ME WHAT YOU'RE TO DO! NOW PUT ON YOUR BONNET AND LETS TODDLE ALONG!
IN A BEAUTY PARLOR--
THIS IS VIOLA VANE. GIVE HER THE WORKS!
AH, MISS VANE. WE'VE HEARD ALL ABOUT YOU. COME THIS WAY, PLEASE!
YOU--YOU HEARD ALL ABOUT ME?
LATER---SHE IS TAKEN TO THE PENTHOUSE SUITE OF A FAMOUS HOTEL!
THE KEYS TO YOUR SUITE, MISS VANE!
YOUR FROCKS, MISS VANE!
YOUR FURS FROM KNOX FURRIERS, MISS VANE!
YOUR JEWELRY FROM MARTIERS, MISS VANE!
HATS
AFTER THEY HAVE GONE, BRUCE EXPLAINS--
YOU SEE, THIS BATMAN CHAP HAS BEEN SCOUTING AROUND TOWN TELLING EVERYBODY ABOUT YOU-SO-O-O EVERYBODY IS CONTRIBUTING TO YOUR CAUSE. YOU'LL BE A STAR-- AT LEAST WHILE YOUR PARENTS ARE HERE! HEY---WHAT ARE YOU BAWLING ABOUT?
EVERYONE HAS BEEN SO NICE TO ME! I'M SO HA-P-PY!

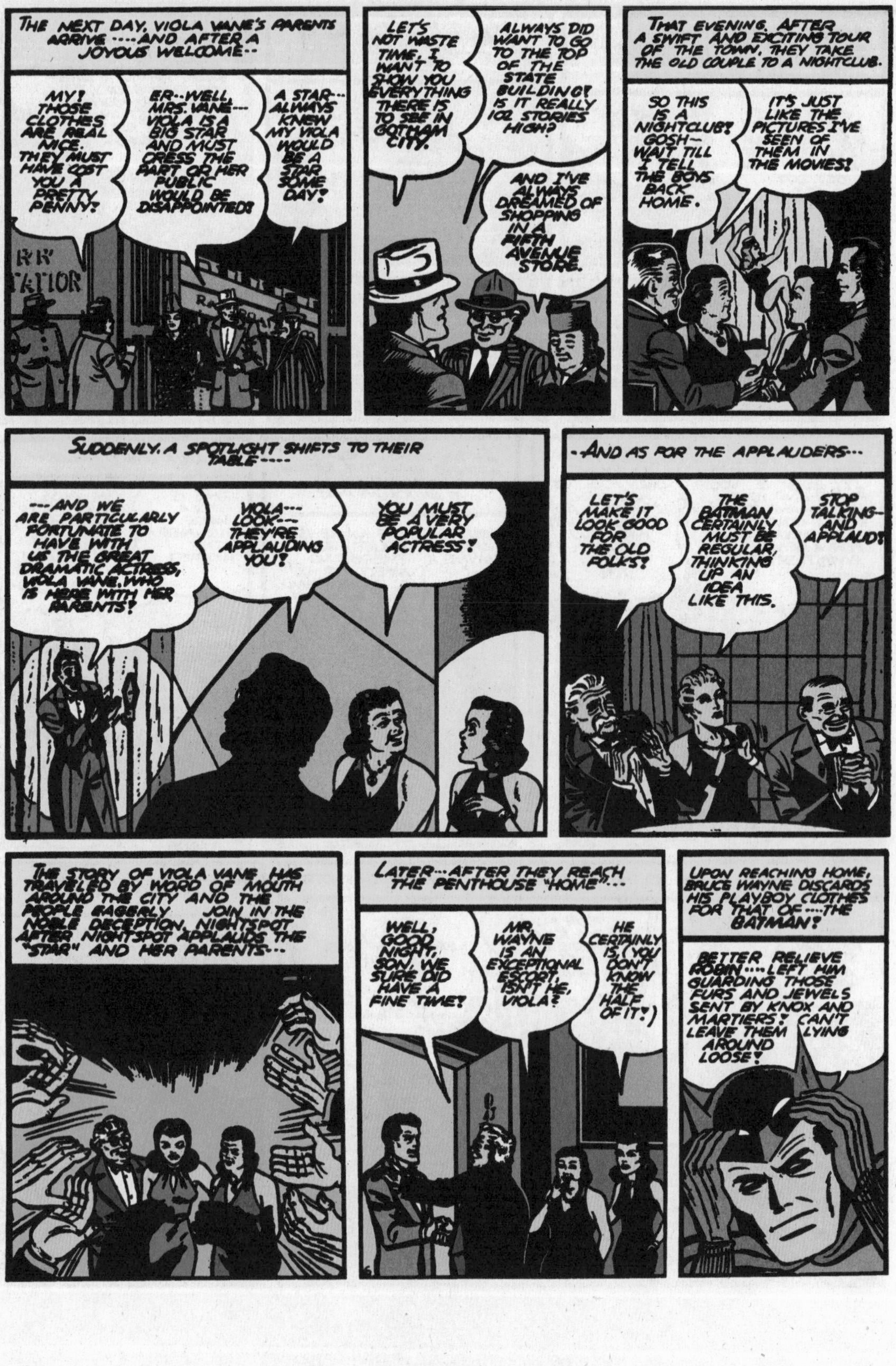
THE NEXT DAY, VIOLA VANE'S PARENTS ARRIVE ----AND AFTER A JOYOUS WELCOME--
MY! THOSE CLOTHES ARE REAL NICE. THEY MUST HAVE COST YOU A PRETTY PENNY!
ER--WELL, MRS. VANE--- VIOLA IS A BIG STAR AND MUST DRESS THE PART OR HER PUBLIC WOULD BE DISAPPOINTED!
A STAR--- ALWAYS KNEW MY VIOLA WOULD BE A STAR SOME DAY!
LET'S NOT WASTE TIME. I WANT TO SHOW YOU EVERYTHING THERE IS TO SEE IN GOTHAM CITY.
ALWAYS DID WANT TO GO TO THE TOP OF THE STATE BUILDING! IS IT REALLY 102 STORIES HIGH?
AND I'VE ALWAYS DREAMED OF SHOPPING IN A FIFTH AVENUE STORE.
THAT EVENING, AFTER A SWIFT AND EXCITING TOUR OF THE TOWN, THEY TAKE THE OLD COUPLE TO A NIGHTCLUB.
SO THIS IS A NIGHTCLUB! GOSH— WAIT TILL I TELL THE BOYS BACK HOME.
IT'S JUST LIKE THE PICTURES I'VE SEEN OF THEM IN THE MOVIES!
SUDDENLY, A SPOTLIGHT SHIFTS TO THEIR TABLE----
---AND WE ARE PARTICULARLY FORTUNATE TO HAVE WITH US THE GREAT DRAMATIC ACTRESS, VIOLA VANE, WHO IS HERE WITH HER PARENTS!
VIOLA--- LOOK--- THEY'RE APPLAUDING YOU!
YOU MUST BE A VERY POPULAR ACTRESS!
-AND AS FOR THE APPLAUDERS---
LET'S MAKE IT LOOK GOOD FOR THE OLD FOLKS!
THE BATMAN CERTAINLY MUST BE REGULAR, THINKING UP AN IDEA LIKE THIS.
STOP TALKING— AND APPLAUD!
THE STORY OF VIOLA VANE HAS TRAVELED BY WORD OF MOUTH AROUND THE CITY AND THE PEOPLE EAGERLY JOIN IN THE NOBLE DECEPTION. NIGHTSPOT AFTER NIGHTSPOT APPLAUDS THE "STAR" AND HER PARENTS---
LATER---AFTER THEY REACH THE PENTHOUSE "HOME"---
WELL, GOOD NIGHT, SON. WE SURE DID HAVE A FINE TIME!
MR. WAYNE IS AN EXCEPTIONAL ESCORT, ISN'T HE, VIOLA?
HE CERTAINLY IS. (YOU DON'T KNOW THE HALF OF IT!)
UPON REACHING HOME, BRUCE WAYNE DISCARDS HIS PLAYBOY CLOTHES FOR THAT OF----THE BATMAN!
BETTER RELIEVE ROBIN----LEFT HIM GUARDING THOSE FURS AND JEWELS SENT BY KNOX AND MARTIERS! CAN'T LEAVE THEM LYING AROUND LOOSE!

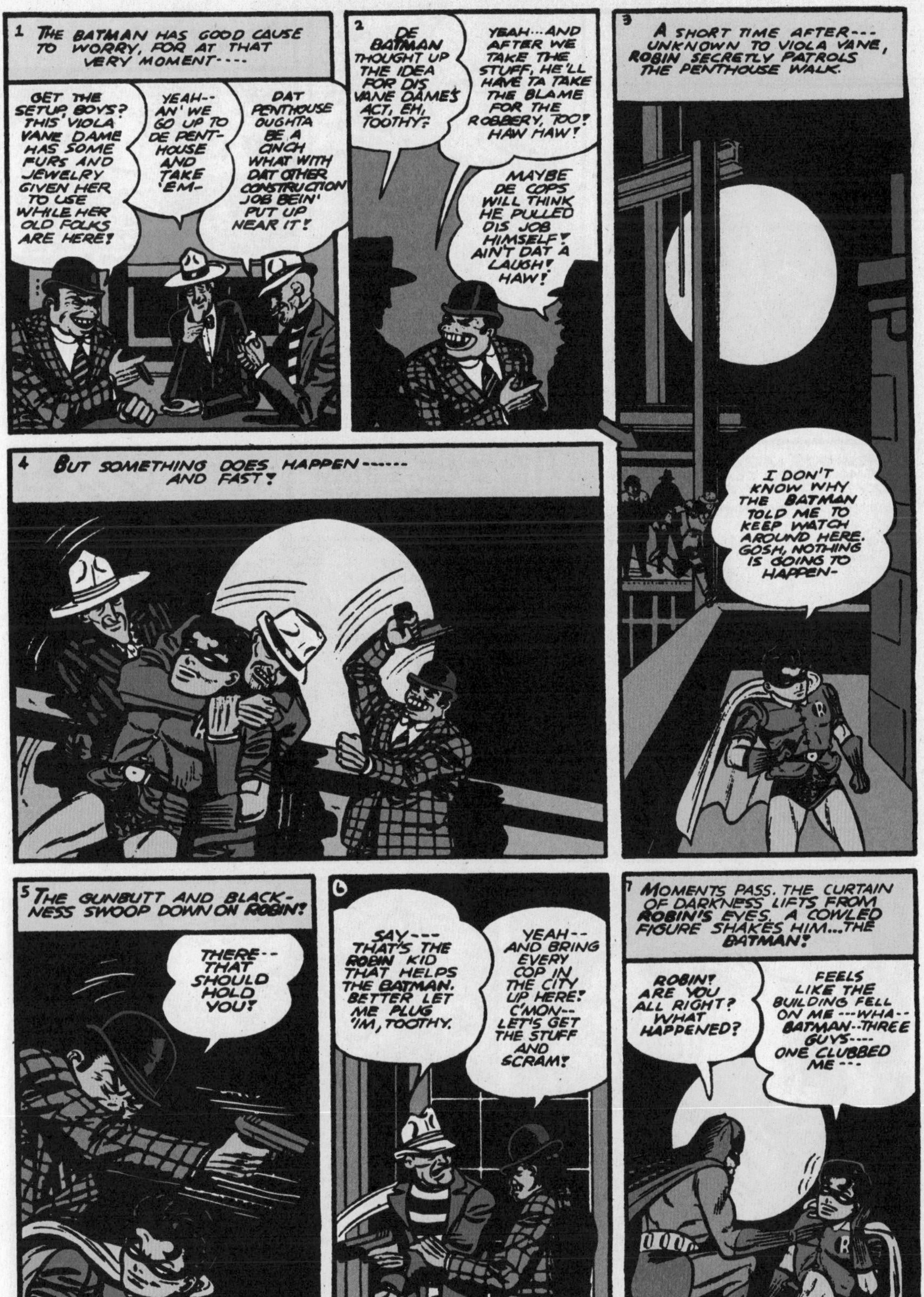
1 THE BATMAN HAS GOOD CAUSE TO WORRY, FOR AT THAT VERY MOMENT----
GET THE SETUP, BOYS? THIS VIOLA VANE DAME HAS SOME FURS AND JEWELRY GIVEN HER TO USE WHILE HER OLD FOLKS ARE HERE!
YEAH-- AN' WE GO UP TO DE PENT-HOUSE AND TAKE 'EM-
DAT PENTHOUSE OUGHTA BE A CINCH WHAT WITH DAT OTHER CONSTRUCTION JOB BEIN' PUT UP NEAR IT!
2
DE BATMAN THOUGHT UP THE IDEA FOR DIS VANE DAME'S ACT, EH, TOOTHY?
YEAH...AND AFTER WE TAKE THE STUFF, HE'LL HAVE TA TAKE THE BLAME FOR THE ROBBERY, TOO! HAW HAW!
MAYBE DE COPS WILL THINK HE PULLED DIS JOB HIMSELF! AIN'T DAT A LAUGH! HAW!
3 A SHORT TIME AFTER--- UNKNOWN TO VIOLA VANE, ROBIN SECRETLY PATROLS THE PENTHOUSE WALK.
I DON'T KNOW WHY THE BATMAN TOLD ME TO KEEP WATCH AROUND HERE. GOSH, NOTHING IS GOING TO HAPPEN-
4 BUT SOMETHING DOES HAPPEN------ AND FAST!
5 THE GUNBUTT AND BLACK-NESS SWOOP DOWN ON ROBIN!
THERE-- THAT SHOULD HOLD YOU!
6
SAY--- THAT'S THE ROBIN KID THAT HELPS THE BATMAN. BETTER LET ME PLUG 'IM, TOOTHY.
YEAH-- AND BRING EVERY COP IN THE CITY UP HERE! C'MON-- LET'S GET THE STUFF AND SCRAM!
7 MOMENTS PASS. THE CURTAIN OF DARKNESS LIFTS FROM ROBIN'S EYES. A COWLED FIGURE SHAKES HIM...THE BATMAN!
ROBIN! ARE YOU ALL RIGHT? WHAT HAPPENED?
FEELS LIKE THE BUILDING FELL ON ME ---WHA-- BATMAN--THREE GUYS---- ONE CLUBBED ME---

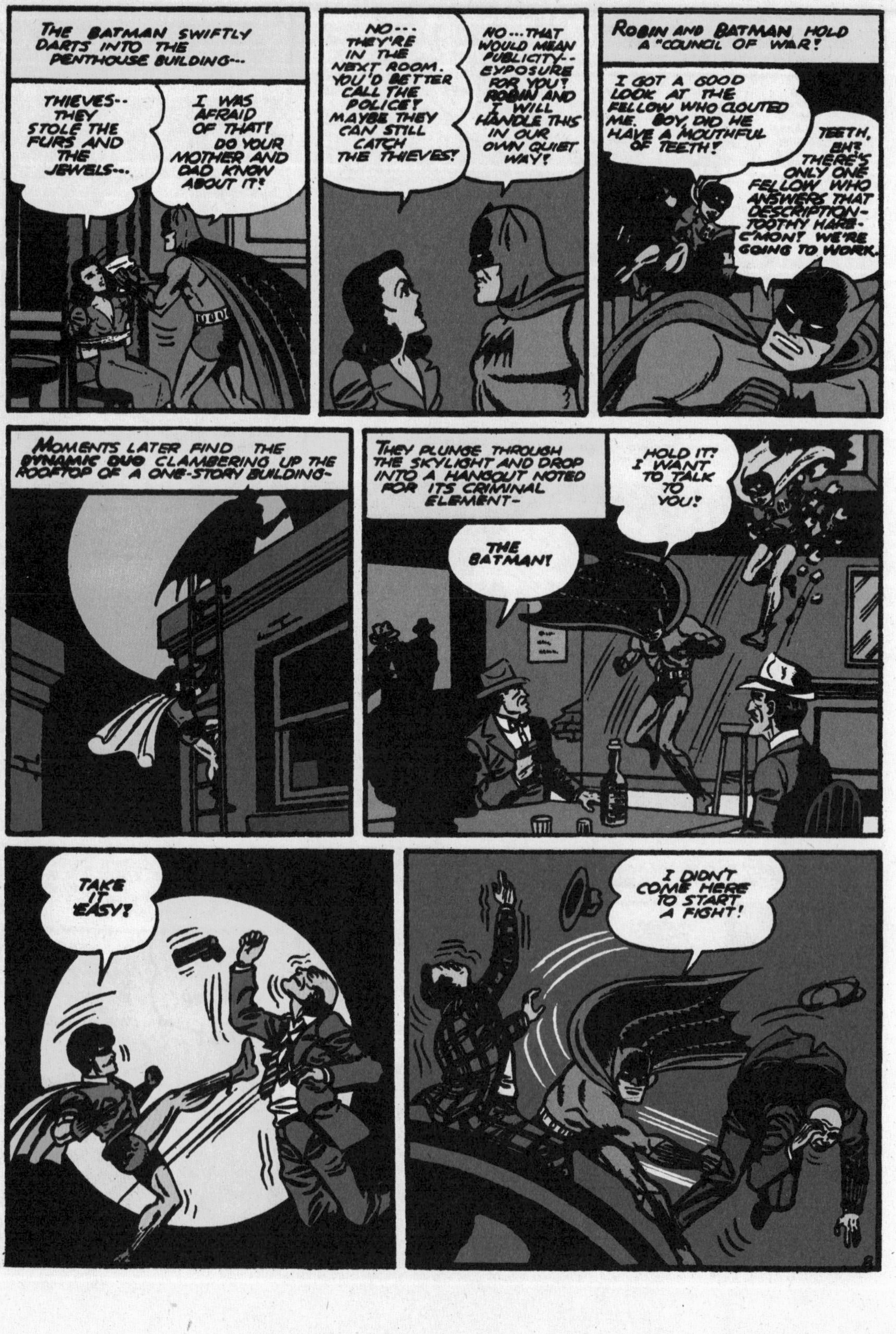
THE BATMAN SWIFTLY DARTS INTO THE PENTHOUSE BUILDING---
THIEVES-- THEY STOLE THE FURS AND THE JEWELS---
I WAS AFRAID OF THAT! DO YOUR MOTHER AND DAD KNOW ABOUT IT?
NO--- THEY'RE IN THE NEXT ROOM. YOU'D BETTER CALL THE POLICE! MAYBE THEY CAN STILL CATCH THE THIEVES!
NO...THAT WOULD MEAN PUBLICITY-- EXPOSURE FOR YOU! ROBIN AND I WILL HANDLE THIS IN OUR OWN QUIET WAY!
ROBIN AND BATMAN HOLD A "COUNCIL OF WAR!
I GOT A GOOD LOOK AT THE FELLOW WHO CLOUTED ME. BOY, DID HE HAVE A MOUTHFUL OF TEETH!
TEETH, EH? THERE'S ONLY ONE FELLOW WHO ANSWERS THAT DESCRIPTION- TOOTHY HARE- C'MON! WE'RE GOING TO WORK.
MOMENTS LATER FIND THE DYNAMIC DUO CLAMBERING UP THE ROOFTOP OF A ONE-STORY BUILDING-
THEY PLUNGE THROUGH THE SKYLIGHT AND DROP INTO A HANGOUT NOTED FOR ITS CRIMINAL ELEMENT-
HOLD IT! I WANT TO TALK TO YOU!
THE BATMAN!
TAKE IT EASY!
I DIDN'T COME HERE TO START A FIGHT!
8

FOR GOSH SAKES, DON'T YOU FELLOWS---

UNDERSTAND ENGLISH?

THE BATMAN FIGHTS WITH THE WILD FURY OF AN UNLEASHED TORNADO!

BY HEAVEN, I'LL MAKE YOU LISTEN TO ME, OR I'LL BREAK A COUPLE OF JAWS IN THE ATTEMPT!

CRACK!

AFTER A FEW MOMENTS OF THE BATMAN AND ROBIN, THE CRIMINALS ARE ONLY TOO ANXIOUS TO LISTEN---

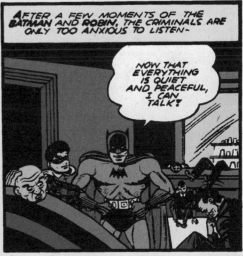

NOW THAT EVERYTHING IS QUIET AND PEACEFUL, I CAN TALK!

THE BATMAN TELLS OF TOOTHY'S LOOTINGS OF THE VIOLA VANE PENTHOUSE--

SO YOU SEE WHAT A ROTTEN TRICK IT IS ON THIS VIOLA VANE GIRL? I WANT TO FIND TOOTHY. HAVE ANY OF YOU ANY IDEA WHERE HE MIGHT BE HIDING OUT?

ER-- NAW--WE DON'T KNOW NOTHIN'

YEAH-- WE AIN'T TALKIN'!

SEEING HE CAN'T SECURE ANY INFORMATION, THE BATMAN LEAVES. AS HE DOES SO A FUGITIVE FIGURE SIDLES UP TO HIM---

PSST···I MAY BE A CROOK, BUT I NEVER PULLED A DOITY STUNT LIKE TOOTHY DONE-- ME USUALLY HIDES OUT IN THE SHACKS AFTER A JOB! ROOM 31!

THANKS!

THE SHACKS! A CROOKED ROW OF WEATHER-BEATEN OLD HOUSES THAT SERVE AS A CRIMINAL HIDEOUT ON THE EDGE OF THE WATERFRONT!

NOT EXACTLY CHEERFUL-LOOKING, ARE THEY?

THEY'RE DANGEROUS RATHOLES FILLED WITH HUMAN RODENTS! ONCE WE WALK IN THERE, WE WALK INTO TROUBLE!

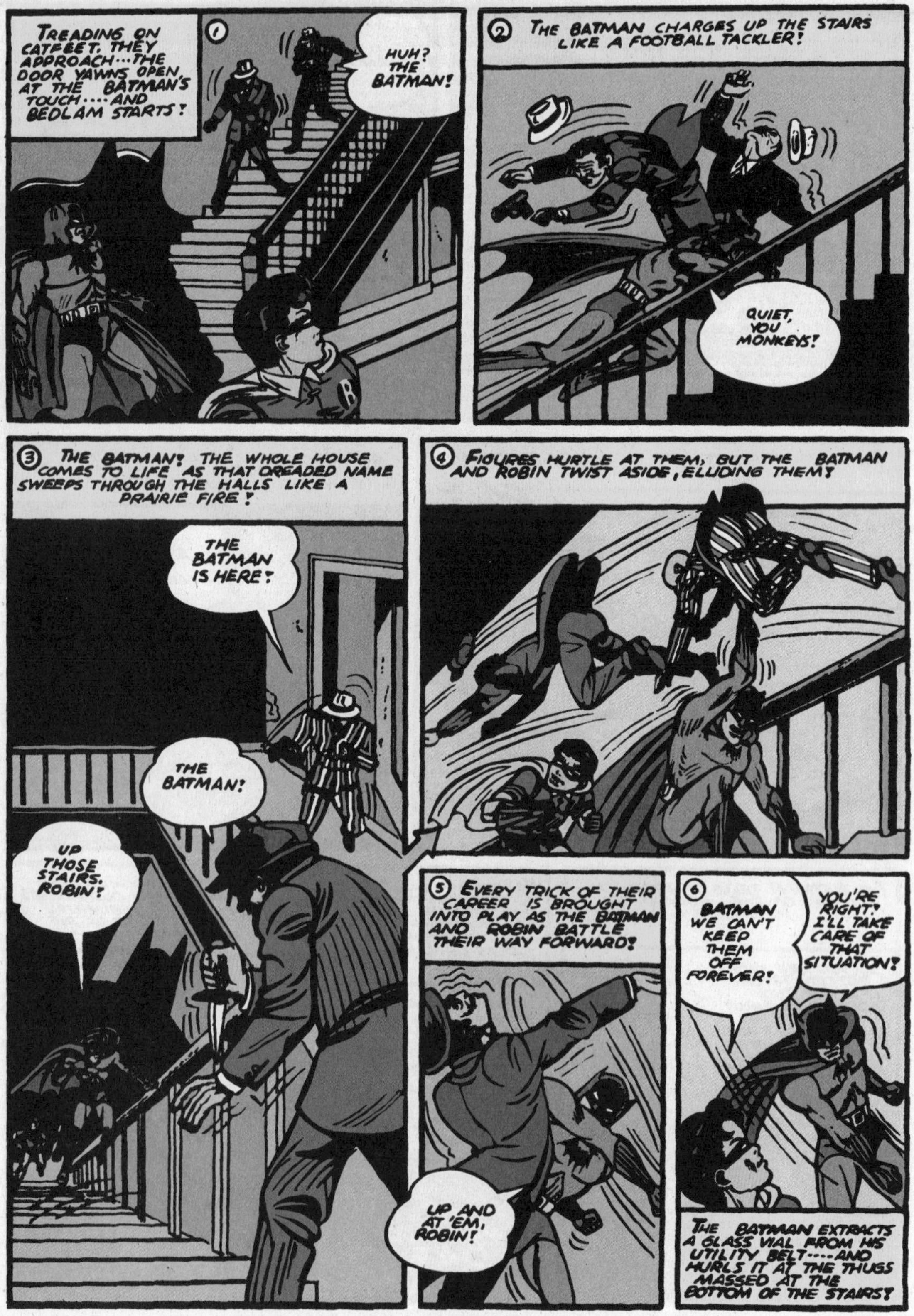
TREADING ON CATFEET, THEY APPROACH...THE DOOR YAWNS OPEN AT THE BATMAN'S TOUCH....AND BEDLAM STARTS!
HUH? THE BATMAN!
THE BATMAN CHARGES UP THE STAIRS LIKE A FOOTBALL TACKLER!
QUIET, YOU MONKEYS!
THE BATMAN! THE WHOLE HOUSE COMES TO LIFE AS THAT DREADED NAME SWEEPS THROUGH THE HALLS LIKE A PRAIRIE FIRE!
THE BATMAN IS HERE!
THE BATMAN!
UP THOSE STAIRS, ROBIN!
FIGURES HURTLE AT THEM, BUT THE BATMAN AND ROBIN TWIST ASIDE, ELUDING THEM!
EVERY TRICK OF THEIR CAREER IS BROUGHT INTO PLAY AS THE BATMAN AND ROBIN BATTLE THEIR WAY FORWARD!
UP AND AT 'EM, ROBIN!
BATMAN WE CAN'T KEEP THEM OFF FOREVER!
YOU'RE RIGHT! I'LL TAKE CARE OF THAT SITUATION!
THE BATMAN EXTRACTS A GLASS VIAL FROM HIS UTILITY BELT----AND HURLS IT AT THE THUGS MASSED AT THE BOTTOM OF THE STAIRS!

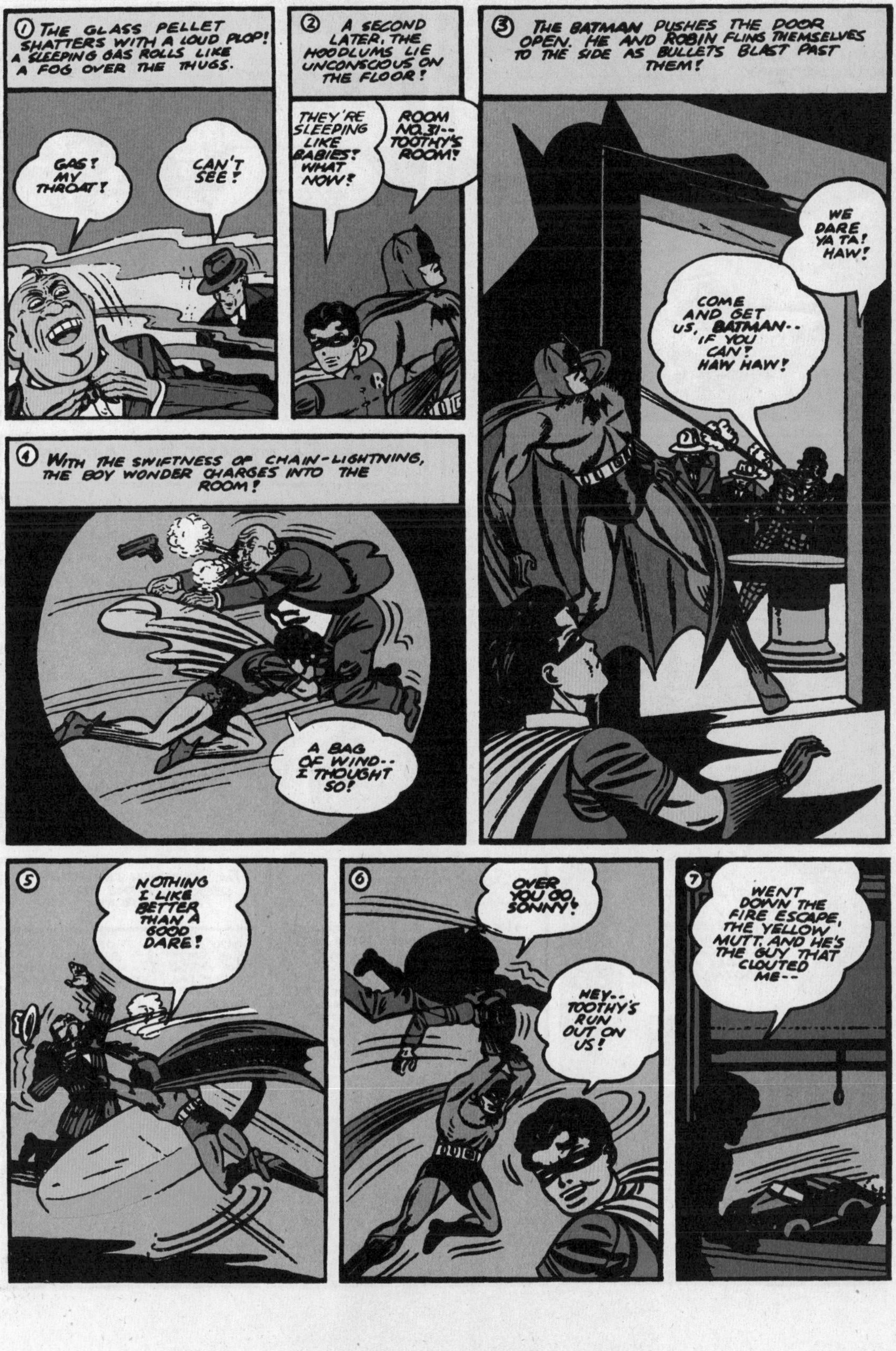

1 THE GLASS PELLET SHATTERS WITH A LOUD PLOP! A SLEEPING GAS ROLLS LIKE A FOG OVER THE THUGS.
GAS! MY THROAT!
CAN'T SEE!
2 A SECOND LATER, THE HOODLUMS LIE UNCONSCIOUS ON THE FLOOR!
THEY'RE SLEEPING LIKE BABIES! WHAT NOW?
ROOM NO. 31-- TOOTHY'S ROOM!
3 THE BATMAN PUSHES THE DOOR OPEN. HE AND ROBIN FLING THEMSELVES TO THE SIDE AS BULLETS BLAST PAST THEM!
WE DARE YA TA! HAW!
COME AND GET US, BATMAN-- IF YOU CAN! HAW HAW!
4 WITH THE SWIFTNESS OF CHAIN-LIGHTNING, THE BOY WONDER CHARGES INTO THE ROOM!
A BAG OF WIND-- I THOUGHT SO!
5
NOTHING I LIKE BETTER THAN A GOOD DARE!
6
OVER YOU GO, SONNY!
HEY-- TOOTHY'S RUN OUT ON US!
7
WENT DOWN THE FIRE ESCAPE, THE YELLOW MUTT, AND HE'S THE GUY THAT CLOUTED ME--

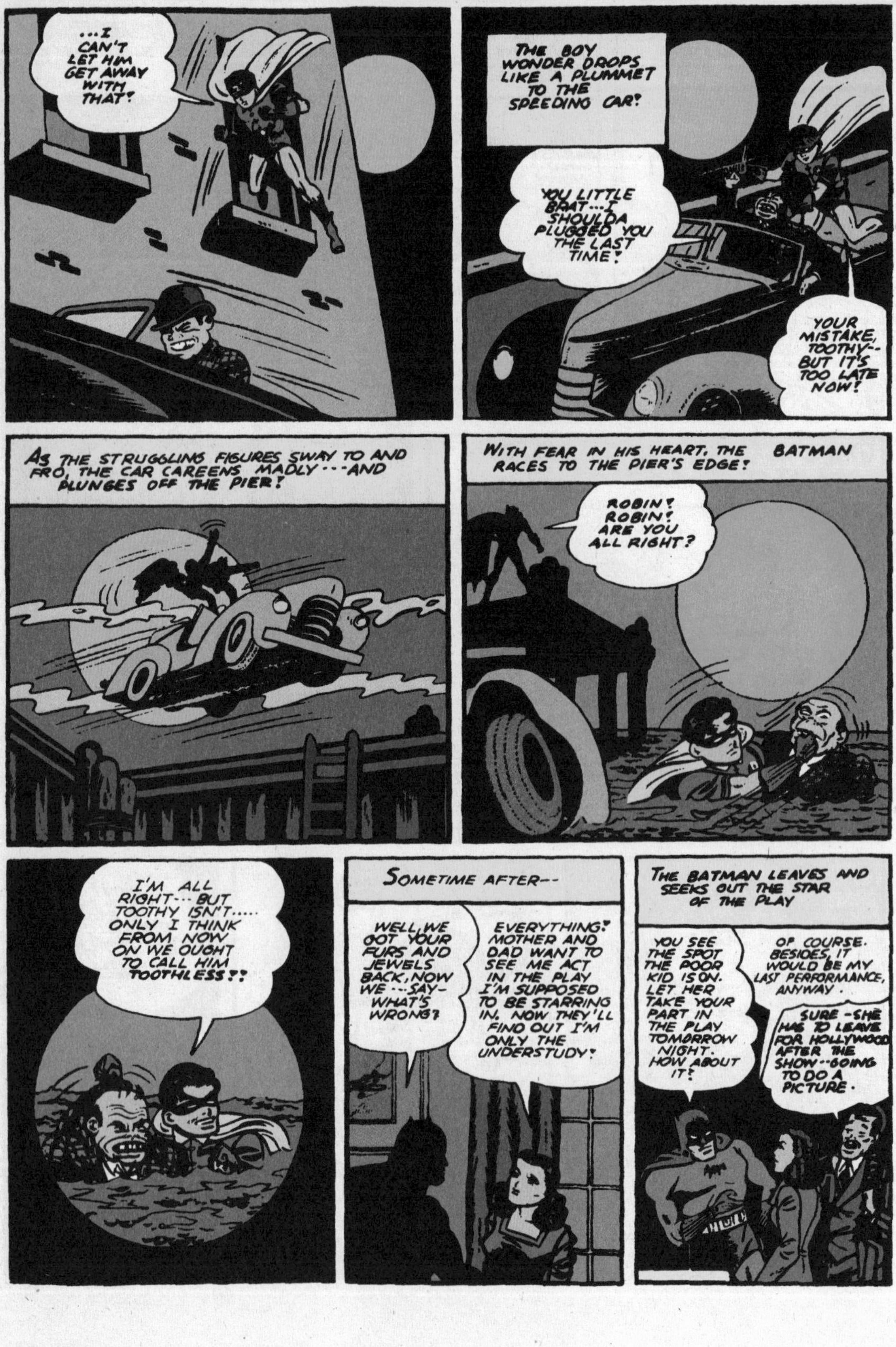
...I CAN'T LET HIM GET AWAY WITH THAT!
THE BOY WONDER DROPS LIKE A PLUMMET TO THE SPEEDING CAR!
YOU LITTLE BRAT...I SHOULDA PLUGGED YOU THE LAST TIME!
YOUR MISTAKE, TOOTHY-- BUT IT'S TOO LATE NOW!
AS THE STRUGGLING FIGURES SWAY TO AND FRO, THE CAR CAREENS MADLY---AND PLUNGES OFF THE PIER!
WITH FEAR IN HIS HEART, THE BATMAN RACES TO THE PIER'S EDGE!
ROBIN! ROBIN! ARE YOU ALL RIGHT?
I'M ALL RIGHT--- BUT TOOTHY ISN'T..... ONLY I THINK FROM NOW ON WE OUGHT TO CALL HIM TOOTHLESS!?
SOMETIME AFTER--
WELL, WE GOT YOUR FURS AND JEWELS BACK, NOW WE ---SAY-- WHAT'S WRONG?
EVERYTHING! MOTHER AND DAD WANT TO SEE ME ACT IN THE PLAY I'M SUPPOSED TO BE STARRING IN. NOW THEY'LL FIND OUT I'M ONLY THE UNDERSTUDY!
THE BATMAN LEAVES AND SEEKS OUT THE STAR OF THE PLAY
YOU SEE THE SPOT THE POOR KID IS ON. LET HER TAKE YOUR PART IN THE PLAY TOMORROW NIGHT. HOW ABOUT IT?
OF COURSE. BESIDES, IT WOULD BE MY LAST PERFORMANCE, ANYWAY.
SURE -SHE HAS TO LEAVE FOR HOLLYWOOD AFTER THE SHOW--GOING TO DO A PICTURE.

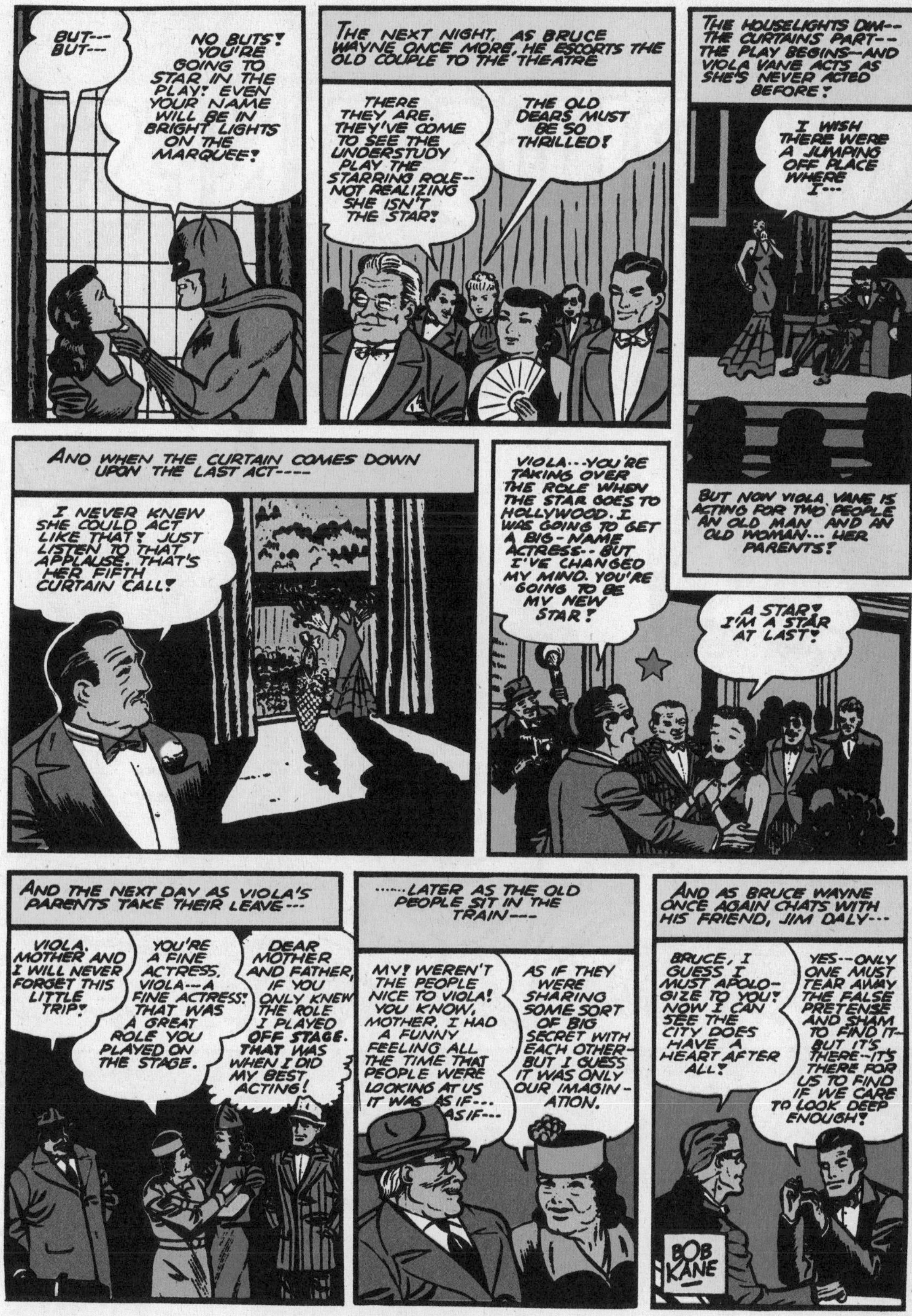
BUT--- BUT---
NO BUTS! YOU'RE GOING TO STAR IN THE PLAY! EVEN YOUR NAME WILL BE IN BRIGHT LIGHTS ON THE MARQUEE!
THE NEXT NIGHT, AS BRUCE WAYNE ONCE MORE, HE ESCORTS THE OLD COUPLE TO THE THEATRE
THERE THEY ARE. THEY'VE COME TO SEE THE UNDERSTUDY PLAY THE STARRING ROLE-- NOT REALIZING SHE ISN'T THE STAR!
THE OLD DEARS MUST BE SO THRILLED!
THE HOUSELIGHTS DIM-- THE CURTAINS PART-- THE PLAY BEGINS--AND VIOLA VANE ACTS AS SHE'S NEVER ACTED BEFORE!
I WISH THERE WERE A JUMPING OFF PLACE WHERE I---
BUT NOW VIOLA VANE IS ACTING FOR TWO PEOPLE AN OLD MAN AND AN OLD WOMAN... HER PARENTS!
AND WHEN THE CURTAIN COMES DOWN UPON THE LAST ACT----
I NEVER KNEW SHE COULD ACT LIKE THAT! JUST LISTEN TO THAT APPLAUSE. THAT'S HER FIFTH CURTAIN CALL!
VIOLA---YOU'RE TAKING OVER THE ROLE WHEN THE STAR GOES TO HOLLYWOOD. I WAS GOING TO GET A BIG-NAME ACTRESS-- BUT I'VE CHANGED MY MIND. YOU'RE GOING TO BE MY NEW STAR!
A STAR! I'M A STAR AT LAST!
AND THE NEXT DAY AS VIOLA'S PARENTS TAKE THEIR LEAVE---
VIOLA. MOTHER AND I WILL NEVER FORGET THIS LITTLE TRIP!
YOU'RE A FINE ACTRESS, VIOLA---A FINE ACTRESS! THAT WAS A GREAT ROLE YOU PLAYED ON THE STAGE.
DEAR MOTHER AND FATHER, IF YOU ONLY KNEW THE ROLE I PLAYED OFF STAGE. THAT WAS WHEN I DID MY BEST ACTING!
......LATER AS THE OLD PEOPLE SIT IN THE TRAIN---
MY! WEREN'T THE PEOPLE NICE TO VIOLA! YOU KNOW, MOTHER, I HAD A FUNNY FEELING ALL THE TIME THAT PEOPLE WERE LOOKING AT US IT WAS AS IF--- AS IF---
AS IF THEY WERE SHARING SOME SORT OF BIG SECRET WITH EACH OTHER- BUT I GUESS IT WAS ONLY OUR IMAGIN-ATION.
AND AS BRUCE WAYNE CHATS WITH HIS FRIEND, JIM DALY---
BRUCE, I GUESS I MUST APOLO-GIZE TO YOU! NOW I CAN SEE THE CITY DOES HAVE A HEART AFTER ALL!
YES--ONLY ONE MUST TEAR AWAY THE FALSE PRETENSE AND SHAM TO FIND IT-- BUT IT'S THERE--IT'S THERE FOR US TO FIND IF WE CARE TO LOOK DEEP ENOUGH!
BOB KANE

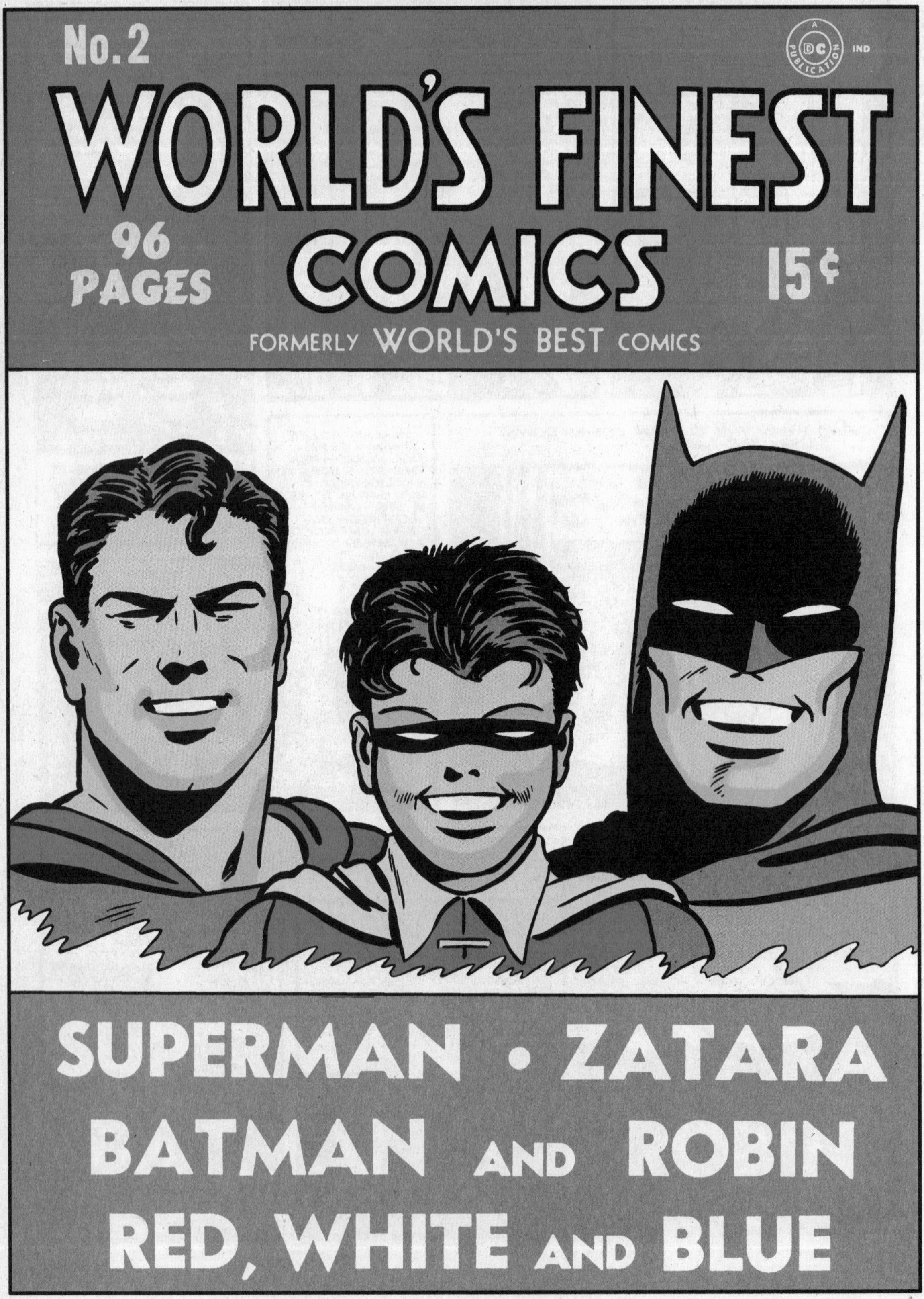
No. 2
A DC PUBLICATION
IND
WORLD'S FINEST
96 PAGES
COMICS
15¢
FORMERLY WORLD'S BEST COMICS
SUPERMAN • ZATARA
BATMAN AND ROBIN
RED, WHITE AND BLUE

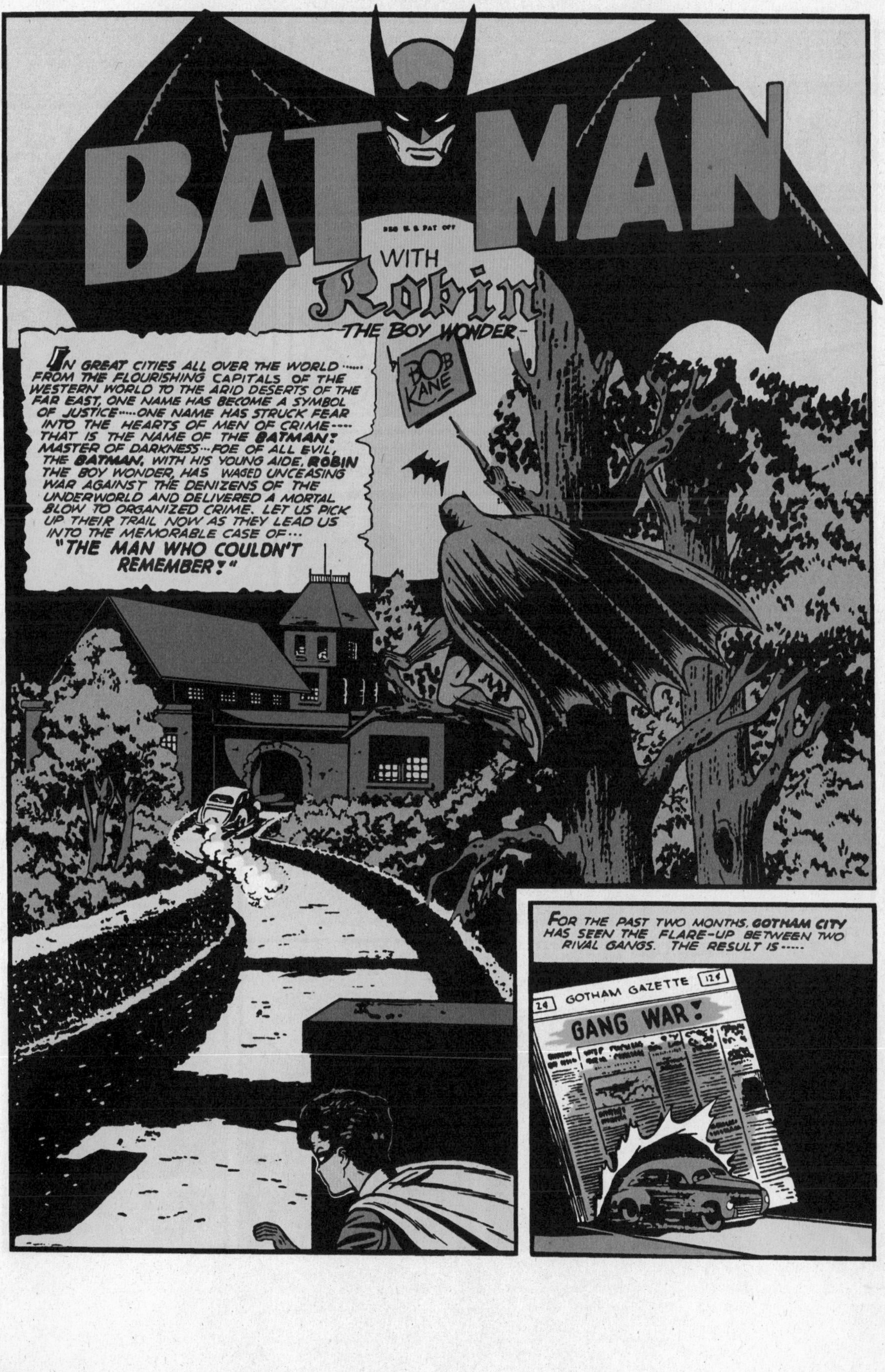
BATMAN
WITH
Robin
THE BOY WONDER
BOB KANE
IN GREAT CITIES ALL OVER THE WORLD...... FROM THE FLOURISHING CAPITALS OF THE WESTERN WORLD TO THE ARID DESERTS OF THE FAR EAST, ONE NAME HAS BECOME A SYMBOL OF JUSTICE.....ONE NAME HAS STRUCK FEAR INTO THE HEARTS OF MEN OF CRIME.... THAT IS THE NAME OF THE BATMAN! MASTER OF DARKNESS...FOE OF ALL EVIL, THE BATMAN, WITH HIS YOUNG AIDE, ROBIN THE BOY WONDER, HAS WAGED UNCEASING WAR AGAINST THE DENIZENS OF THE UNDERWORLD AND DELIVERED A MORTAL BLOW TO ORGANIZED CRIME. LET US PICK UP THEIR TRAIL NOW AS THEY LEAD US INTO THE MEMORABLE CASE OF...
"THE MAN WHO COULDN'T REMEMBER!"
FOR THE PAST TWO MONTHS, GOTHAM CITY HAS SEEN THE FLARE-UP BETWEEN TWO RIVAL GANGS. THE RESULT IS.....
GOTHAM GAZETTE
GANG WAR!

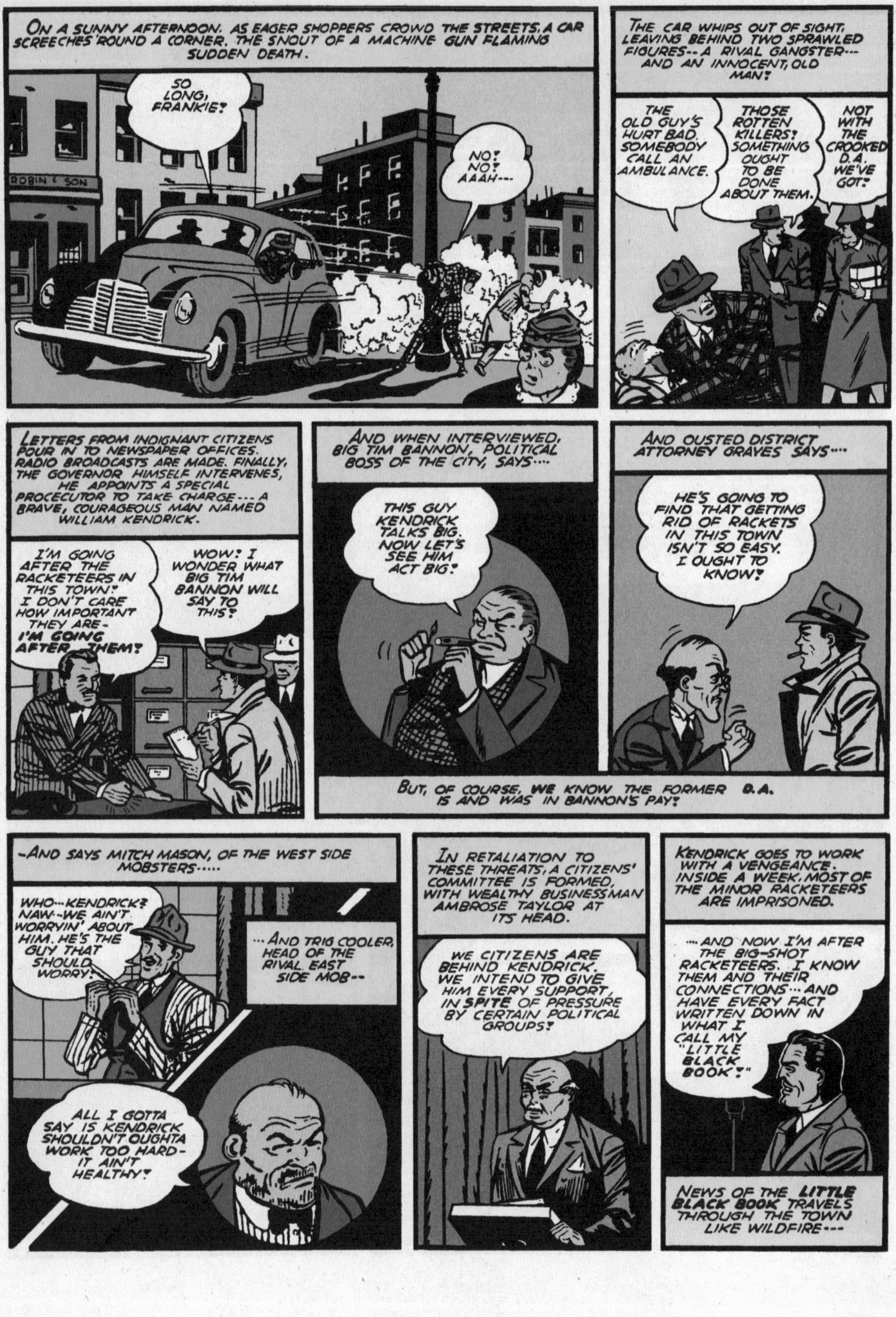
ON A SUNNY AFTERNOON, AS EAGER SHOPPERS CROWD THE STREETS, A CAR SCREECHES 'ROUND A CORNER, THE SNOUT OF A MACHINE GUN FLAMING SUDDEN DEATH.
SO LONG, FRANKIE!
NO! NO! AAAH---
ROBIN & SON
THE CAR WHIPS OUT OF SIGHT, LEAVING BEHIND TWO SPRAWLED FIGURES-- A RIVAL GANGSTER--- AND AN INNOCENT, OLD MAN!
THE OLD GUY'S HURT BAD. SOMEBODY CALL AN AMBULANCE.
THOSE ROTTEN KILLERS! SOMETHING OUGHT TO BE DONE ABOUT THEM.
NOT WITH THE CROOKED D.A. WE'VE GOT!
LETTERS FROM INDIGNANT CITIZENS POUR IN TO NEWSPAPER OFFICES. RADIO BROADCASTS ARE MADE. FINALLY, THE GOVERNOR HIMSELF INTERVENES, HE APPOINTS A SPECIAL PROCECUTOR TO TAKE CHARGE--- A BRAVE, COURAGEOUS MAN NAMED WILLIAM KENDRICK.
I'M GOING AFTER THE RACKETEERS IN THIS TOWN! I DON'T CARE HOW IMPORTANT THEY ARE- I'M GOING AFTER THEM!
WOW! I WONDER WHAT BIG TIM BANNON WILL SAY TO THIS!
AND WHEN INTERVIEWED, BIG TIM BANNON, POLITICAL BOSS OF THE CITY, SAYS....
THIS GUY KENDRICK TALKS BIG. NOW LET'S SEE HIM ACT BIG!
AND OUSTED DISTRICT ATTORNEY GRAVES SAYS....
HE'S GOING TO FIND THAT GETTING RID OF RACKETS IN THIS TOWN ISN'T SO EASY. I OUGHT TO KNOW!
BUT, OF COURSE, WE KNOW THE FORMER D.A. IS AND WAS IN BANNON'S PAY!
-AND SAYS MITCH MASON, OF THE WEST SIDE MOBSTERS.....
WHO...KENDRICK? NAW.-WE AIN'T WORRYIN' ABOUT HIM. HE'S THE GUY THAT SHOULD WORRY!
...AND TRIG COOLER, HEAD OF THE RIVAL EAST SIDE MOB--
ALL I GOTTA SAY IS KENDRICK SHOULDN'T OUGHTA WORK TOO HARD- IT AIN'T HEALTHY!
IN RETALIATION TO THESE THREATS, A CITIZENS' COMMITTEE IS FORMED, WITH WEALTHY BUSINESSMAN AMBROSE TAYLOR AT ITS HEAD.
WE CITIZENS ARE BEHIND KENDRICK. WE INTEND TO GIVE HIM EVERY SUPPORT, IN SPITE OF PRESSURE BY CERTAIN POLITICAL GROUPS!
KENDRICK GOES TO WORK WITH A VENGEANCE. INSIDE A WEEK, MOST OF THE MINOR RACKETEERS ARE IMPRISONED.
...AND NOW I'M AFTER THE BIG-SHOT RACKETEERS. I KNOW THEM AND THEIR CONNECTIONS...AND HAVE EVERY FACT WRITTEN DOWN IN WHAT I CALL MY "LITTLE BLACK BOOK!"
NEWS OF THE LITTLE BLACK BOOK TRAVELS THROUGH THE TOWN LIKE WILDFIRE---

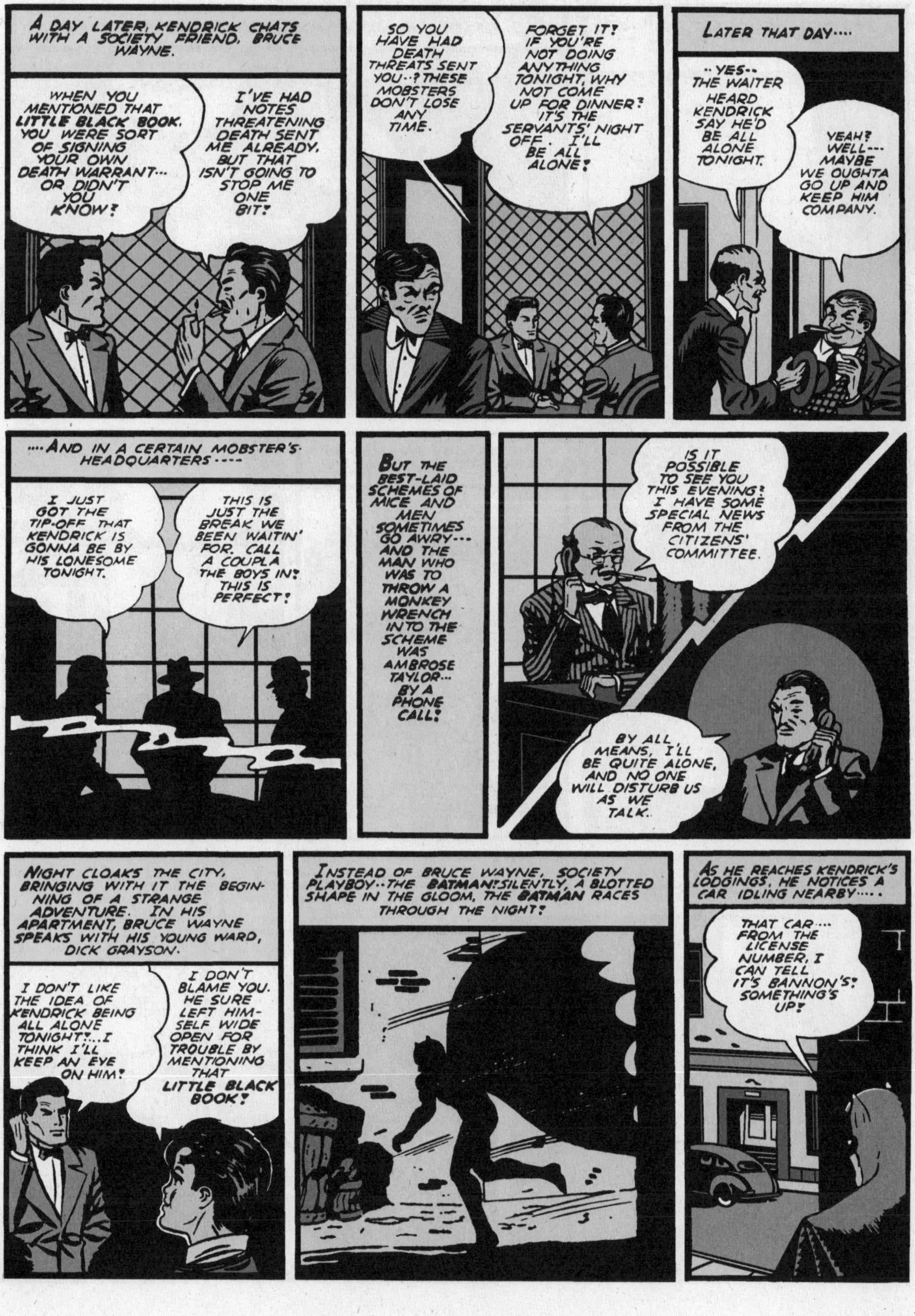
A DAY LATER, KENDRICK CHATS WITH A SOCIETY FRIEND, BRUCE WAYNE.
WHEN YOU MENTIONED THAT LITTLE BLACK BOOK, YOU WERE SORT OF SIGNING YOUR OWN DEATH WARRANT... OR DIDN'T YOU KNOW?
I'VE HAD NOTES THREATENING DEATH SENT ME ALREADY, BUT THAT ISN'T GOING TO STOP ME ONE BIT!
SO YOU HAVE HAD DEATH THREATS SENT YOU..? THESE MOBSTERS DON'T LOSE ANY TIME.
FORGET IT! IF YOU'RE NOT DOING ANYTHING TONIGHT, WHY NOT COME UP FOR DINNER? IT'S THE SERVANTS' NIGHT OFF. I'LL BE ALL ALONE!
LATER THAT DAY....
..YES.. THE WAITER HEARD KENDRICK SAY HE'D BE ALL ALONE TONIGHT.
YEAH? WELL--- MAYBE WE OUGHTA GO UP AND KEEP HIM COMPANY.
....AND IN A CERTAIN MOBSTER'S HEADQUARTERS----
I JUST GOT THE TIP-OFF THAT KENDRICK IS GONNA BE BY HIS LONESOME TONIGHT.
THIS IS JUST THE BREAK WE BEEN WAITIN' FOR. CALL A COUPLA THE BOYS IN! THIS IS PERFECT!
BUT THE BEST-LAID SCHEMES OF MICE AND MEN SOMETIMES GO AWRY--- AND THE MAN WHO WAS TO THROW A MONKEY WRENCH INTO THE SCHEME WAS AMBROSE TAYLOR... BY A PHONE CALL!
IS IT POSSIBLE TO SEE YOU THIS EVENING? I HAVE SOME SPECIAL NEWS FROM THE CITIZENS' COMMITTEE.
BY ALL MEANS, I'LL BE QUITE ALONE, AND NO ONE WILL DISTURB US AS WE TALK.
NIGHT CLOAKS THE CITY, BRINGING WITH IT THE BEGINNING OF A STRANGE ADVENTURE. IN HIS APARTMENT, BRUCE WAYNE SPEAKS WITH HIS YOUNG WARD, DICK GRAYSON.
I DON'T LIKE THE IDEA OF KENDRICK BEING ALL ALONE TONIGHT!...I THINK I'LL KEEP AN EYE ON HIM!
I DON'T BLAME YOU. HE SURE LEFT HIMSELF WIDE OPEN FOR TROUBLE BY MENTIONING THAT LITTLE BLACK BOOK!
INSTEAD OF BRUCE WAYNE, SOCIETY PLAYBOY..THE BATMAN! SILENTLY, A BLOTTED SHAPE IN THE GLOOM, THE BATMAN RACES THROUGH THE NIGHT!
AS HE REACHES KENDRICK'S LODGINGS, HE NOTICES A CAR IDLING NEARBY.....
THAT CAR.... FROM THE LICENSE NUMBER, I CAN TELL IT'S BANNON'S! SOMETHING'S UP!

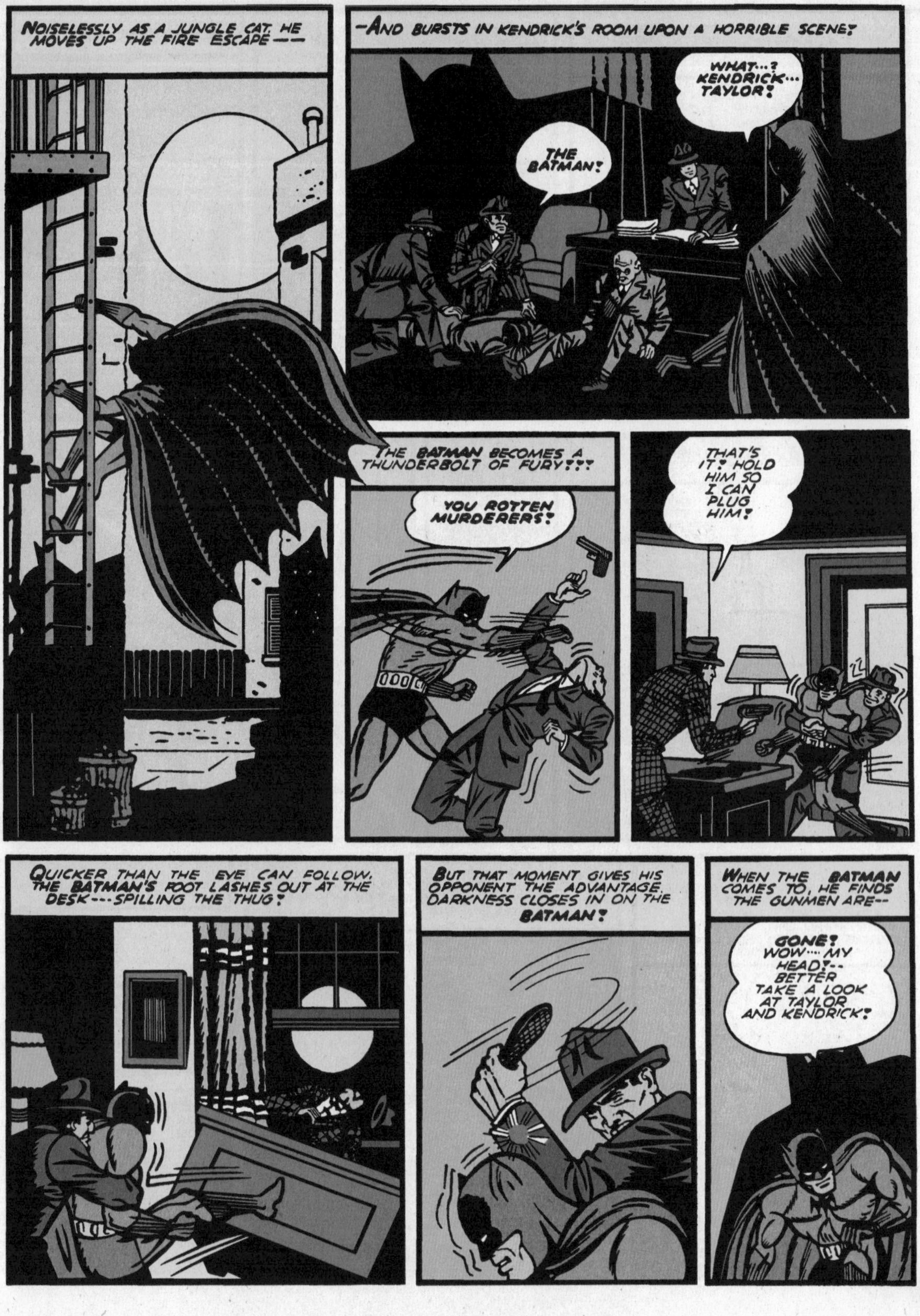
NOISELESSLY AS A JUNGLE CAT, HE MOVES UP THE FIRE ESCAPE---
-AND BURSTS IN KENDRICK'S ROOM UPON A HORRIBLE SCENE!
WHAT...? KENDRICK... TAYLOR!
THE BATMAN!
THE BATMAN BECOMES A THUNDERBOLT OF FURY!!!
YOU ROTTEN MURDERERS!
THAT'S IT! HOLD HIM SO I CAN PLUG HIM!
QUICKER THAN THE EYE CAN FOLLOW, THE BATMAN'S FOOT LASHES OUT AT THE DESK---SPILLING THE THUG!
BUT THAT MOMENT GIVES HIS OPPONENT THE ADVANTAGE. DARKNESS CLOSES IN ON THE BATMAN!
WHEN THE BATMAN COMES TO, HE FINDS THE GUNMEN ARE--
GONE! WOW.... MY HEAD!-- BETTER TAKE A LOOK AT TAYLOR AND KENDRICK!

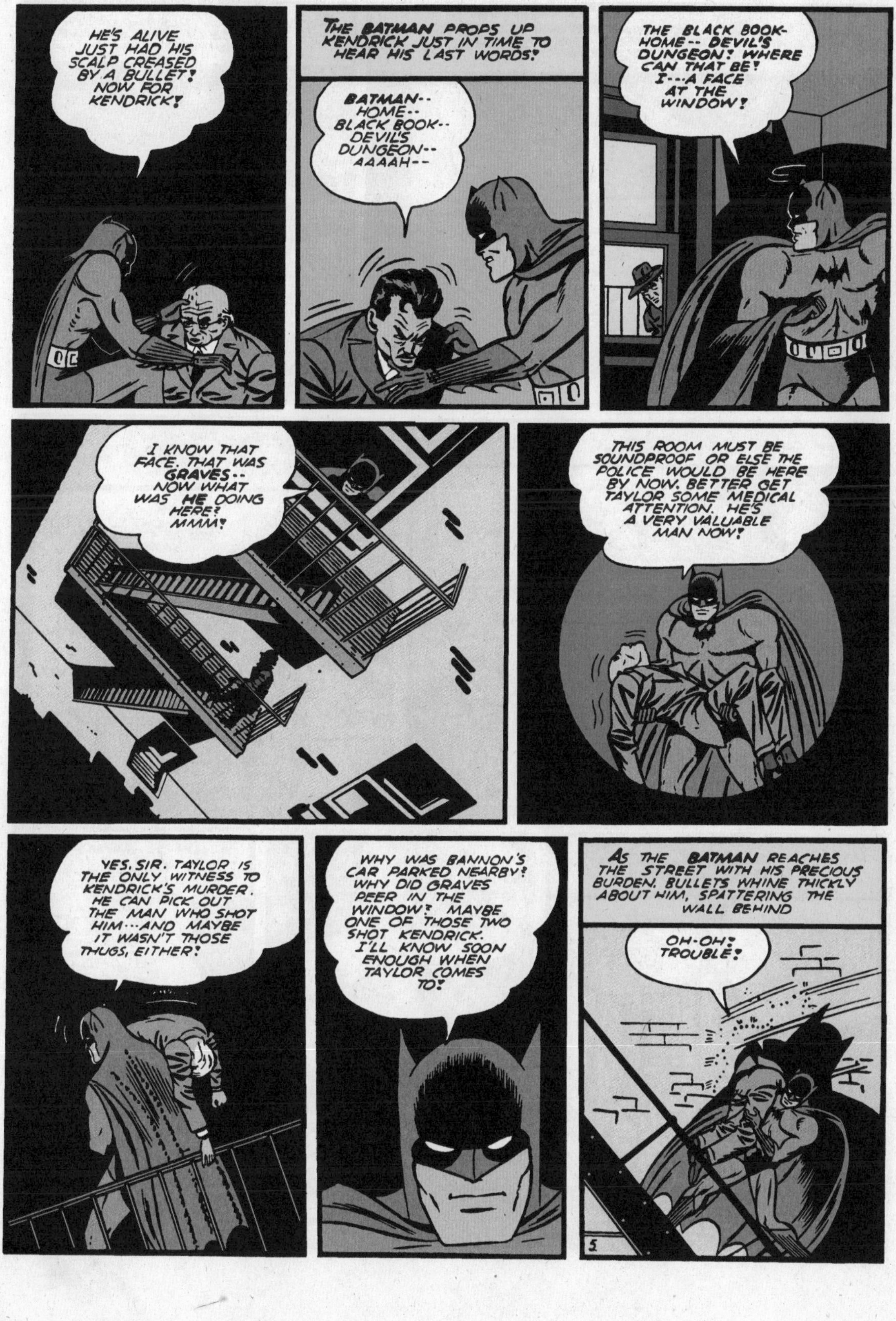
HE'S ALIVE JUST HAD HIS SCALP CREASED BY A BULLET! NOW FOR KENDRICK!
THE BATMAN PROPS UP KENDRICK JUST IN TIME TO HEAR HIS LAST WORDS!
BATMAN-- HOME-- BLACK BOOK-- DEVIL'S DUNGEON-- AAAAH--
THE BLACK BOOK- HOME-- DEVIL'S DUNGEON! WHERE CAN THAT BE! I---A FACE AT THE WINDOW!
I KNOW THAT FACE. THAT WAS GRAVES-- NOW WHAT WAS HE DOING HERE? MMM!
THIS ROOM MUST BE SOUNDPROOF OR ELSE THE POLICE WOULD BE HERE BY NOW. BETTER GET TAYLOR SOME MEDICAL ATTENTION. HE'S A VERY VALUABLE MAN NOW!
YES, SIR. TAYLOR IS THE ONLY WITNESS TO KENDRICK'S MURDER. HE CAN PICK OUT THE MAN WHO SHOT HIM---AND MAYBE IT WASN'T THOSE THUGS, EITHER!
WHY WAS BANNON'S CAR PARKED NEARBY? WHY DID GRAVES PEER IN THE WINDOW? MAYBE ONE OF THOSE TWO SHOT KENDRICK. I'LL KNOW SOON ENOUGH WHEN TAYLOR COMES TO!
AS THE BATMAN REACHES THE STREET WITH HIS PRECIOUS BURDEN, BULLETS WHINE THICKLY ABOUT HIM, SPATTERING THE WALL BEHIND
OH-OH! TROUBLE!
5

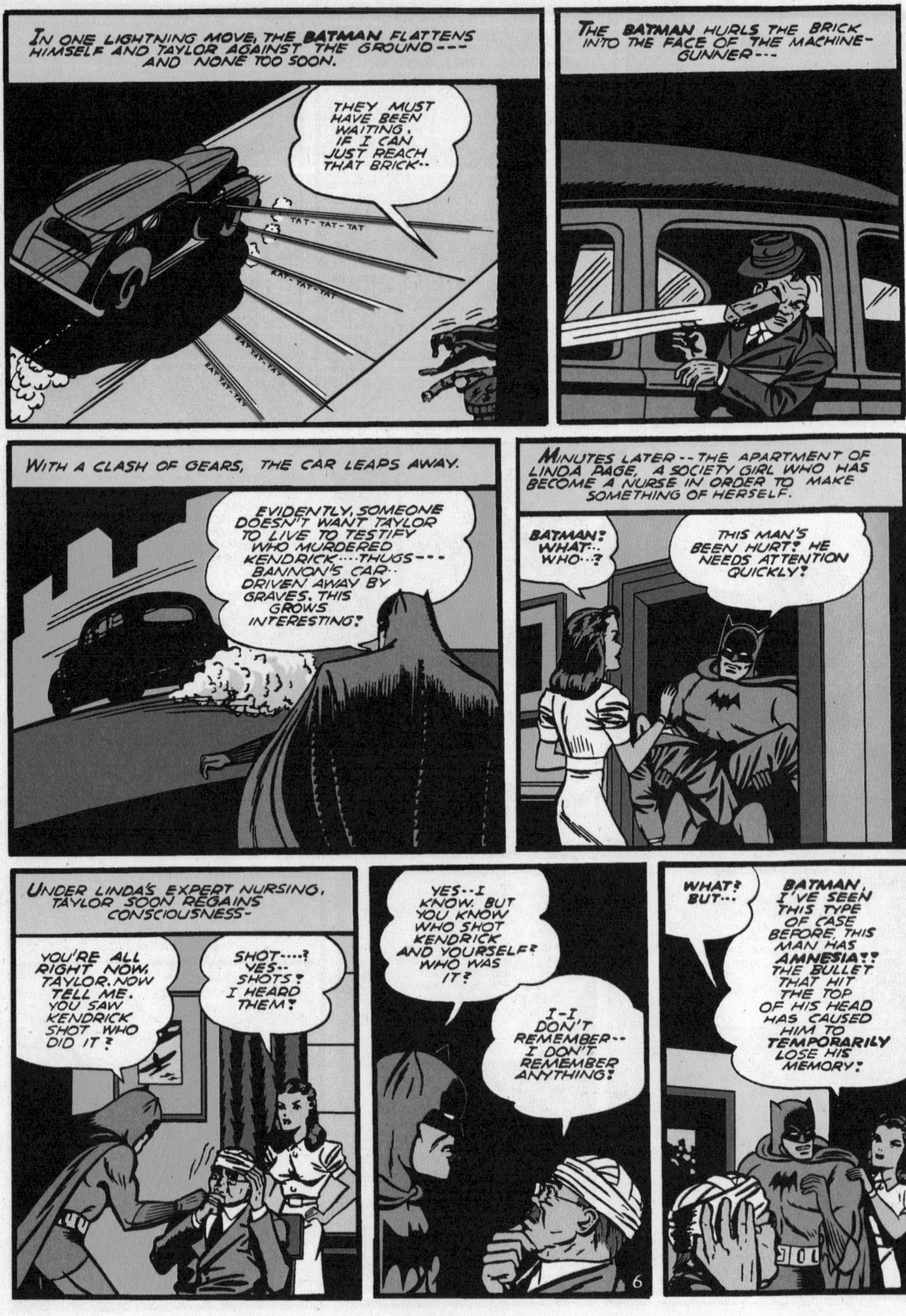
IN ONE LIGHTNING MOVE, THE BATMAN FLATTENS HIMSELF AND TAYLOR AGAINST THE GROUND--- AND NONE TOO SOON.
THEY MUST HAVE BEEN WAITING. IF I CAN JUST REACH THAT BRICK..
TAT-TAT-TAT
RAT-TAT-TAT
RAT-TAT-TAT
RAT-TAT-TAT
THE BATMAN HURLS THE BRICK INTO THE FACE OF THE MACHINE-GUNNER---
WITH A CLASH OF GEARS, THE CAR LEAPS AWAY.
EVIDENTLY, SOMEONE DOESN'T WANT TAYLOR TO LIVE TO TESTIFY WHO MURDERED KENDRICK....THUGS--- BANNON'S CAR.. DRIVEN AWAY BY GRAVES. THIS GROWS INTERESTING!
MINUTES LATER--THE APARTMENT OF LINDA PAGE, A SOCIETY GIRL WHO HAS BECOME A NURSE IN ORDER TO MAKE SOMETHING OF HERSELF.
BATMAN! WHAT.. WHO..?
THIS MAN'S BEEN HURT! HE NEEDS ATTENTION QUICKLY!
UNDER LINDA'S EXPERT NURSING, TAYLOR SOON REGAINS CONSCIOUSNESS-
YOU'RE ALL RIGHT NOW, TAYLOR. NOW TELL ME. YOU SAW KENDRICK SHOT. WHO DID IT?
SHOT....? YES.. SHOTS! I HEARD THEM!
YES..I KNOW. BUT YOU KNOW WHO SHOT KENDRICK AND YOURSELF? WHO WAS IT?
I-I DON'T REMEMBER.. I DON'T REMEMBER ANYTHING!
6
WHAT? BUT..?
BATMAN, I'VE SEEN THIS TYPE OF CASE BEFORE. THIS MAN HAS AMNESIA!! THE BULLET THAT HIT THE TOP OF HIS HEAD HAS CAUSED HIM TO TEMPORARILY LOSE HIS MEMORY!

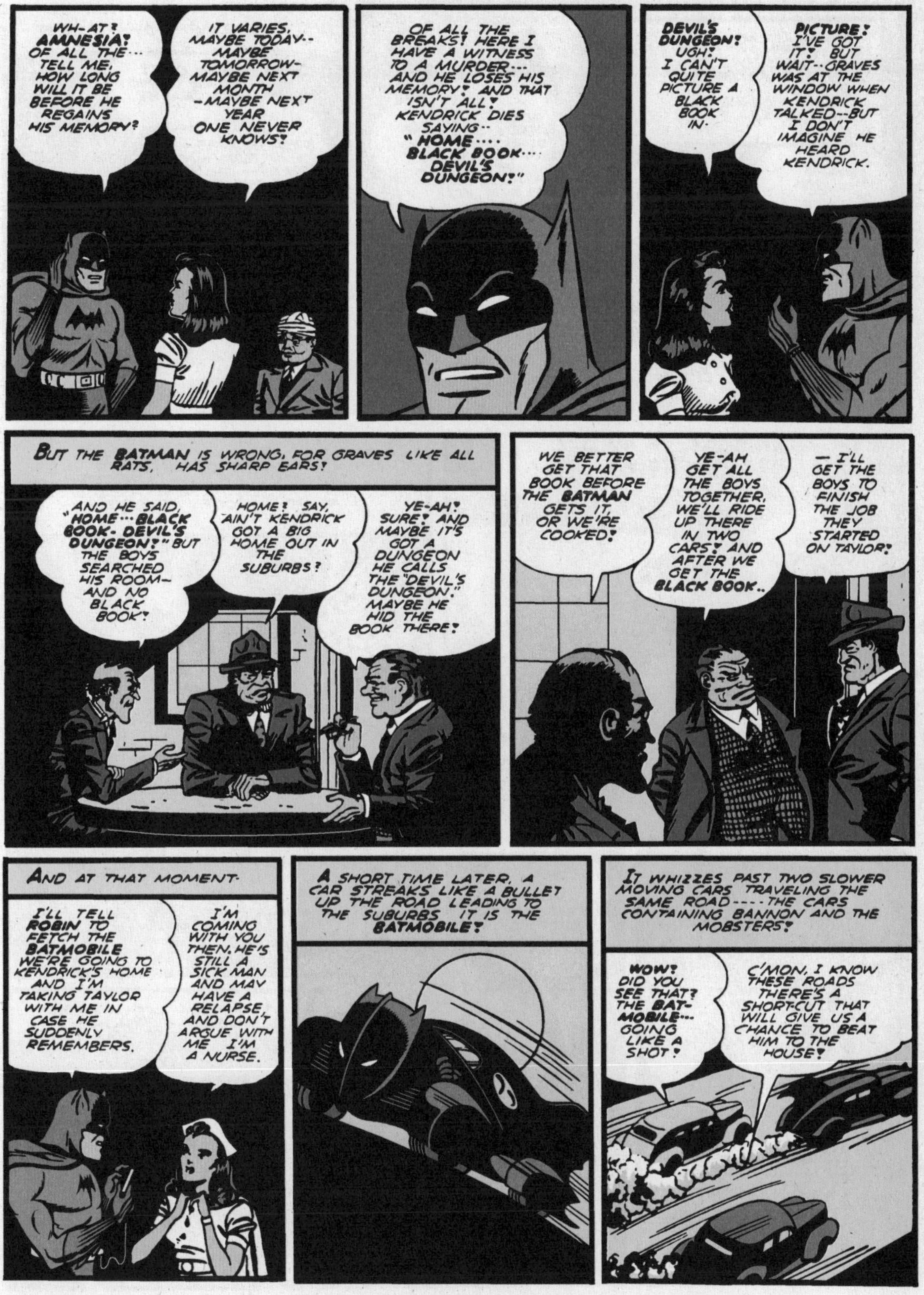

WH-AT! AMNESIA! OF ALL THE... TELL ME, HOW LONG WILL IT BE BEFORE HE REGAINS HIS MEMORY?
IT VARIES. MAYBE TODAY-- MAYBE TOMORROW-- MAYBE NEXT MONTH --MAYBE NEXT YEAR ONE NEVER KNOWS!
OF ALL THE BREAKS! HERE I HAVE A WITNESS TO A MURDER--- AND HE LOSES HIS MEMORY! AND THAT ISN'T ALL! KENDRICK DIES SAYING-- "HOME.... BLACK BOOK.... DEVIL'S DUNGEON!"
DEVIL'S DUNGEON! UGH! I CAN'T QUITE PICTURE A BLACK BOOK IN-
PICTURE! I'VE GOT IT! BUT WAIT--GRAVES WAS AT THE WINDOW WHEN KENDRICK TALKED--BUT I DON'T IMAGINE HE HEARD KENDRICK.
BUT THE BATMAN IS WRONG, FOR GRAVES LIKE ALL RATS, HAS SHARP EARS!
AND HE SAID, "HOME...BLACK BOOK--DEVIL'S DUNGEON!" BUT THE BOYS SEARCHED HIS ROOM-- AND NO BLACK BOOK!
HOME! SAY, AIN'T KENDRICK GOT A BIG HOME OUT IN THE SUBURBS?
YE-AH! SURE! AND MAYBE IT'S GOT A DUNGEON HE CALLS THE "DEVIL'S DUNGEON." MAYBE HE HID THE BOOK THERE!
WE BETTER GET THAT BOOK BEFORE THE BATMAN GETS IT, OR WE'RE COOKED!
YE-AH GET ALL THE BOYS TOGETHER. WE'LL RIDE UP THERE IN TWO CARS! AND AFTER WE GET THE BLACK BOOK..
--I'LL GET THE BOYS TO FINISH THE JOB THEY STARTED ON TAYLOR!
AND AT THAT MOMENT-
I'LL TELL ROBIN TO FETCH THE BATMOBILE WE'RE GOING TO KENDRICK'S HOME AND I'M TAKING TAYLOR WITH ME IN CASE HE SUDDENLY REMEMBERS.
I'M COMING WITH YOU THEN. HE'S STILL A SICK MAN AND MAY HAVE A RELAPSE, AND DON'T ARGUE WITH ME I'M A NURSE.
A SHORT TIME LATER, A CAR STREAKS LIKE A BULLET UP THE ROAD LEADING TO THE SUBURBS IT IS THE BATMOBILE!
IT WHIZZES PAST TWO SLOWER MOVING CARS TRAVELING THE SAME ROAD----THE CARS CONTAINING BANNON AND THE MOBSTERS!
WOW! DID YOU SEE THAT? THE BAT-MOBILE--- GOING LIKE A SHOT!
C'MON, I KNOW THESE ROADS THERE'S A SHORT-CUT THAT WILL GIVE US A CHANCE TO BEAT HIM TO THE HOUSE!

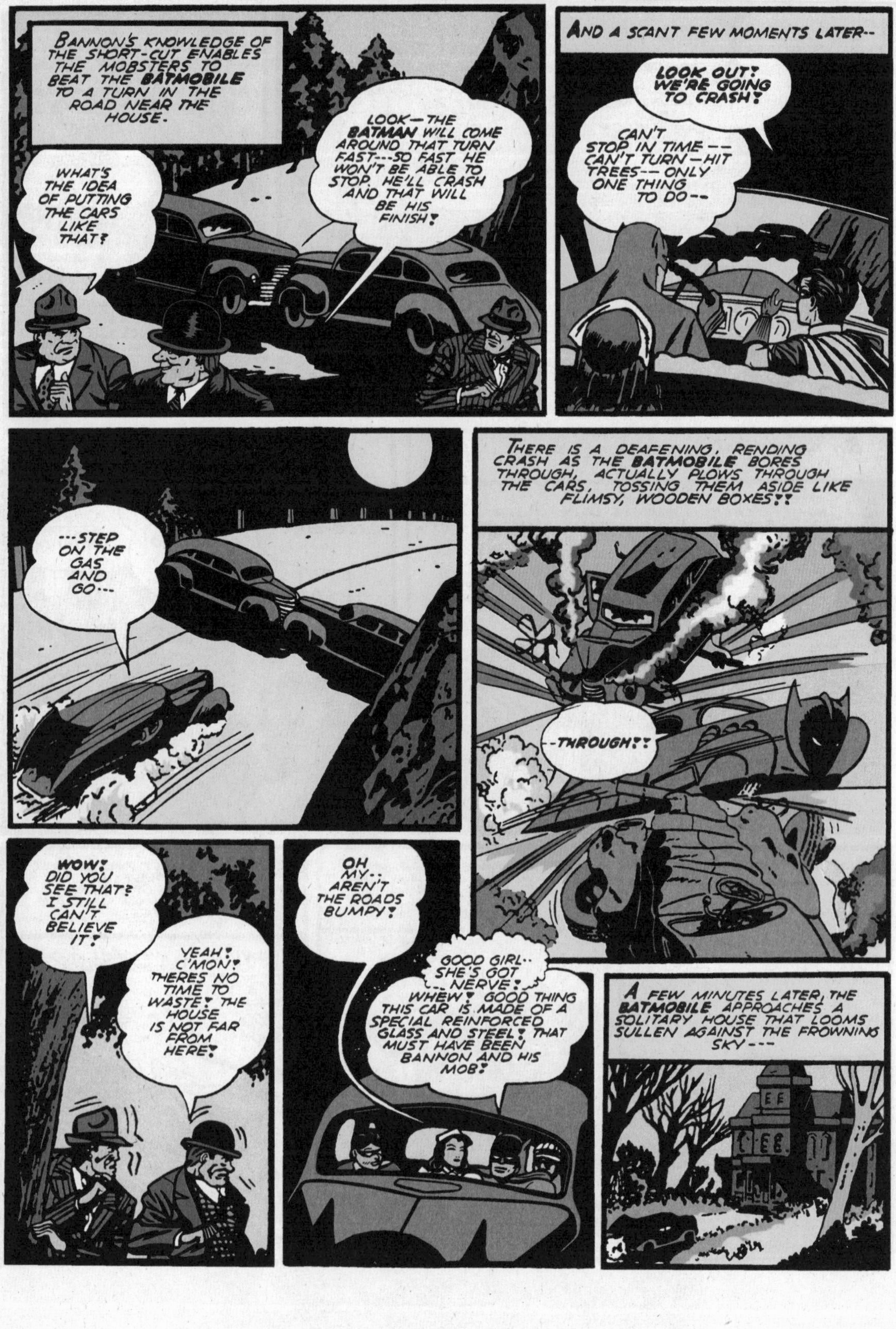

BANNON'S KNOWLEDGE OF THE SHORT-CUT ENABLES THE MOBSTERS TO BEAT THE BATMOBILE TO A TURN IN THE ROAD NEAR THE HOUSE.
WHAT'S THE IDEA OF PUTTING THE CARS LIKE THAT?
LOOK—THE BATMAN WILL COME AROUND THAT TURN FAST---SO FAST HE WON'T BE ABLE TO STOP. HE'LL CRASH AND THAT WILL BE HIS FINISH!
AND A SCANT FEW MOMENTS LATER--
LOOK OUT! WE'RE GOING TO CRASH!
CAN'T STOP IN TIME -- CAN'T TURN—HIT TREES-- ONLY ONE THING TO DO--
---STEP ON THE GAS AND GO---
THERE IS A DEAFENING, RENDING CRASH AS THE BATMOBILE BORES THROUGH, ACTUALLY PLOWS THROUGH THE CARS, TOSSING THEM ASIDE LIKE FLIMSY, WOODEN BOXES!!
--THROUGH!!
WOW! DID YOU SEE THAT? I STILL CAN'T BELIEVE IT!
YEAH! C'MON! THERES NO TIME TO WASTE! THE HOUSE IS NOT FAR FROM HERE!
OH MY.. AREN'T THE ROADS BUMPY!
GOOD GIRL.. SHE'S GOT NERVE!
WHEW! GOOD THING THIS CAR IS MADE OF A SPECIAL REINFORCED GLASS AND STEEL! THAT MUST HAVE BEEN BANNON AND HIS MOB!
A FEW MINUTES LATER, THE BATMOBILE APPROACHES A SOLITARY HOUSE THAT LOOMS SULLEN AGAINST THE FROWNING SKY---

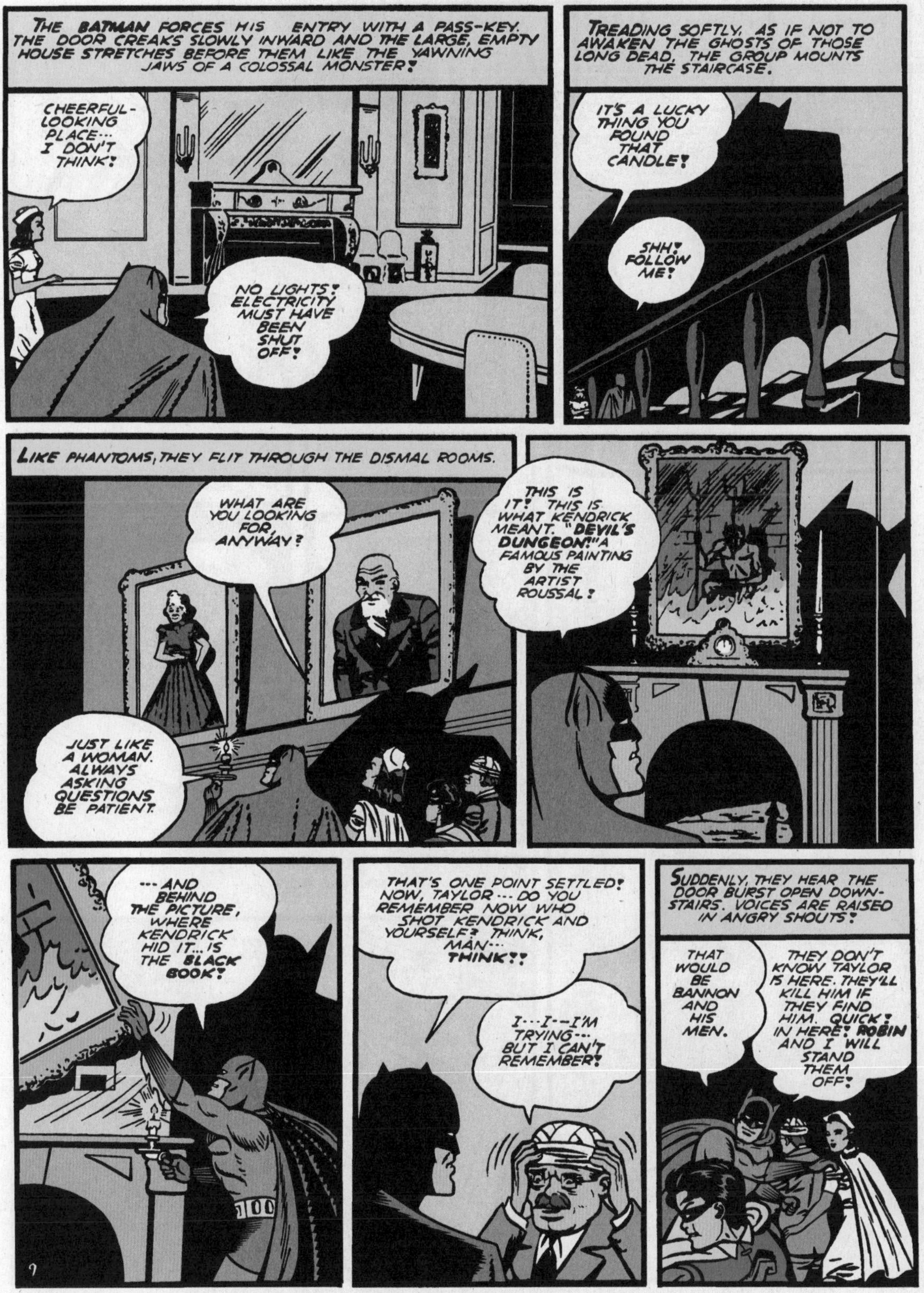
THE BATMAN FORCES HIS ENTRY WITH A PASS-KEY. THE DOOR CREAKS SLOWLY INWARD AND THE LARGE, EMPTY HOUSE STRETCHES BEFORE THEM LIKE THE YAWNING JAWS OF A COLOSSAL MONSTER!
CHEERFUL-LOOKING PLACE... I DON'T THINK!
NO LIGHTS! ELECTRICITY MUST HAVE BEEN SHUT OFF!
TREADING SOFTLY, AS IF NOT TO AWAKEN THE GHOSTS OF THOSE LONG DEAD, THE GROUP MOUNTS THE STAIRCASE.
IT'S A LUCKY THING YOU FOUND THAT CANDLE!
SHH! FOLLOW ME!
LIKE PHANTOMS, THEY FLIT THROUGH THE DISMAL ROOMS.
WHAT ARE YOU LOOKING FOR, ANYWAY?
JUST LIKE A WOMAN. ALWAYS ASKING QUESTIONS BE PATIENT.
THIS IS IT! THIS IS WHAT KENDRICK MEANT. "DEVIL'S DUNGEON!" A FAMOUS PAINTING BY THE ARTIST ROUSSAL!
---AND BEHIND THE PICTURE, WHERE KENDRICK HID IT...IS THE BLACK BOOK!
THAT'S ONE POINT SETTLED! NOW, TAYLOR --- DO YOU REMEMBER NOW WHO SHOT KENDRICK AND YOURSELF? THINK, MAN--- THINK!!
I---I--I'M TRYING--- BUT I CAN'T REMEMBER!
SUDDENLY, THEY HEAR THE DOOR BURST OPEN DOWN-STAIRS. VOICES ARE RAISED IN ANGRY SHOUTS!
THAT WOULD BE BANNON AND HIS MEN.
THEY DON'T KNOW TAYLOR IS HERE. THEY'LL KILL HIM IF THEY FIND HIM. QUICK! IN HERE! ROBIN AND I WILL STAND THEM OFF!

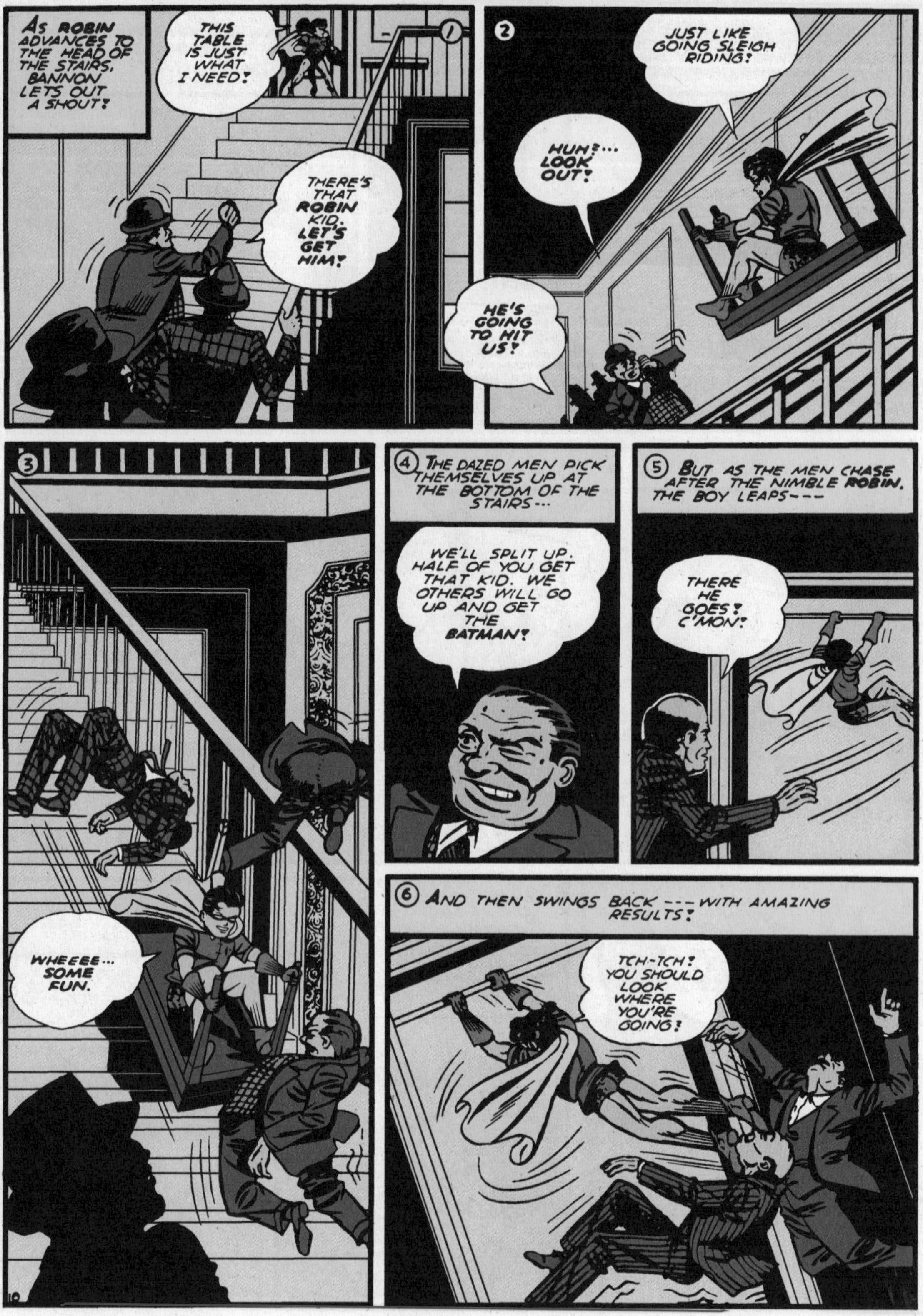
AS ROBIN ADVANCES TO THE HEAD OF THE STAIRS, BANNON LETS OUT A SHOUT!
THIS TABLE IS JUST WHAT I NEED!
THERE'S THAT ROBIN KID. LET'S GET HIM!
JUST LIKE GOING SLEIGH RIDING!
HUH?... LOOK OUT!
HE'S GOING TO HIT US!
WHEEEE... SOME FUN.
THE DAZED MEN PICK THEMSELVES UP AT THE BOTTOM OF THE STAIRS...
WE'LL SPLIT UP. HALF OF YOU GET THAT KID. WE OTHERS WILL GO UP AND GET THE BATMAN!
BUT AS THE MEN CHASE AFTER THE NIMBLE ROBIN, THE BOY LEAPS---
THERE HE GOES! C'MON!
AND THEN SWINGS BACK --- WITH AMAZING RESULTS!
TCH-TCH! YOU SHOULD LOOK WHERE YOU'RE GOING!

MEANWHILE, BANNON AND GRAVES LOSE THEIR WAY IN THE CLOSE-PRESSING DARKNESS.

WE'RE SEPARATED FROM THE MEN!

ANYBODY COULD LOSE HIMSELF IN THIS DARK PLACE. CAN'T SEE A THING!

I CAN'T SEE THEM, BUT THOSE VOICES TELL ME BANNON AND GRAVES ARE HERE!

FROM A POUCH, ESPECIALLY BUILT IN HIS BELT, THE BATMAN TAKES A QUEER-LOOKING PAIR OF GLASSES

NOW I'LL HAVE SOME FUN!

THOUGH HE HIMSELF CANNOT BE SEEN, WITH THESE ESPECIALLY PREPARED GLASSES, THE BATMAN CAN SEE IN THE DARK---AS WOULD A REAL BAT!

I WOULDN'T STRIKE THAT MATCH IF I WERE YOU, BANNON!

THE BATMAN! BUT HOW DID HE KNOW--? IT'S PITCH BLACK IN HERE!

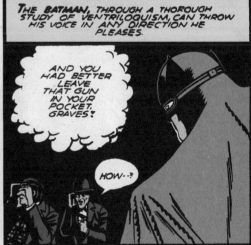

THE BATMAN, THROUGH A THOROUGH STUDY OF VENTRILOQUISM, CAN THROW HIS VOICE IN ANY DIRECTION HE PLEASES.

AND YOU HAD BETTER LEAVE THAT GUN IN YOUR POCKET, GRAVES!

HOW--?

THE MEN SHUDDER IN TERROR AT THE "SUPERNATURAL" POWER OF THE BATMAN!

BANNON! HE CAN SEE! HE CAN SEE IN THE DARK!

IT'S UNCANNY! THAT GUY SEES IN THE DARK LIKE A REAL BAT! LET'S GET OUT OF HERE!

IT'S JUST THAT I DON'T WANT TO SOIL MY HANDS ON YOU TWO!

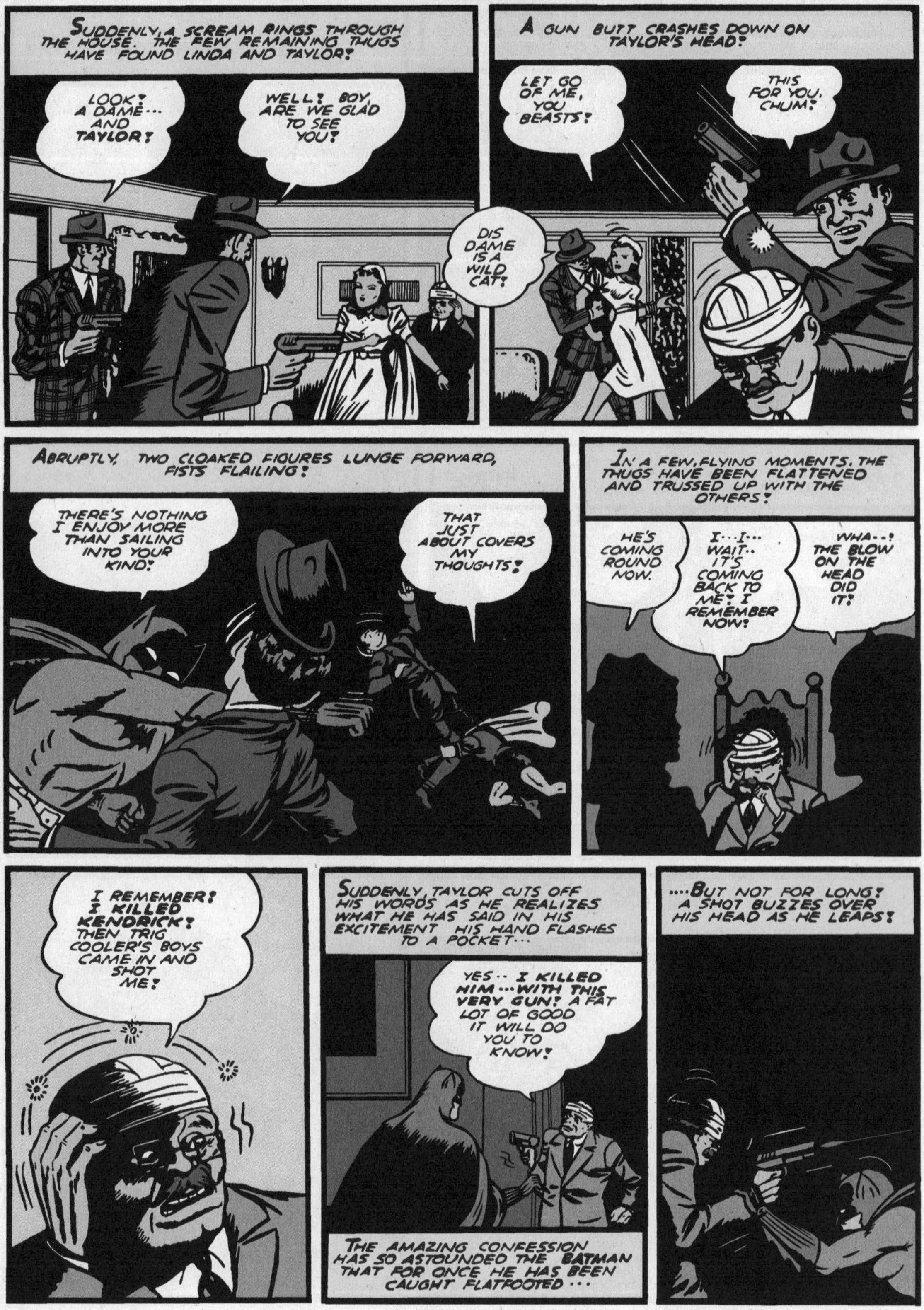
SUDDENLY, A SCREAM RINGS THROUGH THE HOUSE. THE FEW REMAINING THUGS HAVE FOUND LINDA AND TAYLOR!
LOOK! A DAME... AND TAYLOR!
WELL! BOY, ARE WE GLAD TO SEE YOU!
A GUN BUTT CRASHES DOWN ON TAYLOR'S HEAD!
LET GO OF ME, YOU BEASTS!
DIS DAME IS A WILD CAT!
THIS FOR YOU, CHUM!
ABRUPTLY, TWO CLOAKED FIGURES LUNGE FORWARD, FISTS FLAILING!
THERE'S NOTHING I ENJOY MORE THAN SAILING INTO YOUR KIND!
THAT JUST ABOUT COVERS MY THOUGHTS!
IN A FEW, FLYING MOMENTS, THE THUGS HAVE BEEN FLATTENED AND TRUSSED UP WITH THE OTHERS!
HE'S COMING ROUND NOW.
I...I... WAIT.. IT'S COMING BACK TO ME! I REMEMBER NOW!
WHA..! THE BLOW ON THE HEAD DID IT!
I REMEMBER! I KILLED KENDRICK! THEN TRIG COOLER'S BOYS CAME IN AND SHOT ME!
SUDDENLY, TAYLOR CUTS OFF HIS WORDS AS HE REALIZES WHAT HE HAS SAID IN HIS EXCITEMENT. HIS HAND FLASHES TO A POCKET...
YES.. I KILLED HIM ...WITH THIS VERY GUN! A FAT LOT OF GOOD IT WILL DO YOU TO KNOW!
THE AMAZING CONFESSION HAS SO ASTOUNDED THE BATMAN THAT FOR ONCE HE HAS BEEN CAUGHT FLATFOOTED...
....BUT NOT FOR LONG! A SHOT BUZZES OVER HIS HEAD AS HE LEAPS!

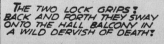

THE TWO LOCK GRIPS! BACK AND FORTH THEY SWAY ONTO THE HALL BALCONY IN A WILD DERVISH OF DEATH!

WITH A TITANIC EFFORT, THE *BATMAN* TEARS A HAND FREE, WINDS IT INTO A FIST... AND CRASHES IT AGAINST TAYLOR'S CHIN!

A SUDDEN SPLINTERING OF WOOD, AND TAYLOR PLUNGES THROUGH THE BALCONY RAILING!

TAYLOR--- THE MURDERER! IT DOESN'T MAKE SENSE!

SURE IT DOES. TAYLOR WAS THE *REAL LEADER* OF THE *WEST SIDE MOBSTERS!* MITCH MASON WAS ONLY HIS LIEUTENANT!

THEN HE SHOT KENDRICK BECAUSE HE THOUGHT HE KNEW--- AND HAD THE INFORMATION IN THE *LITTLE BLACK BOOK!*

WHEN MY BOYS WENT INTO THE ROOM TO FORCE KENDRICK TO GIVE UP THE *BLACK BOOK,* THEY SAW THAT TAYLOR SHOT HIM. THEY TRIED TO GET TAYLOR 'CAUSE HE WAS FROM THE *RIVAL* MOB.

HMM! YOU WERE WORKING WITH BANNON--- GIVING HIM A CUT FOR POLITICAL PROTECTION! BUT, WHY DIDN'T YOU JUST TELL THE POLICE TAYLOR WAS THE MURDERER? YOU'D HAVE RID YOURSELF OF HIM THAT WAY.

IF WE SQUEALED ON TAYLOR, TAYLOR WOULD TALK! HE KNOWS THINGS ABOUT A LOT OF US THAT MIGHT GET *US* IN PRISON CELLS, TOO!

A CASE OF SELF-PROTECTION WELL, NOW ALL THAT'S LEFT TO DO IS GIVE THE BLACK BOOK TO THE POLICE AND LET THEM TAKE OVER.

BOB KANE

LATER--- AFTER THEY HAVE INFORMED THE POLICE, THE TRIO ARE HOMEWARD BOUND---

WHO WOULD HAVE THOUGHT TAYLOR WAS THE MURDERER!

IMAGINE, WE HAD THE MURDERER IN OUR HANDS ALL THE TIME AND DIDN'T KNOW IT!

ROBIN, IF EVER YOU FEEL I'M GETTING TOO COCKSURE OF MY-SELF, I'D APPRECIATE YOUR MENTIONING THIS CASE TO ME! THAT'LL BRING ME DOWN TO EARTH!

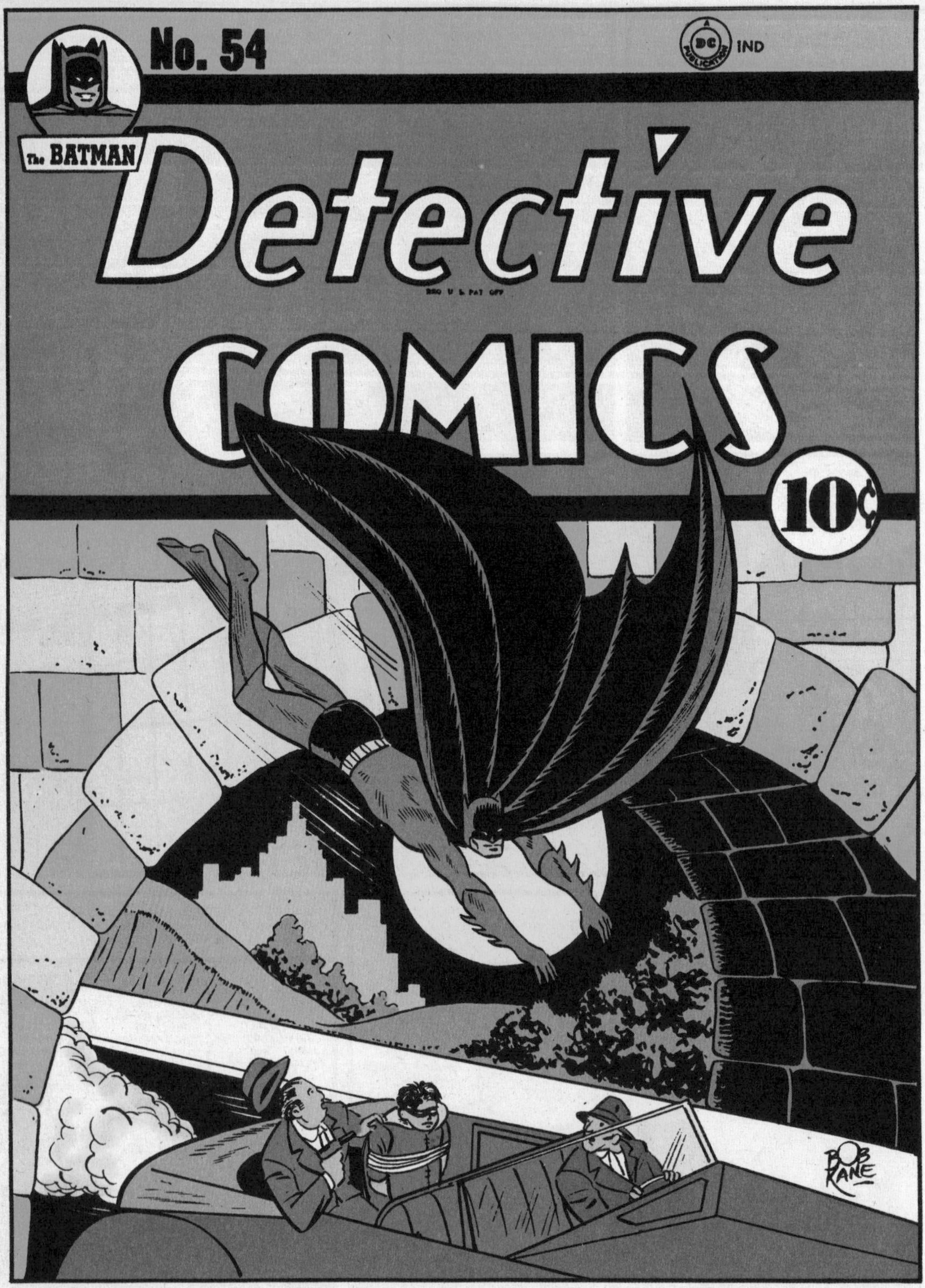
No. 54
A DC PUBLICATION
IND
The BATMAN
Detective
COMICS
10¢
BOB KANE

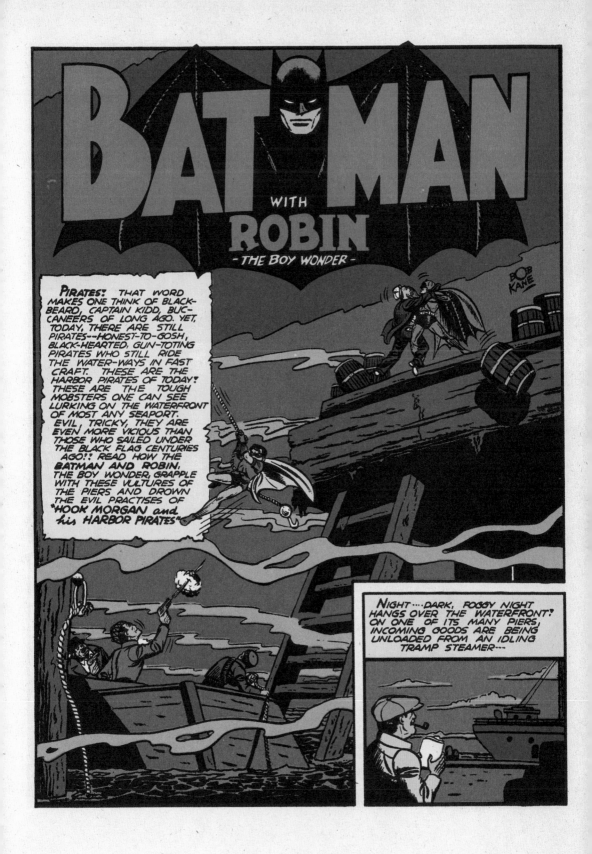

BAT MAN

WITH
ROBIN
- THE BOY WONDER -

BOB KANE

PIRATES! THAT WORD MAKES ONE THINK OF BLACK-BEARD, CAPTAIN KIDD, BUC-CANEERS OF LONG AGO. YET, TODAY, THERE ARE STILL PIRATES--HONEST-TO-GOSH, BLACK-HEARTED, GUN-TOTING PIRATES WHO STILL RIDE THE WATER-WAYS IN FAST CRAFT. THESE ARE THE HARBOR PIRATES OF TODAY! THESE ARE THE TOUGH MOBSTERS ONE CAN SEE LURKING ON THE WATERFRONT OF MOST ANY SEAPORT. EVIL, TRICKY, THEY ARE EVEN MORE VICIOUS THAN THOSE WHO SAILED UNDER THE BLACK FLAG CENTURIES AGO!! READ HOW THE BATMAN AND ROBIN, THE BOY WONDER, GRAPPLE WITH THESE VULTURES OF THE PIERS AND DROWN THE EVIL PRACTISES OF "HOOK MORGAN and his HARBOR PIRATES"

NIGHT----DARK, FOGGY NIGHT HANGS OVER THE WATERFRONT! ON ONE OF ITS MANY PIERS, INCOMING GOODS ARE BEING UNLOADED FROM AN IDLING TRAMP STEAMER---

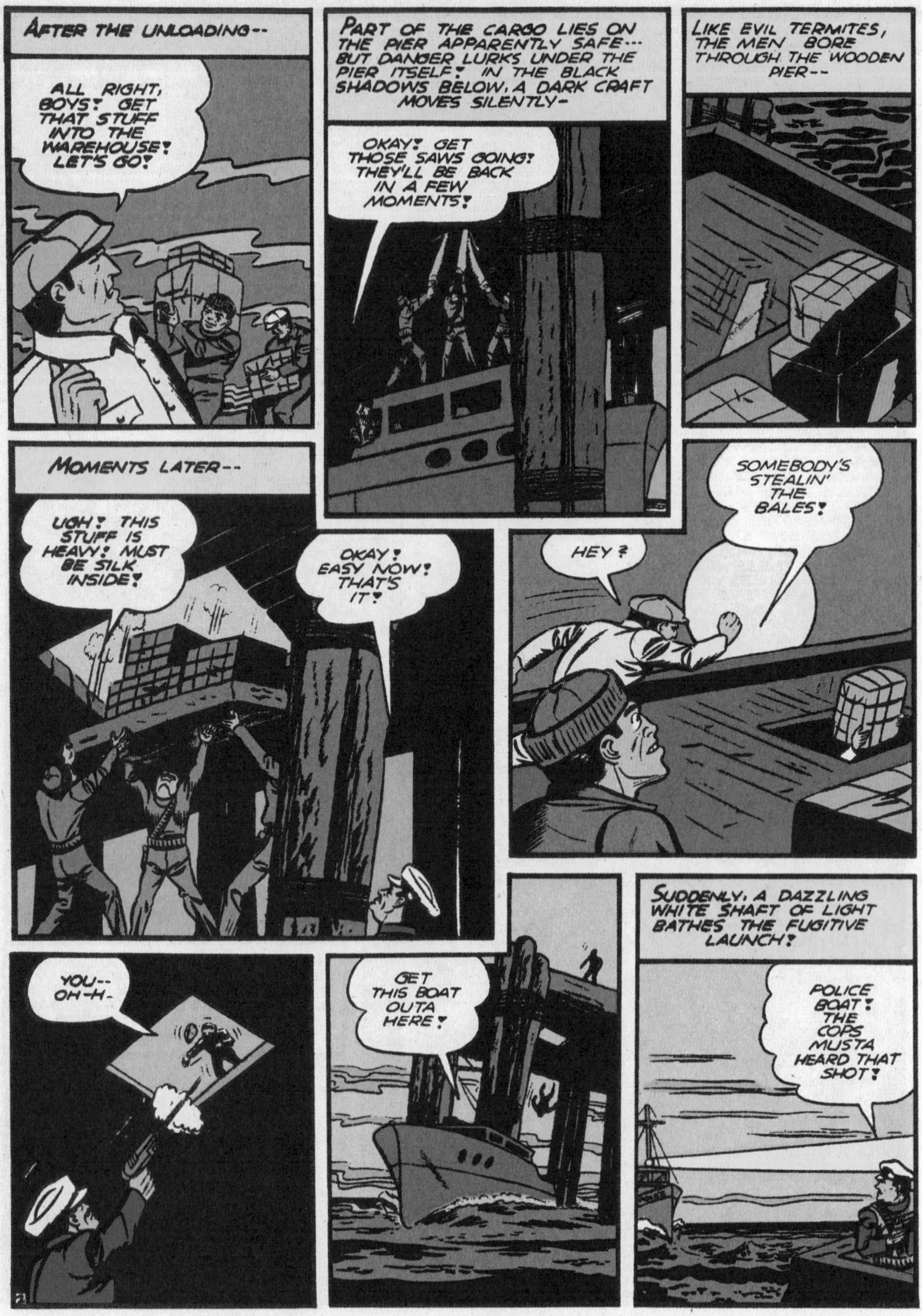
AFTER THE UNLOADING--
ALL RIGHT, BOYS! GET THAT STUFF INTO THE WAREHOUSE! LET'S GO!
PART OF THE CARGO LIES ON THE PIER APPARENTLY SAFE--- BUT DANGER LURKS UNDER THE PIER ITSELF! IN THE BLACK SHADOWS BELOW, A DARK CRAFT MOVES SILENTLY-
OKAY! GET THOSE SAWS GOING! THEY'LL BE BACK IN A FEW MOMENTS!
LIKE EVIL TERMITES, THE MEN BORE THROUGH THE WOODEN PIER--
MOMENTS LATER--
UGH! THIS STUFF IS HEAVY! MUST BE SILK INSIDE!
OKAY! EASY NOW! THAT'S IT!
HEY ?
SOMEBODY'S STEALIN' THE BALES!
YOU-- OH-H-
GET THIS BOAT OUTA HERE!
SUDDENLY, A DAZZLING WHITE SHAFT OF LIGHT BATHES THE FUGITIVE LAUNCH!
POLICE BOAT! THE COPS MUSTA HEARD THAT SHOT!

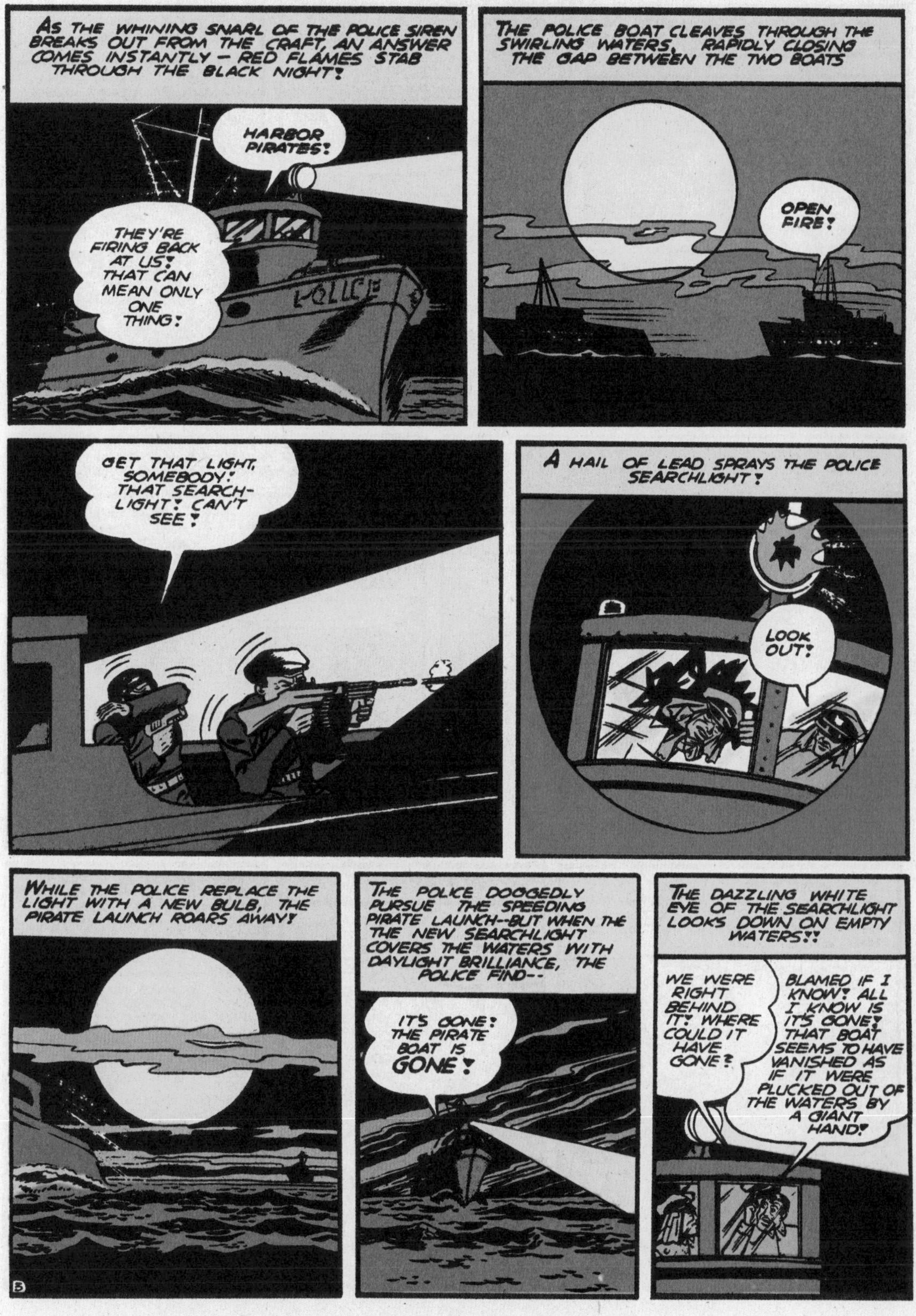
AS THE WHINING SNARL OF THE POLICE SIREN BREAKS OUT FROM THE CRAFT, AN ANSWER COMES INSTANTLY -- RED FLAMES STAB THROUGH THE BLACK NIGHT!
HARBOR PIRATES!
THEY'RE FIRING BACK AT US! THAT CAN MEAN ONLY ONE THING!
POLICE
THE POLICE BOAT CLEAVES THROUGH THE SWIRLING WATERS, RAPIDLY CLOSING THE GAP BETWEEN THE TWO BOATS
OPEN FIRE!
GET THAT LIGHT, SOMEBODY! THAT SEARCH-LIGHT! CAN'T SEE!
A HAIL OF LEAD SPRAYS THE POLICE SEARCHLIGHT!
LOOK OUT!
WHILE THE POLICE REPLACE THE LIGHT WITH A NEW BULB, THE PIRATE LAUNCH ROARS AWAY!
THE POLICE DOGGEDLY PURSUE THE SPEEDING PIRATE LAUNCH--BUT WHEN THE THE NEW SEARCHLIGHT COVERS THE WATERS WITH DAYLIGHT BRILLIANCE, THE POLICE FIND--
IT'S GONE! THE PIRATE BOAT IS GONE!
THE DAZZLING WHITE EYE OF THE SEARCHLIGHT LOOKS DOWN ON EMPTY WATERS!!
WE WERE RIGHT BEHIND IT! WHERE COULD IT HAVE GONE?
BLAMED IF I KNOW! ALL I KNOW IS IT'S GONE! THAT BOAT SEEMS TO HAVE VANISHED AS IF IT WERE PLUCKED OUT OF THE WATERS BY A GIANT HAND!

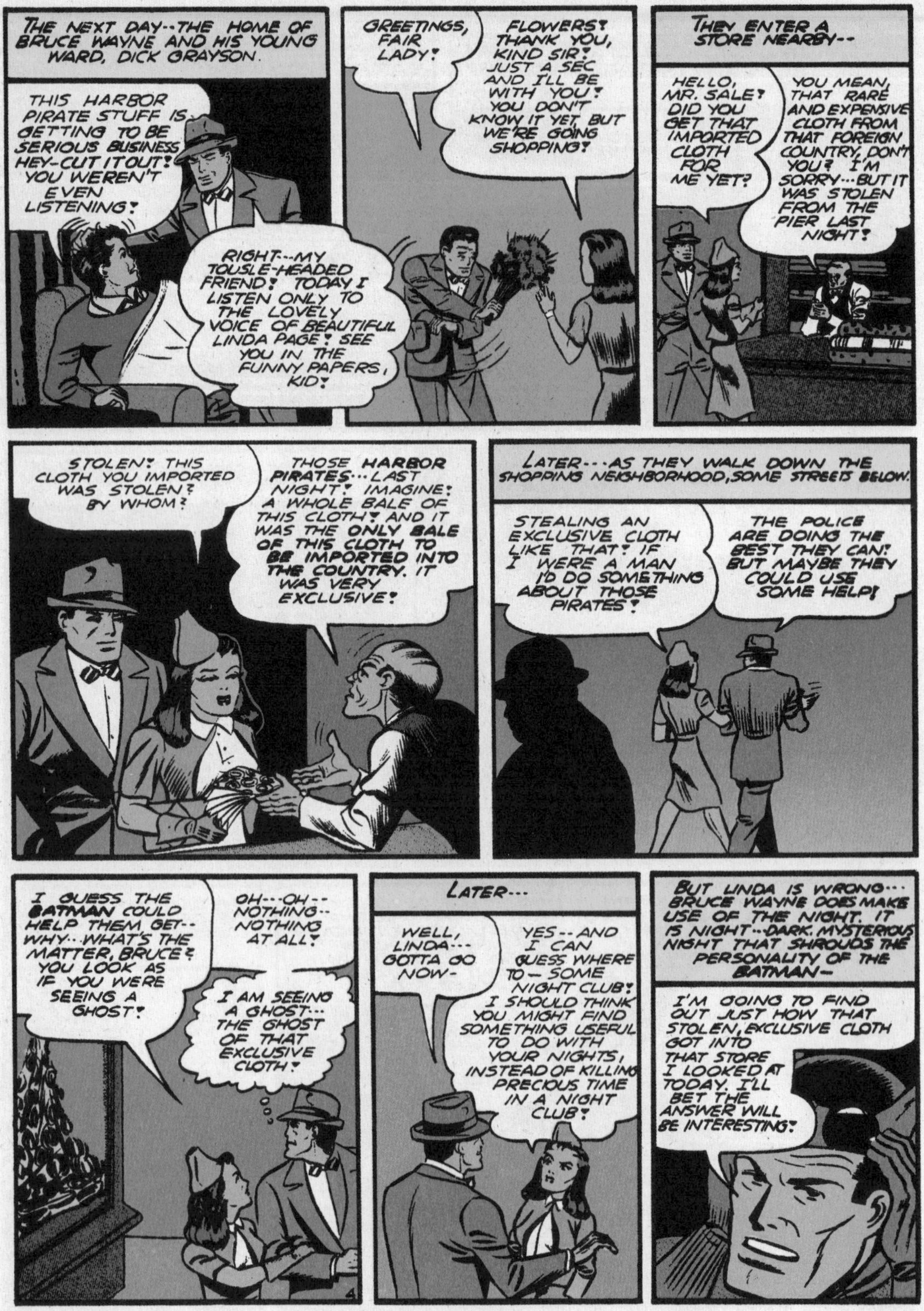

THE NEXT DAY--THE HOME OF BRUCE WAYNE AND HIS YOUNG WARD, DICK GRAYSON.
THIS HARBOR PIRATE STUFF IS GETTING TO BE SERIOUS BUSINESS HEY-CUT IT OUT! YOU WEREN'T EVEN LISTENING!
RIGHT---MY TOUSLE-HEADED FRIEND! TODAY I LISTEN ONLY TO THE LOVELY VOICE OF BEAUTIFUL LINDA PAGE! SEE YOU IN THE FUNNY PAPERS, KID!
GREETINGS, FAIR LADY!
FLOWERS! THANK YOU, KIND SIR! JUST A SEC AND I'LL BE WITH YOU! YOU DON'T KNOW IT YET, BUT WE'RE GOING SHOPPING!
THEY ENTER A STORE NEARBY--
HELLO, MR. SALE! DID YOU GET THAT IMPORTED CLOTH FOR ME YET?
YOU MEAN, THAT RARE AND EXPENSIVE CLOTH FROM THAT FOREIGN COUNTRY, DON'T YOU? I'M SORRY---BUT IT WAS STOLEN FROM THE PIER LAST NIGHT!
STOLEN! THIS CLOTH YOU IMPORTED WAS STOLEN? BY WHOM?
THOSE HARBOR PIRATES---LAST NIGHT! IMAGINE! A WHOLE BALE OF THIS CLOTH! AND IT WAS THE ONLY BALE OF THIS CLOTH TO BE IMPORTED INTO THE COUNTRY. IT WAS VERY EXCLUSIVE!
LATER---AS THEY WALK DOWN THE SHOPPING NEIGHBORHOOD, SOME STREETS BELOW.
STEALING AN EXCLUSIVE CLOTH LIKE THAT! IF I WERE A MAN I'D DO SOMETHING ABOUT THOSE PIRATES!
THE POLICE ARE DOING THE BEST THEY CAN! BUT MAYBE THEY COULD USE SOME HELP!
I GUESS THE BATMAN COULD HELP THEM GET-- WHY--WHAT'S THE MATTER, BRUCE? YOU LOOK AS IF YOU WERE SEEING A GHOST!
OH---OH-- NOTHING-- NOTHING AT ALL!
I AM SEEING A GHOST--- THE GHOST OF THAT EXCLUSIVE CLOTH!
LATER---
WELL, LINDA--- GOTTA GO NOW-
YES--AND I CAN GUESS WHERE TO--SOME NIGHT CLUB! I SHOULD THINK YOU MIGHT FIND SOMETHING USEFUL TO DO WITH YOUR NIGHTS, INSTEAD OF KILLING PRECIOUS TIME IN A NIGHT CLUB!
BUT LINDA IS WRONG--- BRUCE WAYNE DOES MAKE USE OF THE NIGHT. IT IS NIGHT--DARK, MYSTERIOUS NIGHT THAT SHROUDS THE PERSONALITY OF THE BATMAN-
I'M GOING TO FIND OUT JUST HOW THAT STOLEN, EXCLUSIVE CLOTH GOT INTO THAT STORE I LOOKED AT TODAY. I'LL BET THE ANSWER WILL BE INTERESTING!

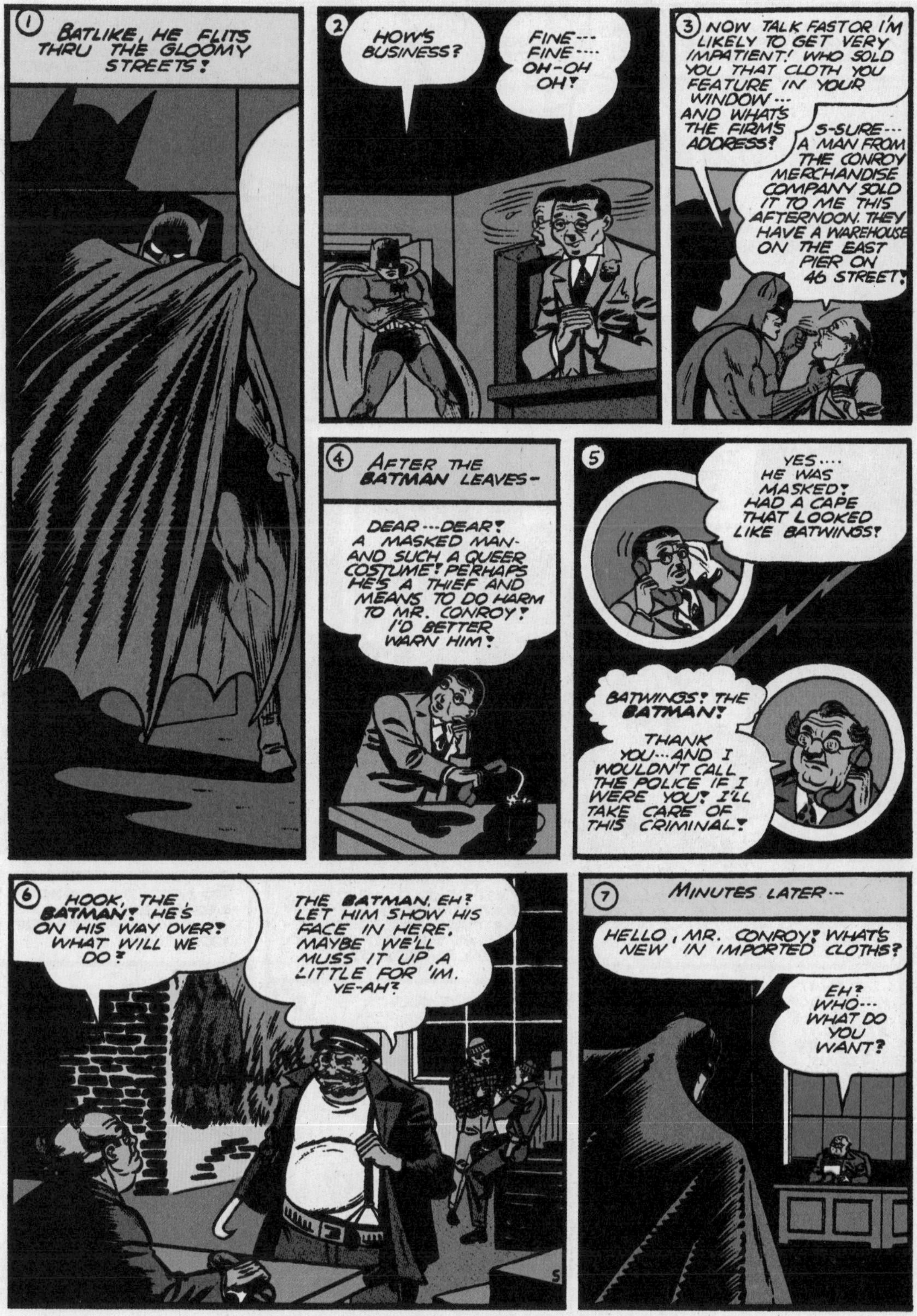
BATLIKE, HE FLITS THRU THE GLOOMY STREETS!
HOW'S BUSINESS?
FINE--- FINE---- OH-OH OH!
NOW TALK FASTOR I'M LIKELY TO GET VERY IMPATIENT! WHO SOLD YOU THAT CLOTH YOU FEATURE IN YOUR WINDOW--- AND WHAT'S THE FIRM'S ADDRESS?
S-SURE--- A MAN FROM THE CONROY MERCHANDISE COMPANY SOLD IT TO ME THIS AFTERNOON. THEY HAVE A WAREHOUSE ON THE EAST PIER ON 46 STREET!
AFTER THE BATMAN LEAVES-
DEAR---DEAR! A MASKED MAN- AND SUCH A QUEER COSTUME! PERHAPS HE'S A THIEF AND MEANS TO DO HARM TO MR. CONROY! I'D BETTER WARN HIM!
YES---- HE WAS MASKED! HAD A CAPE THAT LOOKED LIKE BATWINGS!
BATWINGS? THE BATMAN!
THANK YOU---AND I WOULDN'T CALL THE POLICE IF I WERE YOU! I'LL TAKE CARE OF THIS CRIMINAL!
HOOK, THE BATMAN! HE'S ON HIS WAY OVER! WHAT WILL WE DO?
THE BATMAN, EH? LET HIM SHOW HIS FACE IN HERE. MAYBE WE'LL MUSS IT UP A LITTLE FOR 'IM. YE-AH?
MINUTES LATER--
HELLO, MR. CONROY! WHAT'S NEW IN IMPORTED CLOTHS?
EH? WHO--- WHAT DO YOU WANT?

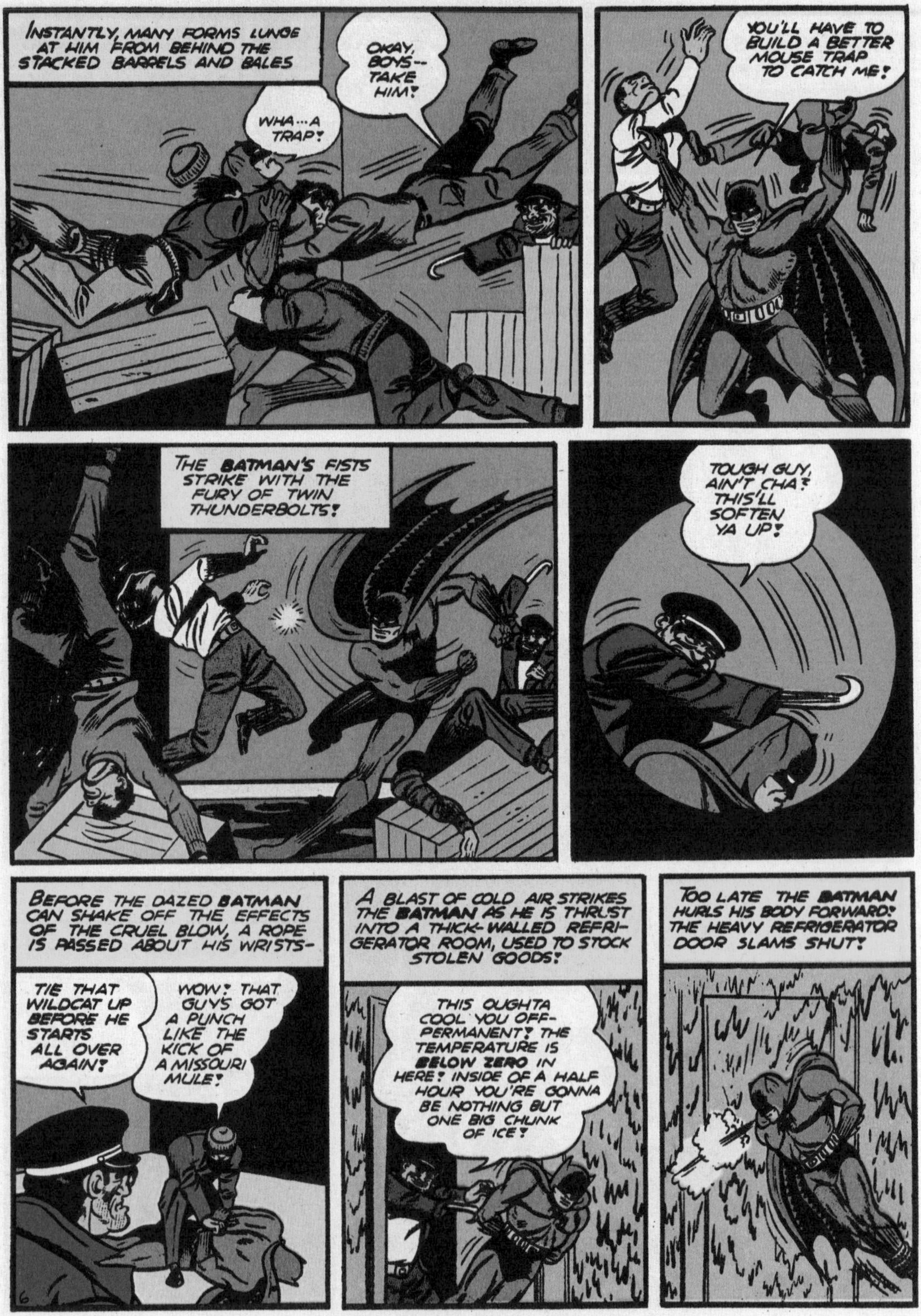
INSTANTLY, MANY FORMS LUNGE AT HIM FROM BEHIND THE STACKED BARRELS AND BALES
WHA...A TRAP!
OKAY, BOYS-- TAKE HIM!
YOU'LL HAVE TO BUILD A BETTER MOUSE TRAP TO CATCH ME!
THE BATMAN'S FISTS STRIKE WITH THE FURY OF TWIN THUNDERBOLTS!
TOUGH GUY, AIN'T CHA? THIS'LL SOFTEN YA UP!
BEFORE THE DAZED BATMAN CAN SHAKE OFF THE EFFECTS OF THE CRUEL BLOW, A ROPE IS PASSED ABOUT HIS WRISTS-
TIE THAT WILDCAT UP BEFORE HE STARTS ALL OVER AGAIN!
WOW! THAT GUY'S GOT A PUNCH LIKE THE KICK OF A MISSOURI MULE!
6
A BLAST OF COLD AIR STRIKES THE BATMAN AS HE IS THRUST INTO A THICK-WALLED REFRIGERATOR ROOM, USED TO STOCK STOLEN GOODS!
THIS OUGHTA COOL YOU OFF-PERMANENT! THE TEMPERATURE IS BELOW ZERO IN HERE! INSIDE OF A HALF HOUR YOU'RE GONNA BE NOTHING BUT ONE BIG CHUNK OF ICE!
TOO LATE THE BATMAN HURLS HIS BODY FORWARD! THE HEAVY REFRIGERATOR DOOR SLAMS SHUT!

AGAIN THE BATMAN'S MUSCULAR FRAME POUNDS, BATTERS AT THE STEEL DOOR IN A FUTILE ATTEMPT TO ESCAPE FROM THE MANTLE OF COLD THAT WRAPS ABOUT HIM!

UGH! NO USE...CAN'T BUDGE IT! GOT TO FIGURE OUT SOMETHING ELSE!

THE BATMAN GROWS NUMB WITH COLD AS INVISIBLE ICE FINGERS TOUCH HIS SHIVERING BODY!

BRRR--B-BETTER GET OUT OF HERE F-FAST OR I'LL F-FREEZE TO DEATH! H-HANDS TIED SO I CAN'T GET AT BOOT-KNIFE BUT THAT B-BULB GIVES M-ME AN IDEA--

THE BATMAN BUTTS HIS HEAD AGAINST THE DANGLING LIGHT BULB---

THIS HAD BETTER W-WORK OR I'M GOING TO BE A J-JACK F-FROST!

...THE BULB SWINGS OUT IN A WIDE ARC!

AGAIN HE BUTTS AT IT--HARDER THIS TIME! IT SWINGS OUT FARTHER IN A WIDER SWEEPING ARC!

BRRR-- G-G-GETTING C-COLDER!

ONE MORE JAB OF THE BATMAN'S HEAD AND THE BULB SWINGS OUT---OUT TILL IT SHATTERS AGAINST A REFRIGERATOR WALL!

THE BATMAN LIES ON THE FLOOR, HIS HANDS PROBING FOR A JAGGED PIECE OF THE SMASHED GLASS BULB!

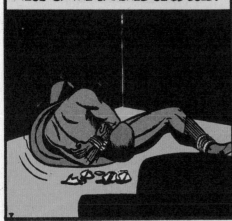

WITH THE RAZOR-SHARP SLIVER BETWEEN FINGERS ALMOST NUMB WITH COLD, HE SAWS AWAY AT HIS BONDS--

FREE! NOW THE BATMAN BRINGS FORTH A VIAL FROM HIS UTILITY BELT--

N-NOW---THE ACID SHOULD EAT AWAY THE L-LOCK!

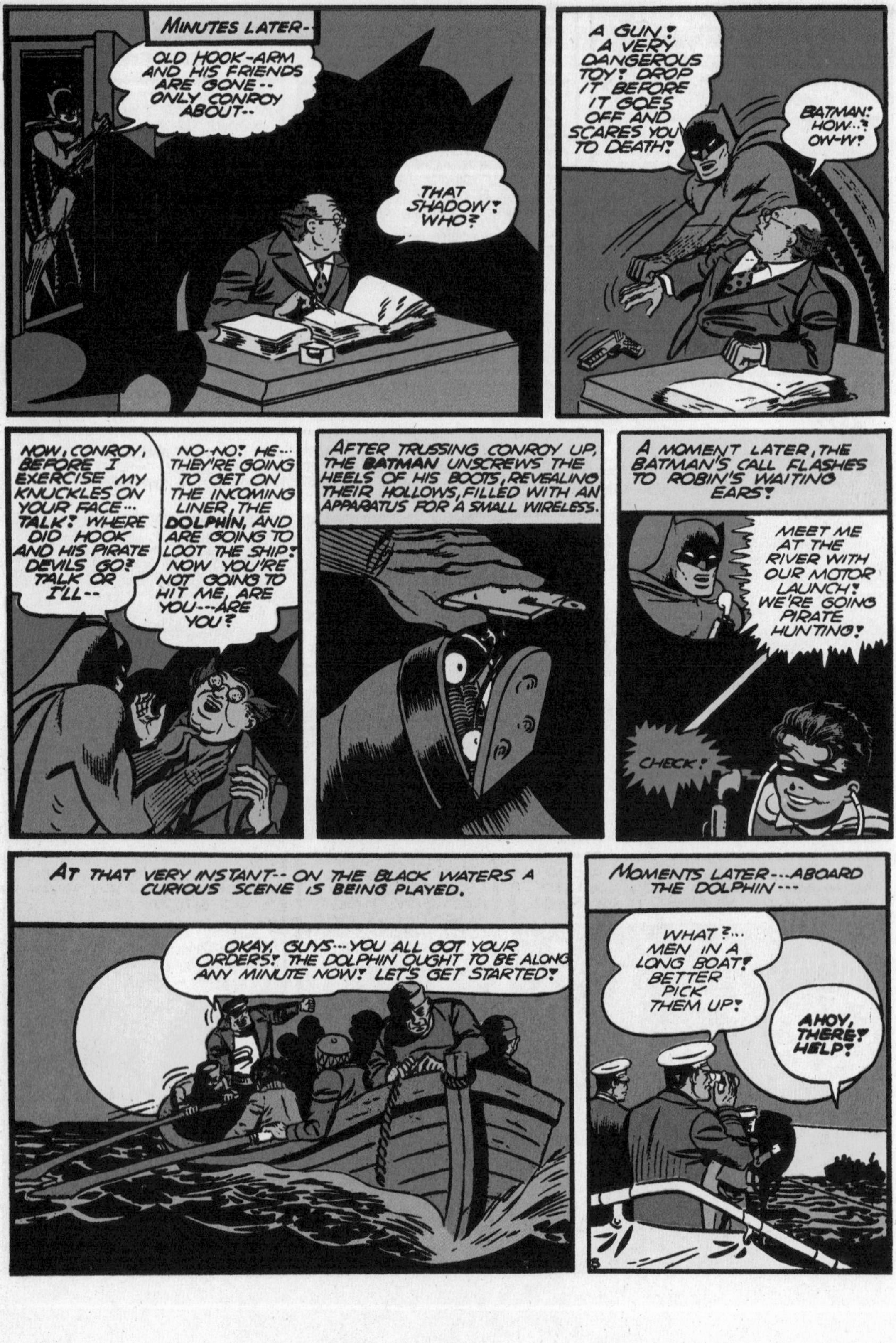
MINUTES LATER--
OLD HOOK-ARM AND HIS FRIENDS ARE GONE -- ONLY CONROY ABOUT--
THAT SHADOW! WHO?
A GUN! A VERY DANGEROUS TOY! DROP IT BEFORE IT GOES OFF AND SCARES YOU TO DEATH!
BATMAN! HOW--? OW-W!
NOW, CONROY, BEFORE I EXERCISE MY KNUCKLES ON YOUR FACE... TALK! WHERE DID HOOK AND HIS PIRATE DEVILS GO? TALK OR I'LL--
NO-NO! HE-- THEY'RE GOING TO GET ON THE INCOMING LINER, THE DOLPHIN, AND ARE GOING TO LOOT THE SHIP! NOW YOU'RE NOT GOING TO HIT ME, ARE YOU---ARE YOU?
AFTER TRUSSING CONROY UP, THE BATMAN UNSCREWS THE HEELS OF HIS BOOTS, REVEALING THEIR HOLLOWS, FILLED WITH AN APPARATUS FOR A SMALL WIRELESS.
A MOMENT LATER, THE BATMAN'S CALL FLASHES TO ROBIN'S WAITING EARS!
MEET ME AT THE RIVER WITH OUR MOTOR LAUNCH! WE'RE GOING PIRATE HUNTING!
CHECK!
AT THAT VERY INSTANT-- ON THE BLACK WATERS A CURIOUS SCENE IS BEING PLAYED.
OKAY, GUYS--- YOU ALL GOT YOUR ORDERS! THE DOLPHIN OUGHT TO BE ALONG ANY MINUTE NOW! LET'S GET STARTED!
MOMENTS LATER---ABOARD THE DOLPHIN---
WHAT?... MEN IN A LONG BOAT! BETTER PICK THEM UP!
AHOY, THERE! HELP!

YOU SAY YOUR FREIGHTER WAS TORPEDOED BY A SUBMARINE?

YES--- WE'VE BEEN DRIFTING FOR HOURS! GOOD THING YOU CAME ALONG!

BUT ONCE UPON THE DECK, THE "SURVIVORS" SUDDENLY WHIP EAGER HANDS INTO THEIR DUFFLE BAGS AND ---

WHY-- WHAT IS THIS?

THIS IS A STICKUP! NOW BE NICE OR ELSE THERE'S GONNA BE A LOT O' STIFFS LAYIN' AROUND!

WHY, YOU-- OH-H!

GET BACK IN LINE BEFORE I RIP YOUR HEAD OFF!

ANYBODY ELSE THAT TRIES ANYTHING GETS THE SAME KIND O' MEDICINE! OKAY, BOYS---TAKE WHAT'S IN THEIR POCKETS AND WHAT YOU SEE ON THIS TUB THAT'S WORTH ANYTHING!

OH, MY FACE-- MY FACE.

WHILE THE PIRATES TAKE OVER THE SHIP, A WEIRD CRAFT SWOOPS DOWN FROM THE BLACK SKY. IT IS THE BATPLANE!

IT GLIDES NOISELESSLY OVER THE LINER AND HANGS THERE MOTIONLESS. TWO MANTLED FIGURES SLIP DOWN A DANGLING ROPE LADDER...

I SET THE ROBOT CONTROLS!

GOOD! NOW LET'S GET 'EM!

THOSE PIRATES MUST BE ALL OVER THE SHIP-- SO WE'LL HAVE TO SEPARATE! YOU TAKE THE LOWER DECK!

RIGHT! HERE'S WHERE WE SEE SOME ACTION!

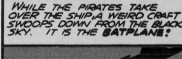

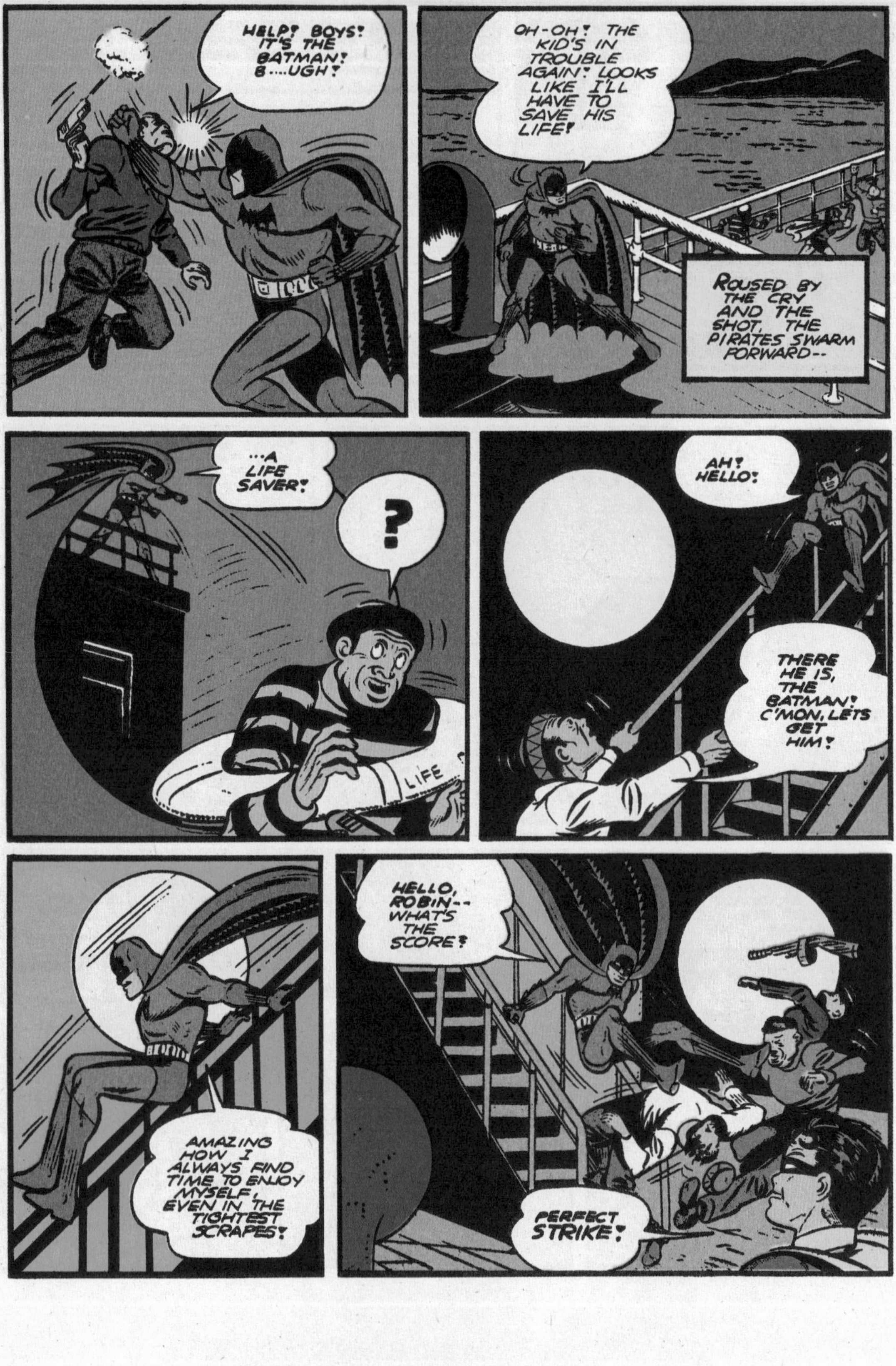
HELP! BOYS! IT'S THE BATMAN! B....UGH!
OH-OH! THE KID'S IN TROUBLE AGAIN! LOOKS LIKE I'LL HAVE TO SAVE HIS LIFE!
ROUSED BY THE CRY AND THE SHOT, THE PIRATES SWARM FORWARD--
...A LIFE SAVER!
?
LIFE
AH! HELLO!
THERE HE IS, THE BATMAN! C'MON, LETS GET HIM!
AMAZING HOW I ALWAYS FIND TIME TO ENJOY MYSELF, EVEN IN THE TIGHTEST SCRAPES!
HELLO, ROBIN-- WHAT'S THE SCORE?
PERFECT STRIKE!

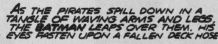

AS THE PIRATES SPILL DOWN IN A TANGLE OF WAVING ARMS AND LEGS, THE BATMAN LEAPS OVER THEM. HIS EYES FASTEN UPON A FALLEN DECK HOSE

THAT'S WHAT I WANT! TURN IT ON, ROBIN!

A VERITABLE NIAGARA ENGULFS THE PIRATES, SENDING THEM ROLLING OVER THE DECK LIKE TUMBLEWEED---

THIS IS PROBABLY THE FIRST BATH YOU'VE HAD IN A LONG TIME!

THE NOW HELPLESS PIRATES ARE HERDED TOGETHER BY THE SHIP'S CREW!

I DON'T SEE HOOK! HE MUST HAVE RUN OUT ON HIS MEN!

LOOK! THERE HE IS...SWIMMING TO THAT LAUNCH!

AS THE LAUNCH ROARS AWAY WITH HOOK, THE BATPLANE DARTS AFTER IT LIKE A PURSUING BIRD AFTER HIS PREY!

THERE'S A HEAVY FOG ROLLING UP!

WE WON'T BE ABLE TO SEE A THING UP HERE IN A FEW MOMENTS! BETTER SET THE PLANE DOWN ON THE WATER!

AS THE BATPLANE HITS THE WATER, THE BATMAN PUSHES A BUTTON. MIRACULOUSLY, THE WHEELS ARE DRAWN IN... THE WINGS FOLD AGAINST THE SIDES--

THE BATPLANE HAS BEEN TRANSFORMED INTO A SPEEDBOAT!!

THE SHORE LINE BECOMES A BLUR AS THE BOATS FLASH PAST AT AMAZING SPEED! MILE AFTER MILE WHIPS BY--

THAT BOAT IS A FAST ONE!

...AND WE CAN'T SEE SO CLEARLY NOW WITH THIS HEAVY FOG!

SUDDENLY, AS THE BATMAN'S BOAT TEARS AROUND A PIER, THE CRIME FIGHTER IS AMAZED TO FIND--

IT'S GONE! THE BOAT'S VANISHED!

BUT HOW--? THAT'S THE QUESTION! WHERE COULD IT HAVE GONE?

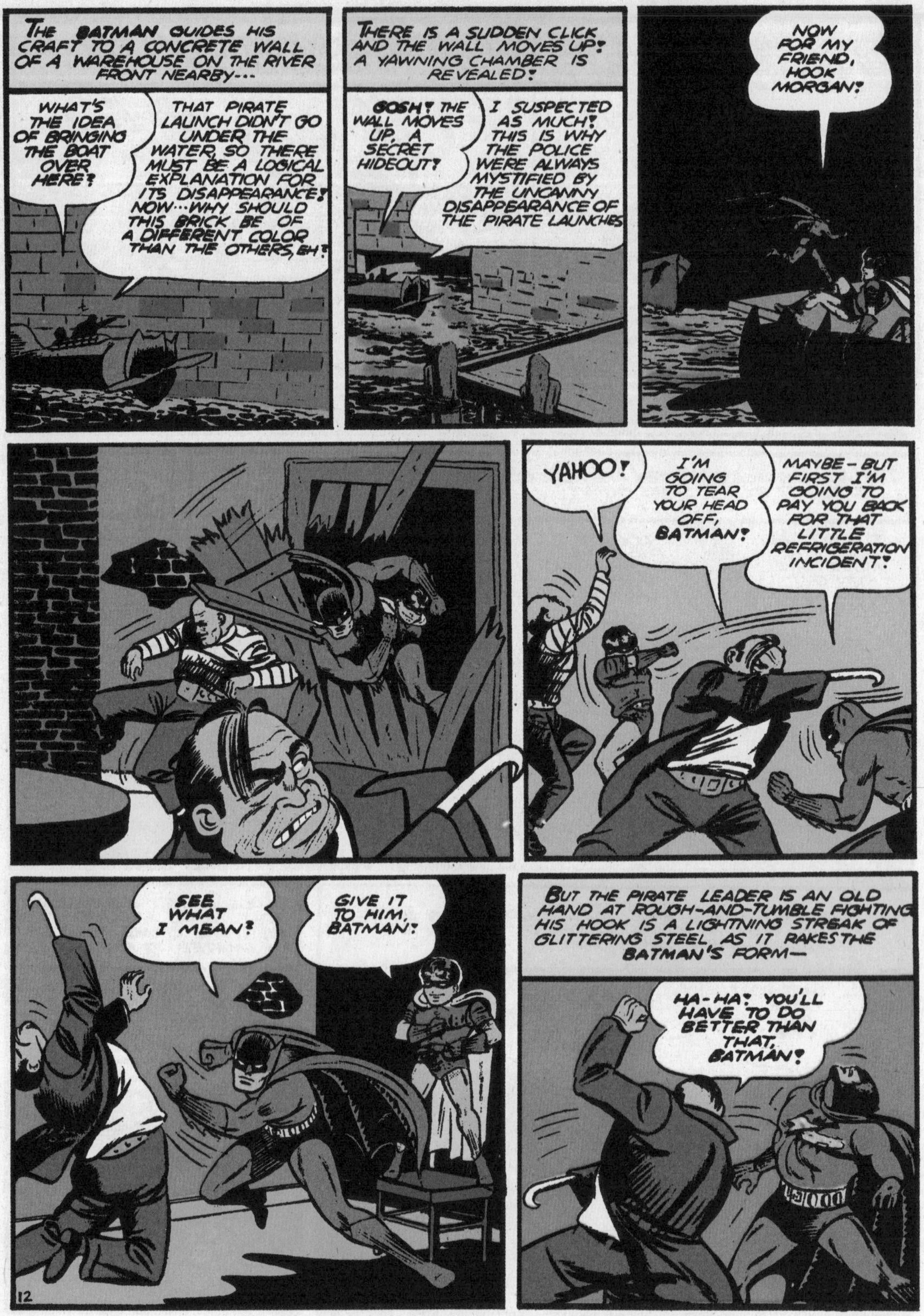
THE BATMAN GUIDES HIS CRAFT TO A CONCRETE WALL OF A WAREHOUSE ON THE RIVER FRONT NEARBY---
WHAT'S THE IDEA OF BRINGING THE BOAT OVER HERE?
THAT PIRATE LAUNCH DIDN'T GO UNDER THE WATER, SO THERE MUST BE A LOGICAL EXPLANATION FOR ITS DISAPPEARANCE! NOW...WHY SHOULD THIS BRICK BE OF A DIFFERENT COLOR THAN THE OTHERS, EH?
THERE IS A SUDDEN CLICK AND THE WALL MOVES UP! A YAWNING CHAMBER IS REVEALED!
GOSH! THE WALL MOVES UP, A SECRET HIDEOUT!
I SUSPECTED AS MUCH! THIS IS WHY THE POLICE WERE ALWAYS MYSTIFIED BY THE UNCANNY DISAPPEARANCE OF THE PIRATE LAUNCHES
NOW FOR MY FRIEND, HOOK MORGAN!
YAHOO!
I'M GOING TO TEAR YOUR HEAD OFF, BATMAN!
MAYBE- BUT FIRST I'M GOING TO PAY YOU BACK FOR THAT LITTLE REFRIGERATION INCIDENT!
SEE WHAT I MEAN?
GIVE IT TO HIM, BATMAN!
12
BUT THE PIRATE LEADER IS AN OLD HAND AT ROUGH-AND-TUMBLE FIGHTING HIS HOOK IS A LIGHTNING STREAK OF GLITTERING STEEL AS IT RAKES THE BATMAN'S FORM—
HA-HA! YOU'LL HAVE TO DO BETTER THAN THAT, BATMAN!

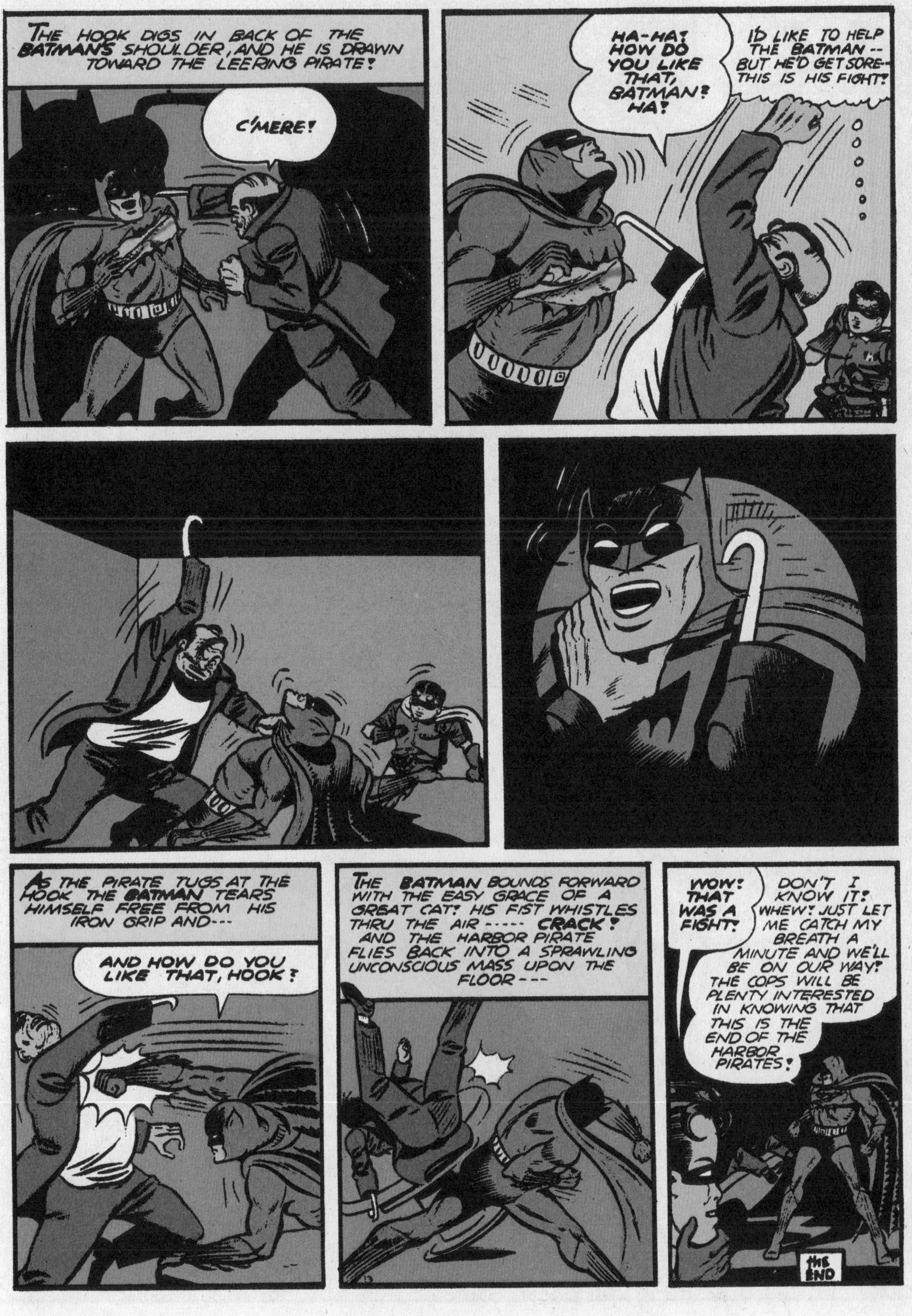
THE HOOK DIGS IN BACK OF THE BATMAN'S SHOULDER, AND HE IS DRAWN TOWARD THE LEERING PIRATE!
C'MERE!
HA-HA! HOW DO YOU LIKE THAT, BATMAN? HA!
I'D LIKE TO HELP THE BATMAN -- BUT HE'D GET SORE-- THIS IS HIS FIGHT!
AS THE PIRATE TUGS AT THE HOOK THE BATMAN TEARS HIMSELF FREE FROM HIS IRON GRIP AND---
AND HOW DO YOU LIKE THAT, HOOK?
THE BATMAN BOUNDS FORWARD WITH THE EASY GRACE OF A GREAT CAT! HIS FIST WHISTLES THRU THE AIR----- CRACK! AND THE HARBOR PIRATE FLIES BACK INTO A SPRAWLING UNCONSCIOUS MASS UPON THE FLOOR---
WOW! THAT WAS A FIGHT!
DON'T I KNOW IT! WHEW! JUST LET ME CATCH MY BREATH A MINUTE AND WE'LL BE ON OUR WAY! THE COPS WILL BE PLENTY INTERESTED IN KNOWING THAT THIS IS THE END OF THE HARBOR PIRATES!
THE END

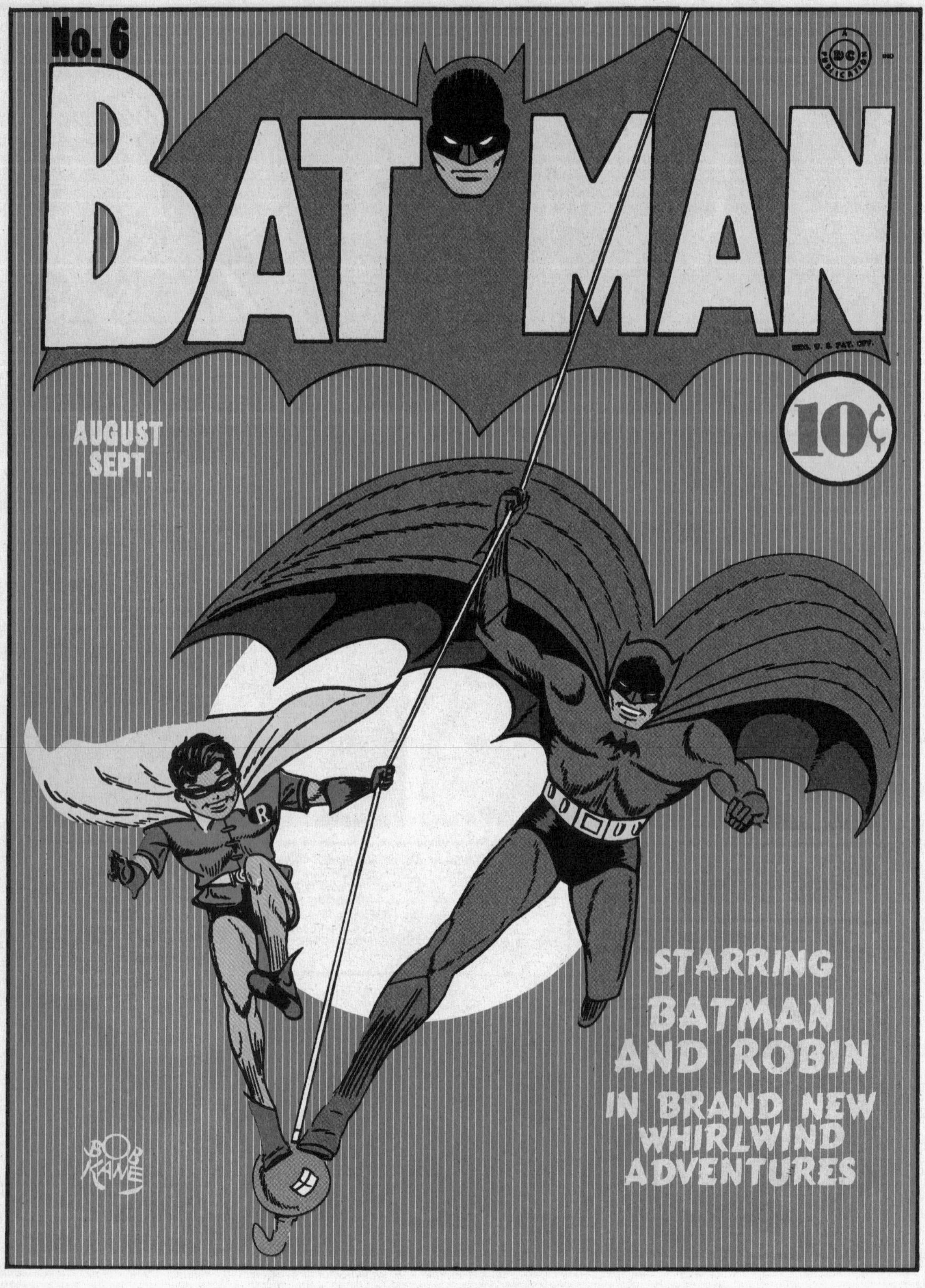
No. 6
BATMAN
AUGUST
SEPT.
10¢
STARRING
BATMAN
AND ROBIN
IN BRAND NEW
WHIRLWIND
ADVENTURES
BOB KANE

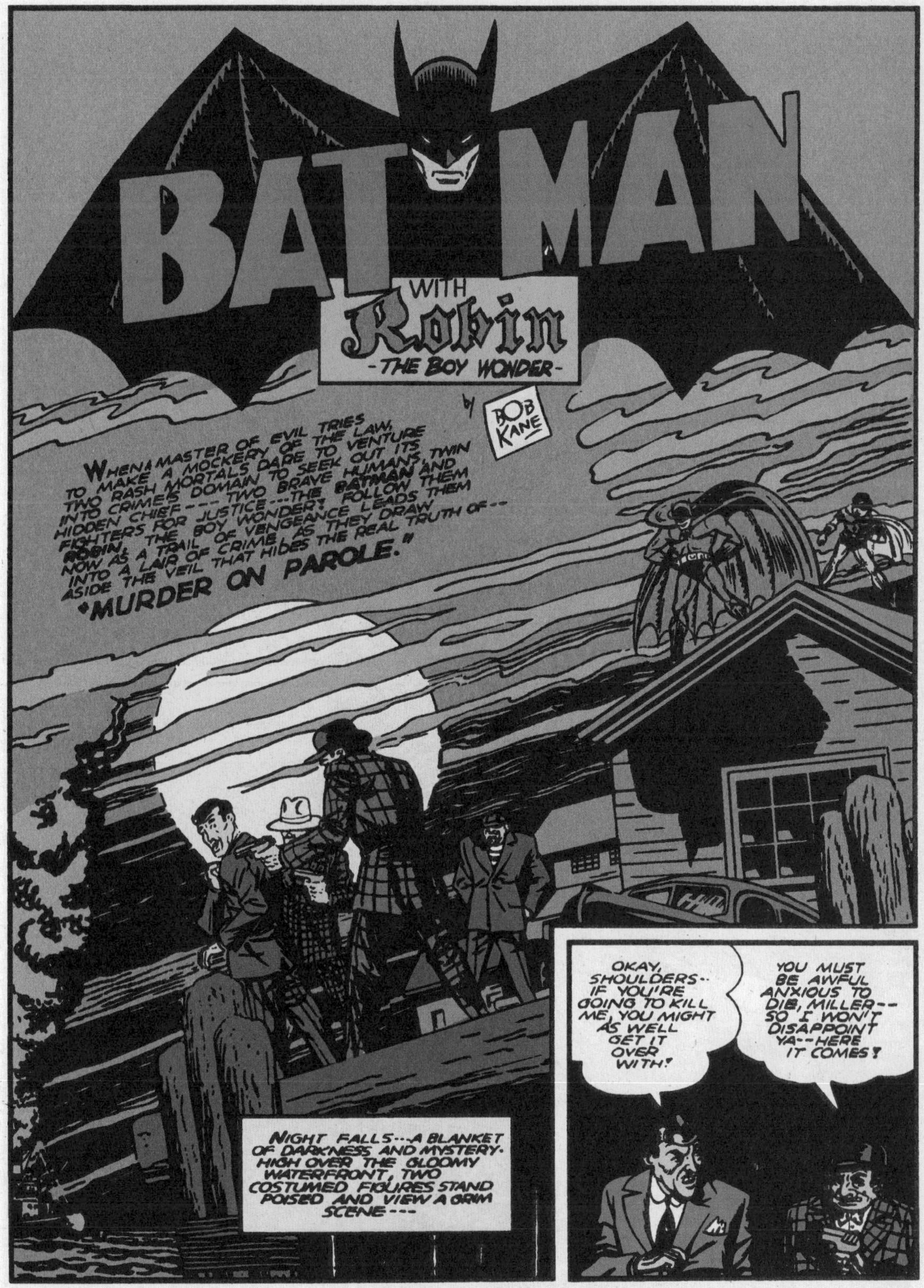
BATMAN
WITH Robin
-THE BOY WONDER-
by BOB KANE
WHEN A MASTER OF EVIL TRIES TO MAKE A MOCKERY OF THE LAW, TWO RASH MORTALS DARE TO VENTURE INTO CRIME'S DOMAIN TO SEEK OUT ITS HIDDEN CHIEF---- TWO BRAVE HUMANS, TWIN FIGHTERS FOR JUSTICE---THE BATMAN AND ROBIN, THE BOY WONDER! FOLLOW THEM NOW AS A TRAIL OF VENGEANCE LEADS THEM INTO A LAIR OF CRIME, AS THEY DRAW ASIDE THE VEIL THAT HIDES THE REAL TRUTH OF--
"MURDER ON PAROLE."
NIGHT FALLS---A BLANKET OF DARKNESS AND MYSTERY. HIGH OVER THE GLOOMY WATERFRONT, TWO COSTUMED FIGURES STAND POISED AND VIEW A GRIM SCENE---
OKAY, SHOULDERS-- IF YOU'RE GOING TO KILL ME, YOU MIGHT AS WELL GET IT OVER WITH!
YOU MUST BE AWFUL ANXIOUS TO DIE, MILLER-- SO I WON'T DISAPPOINT YA--HERE IT COMES!

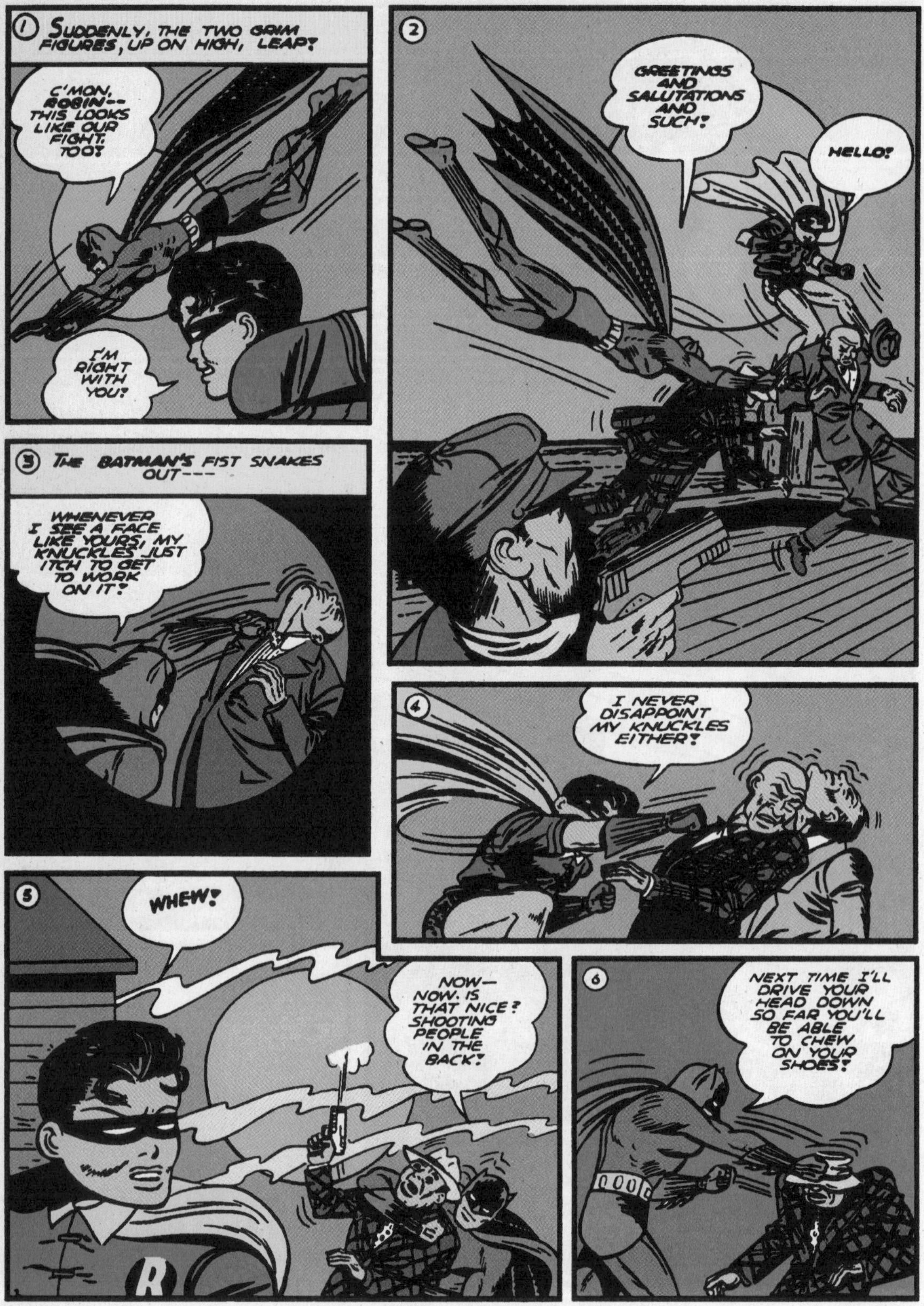
1
SUDDENLY, THE TWO GRIM FIGURES, UP ON HIGH, LEAP!
C'MON, ROBIN-- THIS LOOKS LIKE OUR FIGHT, TOO!
I'M RIGHT WITH YOU!
2
GREETINGS AND SALUTATIONS AND SUCH!
HELLO!
3
THE BATMAN'S FIST SNAKES OUT---
WHENEVER I SEE A FACE LIKE YOURS, MY KNUCKLES JUST ITCH TO GET TO WORK ON IT!
4
I NEVER DISAPPOINT MY KNUCKLES EITHER!
5
WHEW!
NOW-- NOW. IS THAT NICE? SHOOTING PEOPLE IN THE BACK!
6
NEXT TIME I'LL DRIVE YOUR HEAD DOWN SO FAR YOU'LL BE ABLE TO CHEW ON YOUR SHOES!

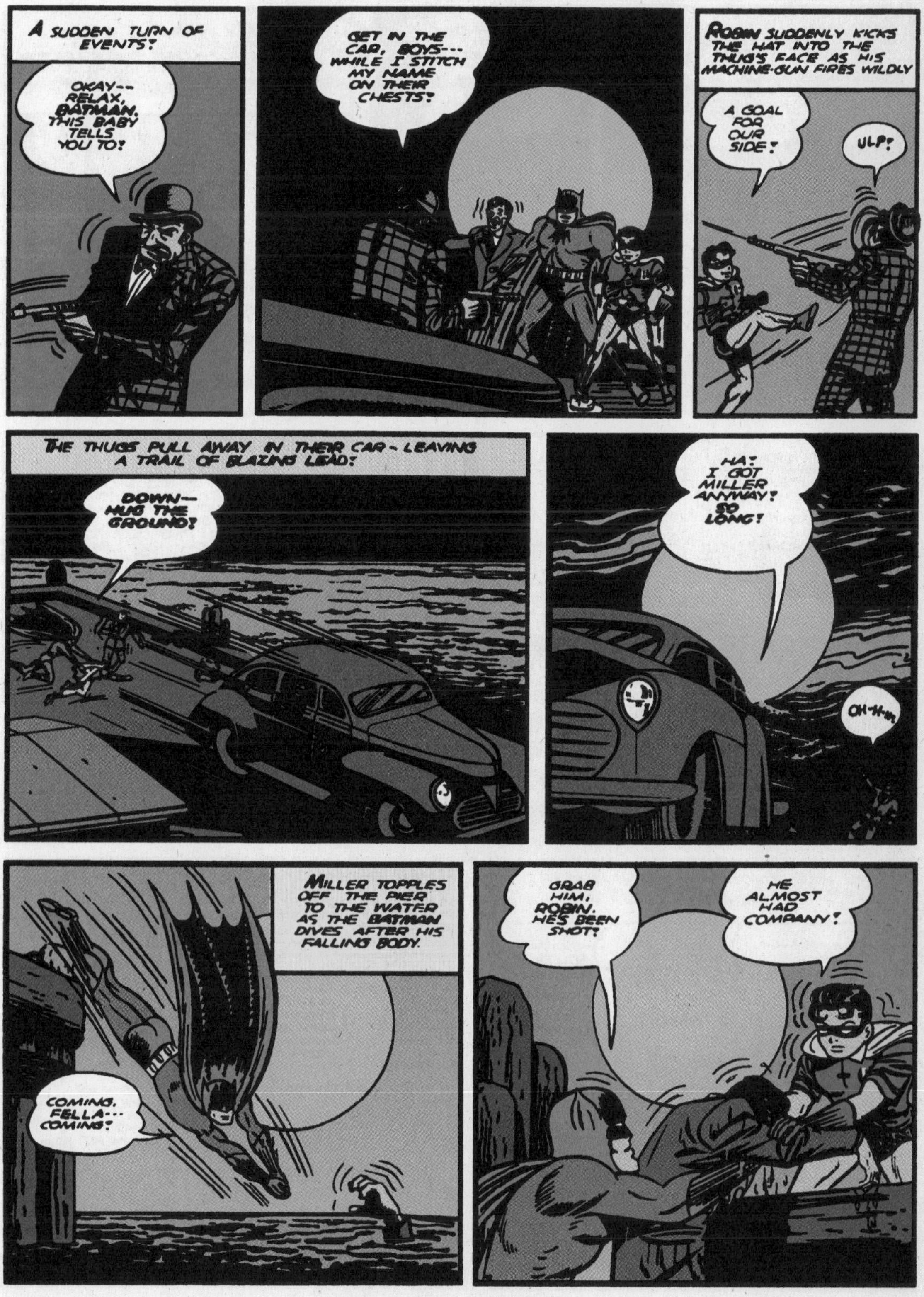
A SUDDEN TURN OF EVENTS!
OKAY-- RELAX, BATMAN. THIS BABY TELLS YOU TO!
GET IN THE CAR, BOYS--- WHILE I STITCH MY NAME ON THEIR CHESTS!
ROBIN SUDDENLY KICKS THE HAT INTO THE THUG'S FACE AS HIS MACHINE-GUN FIRES WILDLY
A GOAL FOR OUR SIDE!
ULP!
THE THUGS PULL AWAY IN THEIR CAR - LEAVING A TRAIL OF BLAZING LEAD!
DOWN-- HUG THE GROUND!
HA! I GOT MILLER ANYWAY! SO LONG!
OH-H-H
MILLER TOPPLES OFF THE PIER TO THE WATER AS THE BATMAN DIVES AFTER HIS FALLING BODY.
COMING, FELLA--- COMING!
GRAB HIM, ROBIN. HE'S BEEN SHOT!
HE ALMOST HAD COMPANY!

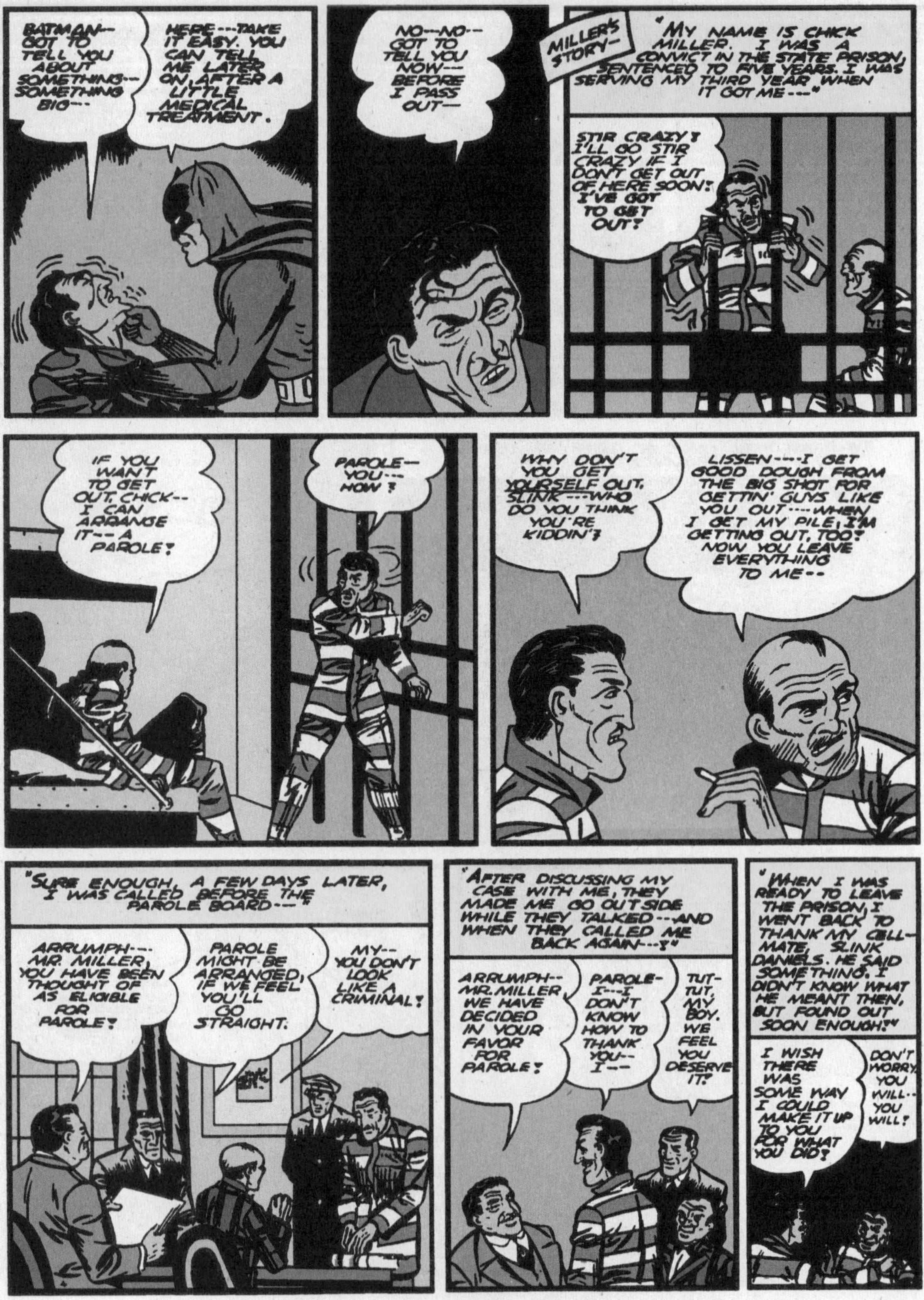
BATMAN-- GOT TO TELL YOU ABOUT SOMETHING-- SOMETHING BIG---
HERE---TAKE IT EASY. YOU CAN TELL ME LATER ON, AFTER A LITTLE MEDICAL TREATMENT.
NO--NO-- GOT TO TELL YOU NOW--- BEFORE I PASS OUT--
MILLER'S STORY--
"MY NAME IS CHICK MILLER. I WAS A CONVICT IN THE STATE PRISON, SENTENCED TO FIVE YEARS. I WAS SERVING MY THIRD YEAR WHEN IT GOT ME---"
STIR CRAZY! I'LL GO STIR CRAZY IF I DON'T GET OUT OF HERE SOON! I'VE GOT TO GET OUT!
IF YOU WANT TO GET OUT, CHICK-- I CAN ARRANGE IT-- A PAROLE!
PAROLE-- YOU--- HOW?
WHY DON'T YOU GET YOURSELF OUT, SLINK---WHO DO YOU THINK YOU'RE KIDDIN'?
LISSEN----I GET GOOD DOUGH FROM THE BIG SHOT FOR GETTIN' GUYS LIKE YOU OUT----WHEN I GET MY PILE, I'M GETTING OUT, TOO! NOW YOU LEAVE EVERYTHING TO ME--
"SURE ENOUGH, A FEW DAYS LATER, I WAS CALLED BEFORE THE PAROLE BOARD---"
ARRUMPH---. MR. MILLER, YOU HAVE BEEN THOUGHT OF AS ELIGIBLE FOR PAROLE!
PAROLE MIGHT BE ARRANGED, IF WE FEEL YOU'LL GO STRAIGHT.
MY-- YOU DON'T LOOK LIKE A CRIMINAL!
"AFTER DISCUSSING MY CASE WITH ME, THEY MADE ME GO OUTSIDE WHILE THEY TALKED---AND WHEN THEY CALLED ME BACK AGAIN---!"
ARRUMPH-- MR. MILLER WE HAVE DECIDED IN YOUR FAVOR FOR PAROLE!
PAROLE-- I---I DON'T KNOW HOW TO THANK YOU-- I---
TUT-TUT, MY BOY. WE FEEL YOU DESERVE IT!
"WHEN I WAS READY TO LEAVE THE PRISON, I WENT BACK TO THANK MY CELL-MATE, SLINK DANIELS. HE SAID SOMETHING. I DIDN'T KNOW WHAT HE MEANT THEN, BUT FOUND OUT SOON ENOUGH!"
I WISH THERE WAS SOME WAY I COULD MAKE IT UP TO YOU FOR WHAT YOU DID!
DON'T WORRY, YOU WILL-- YOU WILL!

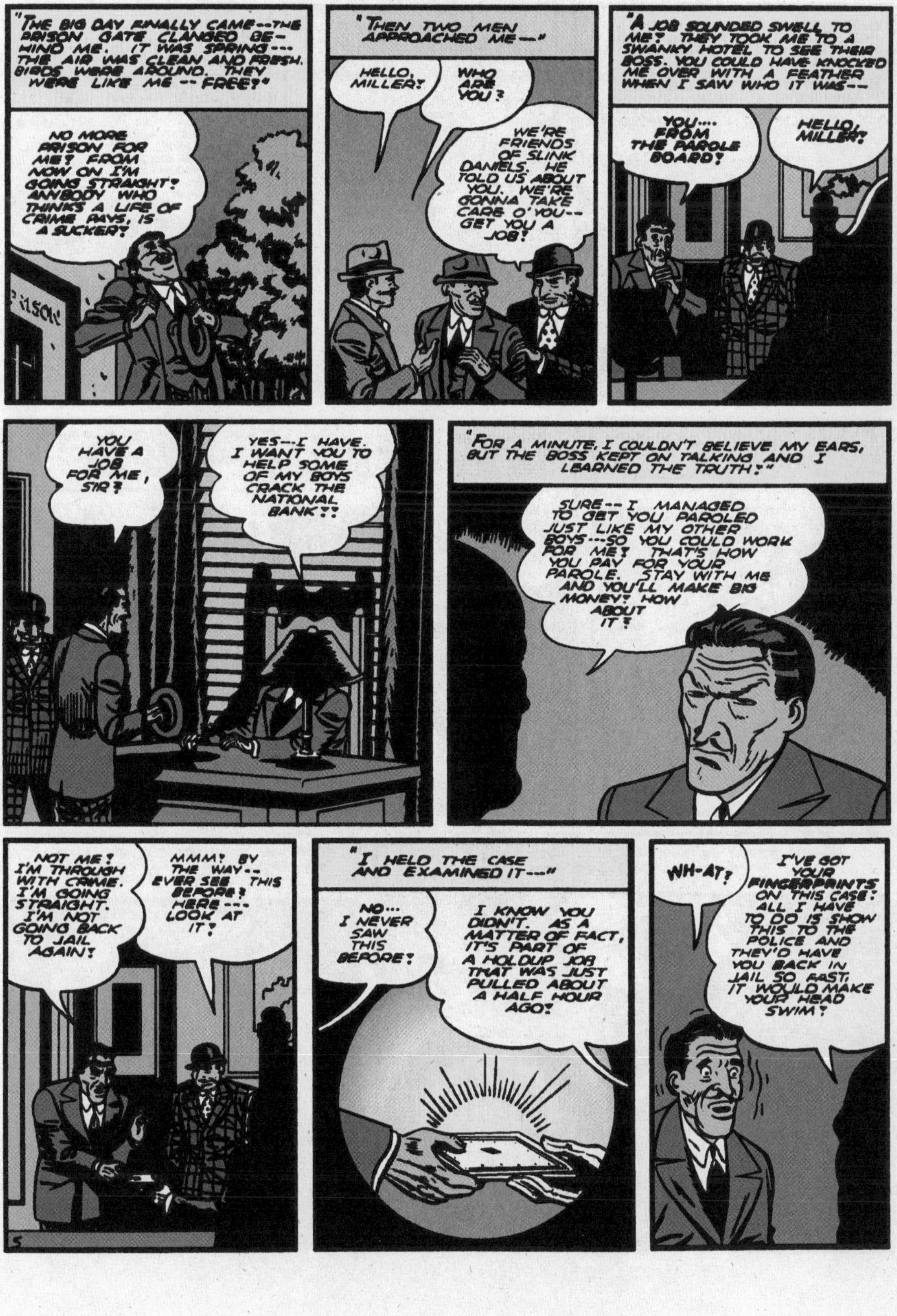
"THE BIG DAY FINALLY CAME--THE PRISON GATE CLANGED BEHIND ME. IT WAS SPRING--- THE AIR WAS CLEAN AND FRESH. BIRDS WERE AROUND. THEY WERE LIKE ME -- FREE!"
NO MORE PRISON FOR ME! FROM NOW ON I'M GOING STRAIGHT! ANYBODY WHO THINKS A LIFE OF CRIME PAYS, IS A SUCKER!
"THEN TWO MEN APPROACHED ME---"
HELLO, MILLER!
WHO ARE YOU?
WE'RE FRIENDS OF SLINK DANIELS. HE TOLD US ABOUT YOU. WE'RE GONNA TAKE CARE O' YOU-- GET YOU A JOB!
"A JOB SOUNDED SWELL TO ME! THEY TOOK ME TO A SWANKY HOTEL TO SEE THEIR BOSS. YOU COULD HAVE KNOCKED ME OVER WITH A FEATHER WHEN I SAW WHO IT WAS--
YOU.... FROM THE PAROLE BOARD!
HELLO, MILLER!
YOU HAVE A JOB FOR ME, SIR?
YES---I HAVE. I WANT YOU TO HELP SOME OF MY BOYS CRACK THE NATIONAL BANK!!
"FOR A MINUTE, I COULDN'T BELIEVE MY EARS, BUT THE BOSS KEPT ON TALKING AND I LEARNED THE TRUTH!"
SURE-- I MANAGED TO GET YOU PAROLED JUST LIKE MY OTHER BOYS---SO YOU COULD WORK FOR ME! THAT'S HOW YOU PAY FOR YOUR PAROLE. STAY WITH ME AND YOU'LL MAKE BIG MONEY! HOW ABOUT IT?
NOT ME! I'M THROUGH WITH CRIME. I'M GOING STRAIGHT. I'M NOT GOING BACK TO JAIL AGAIN!
MMMM! BY THE WAY-- EVER SEE THIS BEFORE? HERE--- LOOK AT IT!
"I HELD THE CASE AND EXAMINED IT---"
NO... I NEVER SAW THIS BEFORE!
I KNOW YOU DIDN'T. AS A MATTER OF FACT, IT'S PART OF A HOLDUP JOB THAT WAS JUST PULLED ABOUT A HALF HOUR AGO!
WH-AT?
I'VE GOT YOUR FINGERPRINTS ON THIS CASE: ALL I HAVE TO DO IS SHOW THIS TO THE POLICE AND THEY'D HAVE YOU BACK IN JAIL SO FAST, IT WOULD MAKE YOUR HEAD SWIM!

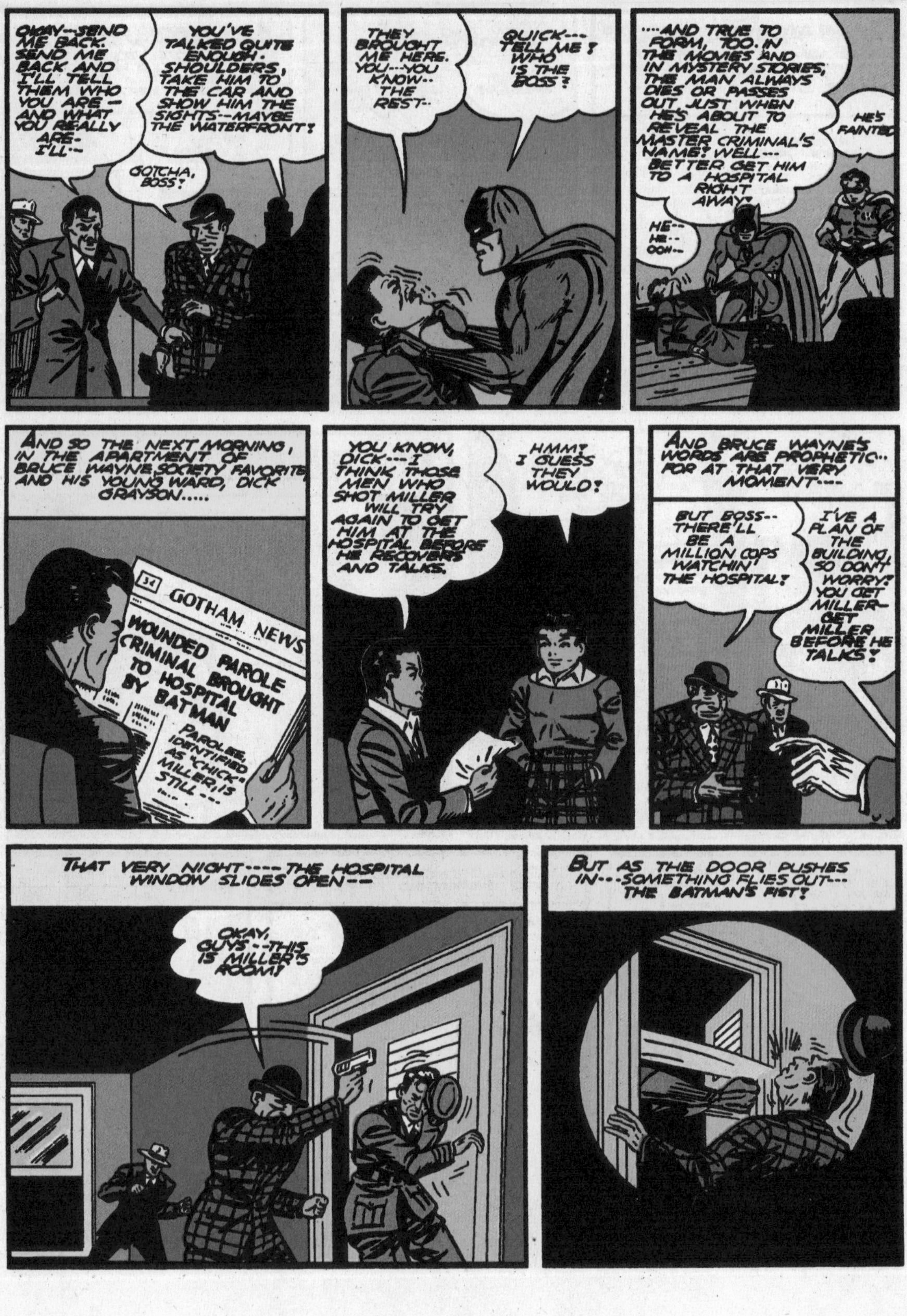

OKAY--SEND ME BACK. SEND ME BACK AND I'LL TELL THEM WHO YOU ARE -- AND WHAT YOU REALLY ARE- I'LL--
YOU'VE TALKED QUITE ENOUGH. SHOULDERS, TAKE HIM TO THE CAR AND SHOW HIM THE SIGHTS--MAYBE THE WATERFRONT!
GOTCHA, BOSS!
THEY BROUGHT ME HERE. YOU---YOU KNOW-- THE REST--
QUICK--- TELL ME! WHO IS THE BOSS?
....AND TRUE TO FORM, TOO. IN THE MOVIES AND IN MYSTERY STORIES, THE MAN ALWAYS DIES OR PASSES OUT JUST WHEN HE'S ABOUT TO REVEAL THE MASTER CRIMINAL'S NAME! WELL--- BETTER GET HIM TO A HOSPITAL RIGHT AWAY!
HE'S FAINTED
HE-- HE-- OOH--
AND SO THE NEXT MORNING, IN THE APARTMENT OF BRUCE WAYNE SOCIETY FAVORITE AND HIS YOUNG WARD, DICK GRAYSON.....
GOTHAM NEWS
WOUNDED PAROLE CRIMINAL BROUGHT TO HOSPITAL BY BATMAN
PAROLEE, IDENTIFIED AS "CHICK" MILLER, IS STILL---
YOU KNOW, DICK---I THINK THOSE MEN WHO SHOT MILLER WILL TRY AGAIN TO GET HIM AT THE HOSPITAL BEFORE HE RECOVERS AND TALKS.
HMM? I GUESS THEY WOULD!
AND BRUCE WAYNE'S WORDS ARE PROPHETIC... FOR AT THAT VERY MOMENT---
BUT BOSS-- THERE'LL BE A MILLION COPS WATCHIN' THE HOSPITAL!
I'VE A PLAN OF THE BUILDING, SO DON'T WORRY! YOU GET MILLER-- GET MILLER BEFORE HE TALKS!
THAT VERY NIGHT----THE HOSPITAL WINDOW SLIDES OPEN--
OKAY, GUYS--THIS IS MILLER'S ROOM!
BUT AS THE DOOR PUSHES IN---SOMETHING FLIES OUT--- THE BATMAN'S FIST!

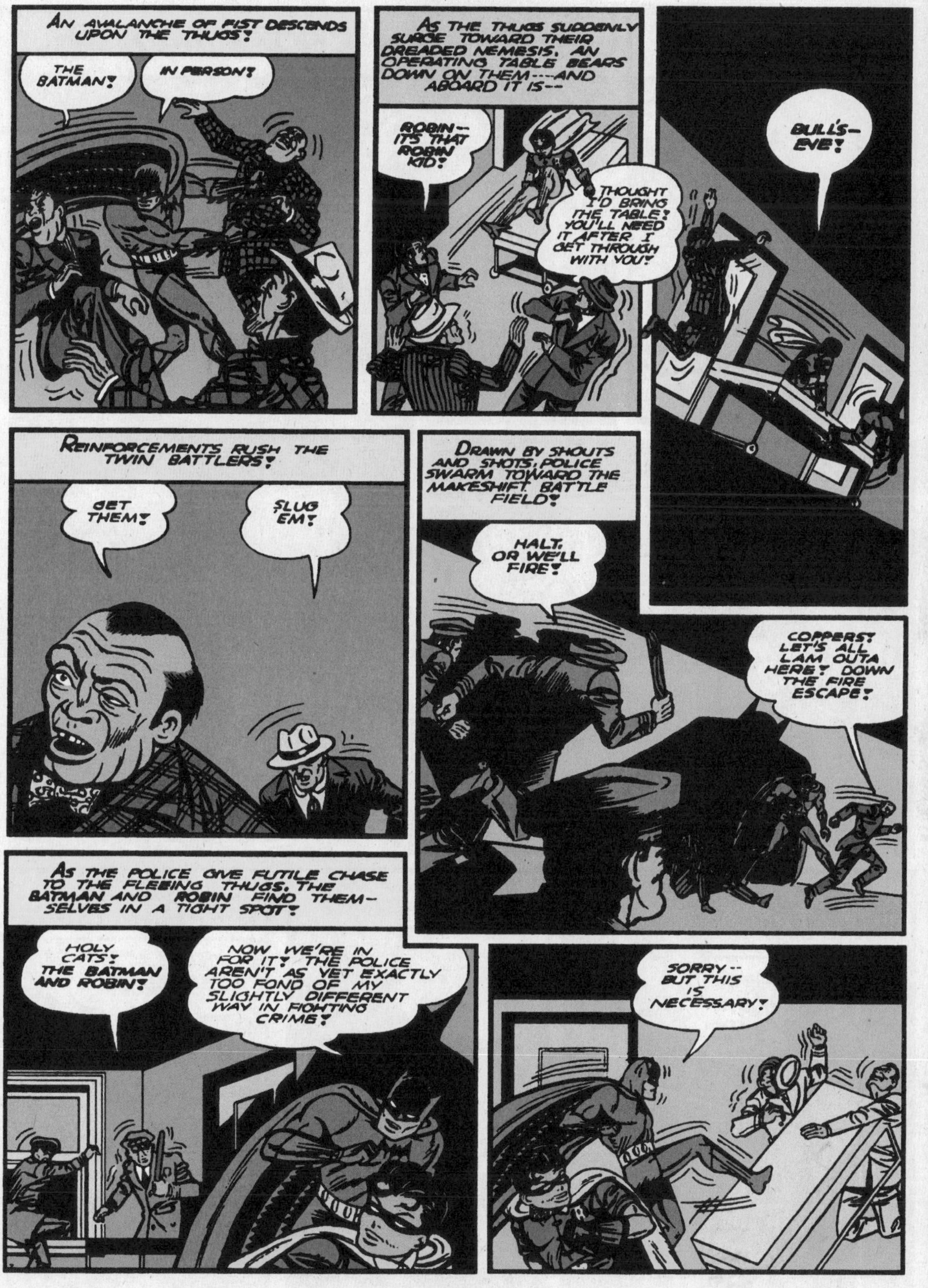
AN AVALANCHE OF FIST DESCENDS UPON THE THUGS!
THE BATMAN!
IN PERSON!
AS THE THUGS SUDDENLY SURGE TOWARD THEIR DREADED NEMESIS, AN OPERATING TABLE BEARS DOWN ON THEM---AND ABOARD IT IS--
ROBIN-- ITS THAT ROBIN KID!
THOUGHT I'D BRING THE TABLE! YOU'LL NEED IT AFTER I GET THROUGH WITH YOU!
BULL'S-EYE!
REINFORCEMENTS RUSH THE TWIN BATTLERS!
GET THEM!
SLUG EM!
DRAWN BY SHOUTS AND SHOTS, POLICE SWARM TOWARD THE MAKESHIFT BATTLE FIELD!
HALT, OR WE'LL FIRE!
COPPERS! LET'S ALL LAM OUTA HERE! DOWN THE FIRE ESCAPE!
AS THE POLICE GIVE FUTILE CHASE TO THE FLEEING THUGS, THE BATMAN AND ROBIN FIND THEMSELVES IN A TIGHT SPOT!
HOLY CATS! THE BATMAN AND ROBIN!
NOW WE'RE IN FOR IT! THE POLICE AREN'T AS YET EXACTLY TOO FOND OF MY SLIGHTLY DIFFERENT WAY IN FIGHTING CRIME!
SORRY -- BUT THIS IS NECESSARY!

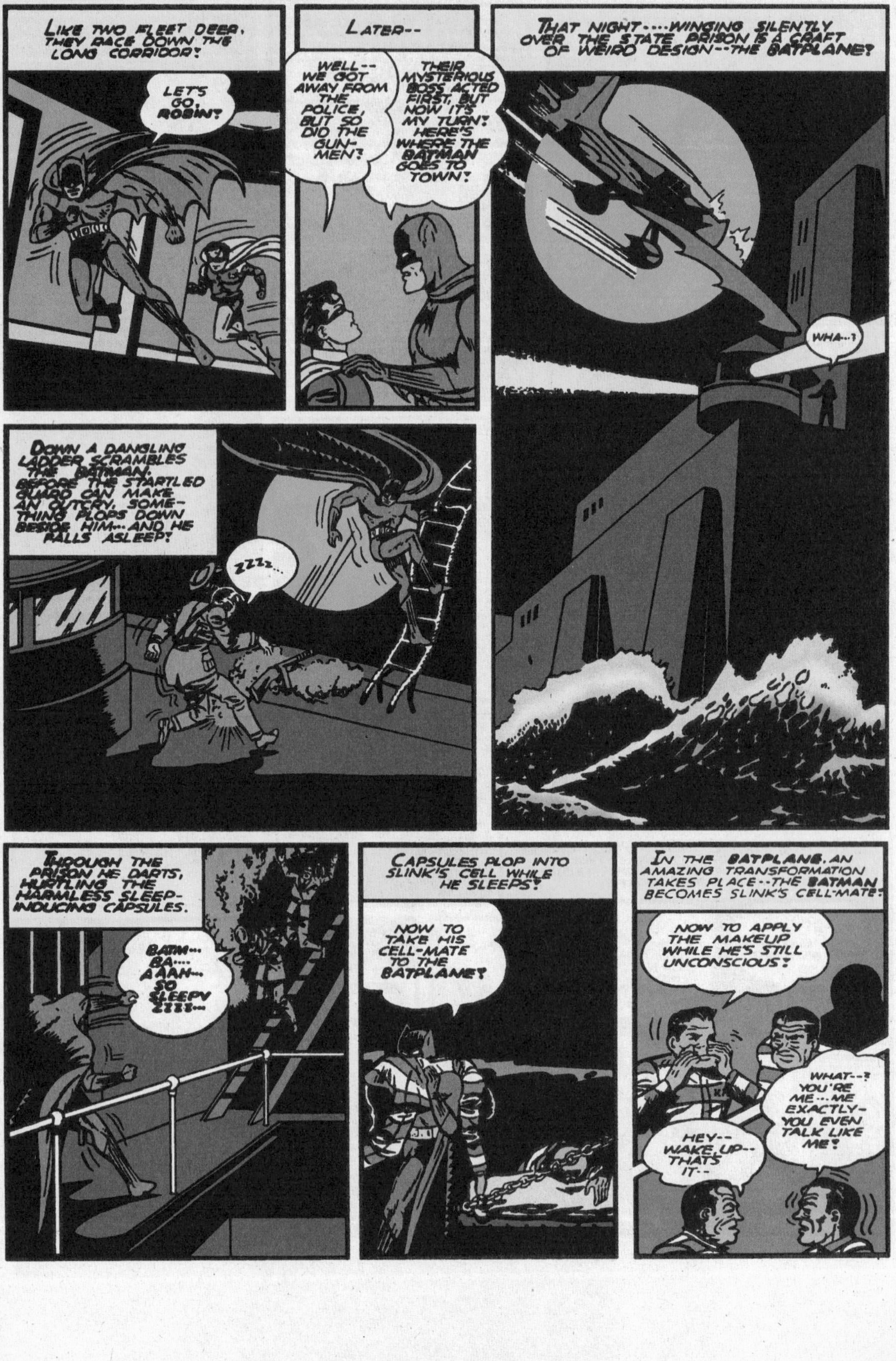
LIKE TWO FLEET DEER, THEY RACE DOWN THE LONG CORRIDOR!
LET'S GO, ROBIN!
LATER--
WELL-- WE GOT AWAY FROM THE POLICE, BUT SO DID THE GUN-MEN!
THEIR MYSTERIOUS BOSS ACTED FIRST, BUT NOW IT'S MY TURN! HERE'S WHERE THE BATMAN GOES TO TOWN!
THAT NIGHT....WINGING SILENTLY OVER THE STATE PRISON IS A CRAFT OF WEIRD DESIGN--THE BATPLANE!
WHA...?
DOWN A DANGLING LADDER SCRAMBLES THE BATMAN. BEFORE THE STARTLED GUARD CAN MAKE AN OUTCRY, SOME-THING PLOPS DOWN BESIDE HIM...AND HE FALLS ASLEEP!
ZZZZ...
THROUGH THE PRISON HE DARTS, HURTLING THE HARMLESS SLEEP-INDUCING CAPSULES.
BATM... BA.... AAAH... SO SLEEPY ZZZZ...
CAPSULES PLOP INTO SLINK'S CELL WHILE HE SLEEPS!
NOW TO TAKE HIS CELL-MATE TO THE BATPLANE!
IN THE BATPLANE, AN AMAZING TRANSFORMATION TAKES PLACE--THE BATMAN BECOMES SLINK'S CELL-MATE!
NOW TO APPLY THE MAKEUP WHILE HE'S STILL UNCONSCIOUS!
HEY-- WAKE UP-- THAT'S IT--
WHAT--? YOU'RE ME...ME EXACTLY-- YOU EVEN TALK LIKE ME!

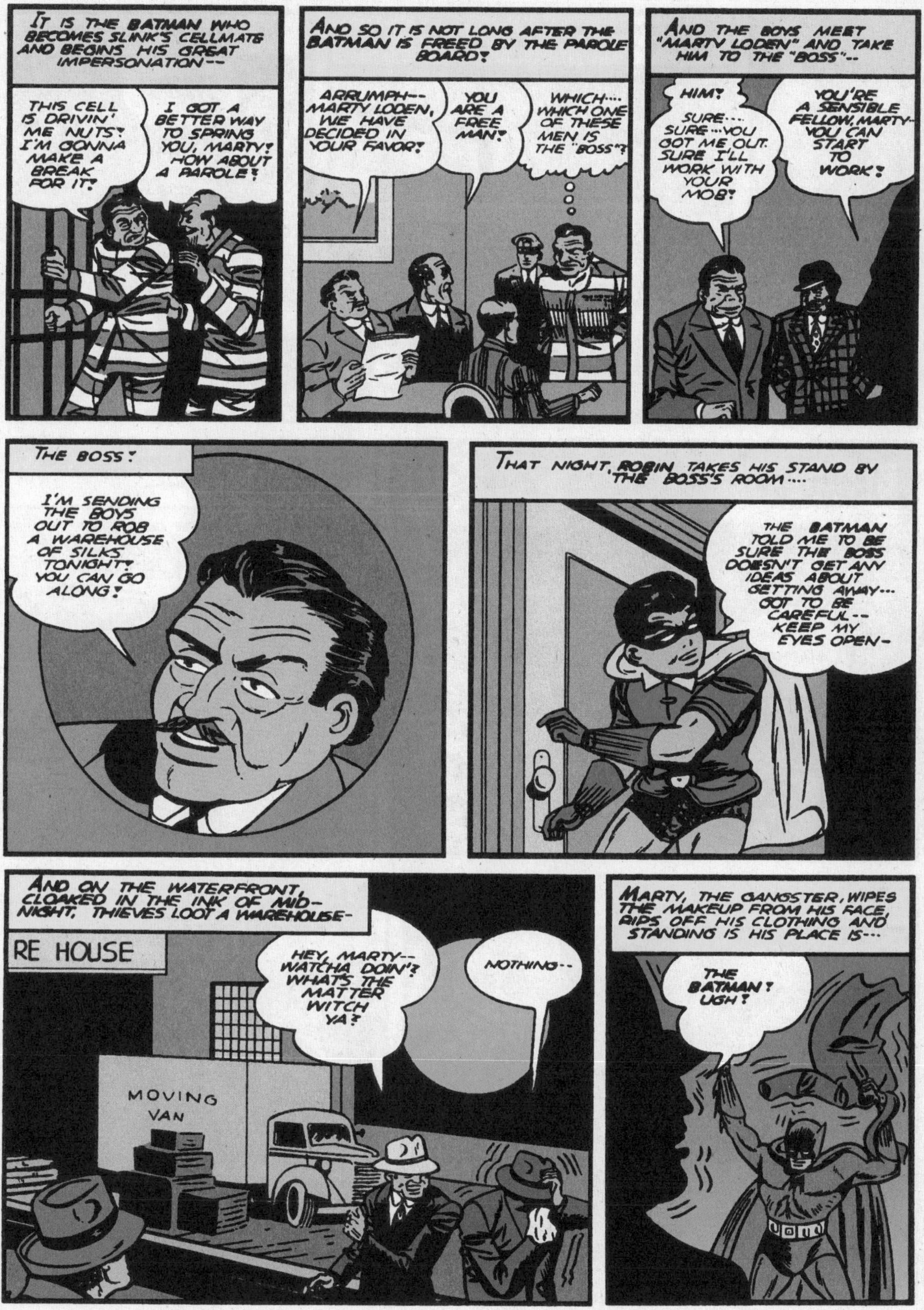
IT IS THE BATMAN WHO BECOMES SLINK'S CELLMATE AND BEGINS HIS GREAT IMPERSONATION--
THIS CELL IS DRIVIN' ME NUTS! I'M GONNA MAKE A BREAK FOR IT!
I GOT A BETTER WAY TO SPRING YOU, MARTY! HOW ABOUT A PAROLE?
AND SO IT IS NOT LONG AFTER THE BATMAN IS FREED BY THE PAROLE BOARD!
ARRUMPH-- MARTY LODEN, WE HAVE DECIDED IN YOUR FAVOR!
YOU ARE A FREE MAN!
WHICH.... WHICH ONE OF THESE MEN IS THE "BOSS"?
AND THE BOYS MEET "MARTY LODEN" AND TAKE HIM TO THE "BOSS"--
HIM!
SURE.... SURE... YOU GOT ME OUT. SURE I'LL WORK WITH YOUR MOB!
YOU'RE A SENSIBLE FELLOW, MARTY-- YOU CAN START TO WORK!
THE BOSS!
I'M SENDING THE BOYS OUT TO ROB A WAREHOUSE OF SILKS TONIGHT! YOU CAN GO ALONG!
THAT NIGHT, ROBIN TAKES HIS STAND BY THE BOSS'S ROOM....
THE BATMAN TOLD ME TO BE SURE THE BOSS DOESN'T GET ANY IDEAS ABOUT GETTING AWAY... GOT TO BE CAREFUL-- KEEP MY EYES OPEN-
AND ON THE WATERFRONT, CLOAKED IN THE INK OF MID-NIGHT, THIEVES LOOT A WAREHOUSE-
RE HOUSE
HEY, MARTY-- WATCHA DOIN'? WHAT'S THE MATTER WITCH YA?
NOTHING--
MOVING VAN
MARTY, THE GANGSTER, WIPES THE MAKEUP FROM HIS FACE, RIPS OFF HIS CLOTHING AND STANDING IS HIS PLACE IS---
THE BATMAN! UGH!

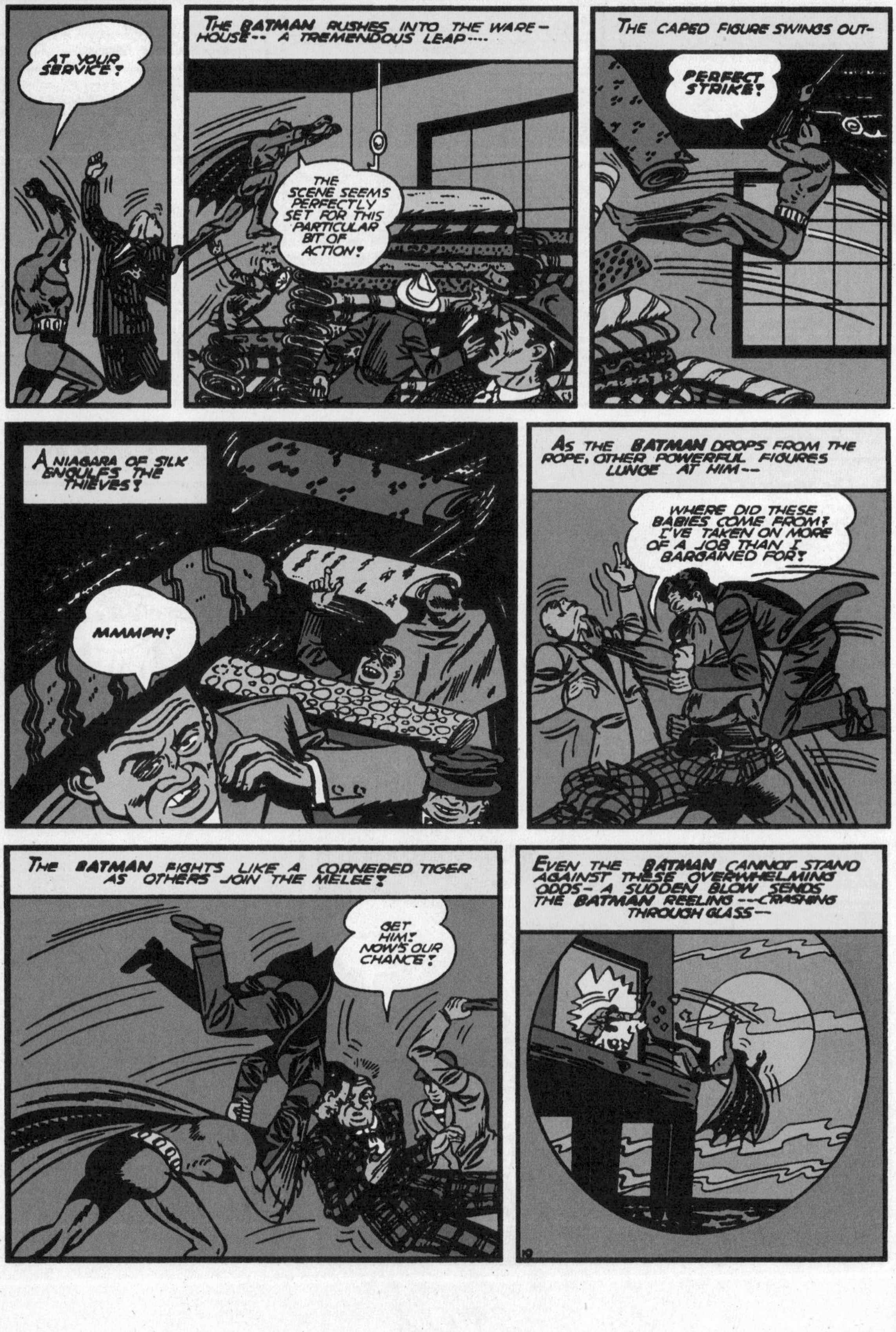
AT YOUR SERVICE!
THE BATMAN RUSHES INTO THE WARE-HOUSE-- A TREMENDOUS LEAP----
THE SCENE SEEMS PERFECTLY SET FOR THIS PARTICULAR BIT OF ACTION!
THE CAPED FIGURE SWINGS OUT-
PERFECT STRIKE!
A NIAGARA OF SILK ENGULFS THE THIEVES!
MMMPH!
AS THE BATMAN DROPS FROM THE ROPE, OTHER POWERFUL FIGURES LUNGE AT HIM--
WHERE DID THESE BABIES COME FROM? I'VE TAKEN ON MORE OF A JOB THAN I BARGAINED FOR!
THE BATMAN FIGHTS LIKE A CORNERED TIGER AS OTHERS JOIN THE MELEE!
GET HIM! NOW'S OUR CHANCE!
EVEN THE BATMAN CANNOT STAND AGAINST THESE OVERWHELMING ODDS- A SUDDEN BLOW SENDS THE BATMAN REELING ---CRASHING THROUGH GLASS--

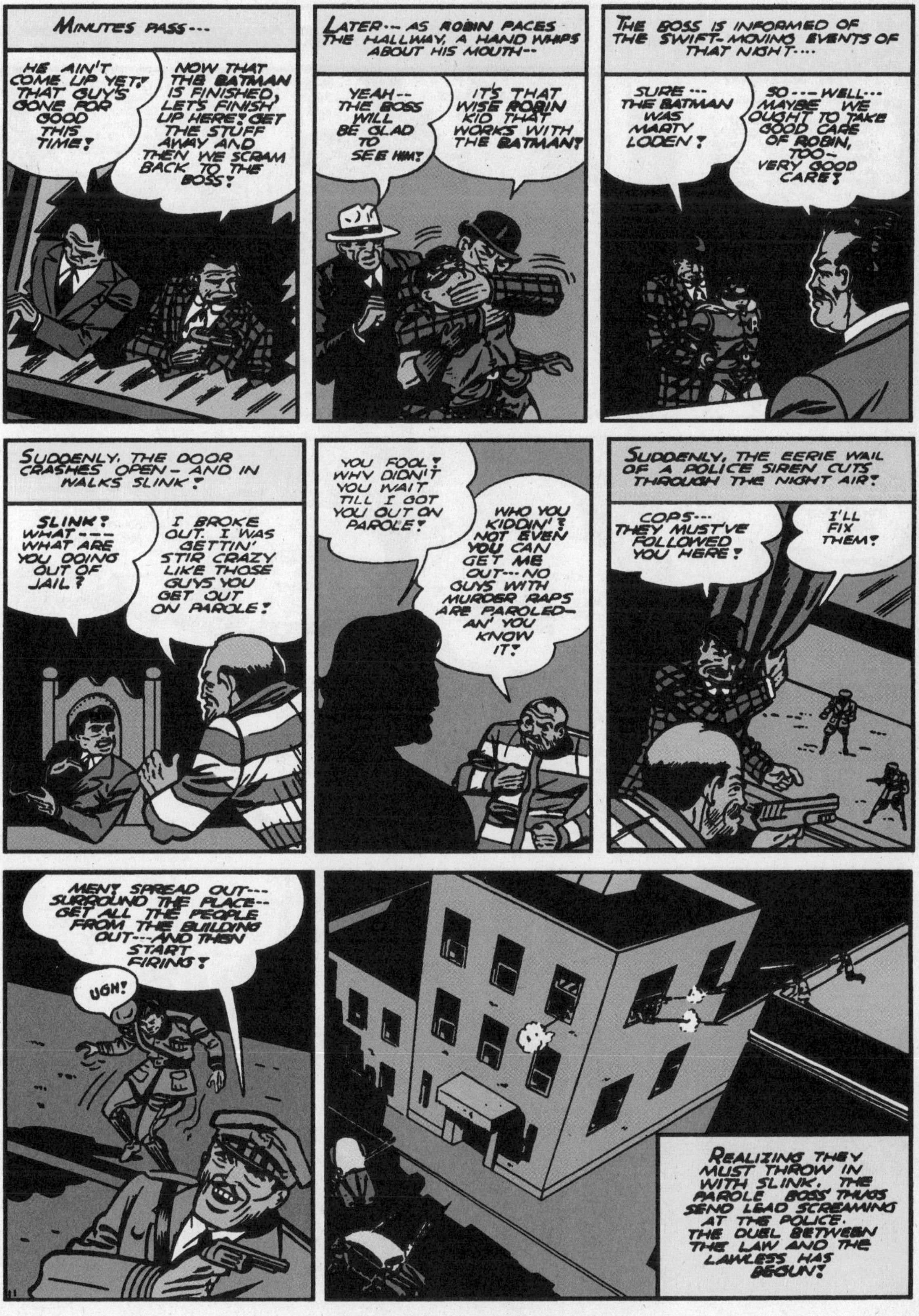
MINUTES PASS---
HE AIN'T COME UP YET! THAT GUY'S GONE FOR GOOD THIS TIME!
NOW THAT THE BATMAN IS FINISHED, LET'S FINISH UP HERE! GET THE STUFF AWAY AND THEN WE SCRAM BACK TO THE BOSS!
LATER-- AS ROBIN PACES THE HALLWAY, A HAND WHIPS ABOUT HIS MOUTH--
YEAH-- THE BOSS WILL BE GLAD TO SEE HIM!
IT'S THAT WISE ROBIN KID THAT WORKS WITH THE BATMAN!
THE BOSS IS INFORMED OF THE SWIFT-MOVING EVENTS OF THAT NIGHT----
SURE --- THE BATMAN WAS MARTY LODEN!
SO --- WELL--- MAYBE WE OUGHT TO TAKE GOOD CARE OF ROBIN, TOO-- VERY GOOD CARE!
SUDDENLY, THE DOOR CRASHES OPEN-- AND IN WALKS SLINK!
SLINK! WHAT --- WHAT ARE YOU DOING OUT OF JAIL?
I BROKE OUT. I WAS GETTIN' STIR CRAZY LIKE THOSE GUYS YOU GET OUT ON PAROLE!
YOU FOOL! WHY DIDN'T YOU WAIT TILL I GOT YOU OUT ON PAROLE!
WHO YOU KIDDIN'! NOT EVEN YOU CAN GET ME OUT--- NO GUYS WITH MURDER RAPS ARE PAROLED-- AN' YOU KNOW IT!
SUDDENLY, THE EERIE WAIL OF A POLICE SIREN CUTS THROUGH THE NIGHT AIR!
COPS--- THEY MUST'VE FOLLOWED YOU HERE!
I'LL FIX THEM!
MEN! SPREAD OUT--- SURROUND THE PLACE-- GET ALL THE PEOPLE FROM THE BUILDING OUT---AND THEN START FIRING!
UGH!
REALIZING THEY MUST THROW IN WITH SLINK, THE PAROLE BOSS' THUGS SEND LEAD SCREAMING AT THE POLICE. THE DUEL BETWEEN THE LAW AND THE LAWLESS HAS BEGUN!

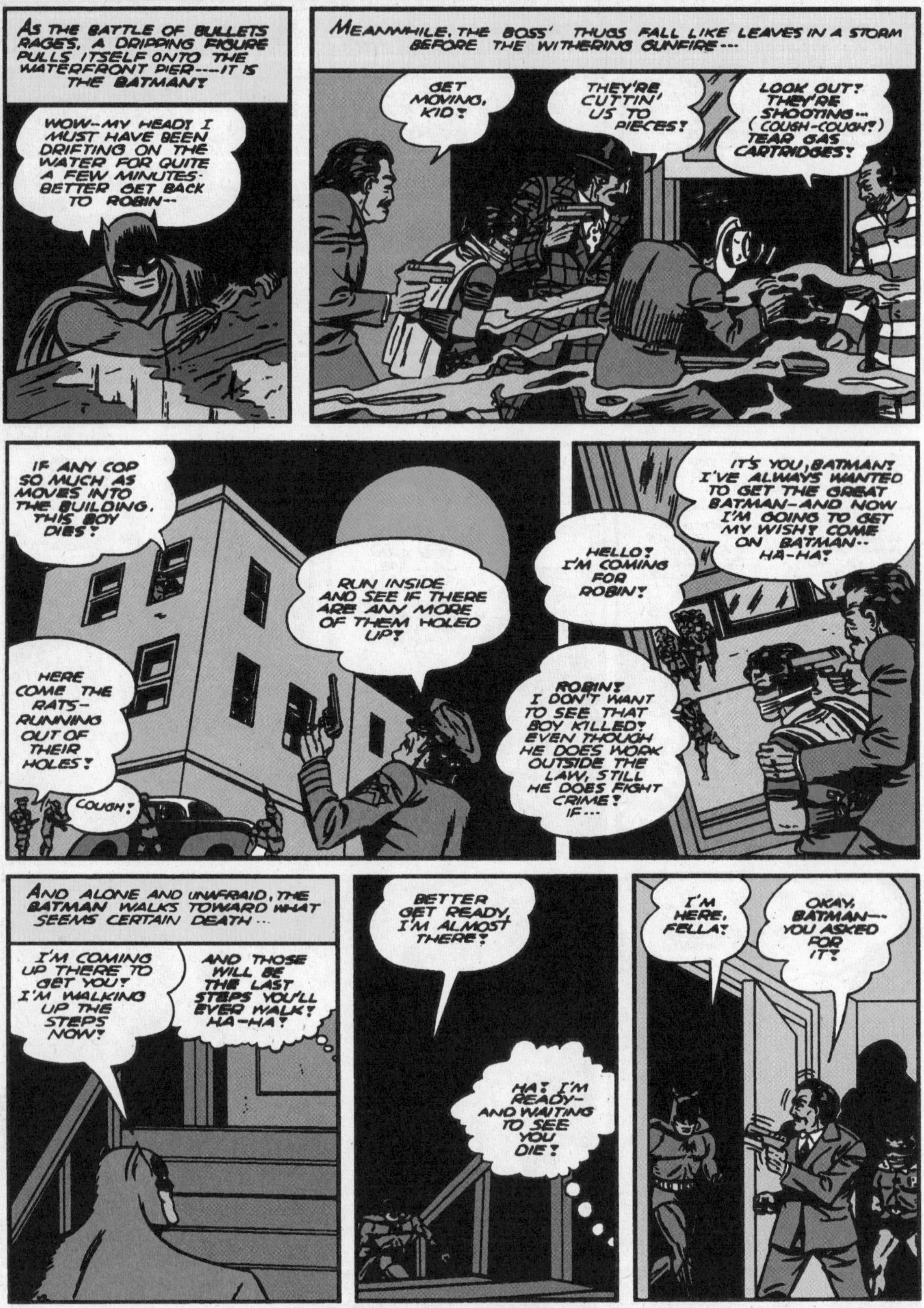
AS THE BATTLE OF BULLETS RAGES, A DRIPPING FIGURE PULLS ITSELF ONTO THE WATERFRONT PIER----IT IS THE BATMAN!
WOW--MY HEAD! I MUST HAVE BEEN DRIFTING ON THE WATER FOR QUITE A FEW MINUTES- BETTER GET BACK TO ROBIN--
MEANWHILE, THE BOSS' THUGS FALL LIKE LEAVES IN A STORM BEFORE THE WITHERING GUNFIRE---
GET MOVING, KID!
THEY'RE CUTTIN' US TO PIECES!
LOOK OUT! THEY'RE SHOOTING--- (COUGH-COUGH!) TEAR GAS CARTRIDGES!
IF ANY COP SO MUCH AS MOVES INTO THE BUILDING, THIS BOY DIES!
RUN INSIDE AND SEE IF THERE ARE ANY MORE OF THEM HOLED UP!
HERE COME THE RATS- RUNNING OUT OF THEIR HOLES!
COUGH!
IT'S YOU, BATMAN! I'VE ALWAYS WANTED TO GET THE GREAT BATMAN-AND NOW I'M GOING TO GET MY WISH! COME ON BATMAN-- HA-HA!
HELLO! I'M COMING FOR ROBIN!
ROBIN! I DON'T WANT TO SEE THAT BOY KILLED! EVEN THOUGH HE DOES WORK OUTSIDE THE LAW, STILL HE DOES FIGHT CRIME! IF---
AND ALONE AND UNAFRAID, THE BATMAN WALKS TOWARD WHAT SEEMS CERTAIN DEATH---
I'M COMING UP THERE TO GET YOU! I'M WALKING UP THE STEPS NOW!
AND THOSE WILL BE THE LAST STEPS YOU'LL EVER WALK! HA-HA!
BETTER GET READY, I'M ALMOST THERE!
HA! I'M READY- AND WAITING TO SEE YOU DIE!
I'M HERE, FELLA!
OKAY, BATMAN--- YOU ASKED FOR IT!

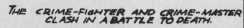

ABRUPTLY--ROBIN ACTS WITH THE SPEED OF THOUGHT...

OOF!

THE CRIME-FIGHTER AND CRIME-MASTER CLASH IN A BATTLE TO DEATH.

A SUDDEN BLOW SENDS THE BATMAN OFF BALANCE AND REELING TOWARD AN OPEN ELEVATOR SHAFT--

NOW I'LL FINISH YOU OFF!

BUT THE MADMAN'S CHARGE CARRIES HIM TOO FAR. BOTH THE BATMAN AND THE PAROLE RACKETEER PLUNGE DOWN THE SHAFT!

WHA--!

EVEN AS HE DROPS, LIKE A LEADEN PLUMMET, THE BATMAN'S HAND CLOSES VISELIKE ABOUT THE OILY ELEVATOR CABLE--BUT THE PAROLE RACKETEER IS NOT SO FORTUNATE! A TRAILING SHRIEK MARKS HIS END!

AAAAAA

BOB KANE

LATER--

WELL, I SUPPOSE ALL THOSE MEN PAROLED BY THEIR BOSS WILL GO BACK TO JAIL!

ALL EXCEPT MILLER! HE EARNED HIS PAROLE. YOU KNOW, IT'S EASY FOR MOST PEOPLE TO UNDERSTAND CRIME DOESN'T PAY, BUT WHEN A CRIMINAL SUDDENLY REALIZES IT, AS MILLER DID, WELL THAT'S ABOUT THE BEST MORAL LESSON THERE CAN BE!

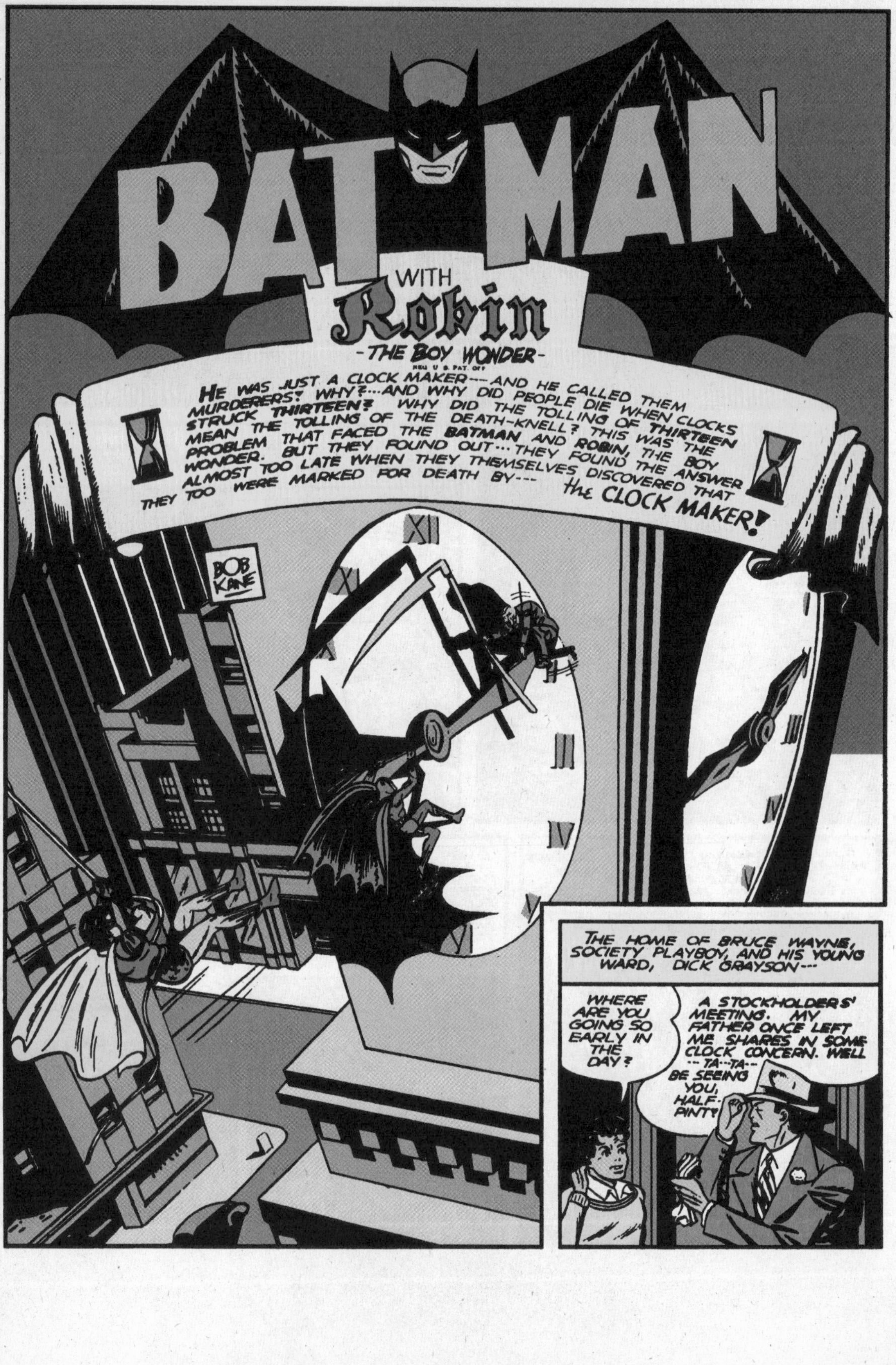
BATMAN
WITH Robin
-THE BOY WONDER-
REG. U. S. PAT. OFF
HE WAS JUST A CLOCK MAKER--- AND HE CALLED THEM MURDERERS! WHY?...AND WHY DID PEOPLE DIE WHEN CLOCKS STRUCK THIRTEEN? WHY DID THE TOLLING OF THIRTEEN MEAN THE TOLLING OF THE DEATH-KNELL? THIS WAS THE PROBLEM THAT FACED THE BATMAN AND ROBIN, THE BOY WONDER. BUT THEY FOUND OUT... THEY FOUND THE ANSWER ALMOST TOO LATE WHEN THEY THEMSELVES DISCOVERED THAT THEY TOO WERE MARKED FOR DEATH BY--- the CLOCK MAKER!
BOB KANE
THE HOME OF BRUCE WAYNE, SOCIETY PLAYBOY, AND HIS YOUNG WARD, DICK GRAYSON---
WHERE ARE YOU GOING SO EARLY IN THE DAY?
A STOCKHOLDERS' MEETING. MY FATHER ONCE LEFT ME SHARES IN SOME CLOCK CONCERN. WELL --TA--TA-- BE SEEING YOU, HALF-PINT!

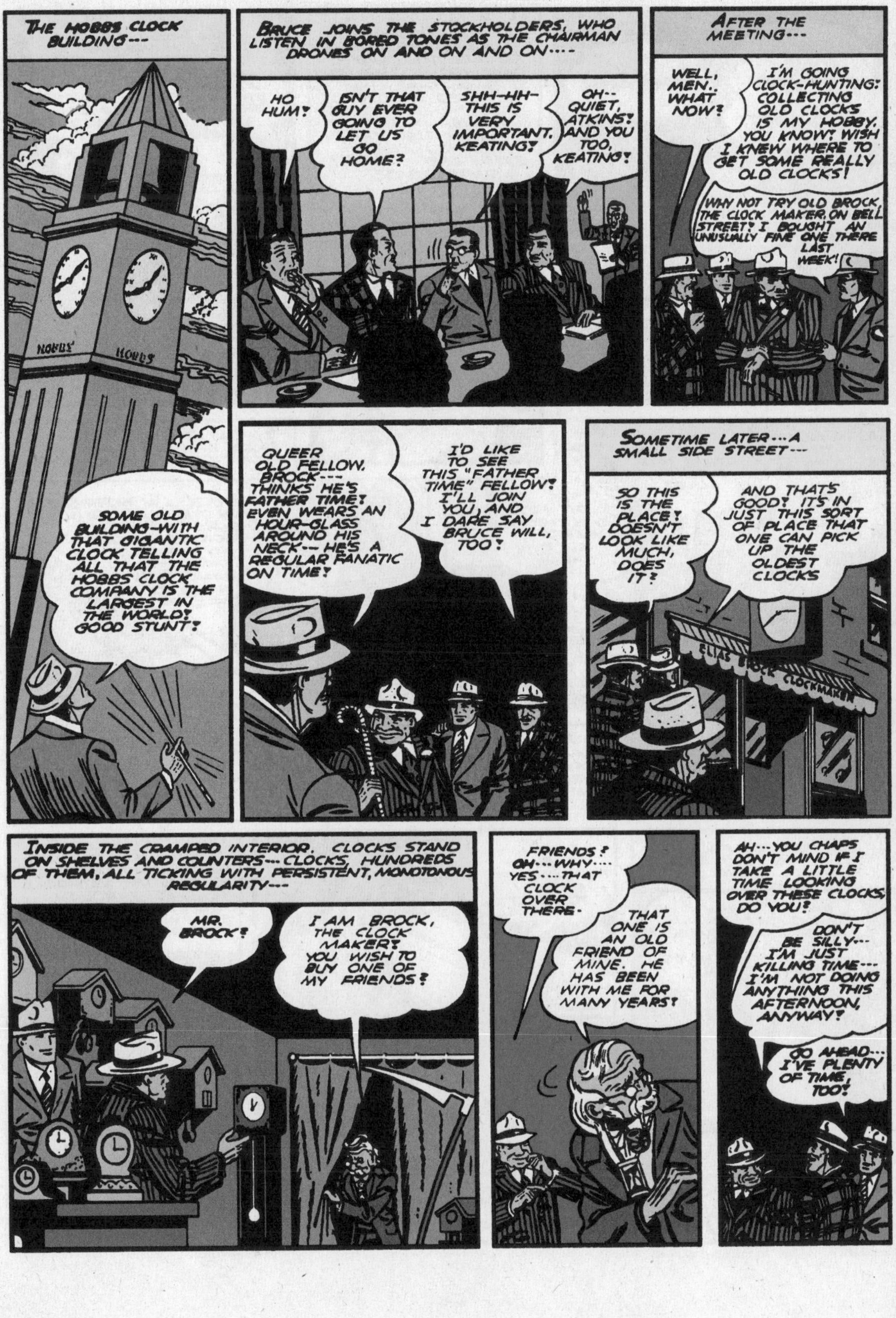

THE HOBBS CLOCK BUILDING---
SOME OLD BUILDING-WITH THAT GIGANTIC CLOCK TELLING ALL THAT THE HOBBS CLOCK COMPANY IS THE LARGEST IN THE WORLD! GOOD STUNT!
HOBBS
HOBBS
BRUCE JOINS THE STOCKHOLDERS, WHO LISTEN IN BORED TONES AS THE CHAIRMAN DRONES ON AND ON AND ON....
HO HUM!
ISN'T THAT GUY EVER GOING TO LET US GO HOME?
SHH-HH- THIS IS VERY IMPORTANT, KEATING!
OH-- QUIET, ATKINS! AND YOU TOO, KEATING!
AFTER THE MEETING---
WELL, MEN.. WHAT NOW?
I'M GOING CLOCK-HUNTING: COLLECTING OLD CLOCKS IS MY HOBBY, YOU KNOW! WISH I KNEW WHERE TO GET SOME REALLY OLD CLOCKS!
WHY NOT TRY OLD BROCK, THE CLOCK MAKER, ON BELL STREET! I BOUGHT AN UNUSUALLY FINE ONE THERE LAST WEEK!
QUEER OLD FELLOW, BROCK--- THINKS HE'S FATHER TIME! EVEN WEARS AN HOUR-GLASS AROUND HIS NECK-- HE'S A REGULAR FANATIC ON TIME!
I'D LIKE TO SEE THIS "FATHER TIME" FELLOW! I'LL JOIN YOU, AND I DARE SAY BRUCE WILL, TOO!
SOMETIME LATER...A SMALL SIDE STREET---
SO THIS IS THE PLACE! DOESN'T LOOK LIKE MUCH, DOES IT?
AND THAT'S GOOD! IT'S IN JUST THIS SORT OF PLACE THAT ONE CAN PICK UP THE OLDEST CLOCKS
ELIAS BROCK CLOCKMAKER
INSIDE THE CRAMPED INTERIOR, CLOCKS STAND ON SHELVES AND COUNTERS--- CLOCKS, HUNDREDS OF THEM, ALL TICKING WITH PERSISTENT, MONOTONOUS REGULARITY---
MR. BROCK!
I AM BROCK, THE CLOCK MAKER! YOU WISH TO BUY ONE OF MY FRIENDS?
FRIENDS? OH...WHY.... YES....THAT CLOCK OVER THERE-
THAT ONE IS AN OLD FRIEND OF MINE. HE HAS BEEN WITH ME FOR MANY YEARS!
AH...YOU CHAPS DON'T MIND IF I TAKE A LITTLE TIME LOOKING OVER THESE CLOCKS, DO YOU?
DON'T BE SILLY--- I'M JUST KILLING TIME--- I'M NOT DOING ANYTHING THIS AFTERNOON, ANYWAY!
GO AHEAD... I'VE PLENTY OF TIME, TOO!

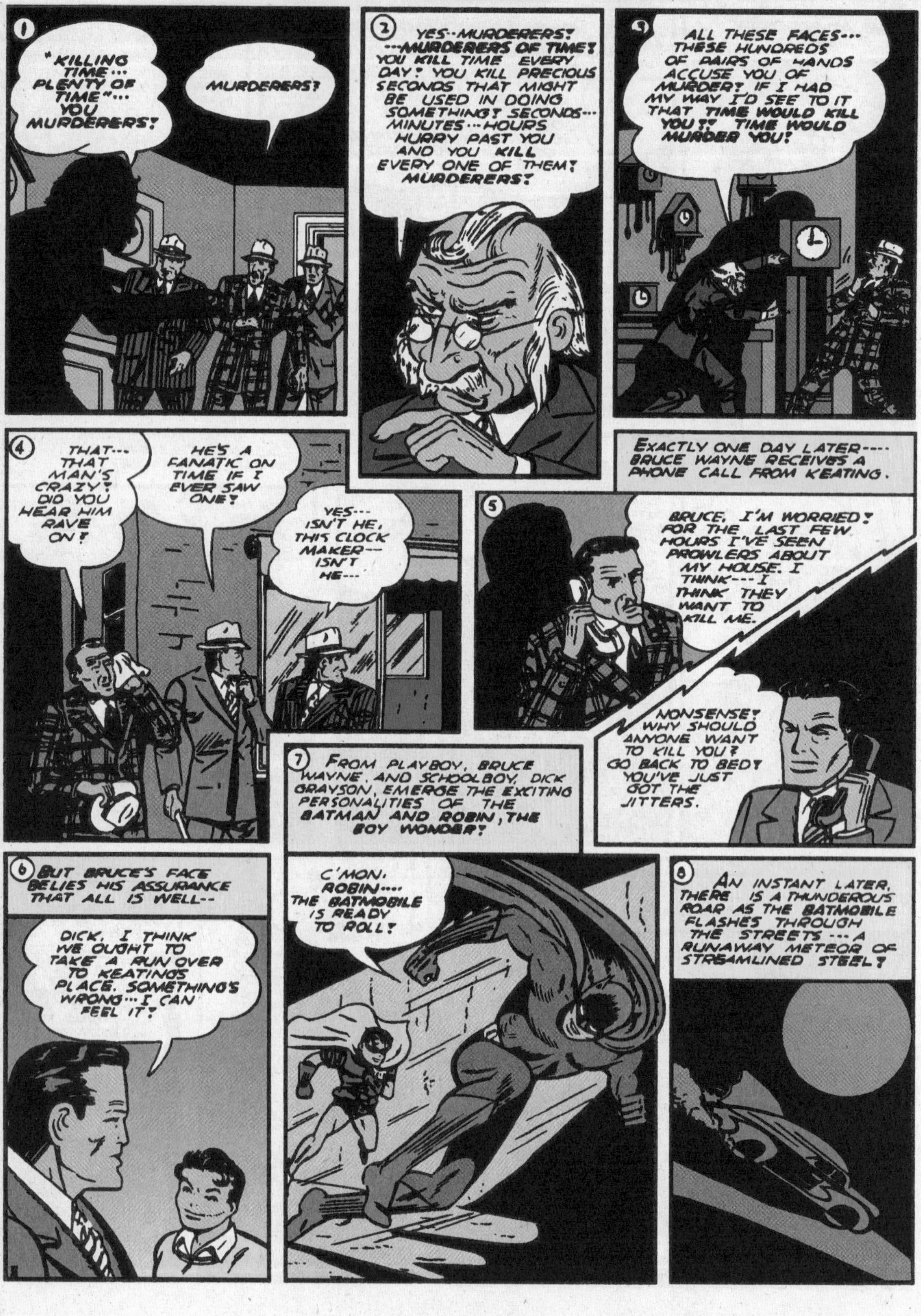
"KILLING TIME... PLENTY OF TIME"... YOU MURDERERS!
MURDERERS?
YES--MURDERERS! ---MURDERERS OF TIME! YOU KILL TIME EVERY DAY! YOU KILL PRECIOUS SECONDS THAT MIGHT BE USED IN DOING SOMETHING! SECONDS--- MINUTES---HOURS HURRY PAST YOU AND YOU KILL EVERY ONE OF THEM! MURDERERS!
ALL THESE FACES--- THESE HUNDREDS OF PAIRS OF HANDS ACCUSE YOU OF MURDER! IF I HAD MY WAY I'D SEE TO IT THAT TIME WOULD KILL YOU!! TIME WOULD MURDER YOU!
THAT--- THAT MAN'S CRAZY! DID YOU HEAR HIM RAVE ON?
HE'S A FANATIC ON TIME IF I EVER SAW ONE!
YES--- ISN'T HE, THIS CLOCK MAKER--- ISN'T HE---
EXACTLY ONE DAY LATER---- BRUCE WAYNE RECEIVES A PHONE CALL FROM KEATING.
BRUCE, I'M WORRIED! FOR THE LAST FEW HOURS I'VE SEEN PROWLERS ABOUT MY HOUSE. I THINK--- I THINK THEY WANT TO KILL ME.
NONSENSE! WHY SHOULD ANYONE WANT TO KILL YOU? GO BACK TO BED! YOU'VE JUST GOT THE JITTERS.
BUT BRUCE'S FACE BELIES HIS ASSURANCE THAT ALL IS WELL--
DICK, I THINK WE OUGHT TO TAKE A RUN OVER TO KEATING'S PLACE. SOMETHING'S WRONG--- I CAN FEEL IT!
FROM PLAYBOY, BRUCE WAYNE, AND SCHOOLBOY, DICK GRAYSON, EMERGE THE EXCITING PERSONALITIES OF THE BATMAN AND ROBIN, THE BOY WONDER!
C'MON, ROBIN---- THE BATMOBILE IS READY TO ROLL!
AN INSTANT LATER, THERE IS A THUNDEROUS ROAR AS THE BATMOBILE FLASHES THROUGH THE STREETS --- A RUNAWAY METEOR OF STREAMLINED STEEL!

THE BATMOBILE RACES TO THE KEATING HOME IN RECORD TIME!

HELP!

C'MON, ROBIN! LOOKS LIKE WE'RE BEING PAGED!

UP THE STEPS AND INTO THE HOUSE DART THE BATMAN AND ROBIN...TWIN AVENGERS OF EVIL!

GREETINGS...!

THE--THE BATMAN!

---AND SALUTATIONS--

...AND ALL THAT SORT OF THING!

HOLD HIM STILL! GIMME A CHANCE TO PLUG 'IM!

YOU HAD YOUR CHANCE, MUGG...BUT YOU MUFFED IT!

OOF!

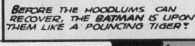

BEFORE THE HOODLUMS CAN RECOVER, THE BATMAN IS UPON THEM LIKE A POUNCING TIGER!

VERY NICE! NOW I DON'T HAVE TO SOIL MY HANDS ON THE BOTH OF YOU!

OUTSIDE, THE THUGS SCRAMBLE TO THEIR FEET AND RUN TO THEIR CAR!

C'MON! LET'S GET OUTA HERE--- BUT FAST!

WAIT-- MITCH IS INSIDE. HE MIGHT TALK!

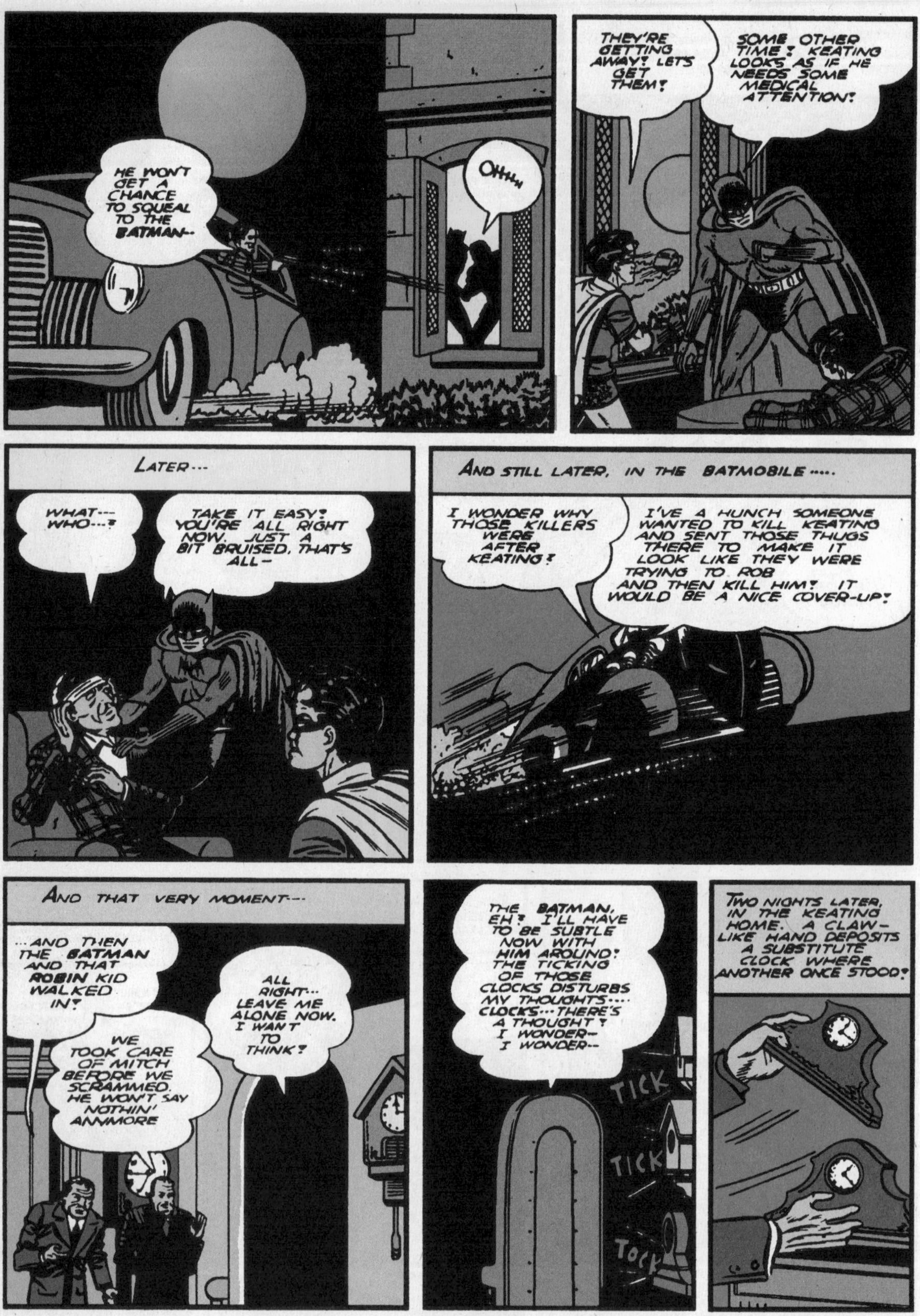
HE WON'T GET A CHANCE TO SQUEAL TO THE BATMAN--
OHHH
THEY'RE GETTING AWAY! LET'S GET THEM!
SOME OTHER TIME! KEATING LOOKS AS IF HE NEEDS SOME MEDICAL ATTENTION!
LATER---
WHAT--- WHO---?
TAKE IT EASY! YOU'RE ALL RIGHT NOW. JUST A BIT BRUISED, THAT'S ALL-
AND STILL LATER, IN THE BATMOBILE.....
I WONDER WHY THOSE KILLERS WERE AFTER KEATING?
I'VE A HUNCH SOMEONE WANTED TO KILL KEATING AND SENT THOSE THUGS THERE TO MAKE IT LOOK LIKE THEY WERE TRYING TO ROB AND THEN KILL HIM! IT WOULD BE A NICE COVER-UP!
AND THAT VERY MOMENT---
...AND THEN THE BATMAN AND THAT ROBIN KID WALKED IN!
WE TOOK CARE OF MITCH BEFORE WE SCRAMMED. HE WON'T SAY NOTHIN' ANYMORE
ALL RIGHT... LEAVE ME ALONE NOW. I WANT TO THINK!
THE BATMAN, EH? I'LL HAVE TO BE SUBTLE NOW WITH HIM AROUND! THE TICKING OF THOSE CLOCKS DISTURBS MY THOUGHTS.... CLOCKS... THERE'S A THOUGHT! I WONDER-- I WONDER--
TICK
TICK
TOCK
TWO NIGHTS LATER, IN THE KEATING HOME. A CLAW-LIKE HAND DEPOSITS A SUBSTITUTE CLOCK WHERE ANOTHER ONCE STOOD!

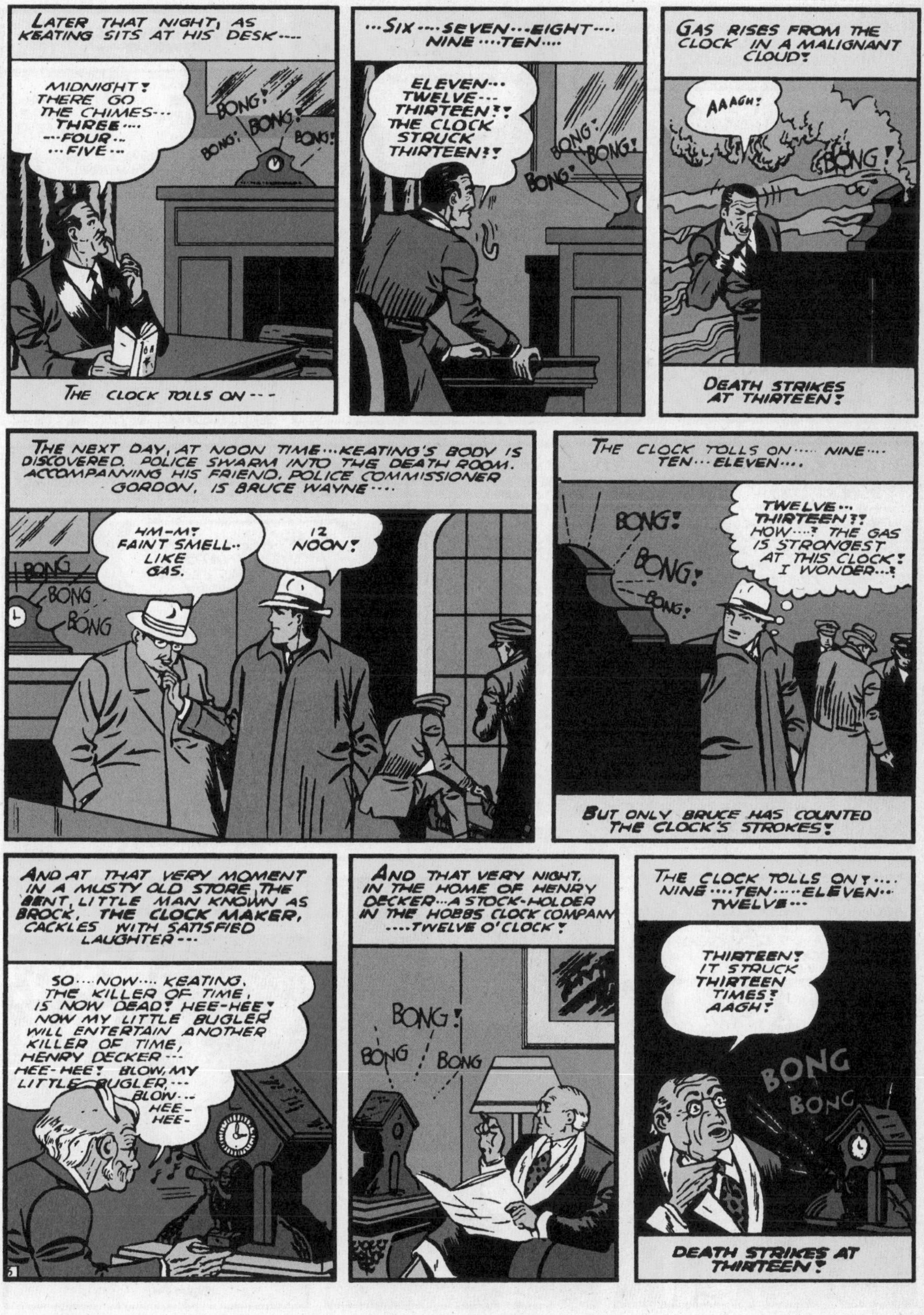
LATER THAT NIGHT, AS KEATING SITS AT HIS DESK----
MIDNIGHT! THERE GO THE CHIMES--- THREE---- ---FOUR--- ---FIVE---
BONG! BONG! BONG! BONG!
THE CLOCK TOLLS ON---
...SIX----SEVEN---EIGHT---- NINE----TEN----
ELEVEN--- TWELVE--- THIRTEEN?! THE CLOCK STRUCK THIRTEEN?!
BONG! BONG! BONG!
GAS RISES FROM THE CLOCK IN A MALIGNANT CLOUD!
AAAGH!
BONG!
DEATH STRIKES AT THIRTEEN!
THE NEXT DAY, AT NOON TIME---KEATING'S BODY IS DISCOVERED. POLICE SWARM INTO THE DEATH ROOM. ACCOMPANYING HIS FRIEND, POLICE COMMISSIONER GORDON, IS BRUCE WAYNE----
HM-M! FAINT SMELL-- LIKE GAS.
12 NOON!
BONG BONG BONG
THE CLOCK TOLLS ON---- NINE---- TEN---ELEVEN----
BONG! BONG! BONG!
TWELVE--- THIRTEEN?! HOW---? THE GAS IS STRONGEST AT THIS CLOCK! I WONDER--?
BUT ONLY BRUCE HAS COUNTED THE CLOCK'S STROKES!
AND AT THAT VERY MOMENT IN A MUSTY OLD STORE THE BENT, LITTLE MAN KNOWN AS BROCK, THE CLOCK MAKER, CACKLES WITH SATISFIED LAUGHTER---
SO----NOW---- KEATING, THE KILLER OF TIME, IS NOW DEAD! HEE-HEE! NOW MY LITTLE BUGLER WILL ENTERTAIN ANOTHER KILLER OF TIME, HENRY DECKER--- HEE-HEE! BLOW, MY LITTLE BUGLER,--- BLOW--- HEE-HEE-
AND THAT VERY NIGHT, IN THE HOME OF HENRY DECKER---A STOCK-HOLDER IN THE HOBBS CLOCK COMPANY ----TWELVE O'CLOCK!
BONG! BONG BONG
THE CLOCK TOLLS ON!---- NINE----TEN-----ELEVEN-- TWELVE---
THIRTEEN! IT STRUCK THIRTEEN TIMES! AAGH!
BONG BONG
DEATH STRIKES AT THIRTEEN!

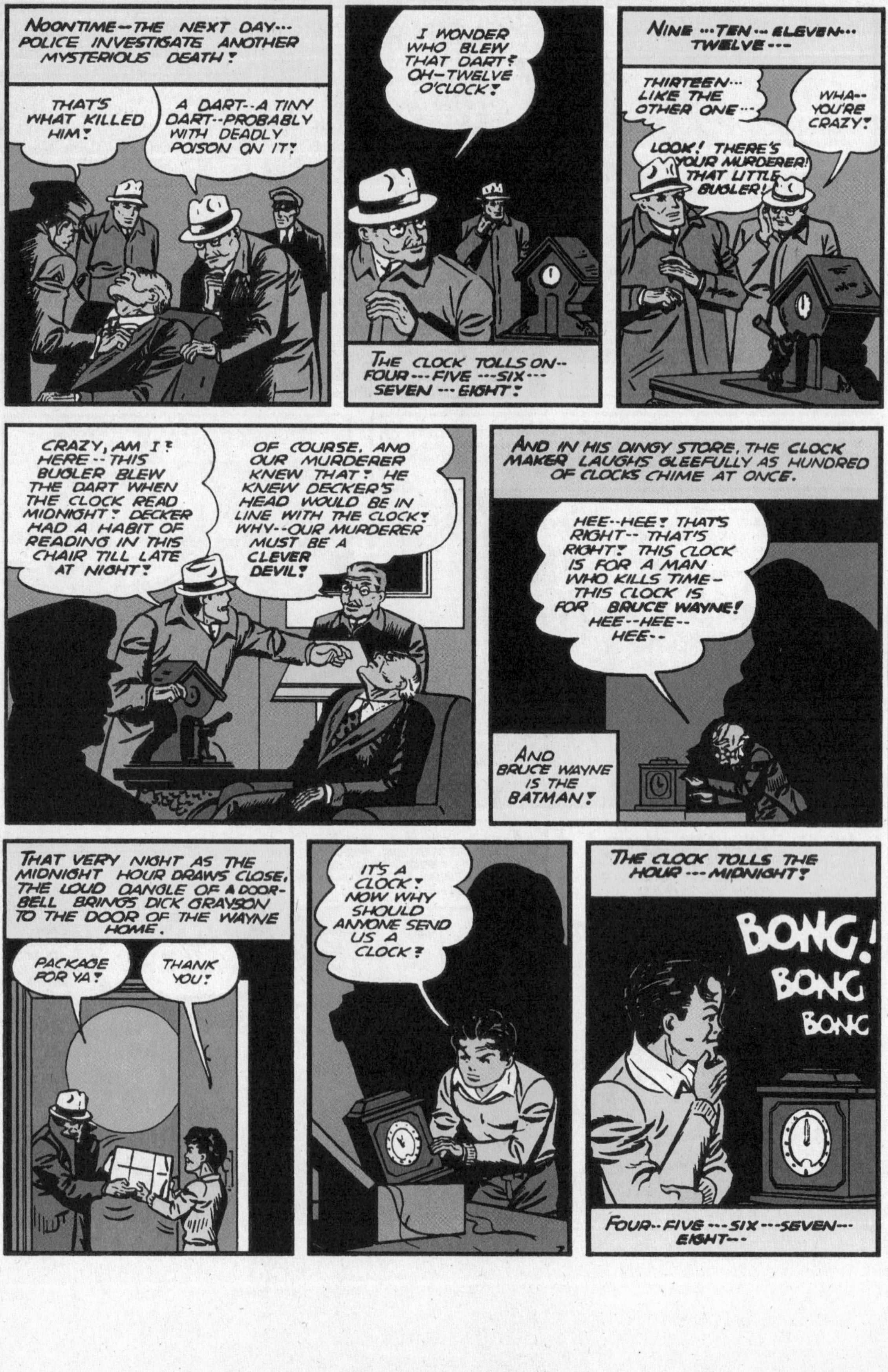
NOONTIME--THE NEXT DAY--- POLICE INVESTIGATE ANOTHER MYSTERIOUS DEATH!
THAT'S WHAT KILLED HIM!
A DART--A TINY DART--PROBABLY WITH DEADLY POISON ON IT!
I WONDER WHO BLEW THAT DART? OH--TWELVE O'CLOCK!
THE CLOCK TOLLS ON-- FOUR --- FIVE --- SIX --- SEVEN --- EIGHT!
NINE --- TEN --- ELEVEN--- TWELVE ---
THIRTEEN--- LIKE THE OTHER ONE---
WHA-- YOU'RE CRAZY!
LOOK! THERE'S YOUR MURDERER! THAT LITTLE BUGLER!
CRAZY, AM I? HERE--THIS BUGLER BLEW THE DART WHEN THE CLOCK READ MIDNIGHT! DECKER HAD A HABIT OF READING IN THIS CHAIR TILL LATE AT NIGHT!
OF COURSE, AND OUR MURDERER KNEW THAT! HE KNEW DECKER'S HEAD WOULD BE IN LINE WITH THE CLOCK! WHY--OUR MURDERER MUST BE A CLEVER DEVIL!
AND IN HIS DINGY STORE, THE CLOCK MAKER LAUGHS GLEEFULLY AS HUNDRED OF CLOCKS CHIME AT ONCE.
HEE--HEE! THAT'S RIGHT-- THAT'S RIGHT! THIS CLOCK IS FOR A MAN WHO KILLS TIME-- THIS CLOCK IS FOR BRUCE WAYNE! HEE--HEE-- HEE--
AND BRUCE WAYNE IS THE BATMAN!
THAT VERY NIGHT AS THE MIDNIGHT HOUR DRAWS CLOSE, THE LOUD DANGLE OF A DOOR-BELL BRINGS DICK GRAYSON TO THE DOOR OF THE WAYNE HOME.
PACKAGE FOR YA!
THANK YOU!
IT'S A CLOCK! NOW WHY SHOULD ANYONE SEND US A CLOCK?
THE CLOCK TOLLS THE HOUR --- MIDNIGHT!
BONG! BONG BONG
FOUR-- FIVE --- SIX --- SEVEN--- EIGHT---

SUDDENLY, A FIGURE HURTLES INTO THE ROOM—PICKS UP THE CLOCK—AND---

BONG, BONG

?

NINE---TEN---ELEVE... THIRTEEN... THEN... BLAST DEAFENS...

BOO...

WHEW!

GOOD THING I HEARD THAT CLOCK START TO CHIME. I KNEW WE HAD NO CLOCKS LIKE THAT! LOOKS LIKE SOMEBODY DOESN'T LIKE US, EH, KID!

THE VERY NEXT NIGHT! ONCE AGAIN BRUCE WAYNE DONS THE INK-HUED GARB OF THE BATMAN!

NOW REMEMBER-- IF I'M NOT BACK WITHIN THE HOUR, COME AND GET ME!

CHECK!

SOMETIME LA... CAPED FIGURE... FILING C...

JUST AS I THOUGHT! BOTH KEATING AND DECKER WERE BOTH STOCKHOLDERS IN THE HOBBS CLOCK COMPANY. THINGS TIE UP! I'D BETTER MAKE A PHONE CALL!

THE BATMAN PHONES THE BANKER, SELBY--

HELLO, SELBY- ARE YOU ALL RIGHT!

OF COURSE I'M ALL RIGHT! WHO IS THIS SPEAKING-- WHA?--THE MAN HUNG UP!

CLICK!

AND IN THE CRAMPED INTERIO... SHOP, THE CLOCK MAKER LIS... A MAN WHO SPEAKS TO...

BRUCE WAYNE IS STILL ALIVE! SOMETHING WENT WRONG. BUT WE'LL GET HIM THE NEXT TIME! NOW, I'VE ANOTHER KILLER OF TIME FOR YOU-- PETER SELBY, THE BANKER!

THAT WON'T... YOU... GOO... ATKI... I KNO... WHY... KILLE... THOSE... HOLDE... AND D... WANTE... HOBBS... COMPA... YOUR...

K...ME
ADDRESS
MAN
MAY
OF
ENDS
AVENUE
TH?

SURE...
SURE...
HIS
ADDRESS
IS...

WHY
DON'T YOU
GIVE HIM
YOUR
ADDRESS...

--ATKINS?

WHO?
--THAT
COSTUME--
YOU'RE
THE
BATMAN!

YOU!

WHOA!
THERE--
FATHER
TIME!

I HATE
TO HIT
AN OLDER
MAN...BUT
I'M AFRAID
THIS TIME
IT'S
NECESSARY!

UN
Y
?
?
CK-
KEATING,
ER! YOU
TO CONTROL
OCK BY
F!

THAT'S RIGHT!
WHEN OLD
HOBBS, THE
FOUNDER OF
THE COMPANY,
DIED, HE LEFT
A WILL
STATING
HIS PERSONAL
STOCK'S
WERE TO
BE DIVIDED
AMONG THE
OTHER
MEMBERS!...

...AND THAT
EACH TIME
ANOTHER
STOCKHOLDER
DIED, HOBBS'
PERSONAL
STOCK WAS
TO BE
DIVIDED
AMONG THE
SURVIVING
MEMBERS! I
HAD MORE
STOCK THAN ANY-
ONE ELSE TO
BEGIN WITH...

AND SO YOU
FIGURED IF
YOU HAD THE
OTHERS KILLED
OFF, YOU ALONE
WOULD SOON
OWN THE
CONTROLLING
SHARES OF
STOCK! A
CLEVER MAN,
BUT A
MAD
ONE!

MAD? HA...IT WAS
CLEVER! I EVEN
PLAYED ON THE
FANATICAL OLD
CLOCK MAKER'S WARPED
SENSES...MADE HIM
THINK THE OTHERS
WERE "MURDERERS
OF TIME" AND SHOULD
BE KILLED -- JUST AS
I'M GOING TO KILL
YOU RIGHT NOW!

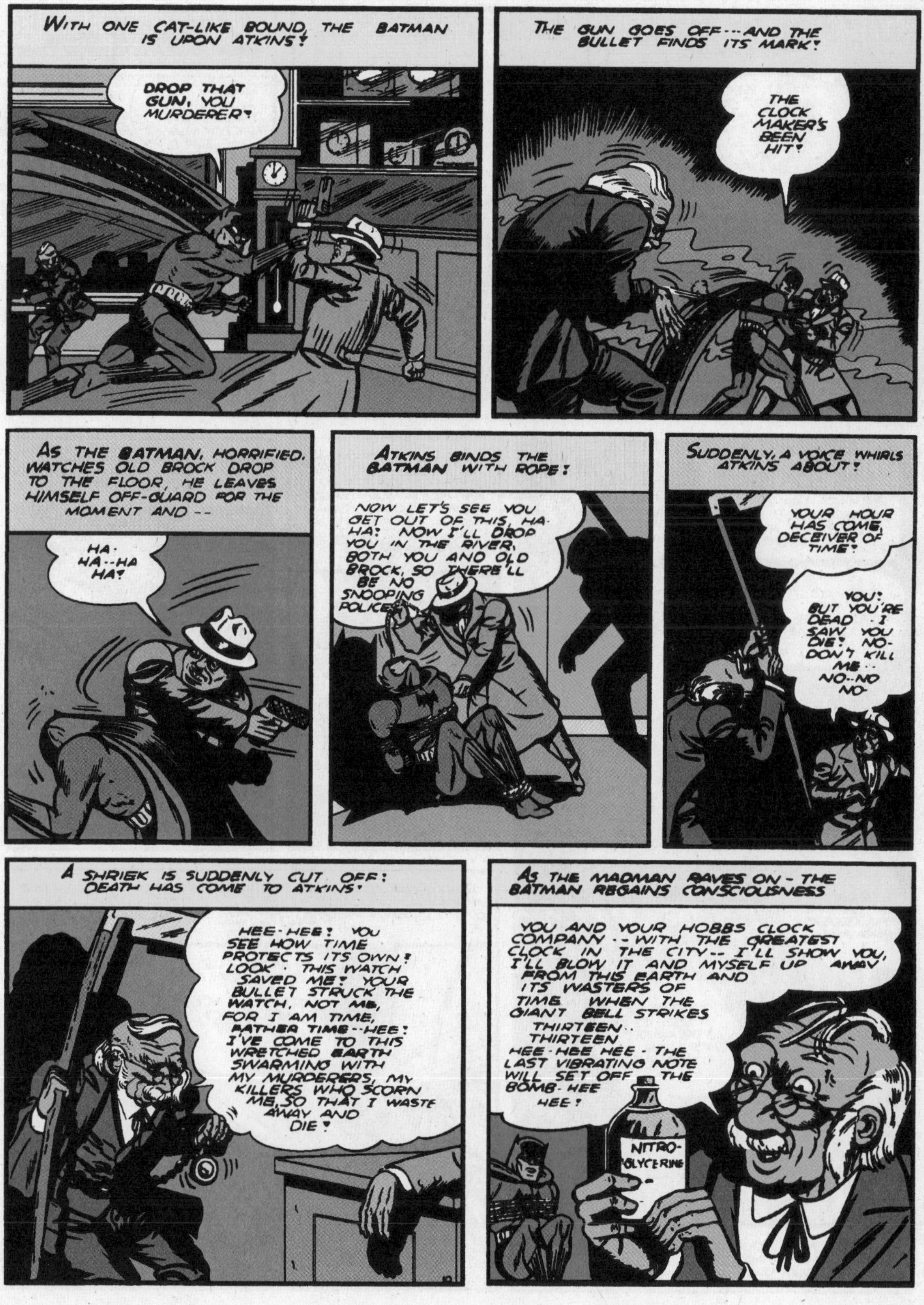
WITH ONE CAT-LIKE BOUND, THE BATMAN IS UPON ATKINS!
DROP THAT GUN, YOU MURDERER!
THE GUN GOES OFF--AND THE BULLET FINDS ITS MARK!
THE CLOCK MAKER'S BEEN HIT!
AS THE BATMAN, HORRIFIED, WATCHES OLD BROCK DROP TO THE FLOOR, HE LEAVES HIMSELF OFF-GUARD FOR THE MOMENT AND --
HA-HA--HA HA!
ATKINS BINDS THE BATMAN WITH ROPE!
NOW LET'S SEE YOU GET OUT OF THIS, HA-HA! NOW I'LL DROP YOU IN THE RIVER, BOTH YOU AND OLD BROCK, SO THERE'LL BE NO SNOOPING POLICE!
SUDDENLY, A VOICE WHIRLS ATKINS ABOUT!
YOUR HOUR HAS COME, DECEIVER OF TIME!
YOU! BUT YOU'RE DEAD - I SAW YOU DIE! NO-DON'T KILL ME.. NO--NO NO-
A SHRIEK IS SUDDENLY CUT OFF: DEATH HAS COME TO ATKINS!
HEE-HEE! YOU SEE HOW TIME PROTECTS ITS OWN! LOOK - THIS WATCH SAVED ME! YOUR BULLET STRUCK THE WATCH, NOT ME, FOR I AM TIME, FATHER TIME--HEE! I'VE COME TO THIS WRETCHED EARTH SWARMING WITH MY MURDERERS, MY KILLERS WHO SCORN ME, SO THAT I WASTE AWAY AND DIE!
AS THE MADMAN RAVES ON - THE BATMAN REGAINS CONSCIOUSNESS
YOU AND YOUR HOBBS CLOCK COMPANY--WITH THE GREATEST CLOCK IN THE CITY-- I'LL SHOW YOU, I'LL BLOW IT AND MYSELF UP AWAY FROM THIS EARTH AND ITS WASTERS OF TIME WHEN THE GIANT BELL STRIKES THIRTEEN.. THIRTEEN HEE-HEE HEE - THE LAST VIBRATING NOTE WILL SET OFF THE BOMB-HEE HEE!
NITRO-GLYCERINE

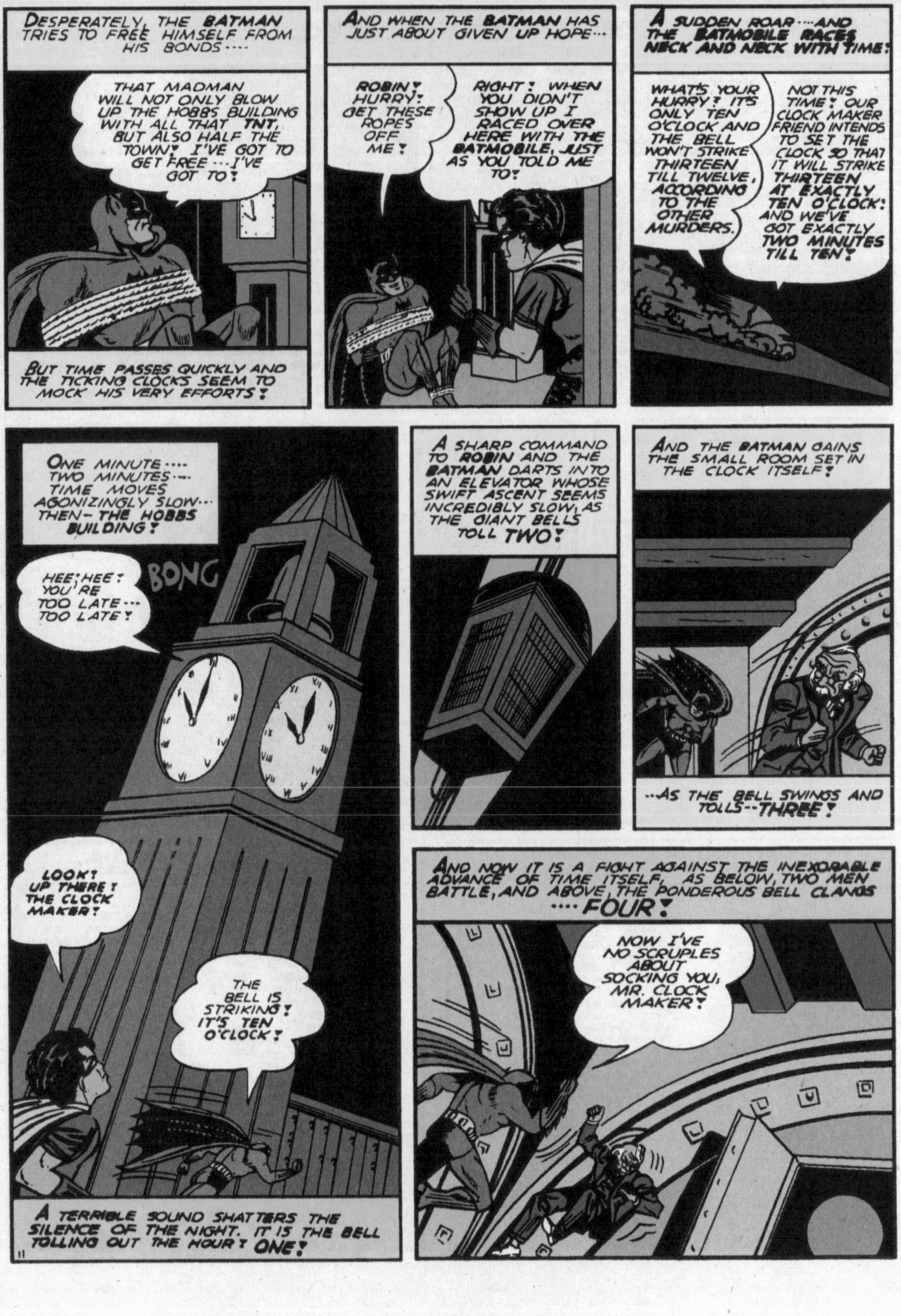
DESPERATELY, THE BATMAN TRIES TO FREE HIMSELF FROM HIS BONDS....
THAT MADMAN WILL NOT ONLY BLOW UP THE HOBBS BUILDING WITH ALL THAT TNT, BUT ALSO HALF THE TOWN! I'VE GOT TO GET FREE ... I'VE GOT TO!
BUT TIME PASSES QUICKLY AND THE TICKING CLOCKS SEEM TO MOCK HIS VERY EFFORTS!
AND WHEN THE BATMAN HAS JUST ABOUT GIVEN UP HOPE...
ROBIN! HURRY! GET THESE ROPES OFF ME!
RIGHT! WHEN YOU DIDN'T SHOW UP I RACED OVER HERE WITH THE BATMOBILE, JUST AS YOU TOLD ME TO!
A SUDDEN ROAR....AND THE BATMOBILE RACES NECK AND NECK WITH TIME!
WHAT'S YOUR HURRY? IT'S ONLY TEN O'CLOCK AND THE BELL WON'T STRIKE THIRTEEN TILL TWELVE, ACCORDING TO THE OTHER MURDERS.
NOT THIS TIME! OUR CLOCK MAKER FRIEND INTENDS TO SET THE CLOCK SO THAT IT WILL STRIKE THIRTEEN AT EXACTLY TEN O'CLOCK: AND WE'VE GOT EXACTLY TWO MINUTES TILL TEN!
ONE MINUTE.... TWO MINUTES.... TIME MOVES AGONIZINGLY SLOW... THEN- THE HOBBS BUILDING!
HEE; HEE! YOU'RE TOO LATE... TOO LATE!
BONG
LOOK! UP THERE! THE CLOCK MAKER!
THE BELL IS STRIKING! IT'S TEN O'CLOCK!
A TERRIBLE SOUND SHATTERS THE SILENCE OF THE NIGHT. IT IS THE BELL TOLLING OUT THE HOUR! ONE!
11
A SHARP COMMAND TO ROBIN AND THE BATMAN DARTS INTO AN ELEVATOR WHOSE SWIFT ASCENT SEEMS INCREDIBLY SLOW, AS THE GIANT BELLS TOLL TWO!
AND THE BATMAN GAINS THE SMALL ROOM SET IN THE CLOCK ITSELF!
...AS THE BELL SWINGS AND TOLLS--THREE!
AND NOW IT IS A FIGHT AGAINST THE INEXORABLE ADVANCE OF TIME ITSELF, AS BELOW, TWO MEN BATTLE, AND ABOVE, THE PONDEROUS BELL CLANGS .... FOUR!
NOW I'VE NO SCRUPLES ABOUT SOCKING YOU, MR. CLOCK MAKER!

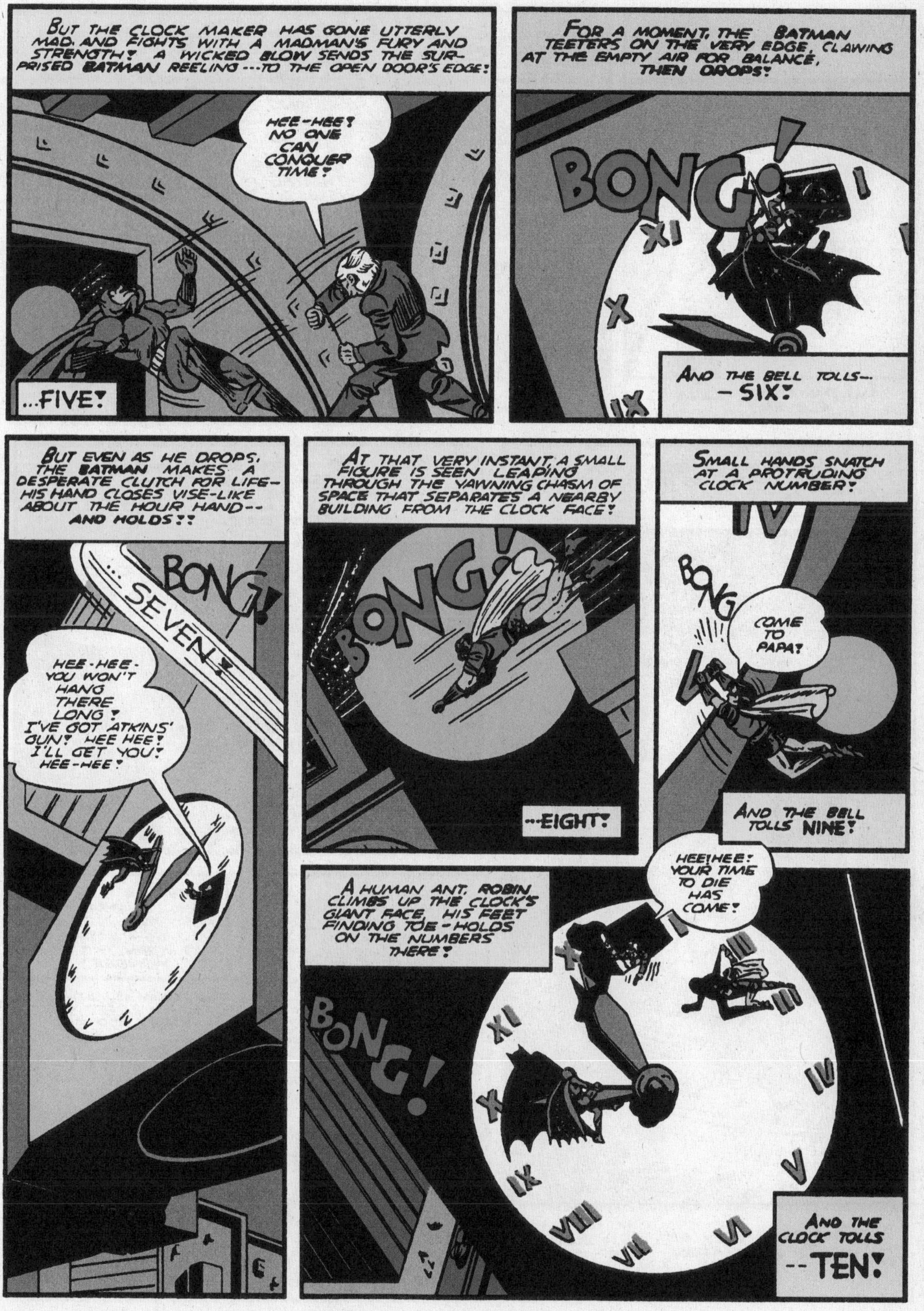

BUT THE CLOCK MAKER HAS GONE UTTERLY MAD, AND FIGHTS WITH A MADMAN'S FURY AND STRENGTH! A WICKED BLOW SENDS THE SURPRISED BATMAN REELING --- TO THE OPEN DOOR'S EDGE!
HEE-HEE! NO ONE CAN CONQUER TIME!
...FIVE!
FOR A MOMENT, THE BATMAN TEETERS ON THE VERY EDGE, CLAWING AT THE EMPTY AIR FOR BALANCE, THEN DROPS!
BONG!
AND THE BELL TOLLS-- -SIX!
BUT EVEN AS HE DROPS, THE BATMAN MAKES A DESPERATE CLUTCH FOR LIFE-- HIS HAND CLOSES VISE-LIKE ABOUT THE HOUR HAND-- AND HOLDS!!
BONG!
...SEVEN!
HEE-HEE- YOU WON'T HANG THERE LONG! I'VE GOT ATKINS' GUN! HEE HEE! I'LL GET YOU! HEE-HEE!
AT THAT VERY INSTANT, A SMALL FIGURE IS SEEN LEAPING THROUGH THE YAWNING CHASM OF SPACE THAT SEPARATES A NEARBY BUILDING FROM THE CLOCK FACE!
BONG!
---EIGHT!
SMALL HANDS SNATCH AT A PROTRUDING CLOCK NUMBER!
BONG
COME TO PAPA!
AND THE BELL TOLLS NINE!
A HUMAN ANT, ROBIN CLIMBS UP THE CLOCK'S GIANT FACE, HIS FEET FINDING TOE-HOLDS ON THE NUMBERS THERE!
HEE! HEE! YOUR TIME TO DIE HAS COME!
BONG!
AND THE CLOCK TOLLS --TEN!

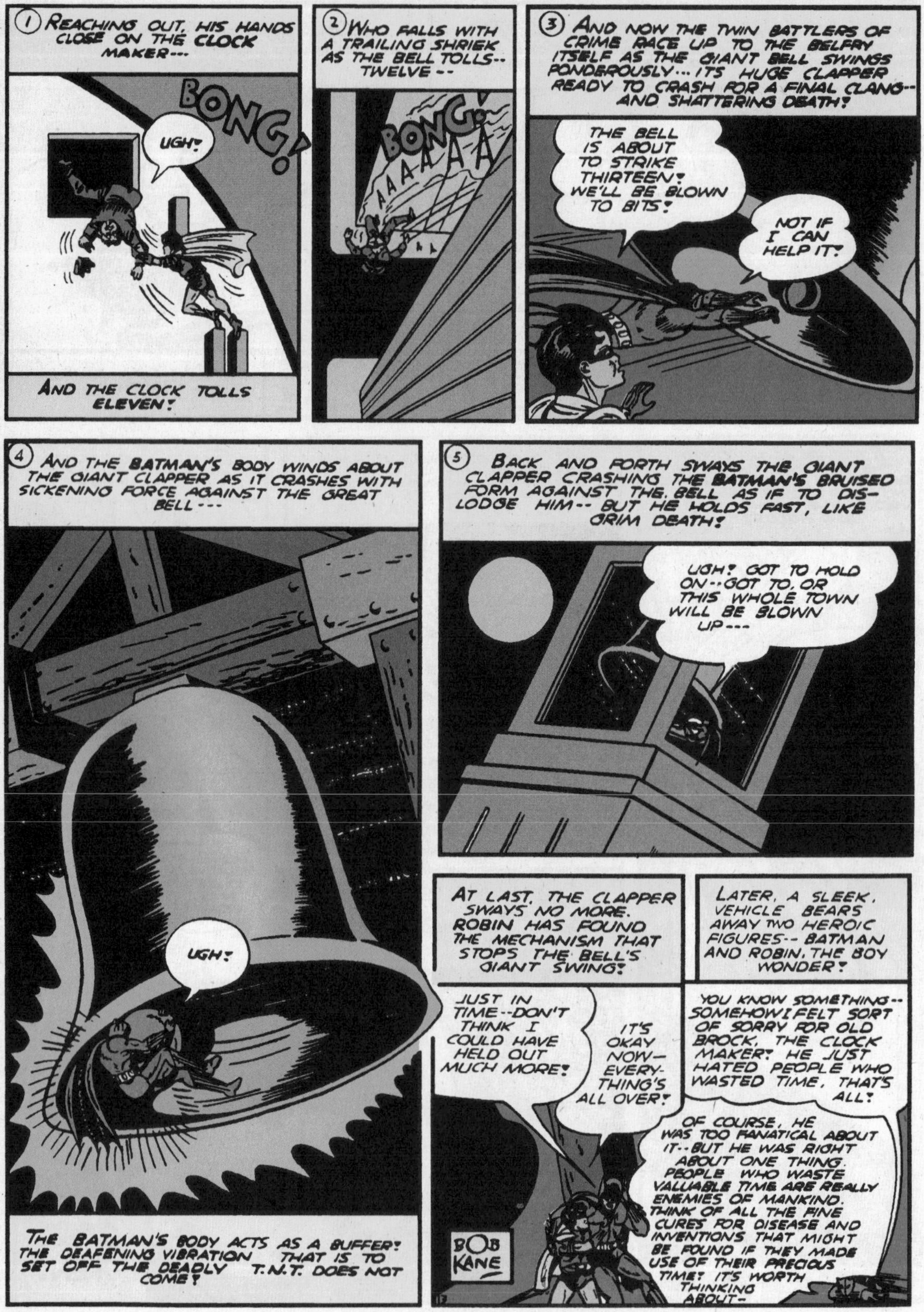
1 REACHING OUT, HIS HANDS CLOSE ON THE CLOCK MAKER---
BONG!
UGH!
AND THE CLOCK TOLLS ELEVEN!
2 WHO FALLS WITH A TRAILING SHRIEK AS THE BELL TOLLS-- TWELVE --
BONG!
AAAAAAA
3 AND NOW THE TWIN BATTLERS OF CRIME RACE UP TO THE BELFRY ITSELF AS THE GIANT BELL SWINGS PONDEROUSLY... ITS HUGE CLAPPER READY TO CRASH FOR A FINAL CLANG-- AND SHATTERING DEATH!
THE BELL IS ABOUT TO STRIKE THIRTEEN! WE'LL BE BLOWN TO BITS!
NOT IF I CAN HELP IT!
4 AND THE BATMAN'S BODY WINDS ABOUT THE GIANT CLAPPER AS IT CRASHES WITH SICKENING FORCE AGAINST THE GREAT BELL---
UGH!
THE BATMAN'S BODY ACTS AS A BUFFER! THE DEAFENING VIBRATION THAT IS TO SET OFF THE DEADLY T.N.T. DOES NOT COME!
5 BACK AND FORTH SWAYS THE GIANT CLAPPER CRASHING THE BATMAN'S BRUISED FORM AGAINST THE BELL AS IF TO DISLODGE HIM-- BUT HE HOLDS FAST, LIKE GRIM DEATH!
UGH! GOT TO HOLD ON--GOT TO, OR THIS WHOLE TOWN WILL BE BLOWN UP---
AT LAST, THE CLAPPER SWAYS NO MORE. ROBIN HAS FOUND THE MECHANISM THAT STOPS THE BELL'S GIANT SWING!
JUST IN TIME--DON'T THINK I COULD HAVE HELD OUT MUCH MORE!
IT'S OKAY NOW-- EVERYTHING'S ALL OVER!
LATER, A SLEEK VEHICLE BEARS AWAY TWO HEROIC FIGURES-- BATMAN AND ROBIN, THE BOY WONDER!
YOU KNOW SOMETHING-- SOMEHOW I FELT SORT OF SORRY FOR OLD BROCK, THE CLOCK MAKER! HE JUST HATED PEOPLE WHO WASTED TIME, THAT'S ALL!
OF COURSE, HE WAS TOO FANATICAL ABOUT IT--BUT HE WAS RIGHT ABOUT ONE THING. PEOPLE WHO WASTE VALUABLE TIME ARE REALLY ENEMIES OF MANKIND. THINK OF ALL THE FINE CURES FOR DISEASE AND INVENTIONS THAT MIGHT BE FOUND IF THEY MADE USE OF THEIR PRECIOUS TIME! IT'S WORTH THINKING ABOUT--
BOB KANE
13

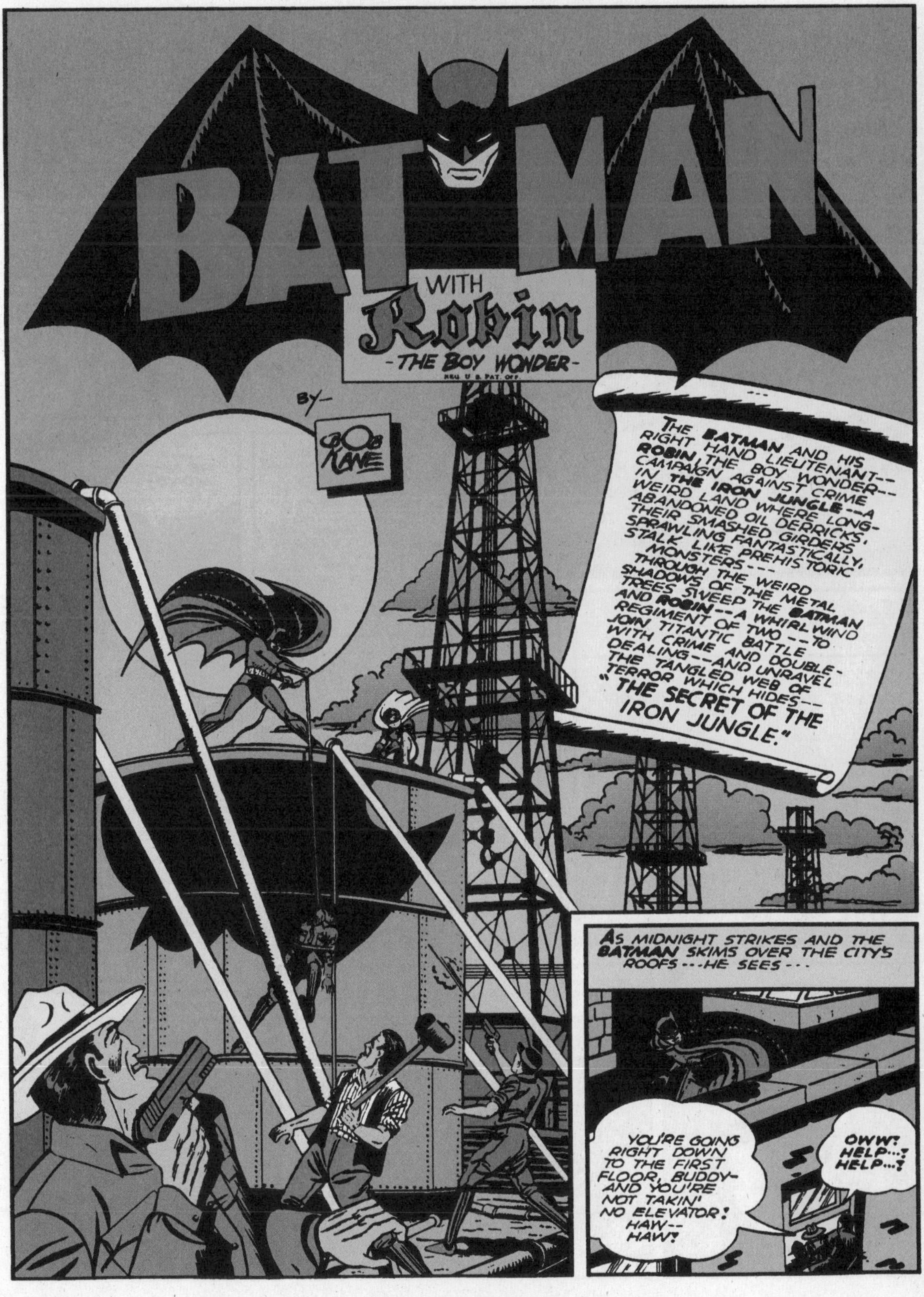
BATMAN
WITH Robin -THE BOY WONDER-
REG. U. S. PAT. OFF.
BY— BOB KANE
THE BATMAN AND HIS RIGHT HAND LIEUTENANT-- ROBIN, THE BOY WONDER-- CAMPAIGN AGAINST CRIME IN THE IRON JUNGLE--A WEIRD LAND WHERE LONG-ABANDONED OIL DERRICKS, THEIR SMASHED GIRDERS SPRAWLING FANTASTICALLY, STALK LIKE PREHISTORIC MONSTERS--- THROUGH THE WEIRD SHADOWS OF THE METAL TREES SWEEP THE BATMAN AND ROBIN--A WHIRLWIND REGIMENT OF TWO--TO JOIN TITANTIC BATTLE WITH CRIME AND DOUBLE-DEALING--AND UNRAVEL THE TANGLED WEB OF TERROR WHICH HIDES-- "THE SECRET OF THE IRON JUNGLE."
AS MIDNIGHT STRIKES AND THE BATMAN SKIMS OVER THE CITY'S ROOFS---HE SEES---
YOU'RE GOING RIGHT DOWN TO THE FIRST FLOOR, BUDDY-AND YOU'RE NOT TAKIN' NO ELEVATOR! HAW--HAW!
OWW! HELP...! HELP...!

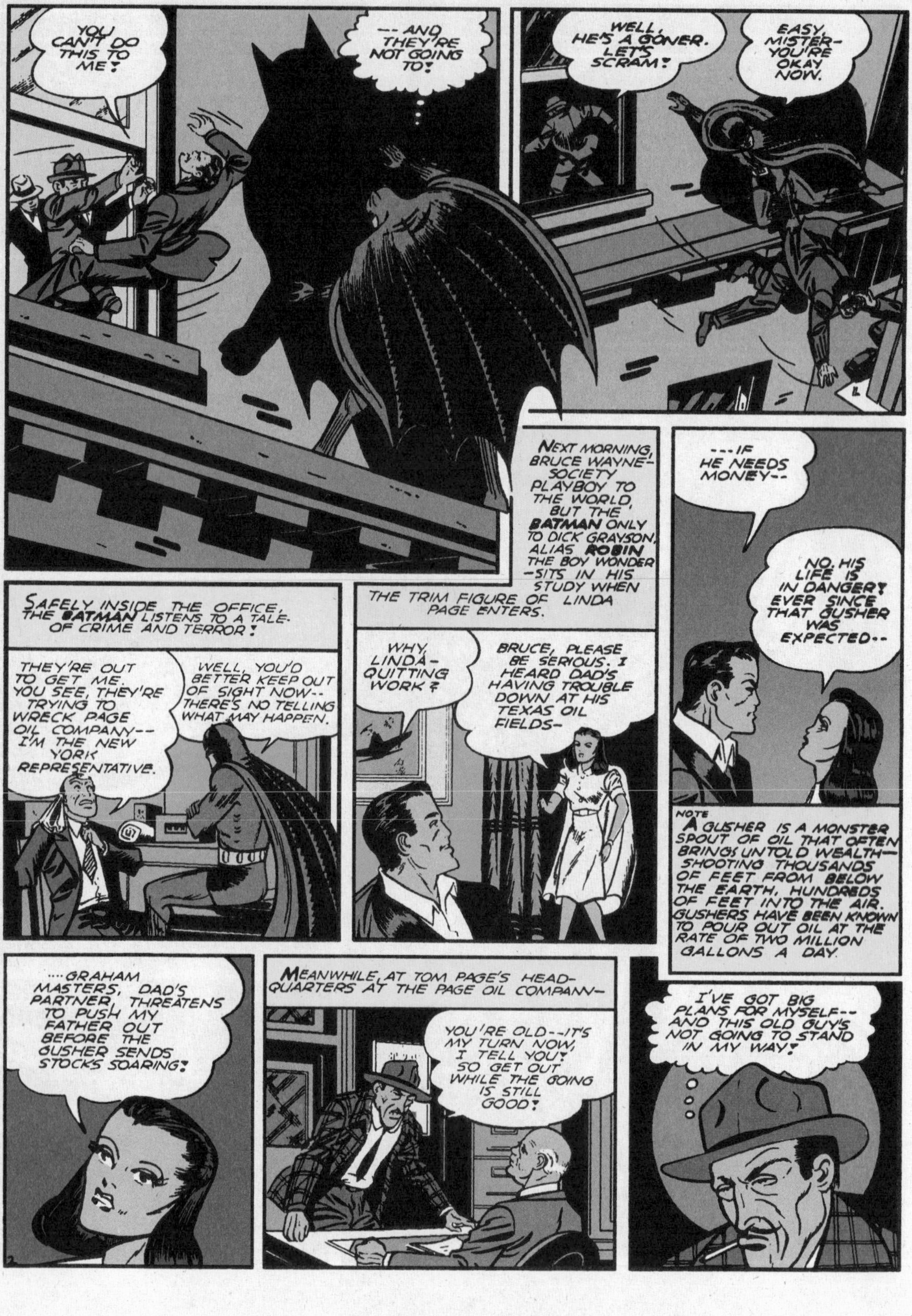

YOU CAN'T DO THIS TO ME!
--AND THEY'RE NOT GOING TO!
WELL, HE'S A GONER. LET'S SCRAM!
EASY, MISTER-YOU'RE OKAY NOW.
NEXT MORNING, BRUCE WAYNE-SOCIETY PLAYBOY TO THE WORLD, BUT THE BATMAN ONLY TO DICK GRAYSON, ALIAS ROBIN THE BOY WONDER -SITS IN HIS STUDY WHEN THE TRIM FIGURE OF LINDA PAGE ENTERS.
SAFELY INSIDE THE OFFICE, THE BATMAN LISTENS TO A TALE OF CRIME AND TERROR!
THEY'RE OUT TO GET ME. YOU SEE, THEY'RE TRYING TO WRECK PAGE OIL COMPANY-- I'M THE NEW YORK REPRESENTATIVE.
WELL, YOU'D BETTER KEEP OUT OF SIGHT NOW--THERE'S NO TELLING WHAT MAY HAPPEN.
WHY, LINDA-QUITTING WORK?
BRUCE, PLEASE BE SERIOUS. I HEARD DAD'S HAVING TROUBLE DOWN AT HIS TEXAS OIL FIELDS-
---IF HE NEEDS MONEY--
NO. HIS LIFE IS IN DANGER! EVER SINCE THAT GUSHER WAS EXPECTED--
NOTE
A GUSHER IS A MONSTER SPOUT OF OIL THAT OFTEN BRINGS UNTOLD WEALTH-SHOOTING THOUSANDS OF FEET FROM BELOW THE EARTH, HUNDREDS OF FEET INTO THE AIR. GUSHERS HAVE BEEN KNOWN TO POUR OUT OIL AT THE RATE OF TWO MILLION GALLONS A DAY.
....GRAHAM MASTERS, DAD'S PARTNER, THREATENS TO PUSH MY FATHER OUT BEFORE THE GUSHER SENDS STOCKS SOARING!
MEANWHILE, AT TOM PAGE'S HEAD-QUARTERS AT THE PAGE OIL COMPANY-
YOU'RE OLD--IT'S MY TURN NOW, I TELL YOU! SO GET OUT WHILE THE GOING IS STILL GOOD!
I'VE GOT BIG PLANS FOR MYSELF--AND THIS OLD GUY'S NOT GOING TO STAND IN MY WAY!

AT THAT VERY MOMENT, LINDA IS TELLING BRUCE WHAT HAS BEEN GOING ON--

---AND ALL KINDS OF STRANGE ACCIDENTS HAVE BEEN HAPPENING---

CHATTING CASUALLY THROUGH THE LIPS OF BRUCE WAYNE-- OUR PLAYBOY PLANS RAPIDLY WITH THE SUREFIRE BRAIN OF THE BATMAN!

OH! THINK I'D LIKE TO SEE TEXAS AGAIN-- I NEED A VACATION.

WELL, WATCH OUT FOR THOSE BIG, HUSKY TEXANS! I'LL BE DOWN LATER TO SEE NOTHING HAPPENS TO YOU.

NO SOONER HAS LINDA LEFT THAN DICK GRAYSON, ALIAS *ROBIN* THE BOY WONDER, DARTS INTO THE ROOM---

I OVER-HEARD EVERYTHING.

LISTEN TO ME, THEN-- WE'VE GOT TO GET TO TEXAS BEFORE SOME-THING HAPPENS TO LINDA'S FATHER.

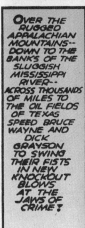

OVER THE RUGGED APPALACHIAN MOUNTAINS-- DOWN TO THE BANKS OF THE SLUGGISH MISSISSIPPI RIVER-- ACROSS THOUSANDS OF MILES TO THE OIL FIELDS OF TEXAS SPEED BRUCE WAYNE AND DICK GRAYSON TO SWING THEIR FISTS IN NEW KNOCKOUT BLOWS AT THE JAWS OF CRIME!

GEE, I'VE ALWAYS WANTED TO SEE THE MISSISSIPPI!

YOU'D BETTER GET BACK IN THE TRUNK NOW. NO ONE MUST SEE YOU.

A DRAMATIC SCENE AWAITS BRUCE AS HIS SWIFT AUTOMOBILE SLIDES BY THE ENTRANCE OF THE *PAGE OIL COMPANY.*

DICK--KEEP YOURSELF OUT OF SIGHT UNTIL THE TIME COMES FOR YOU TO CHANGE PARTS--! ANYTHING CAN HAPPEN AROUND HERE--

PAGE OIL COMPAN

TAP TAP

....AND ANYTHING DOES!

IT'S YOUR LAST CHANCE.

--AND YOURS, TOO!

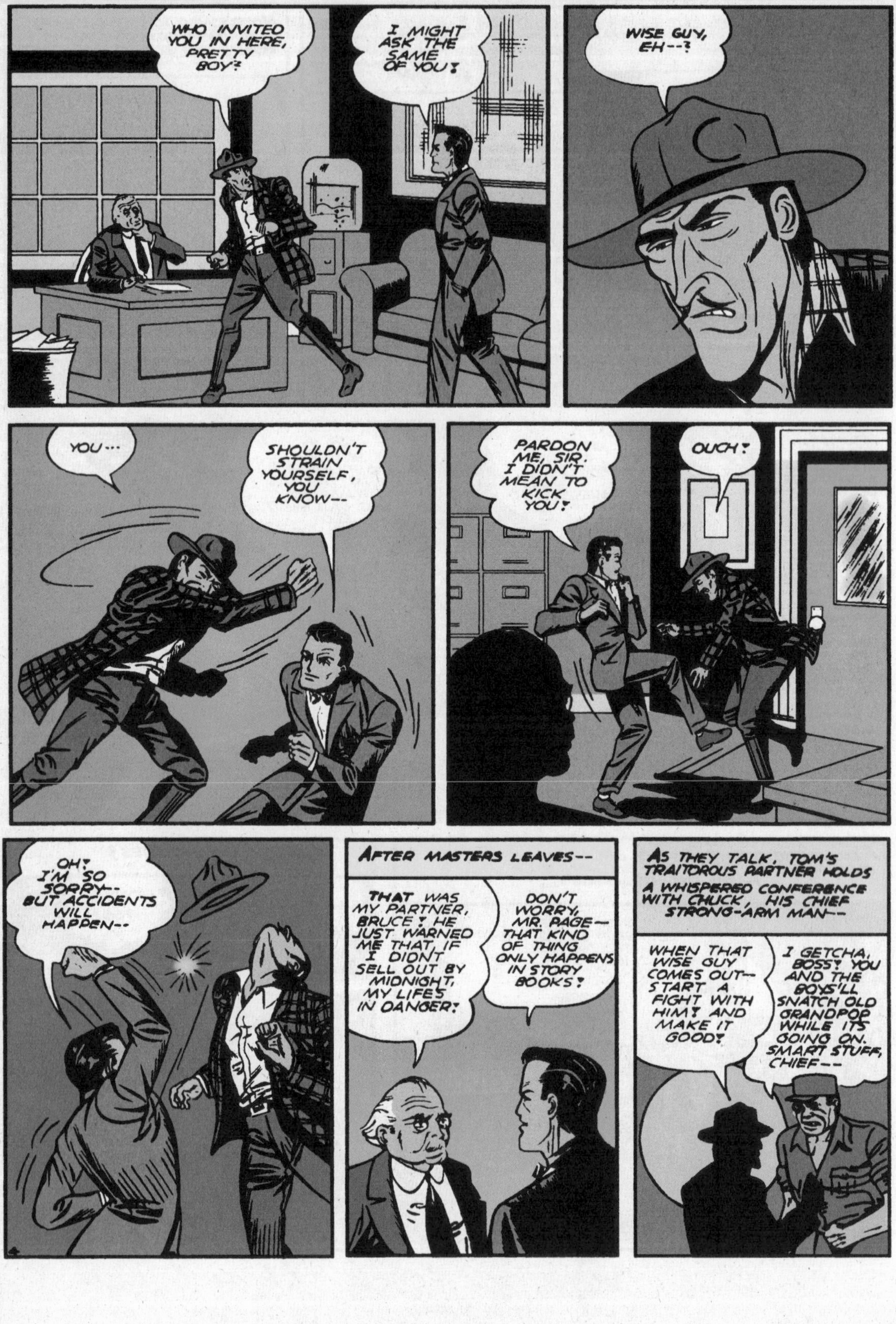
WHO INVITED YOU IN HERE, PRETTY BOY?
I MIGHT ASK THE SAME OF YOU!
WISE GUY, EH--?
YOU...
SHOULDN'T STRAIN YOURSELF, YOU KNOW--
PARDON ME, SIR. I DIDN'T MEAN TO KICK YOU!
OUCH!
OH! I'M SO SORRY-- BUT ACCIDENTS WILL HAPPEN--
AFTER MASTERS LEAVES--
THAT WAS MY PARTNER, BRUCE! HE JUST WARNED ME THAT, IF I DIDNT SELL OUT BY MIDNIGHT, MY LIFES IN DANGER!
DON'T WORRY, MR. PAGE-- THAT KIND OF THING ONLY HAPPENS IN STORY BOOKS!
AS THEY TALK, TOM'S TRAITOROUS PARTNER HOLDS A WHISPERED CONFERENCE WITH CHUCK, HIS CHIEF STRONG-ARM MAN--
WHEN THAT WISE GUY COMES OUT-- START A FIGHT WITH HIM! AND MAKE IT GOOD!
I GETCHA, BOSS! YOU AND THE BOYS'LL SNATCH OLD GRANDPOP WHILE ITS GOING ON. SMART STUFF, CHIEF--

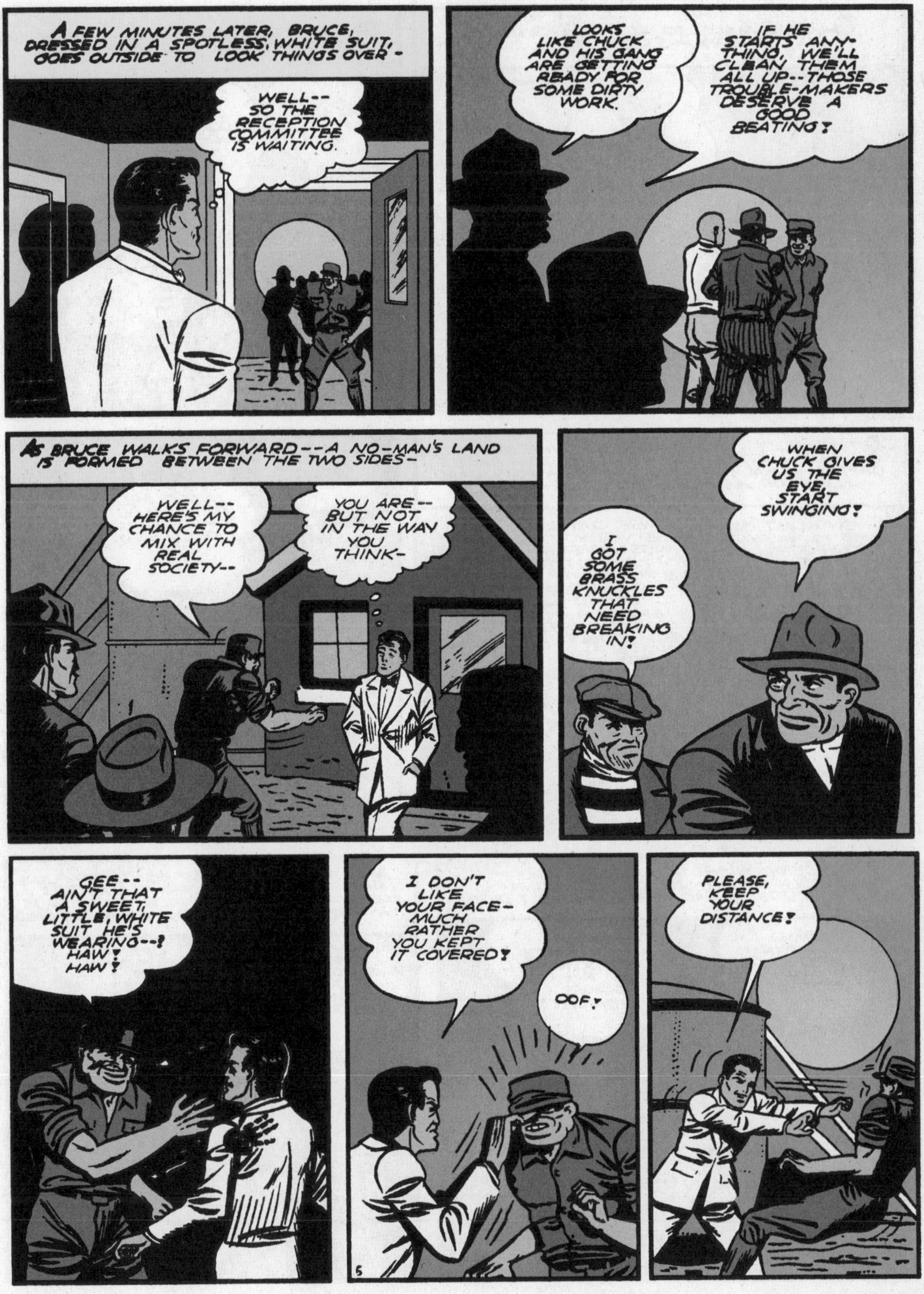
A FEW MINUTES LATER, BRUCE, DRESSED IN A SPOTLESS, WHITE SUIT, GOES OUTSIDE TO LOOK THINGS OVER -
WELL-- SO THE RECEPTION COMMITTEE IS WAITING.
LOOKS LIKE CHUCK AND HIS GANG ARE GETTING READY FOR SOME DIRTY WORK.
IF HE STARTS ANY-THING, WE'LL CLEAN THEM ALL UP--THOSE TROUBLE-MAKERS DESERVE A GOOD BEATING!
AS BRUCE WALKS FORWARD--A NO-MAN'S LAND IS FORMED BETWEEN THE TWO SIDES-
WELL-- HERE'S MY CHANCE TO MIX WITH REAL SOCIETY--
YOU ARE-- BUT NOT IN THE WAY YOU THINK-
WHEN CHUCK GIVES US THE EYE, START SWINGING!
I GOT SOME BRASS KNUCKLES THAT NEED BREAKING IN!
GEE-- AIN'T THAT A SWEET, LITTLE, WHITE SUIT HE'S WEARING--? HAW! HAW!
I DON'T LIKE YOUR FACE-MUCH RATHER YOU KEPT IT COVERED!
OOF!
5
PLEASE, KEEP YOUR DISTANCE!

CHUCK IS MADE TO LOOK RIDICULOUS BEFORE HIS OWN MEN—

DON'T TAKE IT LYING DOWN, CHUCK. HAW HAW—?

BRUCE'S STRATAGEM WORKS—CHUCK, INFURIATED, WADES INTO HIS OWN MEN?

LAUGH AT ME, WILL YA—!

WELL, THEY'RE DOING OUR JOB FOR US VERY NICELY?

CERTAINLY SAVED US A LOT OF TROUBLE. LET'S GET BACK TO WORK.

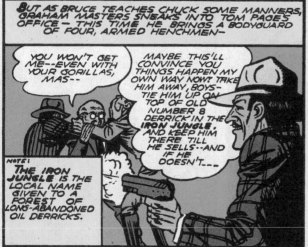

BUT AS BRUCE TEACHES CHUCK SOME MANNERS, GRAHAM MASTERS SNEAKS INTO TOM PAGE'S OFFICE—THIS TIME HE BRINGS A BODYGUARD OF FOUR, ARMED HENCHMEN—

YOU WON'T GET ME—EVEN WITH YOUR GORILLAS, MAS—

MAYBE THIS'LL CONVINCE YOU THINGS HAPPEN MY OWN WAY NOW? TAKE HIM AWAY, BOYS—TIE HIM UP ON TOP OF OLD NUMBER 8 DERRICK IN THE IRON JUNGLE, AND KEEP HIM THERE TILL HE SELLS—AND IF HE DOESN'T—

NOTE: THE IRON JUNGLE IS THE LOCAL NAME GIVEN TO A FOREST OF LONG-ABANDONED OIL DERRICKS.

HE'S SHOT—BOSS?

THE IRON JUNGLE! HE'S NOT HURT BAD. GET HIM OUT OF THE BACK DOOR AND HURRY IT UP.

BUT OUTSIDE, NIGHT IS FALLING, AND BRUCE SLIPS AWAY TO THE OLD BUNK-HOUSE WHERE HE HAD AGREED TO MEET DICK—

COME ON, ROBIN—INTO YOUR WORK CLOTHES?

—I'VE A HUNCH THERE ARE GOING TO BE BIG DOINGS TONIGHT?

MEANWHILE, A YELLOW ROADSTER PULLS UP—AT THE VERY MOMENT MASTERS SNEAKS OUT OF THE OFFICE. LINDA PAGE HAS ARRIVED EARLIER THAN SHE PLANNED.

CHUCK—C'MERE—QUICK—LOOK WHO'S HERE? PAGE'S DAUGHTER—

GET OFF MY CAR AT ONCE?

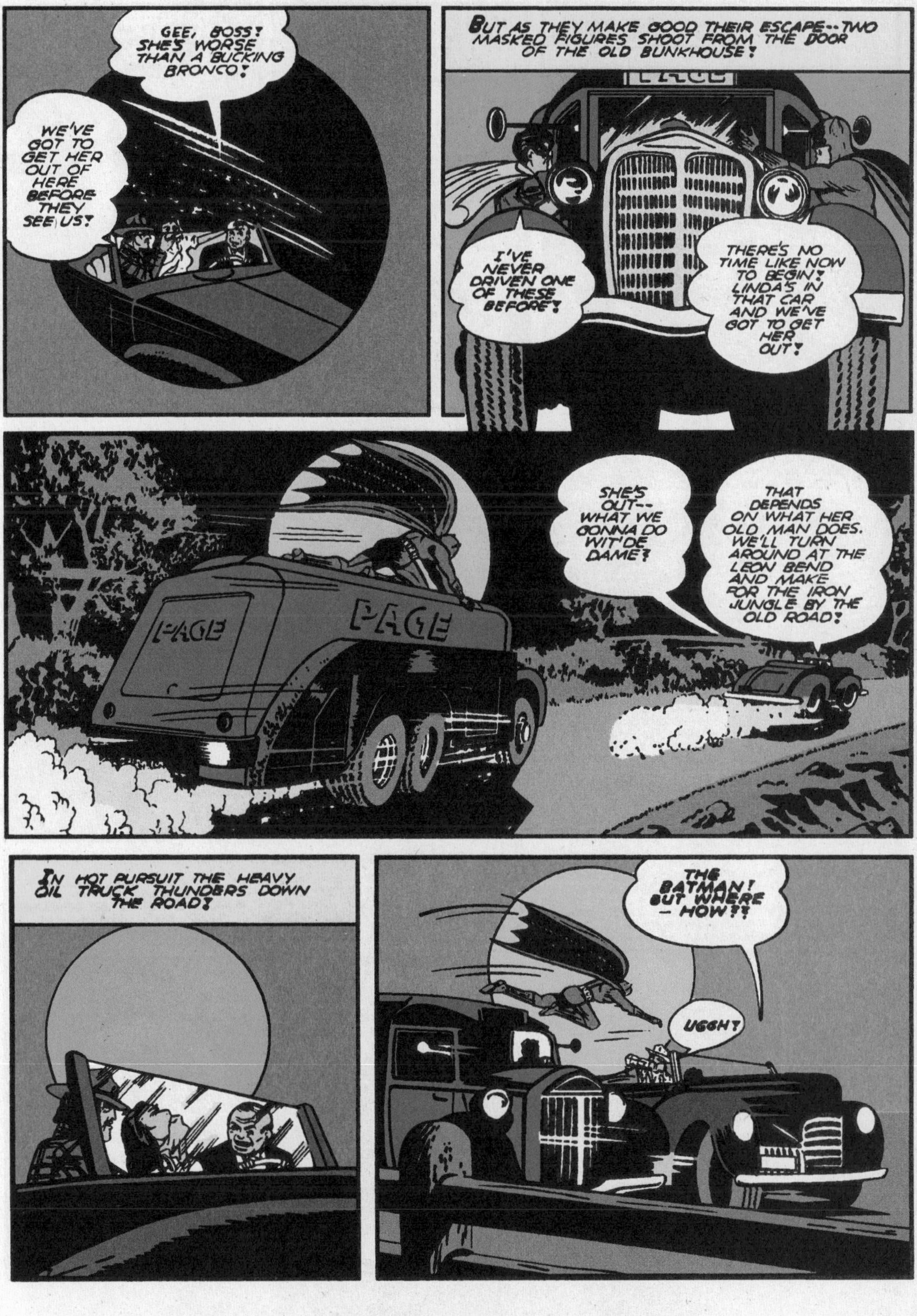
GEE, BOSS! SHE'S WORSE THAN A BUCKING BRONCO!
WE'VE GOT TO GET HER OUT OF HERE BEFORE THEY SEE US!
BUT AS THEY MAKE GOOD THEIR ESCAPE--TWO MASKED FIGURES SHOOT FROM THE DOOR OF THE OLD BUNKHOUSE!
I'VE NEVER DRIVEN ONE OF THESE BEFORE!
THERE'S NO TIME LIKE NOW TO BEGIN! LINDA'S IN THAT CAR AND WE'VE GOT TO GET HER OUT!
PAGE
PAGE
SHE'S OUT-- WHAT WE GONNA DO WIT'DE DAME?
THAT DEPENDS ON WHAT HER OLD MAN DOES. WE'LL TURN AROUND AT THE LEON BEND AND MAKE FOR THE IRON JUNGLE BY THE OLD ROAD!
IN HOT PURSUIT THE HEAVY OIL TRUCK THUNDERS DOWN THE ROAD!
THE BATMAN! BUT WHERE — HOW??
UGGH!

LIKE A BAT ON A SURF BOARD-- THE BATMAN RIDES THE SPEEDING CAR'S MOMENTUM--

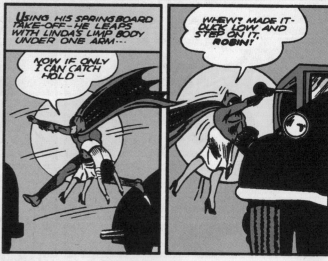

USING HIS SPRINGBOARD TAKE-OFF-- HE LEAPS WITH LINDA'S LIMP BODY UNDER ONE ARM---

NOW IF ONLY I CAN CATCH HOLD--

WHEW! MADE IT-- DUCK LOW AND STEP ON IT, ROBIN!

CHUCK MAKES A SHARP TURN AS MASTERS LOOSES A HAIL OF BULLETS -- AND AS EACH ONE RIPS INTO THE OIL TANK-- FLAMES STAB OUT OF THE BULLET HOLES INTO THE DARKNESS!

THIS'LL FINISH YOU! BURN! HA-HA! YOU'LL BURN TO DEATH! HA-HA

LOOKS LIKE THEY'RE DONE FOR, BOSS! THEY'LL BLOW TO PIECES!

WE'LL GET TO THE IRON JUNGLE THROUGH THE CAMP-- AND THAT OLD GUY'S GOING TO SIGN OVER THEM OIL WELLS MIGHTY PRONTO!

AS MASTERS AND CHUCK SPEED BACK TO THE PAGE OIL COMPANY, ROBIN SWINGS HIS BLAZING TRUCK AROUND-- AND GIVES CHASE LIKE A FIERY COMET ON THE TRAIL OF VENGEANCE! ANY MOMENT THEY FEAR THE TERRIBLE EXPLOSION, WHICH IS BOUND TO COME

WE'VE BEEN IN TIGHT SPOTS BEFORE-- BUT WE'VE NEVER RACED AGAINST FIRE AND DEATH BOTH AT THE SAME MOMENT!

INTO THE LAST LAP SPEEDS THE TRUCK--- A MONSTER BONFIRE LASHING OUT WITH SCARLET OIL FOR WHIPS! AS IT SCREECHES TO A HALT ROBIN AND THE BATMAN, LINDA UNDER THE LATTER'S ARM, LEAP-- AND NONE TOO SOON--

BOOM

WE HAVEN'T A SECOND TO LOSE-- TAKE CARE OF LINDA-- I'M GOING AFTER CHUCK AND MASTERS!

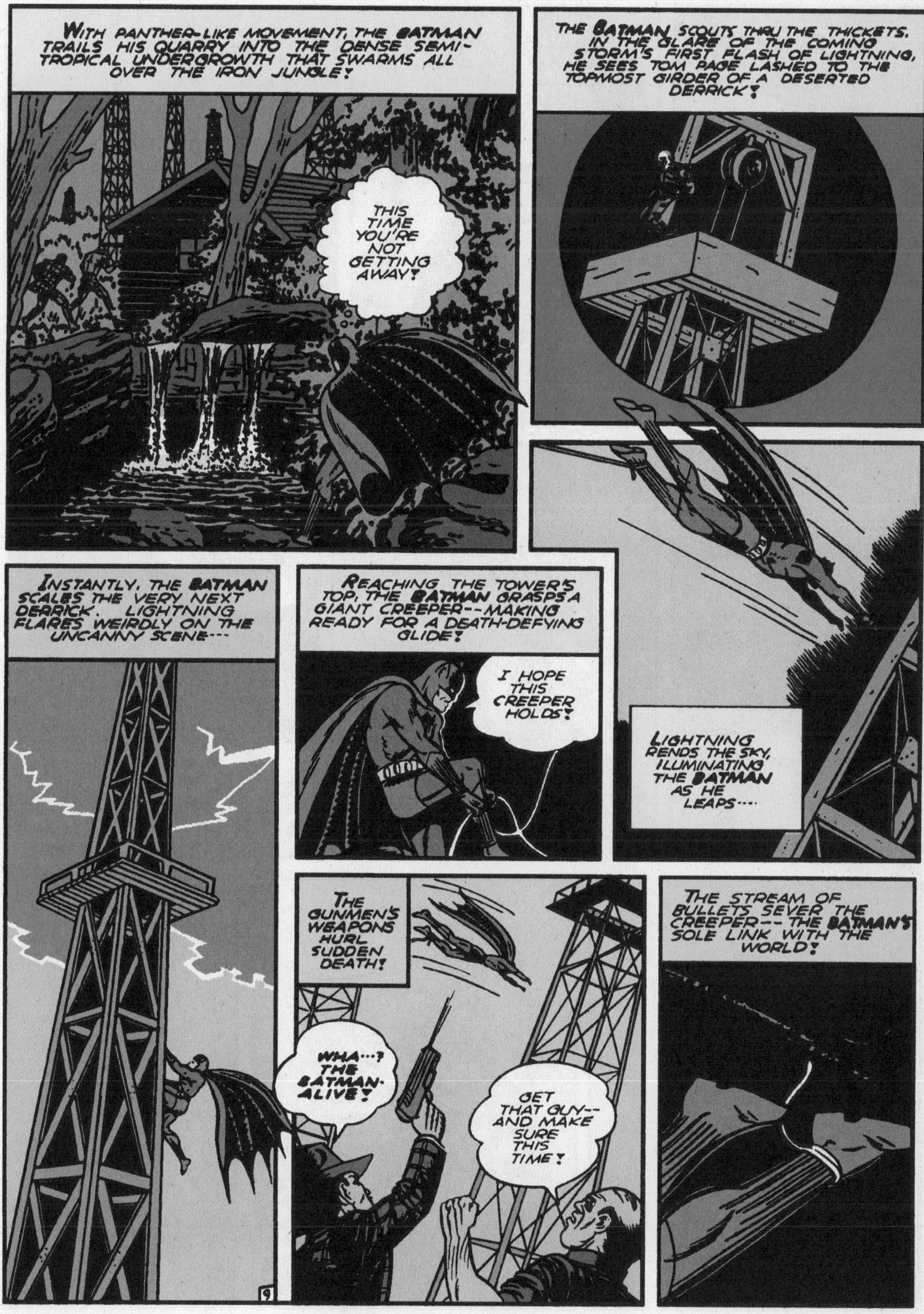
WITH PANTHER-LIKE MOVEMENT, THE BATMAN TRAILS HIS QUARRY INTO THE DENSE SEMI-TROPICAL UNDERGROWTH THAT SWARMS ALL OVER THE IRON JUNGLE!
THIS TIME YOU'RE NOT GETTING AWAY!
THE BATMAN SCOUTS THRU THE THICKETS. IN THE GLARE OF THE COMING STORM'S FIRST FLASH OF LIGHTNING, HE SEES TOM PAGE LASHED TO THE TOPMOST GIRDER OF A DESERTED DERRICK!
INSTANTLY, THE BATMAN SCALES THE VERY NEXT DERRICK. LIGHTNING FLARES WEIRDLY ON THE UNCANNY SCENE---
REACHING THE TOWER'S TOP, THE BATMAN GRASPS A GIANT CREEPER--MAKING READY FOR A DEATH-DEFYING GLIDE!
I HOPE THIS CREEPER HOLDS!
LIGHTNING RENDS THE SKY, ILUMINATING THE BATMAN AS HE LEAPS....
THE GUNMEN'S WEAPONS HURL SUDDEN DEATH!
WHA...? THE BATMAN-ALIVE!
GET THAT GUY--AND MAKE SURE THIS TIME!
THE STREAM OF BULLETS SEVER THE CREEPER-- THE BATMAN'S SOLE LINK WITH THE WORLD!
9

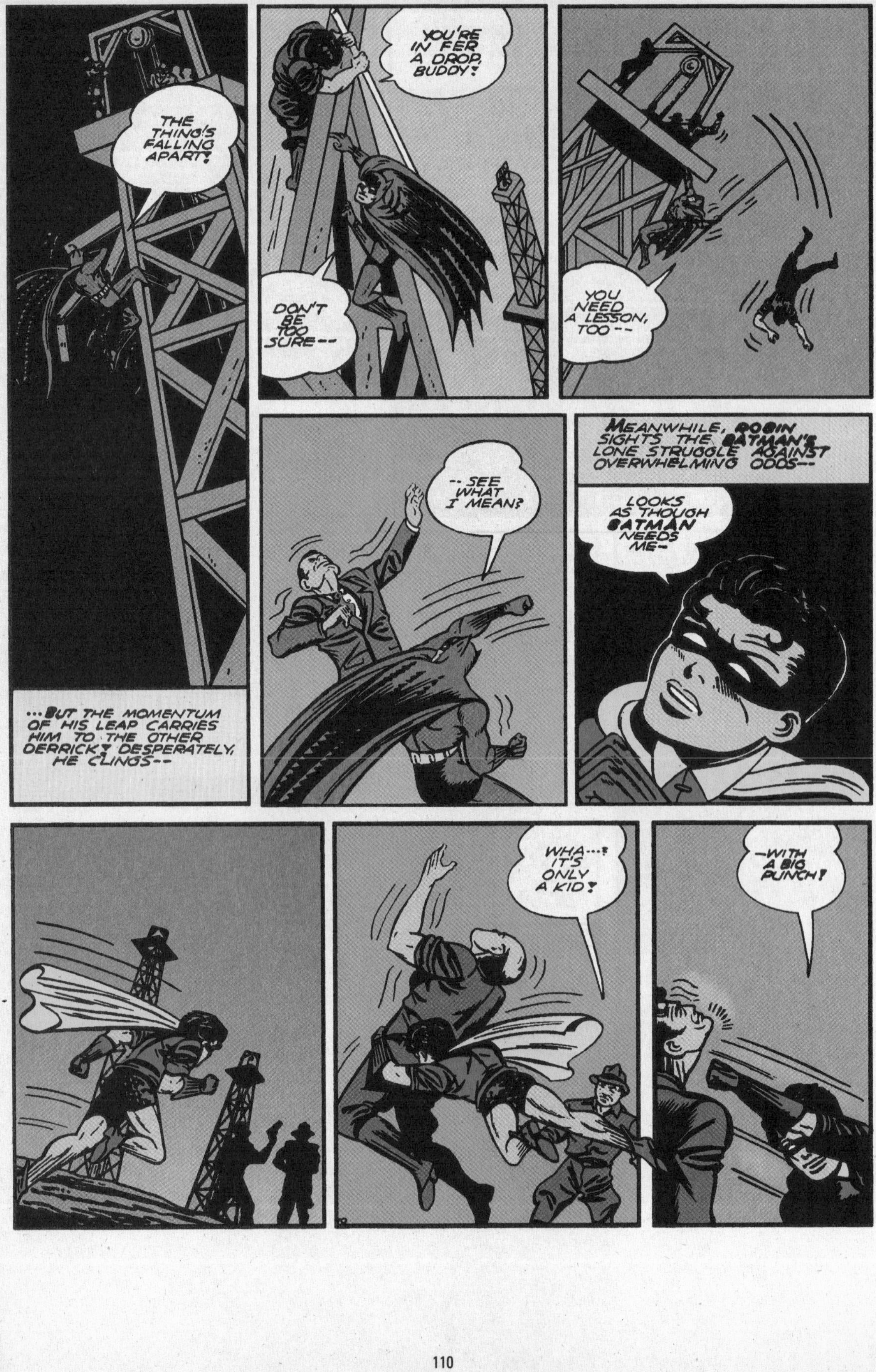
THE THING'S FALLING APART!
...BUT THE MOMENTUM OF HIS LEAP CARRIES HIM TO THE OTHER DERRICK! DESPERATELY, HE CLINGS--
YOU'RE IN FER A DROP, BUDDY!
DON'T BE TOO SURE--
YOU NEED A LESSON, TOO--
--SEE WHAT I MEAN?
MEANWHILE, ROBIN SIGHTS THE BATMAN'S LONE STRUGGLE AGAINST OVERWHELMING ODDS--
LOOKS AS THOUGH BATMAN NEEDS ME-
WHA...! IT'S ONLY A KID!
-WITH A BIG PUNCH!

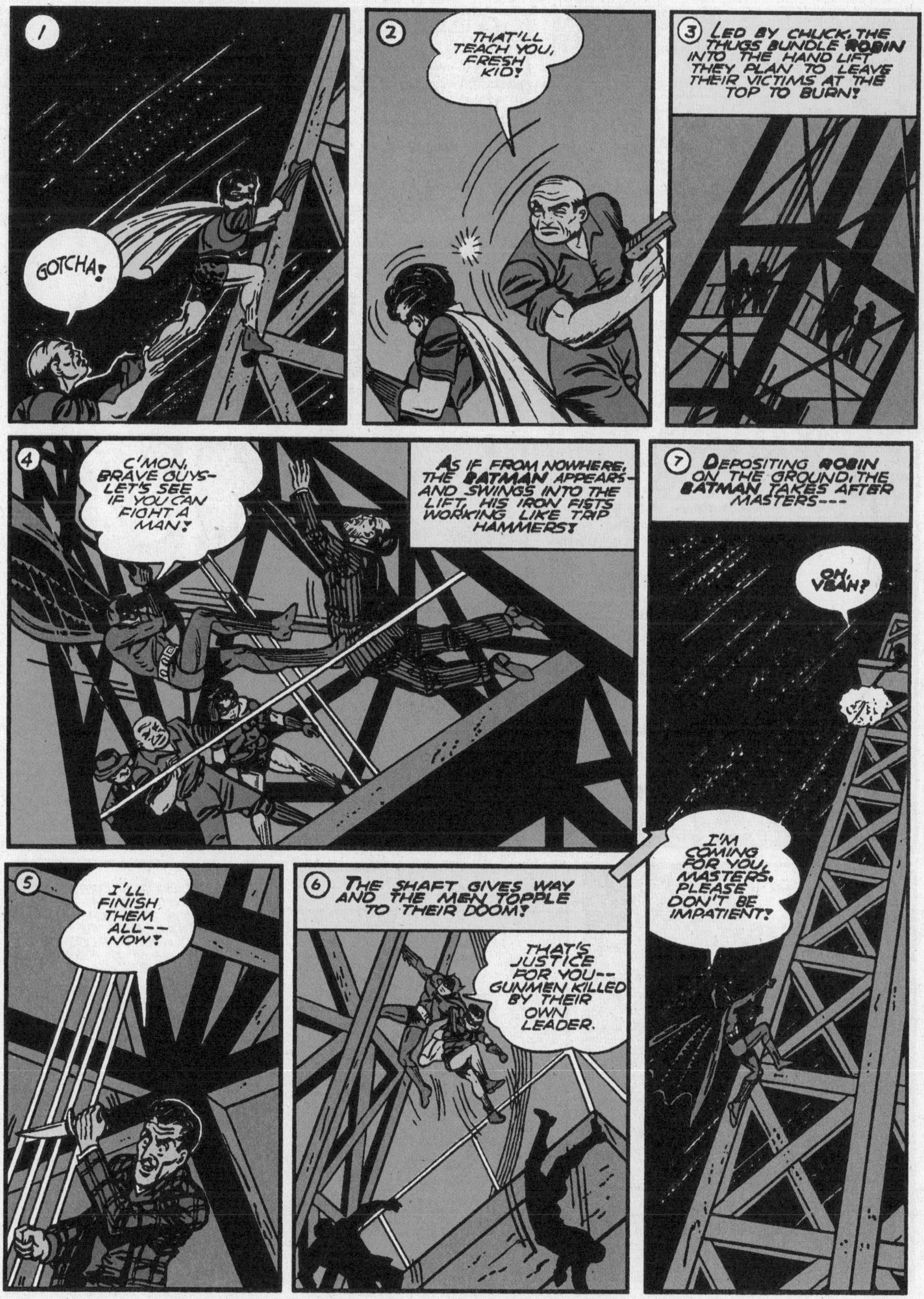
1
GOTCHA!
2
THAT'LL TEACH YOU, FRESH KID!
3
LED BY CHUCK, THE THUGS BUNDLE ROBIN INTO THE HAND LIFT THEY PLAN TO LEAVE THEIR VICTIMS AT THE TOP TO BURN!
4
C'MON, BRAVE GUYS-- LET'S SEE IF YOU CAN FIGHT A MAN!
AS IF FROM NOWHERE, THE BATMAN APPEARS-- AND SWINGS INTO THE LIFT, HIS IRON FISTS WORKING LIKE TRIP HAMMERS!
5
I'LL FINISH THEM ALL-- NOW!
6
THE SHAFT GIVES WAY AND THE MEN TOPPLE TO THEIR DOOM!
THAT'S JUSTICE FOR YOU-- GUNMEN KILLED BY THEIR OWN LEADER.
7
DEPOSITING ROBIN ON THE GROUND, THE BATMAN TAKES AFTER MASTERS---
OH, YEAH?
I'M COMING FOR YOU, MASTERS. PLEASE DON'T BE IMPATIENT!

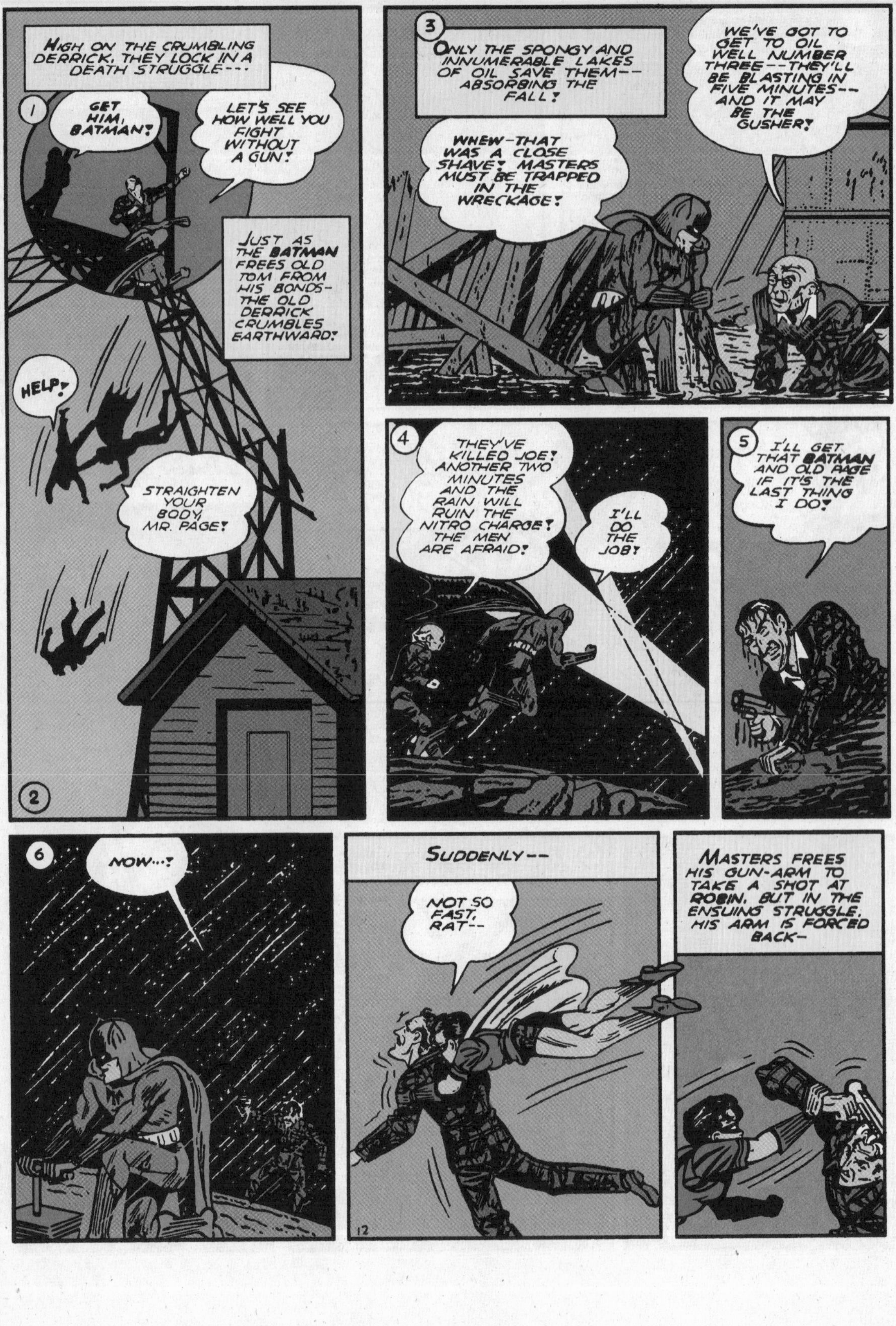
HIGH ON THE CRUMBLING DERRICK, THEY LOCK IN A DEATH STRUGGLE---
GET HIM, BATMAN!
LET'S SEE HOW WELL YOU FIGHT WITHOUT A GUN!
JUST AS THE BATMAN FREES OLD TOM FROM HIS BONDS- THE OLD DERRICK CRUMBLES EARTHWARD!
HELP!
STRAIGHTEN YOUR BODY, MR. PAGE!
ONLY THE SPONGY AND INNUMERABLE LAKES OF OIL SAVE THEM-- ABSORBING THE FALL!
WHEW-THAT WAS A CLOSE SHAVE! MASTERS MUST BE TRAPPED IN THE WRECKAGE!
WE'VE GOT TO GET TO OIL WELL NUMBER THREE--THEY'LL BE BLASTING IN FIVE MINUTES-- AND IT MAY BE THE GUSHER!
THEY'VE KILLED JOE! ANOTHER TWO MINUTES AND THE RAIN WILL RUIN THE NITRO CHARGE! THE MEN ARE AFRAID!
I'LL DO THE JOB!
I'LL GET THAT BATMAN AND OLD PAGE IF IT'S THE LAST THING I DO!
NOW...!
SUDDENLY--
NOT SO FAST, RAT--
MASTERS FREES HIS GUN-ARM TO TAKE A SHOT AT ROBIN, BUT IN THE ENSUING STRUGGLE, HIS ARM IS FORCED BACK-
12

1. ....THE GUN FLAMES—

THE BATMAN IS CERTAINLY RIGHT—CRIME DOES NOT PAY--

2. MEANWHILE, THE BATMAN PUSHES THE PLUNGER--THOUSANDS OF FEET BELOW THE EARTH THERE IS A TREMENDOUS EXPLOSION--AS THE OIL IS UNLEASHED BY THE NITRO'S POWERFUL KICK—

HEADS UP--HERE SHE GOES-

3. MY WORK'S DONE—YOU FINISH THE REST. GOODBYE!

WAIT A MOMENT-YOU SAVED MY LIFE--AND I WANT TO THANK YOU!

4. LOOK AT THAT DARN GUSHER--GOING TO BRING MILLIONS OF GALLONS OF OIL--WHEE--HARRAH!

THE OIL COMPANY'S SAFE AT LAST-

5. WHY, HELLO, LINDA--WHAT BRINGS YOU HERE? I HEARD A LOT OF NOISE AND WONDERED WHAT WAS HAPPENING--

I'M SORRY IT SPOILED YOUR BEAUTY SLEEP.

6. CAN I GIVE YOU A RIDE BACK?

THANKS A LOT--BUT THERE COULDN'T BE ANY EXCITEMENT DRIVING WITH YOU. WEREN'T YOU MAN ENOUGH TO HELP DAD? I'D LIKE YOU A LITTLE BETTER IF YOU TOOK A LEAF OUT OF BATMAN'S BOOK!

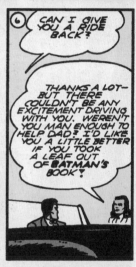

7. BRUCE AND DICK HEAD FOR HOME--

POOR LINDA--SHE'LL NEVER KNOW! SOMETIMES I KIND OF WISH SHE COULD KNOW

AW, GEE! THE BATMAN'S JOB IS TO HUNT CRIMINALS!

13

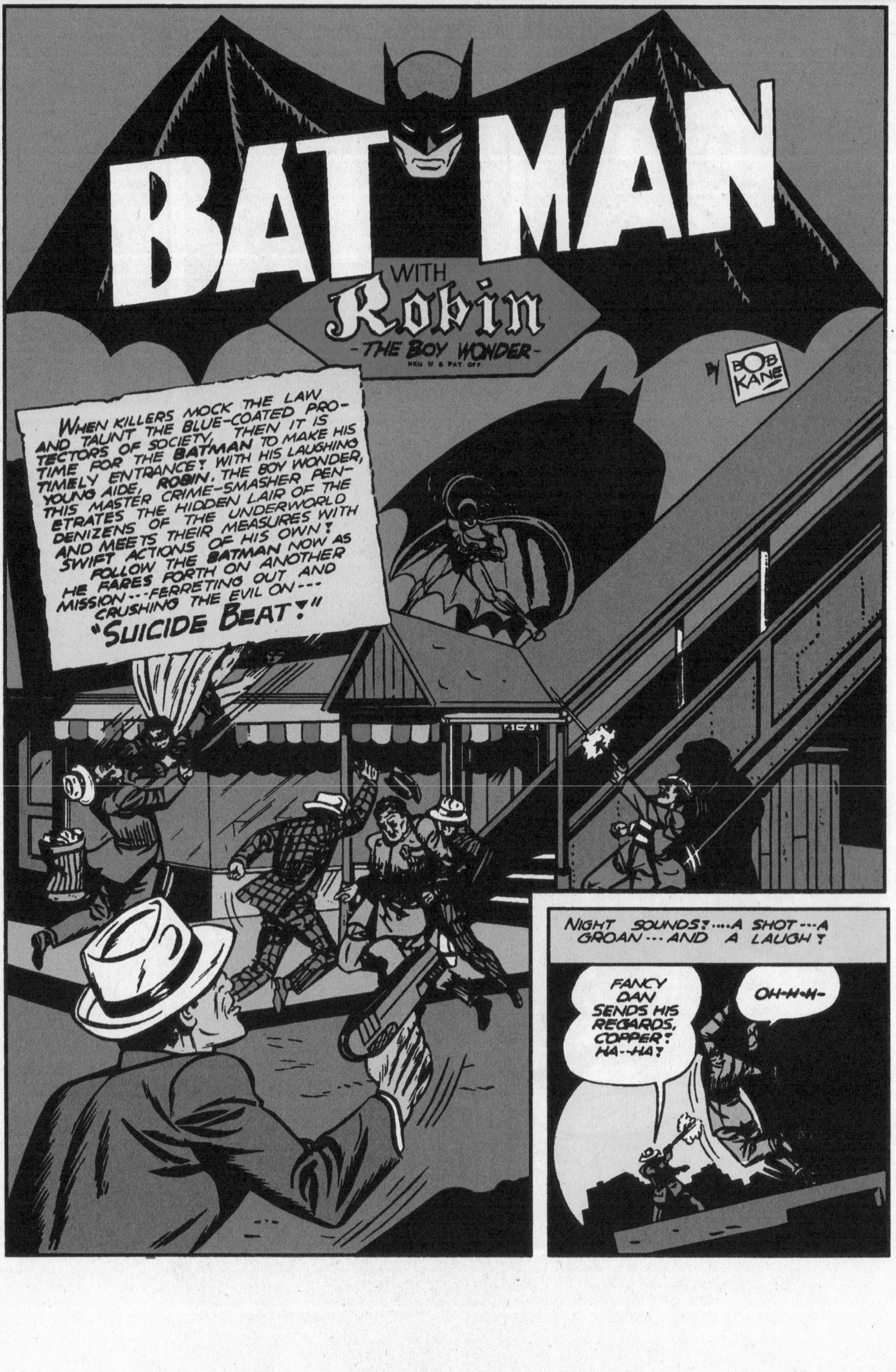
BATMAN
WITH
Robin
-THE BOY WONDER-
BY BOB KANE
WHEN KILLERS MOCK THE LAW AND TAUNT THE BLUE-COATED PROTECTORS OF SOCIETY, THEN IT IS TIME FOR THE BATMAN TO MAKE HIS TIMELY ENTRANCE! WITH HIS LAUGHING YOUNG AIDE, ROBIN, THE BOY WONDER, THIS MASTER CRIME-SMASHER PENETRATES THE HIDDEN LAIR OF THE DENIZENS OF THE UNDERWORLD AND MEETS THEIR MEASURES WITH SWIFT ACTIONS OF HIS OWN! FOLLOW THE BATMAN NOW AS HE FARES FORTH ON ANOTHER MISSION---FERRETING OUT AND CRUSHING THE EVIL ON---
"SUICIDE BEAT!"
NIGHT SOUNDS!....A SHOT---A GROAN---AND A LAUGH!
FANCY DAN SENDS HIS REGARDS, COPPER! HA--HA!
OH-H-H-

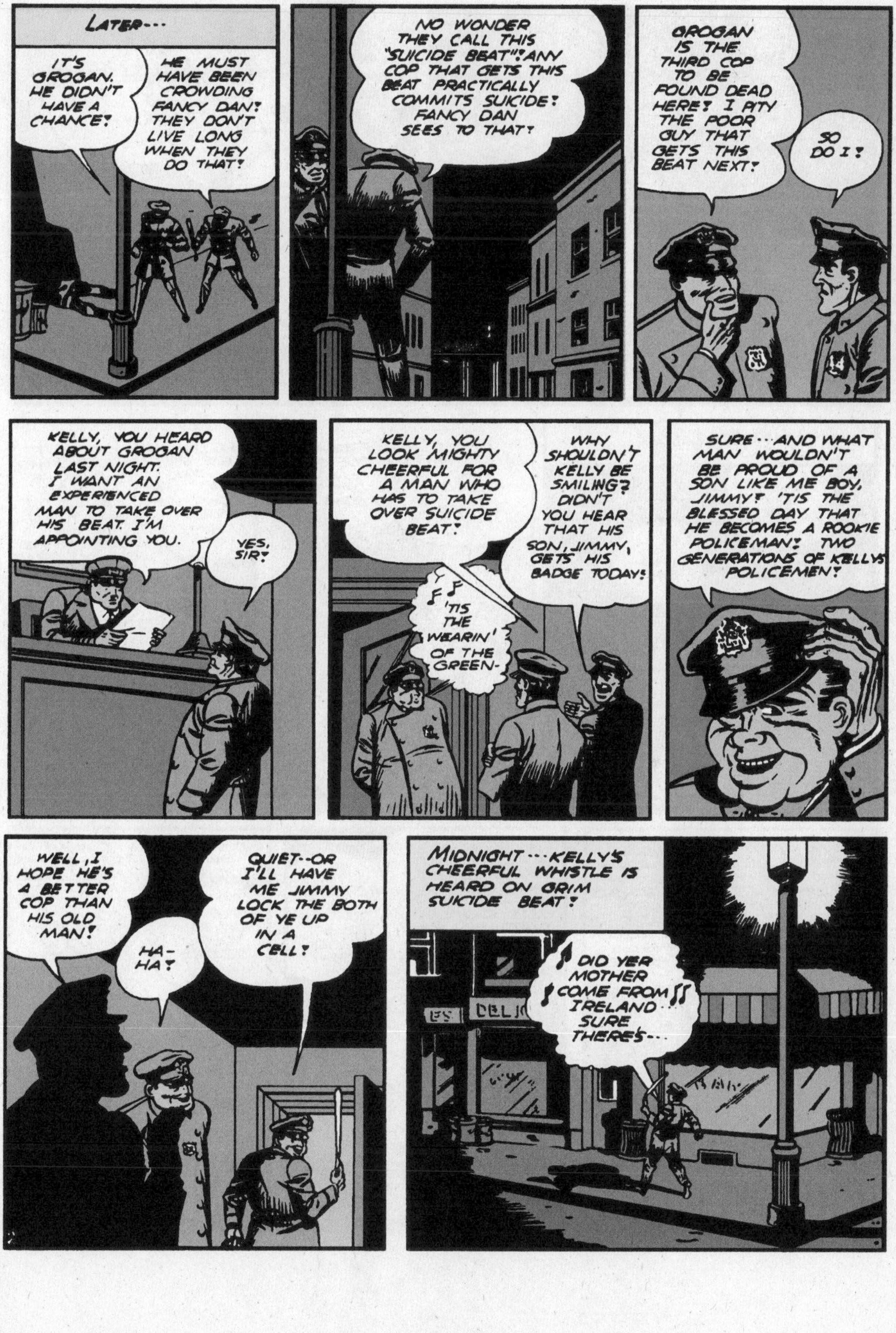
LATER---
IT'S GROGAN. HE DIDN'T HAVE A CHANCE!
HE MUST HAVE BEEN CROWDING FANCY DAN! THEY DON'T LIVE LONG WHEN THEY DO THAT!
NO WONDER THEY CALL THIS "SUICIDE BEAT"! ANY COP THAT GETS THIS BEAT PRACTICALLY COMMITS SUICIDE! FANCY DAN SEES TO THAT!
GROGAN IS THE THIRD COP TO BE FOUND DEAD HERE! I PITY THE POOR GUY THAT GETS THIS BEAT NEXT!
SO DO I!
KELLY, YOU HEARD ABOUT GROGAN LAST NIGHT. I WANT AN EXPERIENCED MAN TO TAKE OVER HIS BEAT. I'M APPOINTING YOU.
YES, SIR!
KELLY, YOU LOOK MIGHTY CHEERFUL FOR A MAN WHO HAS TO TAKE OVER SUICIDE BEAT!
WHY SHOULDN'T KELLY BE SMILING? DIDN'T YOU HEAR THAT HIS SON, JIMMY, GETS HIS BADGE TODAY!
'TIS THE WEARIN' OF THE GREEN-
SURE...AND WHAT MAN WOULDN'T BE PROUD OF A SON LIKE ME BOY, JIMMY! 'TIS THE BLESSED DAY THAT HE BECOMES A ROOKIE POLICEMAN! TWO GENERATIONS OF KELLYS POLICEMEN!
WELL, I HOPE HE'S A BETTER COP THAN HIS OLD MAN!
HA-HA!
QUIET--OR I'LL HAVE ME JIMMY LOCK THE BOTH OF YE UP IN A CELL!
MIDNIGHT...KELLY'S CHEERFUL WHISTLE IS HEARD ON GRIM SUICIDE BEAT!
DID YER MOTHER COME FROM IRELAND... SURE THERE'S---
DELI

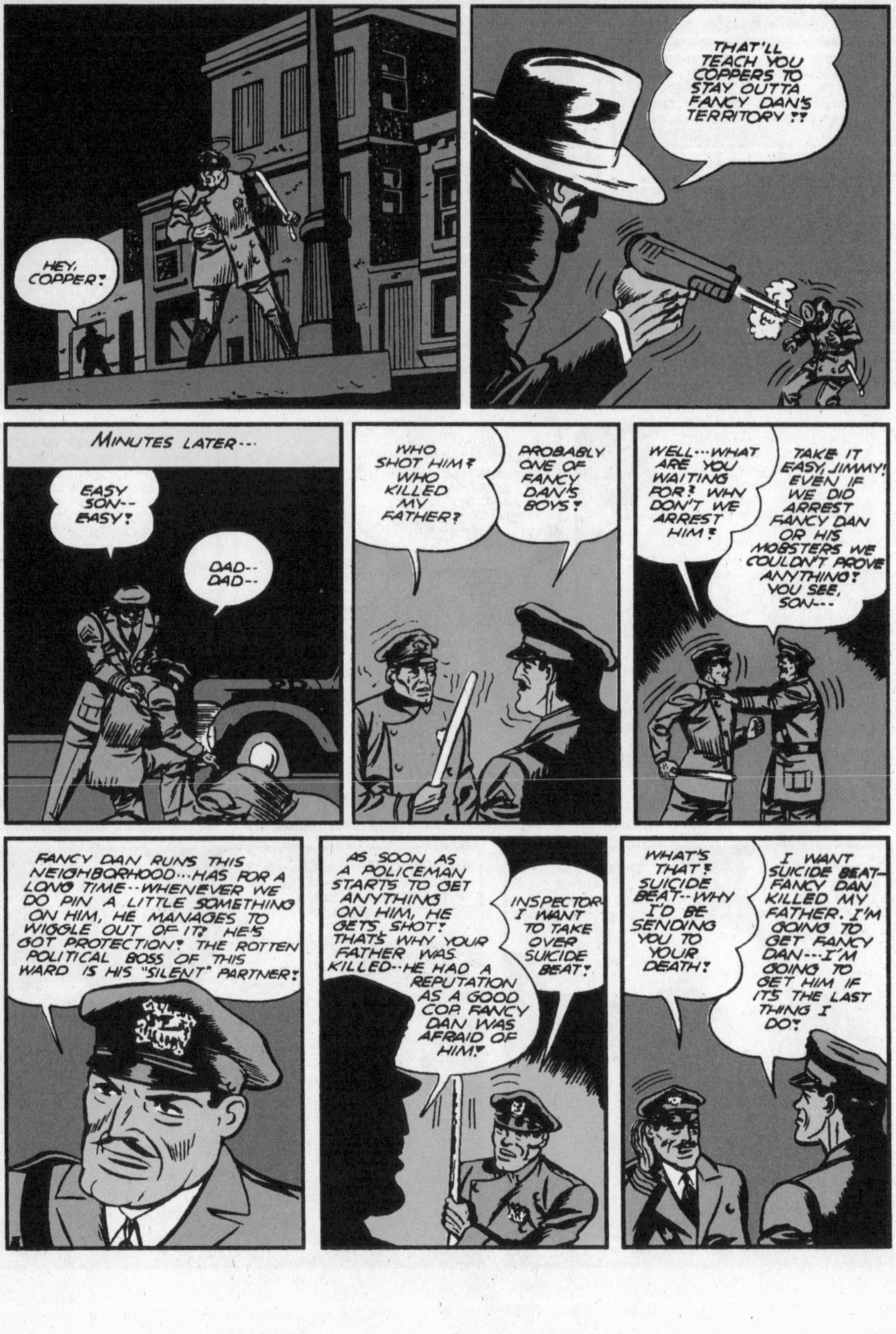

HEY, COPPER!
THAT'LL TEACH YOU COPPERS TO STAY OUTTA FANCY DAN'S TERRITORY !!
MINUTES LATER---
EASY SON-- EASY!
DAD-- DAD--
WHO SHOT HIM? WHO KILLED MY FATHER?
PROBABLY ONE OF FANCY DAN'S BOYS!
WELL---WHAT ARE YOU WAITING FOR? WHY DON'T WE ARREST HIM?
TAKE IT EASY, JIMMY! EVEN IF WE DID ARREST FANCY DAN OR HIS MOBSTERS WE COULDN'T PROVE ANYTHING! YOU SEE, SON---
FANCY DAN RUNS THIS NEIGHBORHOOD---HAS FOR A LONG TIME--WHENEVER WE DO PIN A LITTLE SOMETHING ON HIM, HE MANAGES TO WIGGLE OUT OF IT! HE'S GOT PROTECTION! THE ROTTEN POLITICAL BOSS OF THIS WARD IS HIS "SILENT" PARTNER!
AS SOON AS A POLICEMAN STARTS TO GET ANYTHING ON HIM, HE GETS SHOT! THAT'S WHY YOUR FATHER WAS KILLED--HE HAD A REPUTATION AS A GOOD COP. FANCY DAN WAS AFRAID OF HIM!
INSPECTOR-I WANT TO TAKE OVER SUICIDE BEAT!
WHAT'S THAT? SUICIDE BEAT--WHY I'D BE SENDING YOU TO YOUR DEATH!
I WANT SUICIDE BEAT-FANCY DAN KILLED MY FATHER. I'M GOING TO GET FANCY DAN---I'M GOING TO GET HIM IF IT'S THE LAST THING I DO!

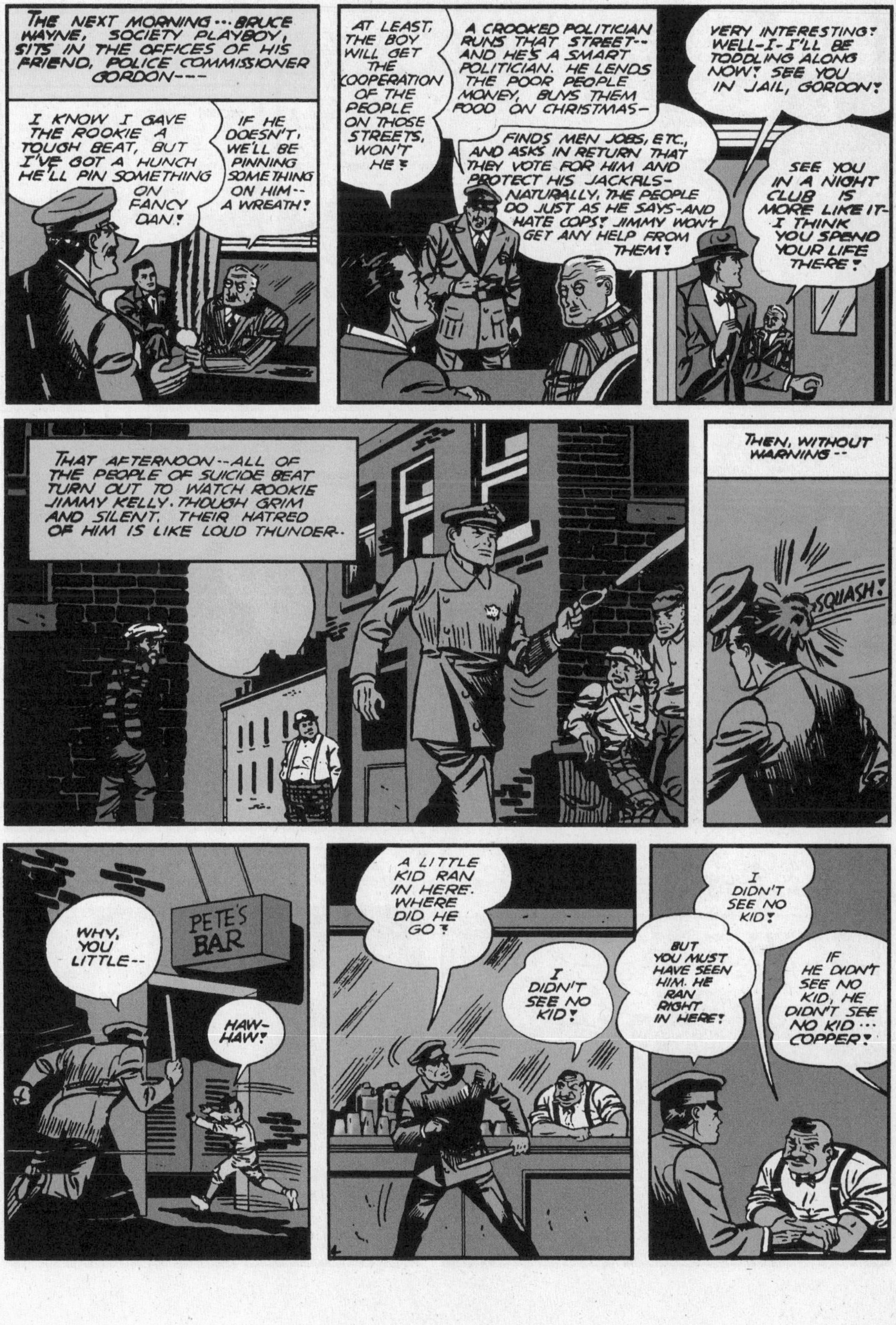
THE NEXT MORNING... BRUCE WAYNE, SOCIETY PLAYBOY, SITS IN THE OFFICES OF HIS FRIEND, POLICE COMMISSIONER GORDON---
I KNOW I GAVE THE ROOKIE A TOUGH BEAT, BUT I'VE GOT A HUNCH HE'LL PIN SOMETHING ON FANCY DAN!
IF HE DOESN'T, WE'LL BE PINNING SOMETHING ON HIM-- A WREATH!
AT LEAST, THE BOY WILL GET THE COOPERATION OF THE PEOPLE ON THOSE STREETS, WON'T HE?
A CROOKED POLITICIAN RUNS THAT STREET-- AND HE'S A SMART POLITICIAN. HE LENDS THE POOR PEOPLE MONEY, BUYS THEM FOOD ON CHRISTMAS-
FINDS MEN JOBS, ETC., AND ASKS IN RETURN THAT THEY VOTE FOR HIM AND PROTECT HIS JACKALS- NATURALLY, THE PEOPLE DO JUST AS HE SAYS-AND HATE COPS! JIMMY WON'T GET ANY HELP FROM THEM!
VERY INTERESTING! WELL-I- I'LL BE TODDLING ALONG NOW! SEE YOU IN JAIL, GORDON!
SEE YOU IN A NIGHT CLUB IS MORE LIKE IT- I THINK YOU SPEND YOUR LIFE THERE!
THAT AFTERNOON--ALL OF THE PEOPLE OF SUICIDE BEAT TURN OUT TO WATCH ROOKIE JIMMY KELLY. THOUGH GRIM AND SILENT, THEIR HATRED OF HIM IS LIKE LOUD THUNDER--
THEN, WITHOUT WARNING--
SQUASH!
PETE'S BAR
WHY, YOU LITTLE--
HAW-HAW!
A LITTLE KID RAN IN HERE. WHERE DID HE GO?
I DIDN'T SEE NO KID!
I DIDN'T SEE NO KID!
BUT YOU MUST HAVE SEEN HIM. HE RAN RIGHT IN HERE!
IF HE DIDN'T SEE NO KID, HE DIDN'T SEE NO KID... COPPER!

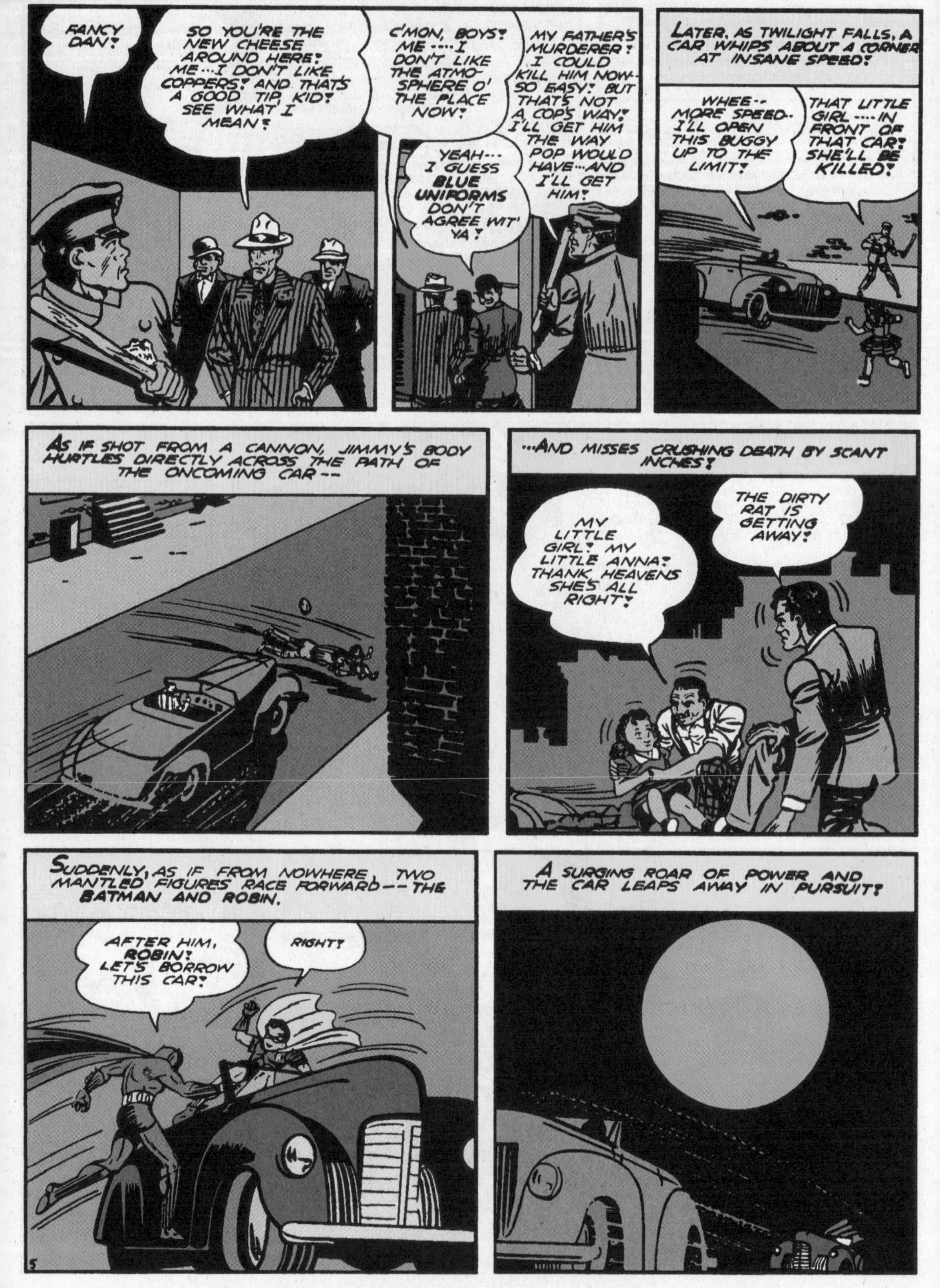
FANCY DAN!
SO YOU'RE THE NEW CHEESE AROUND HERE! ME...I DON'T LIKE COPPERS! AND THAT'S A GOOD TIP, KID! SEE WHAT I MEAN!
C'MON, BOYS! ME....I DON'T LIKE THE ATMOSPHERE O' THE PLACE NOW!
YEAH... I GUESS BLUE UNIFORMS DON'T AGREE WIT' YA!
MY FATHER'S MURDERER! I COULD KILL HIM NOW-- SO EASY! BUT THAT'S NOT A COP'S WAY! I'LL GET HIM THE WAY POP WOULD HAVE...AND I'LL GET HIM!
LATER, AS TWILIGHT FALLS, A CAR WHIPS ABOUT A CORNER AT INSANE SPEED!
WHEE-- MORE SPEED-- I'LL OPEN THIS BUGGY UP TO THE LIMIT!
THAT LITTLE GIRL....IN FRONT OF THAT CAR! SHE'LL BE KILLED!
AS IF SHOT FROM A CANNON, JIMMY'S BODY HURTLES DIRECTLY ACROSS THE PATH OF THE ONCOMING CAR--
...AND MISSES CRUSHING DEATH BY SCANT INCHES!
MY LITTLE GIRL! MY LITTLE ANNA! THANK HEAVENS SHE'S ALL RIGHT!
THE DIRTY RAT IS GETTING AWAY!
SUDDENLY, AS IF FROM NOWHERE, TWO MANTLED FIGURES RACE FORWARD--THE BATMAN AND ROBIN.
AFTER HIM, ROBIN! LET'S BORROW THIS CAR!
RIGHT!
5
A SURGING ROAR OF POWER AND THE CAR LEAPS AWAY IN PURSUIT!

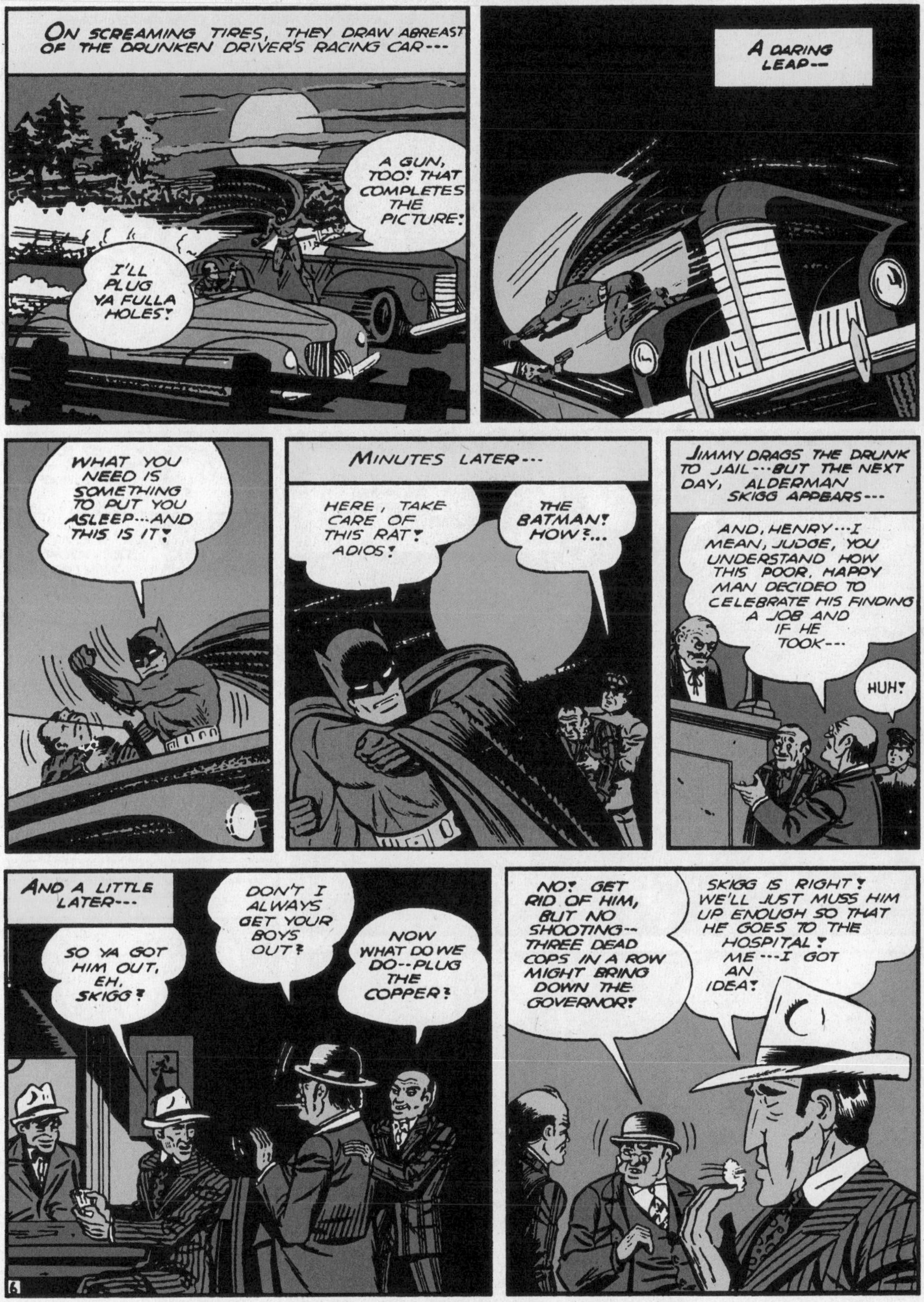
ON SCREAMING TIRES, THEY DRAW ABREAST OF THE DRUNKEN DRIVER'S RACING CAR---
A GUN, TOO! THAT COMPLETES THE PICTURE!
I'LL PLUG YA FULLA HOLES!
A DARING LEAP--
WHAT YOU NEED IS SOMETHING TO PUT YOU ASLEEP---AND THIS IS IT!
MINUTES LATER---
HERE, TAKE CARE OF THIS RAT! ADIOS!
THE BATMAN! HOW?...
JIMMY DRAGS THE DRUNK TO JAIL---BUT THE NEXT DAY, ALDERMAN SKIGG APPEARS---
AND, HENRY---I MEAN, JUDGE, YOU UNDERSTAND HOW THIS POOR, HAPPY MAN DECIDED TO CELEBRATE HIS FINDING A JOB AND IF HE TOOK---
HUH!
AND A LITTLE LATER---
SO YA GOT HIM OUT, EH, SKIGG?
DON'T I ALWAYS GET YOUR BOYS OUT?
NOW WHAT DO WE DO--PLUG THE COPPER?
6
NO! GET RID OF HIM, BUT NO SHOOTING--THREE DEAD COPS IN A ROW MIGHT BRING DOWN THE GOVERNOR!
SKIGG IS RIGHT! WE'LL JUST MUSS HIM UP ENOUGH SO THAT HE GOES TO THE HOSPITAL! ME---I GOT AN IDEA!

THAT VERY NIGHT---SUICIDE BEAT LIES CLOAKED IN SILENCE AND DARKNESS. SUDDENLY---THE SOUND OF A SCUFFLE---

YA DOITY HEEL!

WHY, I'LL PULVERIZE YA!

A FIGHT!

BUT AS JIMMY TRIES TO SEPARATE THE TWO, THEY SUDDENLY TURN ON HIM......AND OUT OF THE SHADOWS LEAP MORE THUGS!

A TRAP!

SOCK THAT COPPER! LET'S GET HIM!

A FIGHT, ROBIN! SHALL WE INTRUDE?

THEN, SWINGING DOWN FROM FIRE ESCAPES COME TWO LITHE FIGURES----

-AND HOW!

NO PARKING

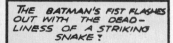

THE BATMAN'S FIST FLASHES OUT WITH THE DEADLINESS OF A STRIKING SNAKE!

MY...YOU MUST SEE YOUR DENTIST MORE OFTEN!

I'LL MOIDER YA!

TSK! TSK!

ASHES TO ASHES!

AND NOW, JIMMY HAS RECOVERED.....

NOW---THIS IS MORE LIKE IT!

SUDDENLY, A CAR SHOOTS FROM BEHIND A CORNER---STOPS LONG ENOUGH TO PICK UP THE HOODLUMS, AND THEN SPEEDS AWAY-----

NO USE TRYING TO GET THOSE RATS!

WELL--WHAT'S THIS? THEY MUST HAVE DROPPED THIS IN THE SCUFFLE!

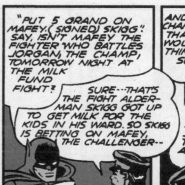

"PUT 5 GRAND ON MAFEY. (SIGNED) SKIGG". SAY, ISN'T MAFEY THE FIGHTER WHO BATTLES JORGAN, THE CHAMP, TOMORROW NIGHT AT THE MILK FUND FIGHT?

SURE---THAT'S THE FIGHT ALDERMAN SKIGG GOT UP TO GET MILK FOR THE KIDS IN HIS WARD. SO SKIGG IS BETTING ON MAFEY, THE CHALLENGER--

AND JORGAN IS THE CHAMP: IF I KNOW SKIGG, THAT CHEAP MISER WOULDN'T BET ON SOMETHING UNLESS HE WAS SURE OF IT!

I'VE GOT A HUNCH THIS FIGHT HAS BEEN FRAMED--IN FACT, I'M ALMOST SURE! I THINK I'M GOING TO PUT THE SKIDS UNDER ALDERMAN SKIGG!

THE NEXT NIGHT---ALDERMAN SKIGG ADDRESSES THE HUGE CROWD IN THE STADIUM....

AND SO, LADIES AND GENTLEMEN, ARUMPH-- I'VE ARRANGED SO THAT THE PROCEEDS WILL BUY GOOD MILK FOR STARVING BABIES ---BLAH BLAH--

AND IN THE CHAMP'S DRESSING ROOM, A SHADOW MOVES ACROSS THE WALL....

WHA...? OH--H-H-H!

IN THE RING ---- THE CHALLENGER, BIFF MAFEY, ACKNOWLEDGES THE PLAUDITS OF THE CROWD.

WHERE'S THE CHAMP? HE SHOULD BE HERE!

SUDDENLY---WALKING DOWN THE AISLE----THE CHAMP'S TRAINER AND MANAGER WITH THE BATMAN....

THE CHAMP HAD AN ACCIDENT-- SO I'M TAKING HIS PLACE! ISN'T THAT RIGHT, BOYS?

YEAH! YEAH, DAT'S RIGHT!

WHAT...? YOU--THAT COWL--YOU'RE THE BATMAN!

BUT YOU CAN'T TAKE HIS PLACE. IT ISN'T...I MEAN--THE CROWD DON'T WANT A SUBSTITUTE!

HOW ABOUT IT, FOLKS? WANT ME TO FIGHT IN THE CHAMP'S PLACE?

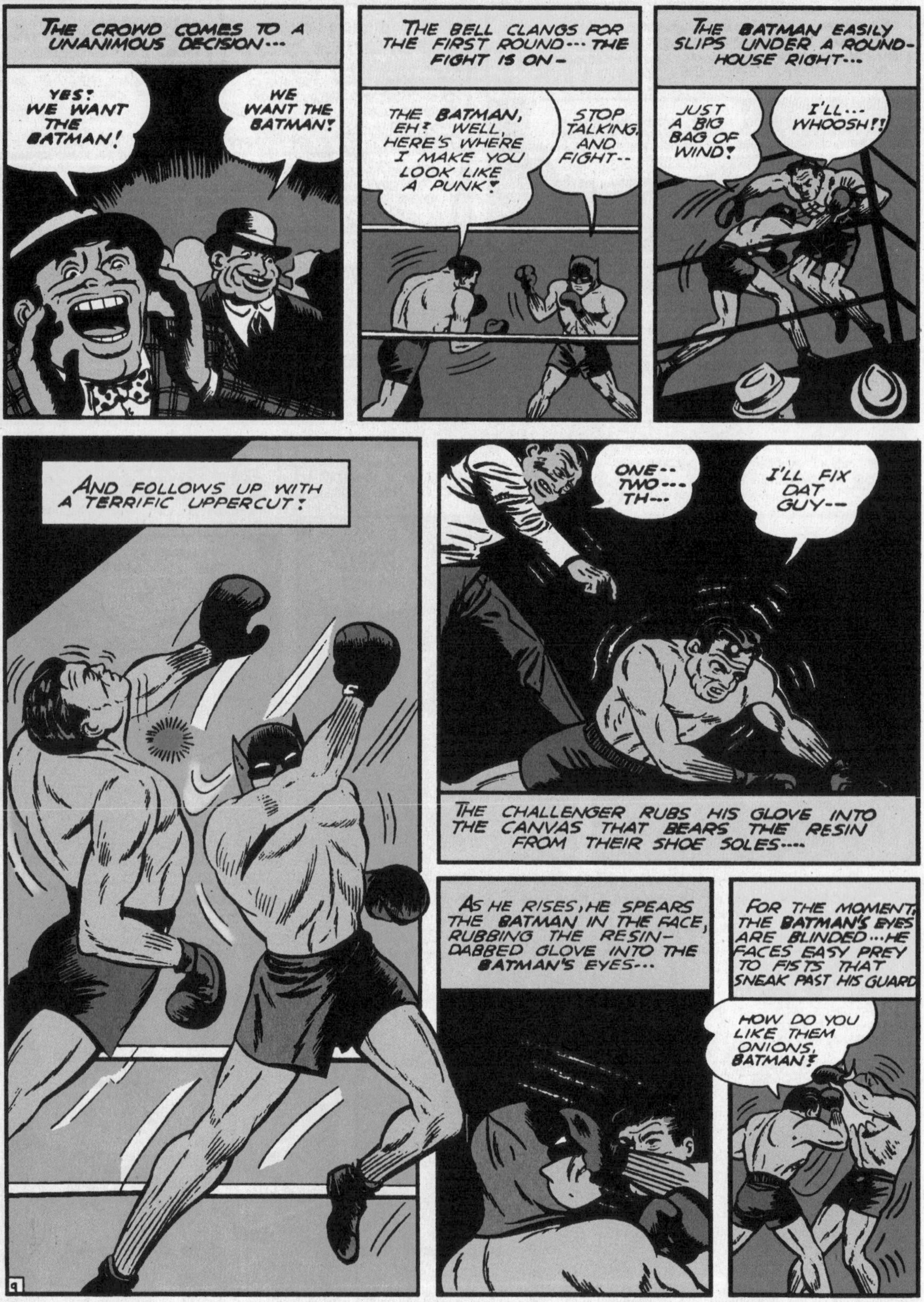

THE CROWD COMES TO A UNANIMOUS DECISION---
YES! WE WANT THE BATMAN!
WE WANT THE BATMAN!
THE BELL CLANGS FOR THE FIRST ROUND--- THE FIGHT IS ON-
THE BATMAN, EH? WELL, HERE'S WHERE I MAKE YOU LOOK LIKE A PUNK!
STOP TALKING, AND FIGHT--
THE BATMAN EASILY SLIPS UNDER A ROUND-HOUSE RIGHT---
JUST A BIG BAG OF WIND!
I'LL--- WHOOSH!!
AND FOLLOWS UP WITH A TERRIFIC UPPERCUT!
9
ONE-- TWO--- TH---
I'LL FIX DAT GUY--
THE CHALLENGER RUBS HIS GLOVE INTO THE CANVAS THAT BEARS THE RESIN FROM THEIR SHOE SOLES----
AS HE RISES, HE SPEARS THE BATMAN IN THE FACE, RUBBING THE RESIN-DABBED GLOVE INTO THE BATMAN'S EYES---
FOR THE MOMENT, THE BATMAN'S EYES ARE BLINDED---HE FACES EASY PREY TO FISTS THAT SNEAK PAST HIS GUARD
HOW DO YOU LIKE THEM ONIONS, BATMAN?

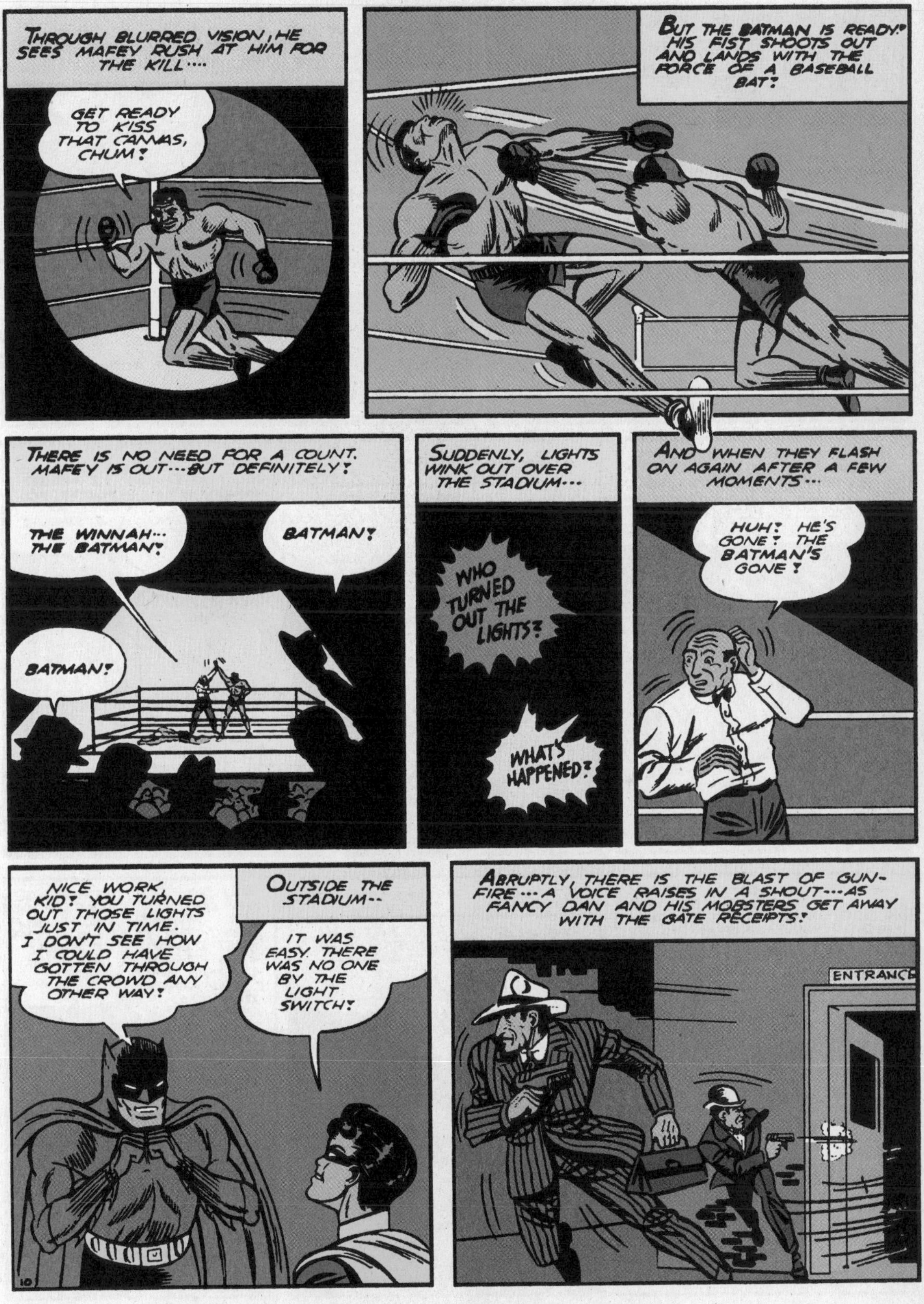
THROUGH BLURRED VISION, HE SEES MAFEY RUSH AT HIM FOR THE KILL....
GET READY TO KISS THAT CANVAS, CHUM!
BUT THE BATMAN IS READY! HIS FIST SHOOTS OUT AND LANDS WITH THE FORCE OF A BASEBALL BAT!
THERE IS NO NEED FOR A COUNT. MAFEY IS OUT---BUT DEFINITELY!
THE WINNAH... THE BATMAN!
BATMAN!
BATMAN!
SUDDENLY, LIGHTS WINK OUT OVER THE STADIUM---
WHO TURNED OUT THE LIGHTS?
WHAT'S HAPPENED?
AND WHEN THEY FLASH ON AGAIN AFTER A FEW MOMENTS---
HUH! HE'S GONE! THE BATMAN'S GONE!
OUTSIDE THE STADIUM--
NICE WORK, KID! YOU TURNED OUT THOSE LIGHTS JUST IN TIME. I DON'T SEE HOW I COULD HAVE GOTTEN THROUGH THE CROWD ANY OTHER WAY!
IT WAS EASY. THERE WAS NO ONE BY THE LIGHT SWITCH!
10
ABRUPTLY, THERE IS THE BLAST OF GUN-FIRE---A VOICE RAISES IN A SHOUT---AS FANCY DAN AND HIS MOBSTERS GET AWAY WITH THE GATE RECEIPTS!
ENTRANCE

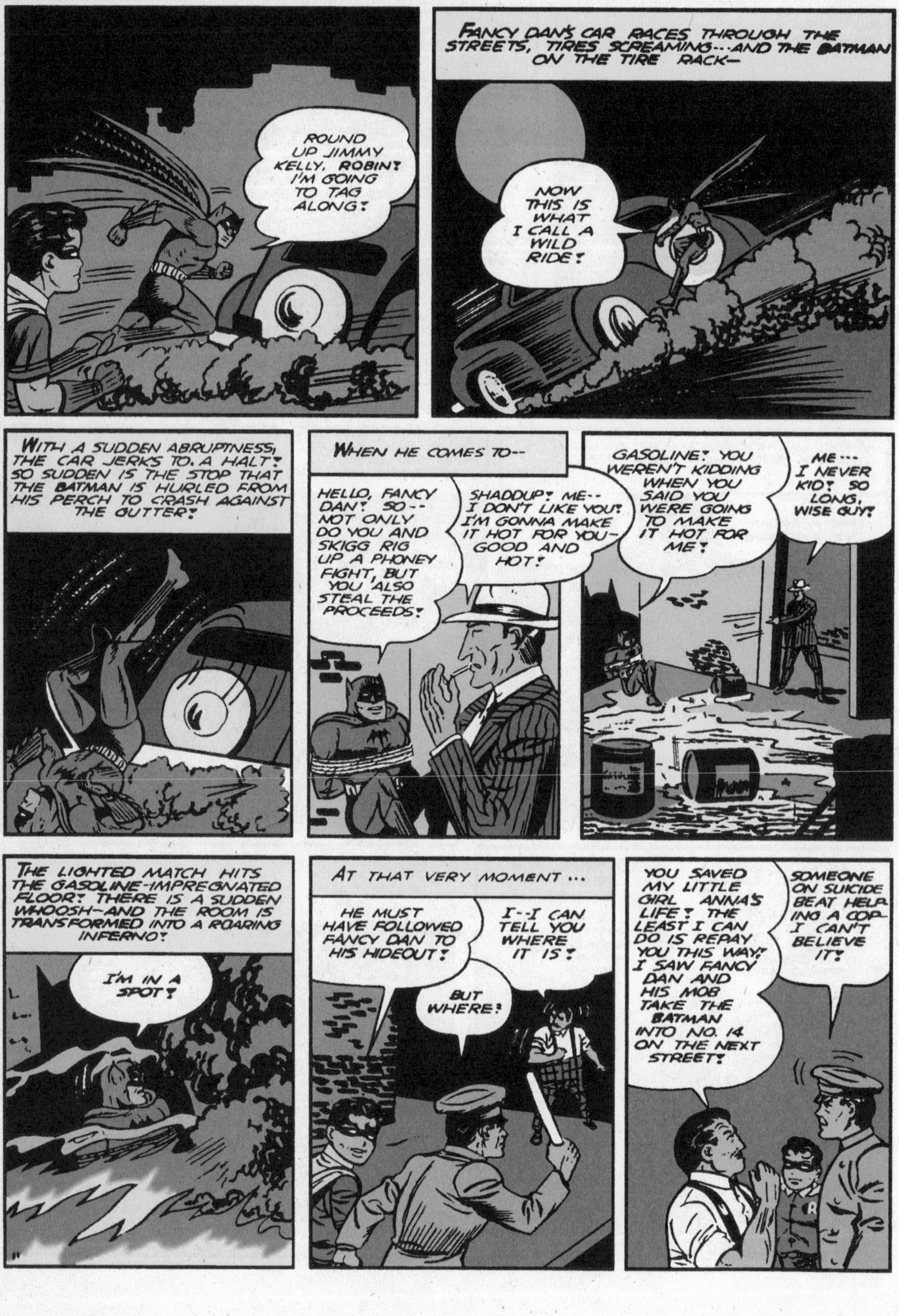
ROUND UP JIMMY KELLY, ROBIN! I'M GOING TO TAG ALONG!
FANCY DAN'S CAR RACES THROUGH THE STREETS, TIRES SCREAMING...AND THE BATMAN ON THE TIRE RACK—
NOW THIS IS WHAT I CALL A WILD RIDE!
WITH A SUDDEN ABRUPTNESS, THE CAR JERKS TO A HALT! SO SUDDEN IS THE STOP THAT THE BATMAN IS HURLED FROM HIS PERCH TO CRASH AGAINST THE GUTTER!
WHEN HE COMES TO—
HELLO, FANCY DAN! SO--NOT ONLY DO YOU AND SKIGG RIG UP A PHONEY FIGHT, BUT YOU ALSO STEAL THE PROCEEDS!
SHADDUP! ME--I DON'T LIKE YOU! I'M GONNA MAKE IT HOT FOR YOU-GOOD AND HOT!
GASOLINE! YOU WEREN'T KIDDING WHEN YOU SAID YOU WERE GOING TO MAKE IT HOT FOR ME!
ME...I NEVER KID! SO LONG, WISE GUY!
THE LIGHTED MATCH HITS THE GASOLINE-IMPREGNATED FLOOR! THERE IS A SUDDEN WHOOSH—AND THE ROOM IS TRANSFORMED INTO A ROARING INFERNO!
I'M IN A SPOT!
AT THAT VERY MOMENT...
HE MUST HAVE FOLLOWED FANCY DAN TO HIS HIDEOUT!
BUT WHERE?
I--I CAN TELL YOU WHERE IT IS!
YOU SAVED MY LITTLE GIRL ANNA'S LIFE! THE LEAST I CAN DO IS REPAY YOU THIS WAY! I SAW FANCY DAN AND HIS MOB TAKE THE BATMAN INTO NO. 14 ON THE NEXT STREET!
SOMEONE ON SUICIDE BEAT HELPING A COP--I CAN'T BELIEVE IT!

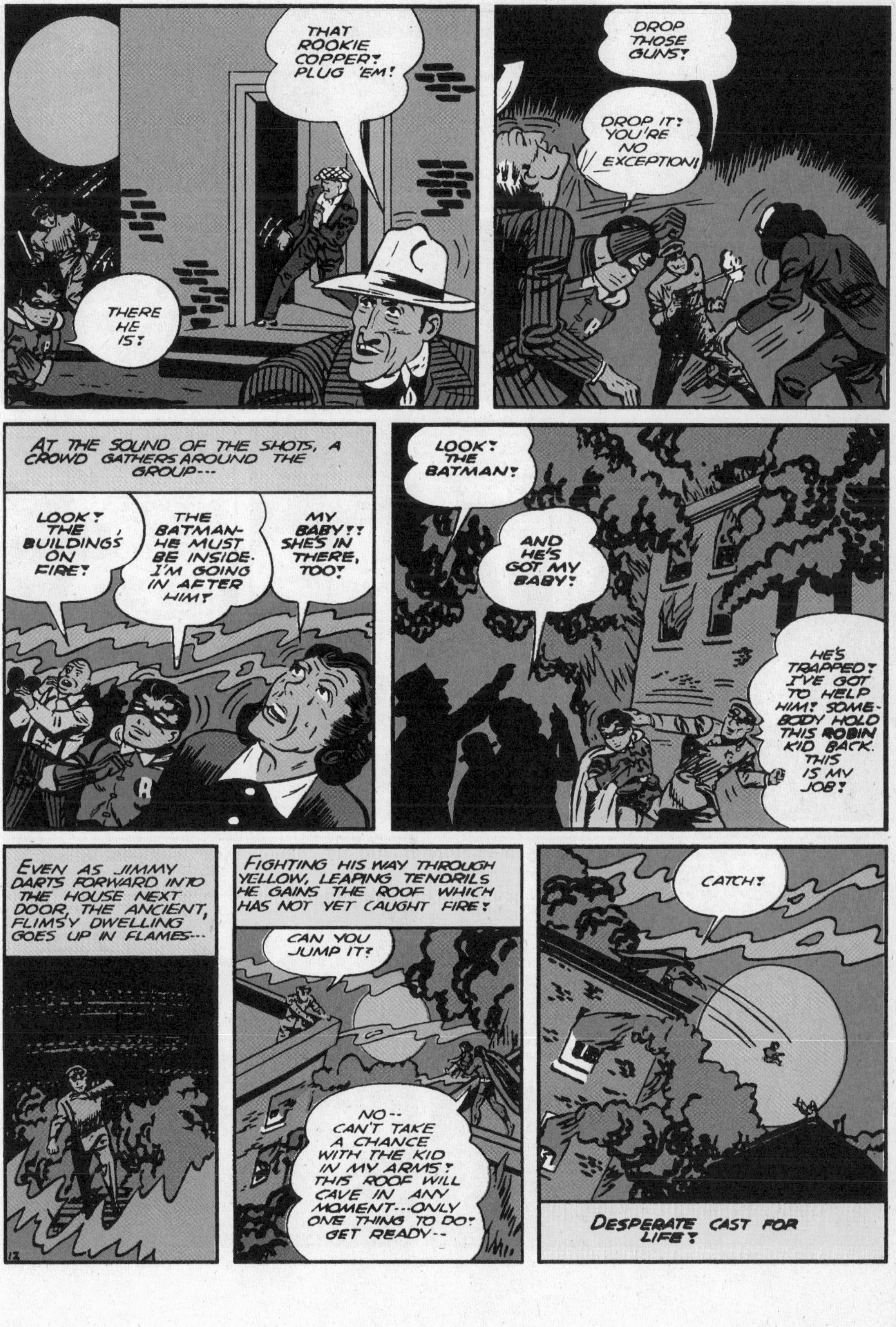
THAT ROOKIE COPPER! PLUG 'EM!
THERE HE IS!
DROP THOSE GUNS!
DROP IT! YOU'RE NO EXCEPTION!
AT THE SOUND OF THE SHOTS, A CROWD GATHERS AROUND THE GROUP---
LOOK! THE BUILDING'S ON FIRE!
THE BATMAN-HE MUST BE INSIDE. I'M GOING IN AFTER HIM!
MY BABY!! SHE'S IN THERE, TOO!
LOOK! THE BATMAN!
AND HE'S GOT MY BABY!
HE'S TRAPPED! I'VE GOT TO HELP HIM! SOMEBODY HOLD THIS ROBIN KID BACK. THIS IS MY JOB!
EVEN AS JIMMY DARTS FORWARD INTO THE HOUSE NEXT DOOR, THE ANCIENT, FLIMSY DWELLING GOES UP IN FLAMES---
FIGHTING HIS WAY THROUGH YELLOW, LEAPING TENDRILS HE GAINS THE ROOF WHICH HAS NOT YET CAUGHT FIRE!
CAN YOU JUMP IT?
NO-- CAN'T TAKE A CHANCE WITH THE KID IN MY ARMS! THIS ROOF WILL CAVE IN ANY MOMENT---ONLY ONE THING TO DO! GET READY--
CATCH!
DESPERATE CAST FOR LIFE!

WHEW! GOT HER!

AT THAT INSTANT, FIREMEN ARRIVE---SPREAD A WIDE NET--AND JIMMY LEAPS TO SAFETY WITH HIS PRECIOUS BURDEN---

AND JUST AS THE BUILDING CRASHES INWARD, THE BATMAN MAKES HIS LEAP THROUGH SPACE TO THAT NET THAT SEEMS SO SMALL BELOW!

JUST IN TIME!

IT'S YOU, SKIGG! WELL--JUST IN TIME FOR ME TO TAKE YOU IN!

WHA-- WHAT IS THAT?

MY BABY!

IT'S JUST THAT YOU NOT ONLY RIGGED UP A PHONEY CHARITY FIGHT, BUT YOU ALSO FIXED IT SO FANCY DAN WOULD STEAL THE GATE RECEIPTS!

...AND THOSE GATE RECEIPTS WOULD HAVE BOUGHT MILK FOR THE KIDS OF THIS NEIGHBORHOOD!

WELL, JIMMY, I GUESS YOU WON'T HAVE ANY MORE TROUBLE ON SUICIDE BEAT!

YES, AND IF I KNOW MY CROOKS, FANCY DAN AND HIS MEN WILL TALK PLENTY DOWN AT HEADQUARTERS--THANKS TO YOU!

LATER--

BUT HOW DID YOU GET FREE?

I MANAGED TO REACH A STEEL BLADE I HAD HIDDEN IN THE HEEL OF MY BOOT! CLOSE CALL THOUGH! SAY, WONDER WHAT THE PEOPLE THINK OF JIMMY NOW?

THE NEXT DAY-- THE ANSWER TO THE BATMAN'S QUESTION!

HELLO, JIMMY!

IT CERTAINLY IS ---- IT CERTAINLY IS A FINE DAY!

FINE DAY!

BOB KANE

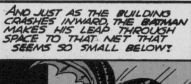

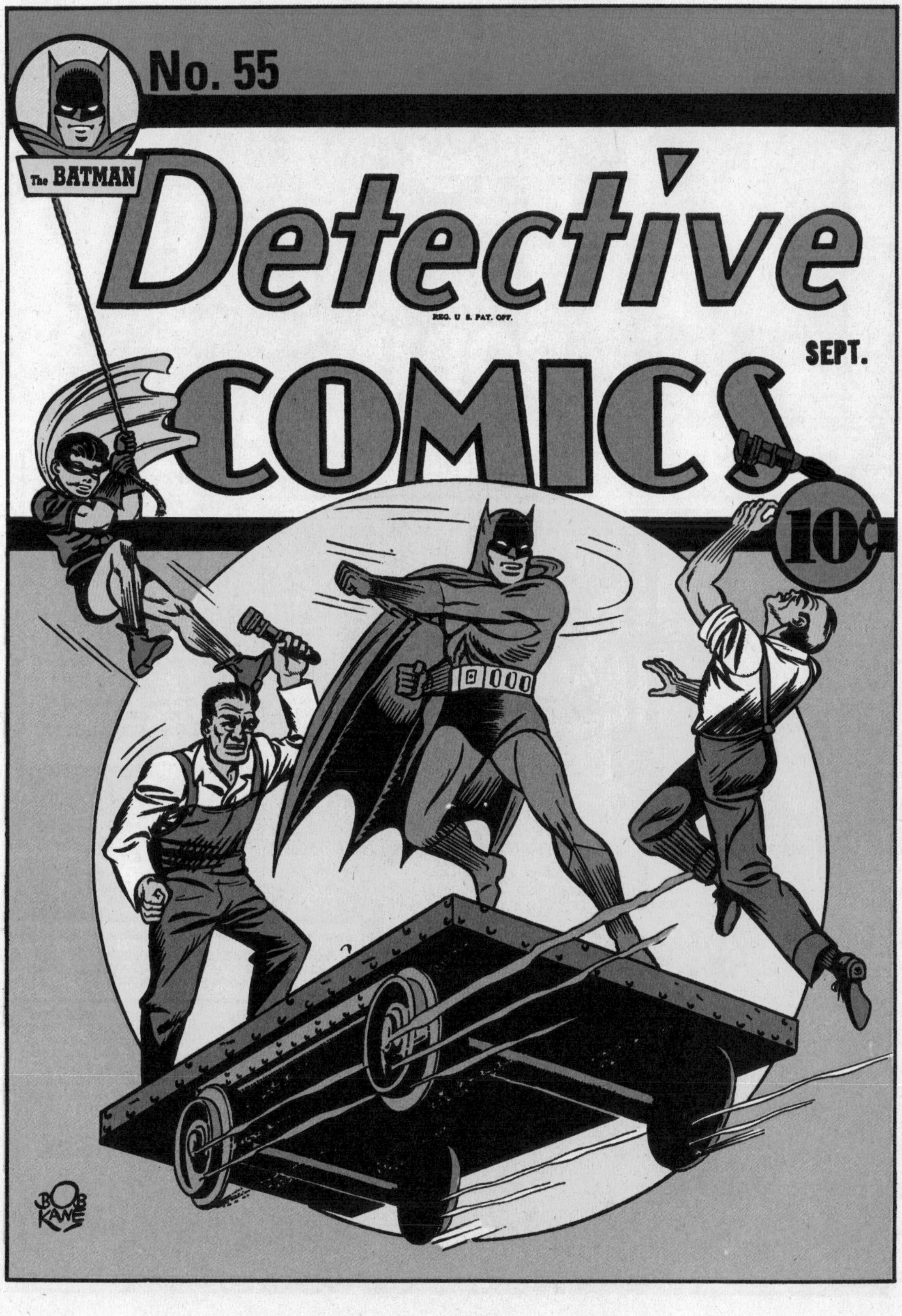
No. 55
The BATMAN
Detective
REG. U. S. PAT. OFF.
SEPT.
COMICS
10¢
BOB KANE

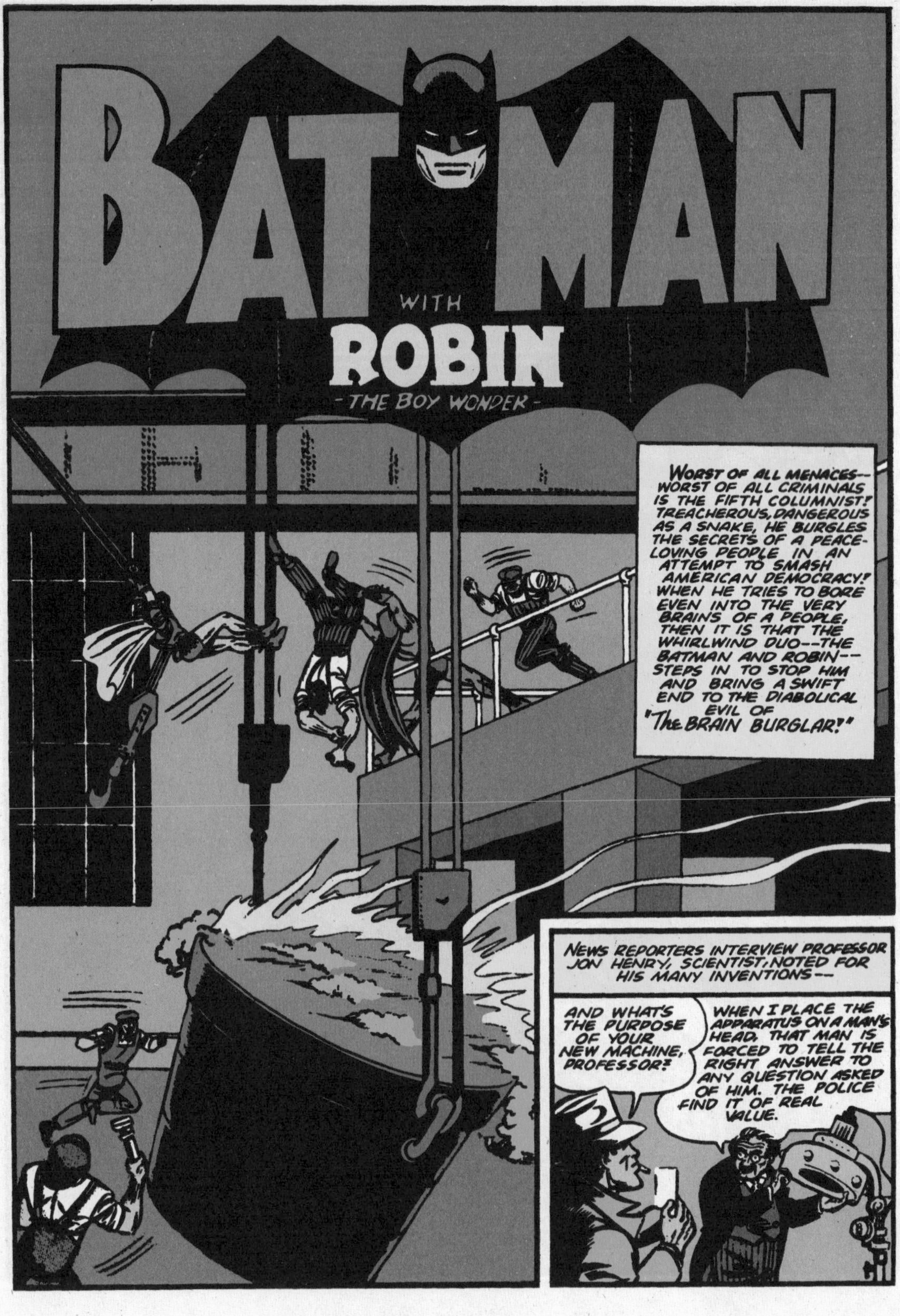

BATMAN
WITH
ROBIN
-THE BOY WONDER-
WORST OF ALL MENACES--WORST OF ALL CRIMINALS IS THE FIFTH COLUMNIST! TREACHEROUS, DANGEROUS AS A SNAKE, HE BURGLES THE SECRETS OF A PEACE-LOVING PEOPLE IN AN ATTEMPT TO SMASH AMERICAN DEMOCRACY! WHEN HE TRIES TO BORE EVEN INTO THE VERY BRAINS OF A PEOPLE, THEN IT IS THAT THE WHIRLWIND DUO--THE BATMAN AND ROBIN--STEPS IN TO STOP HIM AND BRING A SWIFT END TO THE DIABOLICAL EVIL OF "THE BRAIN BURGLAR!"
NEWS REPORTERS INTERVIEW PROFESSOR JON HENRY, SCIENTIST, NOTED FOR HIS MANY INVENTIONS--
AND WHAT'S THE PURPOSE OF YOUR NEW MACHINE, PROFESSOR?
WHEN I PLACE THE APPARATUS ON A MAN'S HEAD, THAT MAN IS FORCED TO TELL THE RIGHT ANSWER TO ANY QUESTION ASKED OF HIM. THE POLICE FIND IT OF REAL VALUE.

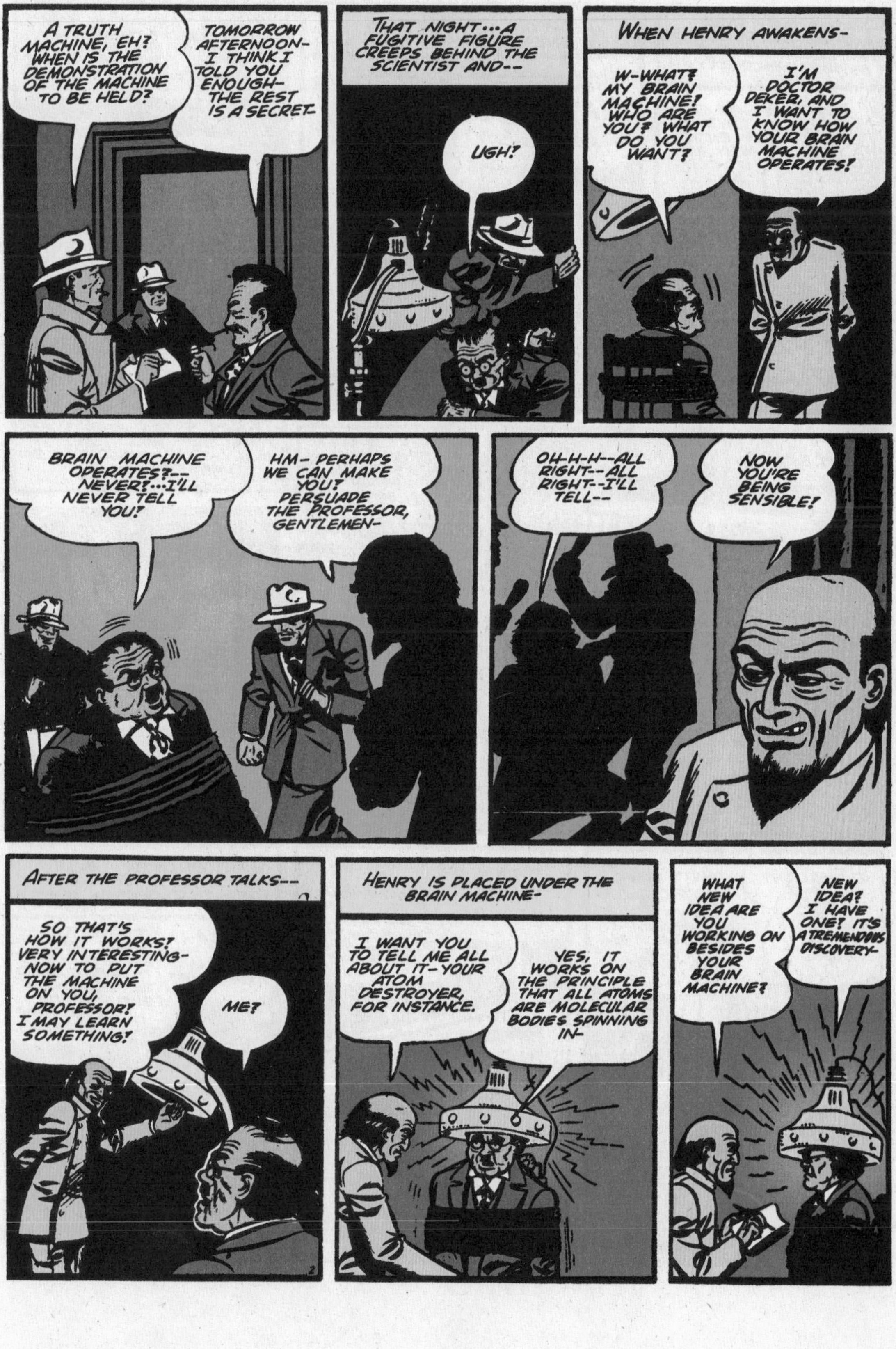
A TRUTH MACHINE, EH? WHEN IS THE DEMONSTRATION OF THE MACHINE TO BE HELD?
TOMORROW AFTERNOON- I THINK I TOLD YOU ENOUGH- THE REST IS A SECRET-
THAT NIGHT...A FUGITIVE FIGURE CREEPS BEHIND THE SCIENTIST AND--
UGH!
WHEN HENRY AWAKENS-
W-WHAT? MY BRAIN MACHINE! WHO ARE YOU? WHAT DO YOU WANT?
I'M DOCTOR DEKER, AND I WANT TO KNOW HOW YOUR BRAIN MACHINE OPERATES!
BRAIN MACHINE OPERATES?-- NEVER!...I'LL NEVER TELL YOU!
HM- PERHAPS WE CAN MAKE YOU! PERSUADE THE PROFESSOR, GENTLEMEN-
OH-H-H--ALL RIGHT--ALL RIGHT--I'LL TELL--
NOW YOU'RE BEING SENSIBLE!
AFTER THE PROFESSOR TALKS--
SO THAT'S HOW IT WORKS! VERY INTERESTING- NOW TO PUT THE MACHINE ON YOU, PROFESSOR! I MAY LEARN SOMETHING!
ME?
HENRY IS PLACED UNDER THE BRAIN MACHINE-
I WANT YOU TO TELL ME ALL ABOUT IT- YOUR ATOM DESTROYER, FOR INSTANCE.
YES, IT WORKS ON THE PRINCIPLE THAT ALL ATOMS ARE MOLECULAR BODIES SPINNING IN-
WHAT NEW IDEA ARE YOU WORKING ON BESIDES YOUR BRAIN MACHINE?
NEW IDEA? I HAVE ONE! IT'S A TREMENDOUS DISCOVERY-

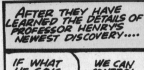

AFTER THEY HAVE LEARNED THE DETAILS OF PROFESSOR HENRY'S NEWEST DISCOVERY....

IF WHAT HE SAYS IS TRUE WE HAVE STUMBLED ONTO SOMETHING THAT IS INDEED TREMENDOUS!

WE CAN -- CONTROL AN ENTIRE ARMY...WITH IT... CALL IN OUR AGENTS. I WANT TO SPEAK TO THEM!

THE ROOM IS FILLED WITH ENEMY AGENTS--

SO, MY COMRADES, I HAVE TOLD YOU EVERYTHING! ARE YOU WILLING TO SUBMIT TO THIS OPERATION?

GLADLY-- WE KNOW WHAT WILL HAPPEN TO US, BUT NO SACRIFICE IS TOO GREAT FOR THE FATHERLAND!

AND SO, THAT NIGHT, MEN SIT AND AWAIT THEIR TURN AS ONE BY ONE THEIR FANATICAL COMRADES SUBMIT TO A MYSTERIOUS OPERATION—

WHAT IS THE PURPOSE? WHAT EVIL WILL IT BRING? ONLY TIME--INSCRUTABLE TIME CAN TELL!

NEXT DAY-

39¢ GOTHAM GAZETTE

PROFESSOR JON HENRY AND BRAIN MACHINE DISAPPEAR!!

THE PRESS WAS AMAZED TO LEARN THIS MORNING OF MYSTIFYING DISAPPEARANCE OF THE NOTED SCIENTIST !!!!

PROFESSOR JON HENRY

AND THAT IS ONLY THE BEGINNING-- FAMOUS SCIENTISTS, KEY MEN IN NATIONAL DEFENSE, INVENTIVE CIRCLES AND OTHERS VANISH, SEEMINGLY PLUCKED AWAY BY INVISIBLE, GHOSTLY HANDS-

I THOUGHT YOU HAD A DATE TODAY WITH LINDA PAGE

THAT'S RIGHT! I HAVE-- BUT THIS LATEST DISAPPEARANCE MADE ME LOSE TRACK OF THE TIME!

WHERE ARE YOU GOING WITH HER, ANYWAY?

TO HER UNCLE'S AVIATION PLANT WHERE THEY'RE MAKING A BOMBER FOR THE ARMY!

MINUTES LATER, BRUCE AND LINDA WALK TOWARD THE GREAT AVIATION PLANT!

BRUCE-- IT'S REALLY INSPIRING!

I SEE YOU WANT ME TO GET INTERESTED IN AVIATION SO I'LL FIND MYSELF SOME SORT OF OCCUPATION! SORRY—

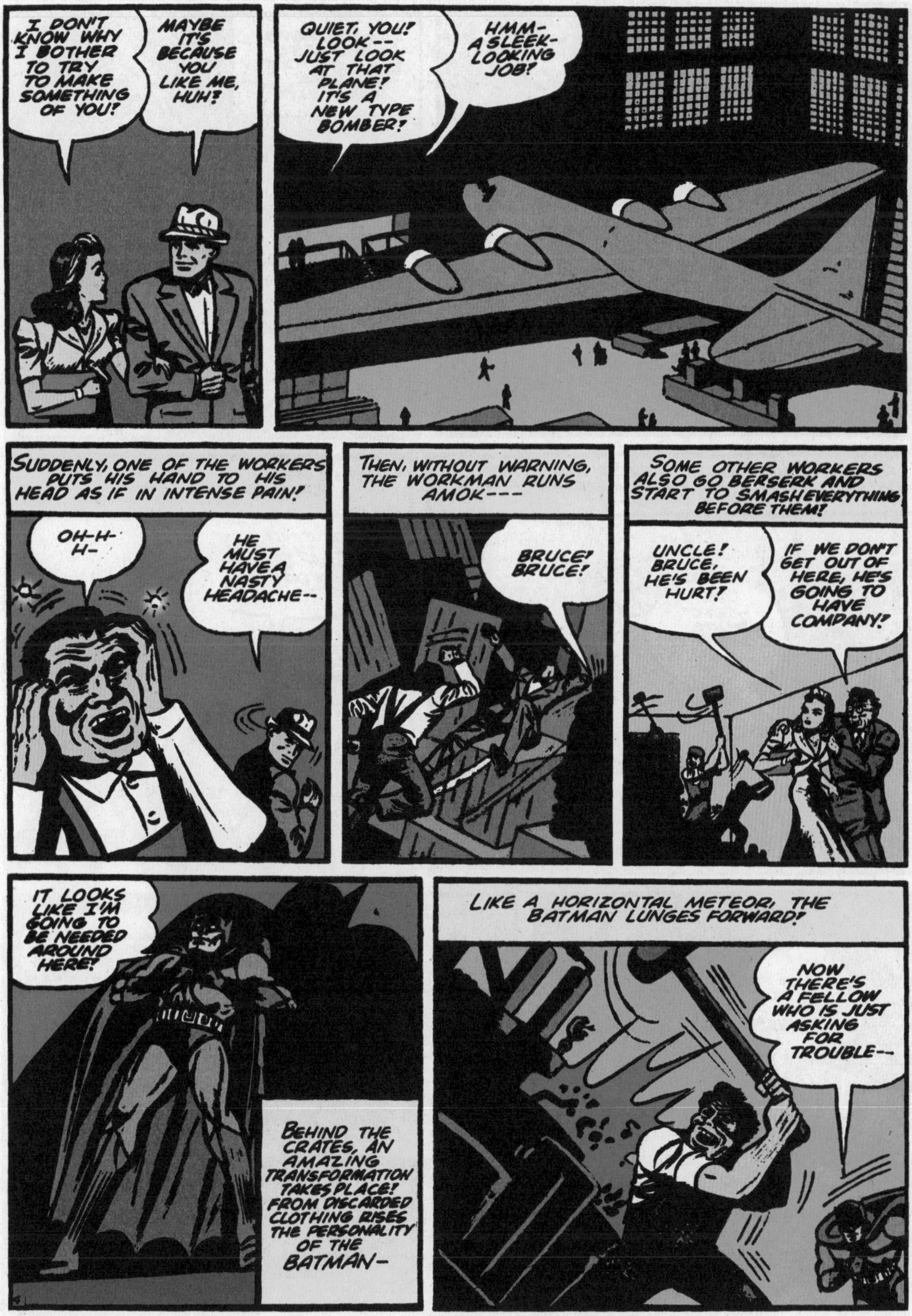

I DON'T KNOW WHY I BOTHER TO TRY TO MAKE SOMETHING OF YOU!
MAYBE IT'S BECAUSE YOU LIKE ME, HUH?
QUIET, YOU! LOOK-- JUST LOOK AT THAT PLANE! IT'S A NEW TYPE BOMBER!
HMM- A SLEEK-LOOKING JOB!
SUDDENLY, ONE OF THE WORKERS PUTS HIS HAND TO HIS HEAD AS IF IN INTENSE PAIN!
OH-H-H-
HE MUST HAVE A NASTY HEADACHE--
THEN, WITHOUT WARNING, THE WORKMAN RUNS AMOK---
BRUCE! BRUCE!
SOME OTHER WORKERS ALSO GO BERSERK AND START TO SMASH EVERYTHING BEFORE THEM!
UNCLE! BRUCE, HE'S BEEN HURT!
IF WE DON'T GET OUT OF HERE, HE'S GOING TO HAVE COMPANY!
IT LOOKS LIKE I'M GOING TO BE NEEDED AROUND HERE!
BEHIND THE CRATES, AN AMAZING TRANSFORMATION TAKES PLACE! FROM DISCARDED CLOTHING RISES THE PERSONALITY OF THE BATMAN-
LIKE A HORIZONTAL METEOR, THE BATMAN LUNGES FORWARD!
NOW THERE'S A FELLOW WHO IS JUST ASKING FOR TROUBLE--

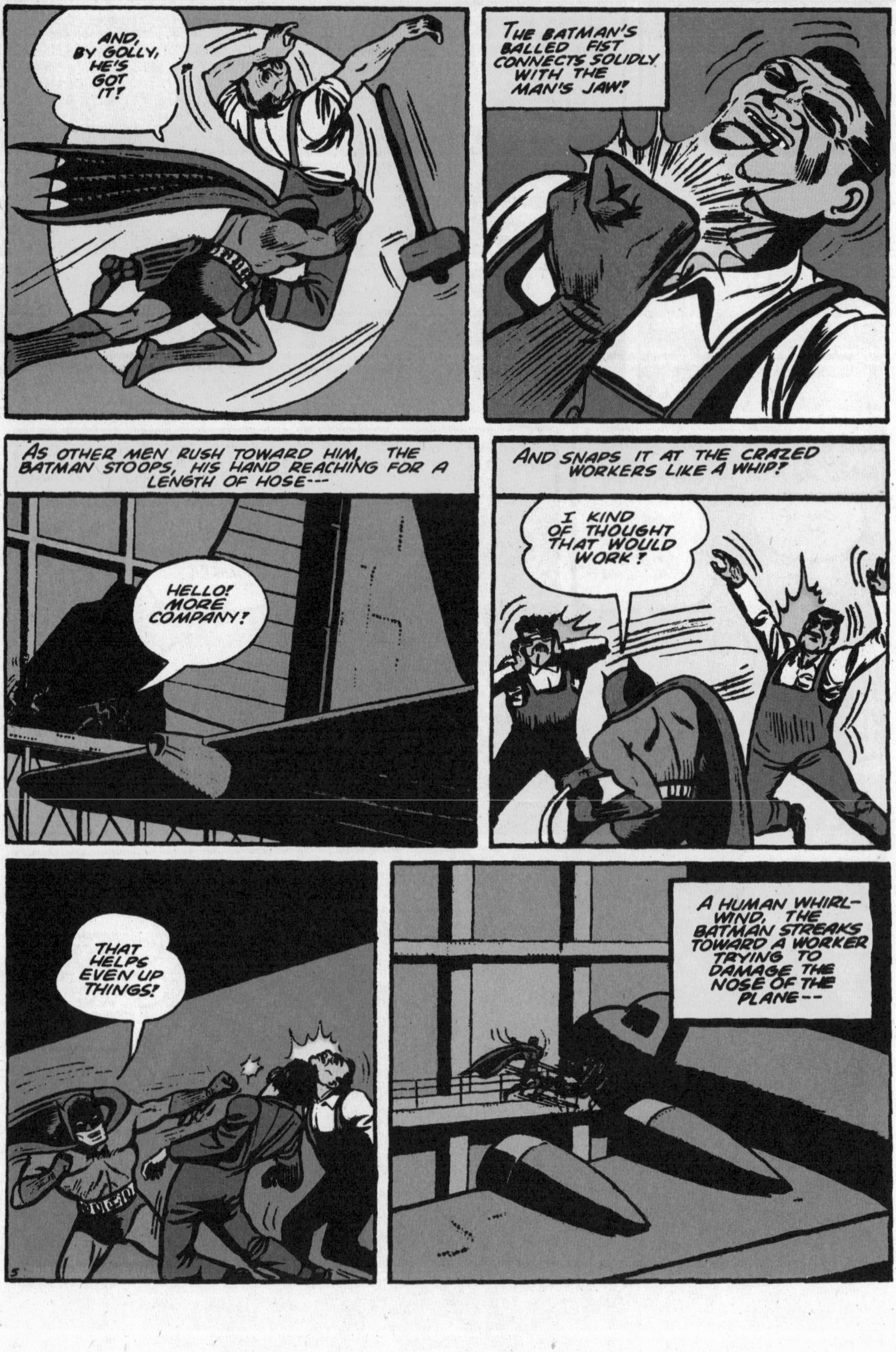
AND, BY GOLLY, HE'S GOT IT!
THE BATMAN'S BALLED FIST CONNECTS SOLIDLY WITH THE MAN'S JAW!
AS OTHER MEN RUSH TOWARD HIM, THE BATMAN STOOPS, HIS HAND REACHING FOR A LENGTH OF HOSE---
HELLO! MORE COMPANY?
AND SNAPS IT AT THE CRAZED WORKERS LIKE A WHIP?
I KIND OF THOUGHT THAT WOULD WORK!
THAT HELPS EVEN UP THINGS!
A HUMAN WHIRL-WIND, THE BATMAN STREAKS TOWARD A WORKER TRYING TO DAMAGE THE NOSE OF THE PLANE--

NOW ONE MORE LITTLE BIT OF STRATEGY AND MY WORK IS DONE!

THE BATMAN SLIDES DOWN THE TOP OF THE SLIPPERY PLANE—

HE SENDS A LARGE TIRE WHEEL TOWARD THE REMAINING GROUP OF MADDENED WORKERS!

THE HUGE TIRE LITERALLY MOWS THEM DOWN!

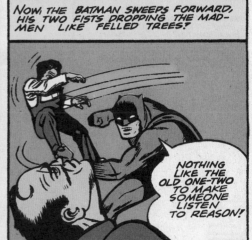

NOW, THE BATMAN SWEEPS FORWARD, HIS TWO FISTS DROPPING THE MAD-MEN LIKE FELLED TREES!

NOTHING LIKE THE OLD ONE-TWO TO MAKE SOMEONE LISTEN TO REASON!

NOW IT'S TIME FOR ME TO GO. THERE'LL BE QUESTIONS AND THAT MIGHT MEAN THE END OF THE BATMAN'S SECRET IDENTITY!

LATER, IT IS BRUCE WAYNE WHO STUMBLES OUT FROM BEHIND THE PACKING CASES!

BRUCE! ARE YOU ALL RIGHT?

OH, MY JAW! WHAT HIT ME? WHAT HAPPENED?

WHAT HAPPENED? ONLY SOME MEN WENT CRAZY AND THE BATMAN CAME OUT OF NOWHERE AND STOPPED THEM—THAT'S ALL—

THE BATMAN—THAT GUY AGAIN?

"THAT GUY" PROBABLY SAVED YOUR LIFE AND MY UNCLE'S PLANT FROM BEING RUINED! WHICH IS MORE THAN YOU DID!

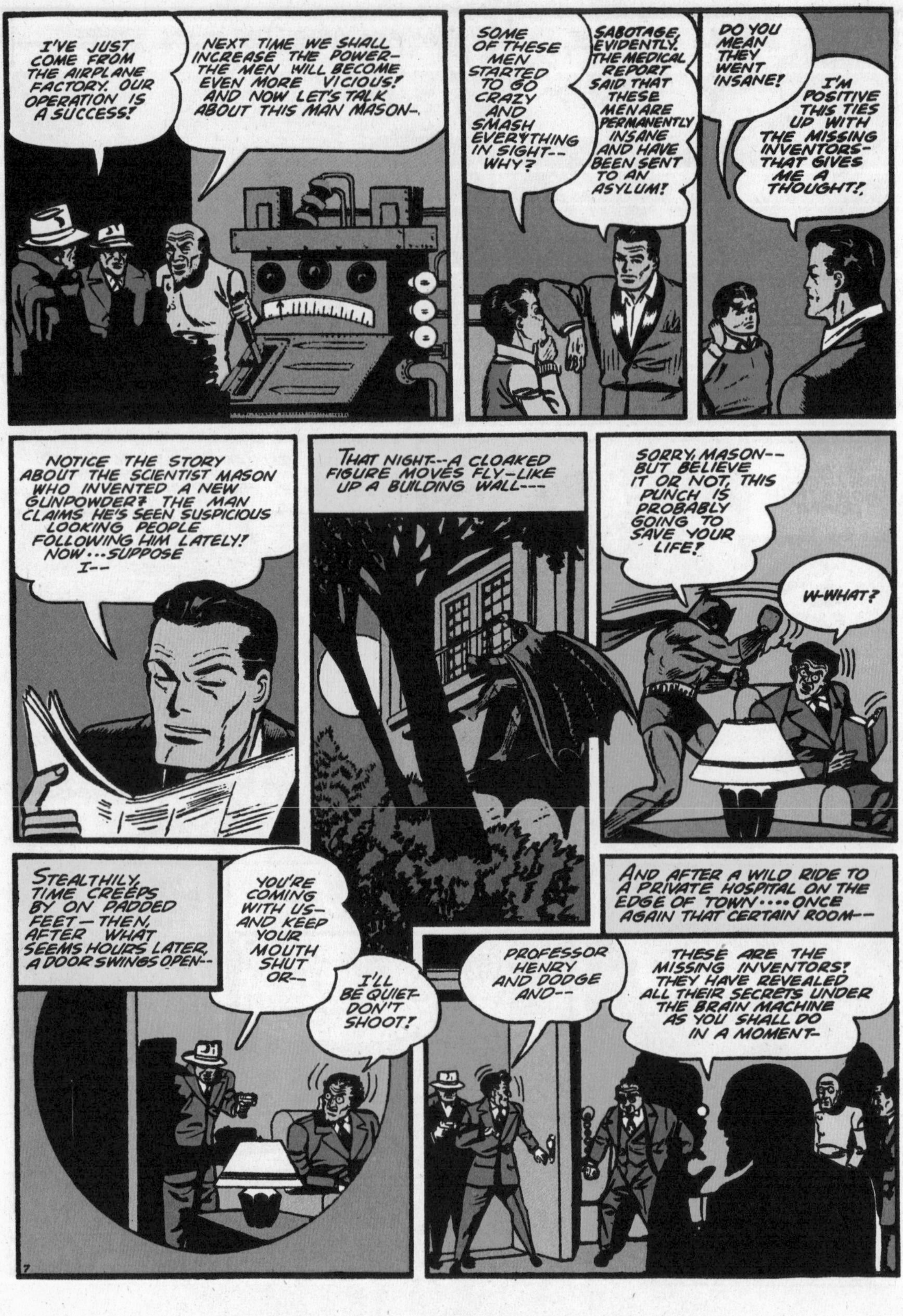
I'VE JUST COME FROM THE AIRPLANE FACTORY. OUR OPERATION IS A SUCCESS!
NEXT TIME WE SHALL INCREASE THE POWER-THE MEN WILL BECOME EVEN MORE VICIOUS! AND NOW LET'S TALK ABOUT THIS MAN MASON-.
SOME OF THESE MEN STARTED TO GO CRAZY AND SMASH EVERYTHING IN SIGHT--WHY?
SABOTAGE, EVIDENTLY. THE MEDICAL REPORT SAID THAT THESE MEN ARE PERMANENTLY INSANE AND HAVE BEEN SENT TO AN ASYLUM!
DO YOU MEAN THEY WENT INSANE!
I'M POSITIVE THIS TIES UP WITH THE MISSING INVENTORS-THAT GIVES ME A THOUGHT!,
NOTICE THE STORY ABOUT THE SCIENTIST MASON WHO INVENTED A NEW GUNPOWDER? THE MAN CLAIMS HE'S SEEN SUSPICIOUS LOOKING PEOPLE FOLLOWING HIM LATELY! NOW...SUPPOSE I--
THAT NIGHT--A CLOAKED FIGURE MOVES FLY-LIKE UP A BUILDING WALL---
SORRY, MASON--BUT BELIEVE IT OR NOT, THIS PUNCH IS PROBABLY GOING TO SAVE YOUR LIFE!
W-WHAT?
STEALTHILY, TIME CREEPS BY ON PADDED FEET-THEN, AFTER WHAT SEEMS HOURS LATER, A DOOR SWINGS OPEN--
YOU'RE COMING WITH US-AND KEEP YOUR MOUTH SHUT OR--
I'LL BE QUIET-DON'T SHOOT!
AND AFTER A WILD RIDE TO A PRIVATE HOSPITAL ON THE EDGE OF TOWN....ONCE AGAIN THAT CERTAIN ROOM--
PROFESSOR HENRY AND DODGE AND--
THESE ARE THE MISSING INVENTORS! THEY HAVE REVEALED ALL THEIR SECRETS UNDER THE BRAIN MACHINE AS YOU SHALL DO IN A MOMENT-
7

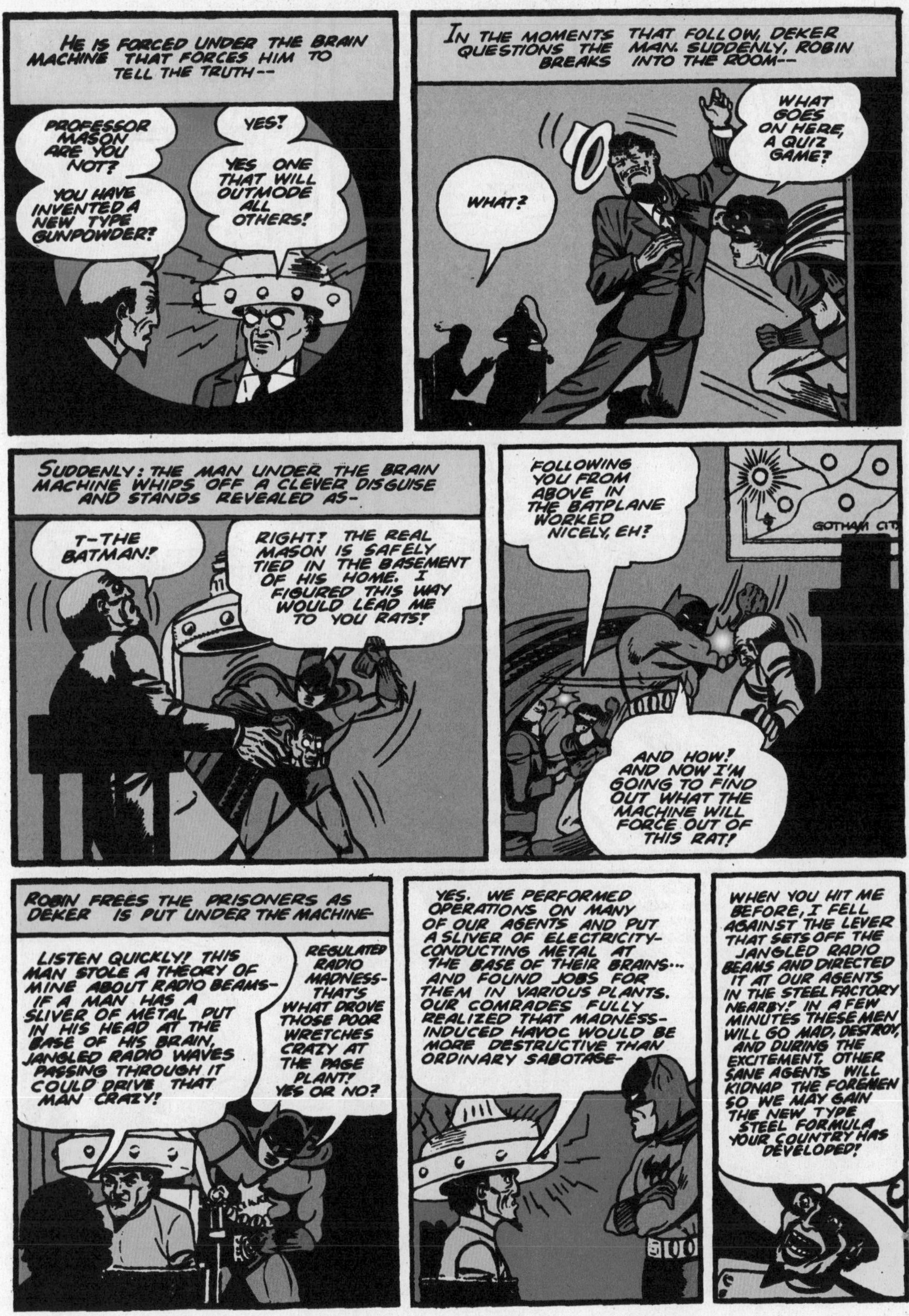
HE IS FORCED UNDER THE BRAIN MACHINE THAT FORCES HIM TO TELL THE TRUTH--
PROFESSOR MASON ARE YOU NOT?
YES!
YOU HAVE INVENTED A NEW TYPE GUNPOWDER?
YES ONE THAT WILL OUTMODE ALL OTHERS!
IN THE MOMENTS THAT FOLLOW, DEKER QUESTIONS THE MAN. SUDDENLY, ROBIN BREAKS INTO THE ROOM--
WHAT GOES ON HERE, A QUIZ GAME?
WHAT?
SUDDENLY: THE MAN UNDER THE BRAIN MACHINE WHIPS OFF A CLEVER DISGUISE AND STANDS REVEALED AS-
T-THE BATMAN!
RIGHT! THE REAL MASON IS SAFELY TIED IN THE BASEMENT OF HIS HOME. I FIGURED THIS WAY WOULD LEAD ME TO YOU RATS!
FOLLOWING YOU FROM ABOVE IN THE BATPLANE WORKED NICELY, EH?
GOTHAM CITY
AND HOW! AND NOW I'M GOING TO FIND OUT WHAT THE MACHINE WILL FORCE OUT OF THIS RAT!
ROBIN FREES THE PRISONERS AS DEKER IS PUT UNDER THE MACHINE-
LISTEN QUICKLY! THIS MAN STOLE A THEORY OF MINE ABOUT RADIO BEAMS- IF A MAN HAS A SLIVER OF METAL PUT IN HIS HEAD AT THE BASE OF HIS BRAIN, JANGLED RADIO WAVES PASSING THROUGH IT COULD DRIVE THAT MAN CRAZY!
REGULATED RADIO MADNESS- THAT'S WHAT DROVE THOSE POOR WRETCHES CRAZY AT THE PAGE PLANT! YES OR NO?
YES. WE PERFORMED OPERATIONS ON MANY OF OUR AGENTS AND PUT A SLIVER OF ELECTRICITY-CONDUCTING METAL AT THE BASE OF THEIR BRAINS... AND FOUND JOBS FOR THEM IN VARIOUS PLANTS. OUR COMRADES FULLY REALIZED THAT MADNESS-INDUCED HAVOC WOULD BE MORE DESTRUCTIVE THAN ORDINARY SABOTAGE-
WHEN YOU HIT ME BEFORE, I FELL AGAINST THE LEVER THAT SETS OFF THE JANGLED RADIO BEAMS AND DIRECTED IT AT OUR AGENTS IN THE STEEL FACTORY NEARBY! IN A FEW MINUTES THESE MEN WILL GO MAD, DESTROY, AND DURING THE EXCITEMENT, OTHER SANE AGENTS WILL KIDNAP THE FOREMEN SO WE MAY GAIN THE NEW TYPE STEEL FORMULA YOUR COUNTRY HAS DEVELOPED!

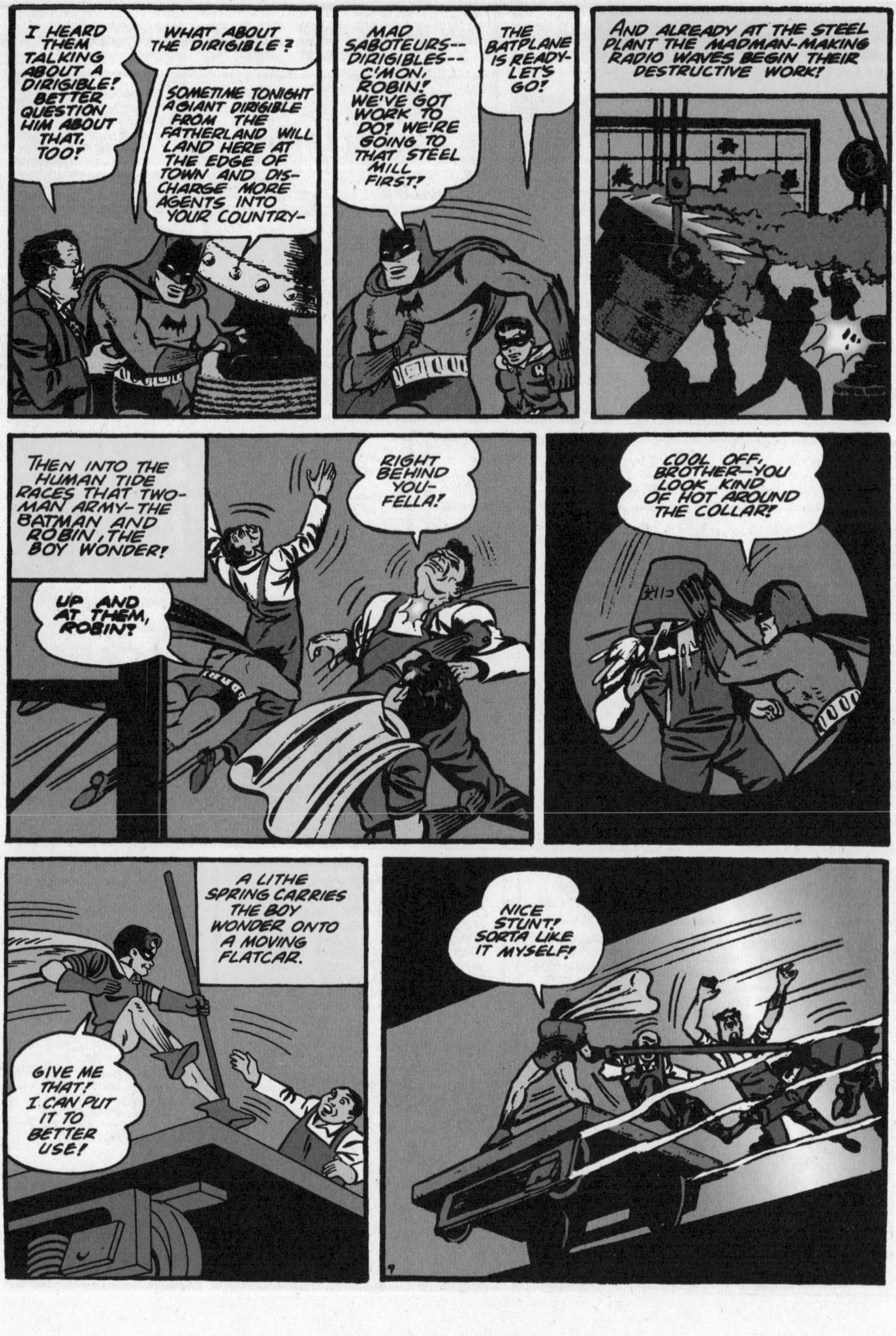
I HEARD THEM TALKING ABOUT A DIRIGIBLE! BETTER QUESTION HIM ABOUT THAT, TOO!
WHAT ABOUT THE DIRIGIBLE?
SOMETIME TONIGHT A GIANT DIRIGIBLE FROM THE FATHERLAND WILL LAND HERE AT THE EDGE OF TOWN AND DISCHARGE MORE AGENTS INTO YOUR COUNTRY-
MAD SABOTEURS-- DIRIGIBLES-- C'MON, ROBIN! WE'VE GOT WORK TO DO! WE'RE GOING TO THAT STEEL MILL FIRST!
THE BATPLANE IS READY- LET'S GO!
AND ALREADY AT THE STEEL PLANT THE MADMAN-MAKING RADIO WAVES BEGIN THEIR DESTRUCTIVE WORK!
THEN INTO THE HUMAN TIDE RACES THAT TWO-MAN ARMY- THE BATMAN AND ROBIN, THE BOY WONDER!
RIGHT BEHIND YOU- FELLA!
UP AND AT THEM, ROBIN!
COOL OFF, BROTHER-YOU LOOK KIND OF HOT AROUND THE COLLAR!
A LITHE SPRING CARRIES THE BOY WONDER ONTO A MOVING FLATCAR.
GIVE ME THAT! I CAN PUT IT TO BETTER USE!
NICE STUNT! SORTA LIKE IT MYSELF!

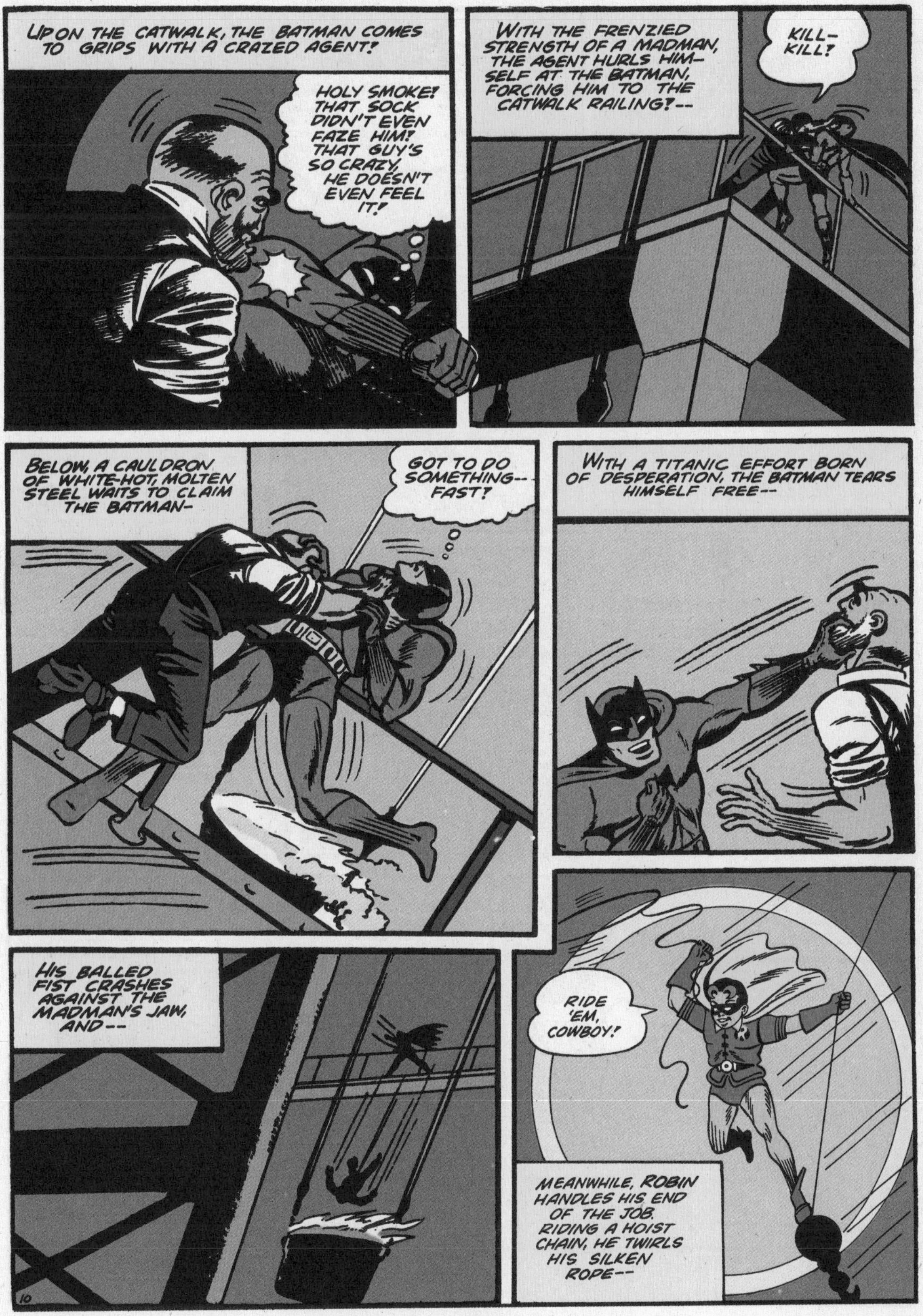
UP ON THE CATWALK, THE BATMAN COMES TO GRIPS WITH A CRAZED AGENT!
HOLY SMOKE! THAT SOCK DIDN'T EVEN FAZE HIM! THAT GUY'S SO CRAZY, HE DOESN'T EVEN FEEL IT!
WITH THE FRENZIED STRENGTH OF A MADMAN, THE AGENT HURLS HIMSELF AT THE BATMAN, FORCING HIM TO THE CATWALK RAILING!--
KILL-KILL!
BELOW, A CAULDRON OF WHITE-HOT, MOLTEN STEEL WAITS TO CLAIM THE BATMAN-
GOT TO DO SOMETHING--FAST!
WITH A TITANIC EFFORT BORN OF DESPERATION, THE BATMAN TEARS HIMSELF FREE--
HIS BALLED FIST CRASHES AGAINST THE MADMAN'S JAW, AND--
10
RIDE 'EM, COWBOY!
MEANWHILE, ROBIN HANDLES HIS END OF THE JOB. RIDING A HOIST CHAIN, HE TWIRLS HIS SILKEN ROPE--

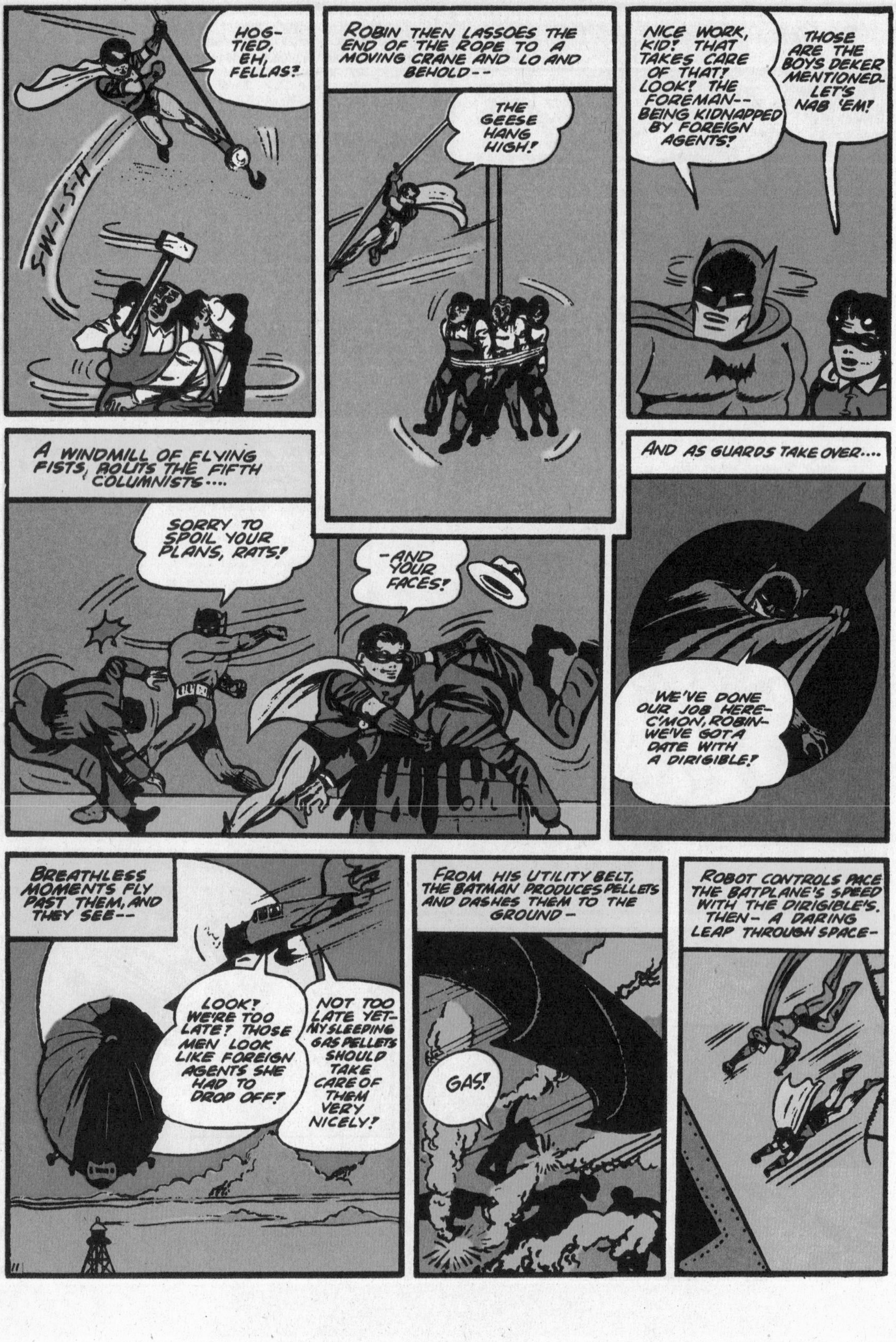
HOG-TIED, EH, FELLAS?
SW-I-S-H
ROBIN THEN LASSOES THE END OF THE ROPE TO A MOVING CRANE AND LO AND BEHOLD--
THE GEESE HANG HIGH!
NICE WORK, KID! THAT TAKES CARE OF THAT! LOOK! THE FOREMAN-- BEING KIDNAPPED BY FOREIGN AGENTS!
THOSE ARE THE BOYS DEKER MENTIONED-LET'S NAB 'EM!
A WINDMILL OF FLYING FISTS, ROUTS THE FIFTH COLUMNISTS....
SORRY TO SPOIL YOUR PLANS, RATS!
-AND YOUR FACES!
AND AS GUARDS TAKE OVER....
WE'VE DONE OUR JOB HERE-C'MON, ROBIN-WE'VE GOT A DATE WITH A DIRIGIBLE!
BREATHLESS MOMENTS FLY PAST THEM, AND THEY SEE--
LOOK! WE'RE TOO LATE! THOSE MEN LOOK LIKE FOREIGN AGENTS SHE HAD TO DROP OFF!
NOT TOO LATE YET-MY SLEEPING GAS PELLETS SHOULD TAKE CARE OF THEM VERY NICELY!
FROM HIS UTILITY BELT, THE BATMAN PRODUCES PELLETS AND DASHES THEM TO THE GROUND-
GAS!
ROBOT CONTROLS PACE THE BATPLANE'S SPEED WITH THE DIRIGIBLE'S. THEN- A DARING LEAP THROUGH SPACE-

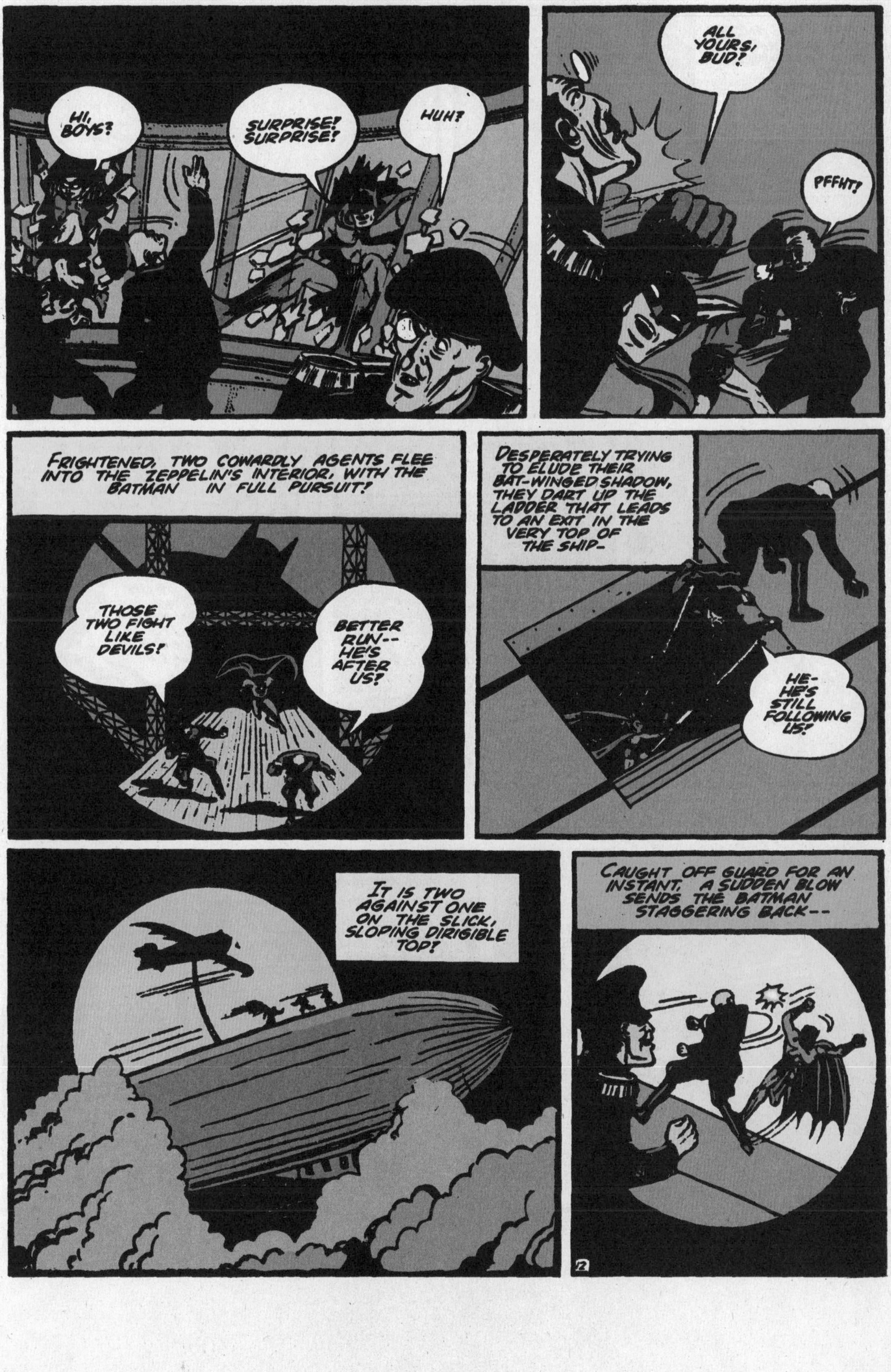
HI, BOYS!
SURPRISE! SURPRISE!
HUH?
ALL YOURS, BUD!
PFFHT!
FRIGHTENED, TWO COWARDLY AGENTS FLEE INTO THE ZEPPELIN'S INTERIOR, WITH THE BATMAN IN FULL PURSUIT!
THOSE TWO FIGHT LIKE DEVILS!
BETTER RUN-- HE'S AFTER US!
DESPERATELY TRYING TO ELUDE THEIR BAT-WINGED SHADOW, THEY DART UP THE LADDER THAT LEADS TO AN EXIT IN THE VERY TOP OF THE SHIP-
HE- HE'S STILL FOLLOWING US!
IT IS TWO AGAINST ONE ON THE SLICK, SLOPING DIRIGIBLE TOP!
CAUGHT OFF GUARD FOR AN INSTANT, A SUDDEN BLOW SENDS THE BATMAN STAGGERING BACK--
12

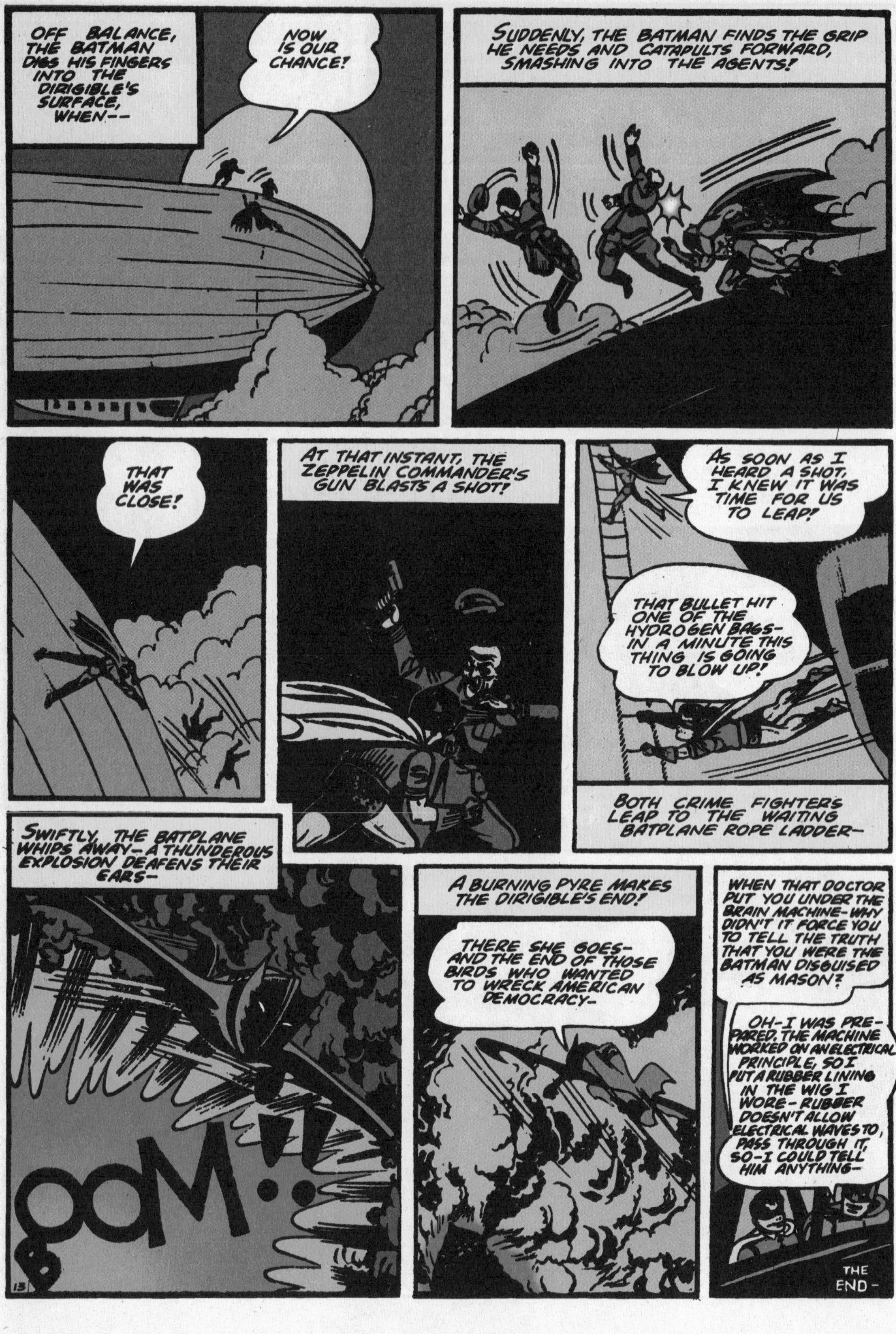

OFF BALANCE, THE BATMAN DIGS HIS FINGERS INTO THE DIRIGIBLE'S SURFACE, WHEN--
NOW IS OUR CHANCE!
SUDDENLY, THE BATMAN FINDS THE GRIP HE NEEDS AND CATAPULTS FORWARD, SMASHING INTO THE AGENTS!
THAT WAS CLOSE!
AT THAT INSTANT, THE ZEPPELIN COMMANDER'S GUN BLASTS A SHOT!
AS SOON AS I HEARD A SHOT, I KNEW IT WAS TIME FOR US TO LEAP!
THAT BULLET HIT ONE OF THE HYDROGEN BAGS- IN A MINUTE THIS THING IS GOING TO BLOW UP!
BOTH CRIME FIGHTERS LEAP TO THE WAITING BATPLANE ROPE LADDER-
SWIFTLY, THE BATPLANE WHIPS AWAY- A THUNDEROUS EXPLOSION DEAFENS THEIR EARS-
BOOM!!
13
A BURNING PYRE MAKES THE DIRIGIBLE'S END!
THERE SHE GOES- AND THE END OF THOSE BIRDS WHO WANTED TO WRECK AMERICAN DEMOCRACY-
WHEN THAT DOCTOR PUT YOU UNDER THE BRAIN MACHINE- WHY DIDN'T IT FORCE YOU TO TELL THE TRUTH THAT YOU WERE THE BATMAN DISGUISED AS MASON?
OH- I WAS PREPARED. THE MACHINE WORKED ON AN ELECTRICAL PRINCIPLE, SO I PUT A RUBBER LINING IN THE WIG I WORE- RUBBER DOESN'T ALLOW ELECTRICAL WAVES TO, PASS THROUGH IT, SO- I COULD TELL HIM ANYTHING-
THE END-

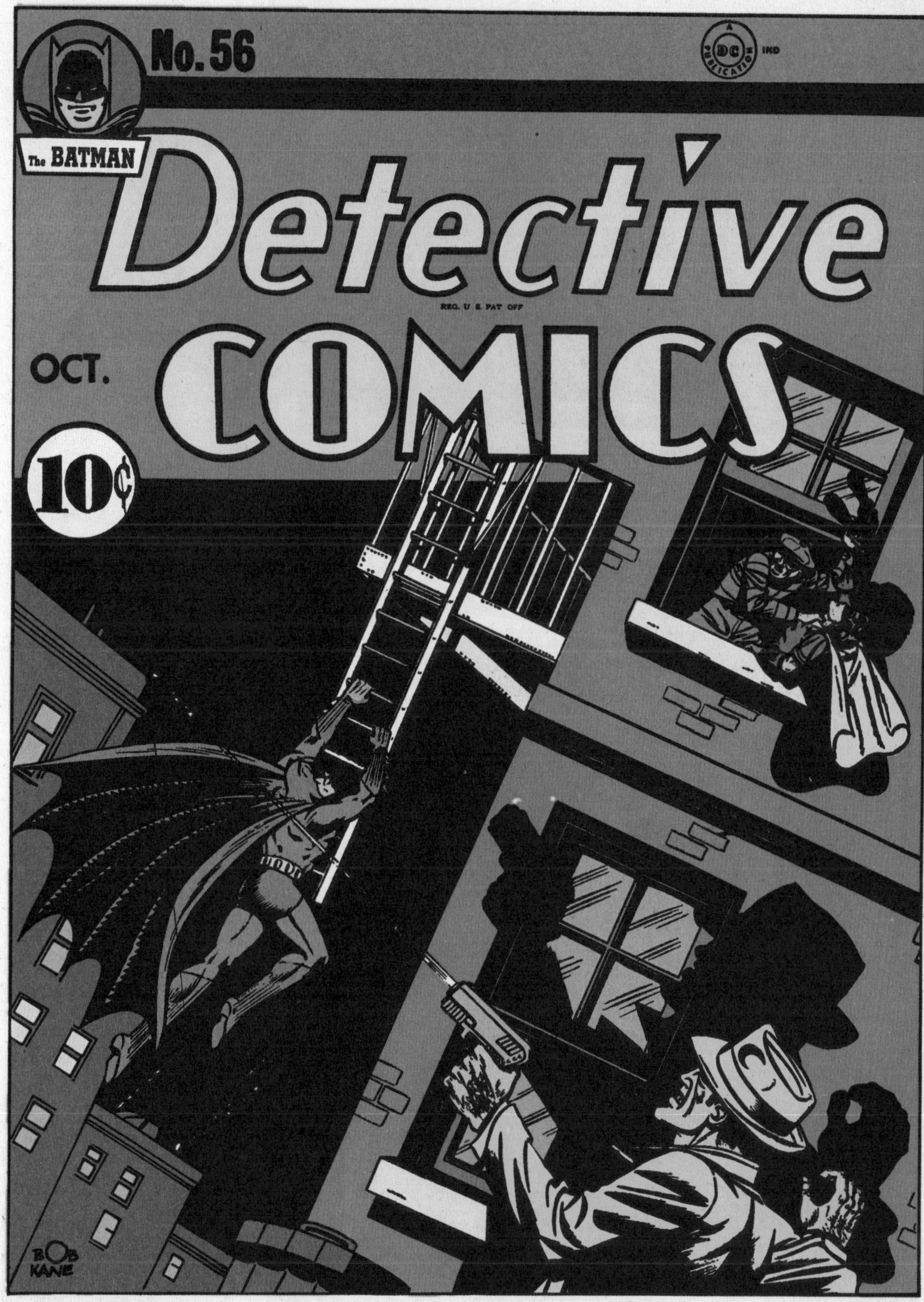
No. 56
A DC PUBLICATION IND
The BATMAN
Detective
REG. U. S. PAT. OFF
COMICS
OCT.
10¢
BOB KANE

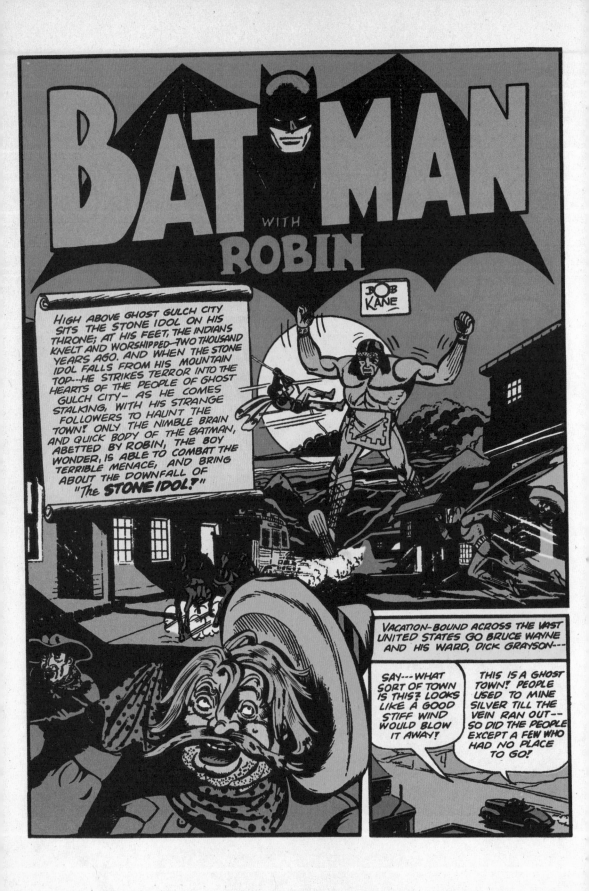

BAT MAN

WITH ROBIN

BOB KANE

HIGH ABOVE GHOST GULCH CITY SITS THE STONE IDOL ON HIS THRONE; AT HIS FEET, THE INDIANS KNELT AND WORSHIPPED—TWO THOUSAND YEARS AGO. AND WHEN THE STONE IDOL FALLS FROM HIS MOUNTAIN TOP—HE STRIKES TERROR INTO THE HEARTS OF THE PEOPLE OF GHOST GULCH CITY— AS HE COMES STALKING, WITH HIS STRANGE FOLLOWERS TO HAUNT THE TOWN! ONLY THE NIMBLE BRAIN AND QUICK BODY OF THE BATMAN, ABETTED BY ROBIN, THE BOY WONDER, IS ABLE TO COMBAT THE TERRIBLE MENACE, AND BRING ABOUT THE DOWNFALL OF "The STONE IDOL?"

VACATION-BOUND ACROSS THE VAST UNITED STATES GO BRUCE WAYNE AND HIS WARD, DICK GRAYSON---

SAY---WHAT SORT OF TOWN IS THIS? LOOKS LIKE A GOOD STIFF WIND WOULD BLOW IT AWAY!

THIS IS A GHOST TOWN! PEOPLE USED TO MINE SILVER TILL THE VEIN RAN OUT-- SO DID THE PEOPLE EXCEPT A FEW WHO HAD NO PLACE TO GO!

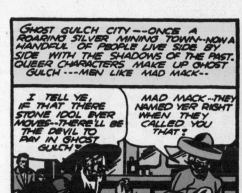

GHOST GULCH CITY--ONCE A ROARING SILVER MINING TOWN--NOW A HANDFUL OF PEOPLE LIVE SIDE BY SIDE WITH THE SHADOWS OF THE PAST. QUEER CHARACTERS MAKE UP GHOST GULCH ---MEN LIKE MAD MACK--

I TELL YE, IF THAT THERE STONE IDOL EVER MOVES--THERE'LL BE THE DEVIL TO PAY IN GHOST GULCH!

MAD MACK--THEY NAMED YER RIGHT WHEN THEY CALLED YOU THAT!

MAYBE HE SPEAKS THE TRUTH!

YOU'RE RIGHT-- DON'T FORGET WHAT I WARNED YA-- WATCH OUT FOR THE STONE IDOL! AND WITH THIS STORM COMIN' ON, HE MAY CRASH AT ANY TIME!

WE'D LIKE A ROOM, PLEASE.

YEP--SURE YOU WOULD! LOOKS LIKE A BAD STORM COMIN'!

AS THE STORM BREAKS OVER THE TOWN, A LARGE TRUCK CRAWLS UP THE ROAD INTO THE MOUNTAINS--

IT'S A NIGHT FOR THE DEVIL!

SHUT UP AND KEEP YOUR EYES ON THE ROAD!

SUDDENLY THE ROAD STARTS GIVING WAY, AND A GIANT HOLE YAWNS AS THE TRUCK SPEEDS FORWARD--

WATCH OUT! THE ROAD'S GONE!

LIGHTNING BLASTS AT THE VERY FEET OF THE STONE IDOL!

AND AFTER A 2000-YEAR REIGN, THE GOD OF STONE PLUNGES FROM HIS MOUNTAIN!

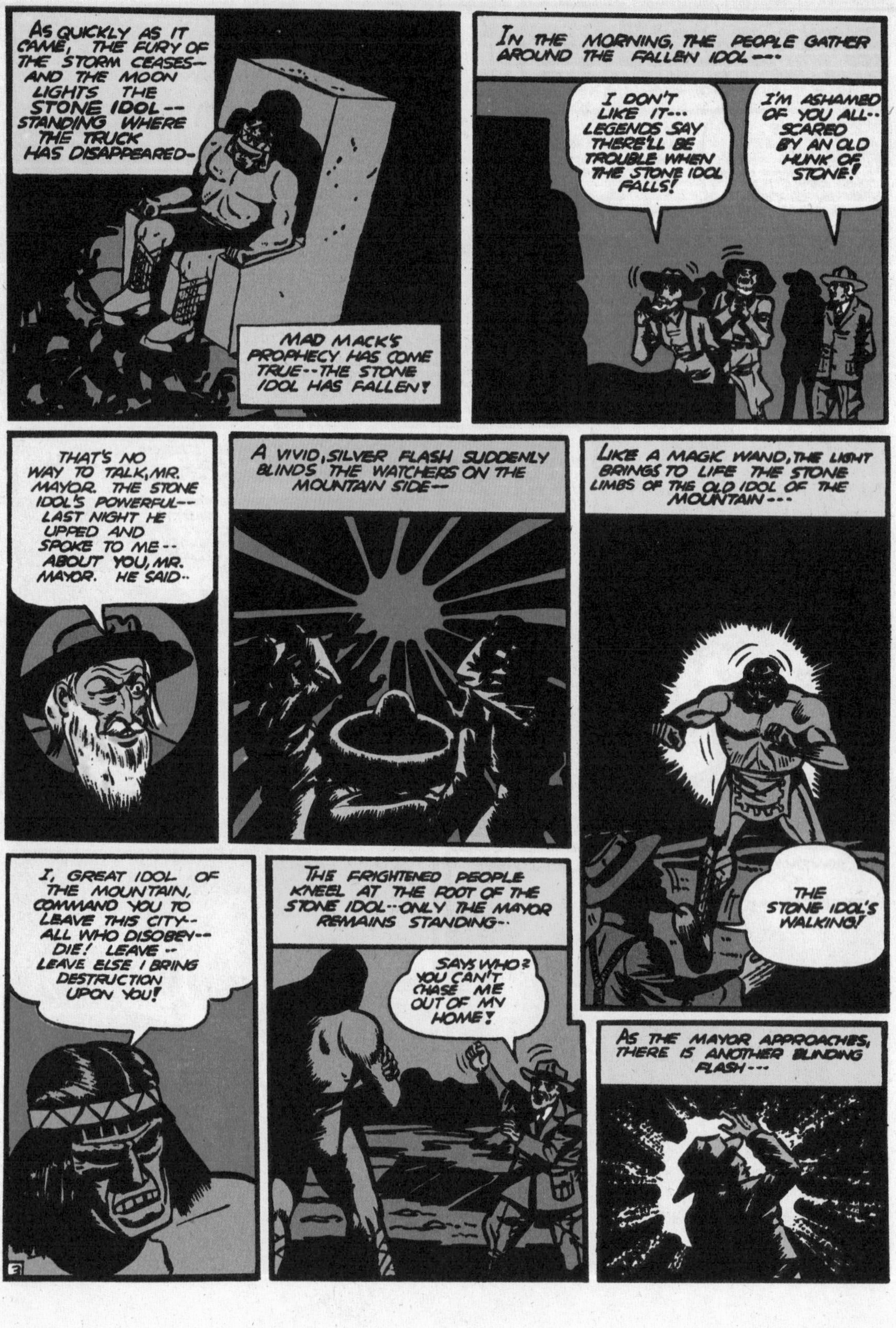
AS QUICKLY AS IT CAME, THE FURY OF THE STORM CEASES-- AND THE MOON LIGHTS THE STONE IDOL-- STANDING WHERE THE TRUCK HAS DISAPPEARED-
MAD MACK'S PROPHECY HAS COME TRUE--THE STONE IDOL HAS FALLEN!
IN THE MORNING, THE PEOPLE GATHER AROUND THE FALLEN IDOL---
I DON'T LIKE IT--- LEGENDS SAY THERE'LL BE TROUBLE WHEN THE STONE IDOL FALLS!
I'M ASHAMED OF YOU ALL-- SCARED BY AN OLD HUNK OF STONE!
THAT'S NO WAY TO TALK, MR. MAYOR. THE STONE IDOL'S POWERFUL-- LAST NIGHT HE UPPED AND SPOKE TO ME-- ABOUT YOU, MR. MAYOR. HE SAID--
A VIVID, SILVER FLASH SUDDENLY BLINDS THE WATCHERS ON THE MOUNTAIN SIDE--
LIKE A MAGIC WAND, THE LIGHT BRINGS TO LIFE THE STONE LIMBS OF THE OLD IDOL OF THE MOUNTAIN---
THE STONE IDOL'S WALKING!
I, GREAT IDOL OF THE MOUNTAIN, COMMAND YOU TO LEAVE THIS CITY-- ALL WHO DISOBEY-- DIE! LEAVE-- LEAVE ELSE I BRING DESTRUCTION UPON YOU!
THE FRIGHTENED PEOPLE KNEEL AT THE FOOT OF THE STONE IDOL--ONLY THE MAYOR REMAINS STANDING--
SAYS WHO? YOU CAN'T CHASE ME OUT OF MY HOME!
AS THE MAYOR APPROACHES, THERE IS ANOTHER BLINDING FLASH---
3

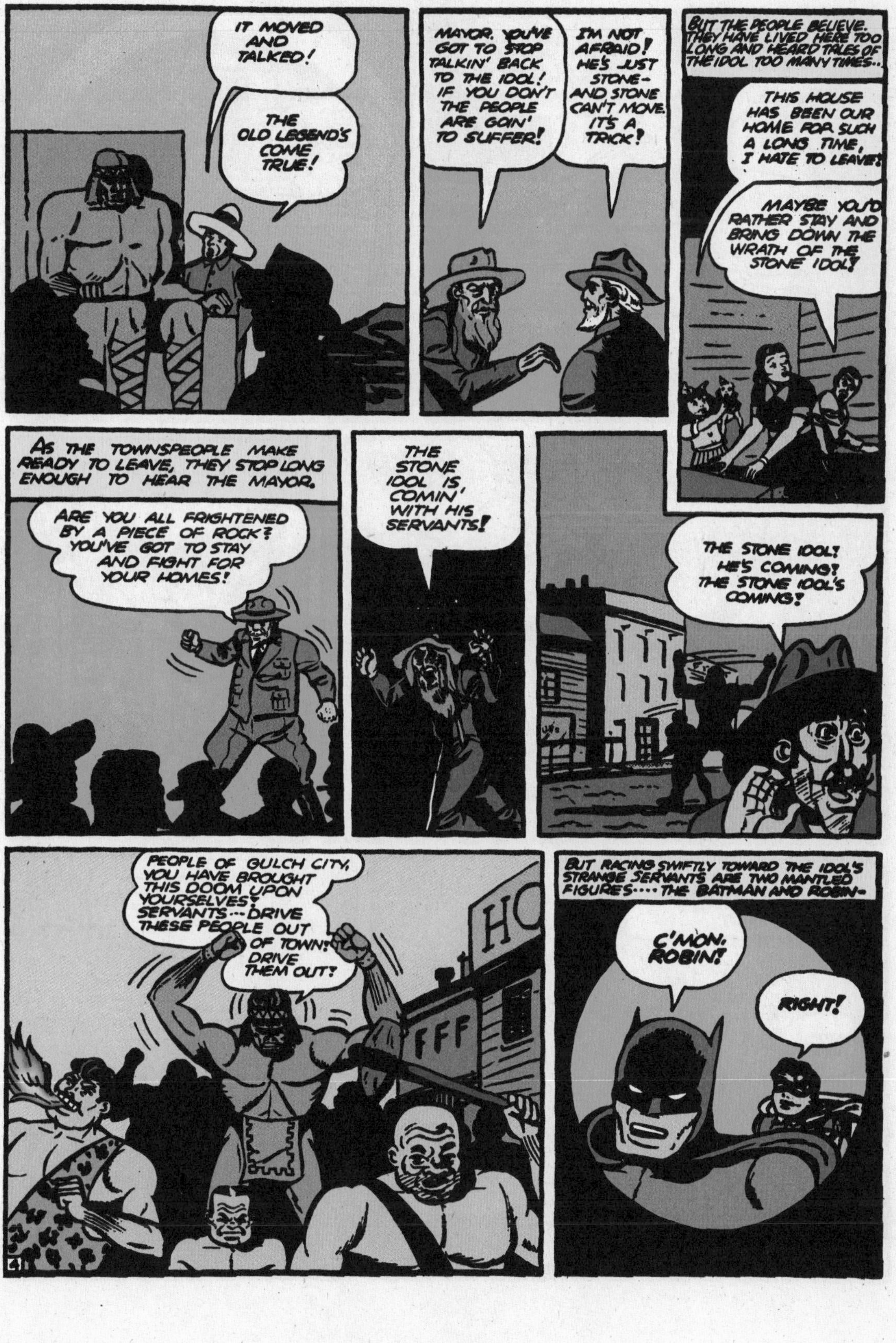
IT MOVED AND TALKED!
THE OLD LEGEND'S COME TRUE!
MAYOR, YOU'VE GOT TO STOP TALKIN' BACK TO THE IDOL! IF YOU DON'T THE PEOPLE ARE GOIN' TO SUFFER!
I'M NOT AFRAID! HE'S JUST STONE-AND STONE CAN'T MOVE. IT'S A TRICK!
BUT THE PEOPLE BELIEVE. THEY HAVE LIVED HERE TOO LONG AND HEARD TALES OF THE IDOL TOO MANY TIMES..
THIS HOUSE HAS BEEN OUR HOME FOR SUCH A LONG TIME, I HATE TO LEAVE!
MAYBE YOU'D RATHER STAY AND BRING DOWN THE WRATH OF THE STONE IDOL!
AS THE TOWNSPEOPLE MAKE READY TO LEAVE, THEY STOP LONG ENOUGH TO HEAR THE MAYOR.
ARE YOU ALL FRIGHTENED BY A PIECE OF ROCK? YOU'VE GOT TO STAY AND FIGHT FOR YOUR HOMES!
THE STONE IDOL IS, COMIN' WITH HIS SERVANTS!
THE STONE IDOL! HE'S COMING! THE STONE IDOL'S COMING!
PEOPLE OF GULCH CITY, YOU HAVE BROUGHT THIS DOOM UPON YOURSELVES! SERVANTS--DRIVE THESE PEOPLE OUT OF TOWN! DRIVE THEM OUT!
HO
FFF
BUT RACING SWIFTLY TOWARD THE IDOL'S STRANGE SERVANTS ARE TWO MANTLED FIGURES.... THE BATMAN AND ROBIN-
C'MON, ROBIN!
RIGHT!

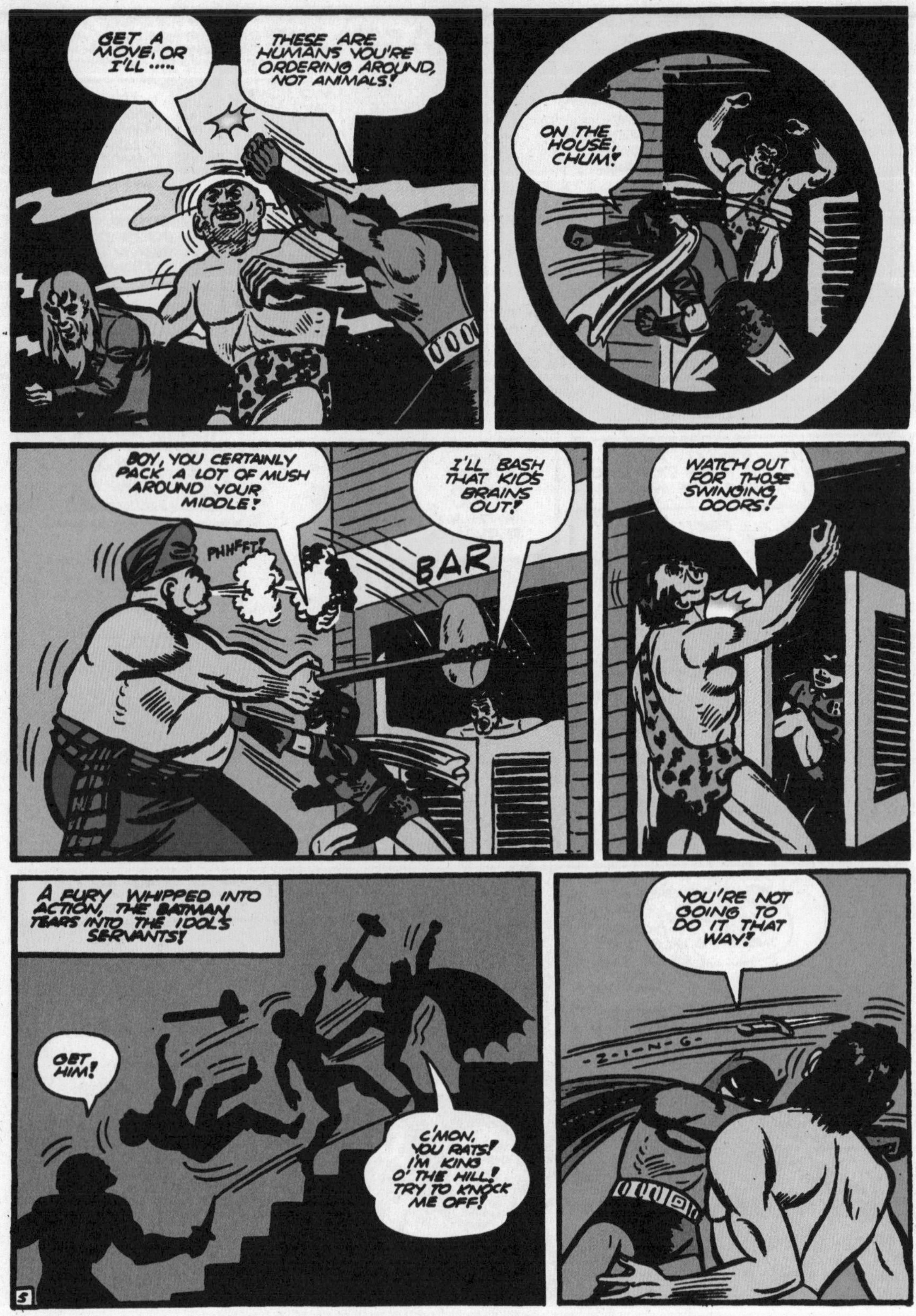
GET A MOVE, OR I'LL.....
THESE ARE HUMANS YOU'RE ORDERING AROUND, NOT ANIMALS!
ON THE HOUSE, CHUM!
BOY, YOU CERTAINLY PACK A LOT OF MUSH AROUND YOUR MIDDLE!
PHHFFT!
I'LL BASH THAT KIDS BRAINS OUT!
BAR
WATCH OUT FOR THOSE SWINGING DOORS!
A FURY WHIPPED INTO ACTION, THE BATMAN TEARS INTO THE IDOL'S SERVANTS!
GET HIM!
C'MON, YOU RATS! I'M KING O' THE HILL! TRY TO KNOCK ME OFF!
5
YOU'RE NOT GOING TO DO IT THAT WAY!
-Z-I-N-G-

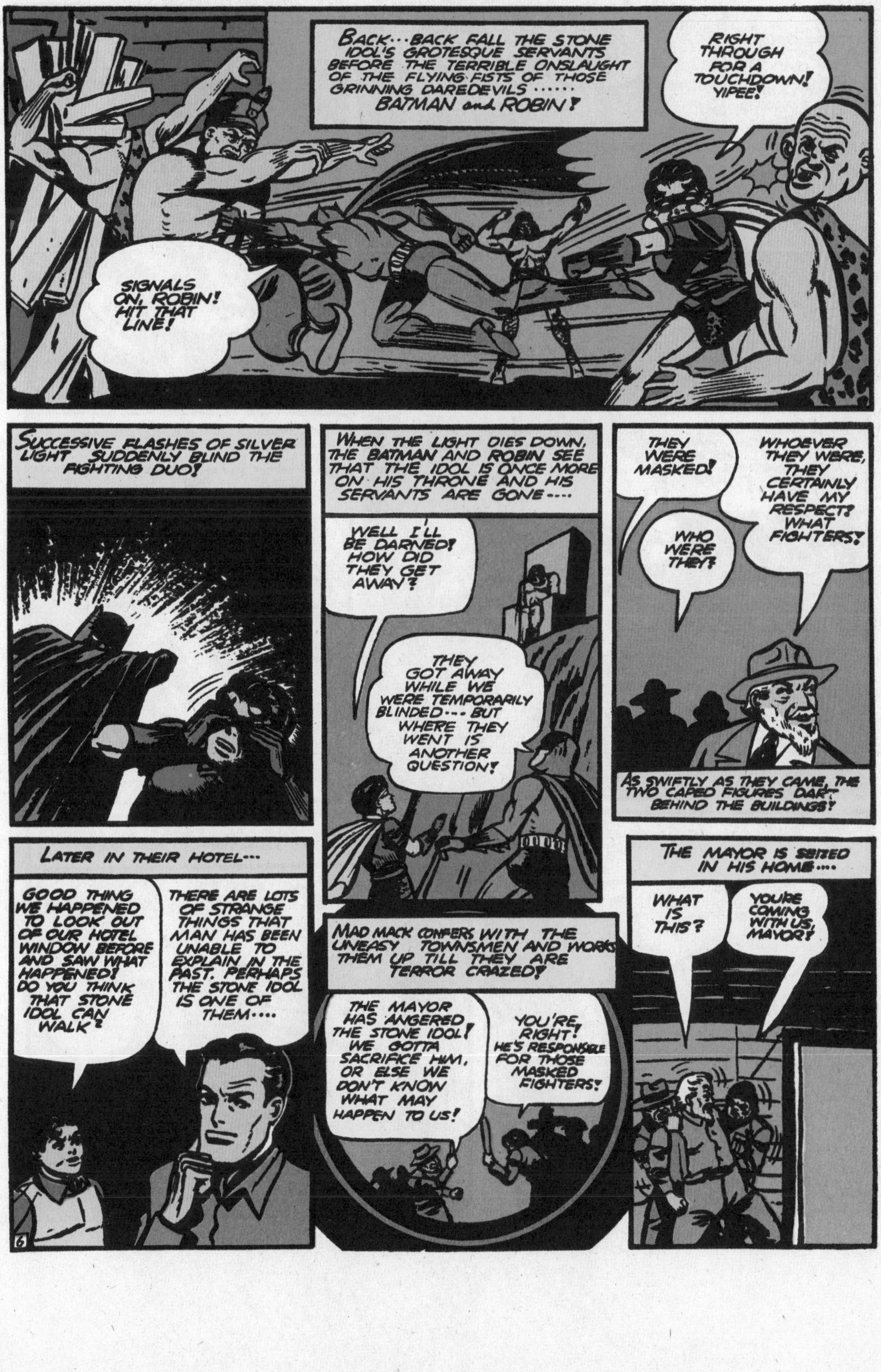

BACK...BACK FALL THE STONE IDOL'S GROTESQUE SERVANTS BEFORE THE TERRIBLE ONSLAUGHT OF THE FLYING FISTS OF THOSE GRINNING DAREDEVILS...... BATMAN and ROBIN!
RIGHT THROUGH FOR A TOUCHDOWN! YIPEE!
SIGNALS ON, ROBIN! HIT THAT LINE!
SUCCESSIVE FLASHES OF SILVER LIGHT SUDDENLY BLIND THE FIGHTING DUO!
WHEN THE LIGHT DIES DOWN, THE BATMAN AND ROBIN SEE THAT THE IDOL IS ONCE MORE ON HIS THRONE AND HIS SERVANTS ARE GONE----
WELL I'LL BE DARNED! HOW DID THEY GET AWAY?
THEY GOT AWAY WHILE WE WERE TEMPORARILY BLINDED--- BUT WHERE THEY WENT IS ANOTHER QUESTION!
THEY WERE MASKED!
WHO WERE THEY?
WHOEVER THEY WERE, THEY CERTAINLY HAVE MY RESPECT? WHAT FIGHTERS!
AS SWIFTLY AS THEY CAME, THE TWO CAPED FIGURES DART BEHIND THE BUILDINGS!
LATER IN THEIR HOTEL---
GOOD THING WE HAPPENED TO LOOK OUT OF OUR HOTEL WINDOW BEFORE AND SAW WHAT HAPPENED! DO YOU THINK THAT STONE IDOL CAN WALK?
THERE ARE LOTS OF STRANGE THINGS THAT MAN HAS BEEN UNABLE TO EXPLAIN IN THE PAST. PERHAPS THE STONE IDOL IS ONE OF THEM....
6
MAD MACK CONFERS WITH THE UNEASY TOWNSMEN AND WORKS THEM UP TILL THEY ARE TERROR CRAZED!
THE MAYOR HAS ANGERED THE STONE IDOL! WE GOTTA SACRIFICE HIM, OR ELSE WE DON'T KNOW WHAT MAY HAPPEN TO US!
YOU'RE RIGHT! HE'S RESPONSIBLE FOR THOSE MASKED FIGHTERS!
THE MAYOR IS SEIZED IN HIS HOME....
WHAT IS THIS?
YOU'RE COMING WITH US, MAYOR!

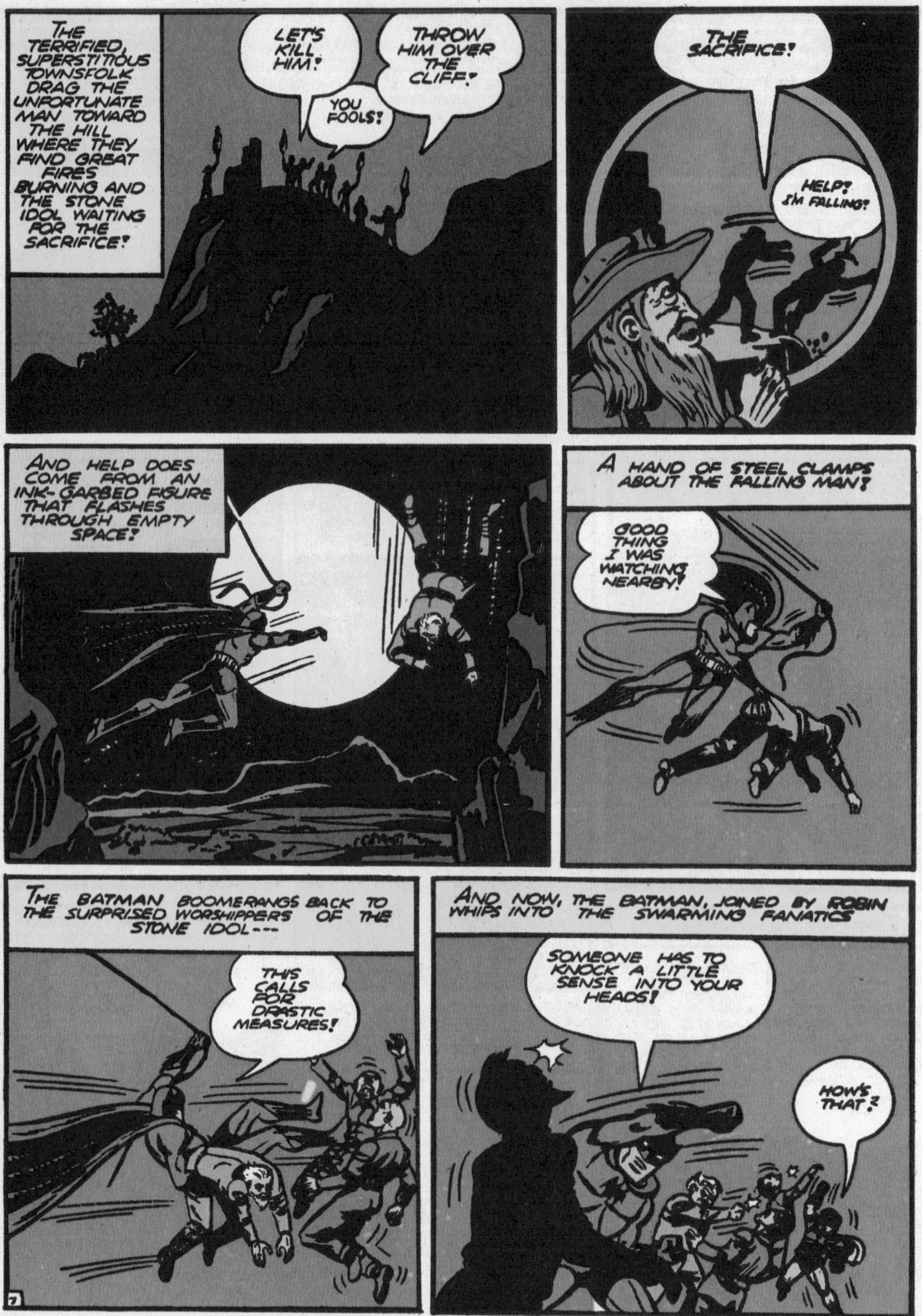
THE TERRIFIED, SUPERSTITIOUS TOWNSFOLK DRAG THE UNFORTUNATE MAN TOWARD THE HILL WHERE THEY FIND GREAT FIRES BURNING AND THE STONE IDOL WAITING FOR THE SACRIFICE!
LET'S KILL HIM!
THROW HIM OVER THE CLIFF!
YOU FOOLS!
THE SACRIFICE!
HELP! I'M FALLING!
AND HELP DOES COME FROM AN INK-GARBED FIGURE THAT FLASHES THROUGH EMPTY SPACE!
A HAND OF STEEL CLAMPS ABOUT THE FALLING MAN!
GOOD THING I WAS WATCHING NEARBY!
THE BATMAN BOOMERANGS BACK TO THE SURPRISED WORSHIPPERS OF THE STONE IDOL---
THIS CALLS FOR DRASTIC MEASURES!
7
AND NOW, THE BATMAN, JOINED BY ROBIN WHIPS INTO THE SWARMING FANATICS
SOMEONE HAS TO KNOCK A LITTLE SENSE INTO YOUR HEADS!
HOW'S THAT?

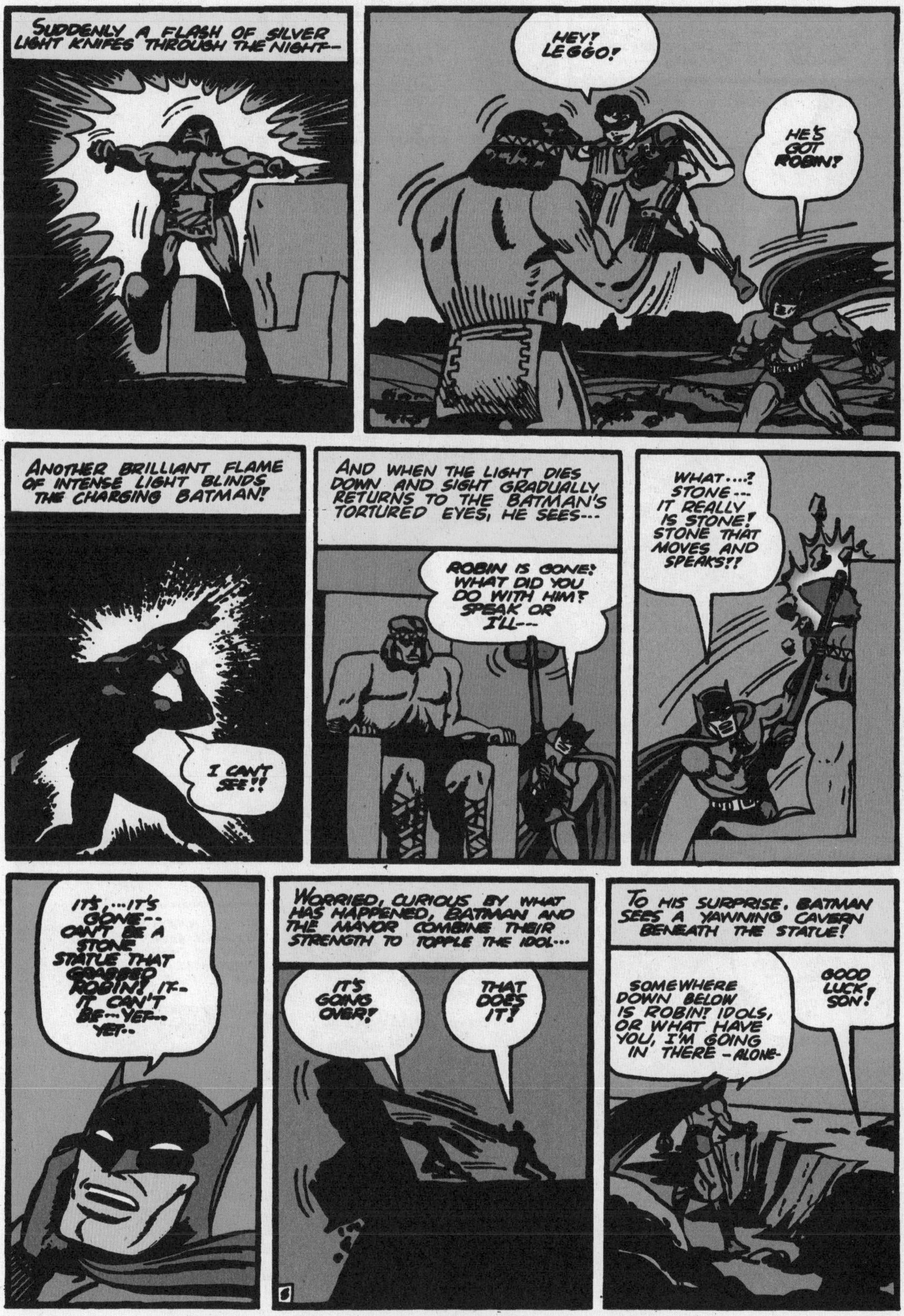
SUDDENLY A FLASH OF SILVER LIGHT KNIFES THROUGH THE NIGHT--
HEY! LEGGO!
HE'S GOT ROBIN!
ANOTHER BRILLIANT FLAME OF INTENSE LIGHT BLINDS THE CHARGING BATMAN!
I CAN'T SEE!!
AND WHEN THE LIGHT DIES DOWN AND SIGHT GRADUALLY RETURNS TO THE BATMAN'S TORTURED EYES, HE SEES---
ROBIN IS GONE! WHAT DID YOU DO WITH HIM? SPEAK OR I'LL--
WHAT....? STONE--- IT REALLY IS STONE! STONE THAT MOVES AND SPEAKS?!
IT'S,...IT'S GONE-- CAN'T BE A STONE STATUE THAT GRABBED ROBIN! IT-- IT CAN'T BE--YET-- YET--
WORRIED, CURIOUS BY WHAT HAS HAPPENED, BATMAN AND THE MAYOR COMBINE THEIR STRENGTH TO TOPPLE THE IDOL...
IT'S GOING OVER!
THAT DOES IT!
TO HIS SURPRISE, BATMAN SEES A YAWNING CAVERN BENEATH THE STATUE!
SOMEWHERE DOWN BELOW IS ROBIN! IDOLS, OR WHAT HAVE YOU, I'M GOING IN THERE -ALONE-
GOOD LUCK SON!

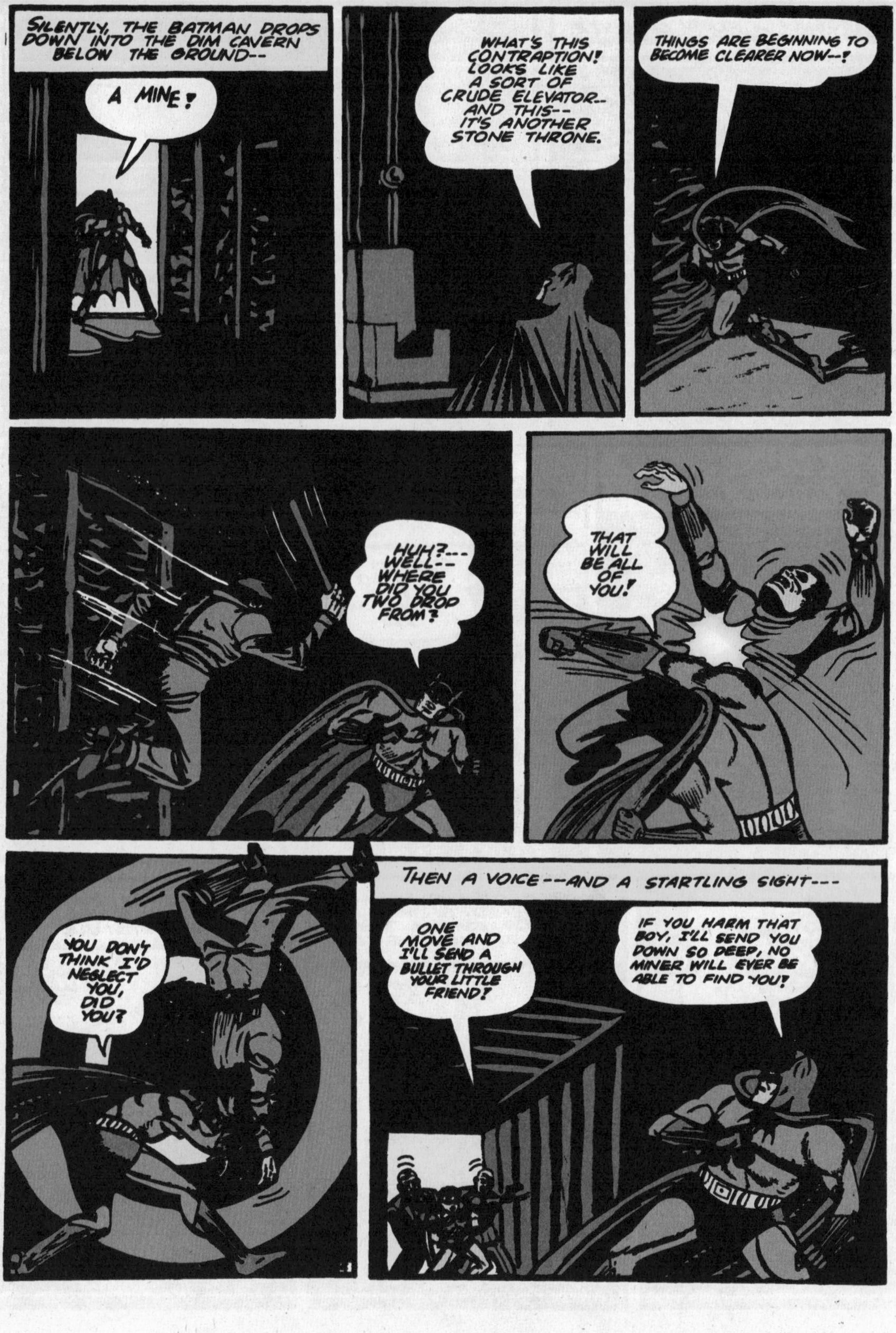
SILENTLY, THE BATMAN DROPS DOWN INTO THE DIM CAVERN BELOW THE GROUND--
A MINE!
WHAT'S THIS CONTRAPTION! LOOKS LIKE A SORT OF CRUDE ELEVATOR-- AND THIS-- IT'S ANOTHER STONE THRONE.
THINGS ARE BEGINNING TO BECOME CLEARER NOW--!
HUH?--- WELL-- WHERE DID YOU TWO DROP FROM?
THAT WILL BE ALL OF YOU!
YOU DON'T THINK I'D NEGLECT YOU, DID YOU?
THEN A VOICE--AND A STARTLING SIGHT---
ONE MOVE AND I'LL SEND A BULLET THROUGH YOUR LITTLE FRIEND!
IF YOU HARM THAT BOY, I'LL SEND YOU DOWN SO DEEP, NO MINER WILL EVER BE ABLE TO FIND YOU!

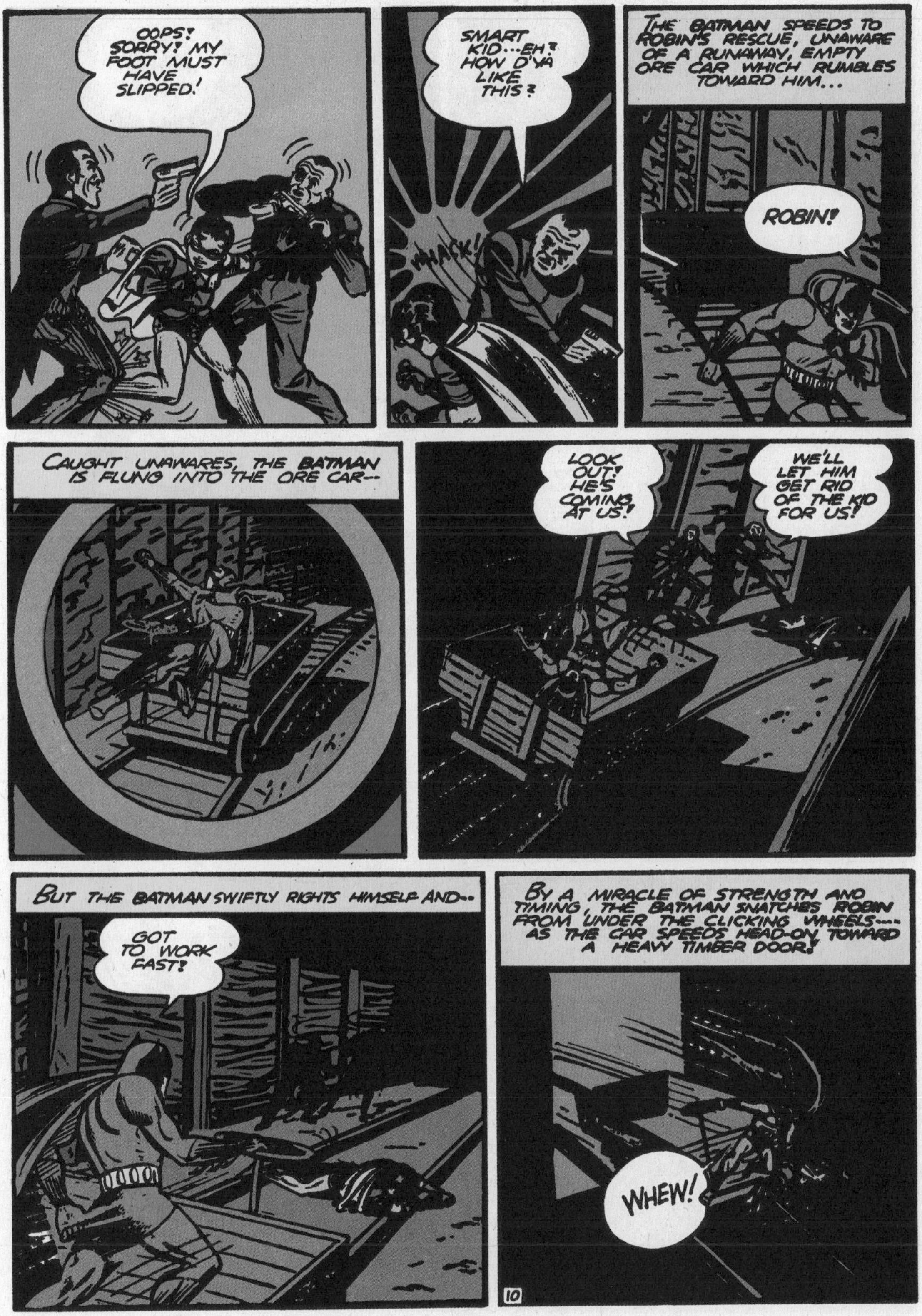
OOPS! SORRY! MY FOOT MUST HAVE SLIPPED!
SMART KID...EH? HOW D'YA LIKE THIS?
WHACK!
THE BATMAN SPEEDS TO ROBIN'S RESCUE, UNAWARE OF A RUNAWAY, EMPTY ORE CAR WHICH RUMBLES TOWARD HIM...
ROBIN!
CAUGHT UNAWARES, THE BATMAN IS FLUNG INTO THE ORE CAR--
LOOK OUT! HE'S COMING AT US!
WE'LL LET HIM GET RID OF THE KID FOR US!
BUT THE BATMAN SWIFTLY RIGHTS HIMSELF AND--
GOT TO WORK FAST!
BY A MIRACLE OF STRENGTH AND TIMING, THE BATMAN SNATCHES ROBIN FROM UNDER THE CLICKING WHEELS.... AS THE CAR SPEEDS HEAD-ON TOWARD A HEAVY TIMBER DOOR!
WHEW!
10

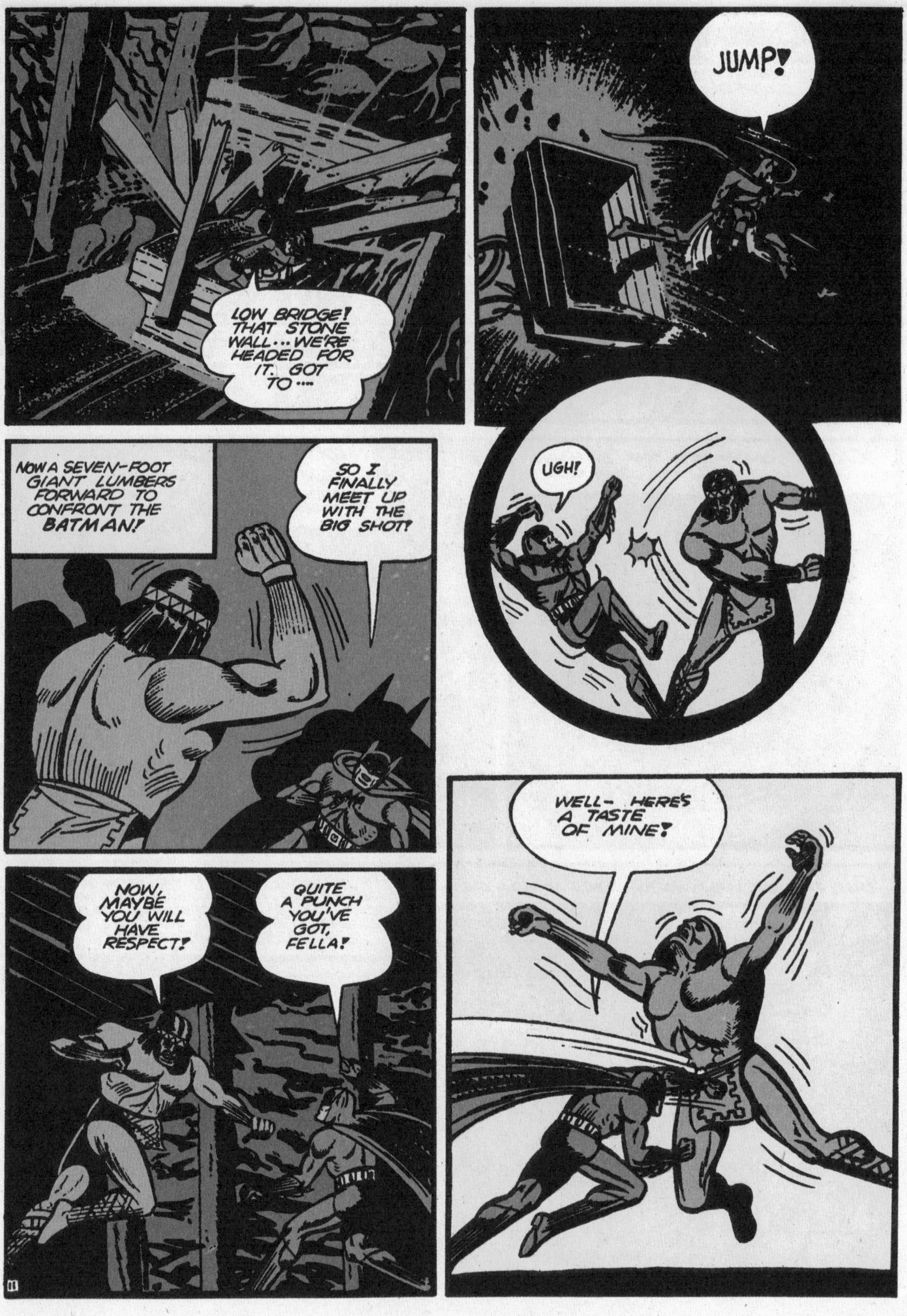
LOW BRIDGE! THAT STONE WALL... WE'RE HEADED FOR IT. GOT TO....
JUMP!
NOW A SEVEN-FOOT GIANT LUMBERS FORWARD TO CONFRONT THE BATMAN!
SO I FINALLY MEET UP WITH THE BIG SHOT?
UGH!
NOW, MAYBE YOU WILL HAVE RESPECT!
QUITE A PUNCH YOU'VE GOT, FELLA!
WELL- HERE'S A TASTE OF MINE!

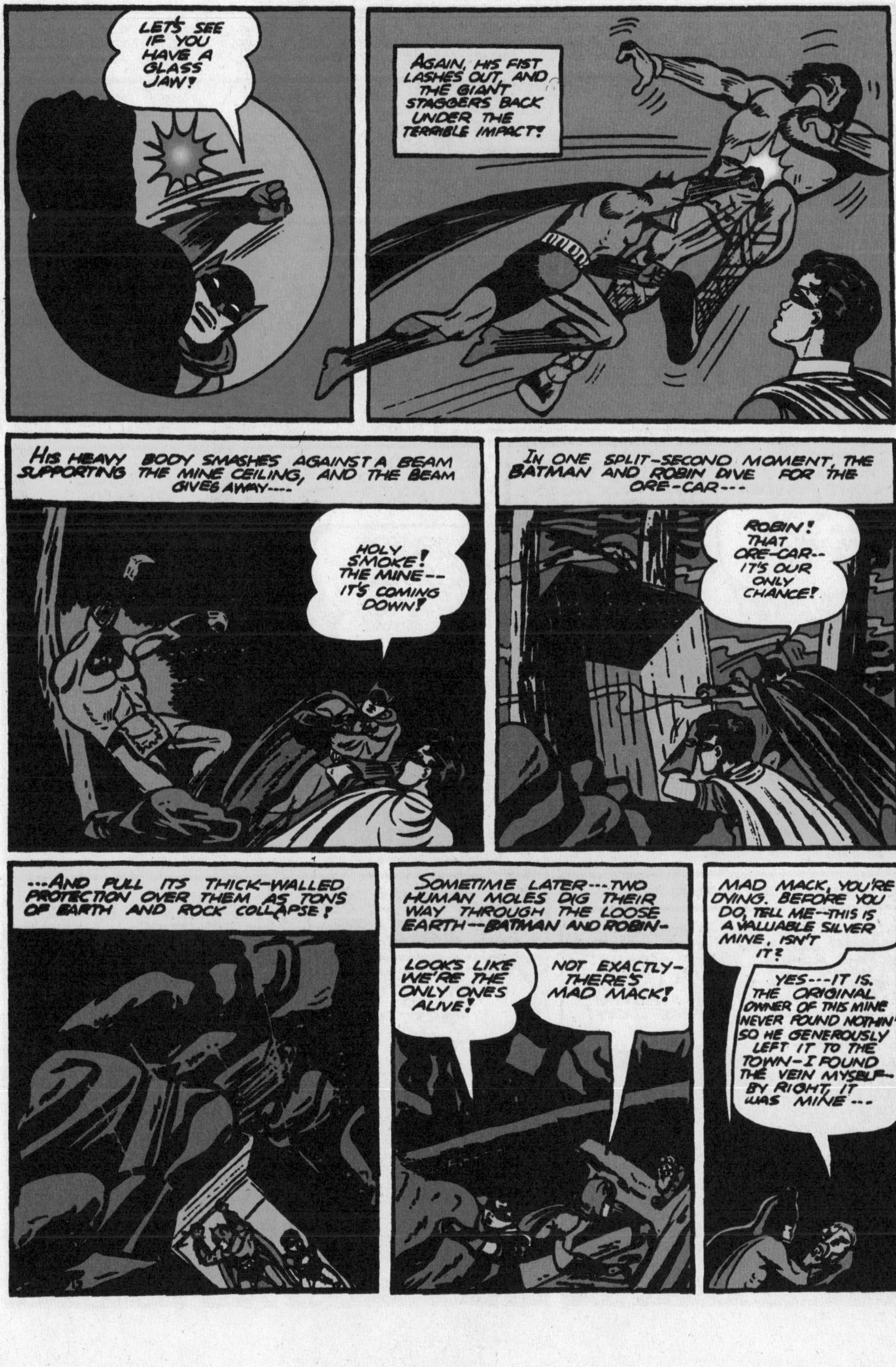

LET'S SEE IF YOU HAVE A GLASS JAW!
AGAIN, HIS FIST LASHES OUT, AND THE GIANT STAGGERS BACK UNDER THE TERRIBLE IMPACT!
HIS HEAVY BODY SMASHES AGAINST A BEAM SUPPORTING THE MINE CEILING, AND THE BEAM GIVES AWAY---
HOLY SMOKE! THE MINE-- IT'S COMING DOWN!
IN ONE SPLIT-SECOND MOMENT, THE BATMAN AND ROBIN DIVE FOR THE ORE-CAR---
ROBIN! THAT ORE-CAR-- IT'S OUR ONLY CHANCE!
...AND PULL ITS THICK-WALLED PROTECTION OVER THEM AS TONS OF EARTH AND ROCK COLLAPSE!
SOMETIME LATER---TWO HUMAN MOLES DIG THEIR WAY THROUGH THE LOOSE EARTH--BATMAN AND ROBIN-
LOOKS LIKE WE'RE THE ONLY ONES ALIVE!
NOT EXACTLY- THERE'S MAD MACK!
MAD MACK, YOU'RE DYING. BEFORE YOU DO, TELL ME--THIS IS A VALUABLE SILVER MINE, ISN'T IT?
YES---IT IS. THE ORIGINAL OWNER OF THIS MINE NEVER FOUND NOTHIN' SO HE GENEROUSLY LEFT IT TO THE TOWN-I FOUND THE VEIN MYSELF-- BY RIGHT, IT WAS MINE---

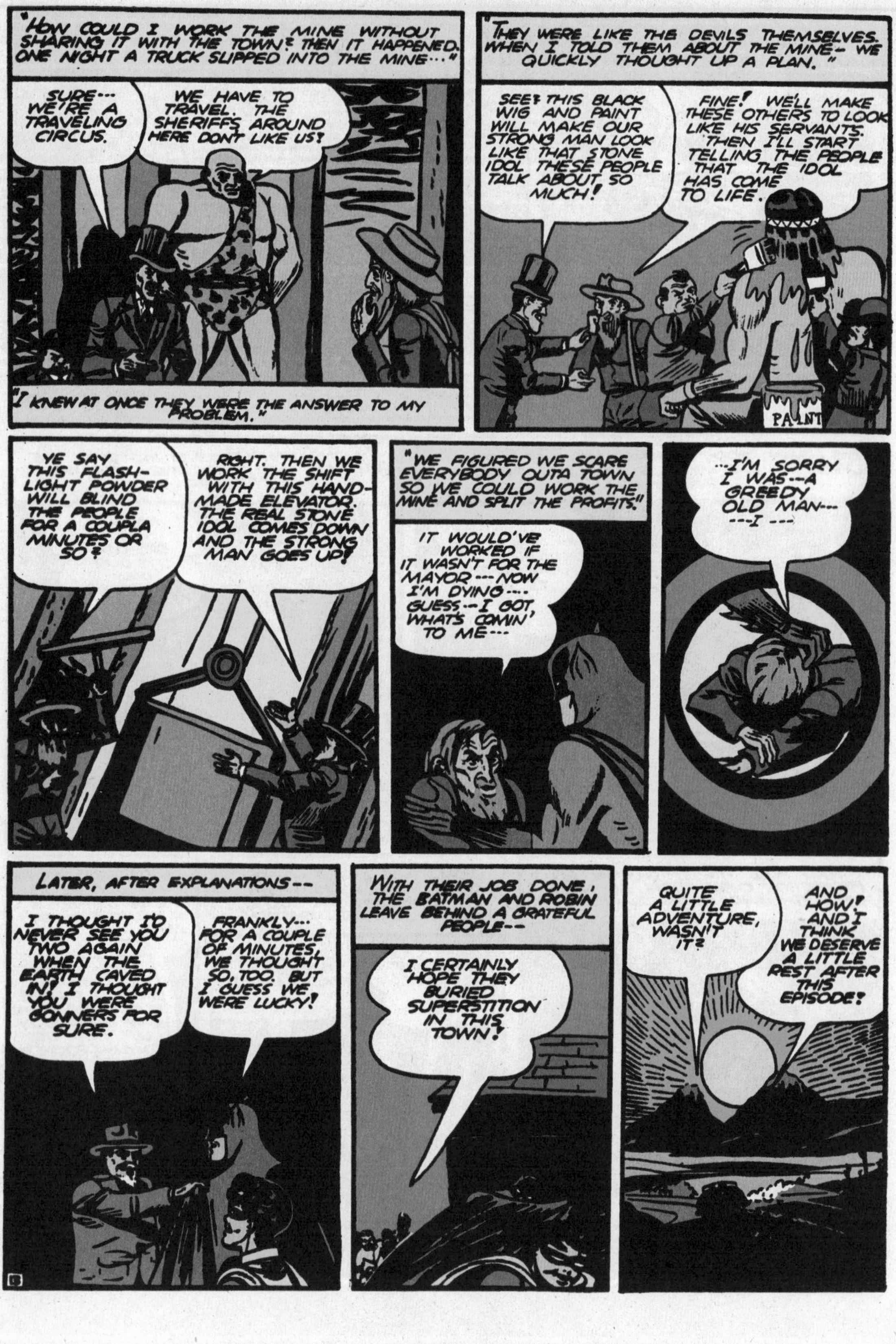
"HOW COULD I WORK THE MINE WITHOUT SHARING IT WITH THE TOWN? THEN IT HAPPENED. ONE NIGHT A TRUCK SLIPPED INTO THE MINE..."
SURE--- WE'RE A TRAVELING CIRCUS.
WE HAVE TO TRAVEL. THE SHERIFFS AROUND HERE DON'T LIKE US!
"I KNEW AT ONCE THEY WERE THE ANSWER TO MY PROBLEM."
"THEY WERE LIKE THE DEVILS THEMSELVES. WHEN I TOLD THEM ABOUT THE MINE-- WE QUICKLY THOUGHT UP A PLAN."
SEE? THIS BLACK WIG AND PAINT WILL MAKE OUR STRONG MAN LOOK LIKE THAT STONE IDOL THESE PEOPLE TALK ABOUT SO MUCH!
FINE! WE'LL MAKE THESE OTHERS TO LOOK LIKE HIS SERVANTS. THEN I'LL START TELLING THE PEOPLE THAT THE IDOL HAS COME TO LIFE.
PAINT
YE SAY THIS FLASH-LIGHT POWDER WILL BLIND THE PEOPLE FOR A COUPLA MINUTES OR SO?
RIGHT. THEN WE WORK THE SHIFT WITH THIS HAND-MADE ELEVATOR. THE REAL STONE IDOL COMES DOWN AND THE STRONG MAN GOES UP!
"WE FIGURED WE SCARE EVERYBODY OUTA TOWN SO WE COULD WORK THE MINE AND SPLIT THE PROFITS."
IT WOULD'VE WORKED IF IT WASN'T FOR THE MAYOR---NOW I'M DYING---. GUESS--I GOT, WHAT'S COMIN' TO ME---
...I'M SORRY I WAS--A GREEDY OLD MAN--- ---I ---
LATER, AFTER EXPLANATIONS--
I THOUGHT I'D NEVER SEE YOU TWO AGAIN WHEN THE EARTH CAVED IN! I THOUGHT YOU WERE GONNERS FOR SURE.
FRANKLY--- FOR A COUPLE OF MINUTES, WE THOUGHT SO, TOO. BUT I GUESS WE WERE LUCKY!
WITH THEIR JOB DONE, THE BATMAN AND ROBIN LEAVE BEHIND A GRATEFUL PEOPLE--
I CERTAINLY HOPE THEY BURIED SUPERSTITION IN THIS TOWN!
QUITE A LITTLE ADVENTURE, WASN'T IT?
AND HOW! AND I THINK WE DESERVE A LITTLE REST AFTER THIS EPISODE!

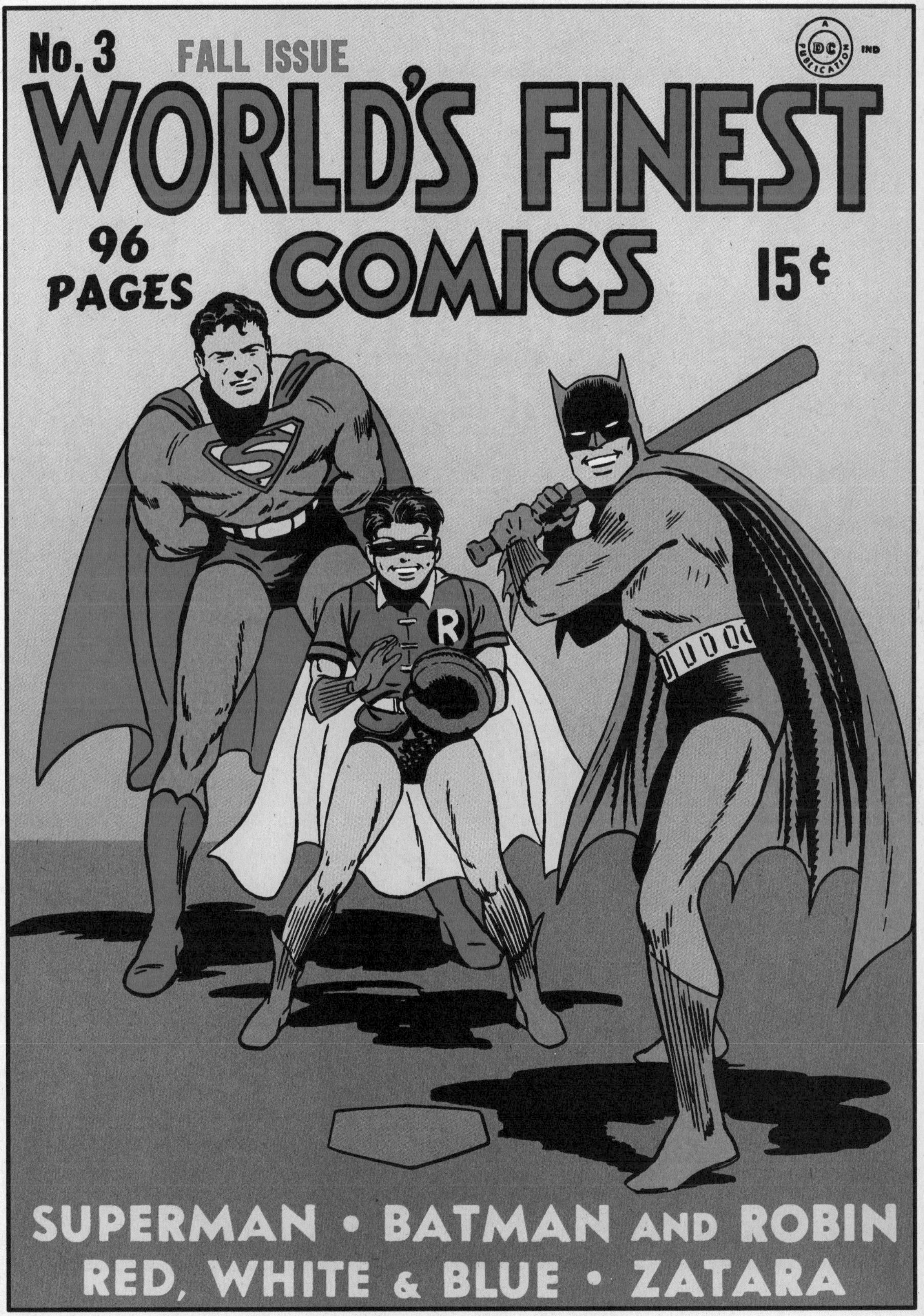
No. 3
FALL ISSUE
A DC PUBLICATION
IND
WORLD'S FINEST
96 PAGES
COMICS
15¢
R
SUPERMAN • BATMAN AND ROBIN
RED, WHITE & BLUE • ZATARA

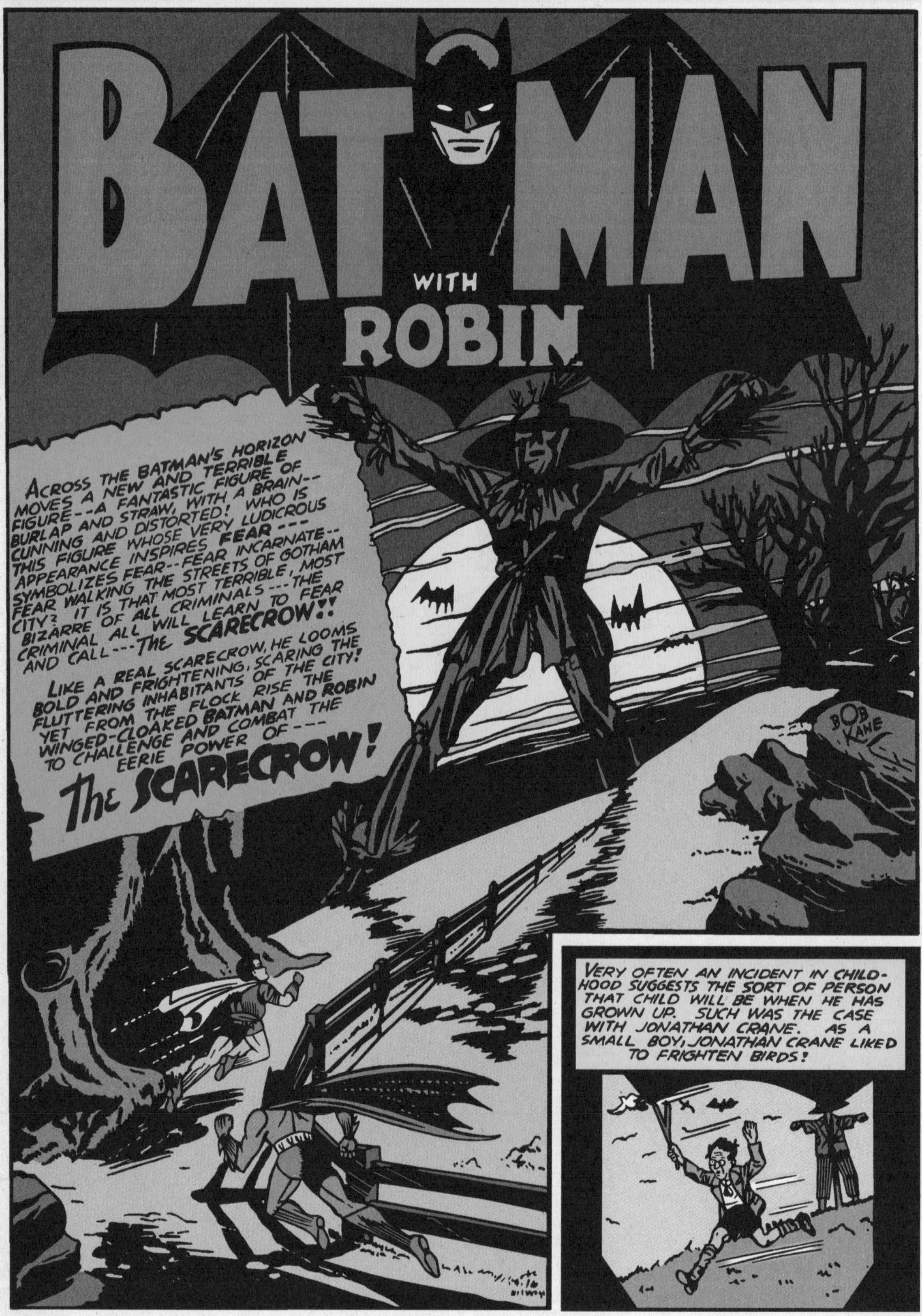
BATMAN
WITH
ROBIN
ACROSS THE BATMAN'S HORIZON MOVES A NEW AND TERRIBLE FIGURE--A FANTASTIC FIGURE OF BURLAP AND STRAW, WITH A BRAIN--CUNNING AND DISTORTED! WHO IS THIS FIGURE WHOSE VERY LUDICROUS APPEARANCE INSPIRES FEAR---SYMBOLIZES FEAR--FEAR INCARNATE--FEAR WALKING THE STREETS OF GOTHAM CITY? IT IS THAT MOST TERRIBLE, MOST BIZARRE OF ALL CRIMINALS---THE CRIMINAL ALL WILL LEARN TO FEAR AND CALL---THE SCARECROW!!
LIKE A REAL SCARECROW, HE LOOMS BOLD AND FRIGHTENING, SCARING THE FLUTTERING INHABITANTS OF THE CITY! YET FROM THE FLOCK RISE THE WINGED-CLOAKED BATMAN AND ROBIN TO CHALLENGE AND COMBAT THE EERIE POWER OF---
The SCARECROW!
BOB KANE
VERY OFTEN AN INCIDENT IN CHILDHOOD SUGGESTS THE SORT OF PERSON THAT CHILD WILL BE WHEN HE HAS GROWN UP. SUCH WAS THE CASE WITH JONATHAN CRANE. AS A SMALL BOY, JONATHAN CRANE LIKED TO FRIGHTEN BIRDS!

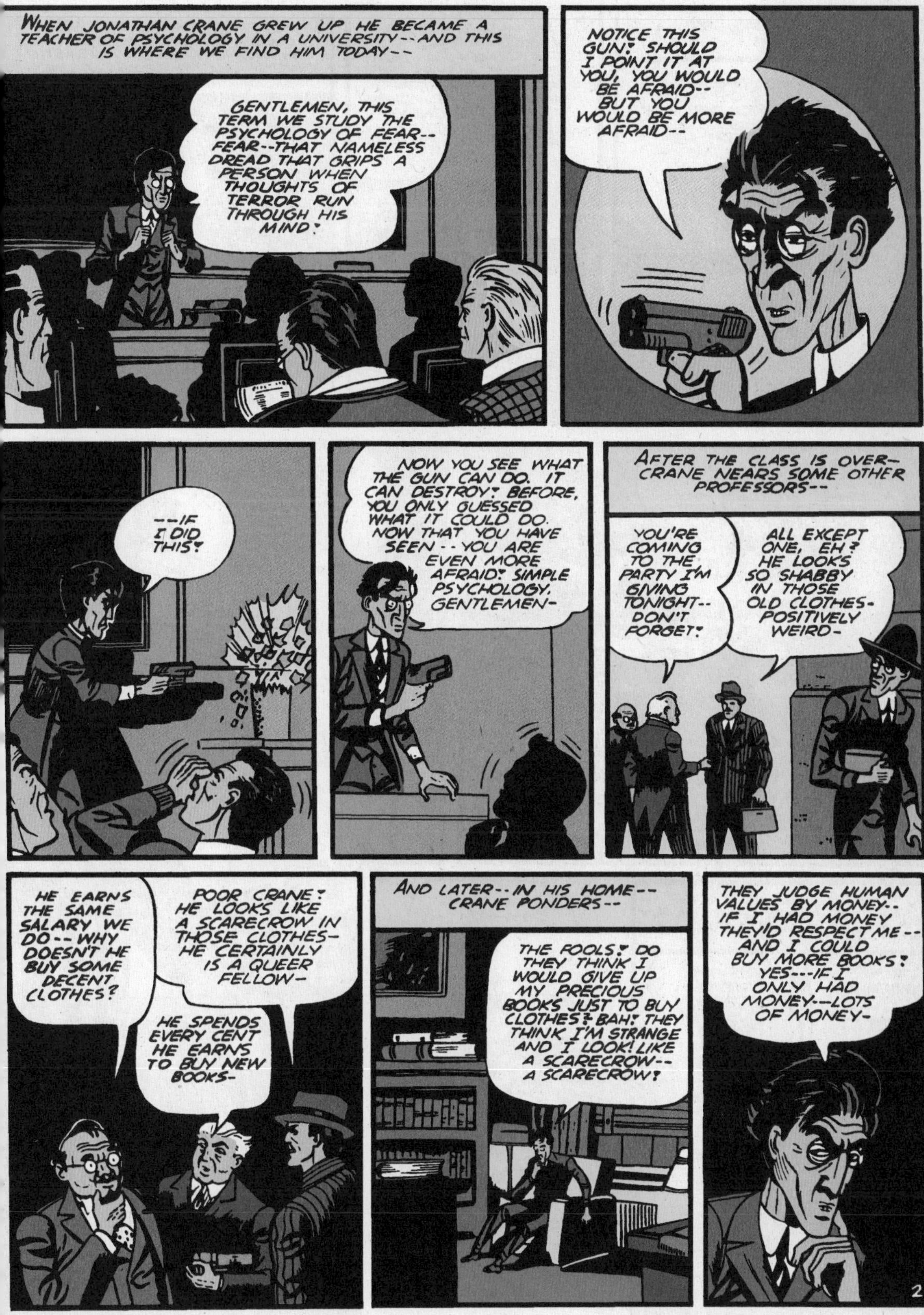
WHEN JONATHAN CRANE GREW UP HE BECAME A TEACHER OF PSYCHOLOGY IN A UNIVERSITY--AND THIS IS WHERE WE FIND HIM TODAY--
GENTLEMEN, THIS TERM WE STUDY THE PSYCHOLOGY OF FEAR--FEAR--THAT NAMELESS DREAD THAT GRIPS A PERSON WHEN THOUGHTS OF TERROR RUN THROUGH HIS MIND!
NOTICE THIS GUN! SHOULD I POINT IT AT YOU, YOU WOULD BE AFRAID--BUT YOU WOULD BE MORE AFRAID--
--IF I DID THIS!
NOW YOU SEE WHAT THE GUN CAN DO. IT CAN DESTROY! BEFORE, YOU ONLY GUESSED WHAT IT COULD DO. NOW THAT YOU HAVE SEEN--YOU ARE EVEN MORE AFRAID! SIMPLE PSYCHOLOGY, GENTLEMEN-
AFTER THE CLASS IS OVER--CRANE NEARS SOME OTHER PROFESSORS--
YOU'RE COMING TO THE PARTY I'M GIVING TONIGHT--DON'T FORGET!
ALL EXCEPT ONE, EH? HE LOOKS SO SHABBY IN THOSE OLD CLOTHES-POSITIVELY WEIRD-
HE EARNS THE SAME SALARY WE DO--WHY DOESN'T HE BUY SOME DECENT CLOTHES?
POOR CRANE! HE LOOKS LIKE A SCARECROW IN THOSE CLOTHES-HE CERTAINLY IS A QUEER FELLOW-
HE SPENDS EVERY CENT HE EARNS TO BUY NEW BOOKS-
AND LATER--IN HIS HOME--CRANE PONDERS--
THE FOOLS! DO THEY THINK I WOULD GIVE UP MY PRECIOUS BOOKS JUST TO BUY CLOTHES? BAH! THEY THINK I'M STRANGE AND I LOOK! LIKE A SCARECROW--A SCARECROW!
THEY JUDGE HUMAN VALUES BY MONEY--IF I HAD MONEY THEY'D RESPECT ME--AND I COULD BUY MORE BOOKS! YES---IF I ONLY HAD MONEY--LOTS OF MONEY-
2

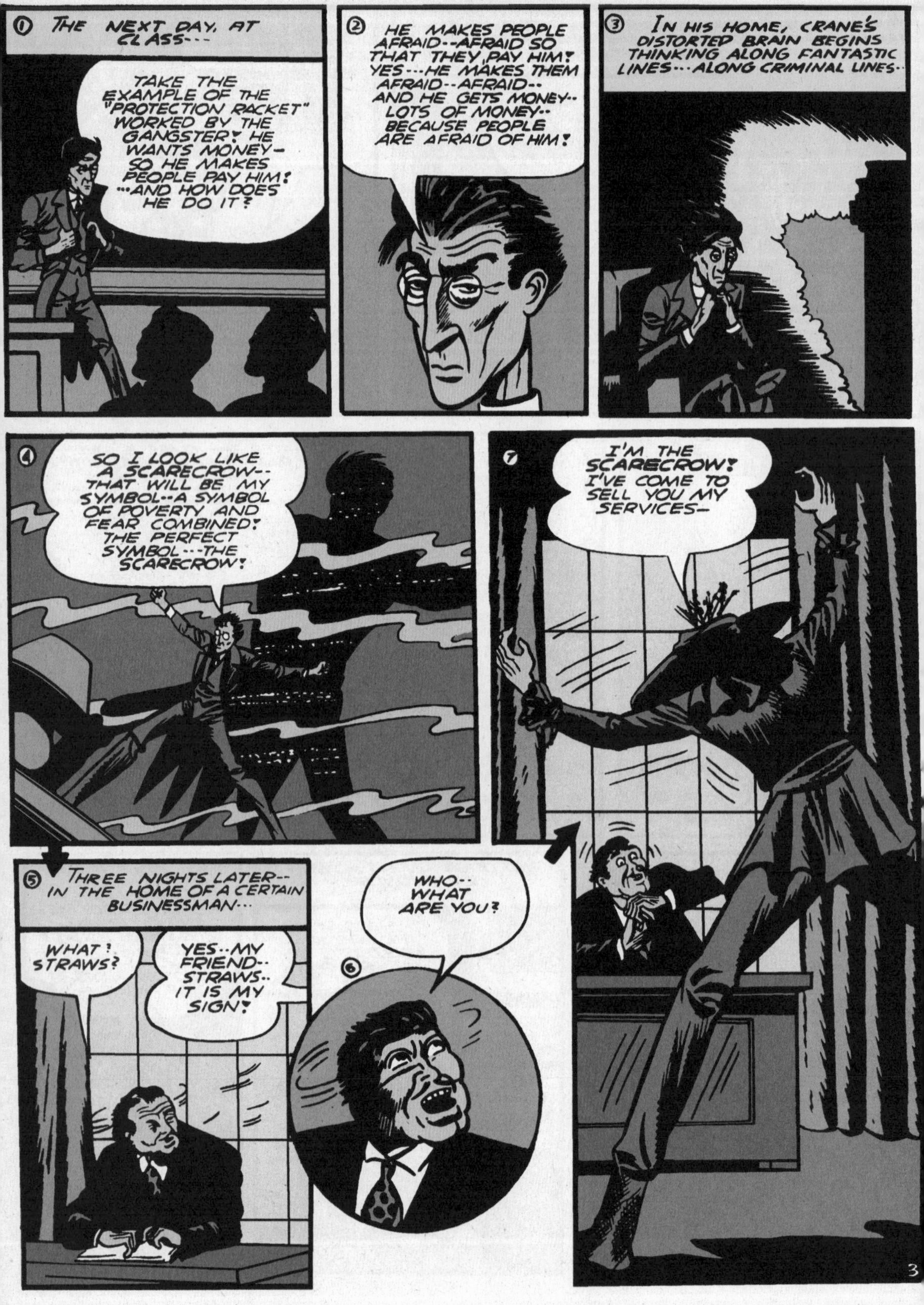
1
THE NEXT DAY, AT CLASS---
TAKE THE EXAMPLE OF THE "PROTECTION RACKET" WORKED BY THE GANGSTER! HE WANTS MONEY- SO HE MAKES PEOPLE PAY HIM! ...AND HOW DOES HE DO IT?
2
HE MAKES PEOPLE AFRAID--AFRAID SO THAT THEY PAY HIM! YES---HE MAKES THEM AFRAID--AFRAID-- AND HE GETS MONEY-- LOTS OF MONEY-- BECAUSE PEOPLE ARE AFRAID OF HIM!
3
IN HIS HOME, CRANE'S DISTORTED BRAIN BEGINS THINKING ALONG FANTASTIC LINES--- ALONG CRIMINAL LINES--
4
SO I LOOK LIKE A SCARECROW-- THAT WILL BE MY SYMBOL--A SYMBOL OF POVERTY AND FEAR COMBINED! THE PERFECT SYMBOL---THE SCARECROW!
5
THREE NIGHTS LATER-- IN THE HOME OF A CERTAIN BUSINESSMAN---
WHAT! STRAWS?
YES--MY FRIEND-- STRAWS-- IT IS MY SIGN!
6
WHO-- WHAT ARE YOU?
7
I'M THE SCARECROW! I'VE COME TO SELL YOU MY SERVICES-
3

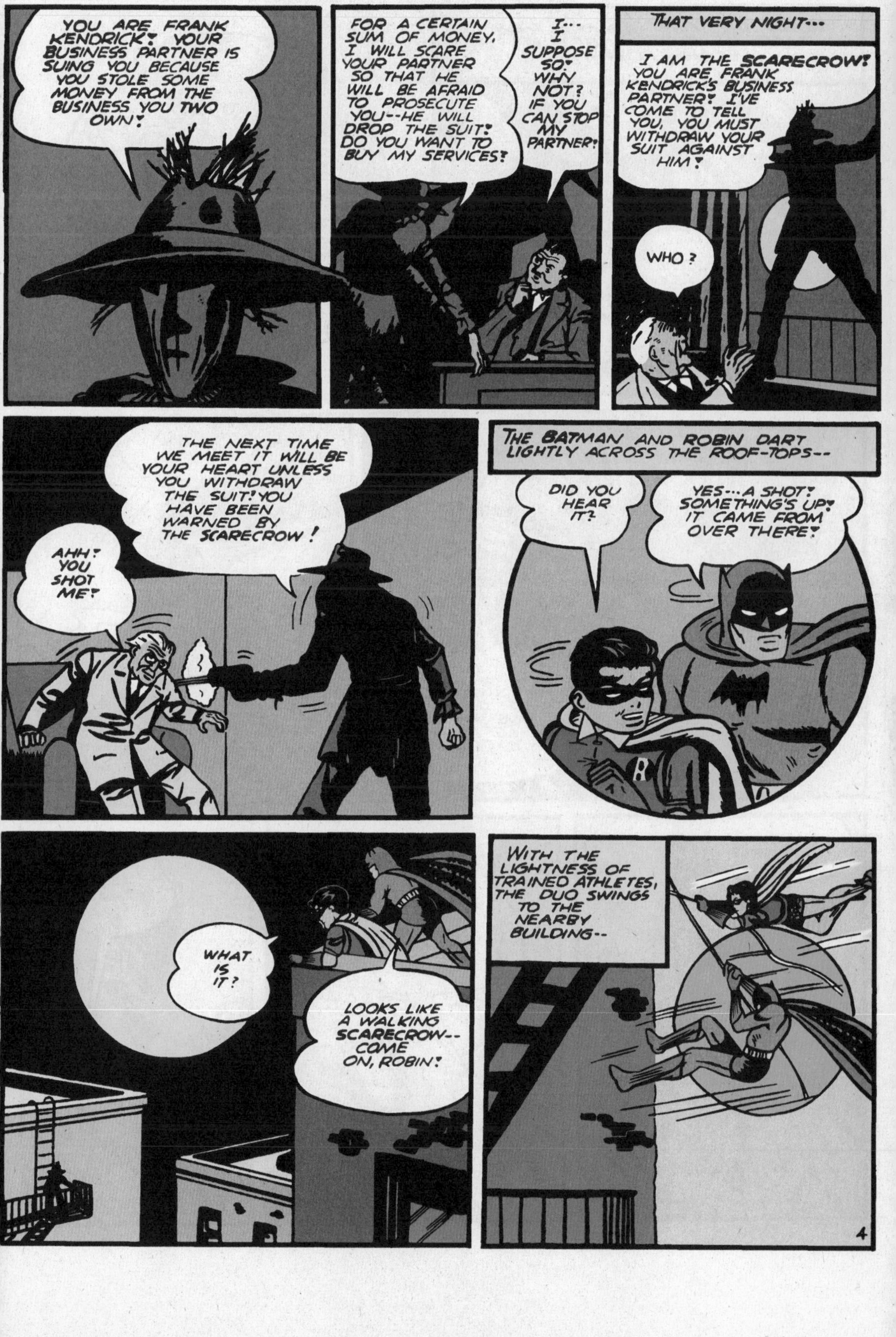
YOU ARE FRANK KENDRICK! YOUR BUSINESS PARTNER IS SUING YOU BECAUSE YOU STOLE SOME MONEY FROM THE BUSINESS YOU TWO OWN!
FOR A CERTAIN SUM OF MONEY, I WILL SCARE YOUR PARTNER SO THAT HE WILL BE AFRAID TO PROSECUTE YOU--HE WILL DROP THE SUIT! DO YOU WANT TO BUY MY SERVICES?
I... I SUPPOSE SO! WHY NOT? IF YOU CAN STOP MY PARTNER!
THAT VERY NIGHT...
I AM THE SCARECROW! YOU ARE FRANK KENDRICK'S BUSINESS PARTNER! I'VE COME TO TELL YOU, YOU MUST WITHDRAW YOUR SUIT AGAINST HIM!
WHO?
THE NEXT TIME WE MEET IT WILL BE YOUR HEART UNLESS YOU WITHDRAW THE SUIT! YOU HAVE BEEN WARNED BY THE SCARECROW!
AHH! YOU SHOT ME!
THE BATMAN AND ROBIN DART LIGHTLY ACROSS THE ROOF-TOPS--
DID YOU HEAR IT?
YES... A SHOT! SOMETHING'S UP! IT CAME FROM OVER THERE!
WHAT IS IT?
LOOKS LIKE A WALKING SCARECROW-- COME ON, ROBIN!
WITH THE LIGHTNESS OF TRAINED ATHLETES, THE DUO SWINGS TO THE NEARBY BUILDING--
4

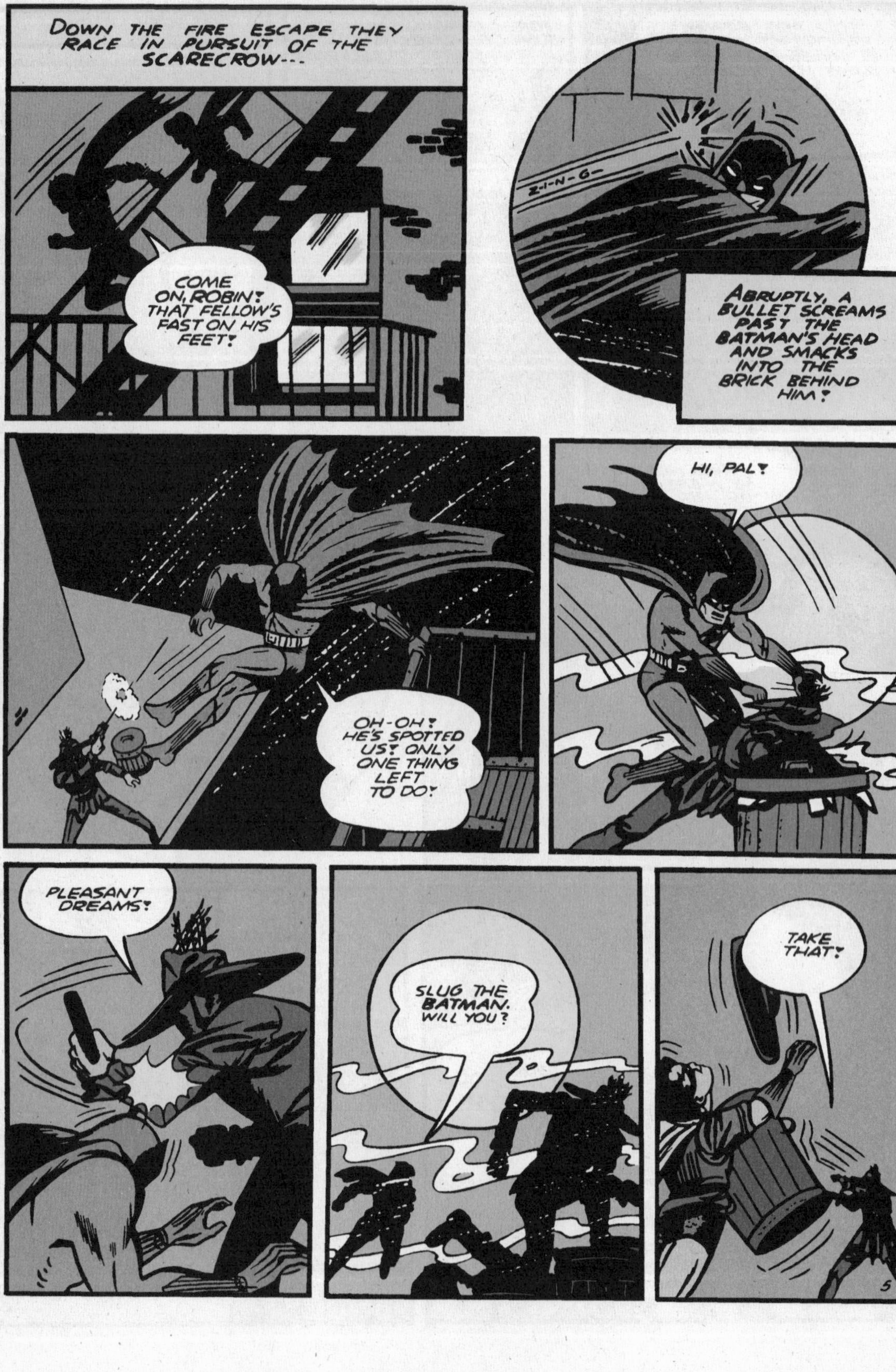
DOWN THE FIRE ESCAPE THEY RACE IN PURSUIT OF THE SCARECROW---
COME ON, ROBIN! THAT FELLOW'S FAST ON HIS FEET!
Z-I-N-G-
ABRUPTLY, A BULLET SCREAMS PAST THE BATMAN'S HEAD AND SMACKS INTO THE BRICK BEHIND HIM!
OH-OH! HE'S SPOTTED US! ONLY ONE THING LEFT TO DO!
HI, PAL!
PLEASANT DREAMS!
SLUG THE BATMAN. WILL YOU?
TAKE THAT!
5

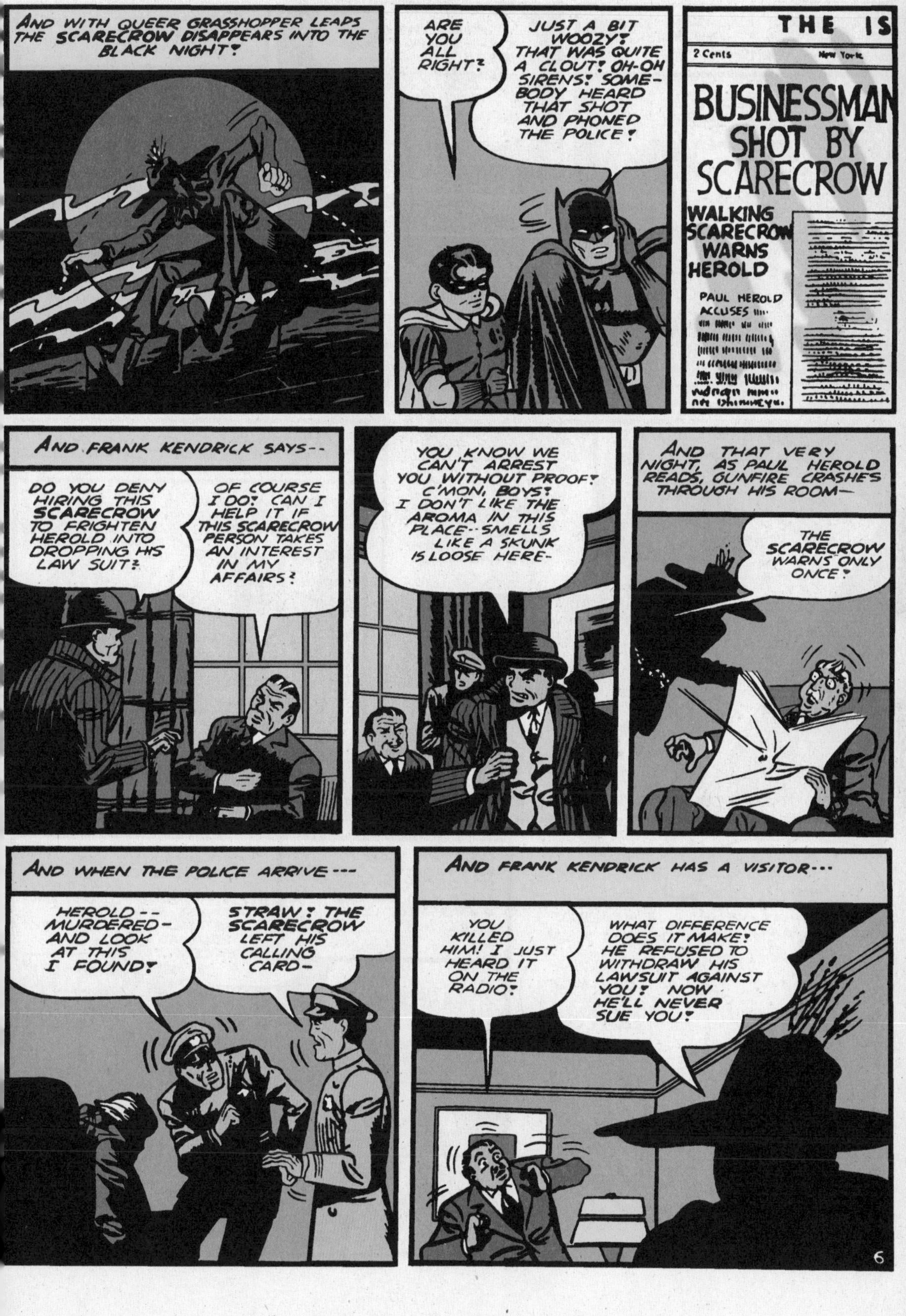
AND WITH QUEER GRASSHOPPER LEAPS THE SCARECROW DISAPPEARS INTO THE BLACK NIGHT!
ARE YOU ALL RIGHT?
JUST A BIT WOOZY! THAT WAS QUITE A CLOUT! OH-OH SIRENS! SOMEBODY HEARD THAT SHOT AND PHONED THE POLICE!
THE IS
2 Cents
New York
BUSINESSMAN SHOT BY SCARECROW
WALKING SCARECROW WARNS HEROLD
PAUL HEROLD ACCUSES
AND FRANK KENDRICK SAYS--
DO YOU DENY HIRING THIS SCARECROW TO FRIGHTEN HEROLD INTO DROPPING HIS LAW SUIT?
OF COURSE I DO! CAN I HELP IT IF THIS SCARECROW PERSON TAKES AN INTEREST IN MY AFFAIRS?
YOU KNOW WE CAN'T ARREST YOU WITHOUT PROOF! C'MON, BOYS! I DON'T LIKE THE AROMA IN THIS PLACE--SMELLS LIKE A SKUNK IS LOOSE HERE-
AND THAT VERY NIGHT, AS PAUL HEROLD READS, GUNFIRE CRASHES THROUGH HIS ROOM—
THE SCARECROW WARNS ONLY ONCE!
AND WHEN THE POLICE ARRIVE---
HEROLD--MURDERED-AND LOOK AT THIS I FOUND!
STRAW! THE SCARECROW LEFT HIS CALLING CARD-
AND FRANK KENDRICK HAS A VISITOR---
YOU KILLED HIM! I JUST HEARD IT ON THE RADIO!
WHAT DIFFERENCE DOES IT MAKE! HE REFUSED TO WITHDRAW HIS LAWSUIT AGAINST YOU! NOW HE'LL NEVER SUE YOU!
6

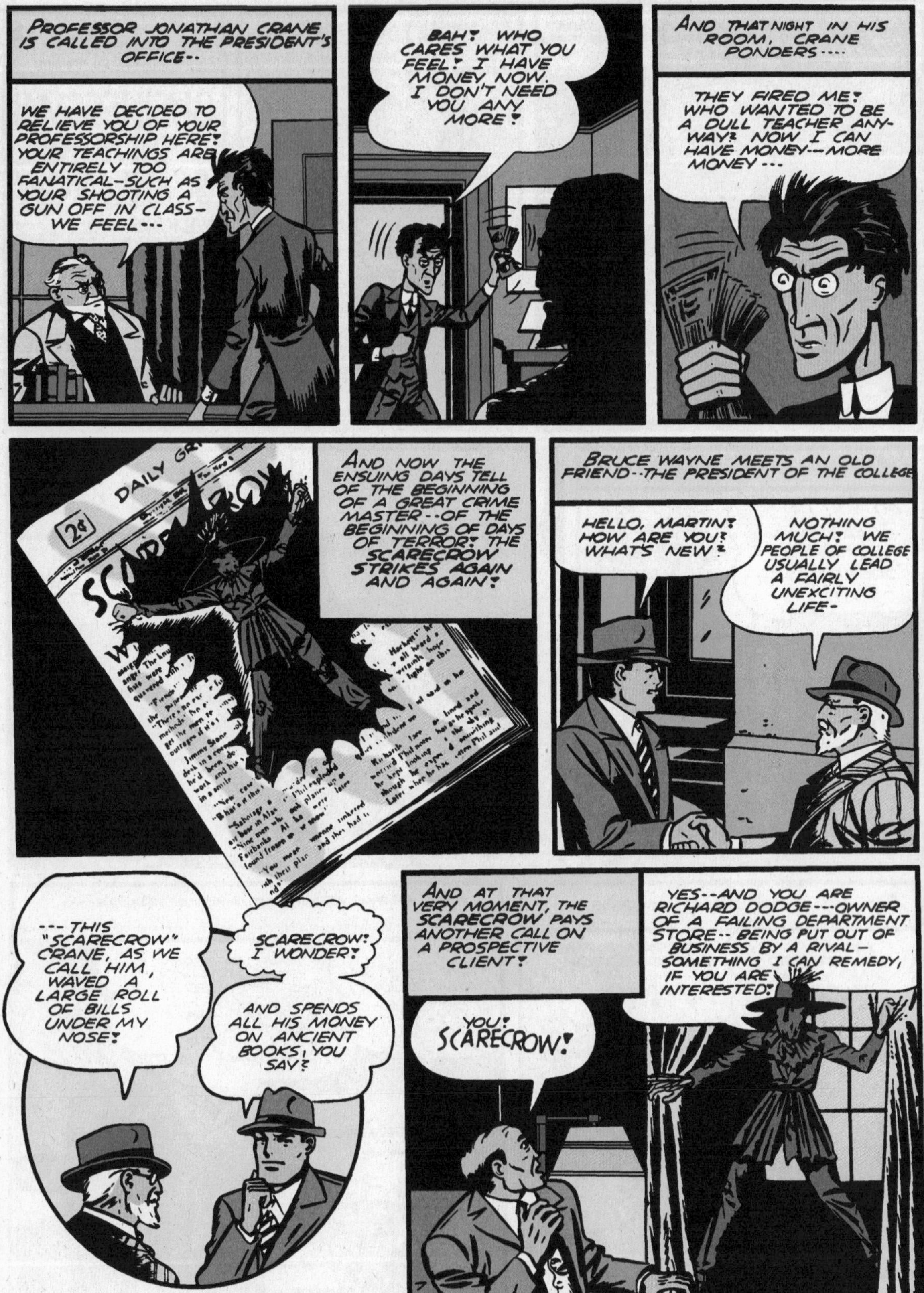
PROFESSOR JONATHAN CRANE IS CALLED INTO THE PRESIDENT'S OFFICE--
WE HAVE DECIDED TO RELIEVE YOU OF YOUR PROFESSORSHIP HERE! YOUR TEACHINGS ARE ENTIRELY TOO FANATICAL-SUCH AS YOUR SHOOTING A GUN OFF IN CLASS-WE FEEL---
BAH! WHO CARES WHAT YOU FEEL! I HAVE MONEY NOW. I DON'T NEED YOU ANY MORE!
AND THAT NIGHT IN HIS ROOM, CRANE PONDERS----
THEY FIRED ME! WHO WANTED TO BE A DULL TEACHER ANY-WAY? NOW I CAN HAVE MONEY--MORE MONEY---
DAILY
2¢
AND NOW THE ENSUING DAYS TELL OF THE BEGINNING OF A GREAT CRIME MASTER--OF THE BEGINNING OF DAYS OF TERROR! THE SCARECROW STRIKES AGAIN AND AGAIN!
BRUCE WAYNE MEETS AN OLD FRIEND--THE PRESIDENT OF THE COLLEGE
HELLO, MARTIN! HOW ARE YOU! WHAT'S NEW?
NOTHING MUCH! WE PEOPLE OF COLLEGE USUALLY LEAD A FAIRLY UNEXCITING LIFE-
---THIS "SCARECROW" CRANE, AS WE CALL HIM, WAVED A LARGE ROLL OF BILLS UNDER MY NOSE!
SCARECROW! I WONDER!
AND SPENDS ALL HIS MONEY ON ANCIENT BOOKS, YOU SAY?
AND AT THAT VERY MOMENT, THE SCARECROW PAYS ANOTHER CALL ON A PROSPECTIVE CLIENT!
YES--AND YOU ARE RICHARD DODGE---OWNER OF A FAILING DEPARTMENT STORE-- BEING PUT OUT OF BUSINESS BY A RIVAL-SOMETHING I CAN REMEDY, IF YOU ARE INTERESTED!
YOU! SCARECROW!

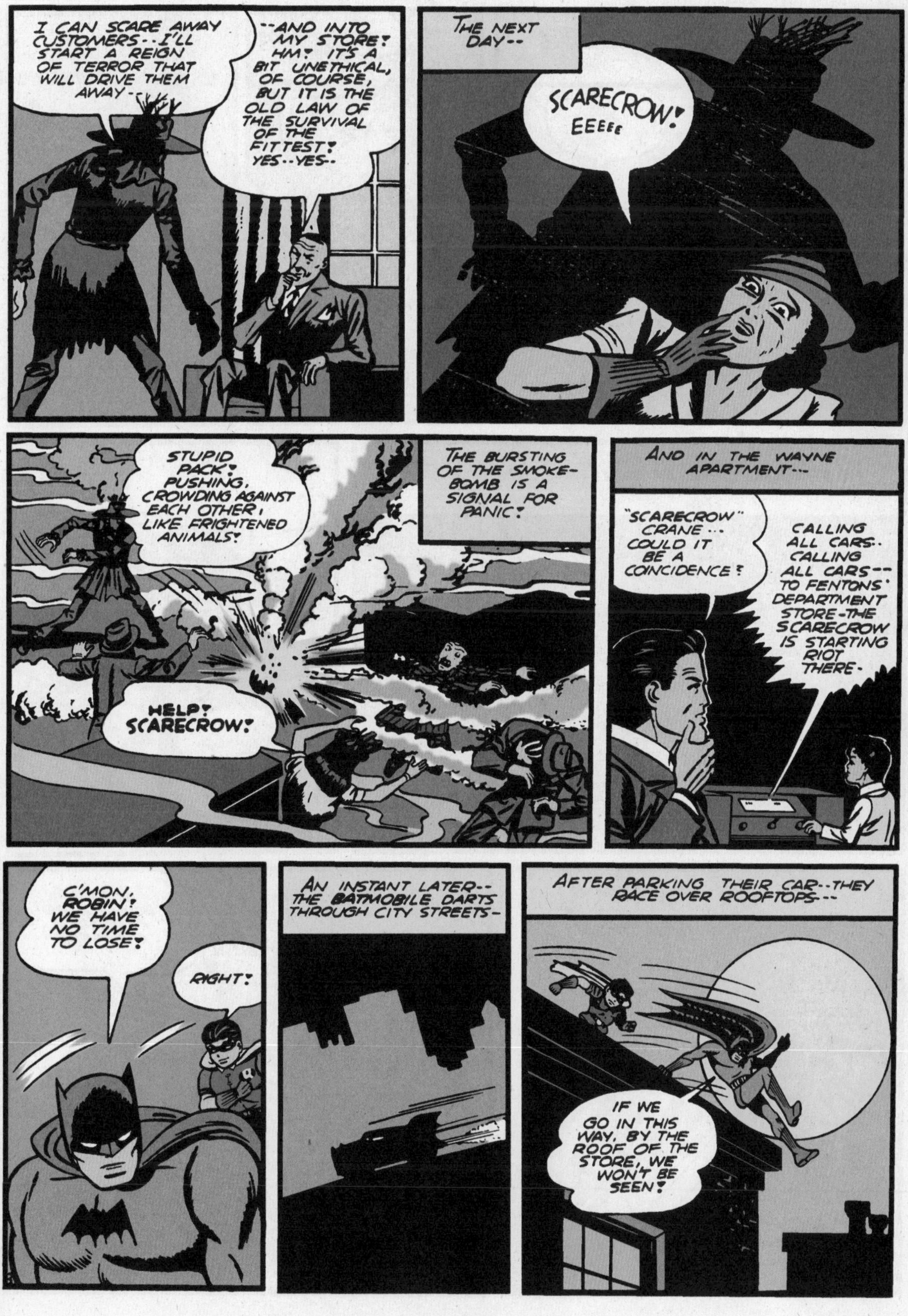
I CAN SCARE AWAY CUSTOMERS--I'LL START A REIGN OF TERROR THAT WILL DRIVE THEM AWAY--
--AND INTO MY STORE! HM! IT'S A BIT UNETHICAL, OF COURSE, BUT IT IS THE OLD LAW OF THE SURVIVAL OF THE FITTEST! YES--YES--
THE NEXT DAY--
SCARECROW! EEEEE
STUPID PACK! PUSHING, CROWDING AGAINST EACH OTHER, LIKE FRIGHTENED ANIMALS!
THE BURSTING OF THE SMOKE-BOMB IS A SIGNAL FOR PANIC!
HELP! SCARECROW!
AND IN THE WAYNE APARTMENT---
"SCARECROW" CRANE... COULD IT BE A COINCIDENCE?
CALLING ALL CARS.. CALLING ALL CARS--- TO FENTONS' DEPARTMENT STORE-THE SCARECROW IS STARTING RIOT THERE-
C'MON, ROBIN! WE HAVE NO TIME TO LOSE!
RIGHT!
AN INSTANT LATER-- THE BATMOBILE DARTS THROUGH CITY STREETS-
AFTER PARKING THEIR CAR--THEY RACE OVER ROOFTOPS---
IF WE GO IN THIS WAY, BY THE ROOF OF THE STORE, WE WON'T BE SEEN!

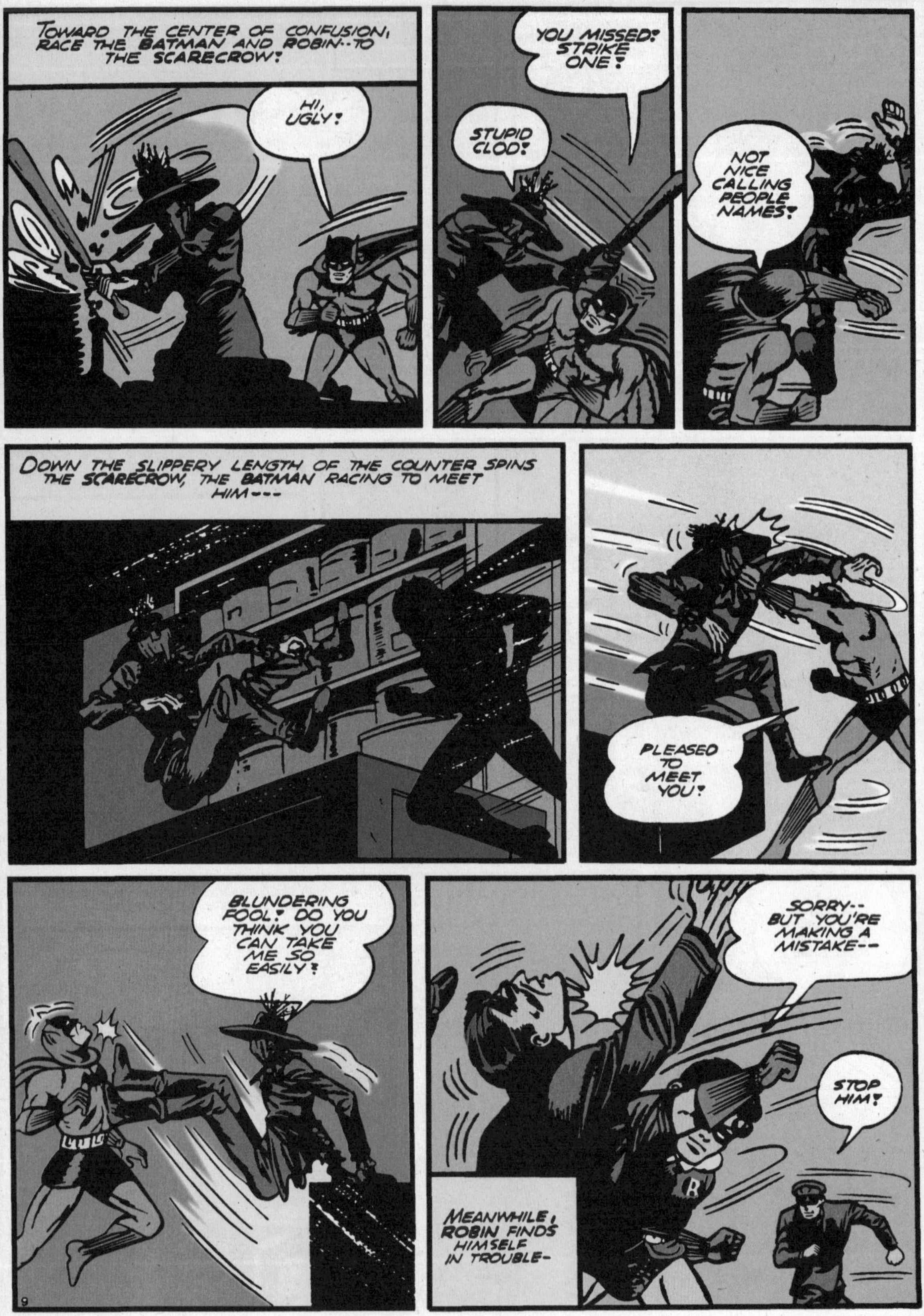
TOWARD THE CENTER OF CONFUSION, RACE THE BATMAN AND ROBIN--TO THE SCARECROW!
HI, UGLY!
YOU MISSED! STRIKE ONE!
STUPID CLOD!
NOT NICE CALLING PEOPLE NAMES!
DOWN THE SLIPPERY LENGTH OF THE COUNTER SPINS THE SCARECROW, THE BATMAN RACING TO MEET HIM---
PLEASED TO MEET YOU!
BLUNDERING FOOL! DO YOU THINK YOU CAN TAKE ME SO EASILY?
SORRY-- BUT YOU'RE MAKING A MISTAKE--
STOP HIM!
MEANWHILE, ROBIN FINDS HIMSELF IN TROUBLE-

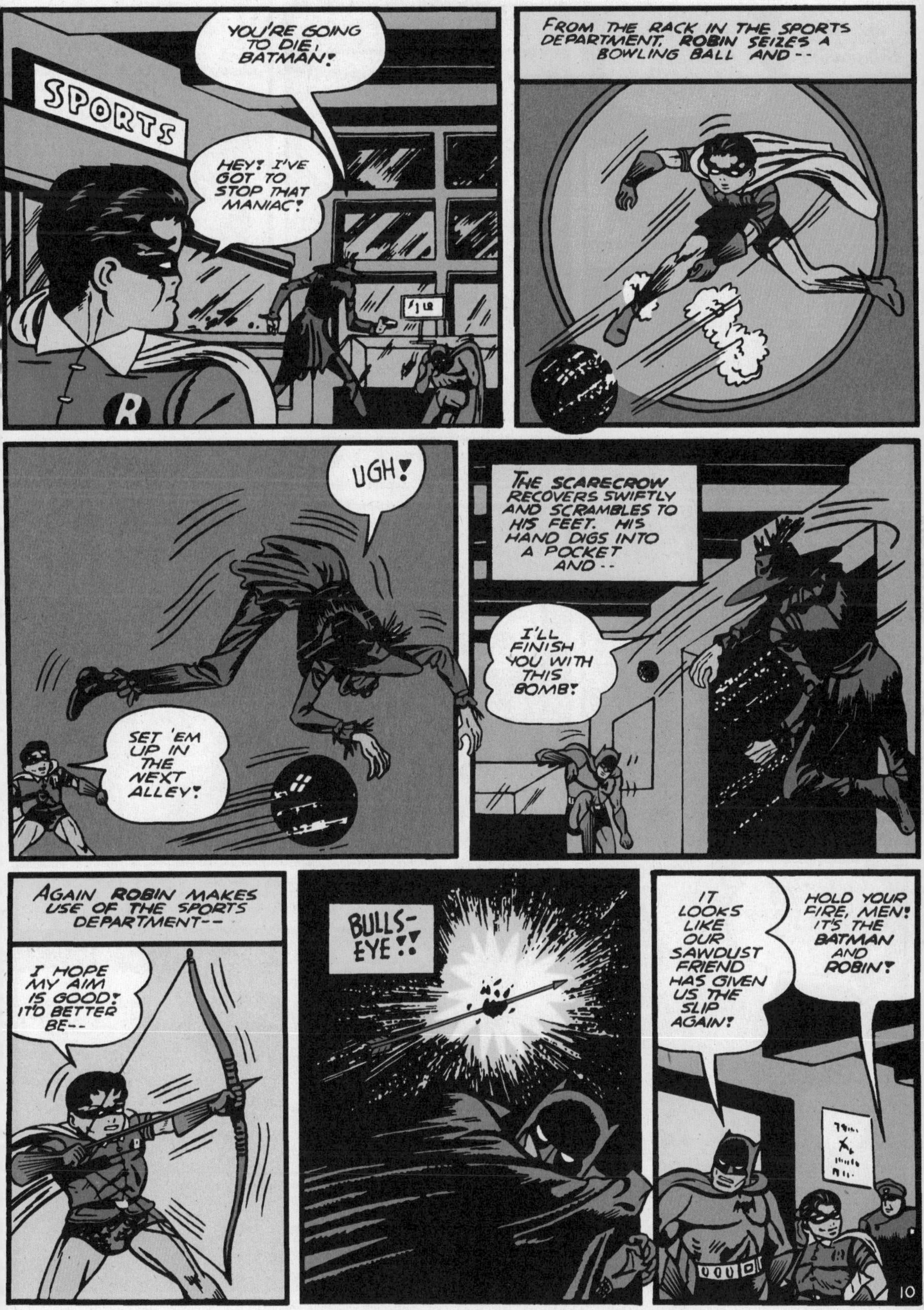
YOU'RE GOING TO DIE, BATMAN!
SPORTS
HEY! I'VE GOT TO STOP THAT MANIAC!
FROM THE RACK IN THE SPORTS DEPARTMENT, ROBIN SEIZES A BOWLING BALL AND--
UGH!
SET 'EM UP IN THE NEXT ALLEY!
THE SCARECROW RECOVERS SWIFTLY AND SCRAMBLES TO HIS FEET. HIS HAND DIGS INTO A POCKET AND--
I'LL FINISH YOU WITH THIS BOMB!
AGAIN ROBIN MAKES USE OF THE SPORTS DEPARTMENT--
I HOPE MY AIM IS GOOD! IT'D BETTER BE--
BULLS-EYE!!
IT LOOKS LIKE OUR SAWDUST FRIEND HAS GIVEN US THE SLIP AGAIN!
HOLD YOUR FIRE, MEN! IT'S THE BATMAN AND ROBIN!
10

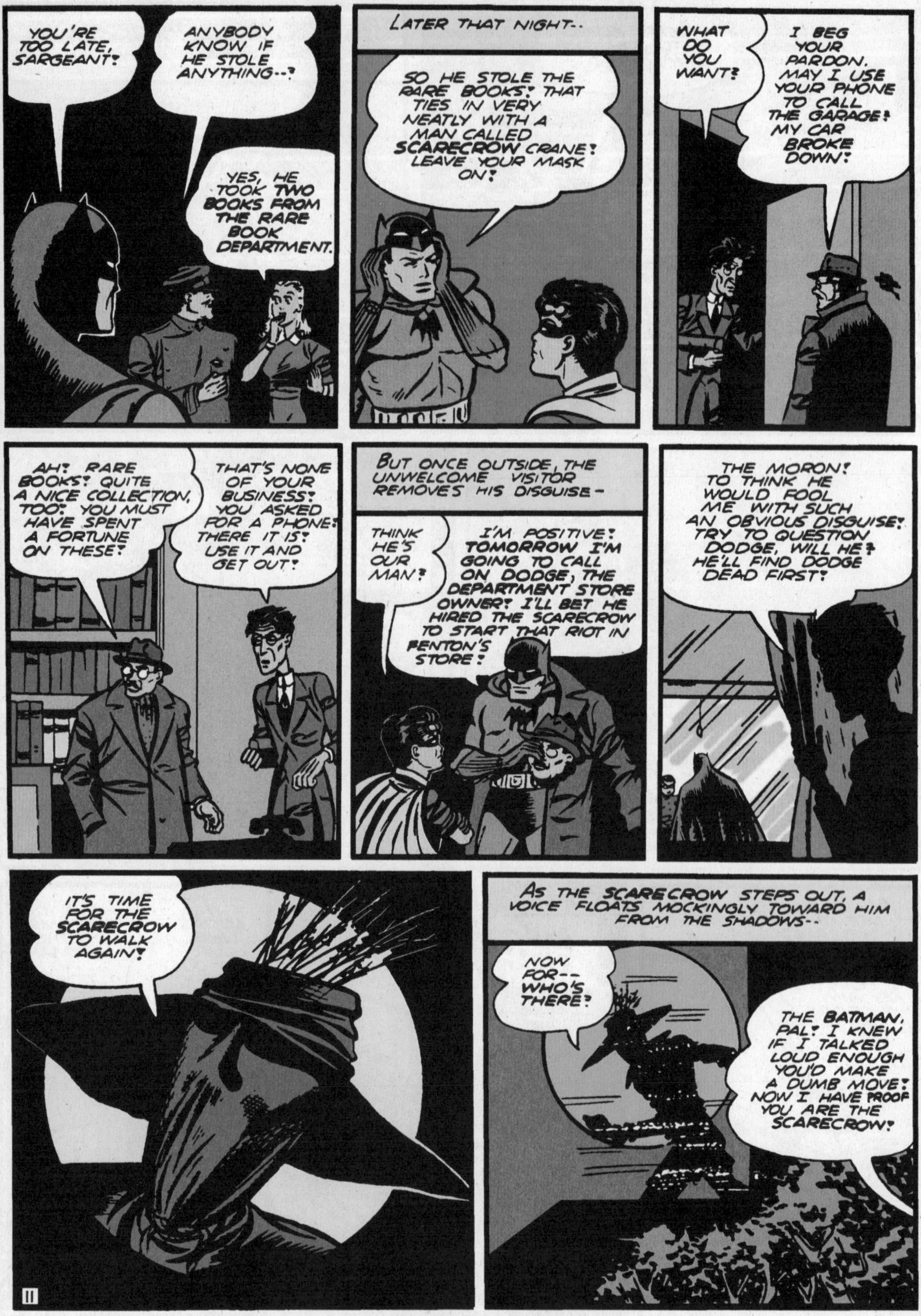
YOU'RE TOO LATE, SARGEANT!
ANYBODY KNOW IF HE STOLE ANYTHING--?
YES, HE TOOK TWO BOOKS FROM THE RARE BOOK DEPARTMENT.
LATER THAT NIGHT--
SO HE STOLE THE RARE BOOKS! THAT TIES IN VERY NEATLY WITH A MAN CALLED SCARECROW CRANE! LEAVE YOUR MASK ON!
WHAT DO YOU WANT?
I BEG YOUR PARDON. MAY I USE YOUR PHONE TO CALL THE GARAGE? MY CAR BROKE DOWN!
AH! RARE BOOKS! QUITE A NICE COLLECTION, TOO! YOU MUST HAVE SPENT A FORTUNE ON THESE!
THAT'S NONE OF YOUR BUSINESS! YOU ASKED FOR A PHONE! THERE IT IS! USE IT AND GET OUT!
BUT ONCE OUTSIDE, THE UNWELCOME VISITOR REMOVES HIS DISGUISE-
THINK HE'S OUR MAN?
I'M POSITIVE! TOMORROW I'M GOING TO CALL ON DODGE, THE DEPARTMENT STORE OWNER! I'LL BET HE HIRED THE SCARECROW TO START THAT RIOT IN FENTON'S STORE!
THE MORON! TO THINK HE WOULD FOOL ME WITH SUCH AN OBVIOUS DISGUISE! TRY TO QUESTION DODGE, WILL HE? HE'LL FIND DODGE DEAD FIRST!
IT'S TIME FOR THE SCARECROW TO WALK AGAIN!
11
AS THE SCARECROW STEPS OUT, A VOICE FLOATS MOCKINGLY TOWARD HIM FROM THE SHADOWS--
NOW FOR-- WHO'S THERE?
THE BATMAN, PAL! I KNEW IF I TALKED LOUD ENOUGH YOU'D MAKE A DUMB MOVE! NOW I HAVE PROOF YOU ARE THE SCARECROW!

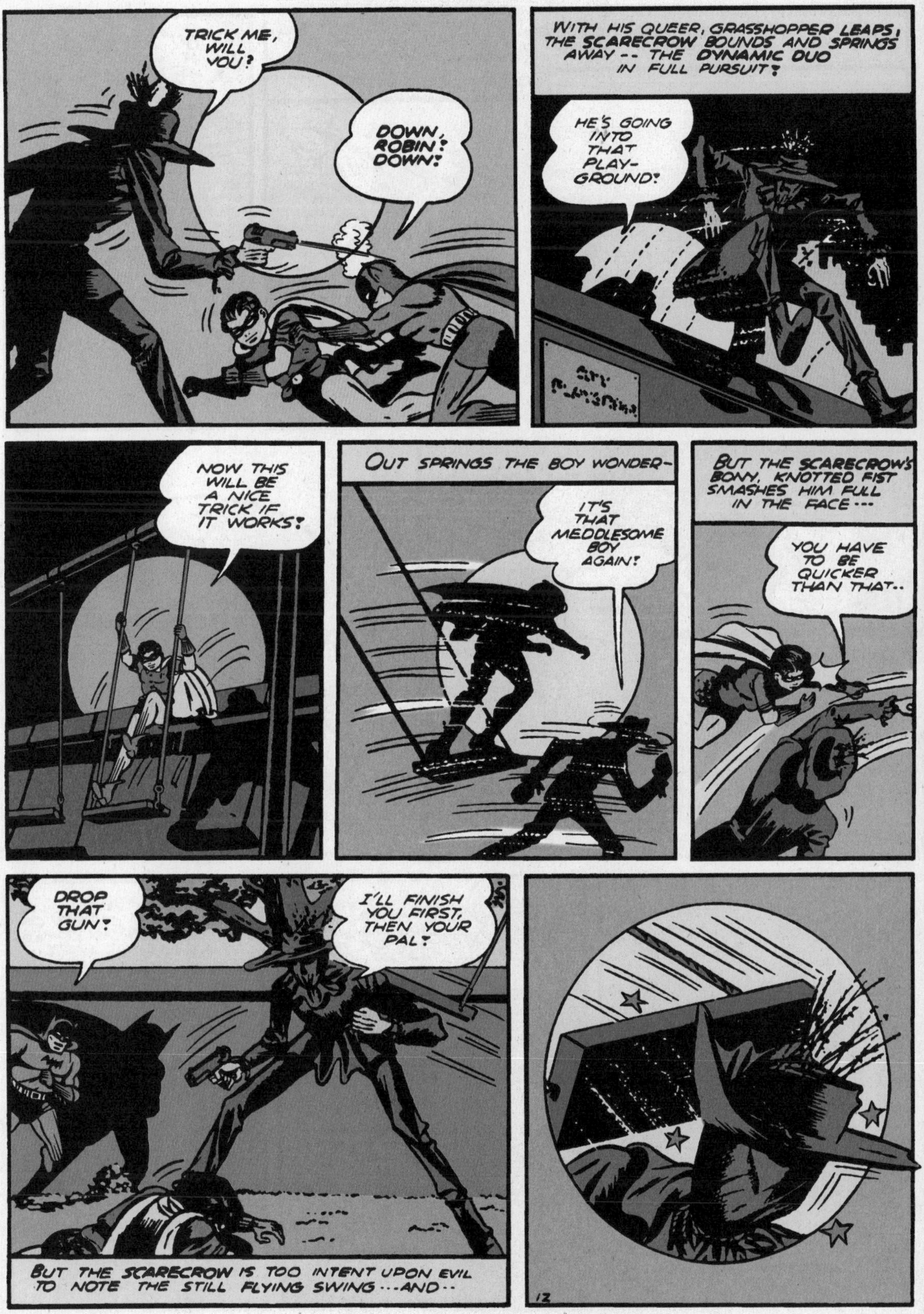
TRICK ME, WILL YOU?
DOWN, ROBIN! DOWN!
WITH HIS QUEER, GRASSHOPPER LEAPS, THE SCARECROW BOUNDS AND SPRINGS AWAY -- THE DYNAMIC DUO IN FULL PURSUIT!
HE'S GOING INTO THAT PLAY-GROUND!
NOW THIS WILL BE A NICE TRICK IF IT WORKS!
OUT SPRINGS THE BOY WONDER-
IT'S THAT MEDDLESOME BOY AGAIN!
BUT THE SCARECROW'S BONY, KNOTTED FIST SMASHES HIM FULL IN THE FACE ---
YOU HAVE TO BE QUICKER THAN THAT..
DROP THAT GUN!
I'LL FINISH YOU FIRST, THEN YOUR PAL!
BUT THE SCARECROW IS TOO INTENT UPON EVIL TO NOTE THE STILL FLYING SWING ---AND--
12

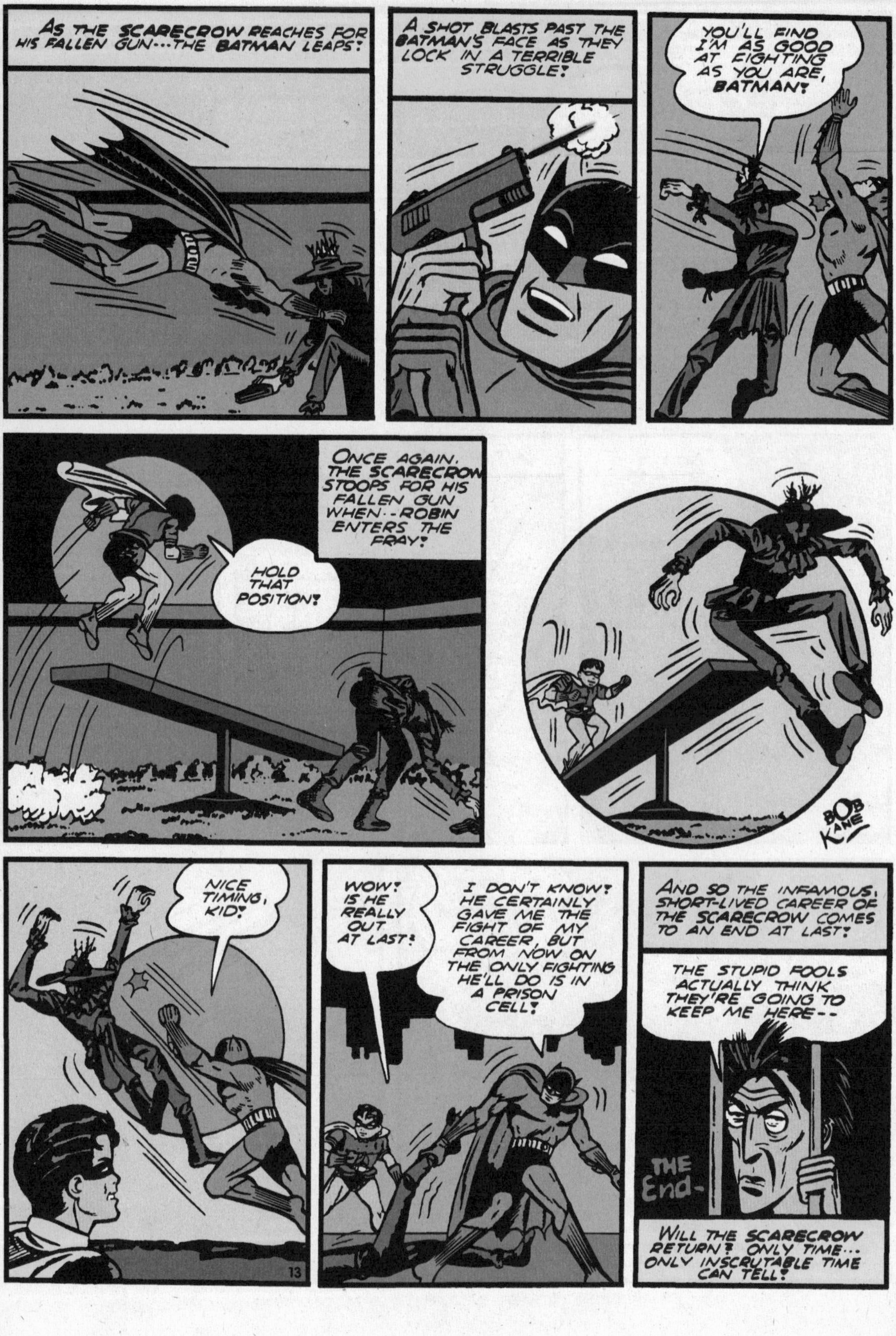
AS THE SCARECROW REACHES FOR HIS FALLEN GUN---THE BATMAN LEAPS!
A SHOT BLASTS PAST THE BATMAN'S FACE AS THEY LOCK IN A TERRIBLE STRUGGLE!
YOU'LL FIND I'M AS GOOD AT FIGHTING AS YOU ARE, BATMAN!
ONCE AGAIN, THE SCARECROW STOOPS FOR HIS FALLEN GUN WHEN--ROBIN ENTERS THE FRAY!
HOLD THAT POSITION!
BOB KANE
NICE TIMING, KID!
13
WOW! IS HE REALLY OUT AT LAST?
I DON'T KNOW! HE CERTAINLY GAVE ME THE FIGHT OF MY CAREER, BUT FROM NOW ON THE ONLY FIGHTING HE'LL DO IS IN A PRISON CELL!
AND SO THE INFAMOUS, SHORT-LIVED CAREER OF THE SCARECROW COMES TO AN END AT LAST!
THE STUPID FOOLS ACTUALLY THINK THEY'RE GOING TO KEEP ME HERE--
THE End-
WILL THE SCARECROW RETURN? ONLY TIME... ONLY INSCRUTABLE TIME CAN TELL!

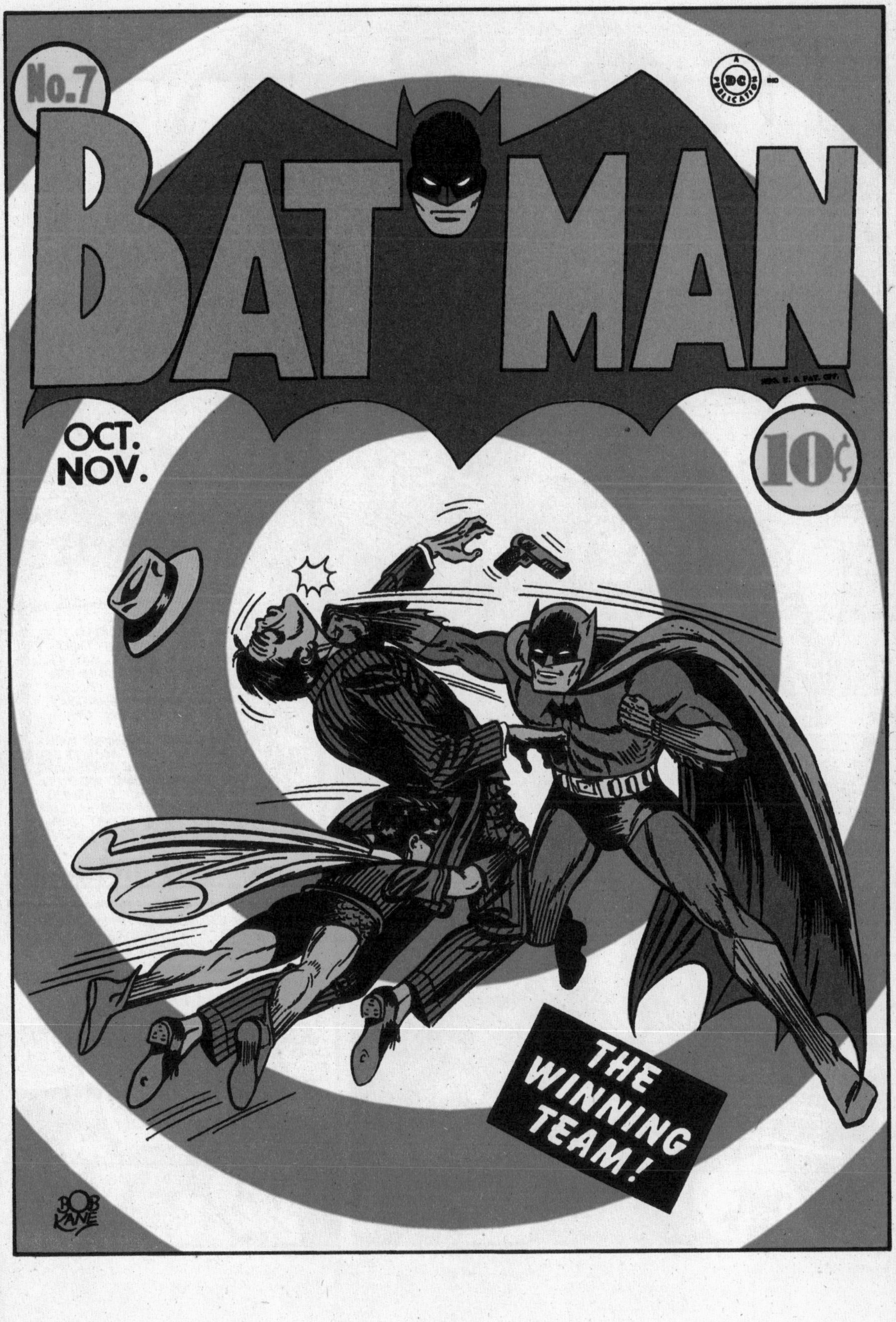
No.7
BATMAN
OCT.
NOV.
10¢
THE WINNING TEAM!
BOB KANE

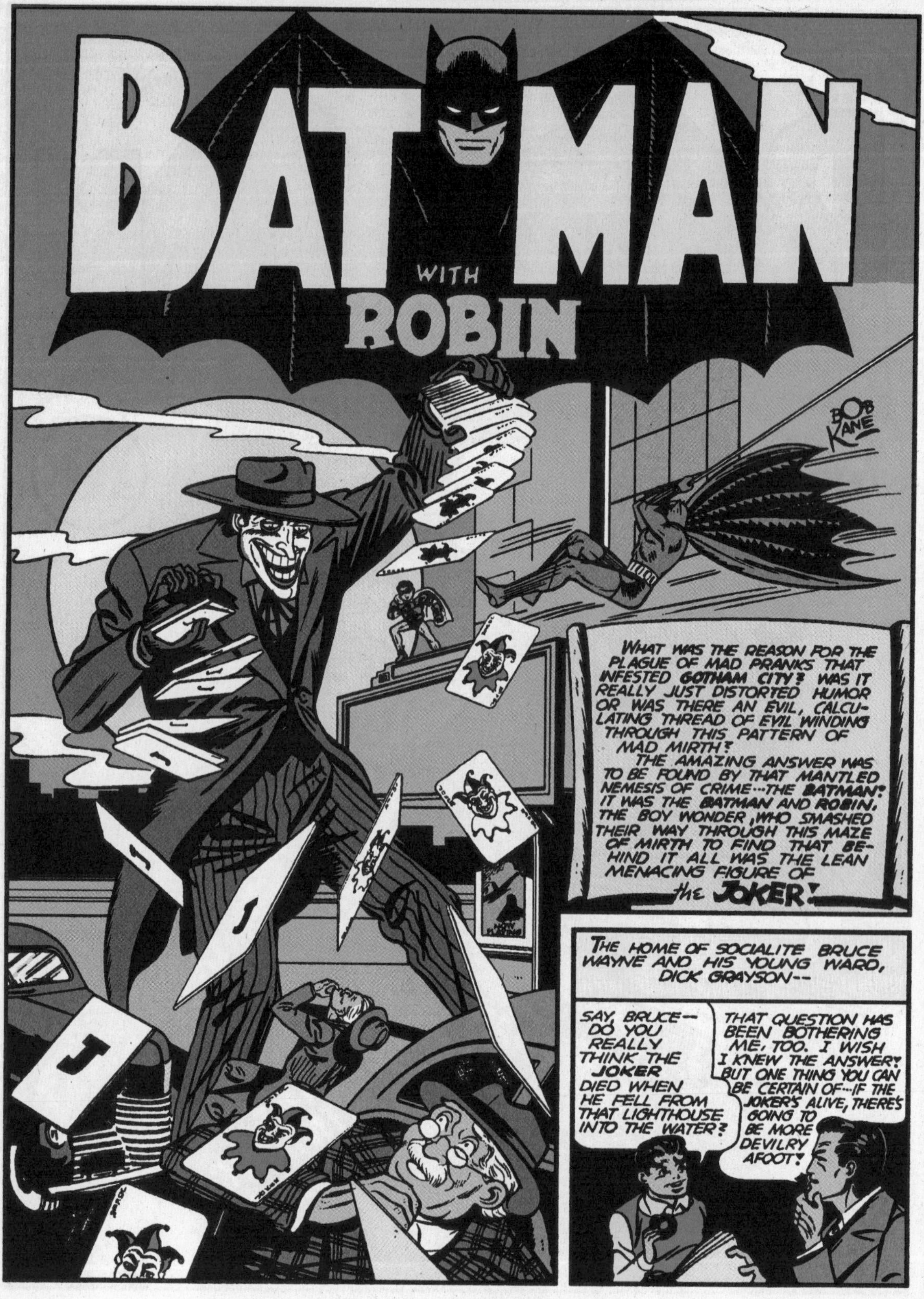

BATMAN
WITH
ROBIN
BOB KANE
WHAT WAS THE REASON FOR THE PLAGUE OF MAD PRANKS THAT INFESTED GOTHAM CITY? WAS IT REALLY JUST DISTORTED HUMOR OR WAS THERE AN EVIL, CALCULATING THREAD OF EVIL WINDING THROUGH THIS PATTERN OF MAD MIRTH? THE AMAZING ANSWER WAS TO BE FOUND BY THAT MANTLED NEMESIS OF CRIME---THE BATMAN! IT WAS THE BATMAN AND ROBIN, THE BOY WONDER, WHO SMASHED THEIR WAY THROUGH THIS MAZE OF MIRTH TO FIND THAT BEHIND IT ALL WAS THE LEAN MENACING FIGURE OF the JOKER!
THE HOME OF SOCIALITE BRUCE WAYNE AND HIS YOUNG WARD, DICK GRAYSON--
SAY, BRUCE-- DO YOU REALLY THINK THE JOKER DIED WHEN HE FELL FROM THAT LIGHTHOUSE INTO THE WATER?
THAT QUESTION HAS BEEN BOTHERING ME, TOO. I WISH I KNEW THE ANSWER! BUT ONE THING YOU CAN BE CERTAIN OF---IF THE JOKER'S ALIVE, THERE'S GOING TO BE MORE DEVILRY AFOOT!

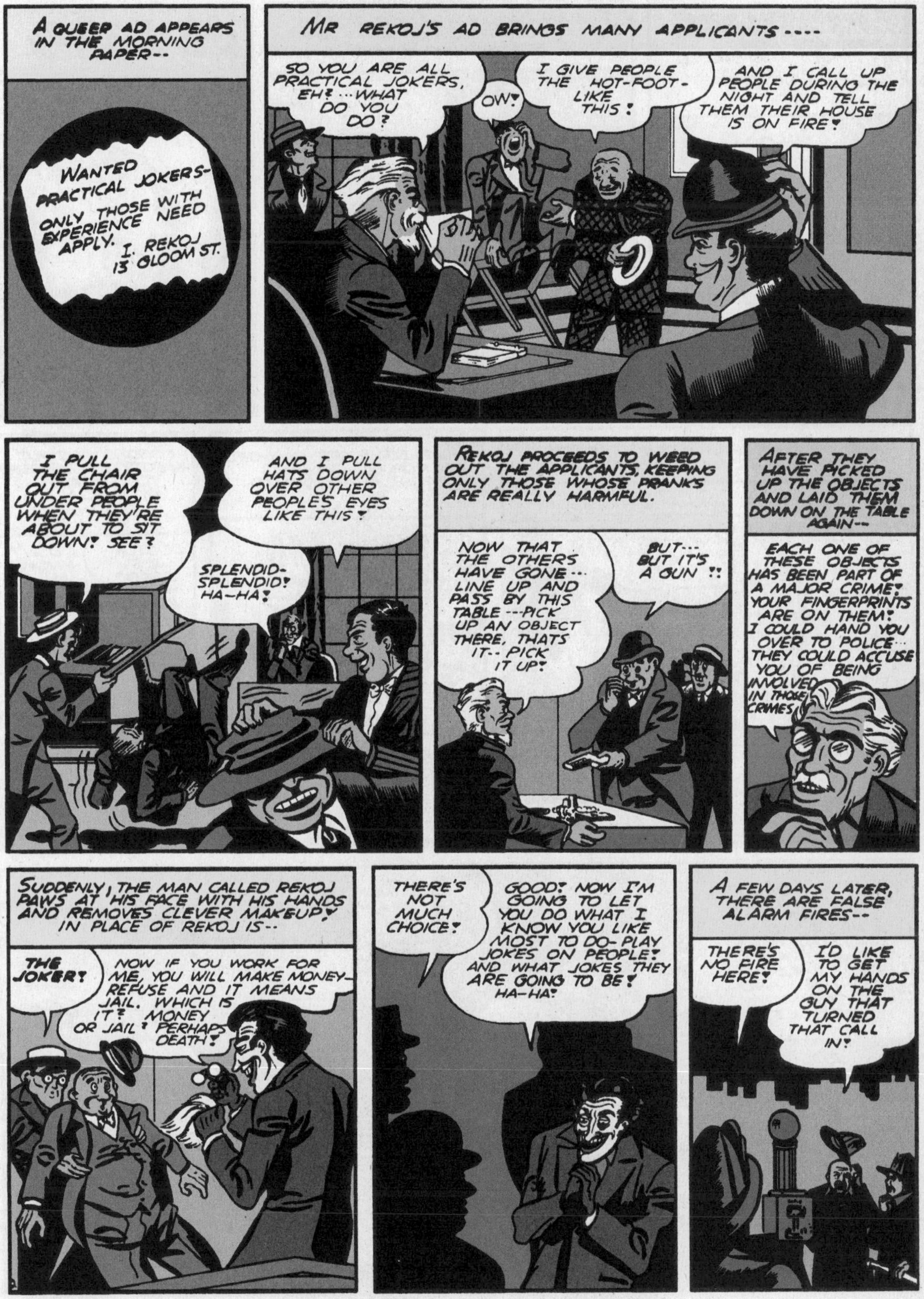
A QUEER AD APPEARS IN THE MORNING PAPER--
WANTED PRACTICAL JOKERS- ONLY THOSE WITH EXPERIENCE NEED APPLY. I. REKOJ 13 GLOOM ST.
MR REKOJ'S AD BRINGS MANY APPLICANTS----
SO YOU ARE ALL PRACTICAL JOKERS, EH? ...WHAT DO YOU DO?
OW!
I GIVE PEOPLE THE HOT-FOOT- LIKE THIS!
AND I CALL UP PEOPLE DURING THE NIGHT AND TELL THEM THEIR HOUSE IS ON FIRE!
I PULL THE CHAIR OUT FROM UNDER PEOPLE WHEN THEY'RE ABOUT TO SIT DOWN! SEE?
AND I PULL HATS DOWN OVER OTHER PEOPLE'S EYES LIKE THIS!
SPLENDID- SPLENDID! HA-HA!
REKOJ PROCEEDS TO WEED OUT THE APPLICANTS, KEEPING ONLY THOSE WHOSE PRANKS ARE REALLY HARMFUL.
NOW THAT THE OTHERS HAVE GONE--- LINE UP AND PASS BY THIS TABLE ---PICK UP AN OBJECT THERE, THATS IT-- PICK IT UP!
BUT--- BUT IT'S A GUN !!
AFTER THEY HAVE PICKED UP THE OBJECTS AND LAID THEM DOWN ON THE TABLE AGAIN--
EACH ONE OF THESE OBJECTS HAS BEEN PART OF A MAJOR CRIME! YOUR FINGERPRINTS ARE ON THEM! I COULD HAND YOU OVER TO POLICE... THEY COULD ACCUSE YOU OF BEING INVOLVED IN THOSE CRIMES
SUDDENLY, THE MAN CALLED REKOJ PAWS AT HIS FACE WITH HIS HANDS AND REMOVES CLEVER MAKEUP! IN PLACE OF REKOJ IS--
THE JOKER!
NOW IF YOU WORK FOR ME, YOU WILL MAKE MONEY- REFUSE AND IT MEANS JAIL. WHICH IS IT? MONEY OR JAIL? PERHAPS DEATH!
THERE'S NOT MUCH CHOICE!
GOOD! NOW I'M GOING TO LET YOU DO WHAT I KNOW YOU LIKE MOST TO DO- PLAY JOKES ON PEOPLE! AND WHAT JOKES THEY ARE GOING TO BE! HA-HA!
A FEW DAYS LATER, THERE ARE FALSE ALARM FIRES--
THERE'S NO FIRE HERE!
I'D LIKE TO GET MY HANDS ON THE GUY THAT TURNED THAT CALL IN!

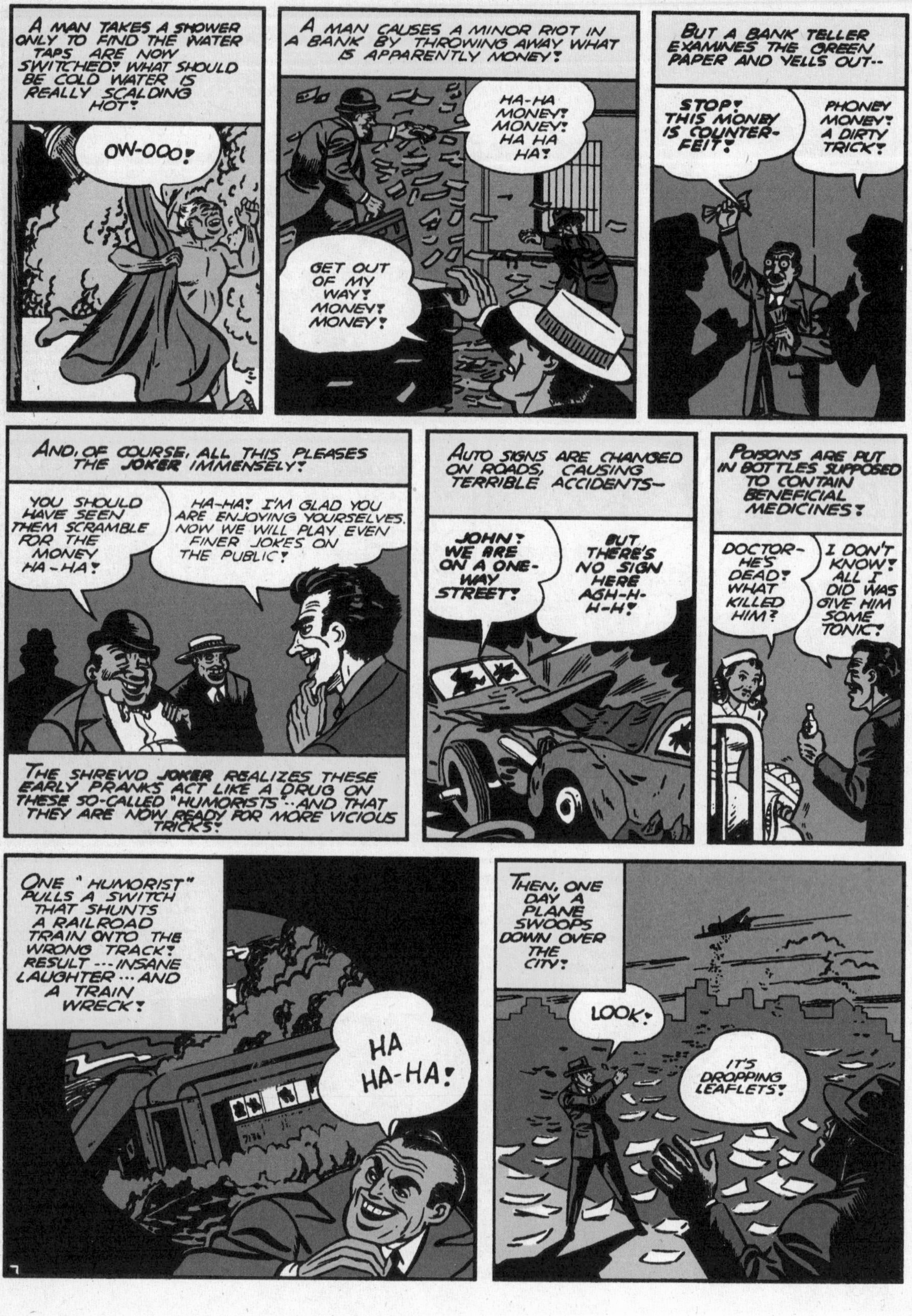
A MAN TAKES A SHOWER ONLY TO FIND THE WATER TAPS ARE NOW SWITCHED! WHAT SHOULD BE COLD WATER IS REALLY SCALDING HOT!
OW-OOO!
A MAN CAUSES A MINOR RIOT IN A BANK BY THROWING AWAY WHAT IS APPARENTLY MONEY!
HA-HA MONEY! MONEY! HA HA HA!
GET OUT OF MY WAY! MONEY! MONEY!
BUT A BANK TELLER EXAMINES THE GREEN PAPER AND YELLS OUT--
STOP! THIS MONEY IS COUNTER-FEIT!
PHONEY MONEY! A DIRTY TRICK!
AND, OF COURSE, ALL THIS PLEASES THE JOKER IMMENSELY!
YOU SHOULD HAVE SEEN THEM SCRAMBLE FOR THE MONEY HA-HA!
HA-HA! I'M GLAD YOU ARE ENJOYING YOURSELVES. NOW WE WILL PLAY EVEN FINER JOKES ON THE PUBLIC!
THE SHREWD JOKER REALIZES THESE EARLY PRANKS ACT LIKE A DRUG ON THESE SO-CALLED "HUMORISTS"--AND THAT THEY ARE NOW READY FOR MORE VICIOUS TRICKS!
AUTO SIGNS ARE CHANGED ON ROADS, CAUSING TERRIBLE ACCIDENTS--
JOHN! WE ARE ON A ONE-WAY STREET!
BUT THERE'S NO SIGN HERE AGH-H-H-H!
POISONS ARE PUT IN BOTTLES SUPPOSED TO CONTAIN BENEFICIAL MEDICINES!
DOCTOR-HE'S DEAD! WHAT KILLED HIM?
I DON'T KNOW! ALL I DID WAS GIVE HIM SOME TONIC!
ONE "HUMORIST" PULLS A SWITCH THAT SHUNTS A RAILROAD TRAIN ONTO THE WRONG TRACK! RESULT---INSANE LAUGHTER...AND A TRAIN WRECK!
HA HA-HA!
THEN, ONE DAY A PLANE SWOOPS DOWN OVER THE CITY!
LOOK!
IT'S DROPPING LEAFLETS!

THE LEAFLET!

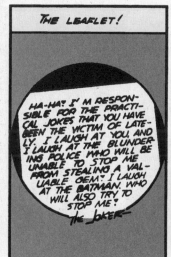

HA-HA! I'M RESPONSIBLE FOR THE PRACTICAL JOKES THAT YOU HAVE BEEN THE VICTIM OF LATELY. I LAUGH AT YOU, AND I LAUGH AT THE BLUNDERING POLICE WHO WILL BE UNABLE TO STOP ME FROM STEALING A VALUABLE GEM! I LAUGH AT THE BATMAN, WHO WILL ALSO TRY TO STOP ME!
The JOKER

PUBLIC FEELING NOW RUNS HIGH! NOBODY LIKES TO BE LAUGHED AT-- ESPECIALLY BY A CRIMINAL!

TAKE IT EASY, GORDON! YOU'RE LIKELY TO BURST A BLOOD VESSEL!

HOW CAN I TAKE IT EASY WHILE THE JOKER LAUGHS AT THE WHOLE POLICE FORCE!

POLICE COMMISSIONER GORDON!

MY NAME IS HENRY VERNE! READ THIS NOTE I RECEIVED THIS MORNING!

"TOMORROW NIGHT I WILL ENTER YOUR HOME AND STEAL THE GREAT DIAMOND YOU POSSESS!
THE JOKER"

WHAT CAN I DO? THE JOKER WILL SURELY STEAL MY DIAMOND!

NO, HE WON'T! YOU STAY AT HOME! WHEN THE JOKER ENTERS YOUR HOUSE, HE'S GOING TO WALK INTO A TRAP!

YOU HOPE!

AND AT THAT MOMENT--

YOU HAVE DONE WELL! THE PUBLIC AND THE POLICE ARE SO AROUSED AGAINST ME THAT OUR PLANS WILL CATCH THEM OFF-GUARD--

THE NEXT NIGHT--- A STRANGE TENSION GRIPS THE POLICEMEN POSTED ABOUT THE VERNE HOME--

I CAN HEAR VERNE PACING UP AND DOWN INSIDE-- BOY, IS HE NERVOUS!

I DON'T BLAME HIM! THIS WAITING AROUND FOR THE JOKER IS GETTING ME, TOO!

AND AT THAT VERY INSTANT, TWO MANTLED FIGURES LOPE SWIFTLY THROUGH GREY CITY STREETS! THEY ARE THE BATMAN AND ROBIN--

C'MON ROBIN, WE'VE GOT A DATE WITH THE JOKER!

LET'S STEP IT UP!

WHEN THEY ARRIVE AT THE VERNE HOME--

LOOK! THEY'RE UNCONSCIOUS!

AND WITH THAT JOKER GRIN ON THEIR FACES! C'MON, LET'S HOPE WE'RE NOT TOO LATE!

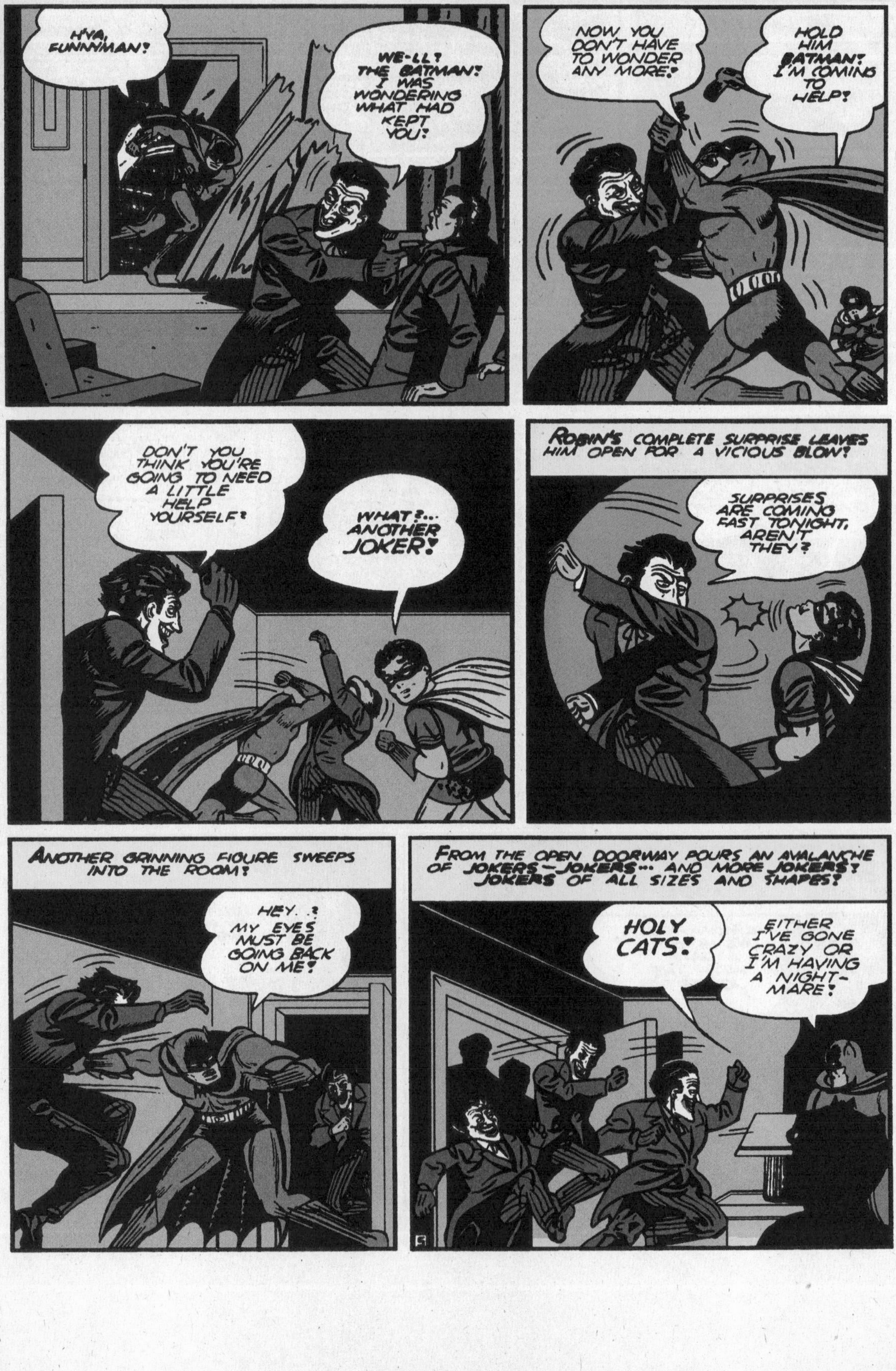
H'YA, FUNNYMAN!
WE-LL! THE BATMAN! I WAS WONDERING WHAT HAD KEPT YOU!
NOW YOU DON'T HAVE TO WONDER ANY MORE!
HOLD HIM BATMAN! I'M COMING TO HELP!
DON'T YOU THINK YOU'RE GOING TO NEED A LITTLE HELP YOURSELF?
WHAT?... ANOTHER JOKER!
ROBIN'S COMPLETE SURPRISE LEAVES HIM OPEN FOR A VICIOUS BLOW!
SURPRISES ARE COMING FAST TONIGHT, AREN'T THEY?
ANOTHER GRINNING FIGURE SWEEPS INTO THE ROOM!
HEY..? MY EYES MUST BE GOING BACK ON ME!
FROM THE OPEN DOORWAY POURS AN AVALANCHE OF JOKERS—JOKERS... AND MORE JOKERS! JOKERS OF ALL SIZES AND SHAPES!
HOLY CATS!
EITHER I'VE GONE CRAZY OR I'M HAVING A NIGHT-MARE!

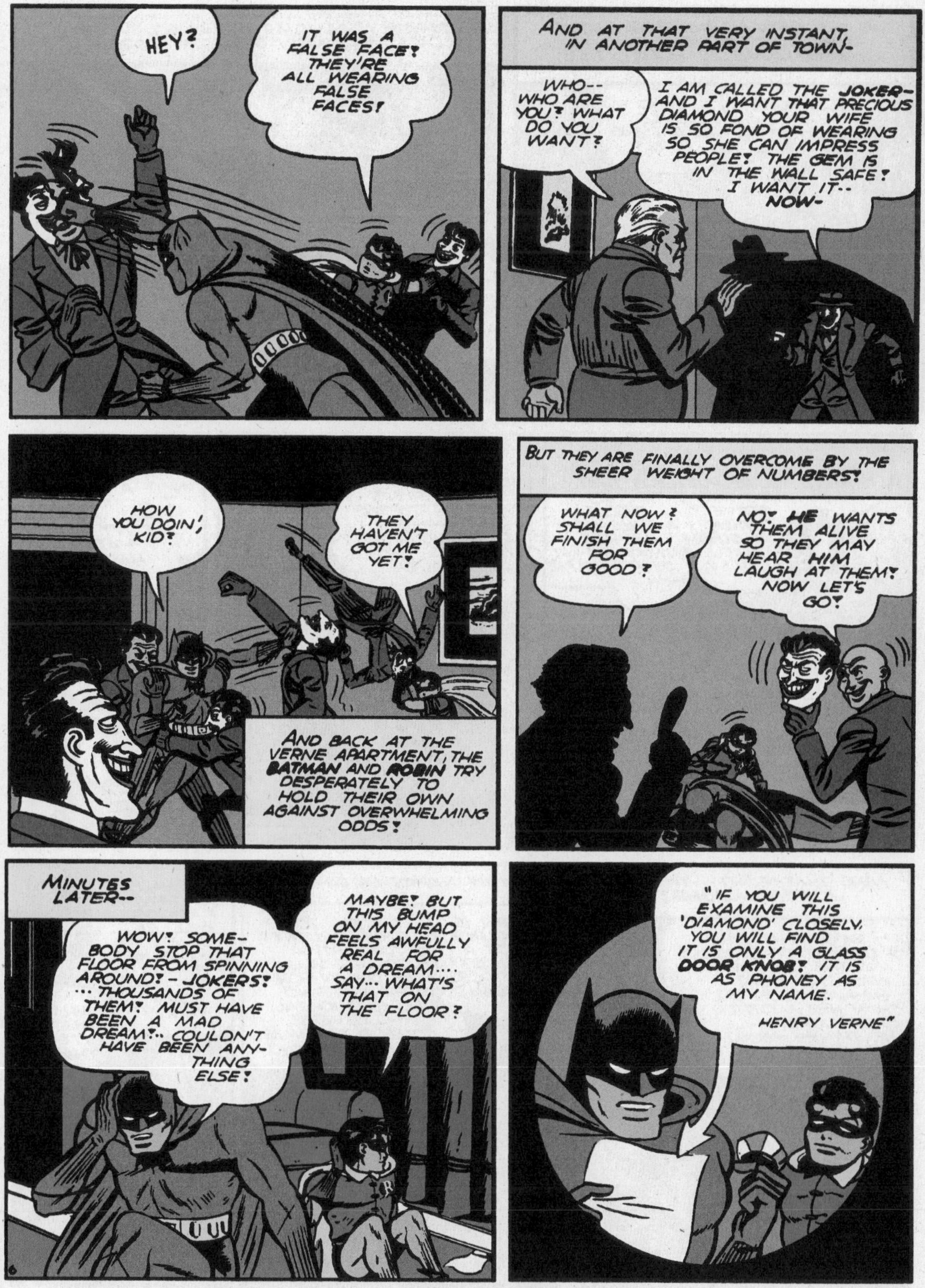
HEY?
IT WAS A FALSE FACE! THEY'RE ALL WEARING FALSE FACES!
AND AT THAT VERY INSTANT, IN ANOTHER PART OF TOWN-
WHO-- WHO ARE YOU? WHAT DO YOU WANT?
I AM CALLED THE JOKER- AND I WANT THAT PRECIOUS DIAMOND YOUR WIFE IS SO FOND OF WEARING SO SHE CAN IMPRESS PEOPLE! THE GEM IS IN THE WALL SAFE! I WANT IT-- NOW-
HOW YOU DOIN', KID?
THEY HAVEN'T GOT ME YET!
AND BACK AT THE VERNE APARTMENT, THE BATMAN AND ROBIN TRY DESPERATELY TO HOLD THEIR OWN AGAINST OVERWHELMING ODDS!
BUT THEY ARE FINALLY OVERCOME BY THE SHEER WEIGHT OF NUMBERS!
WHAT NOW? SHALL WE FINISH THEM FOR GOOD?
NO! HE WANTS THEM ALIVE SO THEY MAY HEAR HIM LAUGH AT THEM! NOW LET'S GO!
MINUTES LATER--
WOW! SOMEBODY STOP THAT FLOOR FROM SPINNING AROUND! - JOKERS! ... THOUSANDS OF THEM! MUST HAVE BEEN A MAD DREAM!.. COULDN'T HAVE BEEN ANYTHING ELSE!
MAYBE! BUT THIS BUMP ON MY HEAD FEELS AWFULLY REAL FOR A DREAM.... SAY... WHAT'S THAT ON THE FLOOR?
"IF YOU WILL EXAMINE THIS 'DIAMOND' CLOSELY, YOU WILL FIND IT IS ONLY A GLASS DOOR KNOB! IT IS AS PHONEY AS MY NAME.
HENRY VERNE"

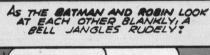
AS THE BATMAN AND ROBIN LOOK AT EACH OTHER BLANKLY, A BELL JANGLES RUDELY!

TELEPHONE!

WHO COULD BE CALLING HERE?

R·I·N·G

A TERRIBLY FAMILIAR, MOURNFUL VOICE FLOATS MOCKINGLY OVER THE WIRE--

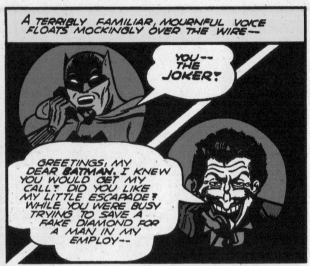

YOU-- THE JOKER?

GREETINGS, MY DEAR BATMAN, I KNEW YOU WOULD GET MY CALL? DID YOU LIKE MY LITTLE ESCAPADE? WHILE YOU WERE BUSY TRYING TO SAVE A FAKE DIAMOND FOR A MAN IN MY EMPLOY--

--- I WAS OUT STEALING A REAL GEM? FUNNY, EH? HA HA? WHILE YOU'RE PUZZLING THAT OUT, YOU MIGHT TRY TO SOLVE THIS RIDDLE-- "WHEN IS A DUKE NOT A DUKE?" HA-HA? ADIEU, BATMAN--HA HA? THINK IT OVER BATMAN? HA-HA

YOU LAUGHING HYENA?

THAT GRINNING DEVIL? I'M GOING TO WIPE THAT SMILE OFF HIS FACE IF IT'S THE LAST THING I DO? WE'LL SEE WHO HAS THE LAST LAUGH YET?

HE HAS A SENSE OF HUMOR-- ONLY IT'S DISTORTED?

"WHEN IS A DUKE NOT A DUKE?" I WONDER WHAT HE MEANT BY THAT? HMM--

AND THAT NIGHT---THE JOKER LAUGHS?

HA-HA-HA? WHAT A COMEDY OF ERRORS? AND THE BATMAN WAS THE GOAT? HA-HA? SOON I'LL SHOW HIM ANOTHER GREAT JOKE WHILE HE THINKS ABOUT THAT RIDDLE? HA HA-HA?

A FEW NIGHTS LATER--

"WHEN IS A DUKE NOT A DUKE?" WHAT DOES IT MEAN?

LISTEN TO THIS, BRUCE? TONIGHT, A DINNER WILL BE GIVEN FOR THE VISITING DUKE MICHEAL, WHO IS HERE COLLECTING FUNDS FOR HIS STARVING PEOPLE?"

"---A VALISE CONTAINING $10,000 WILL BE GIVEN TO DUKE MICHEAL TO AID THE WAR-TORN NATION?"

WHAT? THAT'S IT?... THAT'S IT?

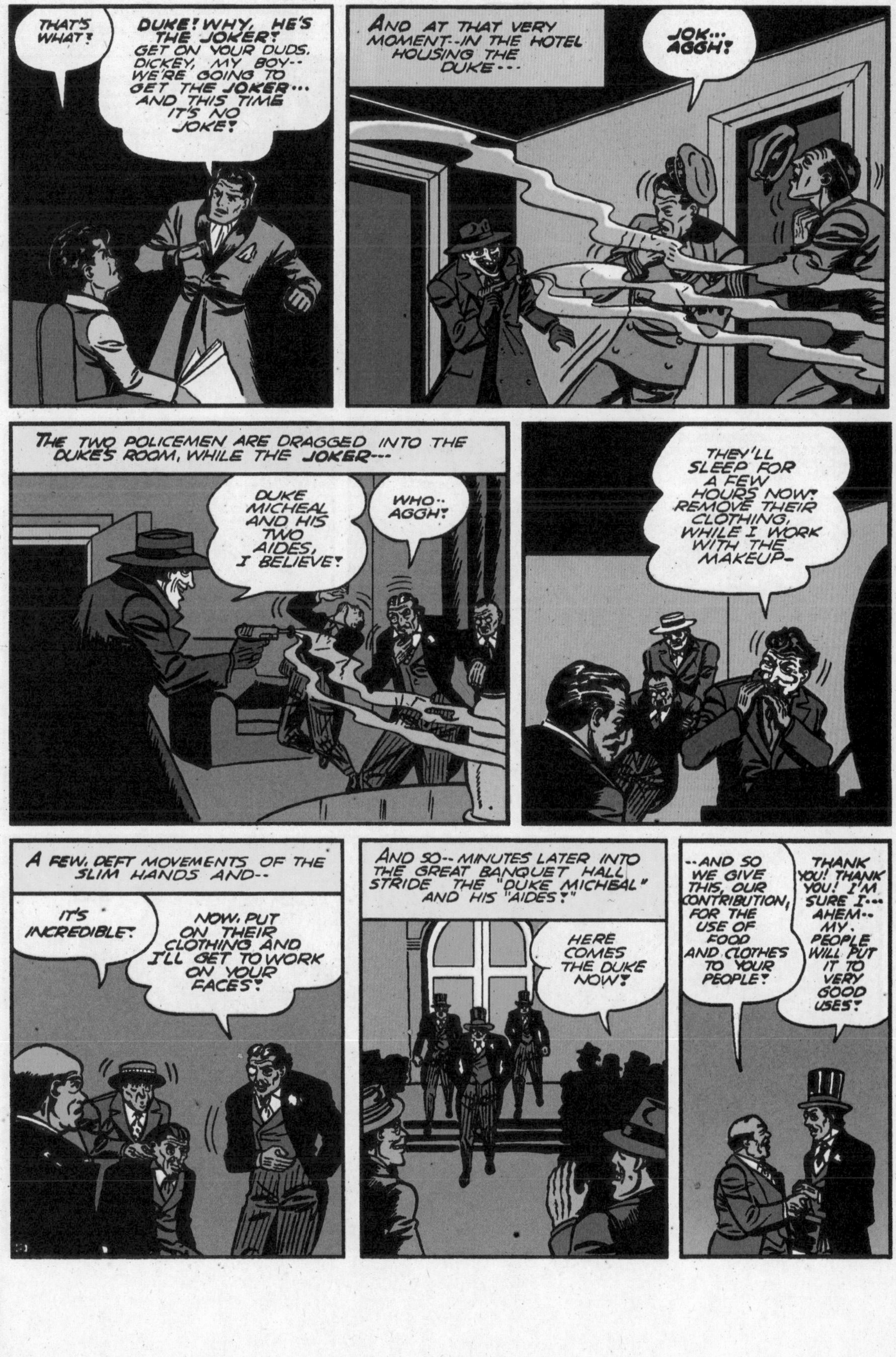
THAT'S WHAT?
DUKE! WHY, HE'S THE JOKER! GET ON YOUR DUDS, DICKEY, MY BOY-- WE'RE GOING TO GET THE JOKER... AND THIS TIME IT'S NO JOKE!
AND AT THAT VERY MOMENT--IN THE HOTEL HOUSING THE DUKE---
JOK... AGGH!
THE TWO POLICEMEN ARE DRAGGED INTO THE DUKE'S ROOM, WHILE THE JOKER---
DUKE MICHEAL AND HIS TWO AIDES, I BELIEVE!
WHO.. AGGH!
THEY'LL SLEEP FOR A FEW HOURS NOW! REMOVE THEIR CLOTHING, WHILE I WORK WITH THE MAKEUP-
A FEW, DEFT MOVEMENTS OF THE SLIM HANDS AND--
IT'S INCREDIBLE!
NOW, PUT ON THEIR CLOTHING AND I'LL GET TO WORK ON YOUR FACES!
AND SO-- MINUTES LATER INTO THE GREAT BANQUET HALL STRIDE THE "DUKE MICHEAL" AND HIS "AIDES!"
HERE COMES THE DUKE NOW!
--AND SO WE GIVE THIS, OUR CONTRIBUTION, FOR THE USE OF FOOD AND CLOTHES TO YOUR PEOPLE!
THANK YOU! THANK YOU! I'M SURE I--- AHEM-- MY PEOPLE WILL PUT IT TO VERY GOOD USES!

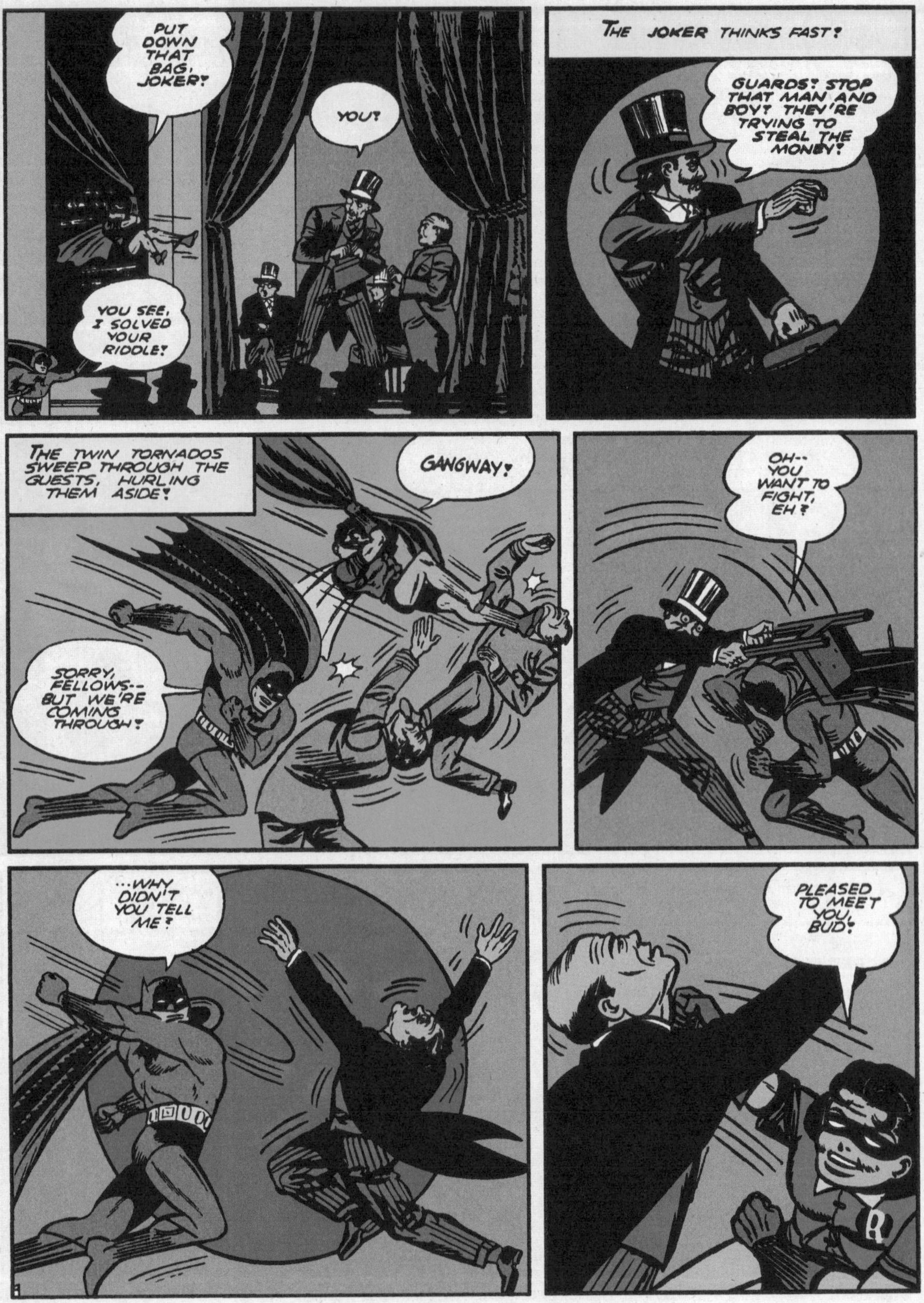
PUT DOWN THAT BAG, JOKER!
YOU!
YOU SEE, I SOLVED YOUR RIDDLE!
THE JOKER THINKS FAST!
GUARDS! STOP THAT MAN AND BOY! THEY'RE TRYING TO STEAL THE MONEY!
THE TWIN TORNADOS SWEEP THROUGH THE GUESTS, HURLING THEM ASIDE!
GANGWAY!
SORRY, FELLOWS-- BUT WE'RE COMING THROUGH!
OH-- YOU WANT TO FIGHT, EH?
...WHY DIDN'T YOU TELL ME?
PLEASED TO MEET YOU, BUD!

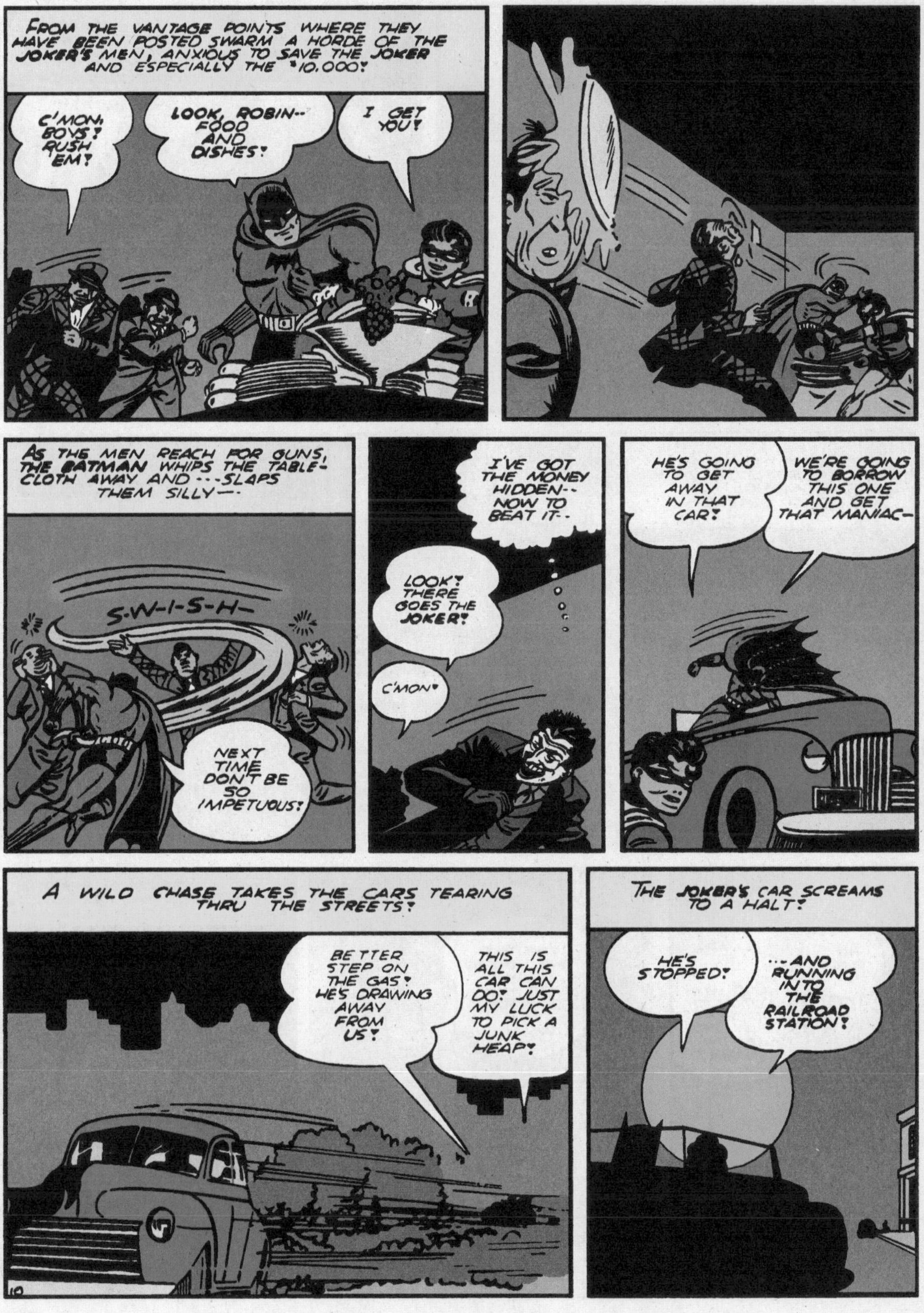
FROM THE VANTAGE POINTS WHERE THEY HAVE BEEN POSTED SWARM A HORDE OF THE JOKER'S MEN, ANXIOUS TO SAVE THE JOKER AND ESPECIALLY THE $10,000!
C'MON, BOYS! RUSH 'EM!
LOOK, ROBIN-- FOOD AND DISHES!
I GET YOU!
AS THE MEN REACH FOR GUNS, THE BATMAN WHIPS THE TABLE-CLOTH AWAY AND---SLAPS THEM SILLY--.
S-W-I-S-H-
NEXT TIME DON'T BE SO IMPETUOUS!
I'VE GOT THE MONEY HIDDEN-- NOW TO BEAT IT--
LOOK! THERE GOES THE JOKER!
C'MON!
HE'S GOING TO GET AWAY IN THAT CAR!
WE'RE GOING TO BORROW THIS ONE AND GET THAT MANIAC--
A WILD CHASE TAKES THE CARS TEARING THRU THE STREETS!
BETTER STEP ON THE GAS! HE'S DRAWING AWAY FROM US!
THIS IS ALL THIS CAR CAN DO! JUST MY LUCK TO PICK A JUNK HEAP!
10
THE JOKER'S CAR SCREAMS TO A HALT!
HE'S STOPPED!
...AND RUNNING INTO THE RAILROAD STATION!

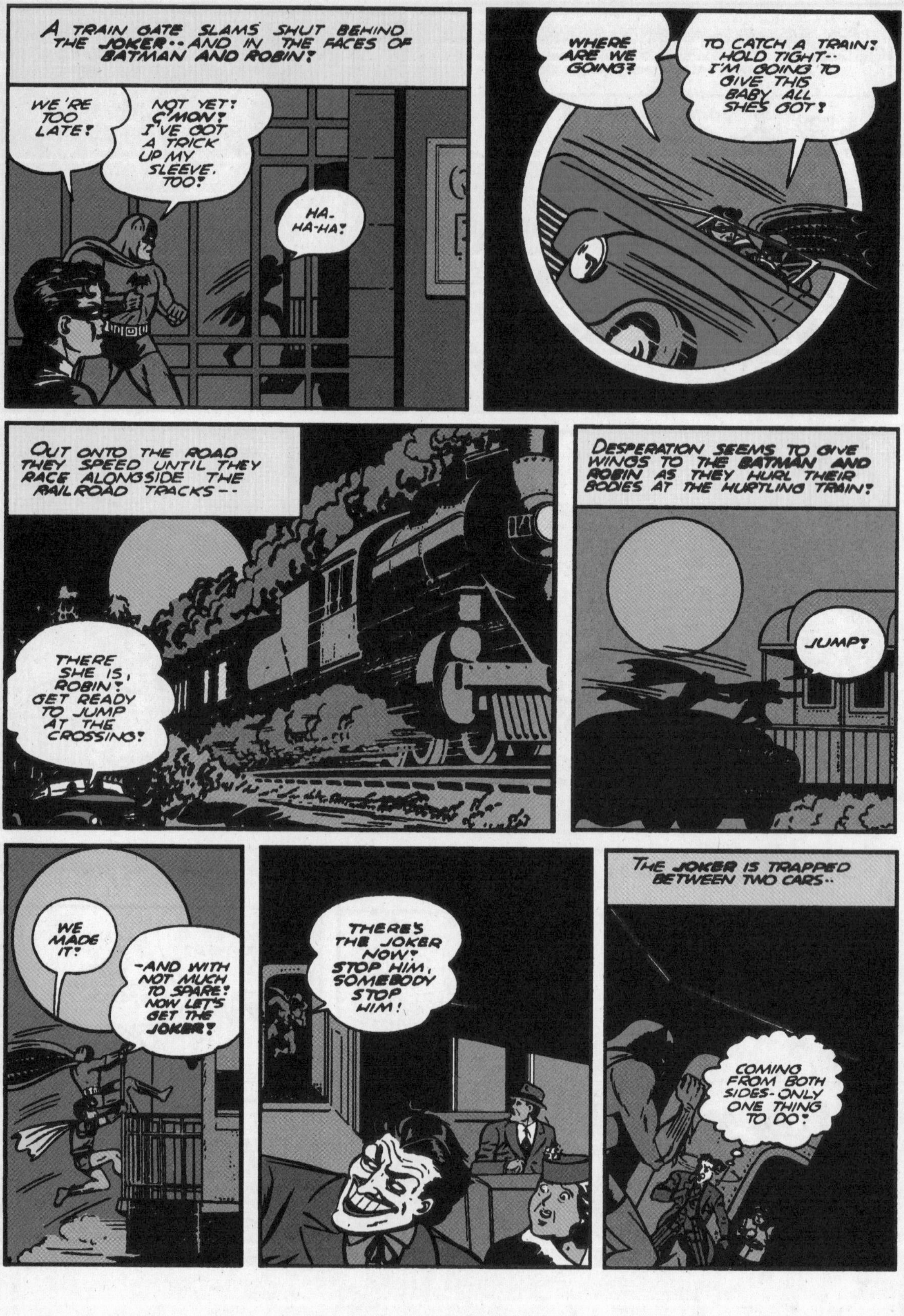

A TRAIN GATE SLAMS SHUT BEHIND THE JOKER--AND IN THE FACES OF BATMAN AND ROBIN!
WE'RE TOO LATE!
NOT YET! C'MON! I'VE GOT A TRICK UP MY SLEEVE, TOO!
HA-HA-HA!
WHERE ARE WE GOING?
TO CATCH A TRAIN! HOLD TIGHT-- I'M GOING TO GIVE THIS BABY ALL SHES GOT!
OUT ONTO THE ROAD THEY SPEED UNTIL THEY RACE ALONGSIDE THE RAILROAD TRACKS--
THERE SHE IS, ROBIN! GET READY TO JUMP AT THE CROSSING!
DESPERATION SEEMS TO GIVE WINGS TO THE BATMAN AND ROBIN AS THEY HURL THEIR BODIES AT THE HURTLING TRAIN!
JUMP!
WE MADE IT!
-AND WITH NOT MUCH TO SPARE! NOW LET'S GET THE JOKER!
THERE'S THE JOKER NOW! STOP HIM, SOMEBODY STOP HIM!
THE JOKER IS TRAPPED BETWEEN TWO CARS..
COMING FROM BOTH SIDES-ONLY ONE THING TO DO!

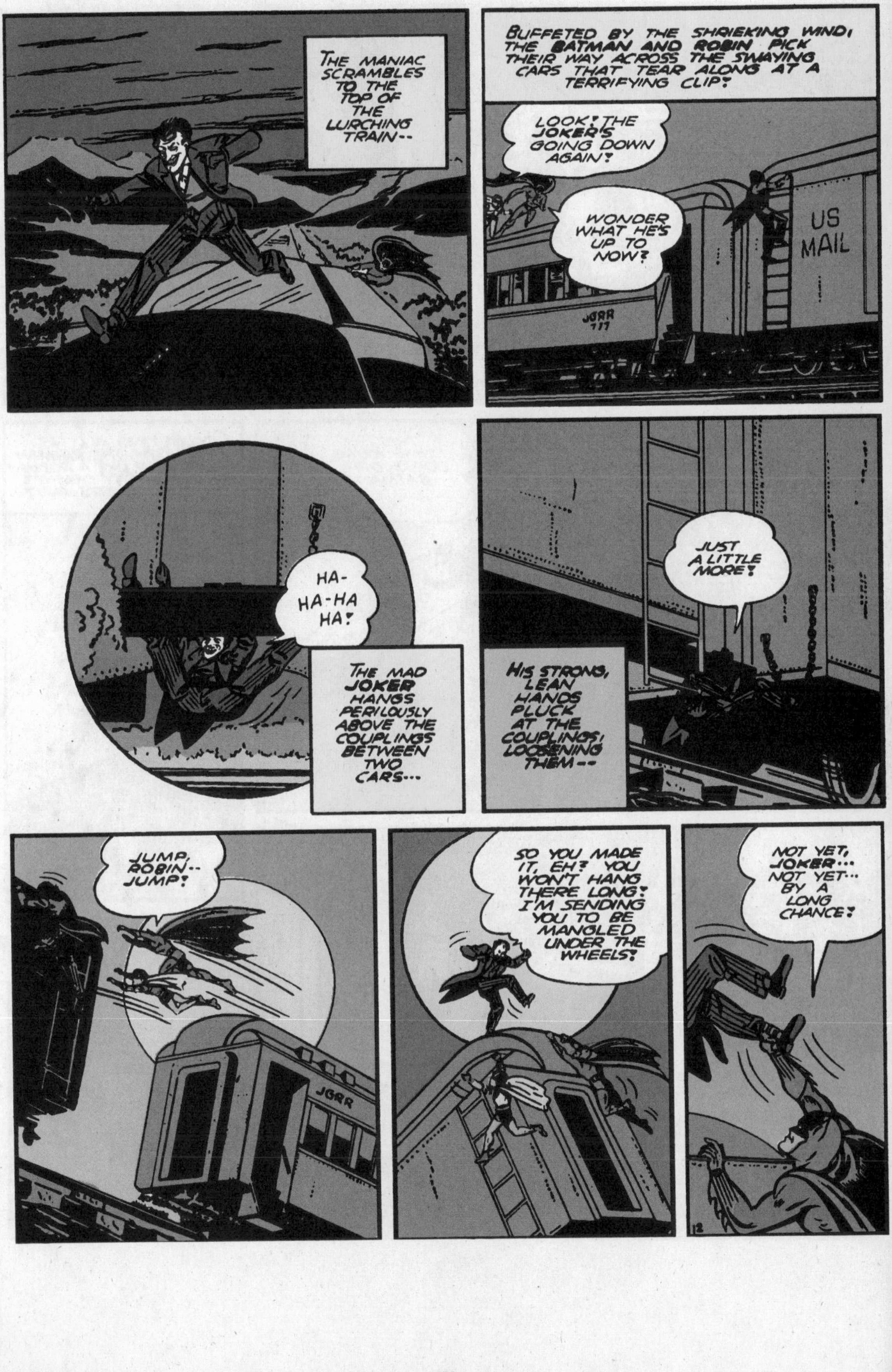
THE MANIAC SCRAMBLES TO THE TOP OF THE LURCHING TRAIN--
BUFFETED BY THE SHRIEKING WIND, THE BATMAN AND ROBIN PICK THEIR WAY ACROSS THE SWAYING CARS THAT TEAR ALONG AT A TERRIFYING CLIP!
LOOK! THE JOKER'S GOING DOWN AGAIN!
WONDER WHAT HE'S UP TO NOW?
US MAIL
JGRR 717
HA-HA-HA HA!
THE MAD JOKER HANGS PERILOUSLY ABOVE THE COUPLINGS BETWEEN TWO CARS...
JUST A LITTLE MORE!
HIS STRONG, LEAN HANDS PLUCK AT THE COUPLINGS, LOOSENING THEM--
JUMP, ROBIN-- JUMP!
JGRR
SO YOU MADE IT, EH? YOU WON'T HANG THERE LONG! I'M SENDING YOU TO BE MANGLED UNDER THE WHEELS!
NOT YET, JOKER... NOT YET... BY A LONG CHANCE!

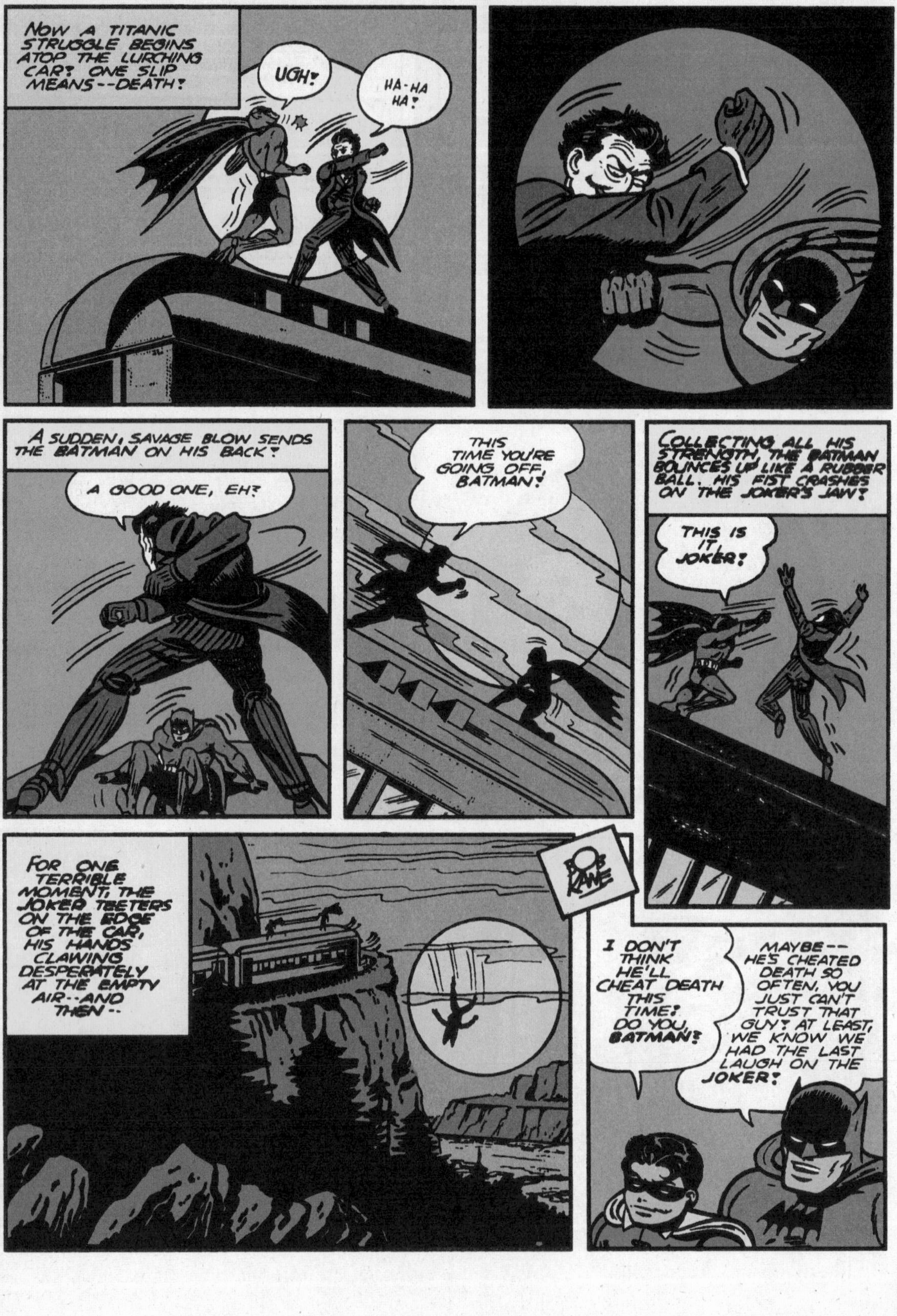
NOW A TITANIC STRUGGLE BEGINS ATOP THE LURCHING CAR! ONE SLIP MEANS--DEATH!
UGH!
HA-HA HA!
A SUDDEN, SAVAGE BLOW SENDS THE BATMAN ON HIS BACK!
A GOOD ONE, EH?
THIS TIME YOU'RE GOING OFF, BATMAN!
COLLECTING ALL HIS STRENGTH, THE BATMAN BOUNCES UP LIKE A RUBBER BALL. HIS FIST CRASHES ON THE JOKER'S JAW!
THIS IS IT, JOKER!
FOR ONE TERRIBLE MOMENT, THE JOKER TEETERS ON THE EDGE OF THE CAR, HIS HANDS CLAWING DESPERATELY AT THE EMPTY AIR--AND THEN--
BOB KANE
I DON'T THINK HE'LL CHEAT DEATH THIS TIME! DO YOU, BATMAN?
MAYBE-- HE'S CHEATED DEATH SO OFTEN, YOU JUST CAN'T TRUST THAT GUY! AT LEAST, WE KNOW WE HAD THE LAST LAUGH ON THE JOKER!

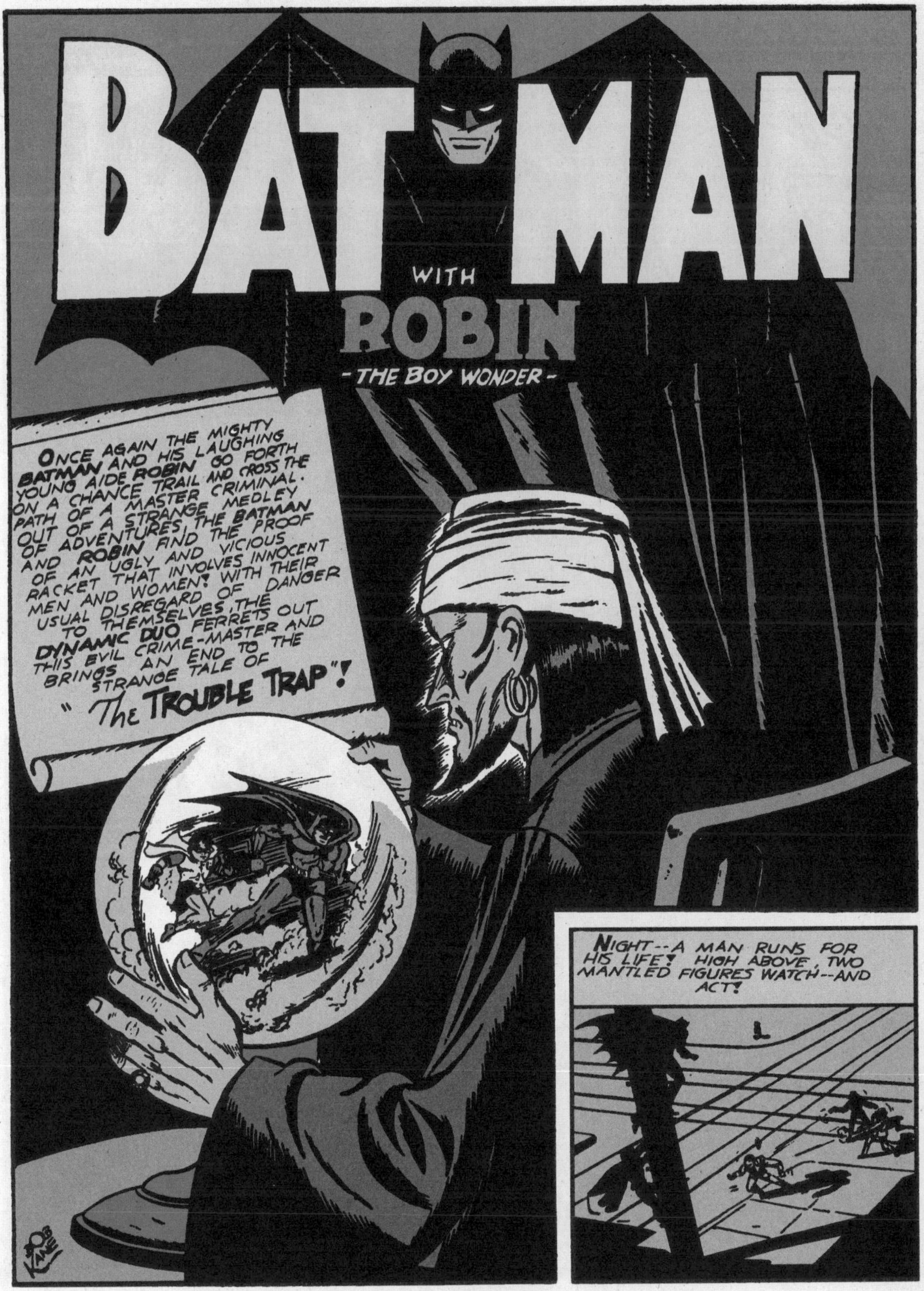
BATMAN
WITH
ROBIN
-THE BOY WONDER-
ONCE AGAIN THE MIGHTY BATMAN AND HIS LAUGHING YOUNG AIDE ROBIN GO FORTH ON A CHANCE TRAIL AND CROSS THE PATH OF A MASTER CRIMINAL. OUT OF A STRANGE MEDLEY OF ADVENTURES, THE BATMAN AND ROBIN FIND THE PROOF OF AN UGLY AND VICIOUS RACKET THAT INVOLVES INNOCENT MEN AND WOMEN! WITH THEIR USUAL DISREGARD OF DANGER TO THEMSELVES, THE DYNAMIC DUO FERRETS OUT THIS EVIL CRIME-MASTER AND BRINGS AN END TO THE STRANGE TALE OF
"The TROUBLE TRAP"!
BOB KANE
NIGHT--A MAN RUNS FOR HIS LIFE! HIGH ABOVE, TWO MANTLED FIGURES WATCH--AND ACT!

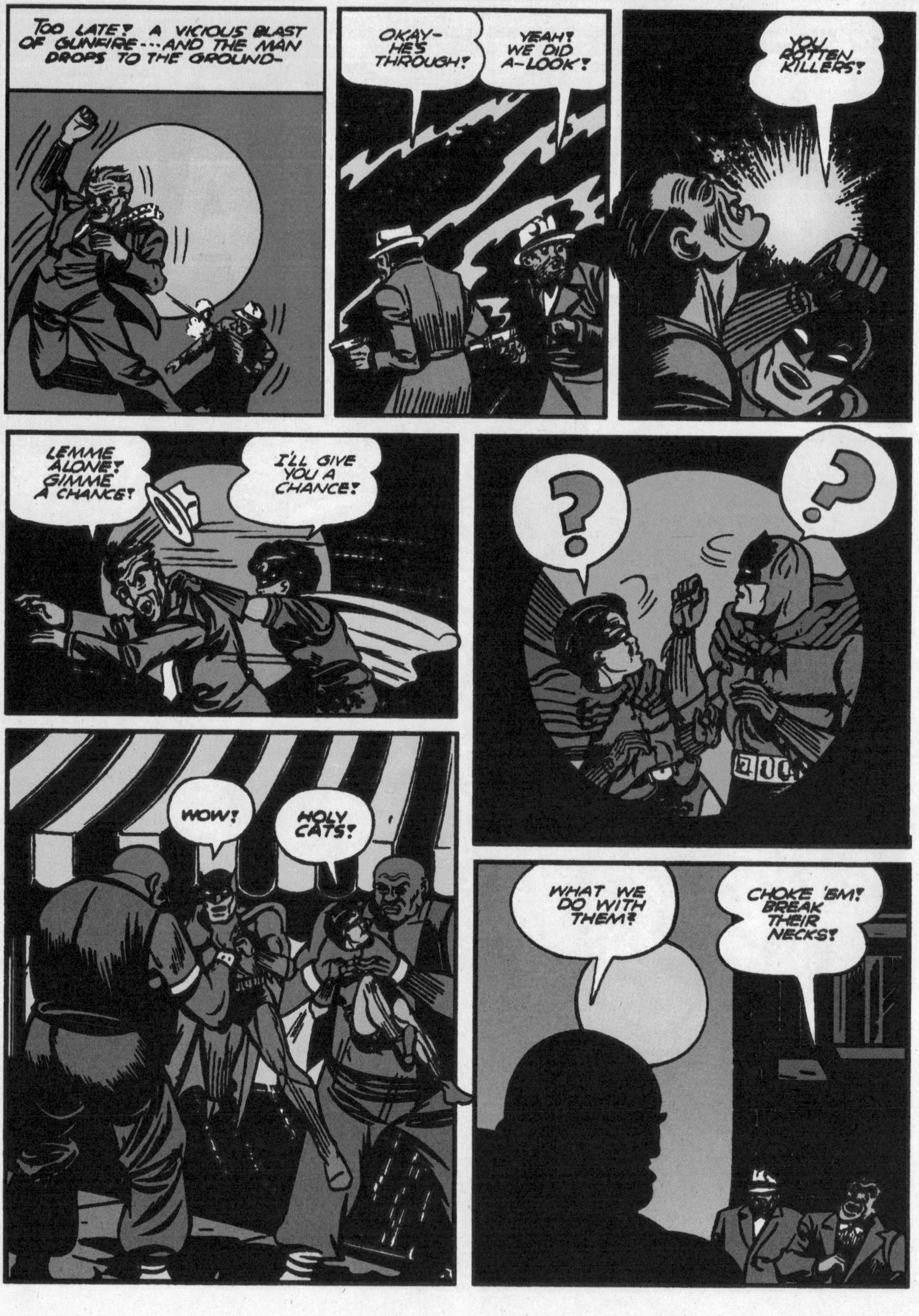
TOO LATE? A VICIOUS BLAST OF GUNFIRE---AND THE MAN DROPS TO THE GROUND-
OKAY- HE'S THROUGH?
YEAH? WE DID A-LOOK?
YOU ROTTEN KILLERS?
LEMME ALONE? GIMME A CHANCE?
I'LL GIVE YOU A CHANCE?
?
?
WOW?
HOLY CATS?
WHAT WE DO WITH THEM?
CHOKE 'EM? BREAK THEIR NECKS?

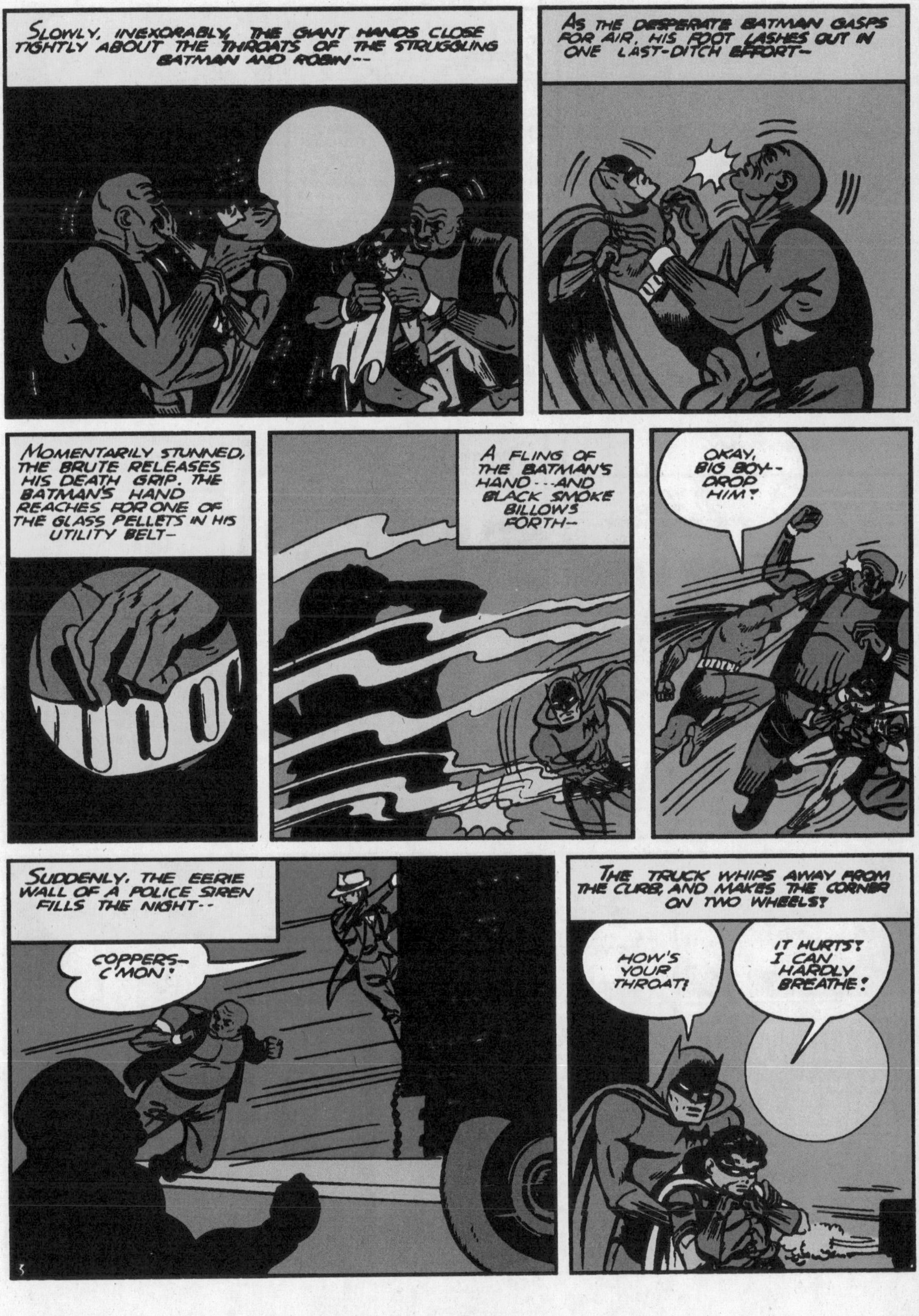
SLOWLY, INEXORABLY, THE GIANT HANDS CLOSE TIGHTLY ABOUT THE THROATS OF THE STRUGGLING BATMAN AND ROBIN--
AS THE DESPERATE BATMAN GASPS FOR AIR, HIS FOOT LASHES OUT IN ONE LAST-DITCH EFFORT--
MOMENTARILY STUNNED, THE BRUTE RELEASES HIS DEATH GRIP. THE BATMAN'S HAND REACHES FOR ONE OF THE GLASS PELLETS IN HIS UTILITY BELT--
A FLING OF THE BATMAN'S HAND---AND BLACK SMOKE BILLOWS FORTH--
OKAY, BIG BOY--DROP HIM!
SUDDENLY, THE EERIE WALL OF A POLICE SIREN FILLS THE NIGHT--
COPPERS--C'MON!
THE TRUCK WHIPS AWAY FROM THE CURB, AND MAKES THE CORNER ON TWO WHEELS!
HOW'S YOUR THROAT?
IT HURTS! I CAN HARDLY BREATHE!

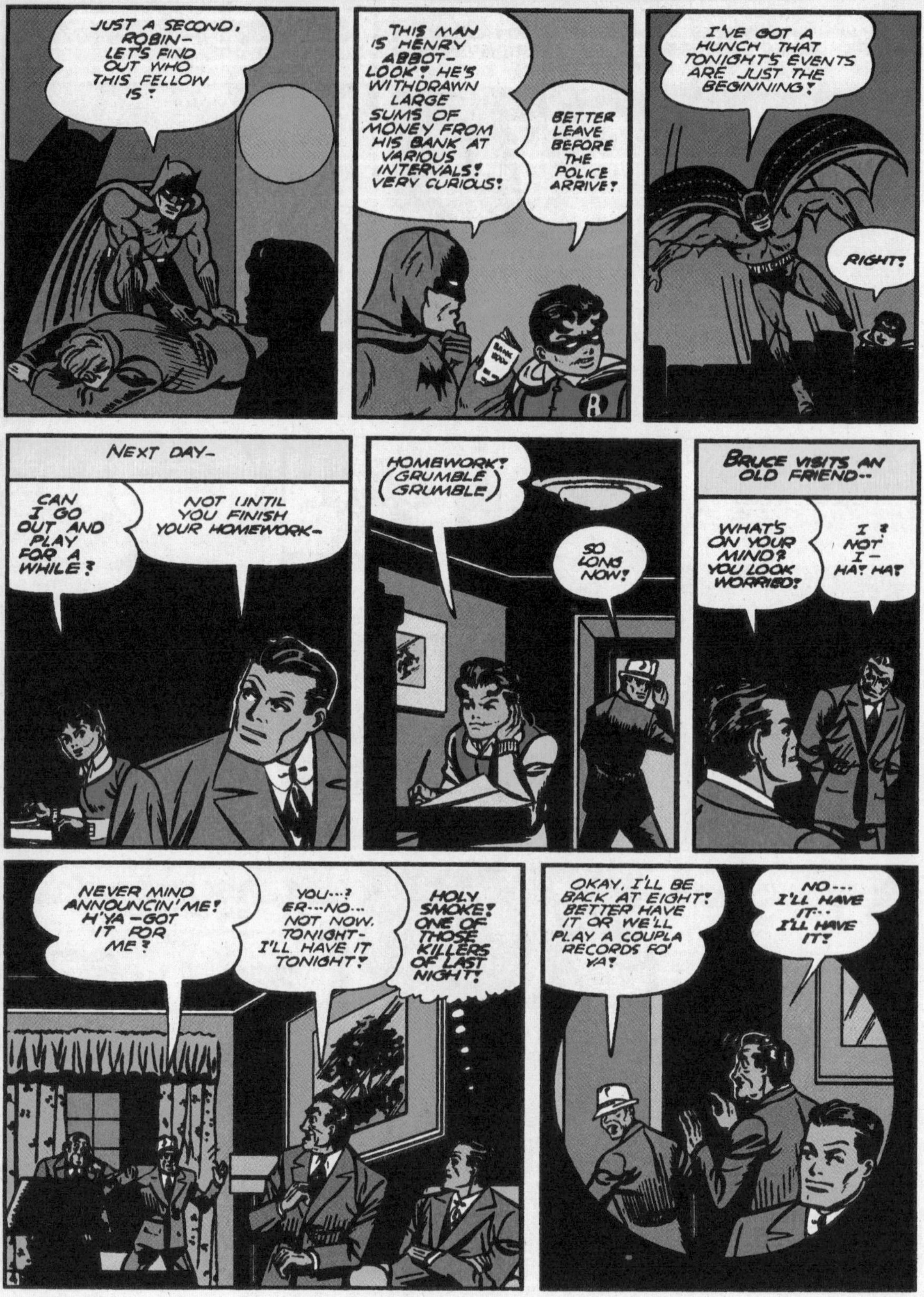
JUST A SECOND, ROBIN- LET'S FIND OUT WHO THIS FELLOW IS!
THIS MAN IS HENRY ABBOT- LOOK! HE'S WITHDRAWN LARGE SUMS OF MONEY FROM HIS BANK AT VARIOUS INTERVALS! VERY CURIOUS!
BETTER LEAVE BEFORE THE POLICE ARRIVE!
I'VE GOT A HUNCH THAT TONIGHT'S EVENTS ARE JUST THE BEGINNING!
RIGHT!
NEXT DAY-
CAN I GO OUT AND PLAY FOR A WHILE?
NOT UNTIL YOU FINISH YOUR HOMEWORK-
HOMEWORK! (GRUMBLE GRUMBLE)
SO LONG NOW!
BRUCE VISITS AN OLD FRIEND--
WHAT'S ON YOUR MIND? YOU LOOK WORRIED!
I? NOT I- HA! HA!
NEVER MIND ANNOUNCIN' ME! H'YA -GOT IT FOR ME?
YOU...? ER---NO... NOT NOW. TONIGHT- I'LL HAVE IT TONIGHT!
HOLY SMOKE! ONE OF THOSE KILLERS OF LAST NIGHT!
OKAY, I'LL BE BACK AT EIGHT! BETTER HAVE IT OR WE'LL PLAY A COUPLA RECORDS FO' YA!
NO--- I'LL HAVE IT-- I'LL HAVE IT!

WHO WAS THAT BOORISH FELLOW? HE WAS VERY IMPATIENT!

NOBODY IMPORTANT-- NOBODY AT ALL! UH, BRUCE, WOULD YOU MIND RUNNING ALONG NOW? I'M VERY BUSY--

SEE YOU AGAIN SOMETIME!

YOU SAID IT-- I'M COMING HERE AT EIGHT OCLOCK AND FIND OUT YOUR BUSINESS WITH THAT KILLER--

RIGHT, CARL!

THAT NIGHT! EIGHT O'CLOCK! A BLOTTED SHAPE MOVES SILENTLY OVER A WINDOW SILL AND INTO CARL DWYER'S HOME--

AND AT THAT VERY MOMENT CARL DWYER OPENS THE FRONT DOOR...

H'YA! GOT IT NOW!

YES! I HAD TO BORROW IT FROM MY FRIENDS! HERE!

YOU PROMISED TO BRING ME THE RECORD! I PAID YOU!

THE RECORD IS YOURS AFTER THE NEXT MONTH'S PAYMENT-- SEE YA NEXT MONTH!

AS THE HOODLUM HURRIES DOWN THE LONELY STREET ---

I SWORE I SAW SOMETHIN' FOLLOWIN' ME!

AND THE HOODLUM IS RIGHT! SOMEONE-- SOMETHING IS FOLLOWING HIM...

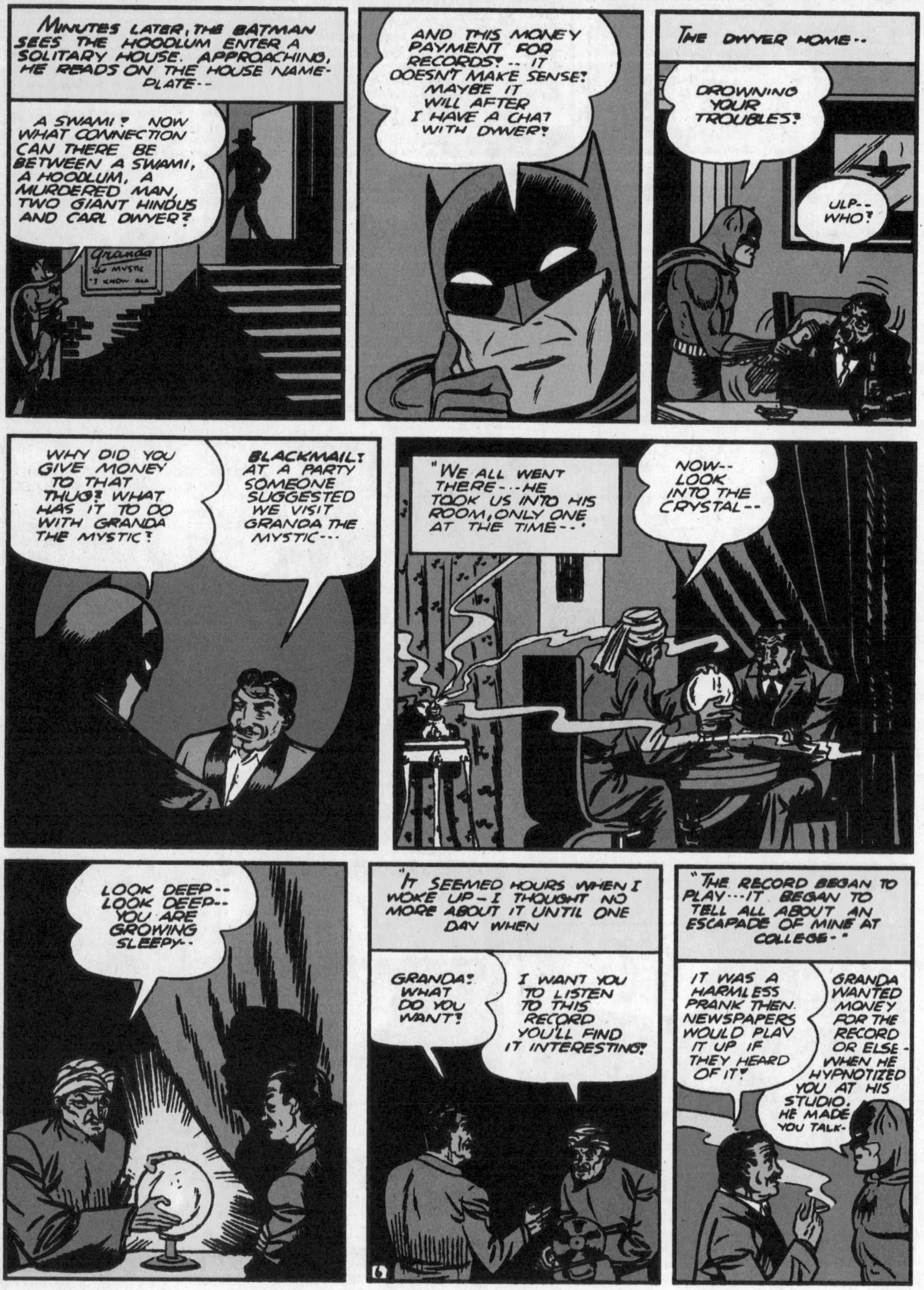
MINUTES LATER, THE BATMAN SEES THE HOODLUM ENTER A SOLITARY HOUSE. APPROACHING, HE READS ON THE HOUSE NAME-PLATE--
A SWAMI! NOW WHAT CONNECTION CAN THERE BE BETWEEN A SWAMI, A HOODLUM, A MURDERED MAN, TWO GIANT HINDUS AND CARL DWYER?
Granda the MYSTIC "I KNOW ALL"
AND THIS MONEY PAYMENT FOR RECORDS! -- IT DOESN'T MAKE SENSE! MAYBE IT WILL AFTER I HAVE A CHAT WITH DWYER!
THE DWYER HOME--
DROWNING YOUR TROUBLES?
ULP-- WHO?
WHY DID YOU GIVE MONEY TO THAT THUG? WHAT HAS IT TO DO WITH GRANDA THE MYSTIC?
BLACKMAIL! AT A PARTY SOMEONE SUGGESTED WE VISIT GRANDA THE MYSTIC---
"WE ALL WENT THERE---HE TOOK US INTO HIS ROOM, ONLY ONE AT THE TIME--"
NOW-- LOOK INTO THE CRYSTAL--
LOOK DEEP-- LOOK DEEP-- YOU ARE GROWING SLEEPY--
"IT SEEMED HOURS WHEN I WOKE UP - I THOUGHT NO MORE ABOUT IT UNTIL ONE DAY WHEN
GRANDA! WHAT DO YOU WANT?
I WANT YOU TO LISTEN TO THIS RECORD YOU'LL FIND IT INTERESTING!
"THE RECORD BEGAN TO PLAY---IT BEGAN TO TELL ALL ABOUT AN ESCAPADE OF MINE AT COLLEGE-"
IT WAS A HARMLESS PRANK THEN. NEWSPAPERS WOULD PLAY IT UP IF THEY HEARD OF IT!
GRANDA WANTED MONEY FOR THE RECORD OR ELSE - WHEN HE HYPNOTIZED YOU AT HIS STUDIO, HE MADE YOU TALK-
6

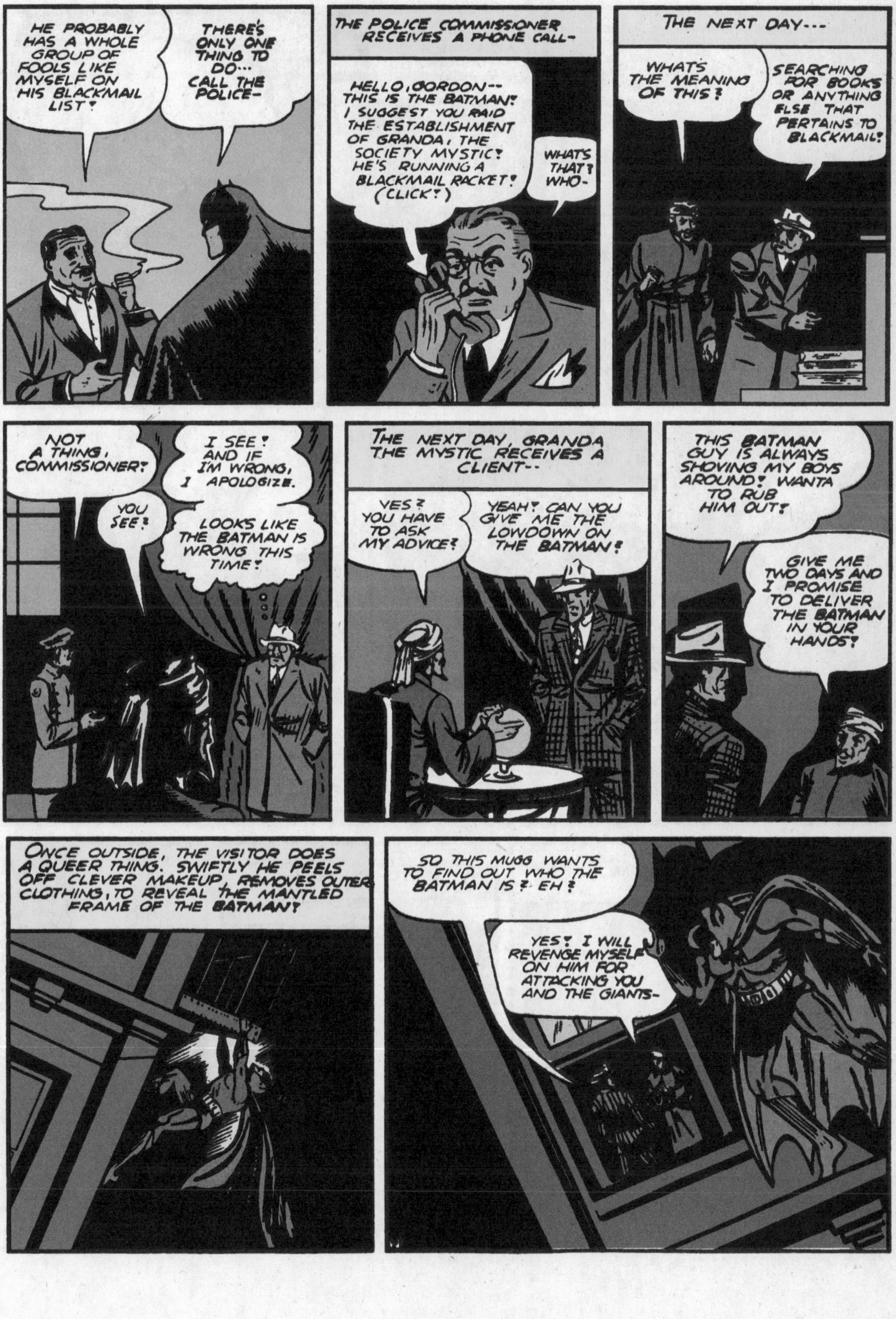
HE PROBABLY HAS A WHOLE GROUP OF FOOLS LIKE MYSELF ON HIS BLACKMAIL LIST!
THERE'S ONLY ONE THING TO DO... CALL THE POLICE-
THE POLICE COMMISSIONER RECEIVES A PHONE CALL-
HELLO, GORDON-- THIS IS THE BATMAN! I SUGGEST YOU RAID THE ESTABLISHMENT OF GRANDA, THE SOCIETY MYSTIC! HE'S RUNNING A BLACKMAIL RACKET! (CLICK!)
WHAT'S THAT? WHO-
THE NEXT DAY---
WHAT'S THE MEANING OF THIS?
SEARCHING FOR BOOKS OR ANYTHING ELSE THAT PERTAINS TO BLACKMAIL!
NOT A THING, COMMISSIONER!
YOU SEE?
I SEE! AND IF I'M WRONG, I APOLOGIZE.
LOOKS LIKE THE BATMAN IS WRONG THIS TIME!
THE NEXT DAY, GRANDA THE MYSTIC RECEIVES A CLIENT--
YES? YOU HAVE TO ASK MY ADVICE?
YEAH! CAN YOU GIVE ME THE LOWDOWN ON THE BATMAN!
THIS BATMAN GUY IS ALWAYS SHOVING MY BOYS AROUND! WANTA TO RUB HIM OUT!
GIVE ME TWO DAYS AND I PROMISE TO DELIVER THE BATMAN IN YOUR HANDS!
ONCE OUTSIDE, THE VISITOR DOES A QUEER THING. SWIFTLY HE PEELS OFF CLEVER MAKEUP, REMOVES OUTER CLOTHING, TO REVEAL THE MANTLED FRAME OF THE BATMAN!
SO THIS MUGG WANTS TO FIND OUT WHO THE BATMAN IS? EH?
YES! I WILL REVENGE MYSELF ON HIM FOR ATTACKING YOU AND THE GIANTS-

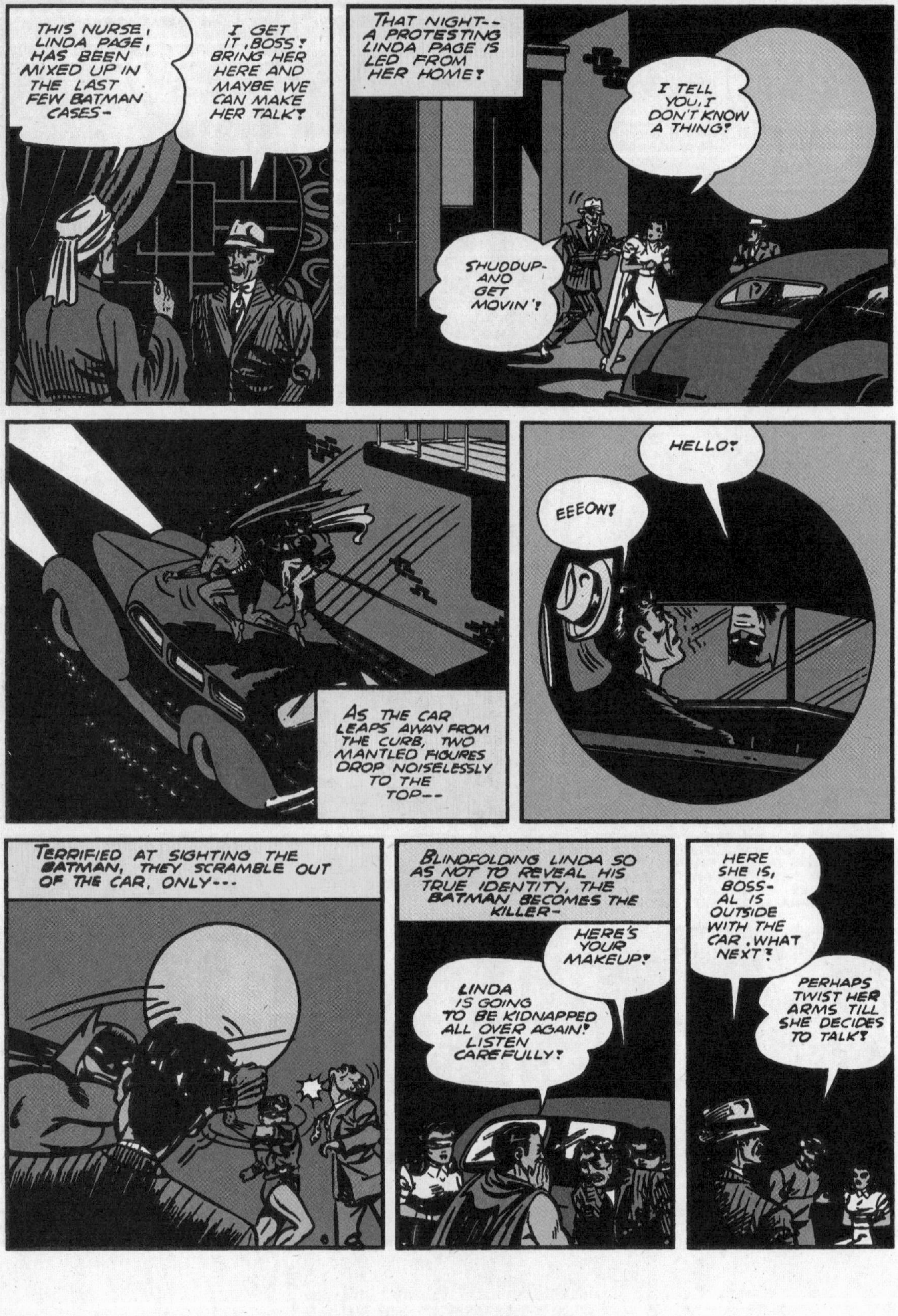
THIS NURSE, LINDA PAGE, HAS BEEN MIXED UP IN THE LAST FEW BATMAN CASES-
I GET IT, BOSS! BRING HER HERE AND MAYBE WE CAN MAKE HER TALK!
THAT NIGHT-- A PROTESTING LINDA PAGE IS LED FROM HER HOME!
I TELL YOU, I DON'T KNOW A THING!
SHUDDUP- AND GET MOVIN'!
AS THE CAR LEAPS AWAY FROM THE CURB, TWO MANTLED FIGURES DROP NOISELESSLY TO THE TOP--
HELLO!
EEEOW!
TERRIFIED AT SIGHTING THE BATMAN, THEY SCRAMBLE OUT OF THE CAR, ONLY---
BLINDFOLDING LINDA SO AS NOT TO REVEAL HIS TRUE IDENTITY, THE BATMAN BECOMES THE KILLER-
HERE'S YOUR MAKEUP!
LINDA IS GOING TO BE KIDNAPPED ALL OVER AGAIN! LISTEN CAREFULLY!
HERE SHE IS, BOSS- AL IS OUTSIDE WITH THE CAR. WHAT NEXT?
PERHAPS TWIST HER ARMS TILL SHE DECIDES TO TALK!

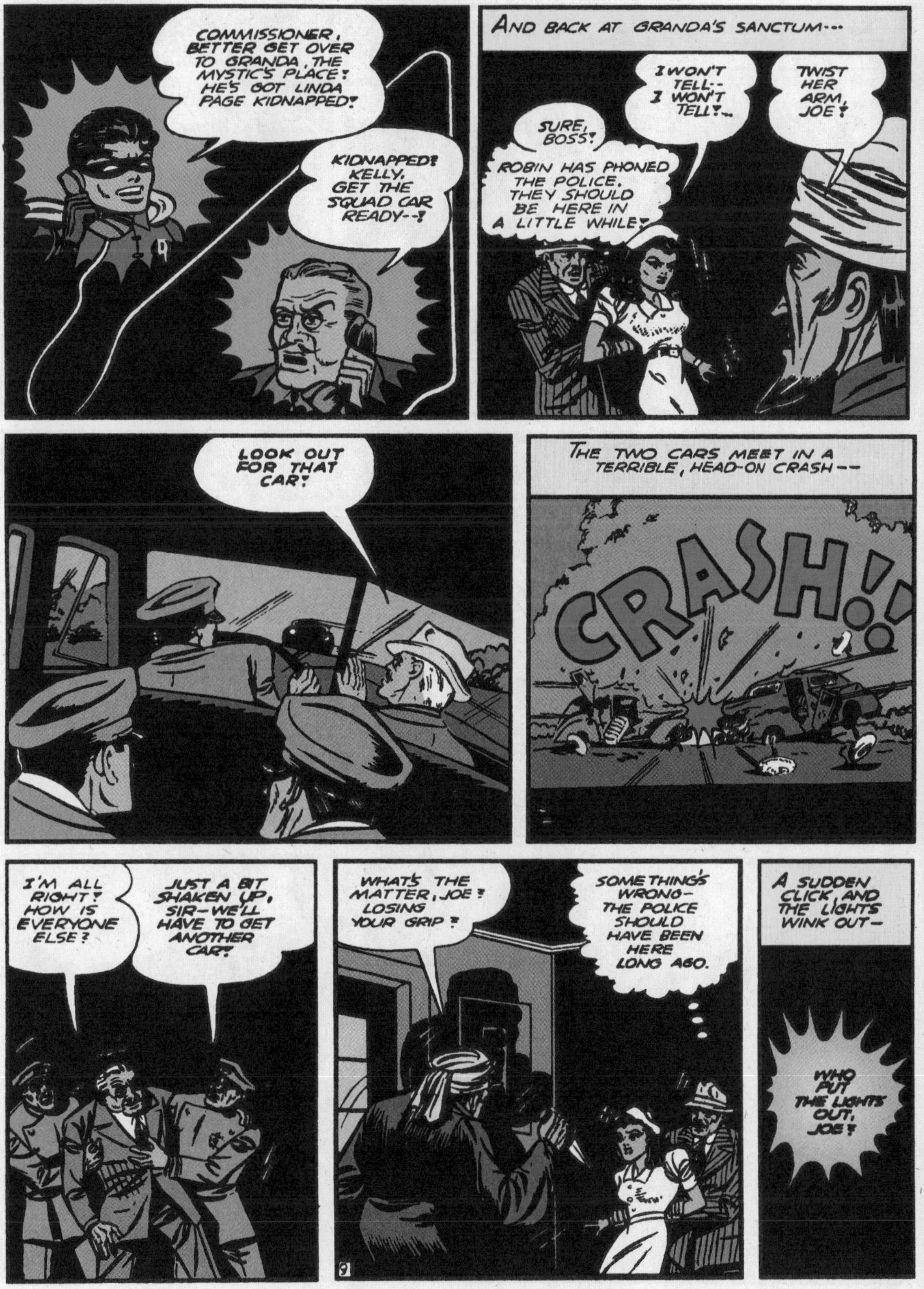
COMMISSIONER, BETTER GET OVER TO GRANDA, THE MYSTIC'S PLACE! HE'S GOT LINDA PAGE KIDNAPPED!
KIDNAPPED! KELLY, GET THE SQUAD CAR READY--!
AND BACK AT GRANDA'S SANCTUM---
I WON'T TELL-- I WON'T TELL!--
TWIST HER ARM, JOE!
SURE, BOSS!
ROBIN HAS PHONED THE POLICE. THEY SHOULD BE HERE IN A LITTLE WHILE!
LOOK OUT FOR THAT CAR!
THE TWO CARS MEET IN A TERRIBLE, HEAD-ON CRASH--
CRASH!!!
I'M ALL RIGHT! HOW IS EVERYONE ELSE?
JUST A BIT SHAKEN UP, SIR--WE'LL HAVE TO GET ANOTHER CAR!
WHAT'S THE MATTER, JOE? LOSING YOUR GRIP?
SOMETHING'S WRONG-- THE POLICE SHOULD HAVE BEEN HERE LONG AGO.
9
A SUDDEN CLICK, AND THE LIGHTS WINK OUT--
WHO PUT THE LIGHTS OUT, JOE?

THE LIGHTS FLASH ON AND STANDING, TOWERING IN THE LIGHT---

THE BATMAN! YOU WERE JOE!

YOU'RE GETTING SMARTER BY THE MINUTE!

EVEN AS THE BATMAN CATAPULTS FORWARD, GRANDA'S FOOT FURTIVELY PRESSES A FLOOR BUTTON, AND--

--THE HINDU GIANTS LUMBER INTO THE ROOM...

HOLY SMOKE! THE BIG BOYS AGAIN--

NIMBLE AS A CAT, THE BATMAN SLIPS BENEATH THE SLASHING BLADE!

THE BATMAN CANNOT AVOID THE SECOND GIANT, WHO TOWERS OVER HIM!

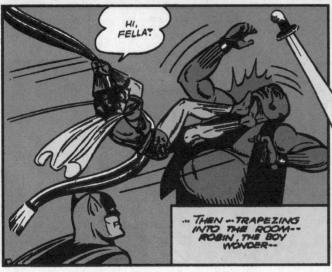

HI, FELLA!

...THEN --TRAPEZING INTO THE ROOM-- ROBIN, THE BOY WONDER--

JUST IN TIME, ROBIN!

OHH-- HERE COMES THE OTHER SHRIMP!

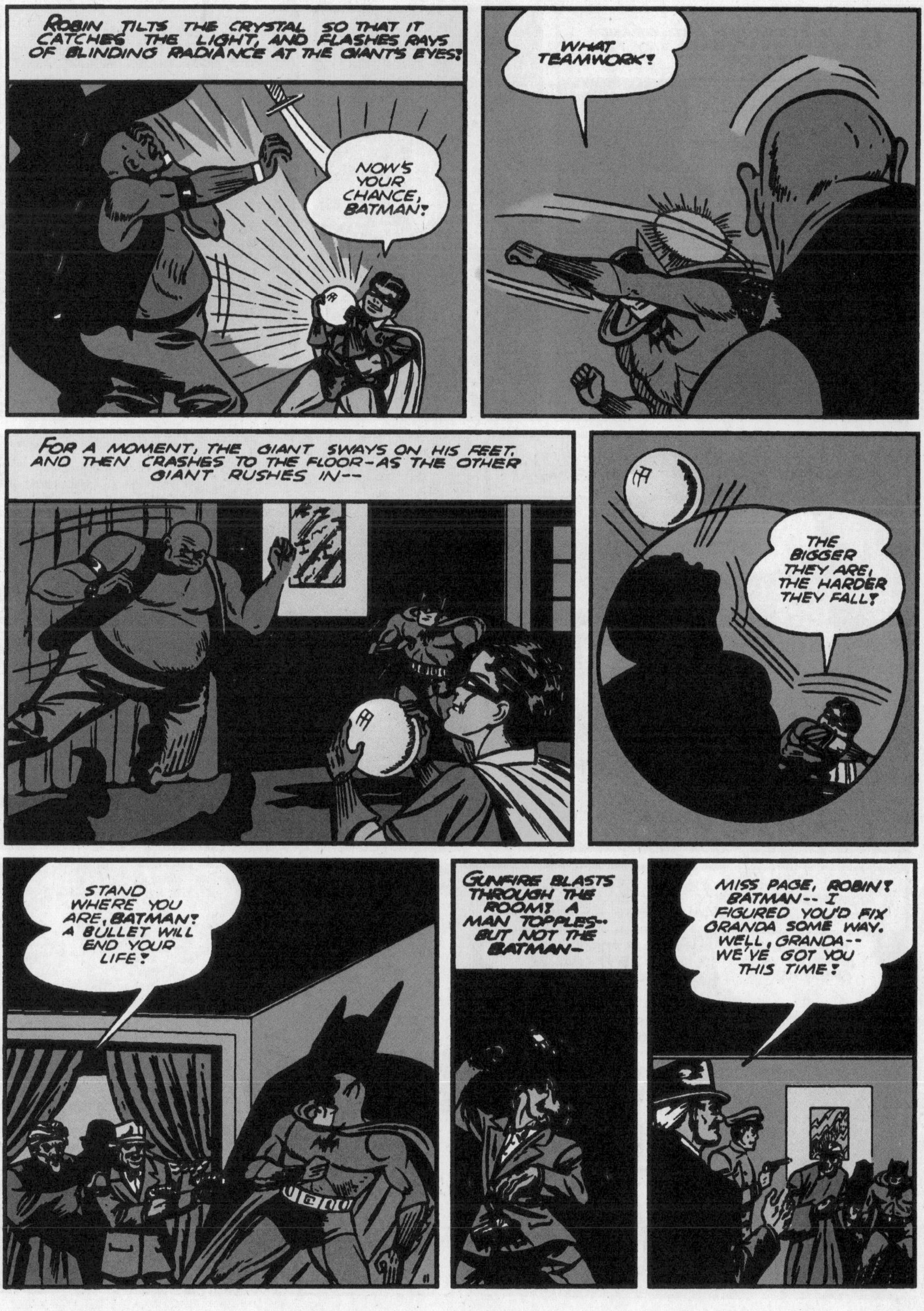
ROBIN TILTS THE CRYSTAL SO THAT IT CATCHES THE LIGHT, AND FLASHES RAYS OF BLINDING RADIANCE AT THE GIANT'S EYES!
NOW'S YOUR CHANCE, BATMAN!
WHAT TEAMWORK!
FOR A MOMENT, THE GIANT SWAYS ON HIS FEET. AND THEN CRASHES TO THE FLOOR--AS THE OTHER GIANT RUSHES IN--
THE BIGGER THEY ARE, THE HARDER THEY FALL!
STAND WHERE YOU ARE, BATMAN! A BULLET WILL END YOUR LIFE!
GUNFIRE BLASTS THROUGH THE ROOM! A MAN TOPPLES-- BUT NOT THE BATMAN-
MISS PAGE, ROBIN! BATMAN-- I FIGURED YOU'D FIX GRANDA SOME WAY. WELL, GRANDA-- WE'VE GOT YOU THIS TIME!

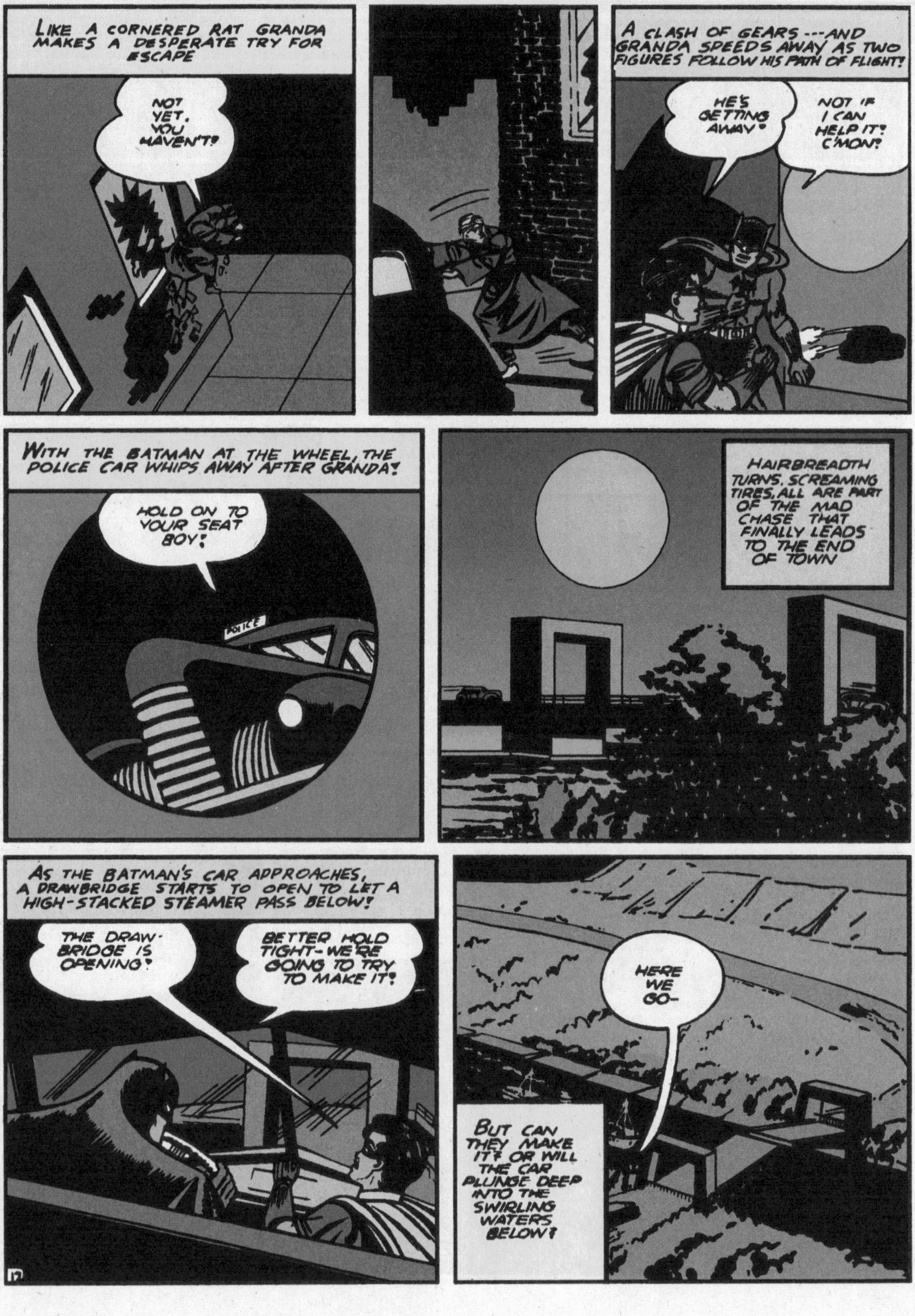
LIKE A CORNERED RAT GRANDA MAKES A DESPERATE TRY FOR ESCAPE
NOT YET, YOU HAVEN'T!
A CLASH OF GEARS ---AND GRANDA SPEEDS AWAY AS TWO FIGURES FOLLOW HIS PATH OF FLIGHT!
HE'S GETTING AWAY!
NOT IF I CAN HELP IT! C'MON!
WITH THE BATMAN AT THE WHEEL, THE POLICE CAR WHIPS AWAY AFTER GRANDA!
HOLD ON TO YOUR SEAT BOY!
POLICE
HAIRBREADTH TURNS, SCREAMING TIRES, ALL ARE PART OF THE MAD CHASE THAT FINALLY LEADS TO THE END OF TOWN
AS THE BATMAN'S CAR APPROACHES, A DRAWBRIDGE STARTS TO OPEN TO LET A HIGH-STACKED STEAMER PASS BELOW!
THE DRAW-BRIDGE IS OPENING!
BETTER HOLD TIGHT-WE'RE GOING TO TRY TO MAKE IT!
17
HERE WE GO-
BUT CAN THEY MAKE IT? OR WILL THE CAR PLUNGE DEEP INTO THE SWIRLING WATERS BELOW?

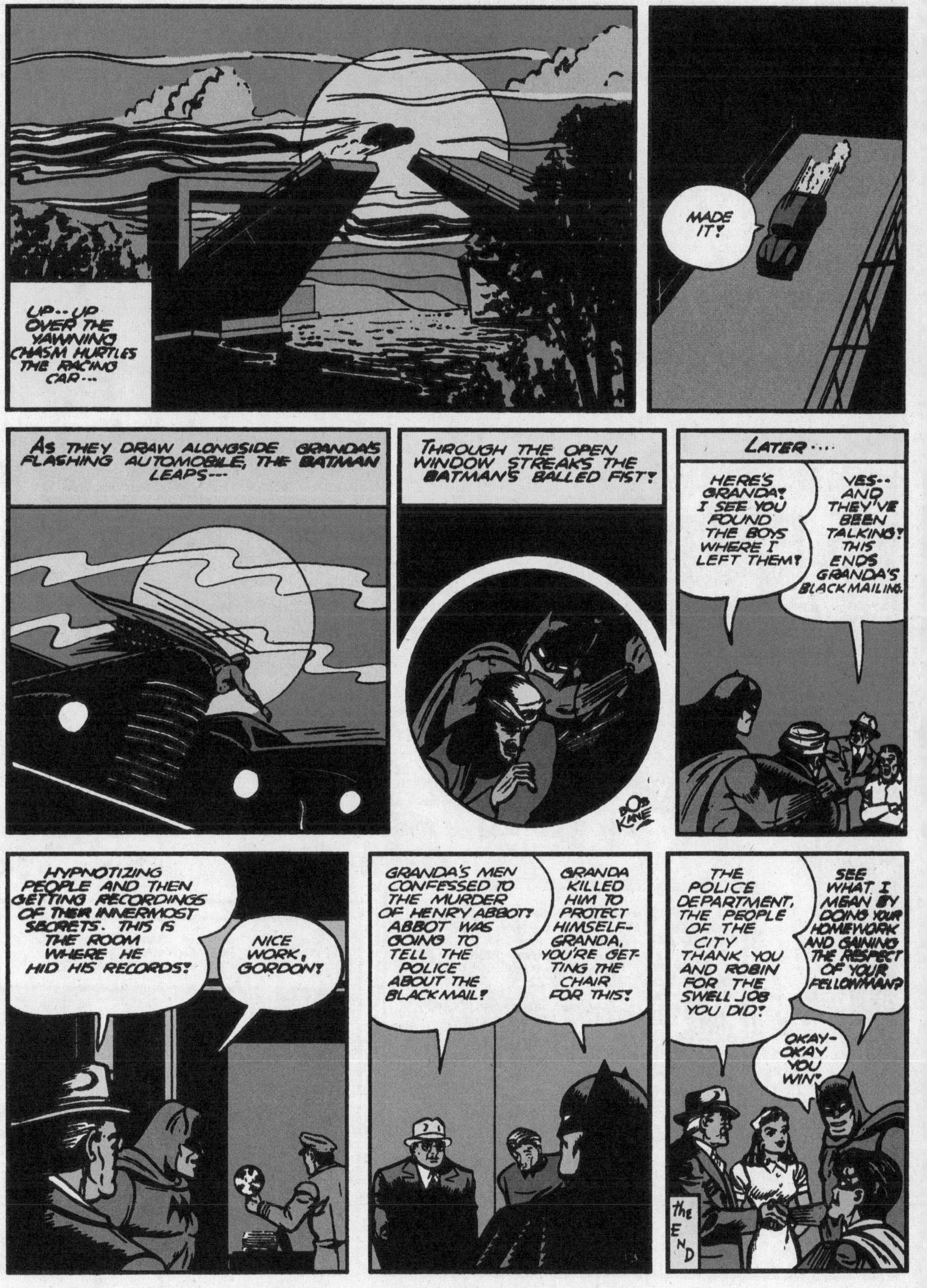

UP...UP OVER THE YAWNING CHASM HURTLES THE RACING CAR...
MADE IT!
AS THEY DRAW ALONGSIDE GRANDA'S FLASHING AUTOMOBILE, THE BATMAN LEAPS---
THROUGH THE OPEN WINDOW STREAKS THE BATMAN'S BALLED FIST!
BOB KANE
LATER....
HERE'S GRANDA! I SEE YOU FOUND THE BOYS WHERE I LEFT THEM!
YES-- AND THEY'VE BEEN TALKING! THIS ENDS GRANDA'S BLACKMAILING.
HYPNOTIZING PEOPLE AND THEN GETTING RECORDINGS OF THEIR INNERMOST SECRETS. THIS IS THE ROOM WHERE HE HID HIS RECORDS!
NICE WORK, GORDON!
GRANDA'S MEN CONFESSED TO THE MURDER OF HENRY ABBOT! ABBOT WAS GOING TO TELL THE POLICE ABOUT THE BLACKMAIL!
GRANDA KILLED HIM TO PROTECT HIMSELF-GRANDA, YOU'RE GETTING THE CHAIR FOR THIS!
THE POLICE DEPARTMENT, THE PEOPLE OF THE CITY THANK YOU AND ROBIN FOR THE SWELL JOB YOU DID!
SEE WHAT I MEAN BY DOING YOUR HOMEWORK AND GAINING THE RESPECT OF YOUR FELLOWMAN?
OKAY-OKAY YOU WIN!
THE END

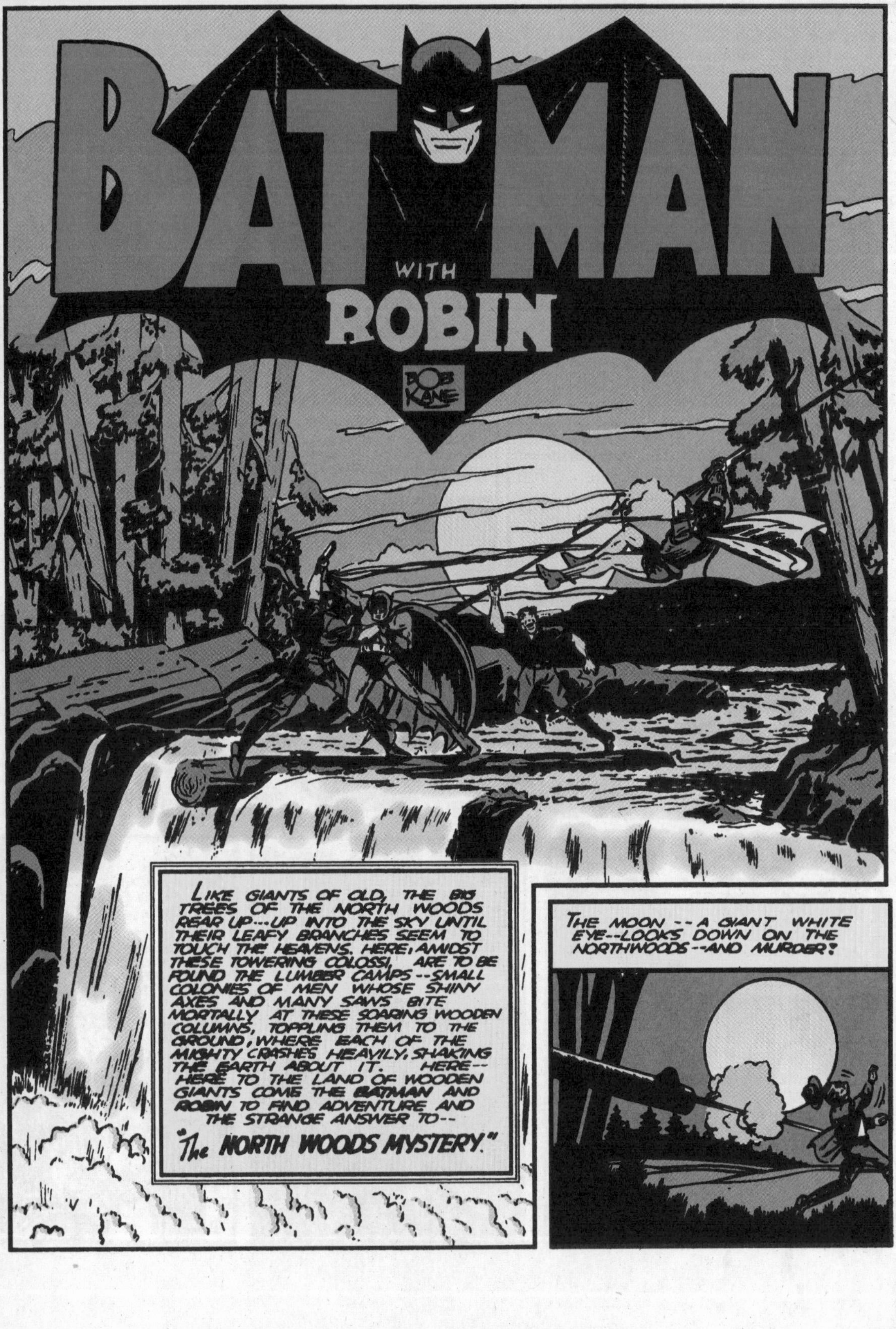
BATMAN
WITH
ROBIN
BOB KANE
LIKE GIANTS OF OLD, THE BIG TREES OF THE NORTH WOODS REAR UP...UP INTO THE SKY UNTIL THEIR LEAFY BRANCHES SEEM TO TOUCH THE HEAVENS. HERE, AMIDST THESE TOWERING COLOSSI, ARE TO BE FOUND THE LUMBER CAMPS--SMALL COLONIES OF MEN WHOSE SHINY AXES AND MANY SAWS BITE MORTALLY AT THESE SOARING WOODEN COLUMNS, TOPPLING THEM TO THE GROUND, WHERE EACH OF THE MIGHTY CRASHES HEAVILY, SHAKING THE EARTH ABOUT IT. HERE--HERE TO THE LAND OF WOODEN GIANTS COME THE BATMAN AND ROBIN TO FIND ADVENTURE AND THE STRANGE ANSWER TO--
"The NORTH WOODS MYSTERY."
THE MOON --A GIANT WHITE EYE--LOOKS DOWN ON THE NORTHWOODS--AND MURDER!

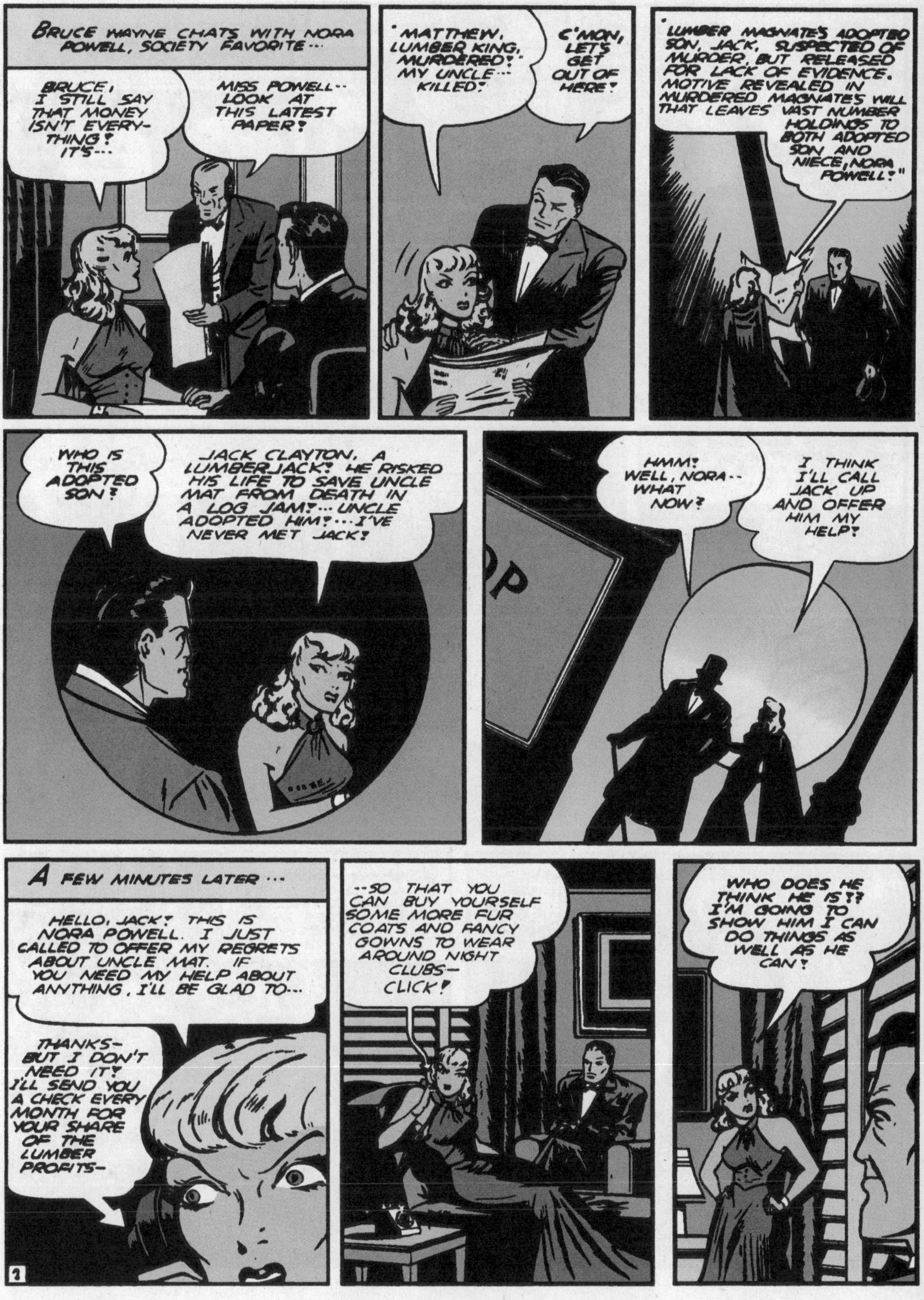
BRUCE WAYNE CHATS WITH NORA POWELL, SOCIETY FAVORITE...
BRUCE, I STILL SAY THAT MONEY ISN'T EVERY-THING! IT'S...
MISS POWELL-- LOOK AT THIS LATEST PAPER!
"MATTHEW, LUMBER KING, MURDERED!" MY UNCLE... KILLED!
C'MON, LET'S GET OUT OF HERE!
"LUMBER MAGNATE'S ADOPTED SON, JACK, SUSPECTED OF MURDER, BUT RELEASED FOR LACK OF EVIDENCE. MOTIVE REVEALED IN MURDERED MAGNATE'S WILL THAT LEAVES VAST NUMBER HOLDINGS TO BOTH ADOPTED SON AND NIECE, NORA POWELL!"
WHO IS THIS ADOPTED SON?
JACK CLAYTON, A LUMBERJACK! HE RISKED HIS LIFE TO SAVE UNCLE MAT FROM DEATH IN A LOG JAM!... UNCLE ADOPTED HIM!... I'VE NEVER MET JACK!
HMM! WELL, NORA-- WHAT NOW?
I THINK I'LL CALL JACK UP AND OFFER HIM MY HELP!
A FEW MINUTES LATER...
HELLO, JACK! THIS IS NORA POWELL. I JUST CALLED TO OFFER MY REGRETS ABOUT UNCLE MAT. IF YOU NEED MY HELP ABOUT ANYTHING, I'LL BE GLAD TO...
THANKS- BUT I DON'T NEED IT! I'LL SEND YOU A CHECK EVERY MONTH FOR YOUR SHARE OF THE LUMBER PROFITS-
--SO THAT YOU CAN BUY YOURSELF SOME MORE FUR COATS AND FANCY GOWNS TO WEAR AROUND NIGHT CLUBS-
CLICK!
WHO DOES HE THINK HE IS?? I'M GOING TO SHOW HIM I CAN DO THINGS AS WELL AS HE CAN!

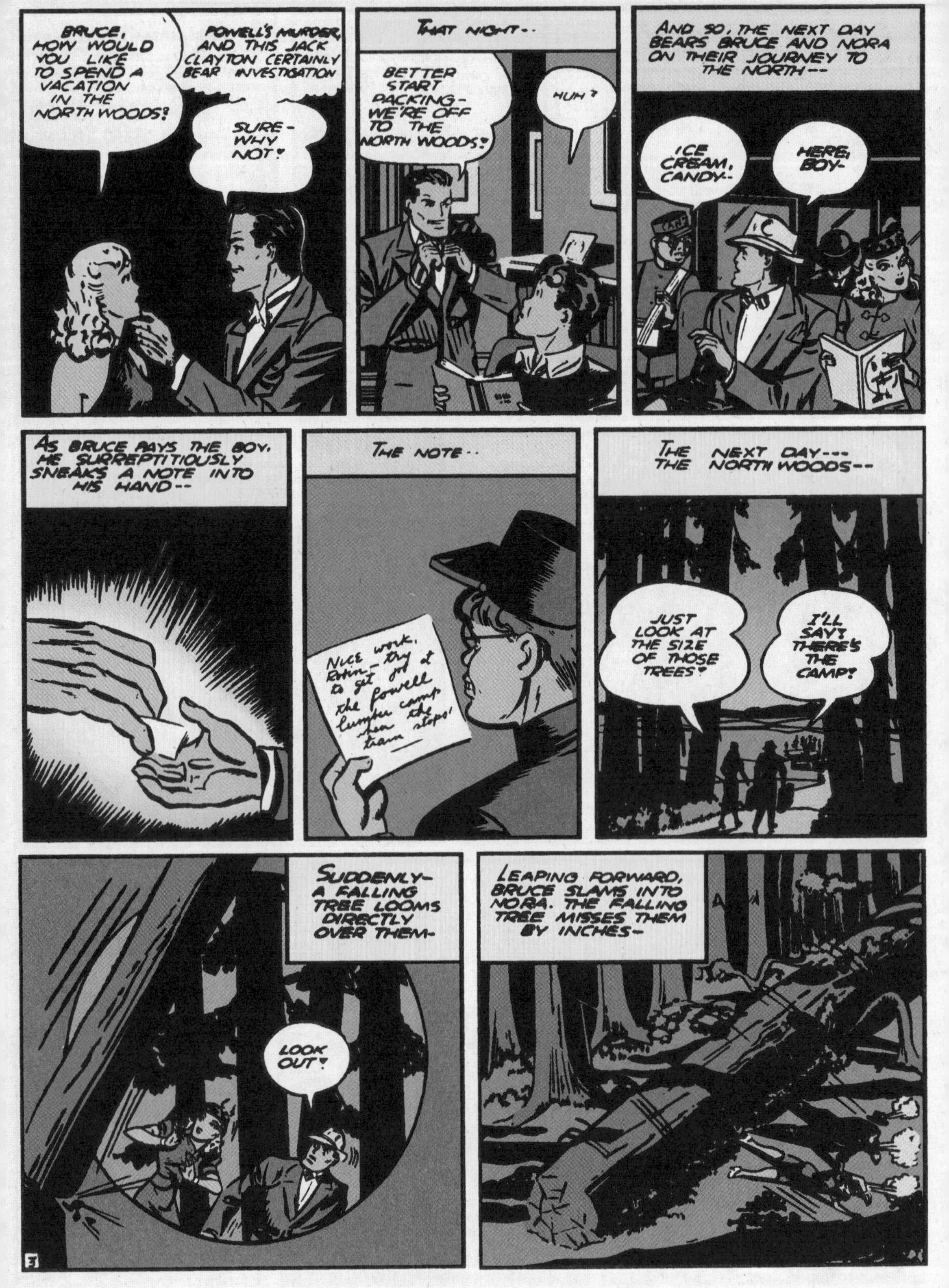
BRUCE, HOW WOULD YOU LIKE TO SPEND A VACATION IN THE NORTH WOODS?
POWELL'S MURDER, AND THIS JACK CLAYTON CERTAINLY BEAR INVESTIGATION
SURE- WHY NOT!
THAT NIGHT--
BETTER START PACKING- WE'RE OFF TO THE NORTH WOODS!
HUH?
AND SO, THE NEXT DAY BEARS BRUCE AND NORA ON THEIR JOURNEY TO THE NORTH--
ICE CREAM, CANDY-
HERE, BOY-
AS BRUCE PAYS THE BOY, HE SURREPTITIOUSLY SNEAKS A NOTE INTO HIS HAND--
THE NOTE--
Nice work, Robin— try to get job at the Powell lumber camp when the train stops!
THE NEXT DAY--- THE NORTH WOODS--
JUST LOOK AT THE SIZE OF THOSE TREES!
I'LL SAY! THERE'S THE CAMP!
SUDDENLY- A FALLING TREE LOOMS DIRECTLY OVER THEM-
LOOK OUT!
LEAPING FORWARD, BRUCE SLAMS INTO NORA. THE FALLING TREE MISSES THEM BY INCHES-

OH-OH THAT WAS CLOSE!

A LOGGER PROBABLY LEFT FOR A MOMENT, LEAVING THE TREE HALF CUT, NOT REALIZING IT WOULD FALL!

THAT WAS NO ACCIDENT-- SOMEONE WANTED TO KILL HER!

A TALL, YOUNG MAN WITH BLACK HAIR, FLASHING EYES AND LOOKING LIKE A VIOLENT STORM, APPROACHES THEM--

I'M NORA POWELL AND THIS IS MY FRIEND, BRUCE WAYNE--I'M LOOKING FOR...

JACK CLAYTON-- SORRY-I DIDN'T WEAR A TUXEDO TO MEET YOU-- THIS MAN WILL SHOW YOU TO YOUR SHACK.

WELL-- OF ALL THE NERVE!

EASY NOW... EASY-

THIS WAY, MISS POWELL!

ABOUT FIVE MINUTES LATER, A YOUNG BOY ENTERS THE CAMP--

I'M KINDA HUNGRY! COULD I SORTA DO ODD JOBS AROUND HERE?

HUNGRY, EH? SURE-- HEY, FRED! GET SOME GRUB FOR THIS KID!

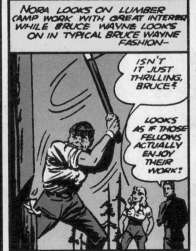

NORA LOOKS ON LUMBER CAMP WORK WITH GREAT INTEREST WHILE BRUCE WAYNE LOOKS ON IN TYPICAL BRUCE WAYNE FASHION--

ISN'T IT JUST THRILLING, BRUCE?

LOOKS AS IF THOSE FELLOWS ACTUALLY ENJOY THEIR WORK!

NORA DOES NOT NOTICE THE LOOK BETWEEN BRUCE AND THE YOUNG BOY--

JUST LOOK AT THE MAGNIFICENCE OF IT ALL! LITTLE MEN CUTTING DOWN THESE WOODEN GIANTS!...

NOTHING BUT TERMITES, THAT'S ALL THEY ARE...

THAT NIGHT...

WISH I KNEW EXACTLY WHY CLAYTON COULD ACT SO HUMAN TO THE BOY AND SO INHUMAN TO US! HE HATES THE GIRL---BUT WHY?

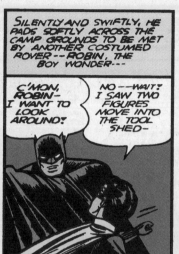

SILENTLY AND SWIFTLY, HE PADS SOFTLY ACROSS THE CAMP GROUNDS TO BE MET BY ANOTHER COSTUMED ROVER -- ROBIN, THE BOY WONDER---

C'MON, ROBIN-- I WANT TO LOOK AROUND!

NO--WAIT! I SAW TWO FIGURES MOVE INTO THE TOOL SHED--

INSIDE THE TOOL SHED--

A LITTLE ACID ON THESE SAWS AND AXES, AND THEY'LL CRACK UP WHEN THEY TRY TO USE THEM ON TIMBER!

THAT'LL SLOW UP THE LUMBER OUTPUT-- AND THAT POWELL DAME WILL BE GLAD TO SELL HER SHARE TO CLAYTON--

NOT QUITE, FELLA, NOT QUITE!

I'LL BATHE YA IN ACID!

SORRY, I PREFER WATER!

OKAY, WISE GUY-- YOU ASKED FOR IT!

BUT IT DOESN'T LOOK LIKE I'M GOING TO GET IT, EH, PAL!

BATMAN, I NEED HELP!

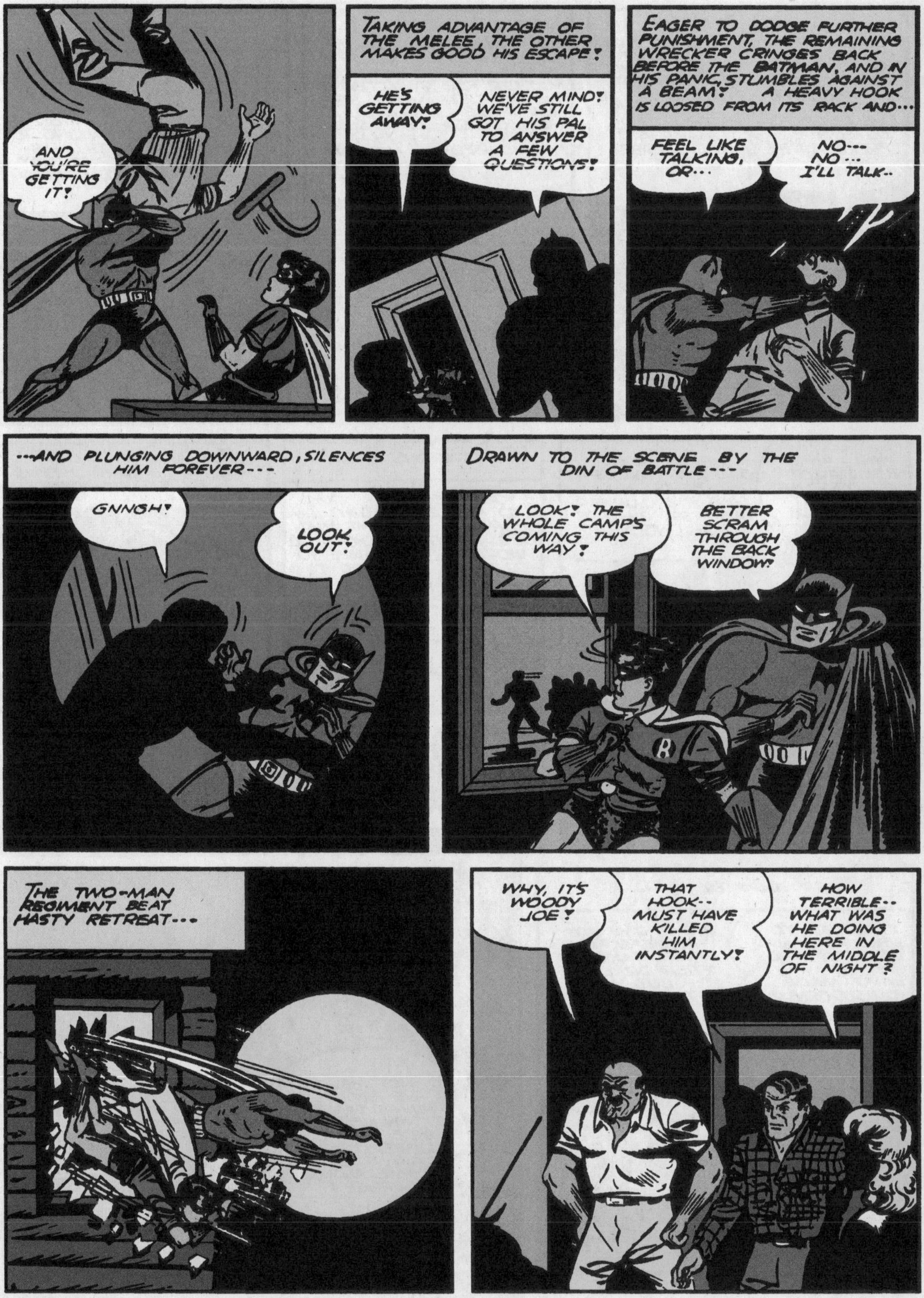
AND YOU'RE GETTING IT!
TAKING ADVANTAGE OF THE MELEE, THE OTHER MAKES GOOD HIS ESCAPE!
HE'S GETTING AWAY!
NEVER MIND! WE'VE STILL GOT HIS PAL TO ANSWER A FEW QUESTIONS!
EAGER TO DODGE FURTHER PUNISHMENT, THE REMAINING WRECKER CRINGES BACK BEFORE THE BATMAN, AND IN HIS PANIC, STUMBLES AGAINST A BEAM! A HEAVY HOOK IS LOOSED FROM ITS RACK AND...
FEEL LIKE TALKING, OR...
NO--- NO... I'LL TALK..
---AND PLUNGING DOWNWARD, SILENCES HIM FOREVER---
GNNGH!
LOOK OUT!
DRAWN TO THE SCENE BY THE DIN OF BATTLE---
LOOK! THE WHOLE CAMP'S COMING THIS WAY!
BETTER SCRAM THROUGH THE BACK WINDOW!
THE TWO-MAN REGIMENT BEAT HASTY RETREAT---
WHY, IT'S WOODY JOE!
THAT HOOK-- MUST HAVE KILLED HIM INSTANTLY!
HOW TERRIBLE-- WHAT WAS HE DOING HERE IN THE MIDDLE OF NIGHT?

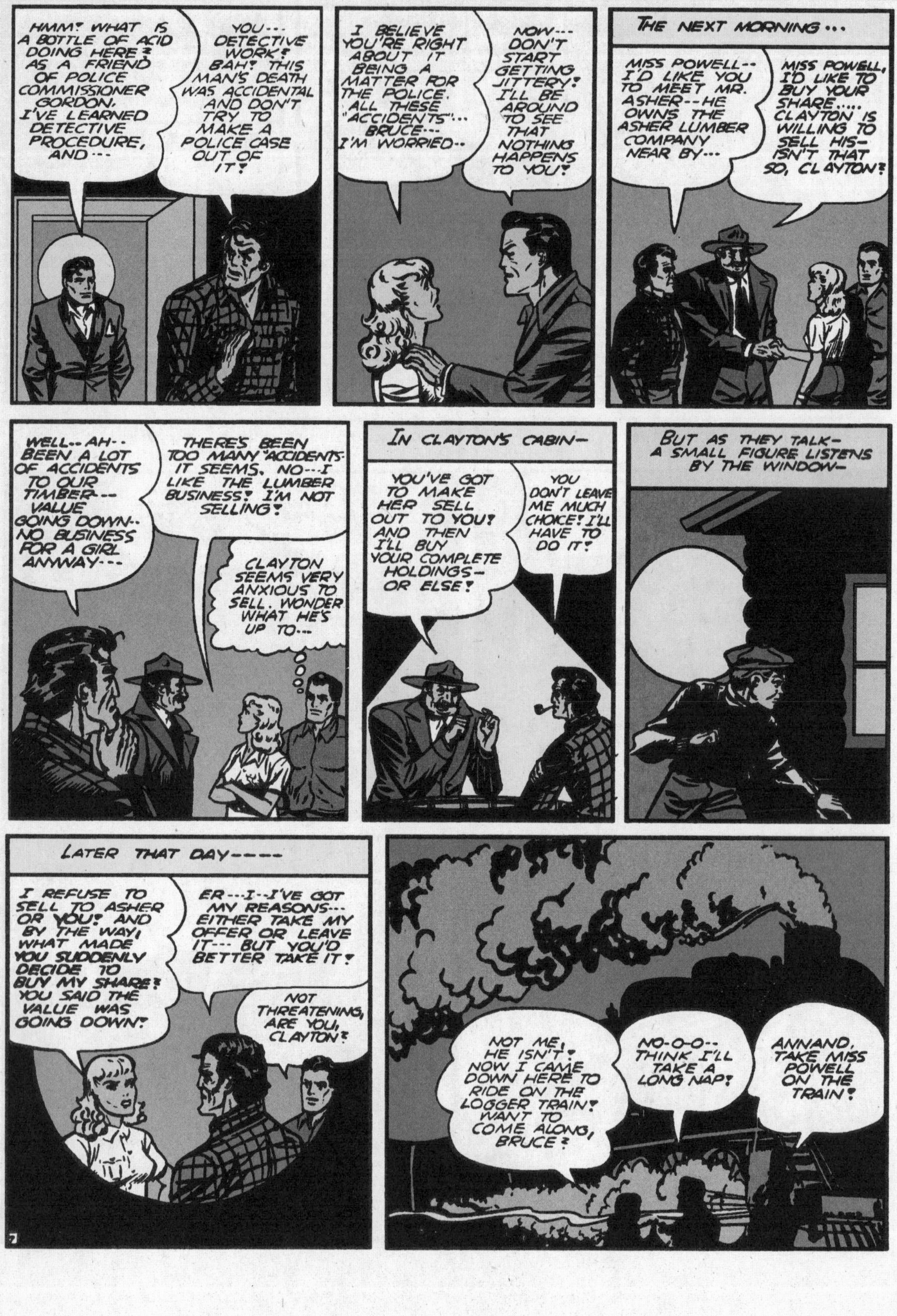
HMM! WHAT IS A BOTTLE OF ACID DOING HERE? AS A FRIEND OF POLICE COMMISSIONER GORDON, I'VE LEARNED DETECTIVE PROCEDURE, AND---
YOU--- DETECTIVE WORK! BAH! THIS MAN'S DEATH WAS ACCIDENTAL AND DON'T TRY TO MAKE A POLICE CASE OUT OF IT!
I BELIEVE YOU'RE RIGHT ABOUT IT BEING A MATTER FOR THE POLICE. ALL THESE "ACCIDENTS"... BRUCE--- I'M WORRIED--
NOW--- DON'T START GETTING JITTERY! I'LL BE AROUND TO SEE THAT NOTHING HAPPENS TO YOU!
THE NEXT MORNING...
MISS POWELL-- I'D LIKE YOU TO MEET MR. ASHER--HE OWNS THE ASHER LUMBER COMPANY NEAR BY...
MISS POWELL, I'D LIKE TO BUY YOUR SHARE..... CLAYTON IS WILLING TO SELL HIS-- ISN'T THAT SO, CLAYTON?
WELL--AH-- BEEN A LOT OF ACCIDENTS TO OUR TIMBER-- VALUE GOING DOWN-- NO BUSINESS FOR A GIRL ANYWAY---
THERE'S BEEN TOO MANY "ACCIDENTS" IT SEEMS. NO---I LIKE THE LUMBER BUSINESS! I'M NOT SELLING!
CLAYTON SEEMS VERY ANXIOUS TO SELL. WONDER WHAT HE'S UP TO---
IN CLAYTON'S CABIN-
YOU'VE GOT TO MAKE HER SELL OUT TO YOU! AND THEN I'LL BUY YOUR COMPLETE HOLDINGS-- OR ELSE!
YOU DON'T LEAVE ME MUCH CHOICE! I'LL HAVE TO DO IT!
BUT AS THEY TALK- A SMALL FIGURE LISTENS BY THE WINDOW-
LATER THAT DAY----
I REFUSE TO SELL TO ASHER OR YOU! AND BY THE WAY, WHAT MADE YOU SUDDENLY DECIDE TO BUY MY SHARE? YOU SAID THE VALUE WAS GOING DOWN!
ER---I--I'VE GOT MY REASONS--- EITHER TAKE MY OFFER OR LEAVE IT--- BUT YOU'D BETTER TAKE IT!
NOT THREATENING, ARE YOU, CLAYTON?
7
NOT ME, HE ISN'T! NOW I CAME DOWN HERE TO RIDE ON THE LOGGER TRAIN! WANT TO COME ALONG, BRUCE?
NO-O-O-- THINK I'LL TAKE A LONG NAP!
ANNAND, TAKE MISS POWELL ON THE TRAIN!

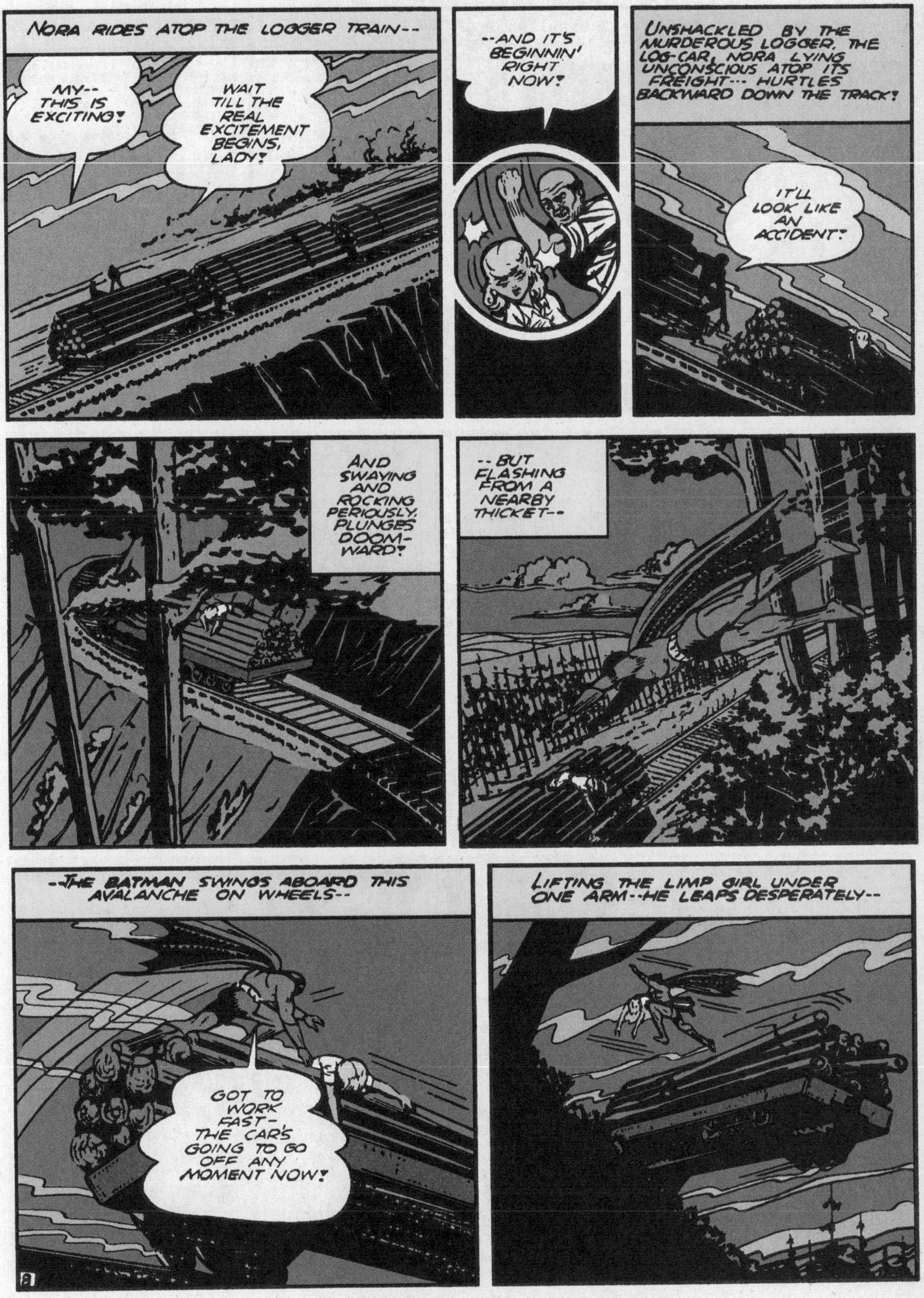
NORA RIDES ATOP THE LOGGER TRAIN--
MY-- THIS IS EXCITING!
WAIT TILL THE REAL EXCITEMENT BEGINS, LADY!
--AND IT'S BEGINNIN' RIGHT NOW!
UNSHACKLED BY THE MURDEROUS LOGGER, THE LOG-CAR, NORA LYING UNCONSCIOUS ATOP ITS FREIGHT--- HURTLES BACKWARD DOWN THE TRACK!
IT'LL LOOK LIKE AN ACCIDENT!
AND SWAYING AND ROCKING PERIOUSLY, PLUNGES DOOM-WARD!
-- BUT FLASHING FROM A NEARBY THICKET--
--THE BATMAN SWINGS ABOARD THIS AVALANCHE ON WHEELS--
GOT TO WORK FAST- THE CAR'S GOING TO GO OFF ANY MOMENT NOW!
LIFTING THE LIMP GIRL UNDER ONE ARM--HE LEAPS DESPERATELY--

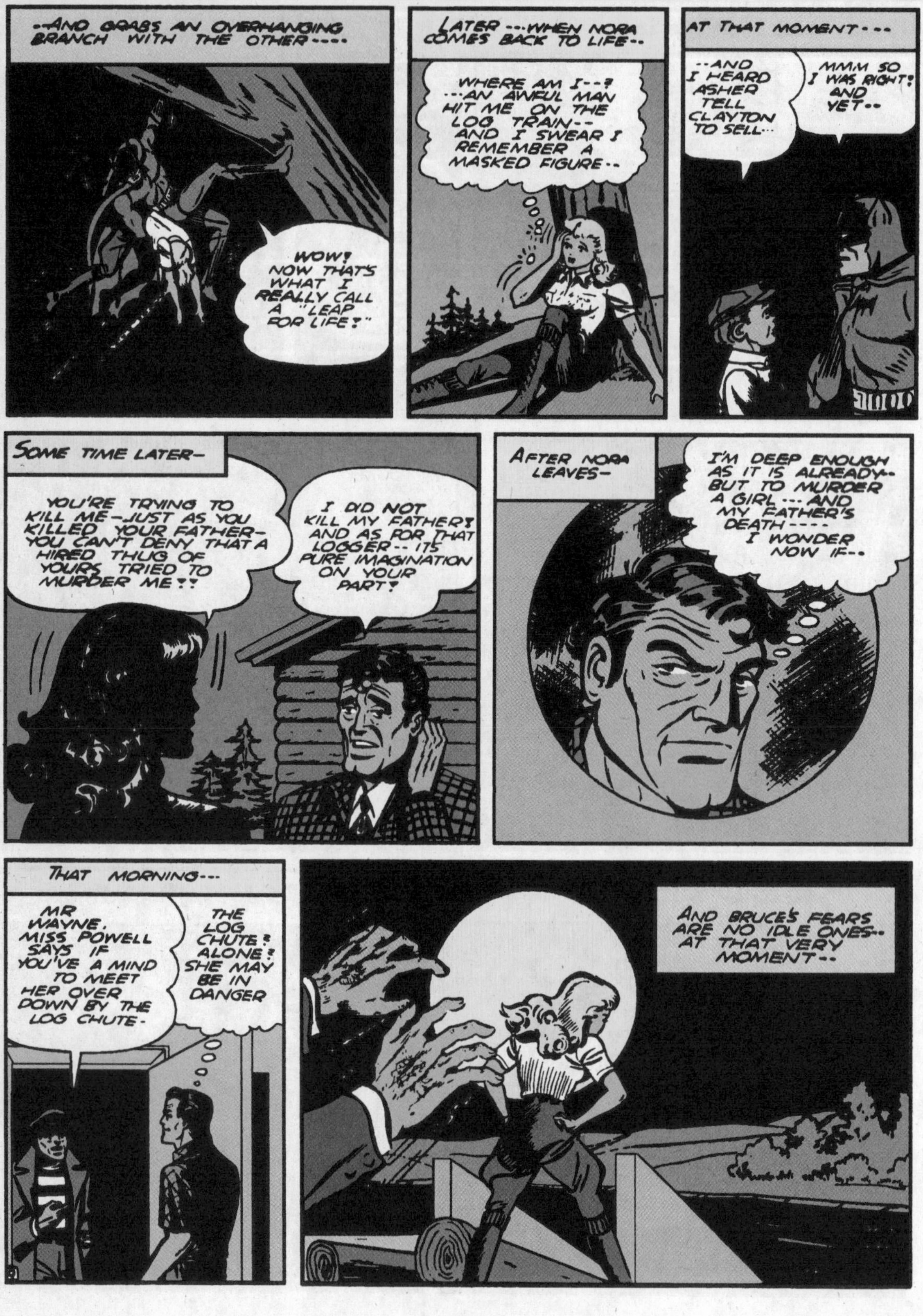
--AND GRABS AN OVERHANGING BRANCH WITH THE OTHER----
WOW! NOW THAT'S WHAT I REALLY CALL A "LEAP FOR LIFE!"
LATER---WHEN NORA COMES BACK TO LIFE--
WHERE AM I--? ---AN AWFUL MAN HIT ME ON THE LOG TRAIN-- AND I SWEAR I REMEMBER A MASKED FIGURE--
AT THAT MOMENT---
--AND I HEARD ASHER TELL CLAYTON TO SELL···
MMM SO I WAS RIGHT! AND YET--
SOME TIME LATER-
YOU'RE TRYING TO KILL ME-JUST AS YOU KILLED YOUR FATHER- YOU CAN'T DENY THAT A HIRED THUG OF YOURS TRIED TO MURDER ME!!
I DID NOT KILL MY FATHER! AND AS FOR THAT LOGGER-- ITS PURE IMAGINATION ON YOUR PART!
AFTER NORA LEAVES-
I'M DEEP ENOUGH AS IT IS ALREADY-BUT TO MURDER A GIRL---AND MY FATHER'S DEATH---- I WONDER NOW IF--.
THAT MORNING---
MR WAYNE, MISS POWELL SAYS IF YOU'VE A MIND TO MEET HER OVER DOWN BY THE LOG CHUTE-
THE LOG CHUTE? ALONE? SHE MAY BE IN DANGER
AND BRUCE'S FEARS ARE NO IDLE ONES-- AT THAT VERY MOMENT--

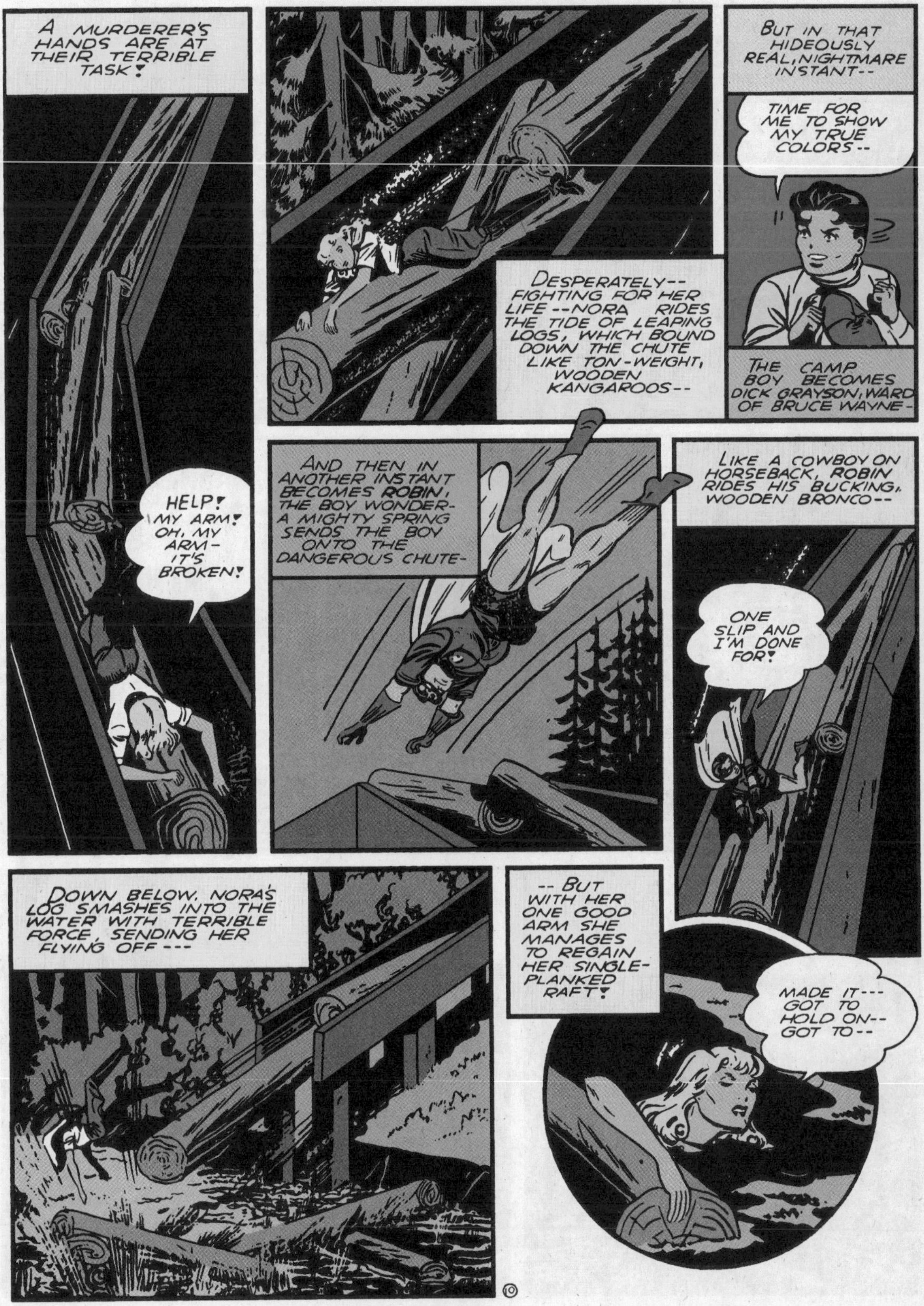
A MURDERER'S HANDS ARE AT THEIR TERRIBLE TASK!
HELP! MY ARM! OH, MY ARM - IT'S BROKEN!
DESPERATELY-- FIGHTING FOR HER LIFE --NORA RIDES THE TIDE OF LEAPING LOGS, WHICH BOUND DOWN THE CHUTE LIKE TON-WEIGHT, WOODEN KANGAROOS--
BUT IN THAT HIDEOUSLY REAL, NIGHTMARE INSTANT--
TIME FOR ME TO SHOW MY TRUE COLORS--
THE CAMP BOY BECOMES DICK GRAYSON, WARD OF BRUCE WAYNE-
AND THEN IN ANOTHER INSTANT BECOMES ROBIN, THE BOY WONDER- A MIGHTY SPRING SENDS THE BOY ONTO THE DANGEROUS CHUTE-
LIKE A COWBOY ON HORSEBACK, ROBIN RIDES HIS BUCKING, WOODEN BRONCO--
ONE SLIP AND I'M DONE FOR!
DOWN BELOW, NORA'S LOG SMASHES INTO THE WATER WITH TERRIBLE FORCE, SENDING HER FLYING OFF ---
-- BUT WITH HER ONE GOOD ARM SHE MANAGES TO REGAIN HER SINGLE-PLANKED RAFT!
MADE IT--- GOT TO HOLD ON-- GOT TO--
10

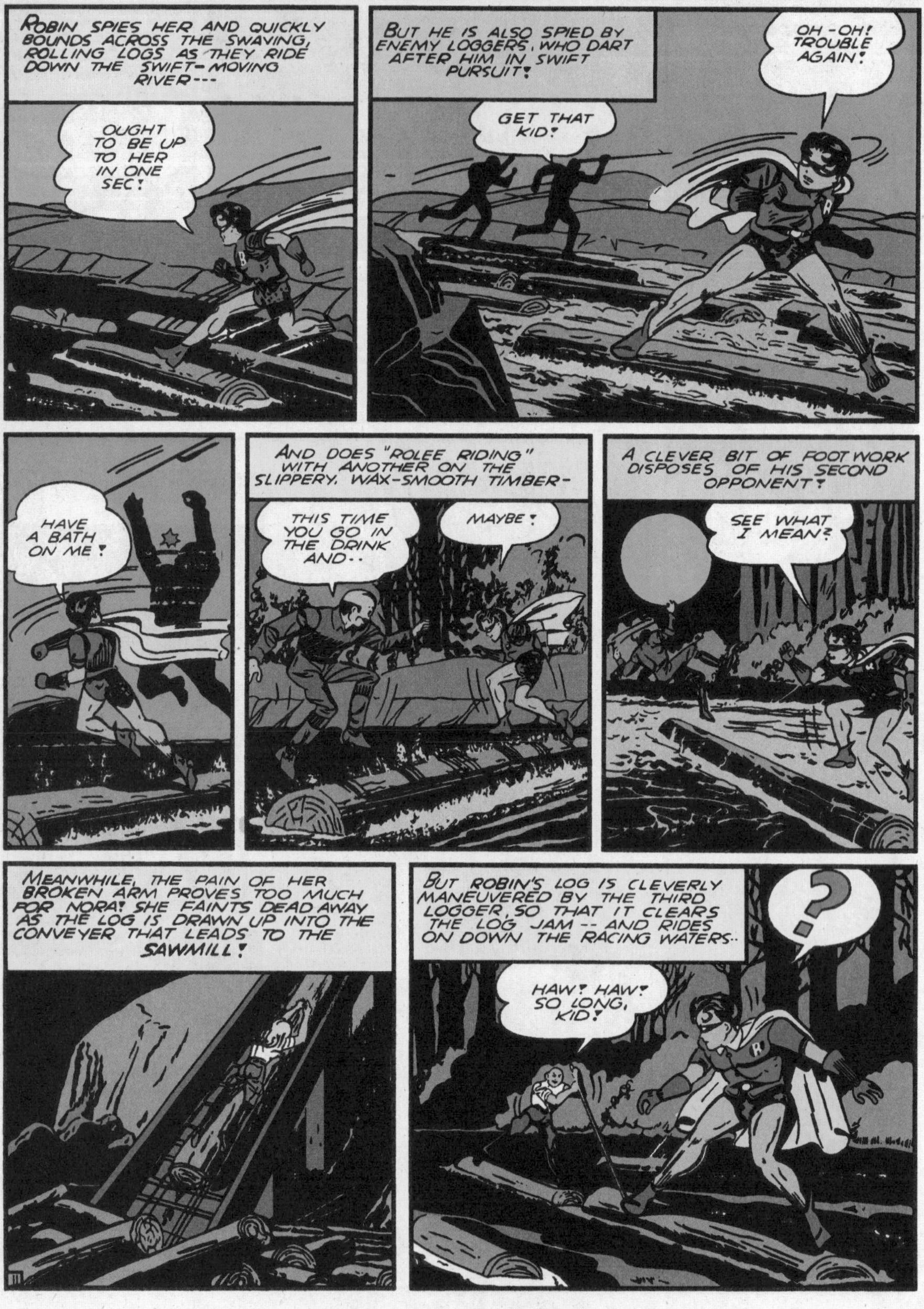
ROBIN SPIES HER AND QUICKLY BOUNDS ACROSS THE SWAYING, ROLLING LOGS AS THEY RIDE DOWN THE SWIFT-MOVING RIVER---
OUGHT TO BE UP TO HER IN ONE SEC!
BUT HE IS ALSO SPIED BY ENEMY LOGGERS, WHO DART AFTER HIM IN SWIFT PURSUIT!
OH-OH! TROUBLE AGAIN!
GET THAT KID!
HAVE A BATH ON ME!
AND DOES "ROLEE RIDING" WITH ANOTHER ON THE SLIPPERY, WAX-SMOOTH TIMBER-
THIS TIME YOU GO IN THE DRINK AND--
MAYBE!
A CLEVER BIT OF FOOTWORK DISPOSES OF HIS SECOND OPPONENT!
SEE WHAT I MEAN?
MEANWHILE, THE PAIN OF HER BROKEN ARM PROVES TOO MUCH FOR NORA! SHE FAINTS DEAD AWAY AS THE LOG IS DRAWN UP INTO THE CONVEYER THAT LEADS TO THE SAWMILL!
BUT ROBIN'S LOG IS CLEVERLY MANEUVERED BY THE THIRD LOGGER, SO THAT IT CLEARS THE LOG JAM -- AND RIDES ON DOWN THE RACING WATERS..
?
HAW! HAW! SO LONG, KID!

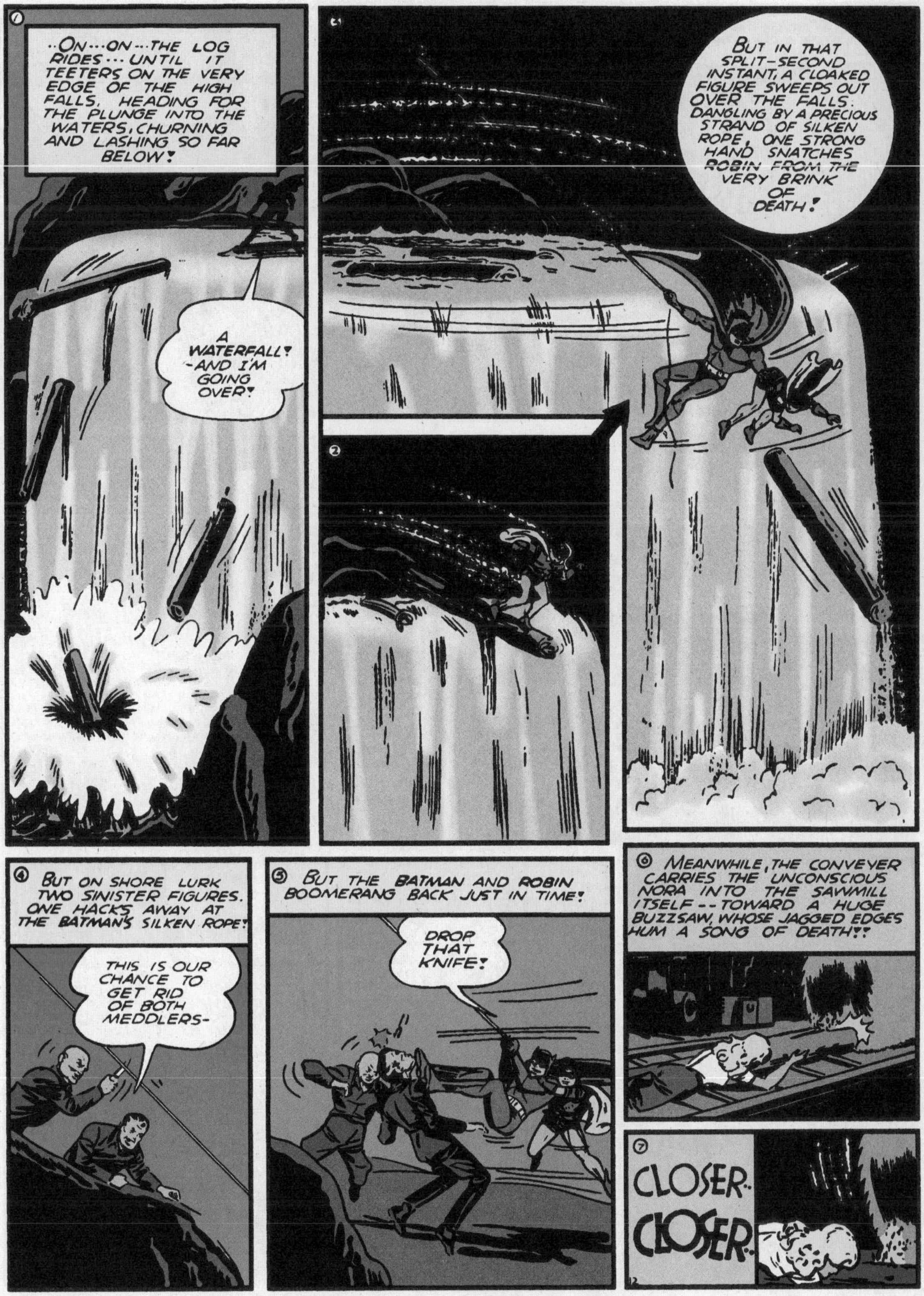
..ON...ON...THE LOG RIDES... UNTIL IT TEETERS ON THE VERY EDGE OF THE HIGH FALLS, HEADING FOR THE PLUNGE INTO THE WATERS, CHURNING AND LASHING SO FAR BELOW!
A WATERFALL! -AND I'M GOING OVER!
BUT IN THAT SPLIT-SECOND INSTANT, A CLOAKED FIGURE SWEEPS OUT OVER THE FALLS: DANGLING BY A PRECIOUS STRAND OF SILKEN ROPE, ONE STRONG HAND SNATCHES ROBIN FROM THE VERY BRINK OF DEATH!
BUT ON SHORE LURK TWO SINISTER FIGURES. ONE HACKS AWAY AT THE BATMAN'S SILKEN ROPE!
THIS IS OUR CHANCE TO GET RID OF BOTH MEDDLERS-
BUT THE BATMAN AND ROBIN BOOMERANG BACK JUST IN TIME!
DROP THAT KNIFE!
MEANWHILE, THE CONVEYER CARRIES THE UNCONSCIOUS NORA INTO THE SAWMILL ITSELF--TOWARD A HUGE BUZZSAW, WHOSE JAGGED EDGES HUM A SONG OF DEATH!!
CLOSER..
CLOSER..

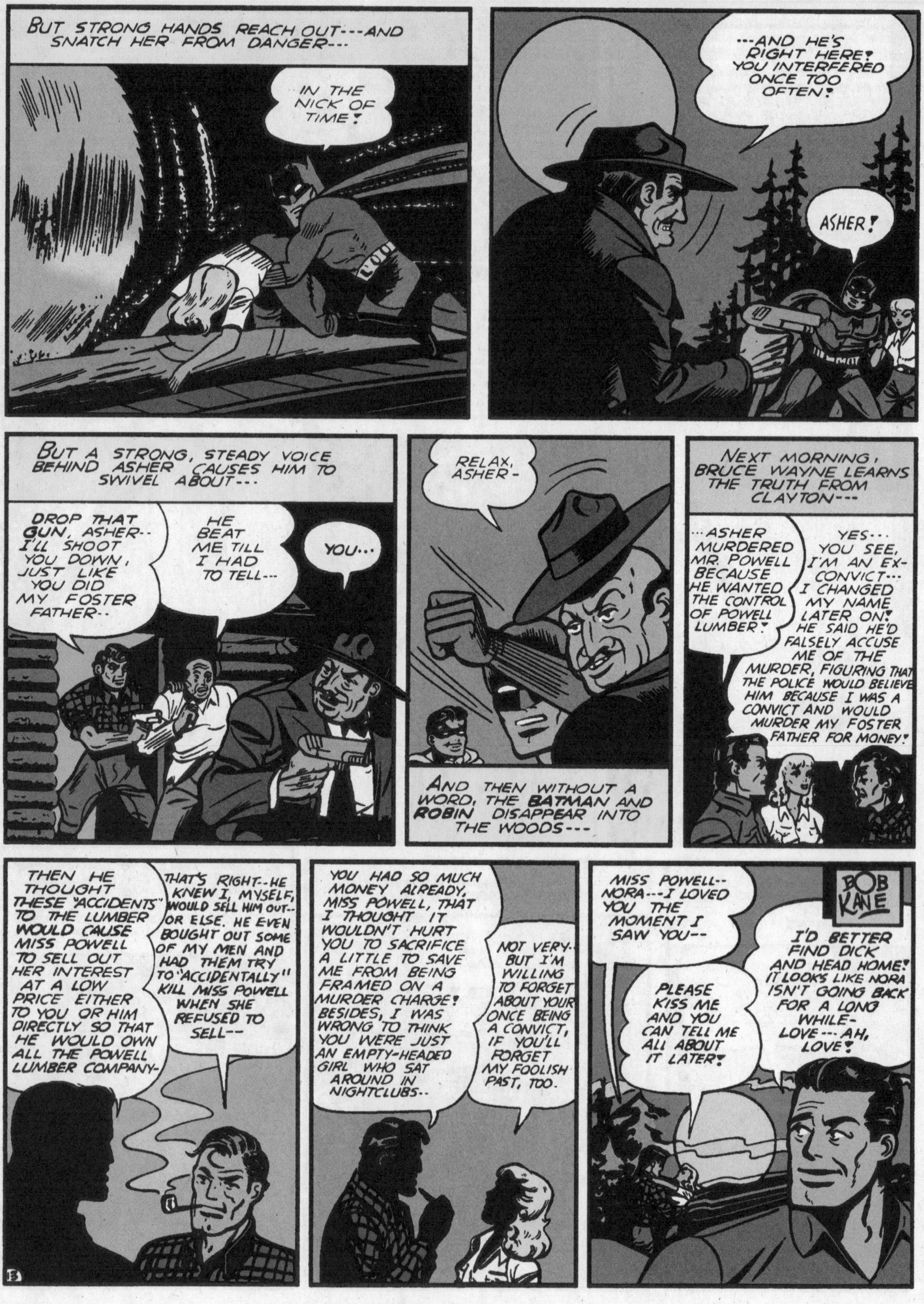
BUT STRONG HANDS REACH OUT---AND SNATCH HER FROM DANGER---
IN THE NICK OF TIME!
---AND HE'S RIGHT HERE! YOU INTERFERED ONCE TOO OFTEN!
ASHER!
BUT A STRONG, STEADY VOICE BEHIND ASHER CAUSES HIM TO SWIVEL ABOUT---
DROP THAT GUN, ASHER-- I'LL SHOOT YOU DOWN, JUST LIKE YOU DID MY FOSTER FATHER--
HE BEAT ME TILL I HAD TO TELL---
YOU...
RELAX, ASHER-
AND THEN WITHOUT A WORD, THE BATMAN AND ROBIN DISAPPEAR INTO THE WOODS---
NEXT MORNING, BRUCE WAYNE LEARNS THE TRUTH FROM CLAYTON---
...ASHER MURDERED MR. POWELL BECAUSE HE WANTED THE CONTROL OF POWELL LUMBER!
YES--- YOU SEE, I'M AN EX-CONVICT--- I CHANGED MY NAME LATER ON! HE SAID HE'D FALSELY ACCUSE ME OF THE MURDER, FIGURING THAT THE POLICE WOULD BELIEVE HIM BECAUSE I WAS A CONVICT AND WOULD MURDER MY FOSTER FATHER FOR MONEY!
THEN HE THOUGHT THESE "ACCIDENTS" TO THE LUMBER WOULD CAUSE MISS POWELL TO SELL OUT HER INTEREST AT A LOW PRICE EITHER TO YOU OR HIM DIRECTLY SO THAT HE WOULD OWN ALL THE POWELL LUMBER COMPANY-
THAT'S RIGHT--HE KNEW I, MYSELF, WOULD SELL HIM OUT--OR ELSE. HE EVEN BOUGHT OUT SOME OF MY MEN AND HAD THEM TRY TO "ACCIDENTALLY" KILL MISS POWELL WHEN SHE REFUSED TO SELL--
YOU HAD SO MUCH MONEY ALREADY, MISS POWELL, THAT I THOUGHT IT WOULDN'T HURT YOU TO SACRIFICE A LITTLE TO SAVE ME FROM BEING FRAMED ON A MURDER CHARGE! BESIDES, I WAS WRONG TO THINK YOU WERE JUST AN EMPTY-HEADED GIRL WHO SAT AROUND IN NIGHTCLUBS--
NOT VERY-- BUT I'M WILLING TO FORGET ABOUT YOUR ONCE BEING A CONVICT, IF YOU'LL FORGET MY FOOLISH PAST, TOO.
MISS POWELL-- NORA---I LOVED YOU THE MOMENT I SAW YOU--
PLEASE KISS ME AND YOU CAN TELL ME ALL ABOUT IT LATER!
BOB KANE
I'D BETTER FIND DICK AND HEAD HOME! IT LOOKS LIKE NORA ISN'T GOING BACK FOR A LONG WHILE-LOVE---AH, LOVE!

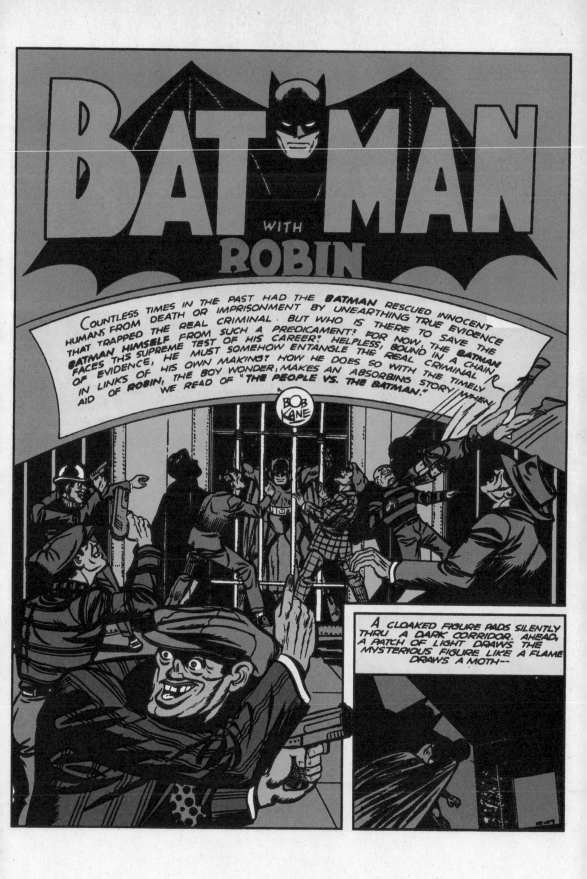

BAT MAN

with ROBIN

Countless times in the past had the BATMAN rescued innocent humans from death or imprisonment by unearthing true evidence that trapped the real criminal. But who is there to save the BATMAN himself from such a predicament? For now, the BATMAN faces this supreme test of his career! Helpless, bound in a chain of evidence, he must somehow entangle the real criminal in links of his own making! How he does so with the timely aid of ROBIN, the boy wonder, makes an absorbing story when we read of "THE PEOPLE VS. THE BATMAN."

BOB KANE

A cloaked figure pads silently thru a dark corridor. Ahead, a patch of light draws the mysterious figure like a flame draws a moth--

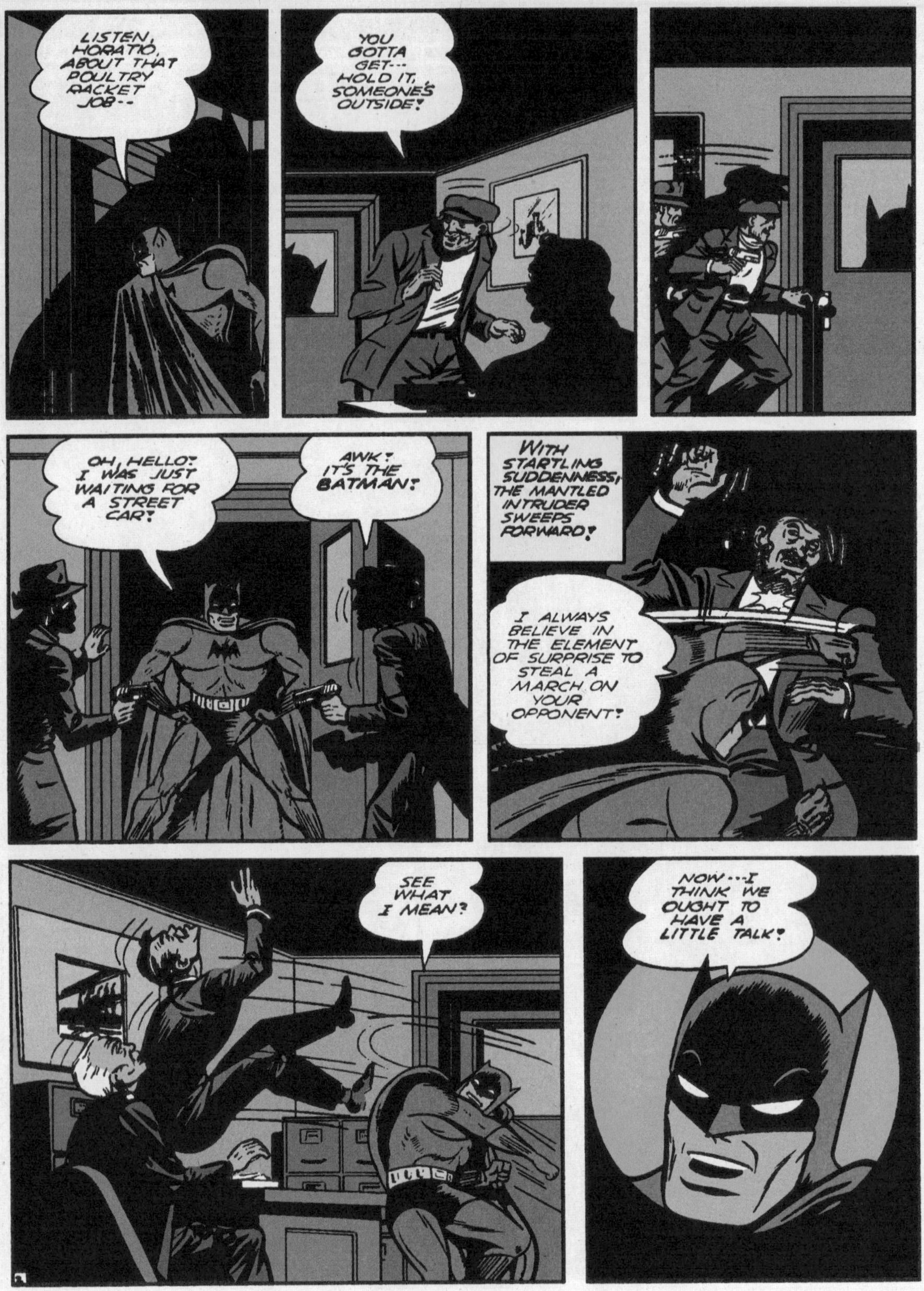

LISTEN, HORATIO, ABOUT THAT POULTRY RACKET JOB--
YOU GOTTA GET--- HOLD IT, SOMEONE'S OUTSIDE!
OH, HELLO! I WAS JUST WAITING FOR A STREET CAR!
AWK! IT'S THE BATMAN!
WITH STARTLING SUDDENNESS, THE MANTLED INTRUDER SWEEPS FORWARD!
I ALWAYS BELIEVE IN THE ELEMENT OF SURPRISE TO STEAL A MARCH ON YOUR OPPONENT!
SEE WHAT I MEAN?
NOW...I THINK WE OUGHT TO HAVE A LITTLE TALK!

BUT AS THE BATMAN TALKS, A THUG'S FURTIVE HAND REACHES FOR THE LIGHT SWITCH---

AND THE LIGHTS WINK OUT!

OKAY, NOW'S OUR CHANCE! SLUG HIM!

BANG BANG!

LET'S SCRAM!

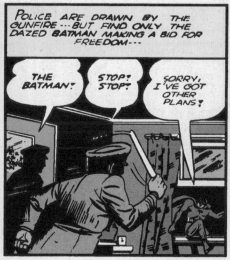

POLICE ARE DRAWN BY THE GUNFIRE---BUT FIND ONLY THE DAZED BATMAN MAKING A BID FOR FREEDOM---

THE BATMAN!

STOP! STOP!

SORRY, I'VE GOT OTHER PLANS!

THE ACROBATIC BATMAN DROPS TO SAFETY!

THERE HE GOES!

I WISH I KNEW WHAT HE WAS DOING HERE!

BECAUSE OF THIS VISIT, THE ENTIRE PHASE OF THE BATMAN'S LIFE IS TO BE AFFECTED!

AND FROM A NEARBY HALLWAY--

THEY'RE GONE NOW!

YEAH!... BUT IT LOOKS LIKE THE BATMAN IS WISE TO YOU!

LATER...THE HOME OF FREDDIE HILL...

I TELL YA, THE BATMAN'S WISE TO THE FACT THAT DELMAR IS REALLY HEAD OF THE RACKETS IN THIS WARD! SUPPOSE HE MAKES DELMAR TALK--THEN WHAT?

WE GOTTA GET RID OF DELMAR BEFORE THAT HAPPENS! I THINK IT'S TIME I RAN THIS MOB MYSELF-- WEASEL, HERE, IS GONNA BUMP OFF DELMAR--

BUT THE COPS WILL PICK ME UP SURE!

NOT THE WAY I FIGURE IT, CAUSE WE'RE GONNA GET SOMEONE TO TAKE THE RAP FOR YA! NOW LISTEN-- YOU GO TO DELMAR'S OFFICE AND WAIT-- WAIT FOR A CLIENT TO SHOW UP--- AND THEN YOU...

AT THAT INSTANT---

WHAT'S UP?

I REALLY DISCOVERED SOMETHING BIG-- THINK I'LL INVESTIGATE TOMORROW AS BRUCE WAYNE-- HE WOULDN'T AROUSE ANY SUSPICION!

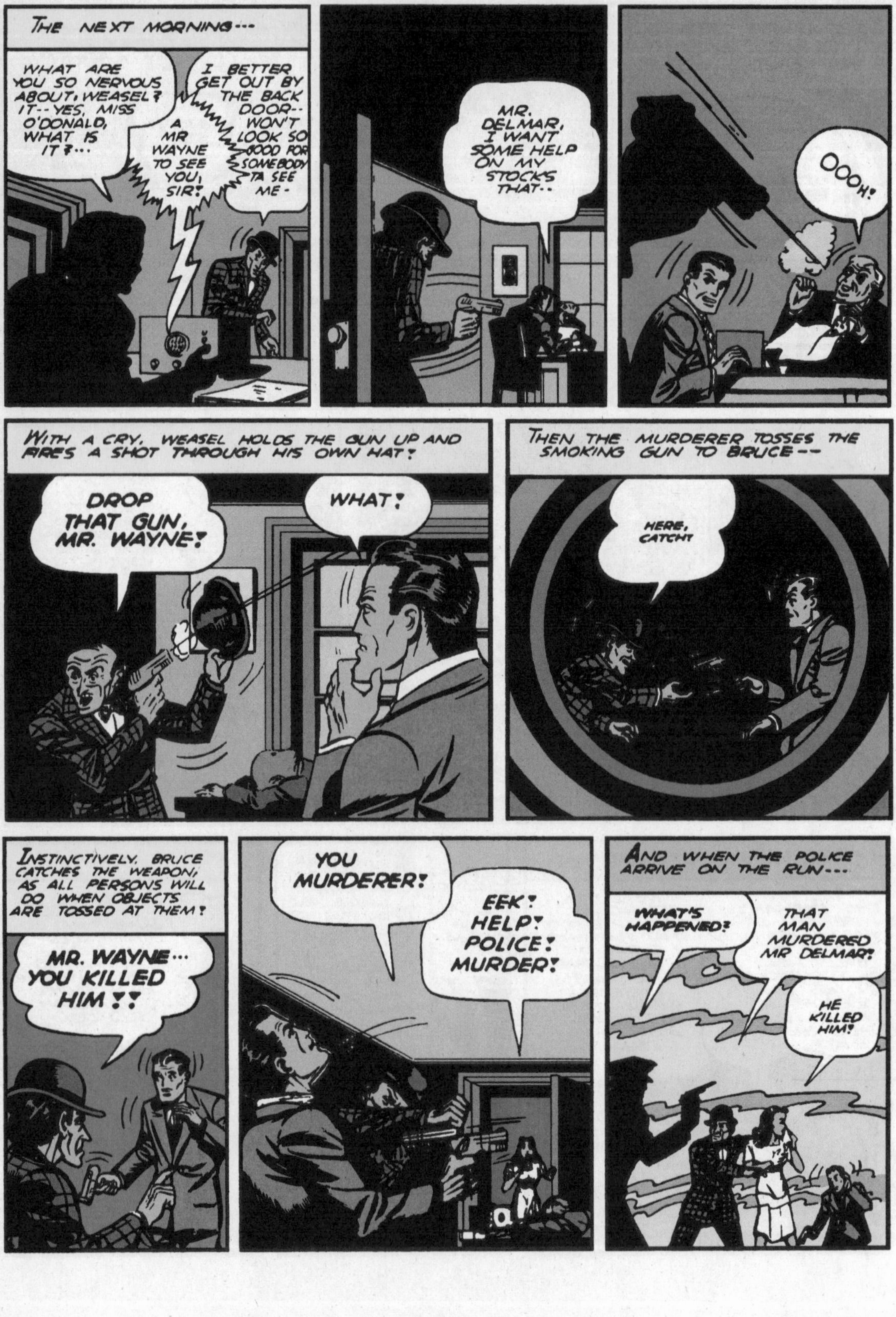
THE NEXT MORNING---
WHAT ARE YOU SO NERVOUS ABOUT, WEASEL? IT--YES, MISS O'DONALD, WHAT IS IT?...
A MR WAYNE TO SEE YOU, SIR!
I BETTER GET OUT BY THE BACK DOOR-- WON'T LOOK SO GOOD FOR SOMEBODY TA SEE ME-
MR. DELMAR, I WANT SOME HELP ON MY STOCKS THAT-.
OOOH!
WITH A CRY, WEASEL HOLDS THE GUN UP AND FIRES A SHOT THROUGH HIS OWN HAT!
DROP THAT GUN, MR. WAYNE!
WHAT!
THEN THE MURDERER TOSSES THE SMOKING GUN TO BRUCE--
HERE, CATCH!
INSTINCTIVELY, BRUCE CATCHES THE WEAPON, AS ALL PERSONS WILL DO WHEN OBJECTS ARE TOSSED AT THEM!
MR. WAYNE... YOU KILLED HIM!!
YOU MURDERER!
EEK! HELP! POLICE! MURDER!
AND WHEN THE POLICE ARRIVE ON THE RUN---
WHAT'S HAPPENED?
THAT MAN MURDERED MR DELMAR!
HE KILLED HIM!

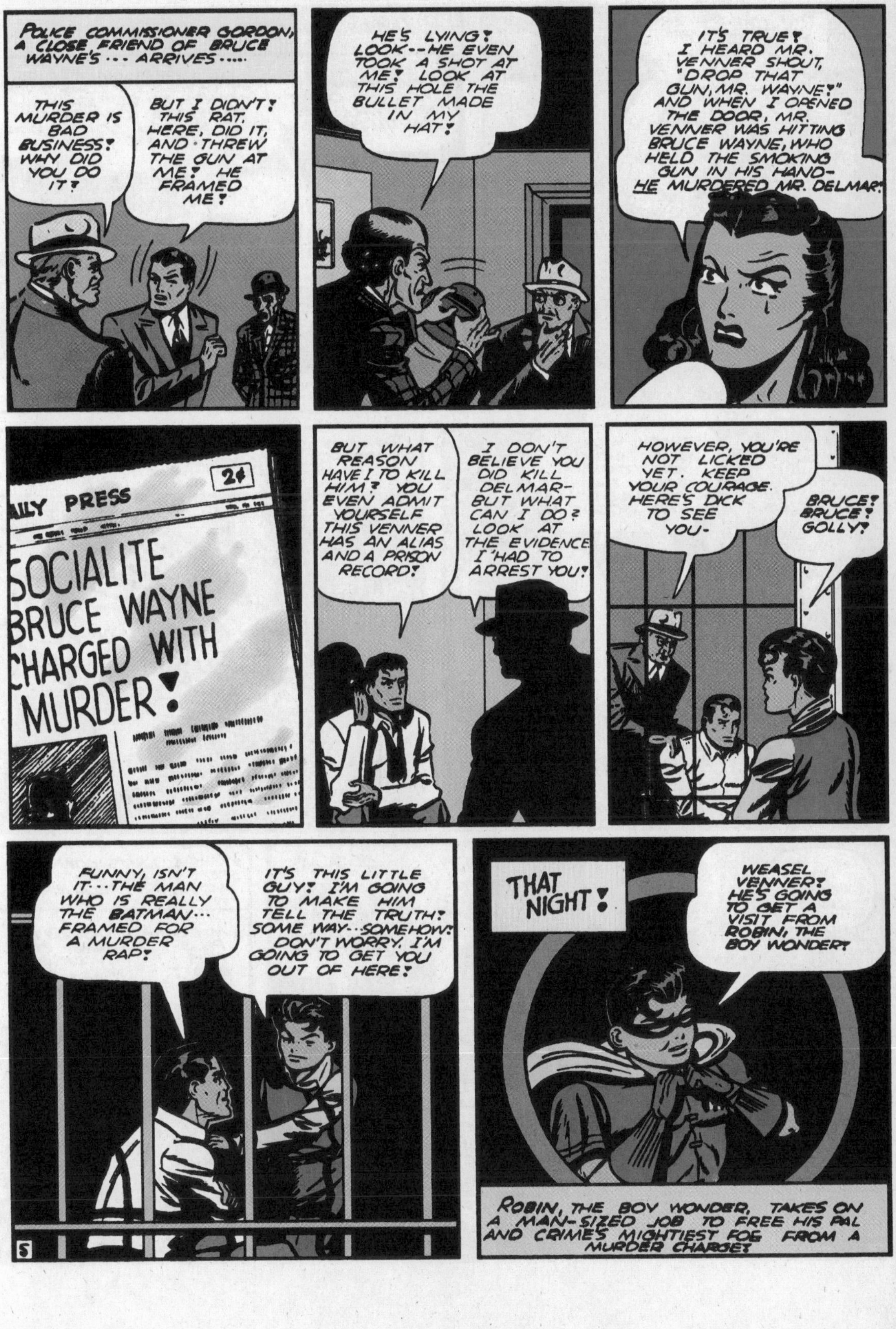
POLICE COMMISSIONER GORDON, A CLOSE FRIEND OF BRUCE WAYNE'S --- ARRIVES ----
THIS MURDER IS BAD BUSINESS! WHY DID YOU DO IT?
BUT I DIDN'T! THIS RAT, HERE, DID IT, AND THREW THE GUN AT ME! HE FRAMED ME!
HE'S LYING! LOOK--HE EVEN TOOK A SHOT AT ME! LOOK AT THIS HOLE THE BULLET MADE IN MY HAT!
IT'S TRUE! I HEARD MR. VENNER SHOUT, "DROP THAT GUN, MR. WAYNE!" AND WHEN I OPENED THE DOOR, MR. VENNER WAS HITTING BRUCE WAYNE, WHO HELD THE SMOKING GUN IN HIS HAND- HE MURDERED MR. DELMAR!
2¢
ILY PRESS
SOCIALITE BRUCE WAYNE CHARGED WITH MURDER!
BUT WHAT REASON HAVE I TO KILL HIM? YOU EVEN ADMIT YOURSELF THIS VENNER HAS AN ALIAS AND A PRISON RECORD!
I DON'T BELIEVE YOU DID KILL DELMAR- BUT WHAT CAN I DO? LOOK AT THE EVIDENCE I HAD TO ARREST YOU!
HOWEVER, YOU'RE NOT LICKED YET. KEEP YOUR COURAGE. HERE'S DICK TO SEE YOU-
BRUCE! BRUCE! GOLLY!
FUNNY, ISN'T IT---THE MAN WHO IS REALLY THE BATMAN--- FRAMED FOR A MURDER RAP!
IT'S THIS LITTLE GUY! I'M GOING TO MAKE HIM TELL THE TRUTH! SOME WAY--SOMEHOW! DON'T WORRY. I'M GOING TO GET YOU OUT OF HERE!
5
THAT NIGHT!
WEASEL VENNER! HE'S GOING TO GET A VISIT FROM ROBIN, THE BOY WONDER!
ROBIN, THE BOY WONDER, TAKES ON A MAN-SIZED JOB TO FREE HIS PAL AND CRIME'S MIGHTIEST FOE FROM A MURDER CHARGE!

THE NEWSPAPERS SAID THIS WAS VENNER'S ADDRESS—

INSIDE VENNER'S APARTMENT—

WELL, HILL, EVERYTHING WORKED OKAY? HEY—WHY THE ARTILLERY?

WE WANTA MAKE SURE, IN CASE YOUR CONSCIENCE STARTS TO BOTHER YOU—SO—WE'RE GONNA FIX IT SO YOU DON'T WORRY ANY MORE!

C'MON, WEASEL, WE'RE TAKIN' YOU FOR A RIDE! THE AIR WILL DO YOU GOOD!

IF THEY KILL HIM HOW AM I EVER GOING TO GET THE TESTIMONY TO FREE BRUCE?

THINKING ONLY OF BRUCE'S PERIL, ROBIN DISREGARDS PERSONAL DANGER AND DIVES HEADLONG—

IT'S ROBIN—UGH!

HOW D'YA GUESS IT?

WAIT TILL I TALK TO—OHH...

OUTA MY WAY! THIS MOB IS AFTER ME—THIS IS MY CHANCE TO BEAT IT—

WEASEL LEAPS DOWN THE STEPS AS HILL AND HIS MOBSTERS RECOVER—

I'M GONNA PLUG THIS BRAT!

FORGET HIM— IT'S WEASEL WE'RE GONNA GET! C'MON!

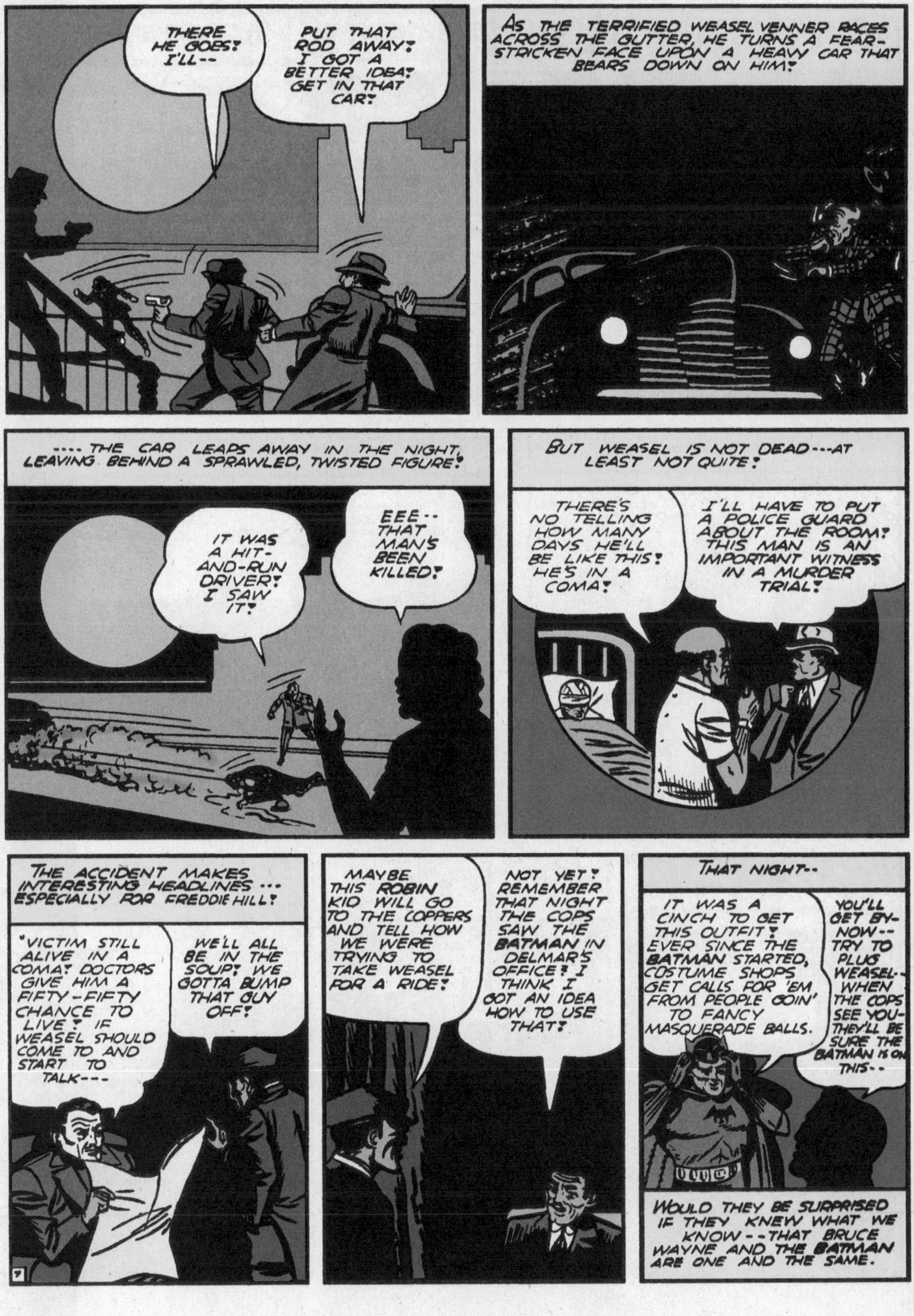
THERE HE GOES! I'LL--
PUT THAT ROD AWAY! I GOT A BETTER IDEA! GET IN THAT CAR!
AS THE TERRIFIED WEASEL VENNER RACES ACROSS THE GUTTER, HE TURNS A FEAR-STRICKEN FACE UPON A HEAVY CAR THAT BEARS DOWN ON HIM!
....THE CAR LEAPS AWAY IN THE NIGHT, LEAVING BEHIND A SPRAWLED, TWISTED FIGURE!
EEE-- THAT MAN'S BEEN KILLED!
IT WAS A HIT-AND-RUN DRIVER! I SAW IT!
BUT WEASEL IS NOT DEAD---AT LEAST NOT QUITE!
THERE'S NO TELLING HOW MANY DAYS HE'LL BE LIKE THIS! HE'S IN A COMA!
I'LL HAVE TO PUT A POLICE GUARD ABOUT THE ROOM! THIS MAN IS AN IMPORTANT WITNESS IN A MURDER TRIAL!
THE ACCIDENT MAKES INTERESTING HEADLINES... ESPECIALLY FOR FREDDIE HILL!
"VICTIM STILL ALIVE IN A COMA! DOCTORS GIVE HIM A FIFTY-FIFTY CHANCE TO LIVE! IF WEASEL SHOULD COME TO AND START TO TALK---
WE'LL ALL BE IN THE SOUP! WE GOTTA BUMP THAT GUY OFF!
7
MAYBE THIS ROBIN KID WILL GO TO THE COPPERS AND TELL HOW WE WERE TRYING TO TAKE WEASEL FOR A RIDE!
NOT YET! REMEMBER THAT NIGHT THE COPS SAW THE BATMAN IN DELMAR'S OFFICE? I THINK I GOT AN IDEA HOW TO USE THAT!
THAT NIGHT--
IT WAS A CINCH TO GET THIS OUTFIT! EVER SINCE THE BATMAN STARTED, COSTUME SHOPS GET CALLS FOR 'EM FROM PEOPLE GOIN' TO FANCY MASQUERADE BALLS.
YOU'LL GET BY-NOW-- TRY TO PLUG WEASEL-- WHEN THE COPS SEE YOU-THEY'LL BE SURE THE BATMAN IS ON THIS--
WOULD THEY BE SURPRISED IF THEY KNEW WHAT WE KNOW--THAT BRUCE WAYNE AND THE BATMAN ARE ONE AND THE SAME.

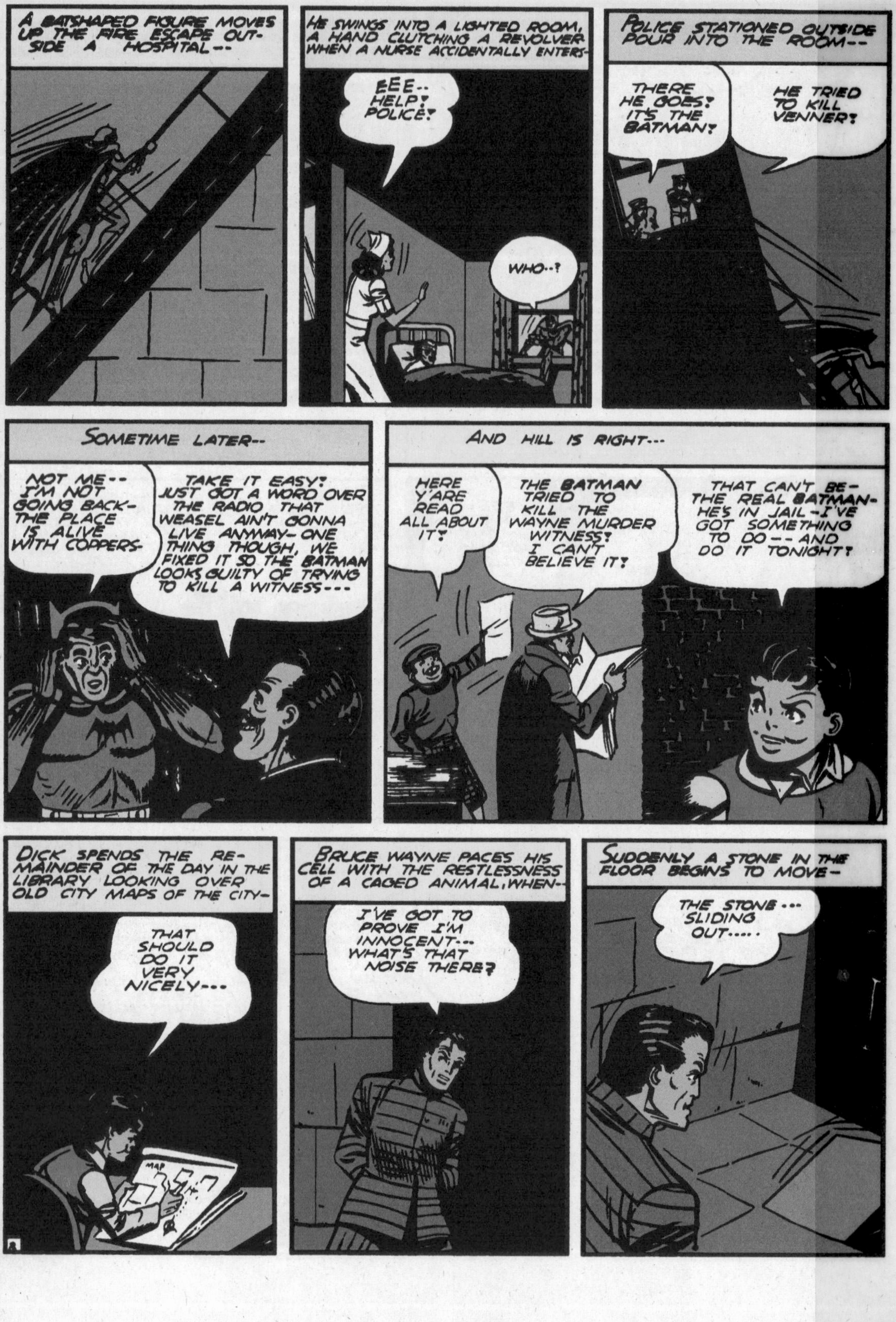
A BATSHAPED FIGURE MOVES UP THE FIRE ESCAPE OUTSIDE A HOSPITAL--
HE SWINGS INTO A LIGHTED ROOM, A HAND CLUTCHING A REVOLVER WHEN A NURSE ACCIDENTALLY ENTERS-
EEE-- HELP! POLICE!
WHO--?
POLICE STATIONED OUTSIDE POUR INTO THE ROOM--
THERE HE GOES! IT'S THE BATMAN!
HE TRIED TO KILL VENNER!
SOMETIME LATER--
NOT ME-- I'M NOT GOING BACK-THE PLACE IS ALIVE WITH COPPERS-
TAKE IT EASY! JUST GOT A WORD OVER THE RADIO THAT WEASEL AIN'T GONNA LIVE ANYWAY- ONE THING THOUGH, WE FIXED IT SO THE BATMAN LOOKS GUILTY OF TRYING TO KILL A WITNESS---
AND HILL IS RIGHT---
HERE Y'ARE READ ALL ABOUT IT!
THE BATMAN TRIED TO KILL THE WAYNE MURDER WITNESS! I CAN'T BELIEVE IT!
THAT CAN'T BE- THE REAL BATMAN-HE'S IN JAIL-I'VE GOT SOMETHING TO DO-- AND DO IT TONIGHT!
DICK SPENDS THE REMAINDER OF THE DAY IN THE LIBRARY LOOKING OVER OLD CITY MAPS OF THE CITY-
THAT SHOULD DO IT VERY NICELY---
MAP
BRUCE WAYNE PACES HIS CELL WITH THE RESTLESSNESS OF A CAGED ANIMAL, WHEN--
I'VE GOT TO PROVE I'M INNOCENT--- WHAT'S THAT NOISE THERE?
SUDDENLY A STONE IN THE FLOOR BEGINS TO MOVE-
THE STONE--- SLIDING OUT.....

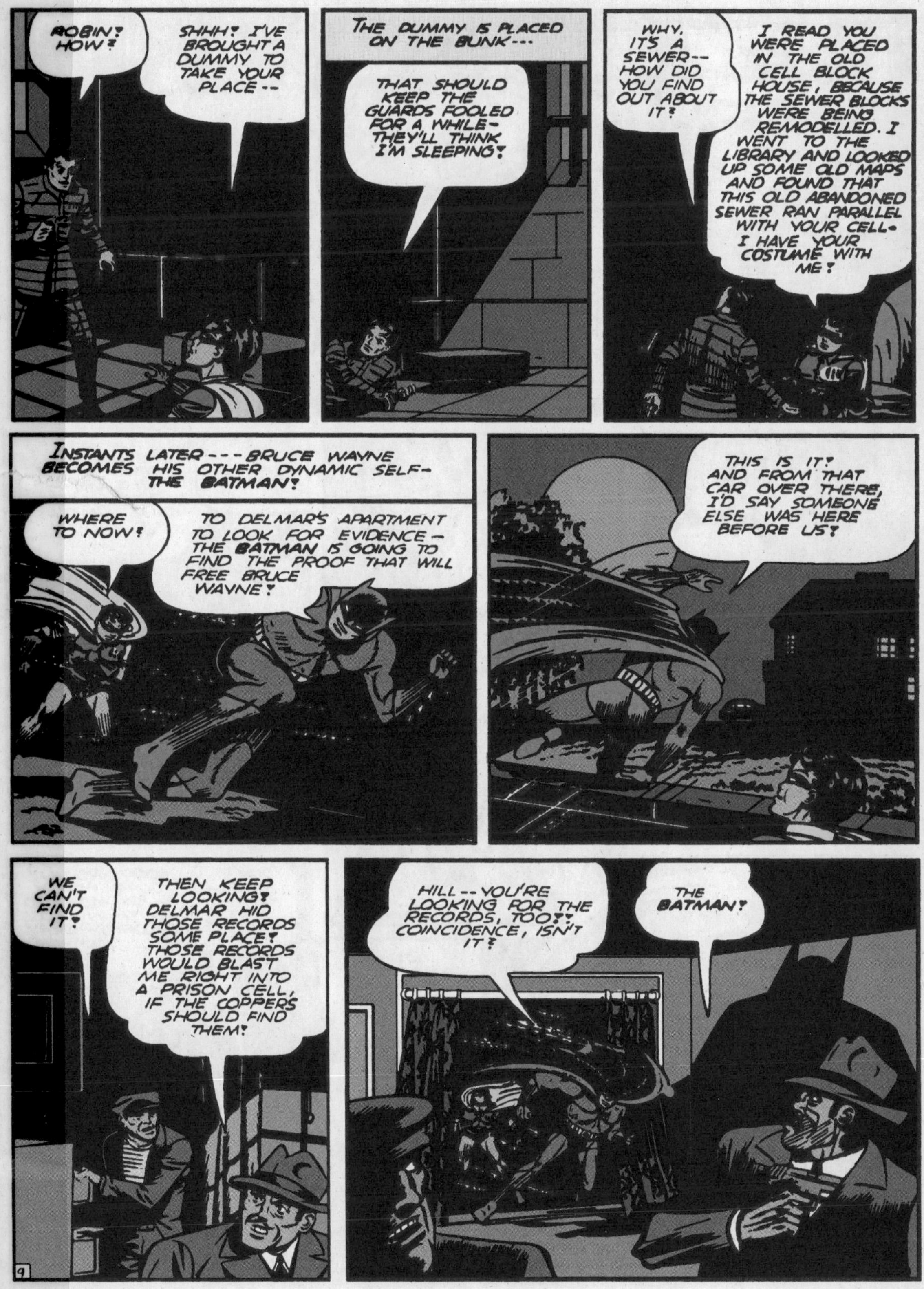

ROBIN? HOW?
SHHH? I'VE BROUGHT A DUMMY TO TAKE YOUR PLACE --
THE DUMMY IS PLACED ON THE BUNK---
THAT SHOULD KEEP THE GUARDS FOOLED FOR A WHILE- THEY'LL THINK I'M SLEEPING?
WHY, IT'S A SEWER-- HOW DID YOU FIND OUT ABOUT IT?
I READ YOU WERE PLACED IN THE OLD CELL BLOCK HOUSE, BECAUSE THE SEWER BLOCKS WERE BEING REMODELLED. I WENT TO THE LIBRARY AND LOOKED UP SOME OLD MAPS AND FOUND THAT THIS OLD ABANDONED SEWER RAN PARALLEL WITH YOUR CELL. I HAVE YOUR COSTUME WITH ME?
INSTANTS LATER---BRUCE WAYNE BECOMES HIS OTHER DYNAMIC SELF- THE BATMAN?
WHERE TO NOW?
TO DELMAR'S APARTMENT TO LOOK FOR EVIDENCE - THE BATMAN IS GOING TO FIND THE PROOF THAT WILL FREE BRUCE WAYNE?
THIS IS IT? AND FROM THAT CAR OVER THERE, I'D SAY SOMEONE ELSE WAS HERE BEFORE US?
WE CAN'T FIND IT?
THEN KEEP LOOKING? DELMAR HID THOSE RECORDS SOME PLACE? THOSE RECORDS WOULD BLAST ME RIGHT INTO A PRISON CELL, IF THE COPPERS SHOULD FIND THEM?
9
HILL--YOU'RE LOOKING FOR THE RECORDS, TOO?? COINCIDENCE, ISN'T IT?
THE BATMAN?

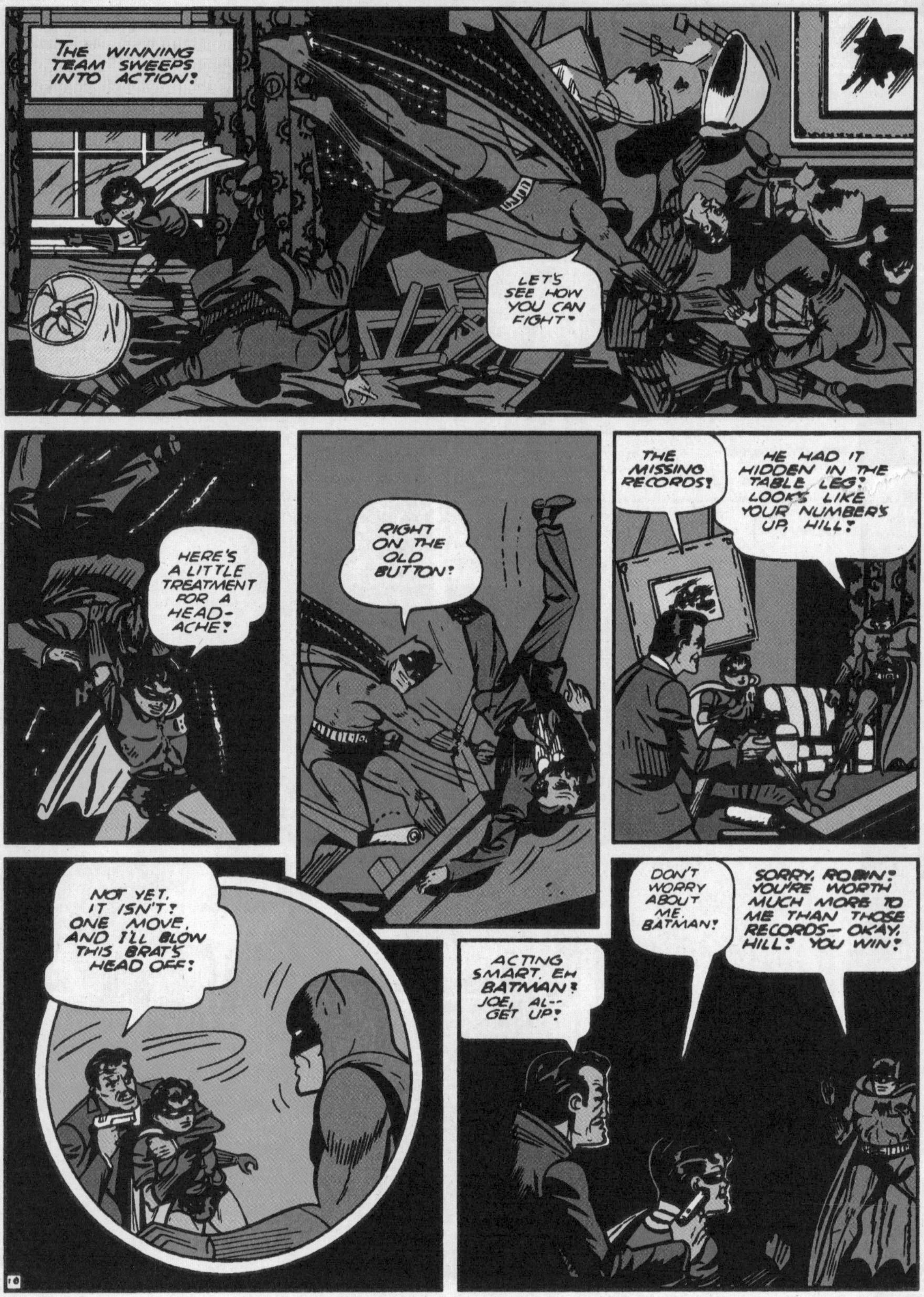
THE WINNING TEAM SWEEPS INTO ACTION!
LET'S SEE HOW YOU CAN FIGHT!
HERE'S A LITTLE TREATMENT FOR A HEAD-ACHE!
RIGHT ON THE OLD BUTTON!
THE MISSING RECORDS!
HE HAD IT HIDDEN IN THE TABLE LEG! LOOKS LIKE YOUR NUMBER'S UP, HILL!
NOT YET, IT ISN'T! ONE MOVE, AND I'LL BLOW THIS BRAT'S HEAD OFF!
ACTING SMART, EH BATMAN? JOE, AL-- GET UP!
DON'T WORRY ABOUT ME, BATMAN!
SORRY, ROBIN! YOU'RE WORTH MUCH MORE TO ME THAN THOSE RECORDS-- OKAY, HILL! YOU WIN!

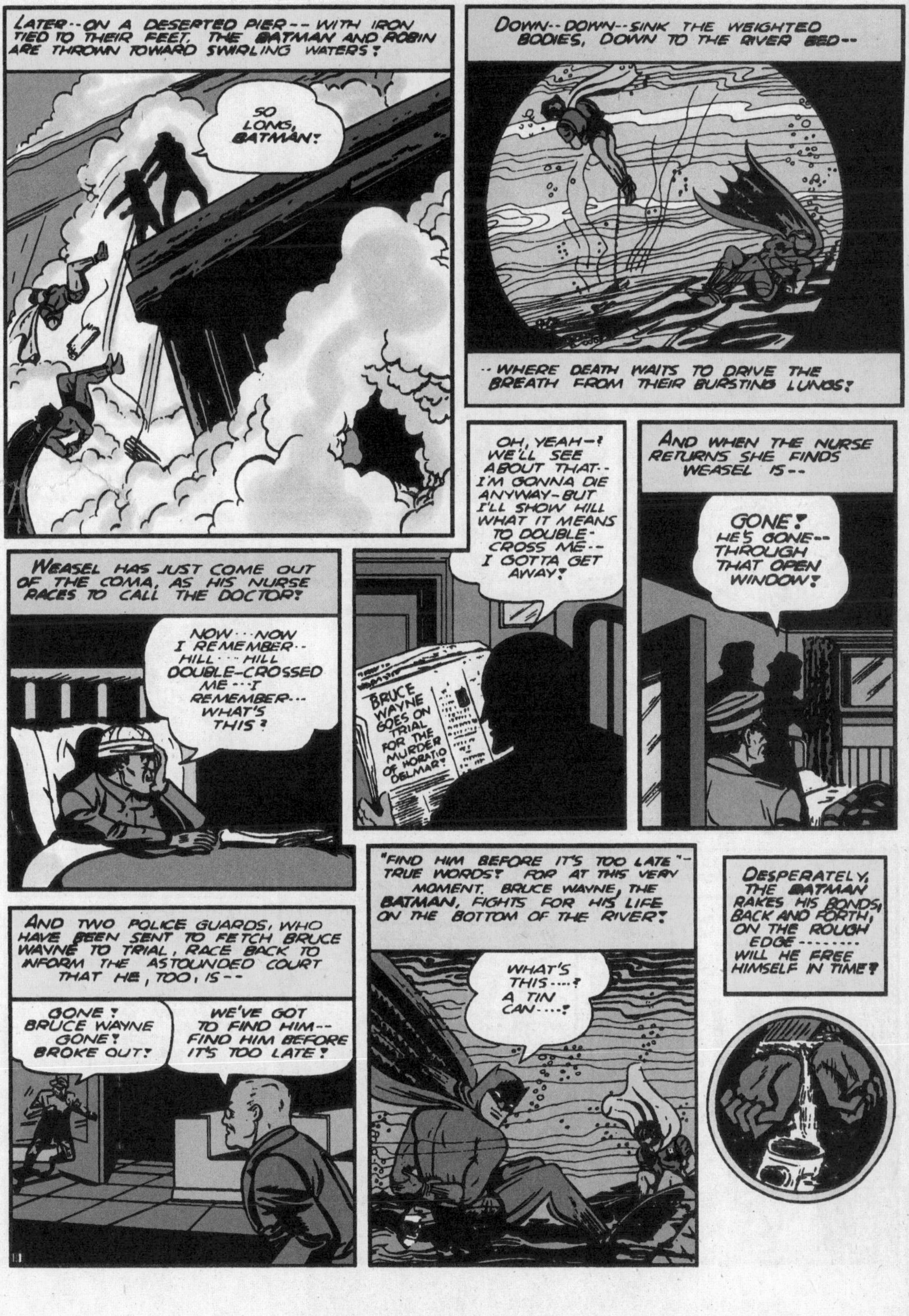
LATER--ON A DESERTED PIER-- WITH IRON TIED TO THEIR FEET, THE BATMAN AND ROBIN ARE THROWN TOWARD SWIRLING WATERS!
SO LONG, BATMAN!
DOWN--DOWN--SINK THE WEIGHTED BODIES, DOWN TO THE RIVER BED--
--WHERE DEATH WAITS TO DRIVE THE BREATH FROM THEIR BURSTING LUNGS!
WEASEL HAS JUST COME OUT OF THE COMA, AS HIS NURSE RACES TO CALL THE DOCTOR!
NOW...NOW I REMEMBER-- HILL...HILL DOUBLE-CROSSED ME...I REMEMBER... WHAT'S THIS?
OH, YEAH--! WE'LL SEE ABOUT THAT-- I'M GONNA DIE ANYWAY- BUT I'LL SHOW HILL WHAT IT MEANS TO DOUBLE-CROSS ME-- I GOTTA GET AWAY!
BRUCE WAYNE GOES ON TRIAL FOR THE MURDER OF HORATIO DELMAR!
AND WHEN THE NURSE RETURNS SHE FINDS WEASEL IS--
GONE! HE'S GONE-- THROUGH THAT OPEN WINDOW!
AND TWO POLICE GUARDS, WHO HAVE BEEN SENT TO FETCH BRUCE WAYNE TO TRIAL, RACE BACK TO INFORM THE ASTOUNDED COURT THAT HE, TOO, IS--
GONE! BRUCE WAYNE GONE! BROKE OUT!
WE'VE GOT TO FIND HIM-- FIND HIM BEFORE IT'S TOO LATE!
"FIND HIM BEFORE IT'S TOO LATE"-- TRUE WORDS! FOR AT THIS VERY MOMENT, BRUCE WAYNE, THE BATMAN, FIGHTS FOR HIS LIFE ON THE BOTTOM OF THE RIVER!
WHAT'S THIS...? A TIN CAN...?
DESPERATELY, THE BATMAN RAKES HIS BONDS, BACK AND FORTH, ON THE ROUGH EDGE-------- WILL HE FREE HIMSELF IN TIME?

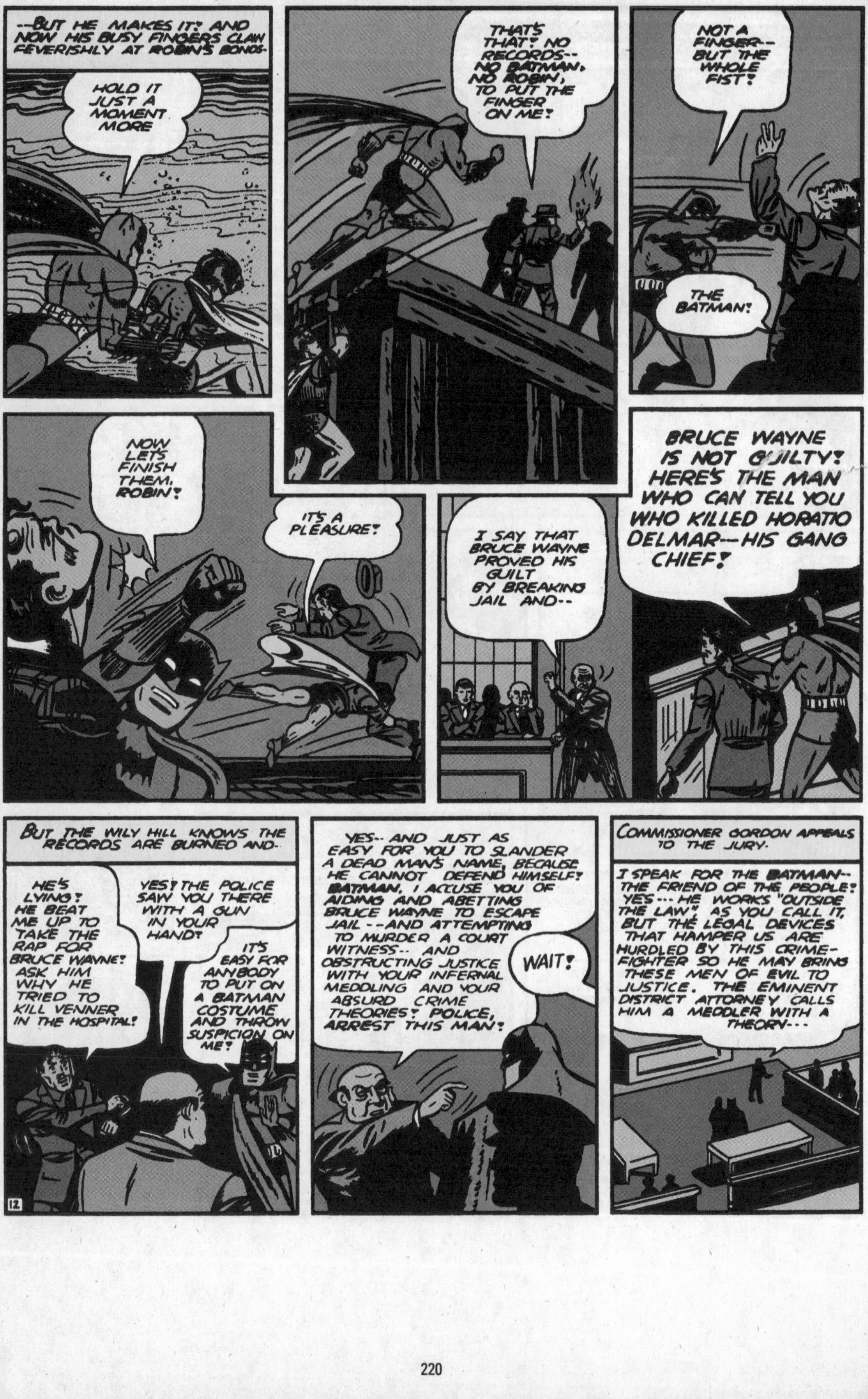
--BUT HE MAKES IT! AND NOW HIS BUSY FINGERS CLAW FEVERISHLY AT ROBIN'S BONDS-
HOLD IT JUST A MOMENT MORE
THAT'S THAT! NO RECORDS-- NO BATMAN, NO ROBIN, TO PUT THE FINGER ON ME!
NOT A FINGER-- BUT THE WHOLE FIST!
THE BATMAN!
NOW LET'S FINISH THEM, ROBIN!
IT'S A PLEASURE!
BRUCE WAYNE IS NOT GUILTY! HERE'S THE MAN WHO CAN TELL YOU WHO KILLED HORATIO DELMAR--HIS GANG CHIEF!
I SAY THAT BRUCE WAYNE PROVED HIS GUILT BY BREAKING JAIL AND--
BUT THE WILY HILL KNOWS THE RECORDS ARE BURNED AND-
HE'S LYING! HE BEAT ME UP TO TAKE THE RAP FOR BRUCE WAYNE! ASK HIM WHY HE TRIED TO KILL VENNER IN THE HOSPITAL!
YES! THE POLICE SAW YOU THERE WITH A GUN IN YOUR HAND!
IT'S EASY FOR ANYBODY TO PUT ON A BATMAN COSTUME AND THROW SUSPICION ON ME!
12
YES-- AND JUST AS EASY FOR YOU TO SLANDER A DEAD MAN'S NAME, BECAUSE HE CANNOT DEFEND HIMSELF! BATMAN, I ACCUSE YOU OF AIDING AND ABETTING BRUCE WAYNE TO ESCAPE JAIL --AND ATTEMPTING TO MURDER A COURT WITNESS-- AND OBSTRUCTING JUSTICE WITH YOUR INFERNAL MEDDLING AND YOUR ABSURD CRIME THEORIES! POLICE, ARREST THIS MAN!
WAIT!
COMMISSIONER GORDON APPEALS TO THE JURY.
I SPEAK FOR THE BATMAN-- THE FRIEND OF THE PEOPLE! YES--- HE WORKS "OUTSIDE THE LAW" AS YOU CALL IT, BUT THE LEGAL DEVICES THAT HAMPER US ARE HURDLED BY THIS CRIME-FIGHTER SO HE MAY BRING THESE MEN OF EVIL TO JUSTICE. THE EMINENT DISTRICT ATTORNEY CALLS HIM A MEDDLER WITH A THEORY---

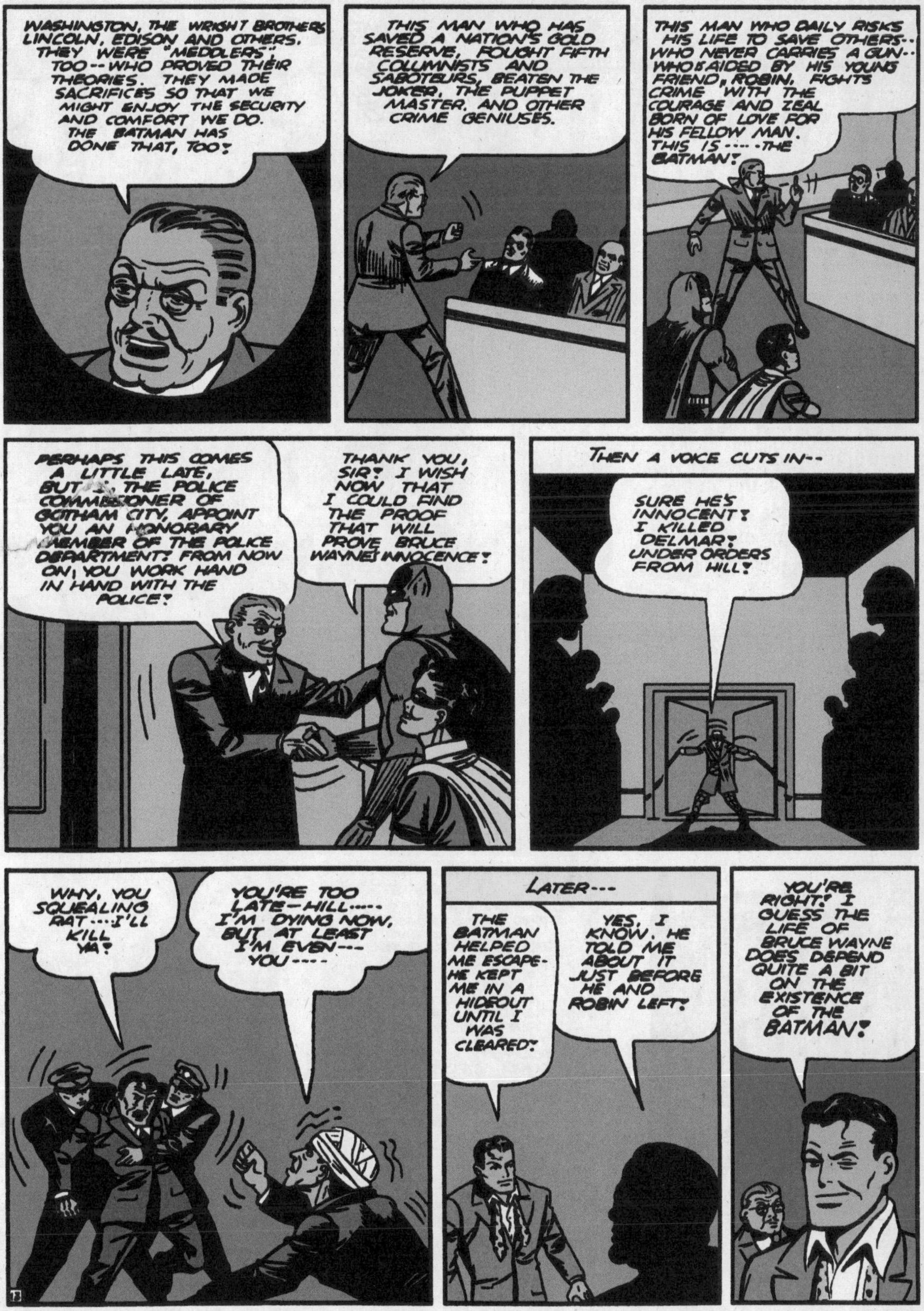

WASHINGTON, THE WRIGHT BROTHERS, LINCOLN, EDISON AND OTHERS. THEY WERE "MEDDLERS" TOO--WHO PROVED THEIR THEORIES. THEY MADE SACRIFICES SO THAT WE MIGHT ENJOY THE SECURITY AND COMFORT WE DO. THE BATMAN HAS DONE THAT, TOO!
THIS MAN WHO HAS SAVED A NATION'S GOLD RESERVE, FOUGHT FIFTH COLUMNISTS AND SABOTEURS, BEATEN THE JOKER, THE PUPPET MASTER, AND OTHER CRIME GENIUSES.
THIS MAN WHO DAILY RISKS HIS LIFE TO SAVE OTHERS-- WHO NEVER CARRIES A GUN-- WHO IS AIDED BY HIS YOUNG FRIEND, ROBIN, FIGHTS CRIME WITH THE COURAGE AND ZEAL BORN OF LOVE FOR HIS FELLOW MAN. THIS IS ----THE BATMAN!
PERHAPS THIS COMES A LITTLE LATE, BUT I, THE POLICE COMMISSIONER OF GOTHAM CITY, APPOINT YOU AN HONORARY MEMBER OF THE POLICE DEPARTMENT! FROM NOW ON, YOU WORK HAND IN HAND WITH THE POLICE!
THANK YOU, SIR! I WISH NOW THAT I COULD FIND THE PROOF THAT WILL PROVE BRUCE WAYNE'S INNOCENCE!
THEN A VOICE CUTS IN--
SURE HE'S INNOCENT! I KILLED DELMAR! UNDER ORDERS FROM HILL!
WHY, YOU SQUEALING RAT----I'LL KILL YA!
YOU'RE TOO LATE--HILL---- I'M DYING NOW, BUT AT LEAST I'M EVEN--- YOU----
LATER---
THE BATMAN HELPED ME ESCAPE-HE KEPT ME IN A HIDEOUT UNTIL I WAS CLEARED!
YES, I KNOW. HE TOLD ME ABOUT IT JUST BEFORE HE AND ROBIN LEFT!
YOU'RE RIGHT! I GUESS THE LIFE OF BRUCE WAYNE DOES DEPEND QUITE A BIT ON THE EXISTENCE OF THE BATMAN!

READ MORE OF THE DARK KNIGHT DETECTIVE'S ADVENTURES IN THESE COLLECTIONS FROM DC COMICS:

BATMAN

BATMAN
HUSH
JEPH LOEB
JIM LEE
SCOTT WILLIAMS
VOLUME ONE

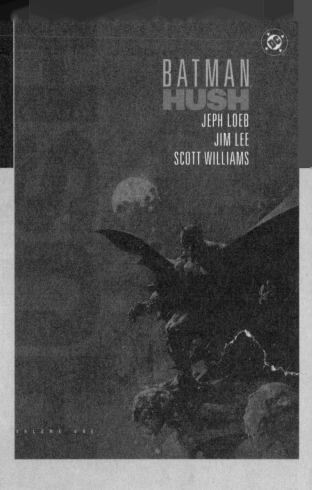

BATMAN: HUSH VOLUME 1

Jeph Loeb, Jim Lee and **Scott Williams** tell an epic tale of friendship, trust and betrayal, in the first volume of a tale that spans a lifetime of the Dark Knight.

"THE ACTION IS EXCITING AND THE DETAIL IS METICULOUS."
— CRITIQUES ON INFINITE EARTHS

BATMAN: THE DARK KNIGHT RETURNS

BATMAN: THE DARK KNIGHT RETURNS
FRANK MILLER
with KLAUS JANSON and LYNN VARLEY

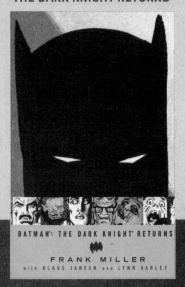

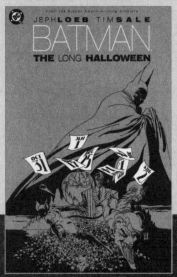

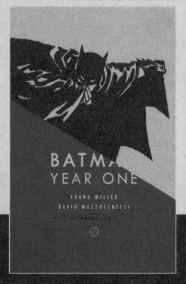

FRANK MILLER
KLAUS JANSON
LYNN VARLEY

BATMAN: THE LONG HALLOWEEN

JEPH LOEB TIM SALE
BATMAN
THE LONG HALLOWEEN

JEPH LOEB
TIM SALE

BATMAN: YEAR ONE

YEAR ONE
FRANK MILLER
DAVID MAZZUCCHELLI

FRANK MILLER
DAVID MAZZUCCHELLI

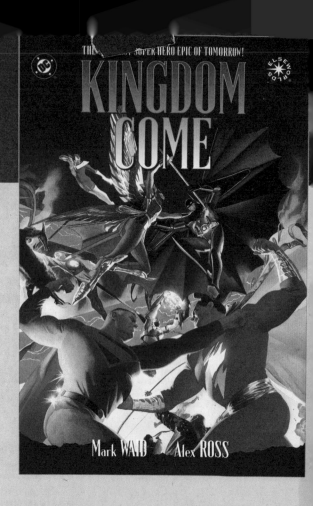